W9-BRI-601

CRITICAL SURVEY
OF GRAPHIC NOVELS

INDEPENDENTS AND
UNDERGROUND CLASSICS

CRITICAL SURVEY OF GRAPHIC NOVELS

INDEPENDENTS AND UNDERGROUND CLASSICS

Volume 1
A.D.: New Orleans After the Deluge – Houdini: The Handcuff King

Editors

Bart H. Beaty
University of Calgary

Stephen Weiner
Maynard, Massachusetts

SALEM PRESS
Ipswich, Massachusetts   Hackensack, New Jersey

Cover images: Top Left: *My Mommy Is in America and She Met Buffalo Bill* (Ponet Mon S.L.) Top Right: *Blueberry* (Editions Darguard) Bottom Right: *Strangers in Paradise* (Abstract Studios) Bottom Left: *Flaming Carrot* (Dark Horse)

Critical survey of graphic novels : independents and underground classics / editors, Bart H. Beaty, Stephen Weiner.
   p. cm.
 Includes bibliographical references and index.
 ISBN 978-1-58765-950-8 (set) -- ISBN 978-1-58765-951-5 (vol. 1) -- ISBN 978-1-58765-952-2 (vol. 2) -- ISBN 978-1-58765-953-9 (vol. 3)
 1. Graphic novels. 2. Comic books, strips, etc. I. Beaty, Bart. II. Weiner, Stephen, 1955-
PN6725.C754 2012
741.5'0973--dc23
                                               2011051380

First Printing

Printed in the United States of America

CONTENTS

MASTER LIST OF CONTENTS

Volume 1

Volume 2

Contents v

Volume 3

PUBLISHER'S NOTE

Graphic novels have spawned a body of literary criticism since their emergence as a specific category in the publishing field, attaining a level of respect and permanence in academia previously held by their counterparts in prose. Salem Press's *Critical Survey of Graphic Novels* series aims to collect the preeminent graphic novels and core comics series that form today's canon for academic coursework and library collection development, offering clear, concise, and accessible analysis of not only the historic and current landscape of the interdisciplinary medium and its consumption, but the wide range of genres, themes, devices, and techniques that the graphic novel medium encompasses.

The combination of visual images and text, the emphasis of art over written description, the coupling of mature themes with the comic form—these elements appeal to the graphic novel enthusiast but remain a source of reluctance to other readers. Designed for both popular and scholarly arenas and collections, the series provides unique insight and analysis into the most influential and widely read graphic novels with an emphasis on establishing the medium as an important academic discipline. We hope researchers and the common reader alike will gain a deeper understanding of these works, as the literary nature is presented in critical format by leading writers in the field of study.

Independents and Underground Classics is the second title of the *Critical Survey of Graphic Novels* series, in conjunction with *Heroes and Superheroes*; *Manga*; and *History, Theme, and Technique*. This title collects more than two hundred graphic novels, the majority of which were published since the emergence of the underground comics—or comix—movement of the 1960's. The current volume provides detailed analyses of the major works that have defined the independent and underground graphic novel movement as it has developed over more than half a century, and stories have been compiled and dissected to provide viewpoints that are easily missed during initial readings.

SCOPE AND COVERAGE

This three-volume set covers over 215 well-regarded works of the independent and underground genre, summarizing plots and analyzing the works in terms of their literary integrity and overall contribution to the graphic novel landscape. It contains works that are self-published or are from independent houses. The entries in this encyclopedic set also cover a wide range of periods and trends in the medium, from the influential early twentieth-century woodcuts—"novels in pictures"—of Frans Masereel to the alternative comics revolution of the 1980's, spearheaded by such works as *Love and Rockets* by the Hernandez brothers; from the anthropomorphic historical fiction of *Maus*, which attempted to humanize the full weight of the Holocaust, to the unglamorous autobiographical *American Splendor* series and its celebration of the mundane; and from Robert Crumb's faithful and scholarly illustrative interpretation of the *Book of Genesis*, to the tongue-in-cheek subversiveness of the genre mashup *Zombies vs. Robots*.

In writing these essays, contributors worked from original sources, providing new criticism and content aimed at deconstructing both centuries-old themes and concepts as well as nontraditional genres and styles, and portraying the graphic novel as literature. To that end, essays look beyond the popular-culture aspects of the medium to show the wide range of literary devices and overarching themes and styles used to convey beliefs and conflicts. Furthermore, critical attention was paid to panel selection and relevancy, and a particular work's influence on the creators' careers, other graphic novels, or literature as a whole.

The graphic novels field is defined by tremendous complexity; to that end, many important works and creators have been omitted. Lastly, while the series has an international scope, attention has been focused on translated works that have been influential in the development of a specific graphic novel tradition.

ORGANIZATION AND FORMAT

The essays in *Independents and Underground Classics* appear alphabetically and are approximately 3 to 4 pages in length. Each essay is heavily formatted and begins with full ready-reference top matter that includes the primary author or authors; illustrators and other artists who contributed to the work; and the first serial and book publication. This is followed by the main text, which is divided into "Publication History," "Plot," "Volumes," "Characters," "Artistic Style,"

"Themes," and "Impact." A list of adaptations of the graphic novel into film and television are also noted, and a user-friendly bibliography completes the essay. Cross-references direct readers to related topics, and further reading suggestions accompany all articles.

Publication History presents an overview of the work's origin and publication chronology. Specifically, dates of first serial publication, first book publication, and first translation into English are provided. Many graphic novels were first serialized in comic book form, often as a limited series, and were later collected or republished in book format, while other graphic novels were conceptualized as novelistic works. In addition, details about the significant awards and honors won by each work are listed.

Plot provides an in-depth synopsis of the main story progression and other story arcs. As an aid to students, this section focuses on the most critically important plot turns in the series or work and why these were important.

Where applicable, *Volumes* orients the reader or researcher to the accepted reading order of the work. For series, it lists individual volumes or collections, often comprising different story arcs. The year when each collection was published is provided. Also identified are the issues that were collected within a volume, a synopsis of the volume's main focus, and its significance within the entire collection.

Characters presents detailed descriptions of major characters in the story, beginning with the main protagonists and antagonists. The section discusses physical description, character traits and significant characteristics, the character's relationship with others, and the primary role a character plays in advancing the plot of the work or series. To aid readers, descriptions include "also known as" names and monikers.

Artistic Style provides analysis of the work's visual content, especially as it relates to characterization, plot, and mood; analysis of the illustrative use of color versus black and white; discussion of any changes in style as the story progresses; and the use of elements and devices such as dialogue, captions, panels, penciling, inking, and backgrounds.

Themes identifies the central themes in the work, how they are expressed—for example, through plot or layout—and how they relate to characterization and style. It also discusses, when applicable, whether a major thematic point is a chronicle of the author's personal development, or a projection of it, and how this may resonate with readers.

Impact covers the work's influence on the creators' careers, publishing houses, the medium of graphic novels itself, and literature in general. The section also analyzes the impact of the creation of new characters or series. Of focus is the critical reception of the work or series and whether it was atypical for its historical period.

Bibliography lists secondary print sources for further study and examination, annotated to assist readers in evaluating focus and usefulness.

APPENDIXES AND OTHER SPECIAL FEATURES

Special features help to further distinguish this reference series from other works on graphic novels. This includes appendixes listing major graphic novel awards and a general bibliography. These resources are complimented by a timeline discussing significant events and influential graphic novel predecessors which spans the ancient world through the Middle Ages and the Renaissance to the present. Another key feature of the essays in this publication is a biographical sidebar on an author or illustrator related to the work profiled. Additionally, the three-volume set features over 250 pictures, including full-page images and panels from the actual work. Four indexes round out the set, illustrating the breadth of the reference work's coverage: Works by Publisher, Works by Author, Works by Artist, and a subject index.

ACKNOWLEDGMENTS

Many hands went into the creation of this work, and Salem Press is grateful for the effort of all involved. This includes the original contributors of these essays, whose names can be found at the end of each essay and in the "Contributors List" that follows the Introduction. Special mention must be paid to Lisa Schimmer, who played an invaluable role in shaping some of the reference content. Finally, we are indebted to our editors, Bart Beaty, Professor of English at the University of Calgary, and Stephen Weiner, Director of Maynard Public Library in Maynard, Massachusetts, for their advice in selecting works and their writing contributions. Both are published in the field of comics and graphic novels studies. Beaty is the author of *Fredric Wertham* and the Critique of Mass Culture, *Unpopular Culture: Transforming the European Comic Book in the 1990s*, and *David Cronenberg's "A History of Violence."* Weiner is the author or co-author of *The 101 Best Graphic Novels*, *Faster Than a Speeding Bullet: The Rise of the Graphic Novel*, *The Hellboy Companion*, *The Will Eisner Companion*, and *Using Graphic Novels in the Classroom*. Their efforts in making this resource a comprehensive and indispensible tool for students, researchers, and general readers alike is gratefully acknowledged.

INTRODUCTION

The factors that shaped the development of the graphic novel are diverse and multifaceted, but one thing is clear: without the intervention of the cartoonists who constituted the American underground in the 1960's, the graphic novel would not exist as it does today. While it is true that newspaper comic strip artists and comic book creators had produced many well-crafted works prior to the rise of the undergrounds, their efforts had been—with only very occasional exceptions—constrained by an industry that imagined comics as disposable entertainment for children. The publishing business that built comics into a global media phenomenon in the first half of the twentieth century placed far greater emphasis on profit than on artistry, churning out a seemingly endless stream of titles that copycatted the slightest successes. The underground artists, with their close connection to the burgeoning counterculture of the Vietnam War era, saw the form differently, as an outlet for personal and political expression where anything goes. These artists pushed comics toward places they had never been before, experimenting with form and content, and establishing an entirely new way to communicate thoughts, beliefs, and ideas.

Tied as it was to the youth movement of the 1960's, the underground comics—or comix—movement inevitably ran out of gas. Crackdowns on "head shops" by law enforcement and the atrophying of the alternative press led to diminishing opportunities for many artists to publish. An entire generation of talented creators drifted out of the scene, and a new one arose to take its place. Supported by the growing "direct market" of comic book shops around the world, independent comics production ramped up at the end of the 1970s. Distinguished from Marvel Comics and DC Comics, the two largest publishers of mainstream superhero and adventure titles like *The Amazing Spider-Man* and *Superman*, these independent artists and publishers pursued non-traditional genres and styles, catering to the interests of a well-developed comic book fandom. Independent, or alternative, comics were sometimes a hybrid of the underground and mainstream traditions, offering fantasy and adventure comics with some of the adult sensibility that had characterized comix. Over time, alternative and independent comics developed their own genres and traditions including autobiography, historical fiction, and off-the-wall humor.

The graphic novel tradition developed globally in fits and starts. In the 1980s and 1990s, the preferred method for presenting independent comics work was the serial comic book. Legendary series of that era—*Love and Rockets* by the Hernandez Brothers, *Eightball* by Dan Clowes, *Yummy Fur* by Chester Brown—often included a number of short pieces in addition to ongoing serials. Only after completion would these serials be collected as graphic novels. The vast majority of the great graphic novels produced during this period, from Art Spiegelman's *Maus* to Alan Moore and Eddie Campbell's *From Hell*, originally appeared episodically over the course of many years, and even from several publishers. Today these works are read as single volumes, and the precarious history of their publication has been largely forgotten. When graphic novels emerged in the 2000s as an important genre in the bookstore market, stand-alone volumes became the norm and serialization gradually faded. Important and lengthy works like Craig Thompson's *Blankets* and David Mazzuchelli's *Asterios Polyp* came to readers as finished books, with the advantage of a firmer footing in existing literary traditions. The graphic novel had finally arrived.

This volume provides in-depth analyses of more than two hundred graphic novels, most of which were published over the course of the past fifty years. While the majority of titles come from the United States, important works from Europe and Asia have also been included. The survey of works is, of course, far from exhaustive, but in focusing on the key graphic novels that helped to shape the underground and independent comics movements we have sought to balance historical importance, cultural influence, and artistic excellence.

This critical survey features a keen attention to detail and a depth of analysis previously absent for works of this kind. Each entry provides a detailed history of the work that will allow readers to navigate the sometimes complex histories of serialization and collection of significant graphic novels, and helps to situate the works in the contexts in which they were created and first read. The plot of the work is the subject of an extensive précis, and, in instances where titles are comprised of multiple volumes, descriptions are offered that will allow readers to quickly navigate to the most pertinent parts of the work. As comics are both a visual and textual art form, significant attention is paid to the artistic style that defines the graphic novel, including drawing style, page layout, and overall design. The themes of the work are encapsulated and considered in depth, and its historical impact is assessed. Each entry ends with recommendations of related entries and a bibliography of important essays and interviews pertaining to the work.

The pages that follow tell the story of the maturing of an entire art form, as comics evolved beyond the repetitive gags of the daily newspaper strip and simple escapist fantasies of four-color superhero comic books. Over the course of the past quarter century, graphic novels have emerged as one of our most compelling art forms. The unique combination of text and image has added new dimensions to storytelling traditions, engaging readers around the world with deeply felt creations that rival the accomplishments of the best poets and novelists working today. For generations, the work of cartoonists, comics artists, and graphic novelists was derided as inconsequential popular entertainment intended for an unsophisticated audience. This volume corrects that erroneous understanding, highlighting, as it does, the incredible diversity that has come to define the contemporary graphic novel. We can only hope that in revealing the rich and dynamic history of an art form that has been too long misunderstood this volume will inspire new generations of readers and students to engage with these incredibly powerful works.

CONTRIBUTORS

Karley Adney
ITT Technical Institute

Maaheen Ahmed
Jacobs University

Linda Alkana
California State University, Long Beach

Ted Anderson
Golden Valley, MN

Stephen Aubrey
Brooklyn College

Bart Beaty
University of Calgary

David A. Berona
Plymouth State University

Adam Bessie
Diablo Valley College

Kyle Bishop
Southern Utah University

Arnold Blumberg
University of Baltimore

Ben Bolling
University of North Carolina, Chapel Hill

Bernadette Bosky
Olympiad Academia

Jenn Brandt
University of Rhode Island

Jacob Brogan
Cornell University

Brian Chappell
Catholic University of America

Daniel Clark
Cedarville University

Brian Cogan
Molloy College

Terry Cole
LaGuardia Community College (CUNY)

Joseph Darowski
Michigan State University

Anita Price Davis
Converse College

Joanna Davis-McElligatt
University of Louisiana, Lafayette

Gail de Vos
University of Alberta

J. Andrew Deman
University of Waterloo

Joseph Dewey
University of Pittsburgh

Christophe Dony
University of Liège

Damian Duffy
University of Illinois at Urbana-Champaign

Lance Eaton
Emerson College

Jack Ewing
Boise, ID

Lydia Ferguson
Clemson University

Theresa Fine-Pawsey
Durham Technical Community College

Rachel Frier
Rockville, MD

Christopher Funkhouser
New Jersey Institute of Technology

Jean-Paul Gabilliet
University of Bordeaux

Elizabeth Galoozis
Bentley University

Margaret Galvan
CUNY Graduate Center

Charles Gramlich
Xavier University of Louisiana

Bettina Grassmann
Concordia University

Joshua Grasso
East Central University

Diana Green
Minneapolis College of Art and Design

Robert Greenberger
Fairfield, CT

Marla Harris
Winchester, MA

Darren Harris-Fain
Auburn University, Montgomery

Benjamin Harvey
Mississippi State University

Forrest C. Helvie
Norwalk Community College

KaaVonia Hinton-Johnson
Old Dominion University

Bob Hodges
University of Mississippi

Susan Honeyman
University of Nebraska, Kearney

David Huxley
Manchester Metropolitan University

Marcy R. Isabella
University of Rhode Island

Patrick D. Johnson
Washington State University

Matt Jones
University of Toronto

Sam Julian
Mountain View, CA

Catherine Kasper
University of Texas at San Antonio

Susan Kirtley
University of Massachusetts, Lowell

Sean Kleefeld
Liberty Township, OH

Thomas Knowlton
Mid-Manhattan Library

Frederik Byrn Kohlert
University of Montreal

Mona Kratzert
Saddleback College Library

Martha Kuhlman
Bryant University

Kathryn Kulpa
University of Rhode Island

Celeste Lempke
University of Nebraska, Kearney

Andrew Lesk
University of Toronto

Hector Fernandez L'Hoeste
Georgia State University

Anna Thompson Lohmeyer
University of Nebraska, Kearney

Bernadette Flynn Low
Community College of Baltimore County, Dundalk

June Madeley
University of New Brunswick, Saint John

Bridget Marshall
University of Massachusetts, Lowell

Michelle Martinez
Sam Houston State University

Greg Matthews
Washington State University Libraries

Bob Matuozzi
Washington State University

Roxanne McDonald
Wilmot, NH

Hannah Means-Shannon
Georgian Court University

Marie-Jade Menni
Concordia University

Julia Meyers
Duquesne University

P. Andrew Miller
Northern Kentucky University

Kari Neely
Middle Tennessee State University

John Nizalowski
Mesa State College

Markus Oppolzer
University of Salzburg

Sam Otterbourg
University of North Carolina, Greensboro

Shannon Oxley
University of Leeds

Marco Pellitteri
London Metropolitan University

Michael Penkas
Chicago, IL

Katharine Polak
University of Cincinnati

Barbara Postema
Ryerson University

Lyndsey Raney
Texas A&M University, College Station

Matt Reingold
York University

Debora J. Richey
California State University, Fullerton

Dore Ripley
Diablo Valley College

Dorothy Dodge Robbins
Louisiana Tech University

Scott Robins
Toronto Public Library

Eddie Robson
Lancaster, UK

Lawrence Howard Rodman
Washington, D.C.

Theresa N. Rojas
Ohio State University

Joseph Romito
University of Pennsylvania

Derek Royal
Philip Roth Studies

Lara Saguisag
Rutgers University, Camden

Wayne Allen Sallee
Burbank, IL

Katherine Sanger
Dickinson, TX

Cord Scott
Loyola University Chicago

David Serchay
Broward County Library System

Richard Shivener
Northern Kentucky University

David Sims
Pennsylvania College of Technology

Kalervo Sinervo
Montreal, Quebec

Shannon Skelton
University of Wisconsin, Madison

Cristine Soliz
Fort Valley State University

Adam Spry
Columbia University

Eric Sterling
Auburn University, Montgomery

Benjamin Stevens
Bard College

Roger Stilling
Appalachian State University

Ryan Stryffeler
Western Nevada College

Shaun Vigil
Harvard University

Shawncey Webb
Taylor University

Janet Weber
Tigard Public Library

Stephen Weiner
Maynard Public Library

Britt White
University at Buffalo (SUNY)

Snow Wildsmith
Mooresville, NC

Joseph Willis
Southern Utah University

Wayne Wise
Chatham University

Frederick Wright
Ursuline College

CRITICAL SURVEY
OF GRAPHIC NOVELS

INDEPENDENTS AND
UNDERGROUND CLASSICS

A

A.D.: *New Orleans After the Deluge*

Author: Neufeld, Josh
Artist: Josh Neufeld (illustrator)
Publisher: Pantheon Books
First serial publication: 2007-2008
First book publication: 2009

Publication History

In 2006, Jeff Newelt, comics editor for the online magazine *Smith*, read a self-published book by Josh Neufeld titled *Katrina Came Calling*. The book centered on Neufeld's volunteer work with the Red Cross in Biloxi, Mississippi, after Hurricane Katrina. Newelt approached Neufeld about telling the story of Katrina and New Orleans in comic format for *Smith* magazine. *A.D.: New Orleans After the Deluge* was serialized as a Web comic from January, 2007, through August, 2008. The online version also included podcasts, videos, and a blog. In 2008, Pantheon Books offered to publish a book version, for which Neufeld expanded the work. He also changed some characters' names and altered other minor details, partly in response to feedback on the Web comic. A hardcover version was published by Pantheon in 2009 and became a *New York Times* best seller. This was followed by a larger-format paperback version, also released by Pantheon in 2009. The print and Web comics are virtually identical except for three characters' names, though only the print version is discussed below.

Plot

Hurricane Katrina struck the Mississippi Gulf coast on August 29, 2005. New Orleans experienced severe winds and then flooded as levees broke. *A.D.: New Orleans After the Deluge* tells of seven real people from New Orleans as they experience the storm's approach, the storm itself or the exodus to avoid it, and the aftermath. The book is divided into five parts: "The Storm,"

A.D.: New Orleans After the Deluge. (Courtesy of Pantheon Books)

"The City," "The Flood," "The Diaspora," and "The Return."

"The Storm" provides an overview of the storm and the days before, beginning August 22, 2005, with clear skies in the Gulf of Mexico, and ending August 31, 2005, with New Orleans devastated and flooded. Images reveal the wind's power as it tears roofs from buildings and pushes a Biloxi casino inland. There is no dialogue. Only a few people, including a floating body, are seen.

"The City" begins August 20, 2005, and introduces the seven main characters: Leo and Michelle, the Doctor, Kwame, Abbas and his friend Darnell, and Denise. All are aware of Katrina's approach but know that the city has been spared many times by hurricanes. However, the mayor of New Orleans calls for an evacuation. Leo and Michelle leave, as do Kwame and his family. Abbas's family evacuates, but Abbas stays to protect his store with the help of Darnell. Denise joins her mother at Memorial Baptist Hospital (Ochsner Baptist Medical Center), where her mother works. The Doctor stays in the city and has a "hurricane party" at his French Quarter home. Denise finds pandemonium at the hospital and returns to her home. The storm worsens, and Denise panics as her house is torn apart. The Doctor manages well, and Abbas and Darnell are battered but safe. Evacuees watching the news realize that the cleanup will take days. As the storm passes, though, most believe the worst is over.

Part 3, "The Flood," begins August 29, 2005. Katrina has passed inland, and the skies are clear over New Orleans. However, levees have collapsed, and the city, which is shaped like a bowl, begins to flood. Abbas and Darnell move to the rooftops to escape the trash- and sewage-filled floodwaters. Denise and her family are taken to the New Orleans convention center, which is horribly overcrowded. Almost no drinking water is available. Denise finds that gang members are keeping order and bringing in water and food taken from local stores. In the relatively dry French Quarter, some bars remain open, though without electricity. The evacuees begin making long-term plans for relocating. Leo and Michelle take refuge with Leo's parents, while Kwame begins to attend high school in California.

In "The Diaspora," the waters have receded and the New Orleans population has been largely evacuated and scattered. Many remain in Houston, Texas, where Abbas finds his family. Denise and her family settle in Baton Rouge, Louisiana. Leo and Michelle return temporarily but find their belongings destroyed; Leo saves only one comic from his massive collection. Kwame finishes high school in California and then enrolls in an Ohio college. Only the Doctor stays in New Orleans.

In "The Return," people returning to New Orleans find a different city. Leo and Michelle are constantly reminded of their losses and feel angry with those who refuse to return and rebuild. Their story ends happily, however, when people start sending Leo replacements for his lost comics. Abbas reopens his store but recognizes the setbacks his business has experienced. Denise finds a job in New Orleans but is aware that many have not returned and perhaps never will.

Characters

- *Denise*, one of seven primary protagonists, is an African American woman with short hair and glasses. Her family has lived in New Orleans for six generations. She has a master's degree in guidance and counseling but is unemployed when Hurricane Katrina hits. She shares an apartment in the Central City neighborhood with her mother, her niece, and her niece's daughter. Her mother works as a surgical technician at Memorial Baptist Hospital. Denise does not evacuate during Katrina and experiences the horrific conditions firsthand.

- *Leo*, a protagonist, is a white male with a beard and glasses. A New Orleans native in his twenties, he edits the independent local music magazine *AntiGravity*. He is an avid comics collector. He lives in the Mid-City neighborhood with Michelle. He evacuates but is committed to the city and returns afterward to reestablish his life.

- *Michelle*, a protagonist, is a white female with short, dark hair. Like Leo, with whom she lives, she is in her twenties and was raised in New Orleans. She works as a gymnastics instructor and a nightclub waitress at TwiRoPa, which closes permanently after Katrina. She evacuates but returns afterward.

- *Abbas* (*Hamid* in the Web comic), a protagonist, is an Iranian man with dark hair, a mustache, and a short beard. He is married, with two children, and lives in Metairie, a suburb of New Orleans. He has lived in the New Orleans area for years and runs a convenience store in the Uptown neighborhood. His family evacuates, but Abbas stays to protect his store and experiences the horrendous flooding.

- *Darnell* (*Mansell* in the Web comic), a protagonist, is an African American man with a bald head. Darnell is curious about hurricanes and weathers the storm with Abbas, his friend. He becomes ill during the story.

- *Kwame* (*Kevin* in the Web comic), a protagonist, is an African American teenager with short, dark hair and a trim mustache and beard. He lives in New Orleans East, which is primarily suburban in appearance. His father is a minister. Kwame evacuates and experiences the displacement faced by many former residents of New Orleans.

- *Doctor Brobson*, a.k.a. *The Doctor*, a protagonist, is an older white male with glasses. He is a medical doctor living in the French Quarter of New Orleans. Knowing that his home has withstood previous hurricanes, the Doctor remains and holds a "hurricane party." He observes the hurricane's aftermath in the French Quarter.

Artistic Style

Both the Web comic and print editions begin with panoramic views of the approaching storm. There is no dialogue, only captions indicating places and dates. People are shown only at long range. The horror is depersonalized, contrasting with the intense personalization of suffering shown later. Characters are the focus in the rest of the work. Backgrounds often have little detail and are sometimes dispensed with altogether. However, depicted backgrounds are realistic and

A.D.: New Orleans After the Deluge. (Courtesy of Pantheon Books)

accurate, as Neufeld worked from photographs or from information supplied by the characters.

The art style is minimalist and owes much to the European "clear-line" drawing style pioneered by Hergé (Georges Prosper Remi), the Belgian comics artist who created *The Adventures of Tintin*. In this style, individual lines have uniform importance. No hatching is used, and contrast is downplayed. Strong colors and illuminated shadows are accompanied by realistic backgrounds. Another of Neufeld's influences is Joe Sacco, who modifies the clear-line technique in his black-and-white comic book work. *A.D.* has the detail of a black-and-white comic, although selective coloration adds much to the story. Sacco also does detailed background research and focuses on human interest stories with larger political ramifications, and his influence in these areas is evident in *A.D.*

In keeping with this clear, simple art style and focus on human stories, Neufeld minimizes the number of lines he uses and accentuates his pencil work with freehand inking. He uses images, such as a Spider-Man action figure floating facedown in a bathtub, to foreshadow coming events. A varying color scheme sets the mood. The prehurricane period is marked by bright oranges and yellows, but the colors shift to purple and yellow-green as fear builds and people evacuate. The storm is depicted in watery blue-greens, while the storm's aftermath is shown with a reddish or sickly yellow-green tint.

Themes

The primary theme of *A.D.* is loss. Neufeld addresses this at the level of individuals, of New Orleans communities, and of the entire city. For the people depicted in the comic, losses include homes, important personal belongings, and livelihoods. Most powerful is the loss of safety and peace of mind. This is poignantly illustrated when Denise's mother resists getting new furniture because she does not want to have "more to lose."

Survival and rebirth are also important themes. Individuals such as Denise, Abbas, and Darnell survive the hurricane itself but pay a physical and psychological toll. Darnell temporarily loses his good health. Though he reopens his store, Abbas remarks that he "lost three years." Denise puts it even more personally

---

Josh Neufeld

Breaking into comics with a series of self-published minicomics and anthology pieces (many of which have been collected in *A Few Perfect Hours and Other Stories from Southeast Asia & Central Europe*), Josh Neufeld is one of the leading exponents of contemporary comics journalism. He is best known for his graphic novel *A.D.: New Orleans After the Deluge*, which was a *New York Times* best seller, based on the time he spent as a Red Cross volunteer in Biloxi, Mississippi, after Hurricane Katrina in 2005. In 2011, he collaborated with journalist Brooke Gladstone on *The Influencing Machine*, a comics essay about the role of news media in shaping popular opinion. Neufeld's comics are characterized by their commitment to everyday reality, and to telling stories about people who are caught up in events beyond their control. His visuals are influenced by the clear-line style, but he tends to use more dramatic close-ups and innovative angles in his drawings than do the classic practitioners of that style.

---

when she says that part of her "was swept away in that hurricane." Even evacuees, such as Leo, lose parts of their personal histories that cannot be replaced.

However, these losses do not prevent rebirth. Abbas does reopen his store. Kwame's family returns to rebuild their home, their church, and their spiritual community. Strangers replace Leo's comics. Denise, unemployed before Katrina, obtains a job and returns to New Orleans. Businesses and cultural centers have closed and the city's population has plummeted, but new opportunities also arise.

Impact

Since the 1960's, underground "comix," such as those produced by Robert Crumb, have shown that comic book-style material could feature adult subject matter and attract sophisticated audiences. This trend began to enter the mainstream in the 1980's. Although *A.D.* does not contain graphic sex or violence, as do many comix and comix-influenced works, it is a literate story that confronts adult issues and adult themes. There is an undercurrent, especially in Denise's story, of criticism of the government's handling of Hurricane Katrina. Thus, the book fits well into the modern comic book period. Some critics have specifically linked Neufeld's work to comix pioneer Crumb, and Neufeld invites the link himself when discussing his influences. He even uses the word "comix" on his Web site to describe his work.

As a Web comic, *A.D.* was widely recognized, including on National Public Radio (NPR), as a work of journalistic excellence. *Newsweek*, and newspapers such as the *New Orleans Times-Picayune*, the *Atlanta Journal-Constitution*, the *Toronto Star*, the *Los Angeles Times*, and *USA Today*, lauded *A.D.* for capturing the pain of the Katrina experience. The hardcover was reviewed favorably in many of the same venues, as well as in the *Wall Street Journal*. *Word Balloon* placed it among the top ten graphic novels of 2009. It was a Salon.com "Critic's Pick" for 2009 and was listed as one of 2009's Top Books by *Mother Jones* magazine. Neil Gaiman included an excerpt in *The Best American Comics 2010*.

Charles Gramlich

Further Reading

Johnson, Mat, and Simon Gane. *Dark Rain: A New Orleans Story* (2010).

Spiegelman, Art. *Maus: A Survivor's Tale* (1986, 1991).

Bibliography

Gustines, George Gene. "Graphic Memories of Katrina's Ordeal." *The New York Times*, August 23, 2009, p. C1.

_____. "Hurricane Katrina: An Illustrated Story of Survival." Interview by Linda Wertheimer. National Public Radio, September 3, 2009. http://www.npr.org/templates/story/story.php?storyId=112506242.

Neufeld, Josh. "Post-Katrina Depicted in Comic Strips." Interview by Farai Chideya. National Public Radio, August 24, 2007. http://www.npr.org/templates/story/story.php?storyId=13928549.

See also: *Maus: A Survivor's Tale; Burma Chronicles*

ADVENTURES OF LUTHER ARKWRIGHT, THE

Author: Talbot, Bryan
Artist: Bryan Talbot (illustrator)
Publisher: Dark Horse Comics
First serial publication: 1978
First book publication: 1997

Publication History

The outlet for Bryan Talbot's work was alternative even for the British science-fiction comics audience. As a point of comparison, the magazine *2000 AD* and its spin-offs were widely distributed, but Galaxy Media, Talbot's original publisher for *The Adventures of Luther Arkwright*, was far less accessible. That circumstance, however, might well have provided the autonomy necessary to create such an intentionally innovative work.

The Adventures of Luther Arkwright started as a serial; its initial installment was featured in the alternative science-fiction title *Near Myths* (1978), issues 1-6, in Britain. All subsequent publications were by British companies until the series was released by Dark Horse Comics. In 1982, a revised and expanded version appeared in the comic publication *Pssst!*, issues 1-5. From 1987 to 1989, the story was serialized over the course of nine issues for Valkyrie Press, which released the complete series in a set of three books. The nine-issue limited series was released through Dark Horse Comics in 1990. A trade paperback edition was published by Dark Horse Comics in 1997. Another trade paperback appeared in 2008.

Plot

In its basic conceptual approach, Talbot's initial work on *The Adventures of Luther Arkwright* was linked to the aesthetics of the politically engaged "new wave" of fantastic British literature (from the late 1950's and early 1960's). This mode may be roughly characterized as an amalgam of psychedelic visual and textual intensity and content informed by savage social commentary.

The action takes place within a grand multiverse; existence itself is composed of an infinite number of

Adventures of Luther Arkwright. (Courtesy of Dark Horse Comics)

parallel Earths, in which conflict and tribulation seem to be the norm. The main flow of events is based in an alternative-reality variant of British history, although the epic scenario jumps to sites throughout Old World Europe and the former Soviet Union. Accordingly, the story's presentation is essentially nonlinear, featuring cumulatively revealed, even impressionistic, plotting. Narrative devices, such as the presence of a narrator and flashbacks, are also woven into the metacontinuity.

Of the multitude of possible Earths, the technologically advanced parallel "zero-zero" exists in harmonious exception to the near-universal human struggle, and its agents enforce zero-zero's objectives throughout the other parallels. Among these agents, only the mystically adept "übermensch" Luther Arkwright possesses the ability to pass between parallels at will. Another exceptional warrior, Rose Wylde, Arkwright's assistant and lover, exists in duplicate form throughout the parallels and can communicate with her other selves.

The London of the novel is a hellhole, in ruins as a result of that particular parallel's extended variation on the English Civil Wars; the country is under Cromwellian rule. The Royalists, revolutionaries under King Charles, oppose this ruling class. While Oliver Cromwell's forces are as ironfisted as they are decadent, their power is not absolute. A malevolent, covert force, the Disruptors, has been manipulating events across parallels and throughout history. Arkwright pits himself against both Cromwell's fascist regime and the Disruptor overlords.

What follows is an intellectually vital spectacle, a showcase for one visual crescendo after another, in which political intrigues, enacted against a backdrop of Old World ceremonial architecture, erupt in hellacious battles.

Arkwright, in his role of reformer, is a remorselessly effective killing machine, becomes a captive, and is then martyred and resurrected. Throughout this work, the reader witnesses his recurring transcendence beyond the confines of the material plane. Moreover, overlain references to Western art history, British history, and mysticism comprise a multilayered allegory on human conflict and the acquisition and misuse of power. This is all on behalf of the questionable cause of a humanity destined to fall somewhat short of redemption.

Characters

- *Luther Arkwright*, the protagonist, is not governed by limitations of time or space; he is "the next stage of human evolution." His motivation appears to be beyond considerations of mere heroism. As a supreme being, he essentially acts to defend the balance of existence itself. It is noted that Arkwright's only personal allegiance is to his women, of whom Rose is his one true emotional connection.

- *Rose Wylde* is parallel zero-zero's field operations section leader; her incarnations are active across multiple parallels (up to seven points at once). Rose exemplifies the inspired woman warrior and is embroiled in a multiparallel conflict characterized on either side by ineffectual or corrupt male leaders.

- *Nathaniel Cromwell*, the antagonist, is a descendant of the Cromwell family and, thus, high lord protector of England. His degenerate private behaviors suggest inbreeding, or at least something equally unholy. His perversity, particularly a nasty streak in regards to women, is a trait passed on to his rampaging Puritan troops.

- *Harry Fairfax* is a major supporting player. He is a sixteenth-century-style throwback, a Royalist operative, and a guttersnipe with a natural gift for vulgarity. He is a good man in a battle and a comic foil for Arkwright, being as earthbound as Arkwright is ethereal. By the end of the novel, he represents the success of the revolution and the ascendance of the common man to the ruling class.

- *Octobriana* is a somewhat bestial woman warrior, a sexually aggressive Ukrainian freedom fighter in league with Arkwright in the struggle against the Disruptors. As is fitting for a graphic novel dealing with alternative histories, she is a previously established character from early 1970's cult comic strips, here appropriated by Talbot.

- *Hiram Kowolsky* is the United Colonies' war artist and a foreign correspondent for *The New Amsterdam Herald*, reporting as a neutral observer, though in hiding because of the danger of the assignment and Cromwell's expulsion of the press. As a journalist, and in interaction with Arkwright, he contextualizes the narrative of events and is engaged in drafting history as it is being made.

- *Princess Anne*, later *Queen Anne*, is to become the ultimate post-Restoration ruler of England and the leader her brother Charles, pretender to the throne, could never have been. She is the third of Arkwright's women and the mother of his twins, born during the novel's cataclysmic final battle at Nasby Circus.

Artistic Style

Talbot employs a meticulous, primarily crosshatched pen-and-ink style for the majority of his illustrations. His rendering and characterization indicate a concern for realism, providing the reader with readily identifiable characters. Some of the key players, notably Rose, are recognizable in their multiple parallel incarnations. The art is in black and white, even to the point of appearing to be composed on scratchboard (an illustration medium featuring a black field, from which white line work must be scratched away with a stylus) and is designed to not be colored but to lend the proceedings a bleak aspect.

Other techniques, such as what appears to have originally been wash but has since been gradated with computer assistance, have been used to indicate flashbacks and cosmic activity fields.

Apart from the role that the book's faithful renditions of historical artwork and architecture play, visual design is used to support characterization. For example, Cromwell's regime considers representational art, such as official portraiture, to be idolatry. They prefer nonrepresentational op-art canvases, which lend an interesting aspect to the set decoration.

Talbot consciously evokes earlier illustrative styles, particularly works from England's history. His hatching is meant to be read as engraving and, to the extent possible, recall printmakers such as William Hogarth, thus borrowing from some of the antique power for the

Adventures of Luther Arkwright. (Courtesy of Dark Horse Comics)

informed reader who might be able to place such an association. In any case, Talbot's artifacts and particular stylistic quotes provide just such a sophisticated platform for his intensive visual storytelling.

Themes

The misuse of power features strongly in the plot. The set pieces, so reminiscent of epic war films, might actually be a distraction from that point. There is more depth to the book's thesis, however. At the least, the narrative carries multiple meanings.

From the beginning of the graphic novel, with the destruction of the Crystal Palace and, with it, the Bayeux tapestry, Talbot employs a dizzying number of cultural associations. The Crystal Palace, the chief architectural wonder at the 1851 Great Exhibition in London, stands for Britain's supremacy as a mercantile center at the peak of the Industrial Revolution. However, its glamour obscured those who might elsewhere be caught in the gears of progress. Blowing it up, as in Talbot's treatment, is tantamount to striking a blow against the class system itself. Likewise, the Bayeux tapestry pulls double duty here. It is a touchstone in the history of sequential art, but, for the sake of the novel, it also represents the universality of violent conflict, another human constant.

Another setting is Karl Marx's tomb, another indication of class consciousness. Does Luther Arkwright, in his perfect messianic mode, represent a force for the liberation of the common man? A parallel can be drawn between Talbot's representation and the time in which he lived, specifically during the era of Margaret Thatcher, prime minister of England from 1979 to 1990, which was a time of popular disenchantment.

Impact

The movement toward socially and politically conscious science fiction was spearheaded by science-fiction writers but influenced the creativity of the era in general, with observable effects on other media, such as comic books and rock music. This movement was both cosmic and grounded in reality, as seen in science-fiction writer Michael Moorcock's collaboration with space rockers Hawkwind, for example.

Moorcock and comics author Alan Moore share a commonality with Talbot in their quest to express the depths of London's mysticism. Talbot has woven supernatural intrigue into the fabric of *The Adventures of Luther Arkwright*.

Having emerged from the underground press, Talbot contributed to the narrative visual-art segment of this new wave. In the epilogue of Valkyrie Press's *Arkwright* editions, he declares that he is striving for a new vocabulary and framework with which to create an uncharacteristically adult, multitextured tale.

Lawrence Howard Rodman

Further Reading

Moorcock, Michael, and Walter Simonson. *Michael Moorcock's Elric: The Making of a Sorcerer* (2007).

Moore, Alan, and Eddie Campbell. *From Hell* (1989-1996).

Wagner, John, and Brian Bolland. *Judge Dredd: Featuring Judge Death* (2001).

Bibliography

Groenwegen, David. "Royals Amok." *The Comics Journal* 218 (December, 1999): 31.

Sabin, Roger. *Comics, Comix, and Graphic Novels: A History of Comic Art*. London: Phaidon Press, 1996.

Talbot, Bryan. *The Adventures of Luther Arkwright*. Milwaukie, Ore.: Dark Horse Books, 2007.

Tong, Ng Suat. "Flopsy, Mopsy, Cotton-tail, and Helen." *The Comics Journal*, no. 1777 (May, 1995): 50-52.

See also: *From Hell; Alice in Sunderland; Zot!*

ADVENTURES OF TINTIN, THE

Author: Hergé

Artist: Hergé (illustrator)

Publisher: Casterman (French); Little, Brown (English)

First serial publication: *Les Aventures de Tintin*, 1929-1976

First book publication: 1930-1976 (English translation, 1958-1991)

Publication History

Belgian comics writer Hergé, born Georges Prosper Remi, created Tintin in 1929 for *Le Petit Vingtième* (*The Little Twentieth*), the children's supplement of *Le Vingtième Siècle* (*The Twentieth Century*), a right-wing Catholic newspaper. At the suggestion of Father Norbert Wallez, the newspaper's managing editor, Tintin's first assignment was to expose the horrors of Soviet Russia; thus, *Tintin in the Land of the Soviets* premiered, first as a black-and-white strip in *Le Petit Vingtième* and next in a newspaper-funded book format. *Le Petit Vingtième* would run Tintin until 1940, but in 1934, beginning with *Cigars of the Pharaoh*, Belgian publisher Casterman took over the book versions and would print all Tintin books thereafter. In 1935, while working on *The Blue Lotus*, Hergé assumed full artistic control of the series.

When Germany invaded Belgium in 1940 and *Le Petit Vingtième* ceased publication, Hergé found a home for Tintin in *Le Soir*, a Nazi-backed Belgium daily. In 1942, Casterman began publishing new Tintin volumes in color and republishing color versions of all the black-and-white volumes.

After Belgium was liberated in 1944, writers who had collaborated with the Nazis were banned from publishing, and this included Hergé, who was halfway through writing *The Seven Crystal Balls*. Two years later, this ban was lifted from Hergé, and he began *Le Journal de Tintin* (*Tintin Magazine*). *Le Journal de Tintin* and Casterman would continue publishing the series right through the last Tintin adventure, *Tintin and the Picaros*, in 1976. During this time, many volumes underwent extensive revisions to update their

(Gamma-Rapho via Getty Images)

Hergé

Born Georges Prosper Remi, the Belgian creator known to the world as Hergé found international acclaim with his series of comics for children about the boy reporter Tintin. His clean-line, cartoony style and sense of wordplay proved a perfect balance to the globe-trotting, action-packed adventures of the title character, which dealt with everything from mystic artifacts to a trip to the moon. Tintin's adventures have remained in print for an all-ages audience to this day.

imagery and rework racially insensitive depictions of non-European races.

When Hergé died in 1983, he was one of the world's most revered and influential cartoonists. In 2007, a century after Hergé's birth, an estimated 200 million copies of Tintin books had sold worldwide.

Plot

The Adventures of Tintin relates the adventures of Tintin, a young Belgian reporter who journeys across the planet with his dog Snowy, untangling plots and conspiracies. Though the series' characters and events are fictional, they are often based on real places and events.

In Hergé's first book, *Tintin in the Land of the Soviets*, Tintin heads for Russia to expose the harsh conditions behind the Communist Party's upbeat propaganda. Next, Tintin's newspaper sends him to the Belgian Congo, where he foils American mobster Al Capone's scheme to control the diamond trade. Tintin then travels to the United States, where he encounters American Indians and takes out Chicago's notorious gangsters.

In *Cigars of the Pharaoh*, Hergé introduces detectives Thomson and Thompson, who, believing Tintin is a drug kingpin, pursue him across south-central Asia. After a series of wild exploits across Egypt and the Red Sea basin, including a brush with notorious gun-runner Captain Allan, Tintin lands in India, where he learns of the drug-smuggling organization responsible for his travails. In *The Blue Lotus*, Tintin travels on to China and goes up against the corrupt head of the Japanese occupational authority, Mr. Mitsuhirato, who is in league with Roberto Rastapopoulos, the drug-smugglers' ringleader.

After returning home, Tintin learns of a mystery involving a stolen South American idol and journeys to San Theodoros, a fictional Latin American country, in search of it. There, Tintin serendipitously becomes a colonel in the regiment of General Alcazar.

In *The Black Island*, Thomson and Thompson accuse Tintin of another crime he did not commit, and he is once again forced to flee. Tintin reaches Scotland and ends up on the Black Island, a hiding place for international counterfeiters led by the evil Doctor Müller. After having the counterfeiters arrested, Tintin is lured to Syldavia, a fictional eastern European country. Soon after, foreign agents steal the scepter of Ottokar, without which the Syldavian king cannot rule. After meeting renowned Milanese opera diva Bianca Castafiore, Tintin returns the scepter, thereby foiling an elaborate conspiracy to bring down the Syldavian

government and allow a takeover by neighboring Borduria, another fictional land.

The Crab with the Golden Claws introduces Captain Haddock, who is so drunk that he is unaware that his cargo hold is filled with Captain Allan's opium. Tintin and Haddock escape the ship in a lifeboat, and after many adventures on the high seas and in the desert, they capture Allan's entire gang.

In *The Shooting Star*, a meteorite with mysterious powers falls into the Arctic Ocean, and Tintin joins the European expedition racing to find it.

The two-part adventure of *The Secret of the Unicorn* and *Red Rackham's Treasure* follows. Tintin buys Haddock a model replica of the ship his ancestor Sir Francis Haddock lost to the pirate Red Rackham, whose treasure sank. Tintin and Haddock set sail to retrieve the treasure, bringing a stowaway, the hearing-impaired inventor Cuthbert Calculus. They unsuccessfully attempt to use Calculus's shark-shaped submarine in their treasure hunt. Heading home, they buy Marlinspike Hall, where they find the treasure had lain hidden all along.

Next, an expedition to the Incan ruins of Peru and Bolivia triumphantly returns to Europe, but one by one, its members succumb to an Incan curse. Soon after, Calculus is kidnapped and taken to Peru, and Tintin and Haddock rush to his rescue. After a dangerous trek across the Peruvian Andes, the would-be rescuers find themselves prisoners of an Incan tribe that survived Spanish colonization unchanged. Only the timely arrival of an eclipse saves the trio from being sacrificed, and Tintin convinces the Incan priests to lift the curse from the expedition members.

Meanwhile, Europe is plunged into crisis when petroleum starts to explode mysteriously. Tintin subsequently travels to Arabia, where he discovers that the nefarious Doctor Müller is tainting oil wells with an explosive chemical.

Back in Marlinspike, Calculus sends Tintin and Haddock a telegram that leads them to Syldavia, where they help build a spaceship that takes them to the moon. Plagued by treachery and sabotage, the team barely makes it back to Earth alive.

In *The Calculus Affair*, nearly deaf scientist Calculus develops a weapon using sound as a destructive force, and the Syldavians and Bordurians take turns kidnapping him to learn its secrets. Tintin and Haddock put an end to these schemes by rescuing Calculus.

Tintin and Haddock then travel to Arabia to help their friend Emir Ben Kalish Ezab, who has been deposed in a coup. This, they discover, is merely a cover for a flourishing slave trade involving their nemesis Rastapopoulos.

Next, Tintin learns that his old friend Chang was aboard an airliner that crashed in the Himalayas and sets out to rescue him. With Chang safe, Tintin returns to Marlinspike Hall, where he solves the case of Castafiore's stolen emerald.

In *Flight 714*, Rastapopoulos and Allan kidnap Tintin and his multimillionaire traveling companion while they are on vacation.

In his last adventure, *Tintin and the Picaros*, Tintin helps General Alcazar reclaim the presidency of San Theodoros from General Tapioca and saves the imprisoned Castafiore and Thompson and Thompson from execution.

Volumes

- *Tintin au pays des Soviets* (1930; *Tintin in the Land of the Soviets*, 1989).
- *Tintin au Congo* (1931; *Tintin in the Congo*, 1991).
- *Tintin en Amérique* (1932; *Tintin in America*, 1978).
- *Les Cigares du pharaon* (1934; *The Cigars of the Pharaoh*, 1971).
- *Le Lotus bleu* (1936; *The Blue Lotus*, 1983).
- *L'Oreille cassée* (1937; *The Broken Ear*, 1975).
- *L'Île noire* (1938; *The Black Island*, 1966).
- *Le Sceptre d'Ottokar* (1939; *King Ottokar's Sceptre*, 1958).
- *Le Crabe aux pinces d'or* (1941; *The Crab with the Golden Claws*, 1958).
- *L'Étoile mystérieuse* (1942; *The Shooting Star*, 1961).
- *Le Secret de la licorne* (1943; *The Secret of the Unicorn*, 1959).
- *Le Trésor de Rackham le Rouge* (1944; *Red Rackham's Treasure*, 1959).

- *Les Sept Boules de cristal* (1948; *The Seven Crystal Balls*, 1963).
- *Le Temple du soleil* (1949; *Prisoners of the Sun*, 1962).
- *Tintin au pays de l'or noir* (1950; *Land of Black Gold*, 1972).
- *Objectif Lune* (1953; *Destination Moon*, 1959).
- *On a marché sur la lune* (1954; *Explorers on the Moon*, 1959).
- *L'Affaire Tournesol* (1956; *The Calculus Affair*, 1960).
- *Coke en stock* (1958; *The Red Sea Sharks*, 1960).
- *Tintin au Tibet* (1960; *Tintin in Tibet*, 1962).
- *Les Bijoux de la Castafiore* (1963; *The Castafiore Emerald*, 1963).
- *Vol 714 pour Sydney* (1968; *Flight 714*, 1968).
- *Tintin et les Picaros* (1976; *Tintin and the Picaros*, 1976).

Characters

- *Tintin*, the protagonist, is a blond-haired teenaged reporter with a characteristic quiff. His inquisitiveness and concern for humanity entangle him in dangerous and complex situations, which he overcomes with ingenuity and bravery.
- *Snowy*, a.k.a. *Milou*, a white fox terrier, is Tintin's constant companion and can talk to his master.
- *Thompson* and *Thompson*, a.k.a. *Dupont* and *Dupond*, are a pair of blundering detectives who dress in matching black suits and bowler hats and have equally bushy moustaches. Often jumping to hasty conclusions, they initially suspect Tintin of being a nefarious criminal but eventually trust Tintin and team up with him.
- *Roberto Rastapopoulos*, the series' chief villain, appears in five adventures, beginning with *Tintin in America*. This bald, large-nosed, monocle-wearing, cigar-smoking schemer uses his cover as a film tycoon to operate international crime rings, involving drug running, slave trading, and kidnapping.
- *Chang Chong-Chen* is a young Chinese boy with dark, parted hair. After Tintin saves him from drowning, he helps Tintin bring down the opium

gang in *The Blue Lotus*. Tintin rescues him later in *Tintin in Tibet*.

- *General Alcazar* is a Latin American with a strong chin, small mustache, and long nose who first appears as president of San Theodoros. Temperamental and headstrong, he leads a rebellion against his rival, General Tapioca.
- *Doctor J. W. Müller*, another of Tintin's nemeses, has an oval face, bald head, and thick black beard. He heads the counterfeiting racket in *The Black Island* and leads the effort to sabotage the world's oil supply in *Land of Black Gold*.
- *Bianca Castafiore*, an opera singer with a beak-like nose, a prominent chin, and curly blond hair, first appears on a Syldavian singing tour in *King Ottokar's Sceptre* and reappears in many of Tintin's adventures thereafter. Tintin restores her lost emerald in *The Castafiore Emerald*.
- *Captain Haddock* is a middle-aged ship's captain with a full black beard and scruffy black hair who sports a blue turtleneck, black pants, and a black sailor's cap. Stubborn, headstrong, and alcoholic, he is deeply faithful to Tintin. He first appears in *The Crab with the Golden Claws* and becomes Tintin's constant companion.
- *Cuthbert Calculus*, a.k.a. *Tryphon Tournesol*, is short, bespectacled man with tufts of curly hair on a bald head and goatee. A brilliant but sensitive inventor, he mishears most statements because he is partially deaf. After helping Tintin and Haddock in *Red Rackham's Treasure*, he joins them at Marlinspike.

Artistic Style

Hergé developed a distinct graphic style called "clear line," which features sharply defined lines, a lack of shadows, and classical concepts of proportion and perspective. Every panel possesses a remarkable level of detail precisely copied from original sources. Also, Hergé, among the first European cartoonists to use speech balloons, made them perfect rectangles with neat, draftsman-quality lettering. When color entered Hergé's art in 1942, he used it to deepen his clear-line style, utilizing bright primary colors and light pastels to create an orderly, familiar world.

Tintin's realism also derived from Hergé's meticulous research. He kept an extensive file of clippings and photographs to be used in Tintin's adventures. When his files did not yield the right image, Hergé would peruse nearby libraries to find the necessary visual texts or visit museums to sketch objects for a particular panel.

In *The Calculus Affair*, Hergé's clear line reached its apex. Many panels in earlier volumes have solid color backdrops or simple walls with minimal embellishment. By *The Calculus Affair*, both the foreground and background of nearly every panel are brimming with detail. By this time, Hergé was also stretching the boundaries of his meticulous layout. For example, *Explorers on the Moon* uses many nearly full-page or page-length horizontal panels to express the vastness of space, and *The Red Sea Sharks* borders on the surreal when a diver's thoughts appear in the bubbles from his diving mask.

In 1942, Hergé hired assistants, Alice Devos and Edgar P. Jacobs, leading to the formation of Hergé Studios in 1950. By 1953, Hergé Studios had fifteen members, who together made *Tintin* an internationally popular graphic series.

Themes

In the beginning, Hergé presented a fundamentally orderly world threatened by forces of corruption and chaos in which, through the efforts of brave, resourceful, and compassionate heroes like Tintin, the chaos is diminished and good triumphs over evil. However, as the twentieth century's geopolitical situation evolved, Hergé's sense of what constituted order and chaos and good and evil changed.

From 1929 to 1940, during Tintin's run in *Le Petit Vingtième*, managing editor Wallez controlled the content of the earliest strips. Thus, the first four volumes present strict Catholic, right-wing values. *Tintin in the Land of the Soviets* is a blistering critique of Russian communism; *Tintin in the Congo* is an unapologetic paean to European colonization of Africa; *Tintin in America* exposes the United States as a materialist nation steeped in sin, greed, and racism; and *Cigars of the Pharaoh* condemns the illegal drug trade.

When Hergé took artistic control of the comic with *The Blue Lotus*, the story's focus shifted. He chose Tintin's destination for the first time and conducted the exhaustive research that became the series' hallmark. For this volume, he relied a great deal on close friend and art student Chang Chong-Chen, who became the basis for Tintin's dear companion in the series and helped redefine the forces of evil Tintin confronts. These forces were no longer solely the opponents of Catholicism but included the more defined political threat of the Japanese occupation in China. This represented Hergé's first open critique of fascism, a theme he took up again in *The Black Island* and *King Ottokar's Sceptre*.

Under Nazi occupation, Hergé avoided antifascist themes, and *Tintin* became more of a pure adventure series, with the only restoration of order coming from Tintin's friends gaining their just rewards. After the war, *Tintin* made its only foray into the paranormal with the *The Seven Crystal Balls* and *Prisoners of the Sun*.

Starting with *Land of Black Gold* in 1950, Hergé's work directly tackled Cold War tensions, often presenting each side of the conflict as mirroring the darkness of the other. This is best exemplified in *The Calculus Affair*, wherein both Syldavia, representing the West, and Borduria, representing the East, try to acquire Calculus's secret sonic weapon.

For a time, Hergé again left the political arena with the straightforward rescue story of *Tintin in Tibet*, the comic mystery of *The Castafiore Emerald*, and the return of Tintin's longtime nemesis Rastapopoulos in *Flight 714*. However, in Tintin's final adventure, Hergé returns to a political theme but with an uncharacteristically cynical twist. In this adventure, Tintin helps General Alcazar retake the presidency of San Theodoros, which ultimately makes no difference to the nation: The nation's dire poverty remains unchanged, and the police have simply switched from the fascist style uniforms of Augusto Pinochet's Chile to the socialist garb of Fidel Castro's Cuba. Nevertheless, the series' overarching theme remains: Although villains in the world will enslave the weak, steal from the righteous, and disrupt the natural order, there are brave, tireless heroes like Tintin to help restore world order.

Impact

When *Tintin* appeared in Belgium in 1929, the strip was an immediate success. The charming illustrations, sense of adventure, assertion of traditional values, and appealing characters made the series a national triumph. Then, as the book editions began to appear in 1930, *Tintin*'s fame spread to France. After World War II, *Tintin*'s fame and influence exploded. Editions began appearing across Europe and the world and became wildly successful in every major market except the United States. An entire genre of adventure comics emerged in the late 1940's directly from *Tintin* and Hergé's clear-line technique. Among these were *Bob et Bobette* (known as *Willy and Wanda* in the United States), *Félix*, *Guy Lefranc*, and *Les Quatre As*. Later French and Belgian comics (*les bandes dessinées*) influenced by Hergé's clear-line approach include *Blake and Mortimer*, *Alix*, *Hassan et Kaddour*, *Cori le Moussaillon*, *Gaspard de la Nuit*, and *Ray Banana*.

Tintin's influence goes well beyond comics. Novelists Frederic Tuten and Françoise Sagan have written novels based on Tintin. Philosopher Michel Serres, anthropologist Claude Lévi-Strauss, and literary critic Jean-Marie Apostolidès have examined *Tintin* as a signifier of twentieth-century European culture. French president Charles de Gaulle once called Tintin his only international rival, and the fourteenth Dalai Lama presented Tintin with the Truth of Light Award.

Films

The Broken Ear. Directed by Karel Van Millegham and Anne-Marie Ullmann. Belvision, 1956. This semi-animated film was the first Tintin movie to debut on Belgian television.

The Crab with the Golden Claws. Directed by Wilfried Bouchery and Cle Keerbergen-Malines Belg. Wilfried Bouchery et Cie, 1947. This animated film adaptation used marionettes and featured the voices of A. Charles and R. Chrus.

Destination Moon. Directed by Yvan Szücs. Belvision, 1959. This full-length feature film was made for French and Belgian television.

King Ottokar's Sceptre. Directed by Karel Van Millegham and Anne-Marie Ullmann. Belvision, 1956.

This film was the second semianimated Tintin movie to debut on Belgian television.

Tintin and the Blue Oranges. Directed by Philippe Condroyer. Alliance de Production, 1964. This live-action film starring Jean-Pierre Talbot as Tintin and Jean Bouise as Captain Haddock follows an original plot rather than any published Tintin books.

Tintin and the Golden Fleece. Directed by Jean-Jacques Vierne. Alliance de Production, 1961. This live-film adaptation starring Jean-Pierre Talbot as Tintin and Georges Wilson as Captain Haddock followed an original script rather than any published Tintin stories. Hergé felt this film and *Tintin and the Blue Oranges* failed to capture the spirit of Tintin, and he refused to place his name on the Casterman publications they inspired.

Tintin and the Lake of Sharks. Directed by Raymond Leblanc. Belvision and Dargaud Films, 1972. This animated film starring Jacques Careuil as the voice of Tintin and Claude Bertrand as Haddock is not based on any Hergé volumes.

Tintin and the Temple of the Sun. Directed by Eddie Lateste. Belvision, 1969. This animated adaptation featured the voices of Philippe Ogouz as Tintin and Claude Bertrand as Haddock. Based on *The Seven Crystal Balls* and *Prisoners of the Sun*, this film condenses the narrative and invents several new characters. Though Hergé worked on this adaptation, he was disappointed with it.

Television Series

Hergé's Adventures of Tintin. Directed by Ray Goossens. Télé Hachette and Belvision, 1958-1962. This series starred Georges Poujouly as the voice of Tintin and Jean Clarieux as Haddock. Plots were sometimes drastically changed; Hergé disavowed the series.

The New Adventures of Tintin. Directed by Stephen Bernasconi. Ellipse and Nelvana, 1991-1992. This series starring Colin O'Meara as the voice of Tintin and David Fox as Haddock in the English version generally follows Hergé's original adventures but differs in their order.

John Nizalowski

Further Reading

Goscinny, René, and Albert Uderzo. *Asterix* (1969-1975).

Jacobs, Edgar P., and Bob de Moor. *Blake and Mortimer* (1946-).

Vandersteen, Willy. *Bob and Bobette* (1945-).

Bibliography

Apostolidès, Jean-Marie. *The Metamorphosis of Tintin, or, Tintin for Adults*. Translated by Jocelyn Hoy. Stanford, Calif.: Stanford University Press, 2010.

Assouline, Pierre. *Hergé: The Man Who Created Tintin*. Translated by Charles Ruas. New York: Oxford University Press, 2009.

McCarthy, Tom. *Tintin and the Secret of Literature*. London: Granta Books, 2006.

Screech, Matthew. "Constructing the Franco-Belgian Hero: Hergé's *Aventures de Tintin*." In *Masters of the Ninth Art: Bandes Dessinées and Franco-Belgian Identity*. Liverpool, England: Liverpool University Press, 2005.

Skilling, Pierre. "The Good Government According to Tintin: Long Live Old Europe?" In *Comics as Philosophy*, edited by Jeff McLaughlin. Jackson: University Press of Mississippi, 2005.

See also: *Asterix; A.D.: New Orleans After the Deluge*

AGE OF BRONZE: THE STORY OF THE TROJAN WAR

Author: Shanower, Eric
Artist: Eric Shanower (illustrator)
Publisher: Image Comics
First serial publication: 1998-
First book publication: 2001-

Publication History

Age of Bronze is published serially as a black-and-white comic book by Image Comics and has been collected in hardcover and trade paperback formats. Serial publication began in November, 1998. Two special issues—*Age of Bronze: Special* (1999), which tells the story of the house of Atreus, and *Age of Bronze: Behind the Scenes* (2002)—have also been published. Publication of collected volumes began in July, 2001; creator Eric Shanower plans to release a total of seven volumes. The comic has been translated into French, Italian, Spanish, Polish, Croatian, and Indonesian.

Shanower was first inspired to use the comics medium to retell the Trojan War in 1991 after listening to an audio version of Barbara W. Tuchman's book *The March of Folly: From Troy to Vietnam* (1985); Tuchman's second chapter covers the Trojan War, focusing on the episode of the Trojan horse.

Shanower's idea was to synthesize every version he could find of the Trojan War story. Thus, his research includes versions of the Trojan War in literature, including ancient and more recent poetry; music, including opera, and the visual arts; architectural and other archaeological remains from the Bronze Age Mediterranean area; and classical scholarship. He decided to have the characters speak "plain, unadorned English" in order to communicate more clearly what he sees as the fascinating interpersonal aspects of the story.

Plot

Out of all of the versions, scholarly investigations, and artistic interpretations of the Trojan War, Shanower's tells not only the general story of the war but also the stories of the political and especially interpersonal

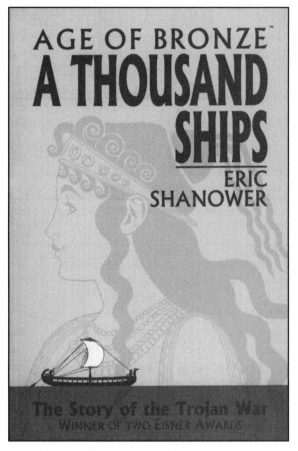

Age of Bronze: The Story of the Trojan War. (Courtesy of Image Comics)

actions leading up to and threaded through the war. The general story is well known: The Greek armies, having assembled as such for the first time, sail to and besiege the city of Troy in order to reverse or avenge the abduction of Helen, rightful wife of the Greek Menelaus, by Paris, prince of Troy. Part of *Age of Bronze*'s appeal is Shanower's depiction of these familiar events in exquisitely researched and drafted detail. The interest in the comic is also generated by its focus on interpersonal relations and actions. These human actions, and their underlying psychological motivations, are especially important in light of Shanower's decision to set his version of the story in a vision of the late Bronze

Age Mediterranean that aims at great historical accuracy; he purposely excludes the Greek gods and goddesses as characters.

The increasing military action, which is the story's most general plot, is enriched by many subplots. These intersecting plots may be conveniently broken down by volume. *A Thousand Ships*, whose title draws on perhaps the most famous line from Christopher Marlowe's *Doctor Faustus* (1604), focuses on Paris's discovery of his identity as a Trojan prince, his abduction of Helen,

the Greeks' discovery of her abduction, and the difficult assembly of their armies and fleet.

Age of Bronze: Sacrifice focuses on the Greek fleet's delays and difficulties in setting sail for Troy. A long final scene, more than one-quarter of the volume, shows the Greeks delayed by heavy winds. So that they may set sail, Agamemnon, as High King of the Achaeans, must fulfill a prophecy by Kalchas, priest of the Delphic oracle, by sacrificing his own daughter Iphigenia; this plot draws freely on ancient versions of

Age of Bronze: The Story of the Trojan War. (Courtesy of Image Comics)

Agamemnon's conflict with his wife and Iphigenia's mother, Klytemnestra.

The final scene culminates in Iphigenia quietly and propitiously giving herself up. Subplots include the deepening involvement of Odysseus, king of Ithaka and great speaker and strategist, with the Greeks' preparations; predictions by the Trojan prophet Kassandra that Troy is doomed as well as Priam's attempt to bolster Troy's defenses; and a deepening love between Achilles and Patroklus that eclipses Achilles' relationship with Deidamia.

Age of Bronze: Betrayal depicts the stepwise advance of the Greek fleet across the Aegean, focusing on landfall, battle, and celebratory feast on the island of Tenedos. Inspired by Achilles' martial valor and courage, the Greeks are successful in battle against the islanders. However, during a celebratory sacrifice, one Greek, Philoktetes, is bitten by the snake of the altar; his incessant cries so disturb his fellows that Odysseus is compelled to leave him on an island. This plot draws heavily on Sophocles' tragedy *Philoktētēs* (409 B.C.E.).

Five issues of the comic book (27-31) have been published serially but not collected into a volume. The primary plot point of these issues is the first battle between the Greeks and the Trojans and its effects on relationships between certain pairs and groups of characters. In that battle, Achilles and Hektor meet, and the Trojans are forced to retreat into the fortress. Relationships continue to develop, now distinctly shadowed by the war: For example, the wedding of Hektor and Andromache is interrupted by Kassandra's cries, signifying the arrival of the Greek armies; Helen is made to leave Troy so as to bear her second child away from the fighting; and Cressida, daughter of Kalchas, marries Troilus, a young prince of Troy, only to find herself involved in an exchange of prisoners of war engineered by her father. Forthcoming issues may be expected to continue telling the general story of the war while focusing on interpersonal relationships complicated by the war as well as on scenes made famous in various other versions.

Volumes

- *Age of Bronze: A Thousand Ships* (2001). Collects issues 1-9. A central theme is the fraught

relationship between individual desire and social, political, or otherwise collective duty; a related theme is the uneven distribution of power in a society, with no necessary correlation between access to power and virtuous action or wisdom.

- *Age of Bronze: Sacrifice* (2004). Collects issues 10-19. A main theme is the human cost of war, as even seemingly incidental and unwarlike individuals are caught up and irrevocably changed by the burgeoning war machine; a related theme is how human action is affected and sometimes limited by tradition.
- *Age of Bronze: Betrayal, Part One* (2007). Collects issues 20-26. A main theme is the "global" effects of a seemingly very "local" conflict, as the war between Greeks (the Achaeans) and the city-state of Troy affects not only their political and military allies but peaceful trading partners and other third parties.

Characters

- *Paris*, the Trojan prince (son of Hektor), is of noble build and features but is inexperienced in politics and battle. His rash abduction of Helen precipitates the war.
- *Helen* is the wife of Menelaus and later the wife of Paris. She is captivatingly beautiful and full of self-interest, seeming not to understand the gravity of the situation or her role in it.
- *Agamemnon* is great king of the Achaeans who assembles the Greek fleet and struggles to maintain control and morale over the years of preparation, journey, and battle.
- *Menelaus* is the brother of Agamemnon and Helen's first husband. He is eager for battle on her behalf and for his own wounded pride.
- *Priam* is the king of the Trojans and father to many princes and princesses. He is appropriately regal in his dealings on behalf of the city, alternately solicitous and uncompromising.
- *Hektor* is Priam's son and the greatest warrior of Troy. He faces Achilles in single combat.
- *Achilles*, son of Thetis and Peleus, is destined from an early age to a tragic choice between either a long life of peaceful obscurity or immortal

fame as the result of a life cut short in battle. Headstrong, proud, and the Achaeans' greatest warrior, he faces Hektor in single combat.

- *Odysseus*, king of Ithaka, is reluctant to join the Greek fleet. He serves as its greatest strategic and tactical advisor because of his good-natured cunning and convincing rhetoric.
- *Kassandra* is the daughter of Priam. Her prophetic abilities confine her to the palace and discomfit her family and city; she serves as a voice of foreboding and represents a missed opportunity for peace.
- *Iphigenia* is the daughter of Agamemnon and must be sacrificed so that he may fulfill his obligation to the gods and, thus, guarantee the Greek fleet a safe departure for Troy.

Artistic Style

Shanower is responsible for all of the series' art, including covers for issues and collected volumes. Color is reserved for covers, while interiors are entirely black and white. The style may be generally described as highly realistic, even "photorealistic." Characters, actions, and settings are almost all depicted at that same level of highest realism. Little space is given to superfluous fantastical imagery, which is limited to depicting things like characters' memories and some dreams or fantasies, as well as some mythological stories. Even less use is made of the sorts of imagery that may be considered traditional or conventional to comics or cartoons, although Shanower does use some traditional devices, including motion lines, onomatopoeia, and different thickness of line in fonts for speech at various volumes and emotional pitches.

More particularly, the style is clean and uncluttered. Shanower reports that his favorite artist is John R. Neill, who illustrated more than forty books set in the Land of Oz. Through Neill's work, a connection may be made to Winsor McCay (*Little Nemo in Slumberland*, 1907), especially in terms of proficient draftsmanship. Shanower is indeed an expert draftsman, meticulously realizing buildings and household goods; chariots and ships; landscape, including natural features and plants; and even animals.

The series' high realism has remained consistent over the years of publication. Within the framework of that consistent realism, Shanower achieves great dynamism in visual narrative. The dynamic range is great, from visually simple depictions involving few lines (an emotionally revealing close-up on a character's face, for example) to much busier depictions involving many shapes as if in motion (a visually chaotic battle scene, for example). Because of Shanower's clarity of line, even the busiest scenes are not confused but, rather, depict confusion.

The series is given narrative ebb and flow through such devices as careful selection of scenes, deliberate pacing, and framing of "shots," including paneling that varies according to the needs of the narrated moment. Some readers have found the pacing relatively slow; there is a lot of speech, but there is no narration within the story, only in front and back matter.

Themes

Perhaps the central theme of *Age of Bronze* is the fraught relationship between individual desire and collective duty. Similar to the ancient Greek epics

---

Eric Shanower

Breaking into the comics industry shortly after graduating from The Kubert School, Eric Shanower made his reputation in the 1980's and 1990's for his work on the Oz graphic novels, based on the work of L. Frank Baum. The five graphic novels, published by First Comics and Dark Horse Comics, were notable for sophisticated visuals that drew heavily on an aesthetic derived from classic children's books. Shanower is deeply connected to Baum's creation, having written an Oz novel (*The Giant Garden of Oz*) and a collection of short stories (*The Salt Sorcerer of Oz*), as well as collaborating on other Oz projects. In 1991 he began telling the story of the Trojan War as a graphic novel, releasing the first of a proposed seven volumes of *Age of Bronze*. In the three volumes that have been released to date, Shanower depicts Troy's absent gods and mythological figures, bringing a new level of realism to the mythological story. Shanower's clean lines and careful compositions have made him a greatly respected comics illustrator.

---

and tragedies that inspired the comics, Shanower explores how the smallest human actions and interpersonal relations are related to the large-scale events in human history, especially military action. Shanower distinguishes his version of the story by focusing not on a single hero but rather on many characters. Given that shifting focus, the status of any one character as a story's "hero" or protagonist becomes problematic. A central effect of Shanower's wide focus on so many characters, then, is to make ironic the importance accorded by tradition to any single character or even set of characters. In this way, the comic emphasizes that all characters are not merely fulfilling public roles but are people with inner lives.

Although many characters are made to suffer unwillingly as a result of decisions made by traditional heroes, all the characters are depicted as being in full possession of their capacities to think and to act. Their free will is affected not only by larger forces but also by their own personalities and changing moods.

Another central theme is a person's capacity to change. This realistic and modern psychological view distinguishes Shanower's version of the story from those of antiquity, in which characters are subject to emotional forces operating from the outside, including in the form of actions performed by the gods.

Impact

Age of Bronze is an ongoing publication; as a result, any impact is only beginning and, thus, hard to gauge. At the time of its first publication, it was a remarkable departure for Image Comics in content, style, and tone. More generally, it may be considered alongside a trend in comics to adapt classic or otherwise well-known works of literature; it is unclear whether the success of *Age of Bronze* has helped to spur an ongoing revival of interest in that trend. Issue 77 of the original U.S. run of *Classics Illustrated* (1941-1971) adapted the Iliad (c. 750 B.C.E.; English translation, 1611). *Age of Bronze* may also be related to an upswing of interest in Greek and Roman classics in the comics field, which began with Frank Miller's *300* (1998).

Age of Bronze has been received positively, not only by the comics industry and by the press but also in the more specialized market consisting of students and teachers of the classics. Attention paid to *Age of Bronze* by classicists encourages a consideration of the comic as part of "classical reception," less as influencing other works than as itself part of a broader, popular-culture trend toward the adaptation of classical material into various media and genres. From this perspective, *Age of Bronze* may be considered alongside adaptations of the classics not only into comics but also into motion pictures, such as *Troy* (2004) and *Alexander* (2004), and into television, such as *Rome* (2005-2007) and *Spartacus* (2010-).

Benjamin Stevens

Further Reading

Baum, L. Frank, and Eric Shanower. *Adventures in Oz* (2006).

Kanter, Albert. *Classics Illustrated* (1941-1971).

Otomo, Katsuhiro. *Akira* (1982-1990).

Willingham, Bill, et al. *Fables* (2002-).

Bibliography

Kanter, Albert. *Classics Illustrated*. New York: Gilberton, 1941-1971.

Shanower, Eric. "Twenty-First Century Troy." In *Classics and Comics*, edited by George Kovacs and C. W. Marshall. New York: Oxford University Press, 2011.

Sulprizio, Chiara. "*Eros* Conquers All: Sex and Love in Eric Shanower's *Age of Bronze*." In *Classics and Comics*, edited by George Kovacs and C. W. Marshall. New York: Oxford University Press, 2011.

See also: *The Cartoon History of the Universe; Maus: A Survivor's Tale; 300*

AGE OF REPTILES

Author: Delgado, Ricardo

Artist: Ricardo Delgado (illustrator); Jim Campbell (colorist); James Sinclair (colorist)

Publisher: Dark Horse Comics

First serial publication: 1993-2010

First book publication: 1996

Publication History

Dinosaurs rose significantly in popularity in the early 1990's, with James Gurney's illustrated book series *Dinotopia* and the 1993 premiere of the highly successful film *Jurassic Park*, directed by Steven Spielberg and based on the novel by Michael Crichton. In 1993, in the midst of this feverish public interest in dinosaurs, Dark Horse Comics released the first issue in the series *Age of Reptiles* by Ricardo Delgado, later noted for his storyboarding of films like *Species* (1995), *Strange Days* (1995), *Apollo 13* (1995), the *Matrix* series (1999 and 2003), *Elektra* (2005), and *X-Men Origins: Wolverine* (2009). His animation credits include work as the development artist for *WALL-E* (2008) and in visual development for *The Incredibles* (2004). Delgado traces his fascination with dinosaurs to such inspirations as the original *King Kong* (1933), the dinosaur exhibits at the Los Angeles Museum of Natural History, and artist Charles R. Knight's paintings of dinosaurs and other prehistoric animals.

The success of the first four issues of the *Age of Reptiles* resulted in the publication of a trade paperback, subtitled *Tribal Warfare*, in 1996. This was followed by a second collection of five issues, *The Hunt*, published as a trade paperback in 1997. A third collection, *The Journey*, was published in four issues in 2009-2010, but not released as a trade paperback. The *Age of Reptiles Omnibus*, which includes all three collections plus bonus material, was published in 2011.

Plot

Each collection features a different plot, but all generally revolve around the basic need of survival, which Delgado portrays via the wordless interactions of various anthropomorphized dinosaurs. *Tribal Warfare*

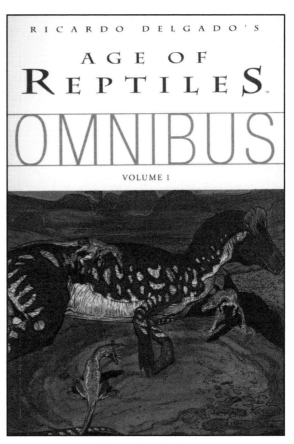

Age of Reptiles. (Courtesy of Dark Horse Comics)

tells the story of an ongoing battle between a family of tyrannosaurs and a gang of deinonychus, which are a type of raptor. After the deinonychus kill a sauropod called Ring Neck, a tyrannosaur called Blue Back frightens them off and takes the kill for himself. Snake Eye, a deinonychus, decides to assault Blue Back, but is not quick enough to escape his clenching jaws and is killed. The other deinonychus quickly flee, though two of the gang, Dark Eye and Leopard, discover where Blue Back is camped. After he and two infant tyrannosaurs fall asleep, Dark Eye and Leopard sneak inside, steal their eggs, and manage to escape Blue Back after he awakens. Blue Back plans his revenge on the deinonychus and waits until the gang is away hunting before he attacks the others in the tribe. When the gang returns home, they discover many of their tribe being ripped apart by Blue Back. Dark Eye manages to escape his wrath and later traps and kills a young tyrannosaur named Short Tail. Long Jaw, the father, is too late to save Short Tail and roars with grief and anger. In a final battle between the deinonychus and the tyrannosaurs, the side of the cliff they are fighting on shears off from the mountain during a storm, and all the dinosaurs except Long Jaw fall to their deaths. When Long Jaw returns to his cave, he is surprised to find a mammal called Proto eating the tribe's eggs.

In *The Hunt*, a young allosaur named Santo watches as ceratosaurs Big Nose, Two Nose, and Broken Nose kill his mother. After Santo escapes and grows into an adult, he is pursued by the same gang of ceratosaurs. Santo and the ceratosaurs survive an earthquake that flushes them into a lush land of water and vegetation. Subsequent subplots focus on battles among other dinosaurs, including a trio of flying dsungaripterus (pterosaurs) that chase a single criorhynchus (another type of pterosaur) through thick layers of clouds. In addition, natural disasters like violent thunderstorms and lightning, earthquakes, and tsunamis are as much of a threat to Santo's survival as the other dinosaurs. Santo survives a final battle with the ceratosaurs, but discovers another family of ceratosaurs hiding in the caves, posing a threat to his future safety.

In the third collection, *The Journey*, the encroachment of evolving birds and mammals on local resources leads to a mass exodus of land-bound dinosaurs, as they travel in search of a new home with adequate water and vegetation. This collection chronicles the struggle of a wide variety of dinosaurs to keep themselves alive in the most inhospitable conditions, while tyrannosaurs and other carnivores feed off the weak and dying. As the herds travel through an arid region, a pack of deinonychus, numbering in the hundreds, takes down and feasts on the massive body of a brontosaurus. After they reach fertile land, the migrating herds are crossing a deep river when they are attacked by hundreds of crocodiles, which kill many of the dinosaurs before they can make it to shore. A mother and her two young tyrannosaurs continue to follow the survivors and feed off any stragglers. The migration moves through the jungle and along a coastline, and when the young

Age of Reptiles. (Courtesy of Dark Horse Comics)

tyrannosaurs chase their prey too close to the water, a marine-dwelling plesiosaur attacks. The mother jumps into the water and engages in a lengthy and ferocious battle before she overpowers the plesiosaur, which escapes and swims out to sea. After many trials, the migrating dinosaurs finally discover a hospitable environment with food and water for the survivors. Apart from the lengthy battle between the plesiosaur and the tyrannosaurs, *The Journey* features no distinct characters; rather, the entire population of dinosaurs is the primary character at risk of extinction.

Volumes

- *Age of Reptiles: Tribal Warfare* (1996). Collects issues 1-4. Set in the Cretaceous period, this collection centers on a deadly battle between a family of tyrannosaurs and a tribe of deinonychus.

- *Age of Reptiles: The Hunt* (1997). Collects issues 1-5. In the Jurassic period, a lone allosaur flees from a pack of pursuing ceratosaurs before turning the tables and becoming the hunter.
- *Age of Reptiles: The Journey* (2009-2010). Collects issues 1-4. In the Cretaceous period, herds of dinosaurs migrate south to reach a more hospitable environment.
- *Age of Reptiles Omnibus* (2011). Collects all issues.

Characters

- *Blue Back* and *Long Jaw*, from *Age of Reptiles: Tribal Warfare*, are tyrannosaurs who try to protect their young and guard their eggs from the malicious deinonychus.
- *Snake Eye, Leopard, Dark Eye, Sina, Maya, One Claw, Quetzal,* and *Three Tooth*, from *Age of Reptiles: Tribal Warfare*, are a family of deinonychus who battle Blue Back and Long Jaw.
- *Proto*, from *Age of Reptiles: Tribal Warfare*, is a mammal, similar in appearance to a tarsier, who feasts on the last of the tyrannosaurs' eggs.
- *Santo*, from *Age of Reptiles: The Hunt*, is an allosaur who plans revenge on the ceratosaurs who killed his mother.
- *Chula*, from *Age of Reptiles: The Hunt*, is Santo's mother, who, despite her size, is overpowered and killed by a gang of ceratosaurs.
- *Big Nose, Broken Nose, Two Nose,* and *One Claw*, from *Age of Reptiles: The Hunt*, are the ceratosaurs who pursue Santo after killing his mother.
- *Oscura*, from *Age of Reptiles: The Hunt*, is Big Nose's mate, who guards her family of young ceratosaurs after Santo kills the last of the adults.
- A *mother tyrannosaur*, from *Age of Reptiles: The Journey*, engages in a fierce battle with a plesiosaur to protect her young.
- A *plesiosaur*, from *Age of Reptiles: The Journey*, attacks a pair of young tyrannosaurs near the edge of the water.

Artistic Style

Delgado is recognized for his extensive work in films, such as cinematic storyboarding, and this background is evident in the cinematic flow of action displayed in the series. He skillfully uses an assortment of panel sizes, including many long shots and panoramic two-page spreads, to present a prehistoric landscape, while close-ups and thumbnail panels within panels show simultaneous reactions of characters during unfolding events. For example, in a page-wide center panel in *Tribal Warfare*, two deinonychus sneak into the tyrannosaurs' cave while they are asleep and steal their eggs. Within this panel, Delgado places two vertical thumbnails. The top thumbnail is a close-up of a sleeping tyrannosaur that, in the lower thumbnail, awakens suddenly with a roar after hearing the intruders.

One challenge for Delgado is to provide the dinosaurs with distinct visual features in order to distinguish them from one another. He achieves this by using color markings, such as the blue stripes on the tyrannosaur named Blue Back. This individuality seems less important in *The Journey*, where the focus is on dinosaurs as a whole; accordingly, Delgado fills the majority of panels with numerous species of dinosaurs, moving the focus from the distinct to the general.

Delgado does not use any word balloons or narration and relies on facial expressions to display emotion; for example, he uses wide eyes to indicate surprise during an attack. Sound, from a roar of aggression to a cry for help, is indicated by thin, radiating red lines. Delgado uses simple directional lines to indicate motion, like a quick turn to catch prey, and a squiggle of his pen to imply frustration when the prey escapes the dinosaur's grasp.

Delgado's artwork depicts the dinosaurs with fine detail and in a wide range of colors. The majority of the panel backgrounds are presented in flat colors, and are sometimes completely white, which concentrates the reader's focus on the dinosaurs and the unfolding action. The panel borders are usually white, except in scenes that Delgado wishes to accentuate, such as the bloody intertribal battle of the raptors, where the borders are red instead. The use of color both in the cover art and on the page, especially in the many one- and two-page spreads, is the visual enticement to the majestic drama that unfolds in each collection.

Themes

Survival is the main theme in this series and is addressed from the perspectives of the individual dinosaur, the family or tribe, and ultimately the entirety of the population. Since the dinosaurs are given human characteristics, it is easy to extend this theme and others to the human world. Another theme, of unity and safety, is expressed clearly in the first two collections, in which the isolated individual is more at risk than one who is closely tied to a family or group. However, the violence among the dinosaurs, even within groups of the same species, prompts a question: If peaceful coexistence is impossible in the dinosaur world, should the reader assume the same of the human world?

In the last collection, *The Journey*, the motif of mass migration can readily be seen as applicable to the human world, in which one can see daily news reports about the growing displacement of refugees from war-torn countries. Developing this theme further, the example of the clash between the plesiosaur and the intruding tyrannosaur provides an analogy for the growing conflict between the population of a host country and unwelcome immigrants, especially during times of economic hardship. Delgado seems to ask, as environmental resources diminish, what impact will a growing population have on the human species as a whole? Will humans, like the various species of dinosaurs, find themselves part of a mass migration of different races and cultures, seeking and fighting over the dwindling resources left on Earth? When those resources vanish, will humans face extinction like the dinosaurs or rise above natural law and work together to sustain the species? Delgado offers hope: At the end of *The Journey*, the surviving dinosaurs reach a hospitable environment.

The *Age of Reptiles* series offers a distinct version of the prehistoric world without any words of explanation or narration, allowing readers the opportunity to visually interpret each savage battle and personally imagine the sound of crashing thunder in a jungle storm or the loud roars of a ravenous dinosaur as it rips apart its prey. Delgado's decision to provide dinosaurs

---

Ricardo Delgado

Coming from a background in Hollywood, where he worked as a storyboard artist and in the art department on a number of blockbusters including *Men in Black*, *Apollo 13*, and *The Incredibles*, Ricardo Delgado is best known in comics as the creator of *Age of Reptiles* for Dark Horse Comics. Launched in 1993, *Tribal Warfare* tells the story of a pack of deinonychus who seek revenge on a tyrannosaurus, while the sequel, *The Hunt*, tells the story of a dinosaur seeking revenge on the ceratosaurs who killed his mother. A third title, *The Journey*, depicts a migration of dinosaurs. Delgado's comics are celebrated for their visual intensity. He uses a large number of page-width panels that provide a cinematic feeling and his action scenes are dramatic and intensely gory. Delgado is also the author of two novels, *Sam Specter and the Book of Spells* and *Warhead*.

---

with human emotions connects the reader with the dinosaurs.

Delgado tackles themes such as the survival of a population in a world of environmental concerns, global warming, and shrinking resources. Despite these strong themes, there is a limit to the number of times interest can be prolonged with dinosaur battles and the predictable deadly results. The use of extended subplots and of several one- and two-page spreads in *The Hunt* breaks up the predictability; however, without a clear connection to the main plot, they serve as little more than intermissions. In addition, the last collection lacks an identifiable hero. While this retreat from character serves to foreground the common plight of dinosaurs as a whole, it also results in the loss of a strong personal connection, which is an essential element in the success of any series. A good example of this important personal connection with a character can be seen in *Gon* (1992-2002), a wordless comic series about dinosaurs by the Japanese artist Masashi Tanaka, the success of which rests entirely on the character development of the tiny tyrannosaur named Gon. Despite these limitations, however, the *Age of Reptiles* is a valuable resource not only in the wordless genre but also as an example of the recurrent and popular association of dinosaurs and comics.

Impact

Dinosaurs played an important role in early adventure comics, such as *Turok, Son of Stone* (1956-1982) and *The War That Time Forgot* (1960-1968). However, these classic comics always depicted humans mysteriously entering the world of dinosaurs. Delgado's comic series explores the world of the dinosaur only, without human interference, and displays the unfolding life-and-death situations from a fictionalized prehistoric world.

David A. Beronä

Further Reading

DuBois, Gaylord, et al. *Turok, Son of Stone* (1956-1982).

Schultz, Mark. *Cadillacs and Dinosaurs* (1989).

Tanaka, Masashi. *Gon* (1992-2002).

Bibliography

Delgado, Ricardo. Afterword to *Age of Reptiles: Tribal Warfare*. Milwaukie, Ore.: Dark Horse Comics, 1996.

Manning, Shaun. "Ricardo Delgado on *Age of Reptiles: The Journey*." Comic Book Resources, September 18, 2009. http://www.comicbookresources.com/?page=article&id=22978.

See also: *Xenozoic Tales*

AIRTIGHT GARAGE OF JERRY CORNELIUS

Author: Moebius

Artist: Moebius (illustrator)

Publisher: Les Humanoïdes Associés (French); Marvel Comics (English)

First serial publication: *Le Garage hérmetique de Jerry Cornelius*, 1976-1980 (English translation, 1993)

First book publication: 1979 (English translation, 1987)

Publication History

In France, *Le Garage hérmetique de Jerry Cornelius* was published in short episodes in *Métal Hurlant*, *France Soir*, and *Fluide Glacial* during a five-year time span. Creator Moebius, whose real name is Jean Giraud, worked on the series late at night, drawing strange stories for several hours before finally falling asleep. The next day, he would wake to find he had created stories and sequences without any logical sense, and he therefore tried to reconstruct them and establish a narrative. Jean-Pierre Dionnet, the editor in chief of *Métal Hurlant*, saw the drawings and asked Moebius to create a coherent plot and to continue and conclude the story. The collected edition of the series, titled *Le Major Fatal*, was published by Les Humanoïdes Associés in 1979.

In English, the work was first published in book format as *Moebius 3: The Airtight Garage* (1987). For this Marvel edition, the name "Jerry Cornelius" was changed to "Lewis Carnelian" in order to avoid copyright issues. "Jerry Cornelius" was a moniker introduced previously by writer Michael Moorcock, who had initially permitted any artist to use the name freely but later revoked such freedom of use.

Plot

One of the fundamental features of *Airtight Garage* is that it was drawn and written without a planned plot. The entire work is articulated in "acts," the events of which follow a chronological order. In the Leo constellation, there is a small, hollow asteroid in which a human, Major Grubert, has created the "airtight

Moebius

One of the legendary figures of French comics for more than a half century, Jean Giraud became an apprentice of the influential artist Jijé in 1961, collaborating on a *Jerry Spring* graphic novel. In 1962, with writer Jean-Michel Charlier, he created *Fort Navajo* for the comics magazine *Pilote*, and the character for whom he is best known, Lt. Blueberry. For his science-fiction work in *Hara-Kiri* and elsewhere, he adopted the pseudonym Moebius. His work under this name for *Métal Hurlant* included *The Incal* (with Alejandro Jodorowsky), *The Airtight Garage*, and *Arzach*. His work has been translated into English, and he also collaborated with writer Stan Lee on a *Silver Surfer* graphic novel. Giraud's contribution to the artistic style of French comics was immense. His western work was defined by its naturalism and realism, and also by its elegant use of a brush. His science-fiction and fantasy work is generally drawn with a pen and features exotic landscapes and scenes. Few artists in the history of comics have been as influential as Giraud.

garage" using twenty-three generator engines. This airtight garage consists of a variety of pocket worlds and contains three levels, created in different moments. The first level contains wild and little-populated worlds, the second level contains densely populated and technologically advanced worlds, and the third level is purely mechanical and contains the engines that have generated the worlds. It is possible to travel between worlds through the use of machines that transfer matter.

The levels and worlds of the airtight garage are home to a variety of humanoid and nonhumanoid, evolved and unevolved races and peoples such as the Bakalites, the Tar'Hai, the Triclos, the Exos, and others. The worlds contain sentient beings, bizarre animals, religious leaders, giant robots, androids, and even a sort of superhero. All acts focus on Jerry Cornelius and on a collective quest to find him.

From a starship in orbit around the asteroid, Major Grubert travels between the fantastic and science-fictional worlds in which the story is set in search of his old friend and former comrade, Jerry Cornelius. The airtight garage isolates the alien worlds contained within it from the "continuum," the open space. Many within the garage believe that Cornelius seeks to destroy the continuum, but he is truly protecting it from the Bakalites, a powerful mystical order that attempts to acquire and control it.

After several episodes featuring chases and explosions, the Bakalites' leader, the Nagual, kills Cornelius in the final confrontation. Major Grubert escapes into the continuum through a multidimensional door and enters the world of the reader, emerging in a Paris subway station.

Characters

- *Jerry Cornelius* (*Lewis Carnelian* in the Marvel publication) is a human for whom everyone in the airtight garage is searching. He first appears while driving a desert car toward the city of Armjourth, helped from a distance by a clumsy mechanical engineer, Barnier.

- *Major Grubert* is a human and former comrade of Jerry Cornelius whose starship, the Ciguri, orbits the asteroid that contains the airtight garage. He was born in 1958 in West Germany and worked as a journalist for the *Di-velt* (*Die Welt*). One day, he accidentally passed through the "Angkor trans-temporal circle," emerging in the nineteenth century, where he was instructed by a Brahman about the secrets of "space magic." While scouring deep space, he and Jerry Cornelius found the wreck of the Otra, the legendary starship of the Ancients, inside which he discovered the secret of immortality. His ultimate mission is to protect the garage, his creation, from the Bakalites.

- *The Bakalites* are members of a powerful religious order that seeks to conquer the garage.

- *Houm Jakin* is the master of a region of the airtight garage, the Carn Finehac. He travels to Bolzedura to find help in order to repair the "junction," which had been interrupted by the magic of the Bakalites.

- *Boaz* is a killer who lives on Syldain-Dolcignus, one of the worlds within the garage.

- *Samuel Mohad* is a spy sent by the officers of the Ciguri. Although Mohad is a human, the spy that is sent is a radio-driven android. The android, in turn, drives a giant robot named Star Billiard that is similar in appearance to the classic comics character the Phantom.

- *Malvina* is the fiancé of Major Grubert. She commands the Ciguri while Grubert is on missions in the airtight garage.

- *Yetchem the Archer* is an emissary of the Tar'Hai who believes that Jerry Cornelius and Major Grubert are threats to the peace and safety of his world. He and his people seek the airtight garage's independence.

- *Larc Dalxtré* is a soldier on the Ciguri who is sent into the garage by Malvina.

- *Graad* is a Triclo, a humanoid being with three horns on his head. He meets Major Grubert in Armjouth and helps him travel from the second level of the garage to the first and highest.

Artistic Style

Moebius's artistic style in *Airtight Garage* is one of the most representative ever used by the artist. This style is a somewhat eclectic mix, combining the clear-line style of Franco-Belgian comics, the eighteenth- and nineteenth-century tradition of xylographies, and the brushwork of American and European serial comics. Most evident when the art is examined in black and white, the lines drawn by Moebius are thin but perfectly refined in their modulation, and his use of hatching is significant.

Panels are usually rectangular in shape, and the pagination is quite regular, giving way to the drawings when necessary. Many individual panels depict large changes or actions, while, in contrast, seemingly simple actions may take many chapters to unfold. Moebius seems equally comfortable depicting massive scenes and miniscule detail, and later printings of the comic accent this artwork with strong colors. While his inventive style makes his influences difficult to trace,

Moebius seems to draw inspiration from the work of such artists as filmmaker Sergio Leone, in terms of his "far West" settings and the "cut" of certain panels and scenes; illustrator and comic artist Winsor McCay, for several elements of design, some perspectives, and the multidimensional games with panels; and painter René Magritte, for numerous surrealist atmospheres.

Themes

Airtight Garage has a relatively simple plot, the quest for a crucial character by several other characters within a strange and artificial world, and its fragmented narrative is not particularly conducive to thematic exploration within the context of the story. The true theme of *Airtight Garage* is an extranarrative metatheme of creation having to do with the ability of a great comics creator to fascinate readers with a story even when it was begun without any real purpose. In this sense, therefore, the comic calls attention to the idea that an exercise of style by an artist, featuring artistically elegant drawings, science-fiction and science-fantasy settings, and a mix of pseudohistorical sensibilities and aesthetic styles, can also create a compelling reading experience.

Impact

The artistic style, narrative atmosphere, and settings of *Airtight Garage* have made a significant impact on European comics, influencing not only auteur comics but also popular comics in France, Italy, and Spain. Moebius's work has also influenced that of several eastern European artists, especially Enki Bilal. In the United States, where the impact of *Airtight Garage* and European comics in general has been relatively limited, Moebius is better known for his Marvel limited series *Silver Surfer: Parable* (1988) and design work for such films as *Alien* (1979), *Tron* (1982), and *The Fifth Element* (1997). Nevertheless, Moebius has been cited as an influence by Geof Darrow, Frank Quitely, James Stokoe, and many other artists working in the U.S.

comics industry. An arc of *New X-Men* (2001-2004), illustrated by Quitely, features characters, scenes, and even panels in direct homage to *Airtight Garage*.

Marco Pellitteri

Further Reading

Druillet, Philippe. *Chaos: Lone Sloane* (2000).

Moebius, and Alejandro Jodorowsky. *The Incal: Classic Collection* (2011).

Moebius, Jean-Marc Lofficier, and Randy Lofficier. *The Man from the Ciguri* (1996).

Bibliography

Boucher, Geoff. "Moebius on His Art, Fading Eyesight, and Legend: 'I Am Like a Unicorn.'" *Los Angeles Times Hero Complex*, April 2, 2011. http://herocomplex.latimes.com/2011/04/02/moebius-on-his-art-fading-eyesight-and-legend-i-am-like-a-unicorn.

Brothers, David. "Jean 'Moebius' Giraud: Your Favorite Artist's Favorite Artist." *Comics Alliance*, April 22, 2011. http://comicsalliance.com/2011/04/22/jean-moebius-giraud-art.

Frauenfelder, Mark. "Moebius." *Wired*, 2009. http://wired.com/wired/archive/2.01/moebius.html.

Seneca, Matt. "Your Monday Panel 15: *Le garage hérmetique de Jerry Cornelius* episode 26 (1988), page 1, panel 1. Drawn by Moebius." *Death to the Universe*, June 7, 2010. http://deathtotheuniverse.blogspot.com/2010/06/your-monday-panel-15.html.

Witzke, Sean. "Emma Peel Sessions 50: Because It's Everything, Though Everything Was Never the Deal." *Supervillain*, February 20, 2011, http://supervillain.wordpress.com/2011/02/20/emma-peel-sessions-50-because-its-everything-though-everything-was-never-the-deal.

See also: *The Adventures of Luther Arkwright; Asterix; The Adventures of Tintin*

ALAN'S WAR: THE MEMORIES OF G.I. ALAN COPE

Author: Guibert, Emmanuel

Artist: Emmanuel Guibert (illustrator); Céline Merrien (letterer)

Publisher: L'Association (French), First Second (English)

First serial publication: *La Guerre d'Alan*, 2000

First book publication: 2000 (English translation, 2008)

Publication History

Alan's War: The Memories of G.I. Alan Cope was originally published in France under the titles *La Guerre d'Alan* (2000), *La Guerre d'Alan 2* (2002), and *La Guerre d'Alan 3* (2008) by L'Association, an independent French comics publisher. L'Association started serializing the project in *Lapin*, its in-house magazine. The American English-language edition was published by First Second in 2008 and translated by Kathryn Pulver.

As he explains in his preface, Emmanuel Guibert met former American G.I. Alan Cope in 1994. Cope was a sixty-nine-year-old retired American living in France; Guibert, thirty, was a French illustrator and graphic novel writer. They agreed to form a partnership in which Cope would tell stories of his life and Guibert would illustrate them, starting a five-year collaboration that ended with Cope's death in 1999. Their project would be a two-part biographical work. The first installment, *Alan's War: The Memories of G.I. Alan Cope*, covers Cope's life from his induction into the military to his death in France; the second, *Alan's Youth*, was planned for later publication and would cover Cope's early days in Pasadena, California, during the Great Depression.

Plot

Cope is working as a newspaper delivery boy in California when Pearl Harbor is bombed in 1941. Drafted into military service, he trains at Fort Knox, Kentucky, where he becomes part of a tank crew, is almost killed in a training accident, and learns radio operations.

(Getty Images)

Emmanuel Guibert

The versatile French artist Emmanuel Guibert works in a wide variety of styles and genres. For children, he's created the silly, cartoony style of the *Sardine in Outer Space* series; for adult readers, he's done a number of more serious, realistic works, including collaborations with a veteran of World War II and a reporter who worked with Doctors Without Borders on a mission. Guibert's artistic style ranges from clean lines to more elaborate visuals employing such techniques as ink wash.

While war wages elsewhere, he teaches radio and discovers classical music in the G.I. recreation hall.

Cope lands in France in 1945 on his twentieth birthday. Although he does not see action, he receives a Purple Heart after falling out of a barn loft.

He remembers destruction and chaos, including two months spent in a Normandy farmhouse because the Army misplaced the weapons and vehicles, speeding through villages in a tank and trying to clip the plaster off the buildings, destroying a farmer's fence to build a fire, and even looting—he steals a watch, though he is not proud of it.

During General George S. Patton's push to Plzeň (Pilsen), Cope witnesses German soldiers being captured and shot by Russian officers. He meets a woman who was once a pianist and now washes clothes to survive. *Alan's War* is full of such encounters; some are fleeting, as with the displaced Slavic Gypsies who share freshly cooked rabbit and a séance with him, or the nine-year-old German orphan whom he wants to adopt.

As a chaplain's assistant in Bavaria at war's end, Cope learns to ski and gets a private tour of Ludwig II's castle and Richard Strauss's house. He meets Gerhart Muench, a German composer and pianist, and his wife, Vera, an American poet. They had been part of a circle of writers, artists, and intellectuals living in Paris and Italy before the war who had subsequently been trapped in Europe once it began. Cope also meets Gisela, a pretty young woman who regrets that Nazism failed.

Following his demobilization, Cope decides to stay in Germany. After six months spent hiking and biking through the Austrian mountains, however, he returns home to his girlfriend Patzi, a life-changing decision he soon regrets. Cope starts training as a Baptist minister while working at a variety of jobs; he tutors spoiled rich children and takes Mexican migrant children out to the countryside. His college friends include the very wealthy, the thoughtful, and the lost. Some are religious, some atheist, and all work at figuring out their lives.

An emotional experience in the California redwood forest leads Cope to ask philosophical and religious questions. The natural world is more real to him than 1950's California. He quits his ministry course, breaks off his engagement, and decides to return to Europe.

In the meantime, Gerhart and Vera contact him, having arrived in the United States penniless. With their artistic and literary connections, they expose Cope to the wealth of Hollywood, but he is unsettled by it, with his memories of wartime Europe still fresh.

The last part of the book recounts Cope's life in France. Cope is vague about these years. He takes classes in pottery, starts a family, and becomes an army civilian employee. His government job gives him time to read, and this starts his next stage of life as a self-proclaimed philosopher, reviewing his life and trying to make sense of it and the choices he has made.

Cope died before Guibert finished their collaboration. Guibert inserts himself into the narrative to relate that Cope left the title of the book to him, and he aptly chose to call it *Alan's War*.

Characters

- *Alan Cope*, the protagonist, recounts his memories of his experiences in World War II Europe and postwar California to illustrator Emmanuel Guibert.
- *Emmanuel Guibert* is not part of the story, but his presence is felt as he edits Cope's words, illustrates Cope's experiences and reminiscences, and appears in the final pages of the book after Cope's death.
- *Gerhart Muench* is a German composer and pianist whom Cope knows in Europe and later in the United States. Drafted into the German army in World War II, he would not play piano for the Oberkommando der Wehrmacht (German High Command). In California, he introduces Cope to a world of wealth and fame that contrasts sharply with the world Cope saw in war-torn Europe.
- *Vera Muench* is an American poet from Boston who stays in Germany with Gerhart, her husband, during the war. Cope loses contact with Vera and her husband, and finding them again plays an important part in his reflections on life.
- *Patzi* is Cope's fiancé. They get engaged by mail during the war. He returns from Europe with the intention of marrying her, which he later considers to be one of his biggest mistakes. Although Cope and Patzi never marry, she becomes a symbol of the conventions that Cope finds constricting.

- *Chaplain Captain Plimey Elliot* was among the first Americans to arrive at a concentration camp near Munich. He offers Cope a job as chaplain's assistant in postwar Austria, mainly because Cope can play the organ. His influence, in part, causes Cope to choose to enter the ministry upon his return to California.

Artistic Style

Guibert uses a distinctive ink-and-water technique for this black-and-white illustrated work. His images capture the uniqueness of individual faces, the darkness and confusion of the war, and the majesty of the California redwoods. The drawings are supplemented occasionally with reproductions of photographs, letters, documents, and even a musical score. Although Guibert's drawing style ranges from abstract to near-photographic realism, it always remains recognizably the work of one individual, lending coherence to Cope's story and melding the narrative with the images. The panels vary in size and are used to good effect, especially in giving a sense of place and of nature. Guibert includes a thirteen-page photo album at the end of the book, featuring snapshots of Cope and his friends, which gives further authority and authenticity to Guibert's interpretation of Cope's life in *Alan's War*.

Guibert's use of the first-person narrative for Cope's story rings true and dominates the work. By using the first person and remaining true to his subject's own words, Guibert captures an innocence of time and place, expressed by one person, which is refreshing in the larger context of the many interpretations of the war that are often defined by modern sensibilities and language. Word balloons are used effectively for the other characters. First Second Books made available on YouTube two brief companion clips, "Drawing with Water: Making the Art for *Alan's War*" and "A Song for Alan, Performed by Emmanuel Guibert." The latter, a song Cope taught Guibert, serves to make Cope as accessible through the Internet as Guibert's illustrations make him in this graphic novel.

Themes

Like most good autobiographies and biographies, *Alan's War* transcends just one person's story. Although the surface theme is about war and its consequences, the dominant theme is more existential, as Cope's reminiscences about the war and the decisions he makes in his life reflect his belief in the limits on individual choices imposed not only by war but also by tradition and religion, and the role these experiences play in human freedom and happiness.

Despite his openness about his life, Cope is ultimately a private person. The book hints at issues of spirituality and sexuality that may have placed him at odds with his surroundings, but his genuine love of music, the arts, and nature also separates him from a more superficial environment. A running theme throughout the book is the importance of nature and the arts. Reading and thinking are ways of figuring out life, and as Cope explains, he becomes a philosopher by doing so.

Another theme that emerges from his decision to reflect on his life is the importance of friends. Throughout his memoir, Cope searches for people he knew at various times of his life and discusses how they influenced him or how his life might have been different had he made different decisions concerning them. Also significant in this regard is Cope's friendship with Guibert; their collaboration and the book it produced were a result of the decisions, thoughts, and friendship that are the themes of this work. Ultimately, *Alan's War* is not about Cope's brief time in the military during World War II, but about his battles with conformity, superficiality, and the social restraints that distance people from nature and limit free will.

Impact

Since its publication in France in 2000, *Alan's War* has never been out of print. It has won numerous local and national awards and was nominated for four Eisner Awards in 2009, honors that suggest the impact of *Alan's War* will long be felt in the world of graphic novels. In addition to the book's notable artistic style, the collaboration between subject and author creates a distinctive model for the genre of biographical and autobiographical writing.

Guibert again employed the format of *Alan's War* in his collaborative project with photojournalist Didier Lefèvre, *The Photographer* (2009). In this book,

Guibert maintains his unique pen-and-water illustrations, this time both in color and in black and white, and adds them to the photographs that Lefèvre took in a Doctors Without Borders expedition to war-torn Afghanistan in 1986. Guibert's work sets a standard for combined media in graphic novels; his mixture of photographs and art in *The Photographer* is praised by the *Los Angeles Times* for allowing "the graphic novel form to flex its muscle to stunning effect."

Linda Kelly Alkana

Further Reading

Brown, Chester. *Louis Riel: A Comic-Strip Biography* (2004).

Guibert, Emmanuel, Didier Lefèvre, and Frédéric Lemercier. *The Photographer: Into War-Torn Afghanistan with Doctors Without Borders* (2009).

Kubert, Joe. *Fax from Sarajevo* (1996).

Neufeld, Josh. *A.D.: New Orleans After the Deluge* (2009).

Pekar, Harvey, and Gary Dumm. *Students for a Democratic Society: A Graphic History* (2008).

Satrapi, Marjane. *The Complete Persepolis* (2007).

Bibliography

Phegley, Keil. "Emmanuel's Travels: Guibert Talks *Alan's War*." Comic Book Resources, May 8, 2009. http://comicbookresources.com?page=article&id=21146.

Watson, Sasha. "The Graphic Reality of a Stricken Land." *Los Angeles Times*, May 31, 2009.

See also: *Louis Riel; Photographer; Fax from Sarajevo; A.D.: New Orleans After the Deluge; Persepolis*

ALEC: THE YEARS HAVE PANTS

Author: Campbell, Eddie
Artist: Eddie Campbell
Publisher: Top Shelf Productions
First serial publication: 1981-
First book publication: 2009

Alec: The Years Have Pants. (Courtesy of Top Shelf Productions)

Publication History

Emerging from the British small-press comics scene of the early 1980's, Eddie Campbell has documented the adventures of his fictional alter ego, Alec MacGarry, for more than three decades and with multiple publishers. Inspired by the autobiographically based fiction of writers Jack Kerouac and Henry Miller, Campbell has tried to create a similar literature in a different medium. Like autobiographical comics writer Harvey Pekar, whose work Campbell soon discovered after creating his first *Alec* comics, Campbell has demonstrated that everyday life can make for extraordinary art. Unlike Pekar, however, Campbell both writes and draws his comics, making the *Alec* series the singular vision of an artist.

Campbell's first work was self-published. Hailing from Scotland, Campbell was living in England when he first turned to his own experiences for source material in the late 1970's with the *In the Days of the Ace Rock'n'Roll Club* stories, centered on a group of rockabilly music fans. With *Alec*, his work turned even more personal, and he used pseudonyms for the characters' names (a device dropped later in favor of real names) as he began publishing the stories in the minicomic *Flick*. When Campbell began meeting fellow cartoonists who also took advantage of the accessibility and affordability of the photocopier to disseminate their comics in small booklets, his *Alec* stories soon became a staple of the *Fast Fiction* anthology. After publishing in numerous fanzines and minicomics of the small-press scene, Campbell began moving into more commercial publishing ventures. Publishing wherever he could get paid for his work, in such anthologies as *Fox Comics* and *Taboo*, Campbell disseminated *Alec* stories as widely as he could. The stories were collected occasionally in such volumes as *The Complete Alec* (1990) and *Little Italy* (1991).

Still having trouble making a living and isolated from the British comics scene by his move to his wife's native Australia in the 1980's, Campbell returned to self-publishing in the 1990's with his *Bacchus* comic book. By forming Eddie Campbell Comics, Campbell was able to collect and present his work in a series of trade paperbacks such as *After the Snooter* (2002). After releasing his most successful work, *From Hell* (1989-1996), a long collaboration with Alan Moore about Jack the Ripper, Campbell tired of publishing and closed down his company in the early 2000's.

Since then, his work has been made available through other publishers. His body of autobiographically based work was collected in 2009 by Top Shelf Comics in a large single volume entitled *Alec: The Years Have Pants—A Life-Sized Omnibus*. Though this collection does not include *The Fate of the Artist* (2006) and stories such as "The History of Humour" have been condensed from their serial publication, it does include unpublished and rare work. Campbell named the volume *The Years Have Pants* after a line in a poem by William Ernest Moenkhaus, a friend of songwriter Hoagy Carmichael. Campbell viewed the line as an apt understanding of how time eventually carries everything into oblivion, while his own work provides some glimpses of the life along the way that might otherwise be overlooked.

Plot

Traditionally appealing to readers looking for down-to-earth comics, *Alec* can be read as a long picaresque novel depicting the everyday life of cartoonist Alec MacGarry (a stand-in for Campbell); however, *The Years Have Pants* can also be read as a collection of short stories. Some of the chapters in the omnibus, which is arranged chronologically according to the lives of the characters, have been regarded as graphic novels on their own in previous publication. As of 2011, however, only *The Fate of the Artist* stood as a separate volume.

"The King Canute Crowd" details the drunken escapades of a twenty-something Alec and his compatriots, who gather at a country pub called the King Canute in late 1970's England. The artistically inclined Alec works at a sheet-metal factory and strikes up a friendship with forklift driver Danny Grey, who serves as a role model of masculinity for Alec as they both endure romantic troubles, workingman blues, and the occasional pub punch-up. The fun ends when the characters mature and drift away from one another.

"Graffiti Kitchen" picks up the story of Alec in 1981, as his relationship with a girlfriend, Penny Moore, is falling apart. He falls into the social circle of Jane and Georgette Maison, a mother and daughter, and he has sexual relations with both, causing metaphorical friction between the generations and literal friction between the sexes. Grey, now married, reappears, and the story turns slightly metafictional as he reads the first *Alec* story.

"Shorts" collects two stories related to *Alec*, though Alec only appears in one of them.

In "How to Be an Artist," Alec attempts to make a living from cartooning after his factory job has ended. He has just started self-publishing his autobiographical comics and meets a number of fellow cartoonists. As a result, the story also serves as a history of the British small-press comics scene of the early 1980's, complete with sampled art from other cartoonists and a treatise on the history of the "graphic novel" (a term about which Campbell has reservations).

The story also introduces the second most important character of the *Alec* stories, Annie, Campbell's future wife, as well as other significant characters such as Alan Moore. Alec starts getting published by others but not paid, so he has to move in with his parents again. Eventually, he marries Annie, and they have their first child; the new family moves to Australia in 1986. The chapter concludes with a meditation on Moore's disastrous experience in self-publishing after the success of *Watchmen* (1986-1987) and the beginning of Campbell's collaboration with him on *From Hell*.

"Little Italy" details Alec's move to Australia, as he explores local history, family life, and nature. "The Dead Muse" includes the portions of an anthology of fellow comics artists compiled by Campbell. In the stories, he attempts to make a living in his adopted country and has little luck doing so.

"The Dance of Lifey Death" begins with Alec traveling around the world to attend comics conventions. He details his obsession with wine, his growing family, the collection of his friend Doc Nodule, a visit from fellow artist Glenn Dakin, and various other anecdotes.

"After the Snooter" shows Campbell in midlife, reflecting on the past and dreading slightly the inevitability of aging and death. He starts his own publishing company and visits his parents and Moore in the United Kingdom, while fellow comics professionals Dave Sim and Neil Gaiman visit him independently in Australia. Later, he starts court sketching on the side, and he and his family buy a house with the money he receives from the film adaptation of *From Hell* (2001).

Then he embarks on "The Millennium World Tour of Eddie Campbell," as he attends comics conventions in Maryland and Spain and visits Bob ("Danny Grey"), his parents, Moore, and Top Shelf publisher Chris Staros. His family, friends, and pets in Australia are the focus of many of the stories in the chapter, and it concludes with a trip to Hollywood for the *From Hell* movie premiere.

"Fragments" includes Campbell's aborted work "The History of Humour" and a couple of shorter stories.

"The Fate of the Artist," the only major story not included in *The Years Have Pants*, is a mystery about the alleged disappearance of Campbell after he has closed down his publishing company. This colorful, postmodern storytelling experiment can be read as a stand-alone graphic novel but also fits comfortably into the later *Alec* stories, especially if one regards it as the artistic representation of a midlife crisis.

"The Years Have Pants" makes its debut in the collection of the same name and is filled with recollections of the past, including a series of stories centered around "Obscure Objects," such as the Lempi International Award that Campbell received for *From Hell* at a Finnish comics convention. Many of the stories were initially composed as blog posts, so some feature Campbell on the computer, providing a portrait of the artist as a middle-aged man, as life goes on.

Characters

- *Alec MacGarry*, a.k.a. *Eddie Campbell*, the protagonist, is usually presented as a bespectacled, dark-haired, mature Caucasian man, though, depending on the story, he is depicted at various ages, from childhood to old age. He is typically amused by the events surrounding him and prone to thoughtful digressions on the nature of art and the meaning of life. The story shows how he grows from his early twenties to his early fifties, with flashbacks showing his childhood and adolescence and occasional imagined visions of his later years.
- *Danny Grey*, a.k.a. *Bob*, is a dark-haired, tattooed, muscular Caucasian man who is intelligent and sociable. He works as a forklift driver in the same factory as Alec, and they start to drink together, leading to numerous drunken escapades and a lifelong friendship. Later in life, he becomes a veterinarian's assistant and continues to be a hero to Campbell.

Alec: The Years Have Pants. (Courtesy of Top Shelf Productions)

- *Penny Moore* is a pretty, blond-haired Caucasian woman who is charming and flirtatious. She is separated from her husband and has a child. She owns a horse and is missing two teeth from an automobile accident. Alec meets her through Grey and becomes romantically involved with her for two tumultuous years.
- *Georgette Maison* is a young Caucasian woman with long, dark hair. She is artistic and precocious. She lives with her mother, Jane, and the two of them become involved in a love triangle with Alec, for whom Georgette serves as a muse. The relationships end when the Maisons move away.
- *Annie Campbell* is a dark-haired, Caucasian woman from Australia. She frequently becomes exasperated with Campbell but loves him nevertheless. She meets him in London, marries him, and serves as a comic foil for him throughout the stories, often in conjunction with their three children: Hayley, Erin, and Callum. Because of her homesickness, she moves to Australia, taking Campbell with her.
- *Alan Moore* is a long-haired, bearded, and dour-looking large Caucasian man, known for his genius, wit, and magical propensity to help Campbell at key moments. He is usually pictured as smoking a cigarette. In addition to trying to find work for Campbell, he becomes a creative partner with him, and they collaborate on several comics.

Artistic Style

The Years Have Pants starts with an illustration of a boy sketching at a bus stop, an apt symbol of the artistic journey on which both artist and reader embark in the book and in the series in general. Campbell's art constantly changes: It includes lush colors, Zip-A-Tone, children's drawings, and photographs as he experiments, but underneath it all remains a core sketchiness that is always idiosyncratically recognizable and charmingly personal. Despite the surface casualness, Campbell is a meticulous craftsperson, and the reader can see his illustration deepen and develop throughout the *Alec* stories, from the kitchen-sink realism of "King Canute" to the more expressionistic work of

"The Years Have Pants." From the beginning, though, Campbell favors nine-panel grids for his page layouts, and in the single-page stories, he typically and masterfully delivers a punch line on the last panel.

Most of his work is in black and white, but *The Fate of the Artist* is in color and is experimental in other ways, with its faux-vintage comic strips, play with typography, and extensive use of photographs. Campbell often likes to reference the work of other artists by sampling it for demonstrative purposes, such as in "How to Be an Artist," in which he provides a miniature history of the comics industry in the 1980's. His panels are often arranged with the narration on top and the illustration on the bottom, and he prefers to have Alec appear in the panels, rather than have the story be told from his point of view visually.

Themes

The major theme of *Alec* is the wonder of life, particularly the small moments that would otherwise go undocumented. Campbell's tone remains whimsical and ironic throughout the series. Campbell laughs along, as he observes how human beings occupy themselves with alcohol, art, death, love, sex, and, most of all, one another. The importance of social bonds seems paramount in the stories, as Alec leaves his parents to form a new family with Annie and their children. In the interim years, his friends, such as Grey, form a surrogate family. Despite the frustrations that come from close interactions with others, Campbell finds such interactions of fundamental importance. Indeed, his art seems to ask the reader to pay attention to her or his own life in a manner similar to how Campbell examines his own.

History emerges as a theme, particularly the history of comics and graphic novels. Strangely enough, humanity's collective history is not much of a concern for Campbell. For example, a reader would hardly know the Cold War ended during the time period documented, though social transformations such as the emergence of women in the workplace and the increasing role of computer technology are reflected in *Alec*. Everything in the book is viewed through the prism of private life, which is precisely the point of the work. While professional historians cover the rise and fall of nations and other major events, Campbell chronicles his personal history and provides a refreshing, individually scaled take on the passage of the decades.

Impact

Like the work of Pekar, Campbell's *Alec* pushed the boundaries of comics further, making everyday life a subject every bit as important as the genre material that typically appeared in comics beforehand. As such, Campbell can be seen as a forerunner of the following generation of independent cartoonists and graphic novelists, particularly those of an autobiographical bent. As a form of comparison, when Campbell's comrade Moore was writing *Watchmen* and bringing new levels of realism to the superhero genre, Campbell had already dispensed with the superhero fantasy and was just focusing on realism. As a result, many comics professionals such as Warren Ellis have cited Campbell as an influence.

Though the *Alec* stories often appeared in serialized form over the years and can be enjoyed individually, with *The Years Have Pants*, many readers are likely to view the *Alec* oeuvre as a whole. Perhaps no one other than Pekar has documented her or his own life in comics for as long a time as Campbell has. For both Campbell and his doppelgänger Alec MacGarry, life and art go on. Though Campbell has always had a love/ hate relationship with the term "graphic novel," he likely will be long identified as one of the masters of the form.

Frederick A. Wright

Further Reading

Bechdel, Alison. *Fun Home* (2006).

Brown, Chester. *I Never Liked You* (1994).

Campbell, Eddie, et al. *Eddie Campbell's Bacchus* (1995).

Moore, Alan, and Eddie Campbell. *From Hell* (1989-1996).

Pekar, Harvey, et al. *American Splendor* (1976-1991).

Bibliography

Campbell, Eddie. "What Is a Graphic Novel?" *World Literature Today* 81, no. 2 (March/April, 2007): 13.

Coale, Mark. *Breaking the Panels: Over Seventy-Five Short Interviews from Around the Comics Industry.* Colora, Md.: O-Goshi Studios, 1998.

Fischer, Craig, and Charles Hatfield. "Teeth, Sticks, and Bricks: Calligraphy, Graphic Focalization, and Narrative Braiding in Eddie Campbell's *Alec*." *SubStance* 40, no. 1 (2011): 70-93.

Wiater, Stanley, and Stephen Bissette. *Comic Book Rebels: Conversations with the Creators of the New Comics.* New York: Donald I. Fine, 1993.

See also: *Fun Home; I Never Liked You; Bacchus; Get a Life; From Hell; American Splendor; Persepolis; It's a Good Life If You Don't Weaken*

ALICE IN SUNDERLAND: AN ENTERTAINMENT

Author: Talbot, Bryan
Artist: Bryan Talbot (illustrator); Jordan Smith (cover artist)
Publisher: Dark Horse Comics
First book publication: 2007

Publication History

Bryan Talbot began his comics career creating underground comics in the early 1970's. Though he has worked for publishers as varied as DC Comics, Tekno Comix, and Paradox Press, his work has always maintained an independent feel. Talbot was never a prolific creator, and his published output declined considerably in the early 2000's as he began work on *Alice in Sunderland.*

According to the book itself, Talbot was struck by the idea during a performance of Peter Ilich Tchaikovsky's *Swan Lake* at the Empire Theatre in Sunderland, England. He conceived of *Alice in Sunderland* as a "dream documentary" to discuss the root idea of storytelling, both as a form of entertainment and as it pertains to crafting one's own history and destiny. Talbot started with Lewis Carroll's two Alice stories, *Alice's Adventures in Wonderland* (1865) and *Through the Looking Glass and What Alice Found There* (1871), and branched out in many different directions to showcase how these tales have been updated and modified over the years, as well as how individuals might later take cues from Carroll's plot and themes to alter their own personal stories.

Talbot worked on *Alice in Sunderland* for several years. The book was first published nearly simultaneously by Dark Horse Comics in the United States and Jonathan Cape in the United Kingdom, and was soon followed by Italian, Spanish, French, and Czech editions. For the third printing of the U.K. edition, Talbot took the opportunity to correct a few typographical errors and make minor adjustments to some of the images.

Plot

Alice in Sunderland opens as the Punter idly wanders into the Empire Theatre, looking to kill some

Alice in Sunderland: An Entertainment. (Courtesy of Dark Horse Comics)

time. The Performer takes the stage and begins discussing the history of the Empire Theatre up to its only original production, a 1970 musical loosely based on Carroll's two Alice books. Joined by the Pilgrim, he then segues into a lengthy history of Sunderland, its inhabitants, Carroll, and the creation of the Alice books. The Performer teases his audience by stating that one of his subsequent tales will be completely false, and it is the job of the audience to figure out which. He traces Sunderland's history from the building of St. Peter's Church in 674 through 2007, with a discussion of how the area has reinvented itself with artist-in-residence Colin Wilbourn and writer-in-residence

Chaz Brenchley. He also touches on the centuries-old rivalry between Sunderland residents, called Mackems, and the Geordies of nearby Newcastle upon Tyne. The Pilgrim closes the first act by concentrating on Carroll's publication of *Alice's Adventures in Wonderland*, including his collaboration with artist John Tenniel and the engravers, and his ultimate success at getting a bound copy into the real Alice's hands, although not before Alice's mother puts an end to the platonic relationship.

During the show's intermission, the Punter tries to figure out which stories are true. Some of the pieces presented sound more like myths and legends than historical fact, and the ghost of actor Sid James goads him on to sort things out for himself.

The performance continues with the Pilgrim's and the Performer's tales still circling around Sunderland. The narratives always seem to come back to the Alice stories, although occasionally in extremely tangential or tenuous ways. Increasingly, the stories become more about telling stories and creating myths, and how they can endure and permeate culture; the tales cited are a varied lot, ranging from the legend of the Lambton Worm to how Carroll first spontaneously concocted Alice's underground adventures while on a boating trip. Also discussed is how the real Alice Hargreaves (née Liddell), in financial trouble following the deaths of her son and her husband, is given a hero's welcome in the United States as part of a centennial celebration of Carroll's birth. This is all copiously documented by a Paramount newsreel, which perpetuates some of the myths around the Alice books.

The Performer finally admits that, despite his original statement to the contrary, everything he has relayed is absolutely accurate as far as anyone is able to determine. He ends his performance with a grand song and dance, featuring fireworks, flying jets, and final cameos by as many of the people he has discussed as can fill the stage, before finally commanding the Punter to go home.

Talbot awakes suddenly in the Empire Theatre. He remains seated with an astonished look on his face as those around him applaud and eventually leave. On their way out of the Empire, his wife scolds him for sleeping through *Swan Lake*.

Characters

- *The Punter* is initially described in the book as simply "this guy" and is presented accordingly. He is past his prime, somewhat overweight, and carries himself with a casual weariness. Initially, he seems to be the audience to whom the Performer speaks, but it soon becomes clear that he represents the reader. His questioning and heckling of the performance often serves to directly address issues the book's readers might have with the main text.

- *The Performer* acts as host to the narrative, trying to keep the Punter entertained with dramatic and sometimes highly emotional flourishes. Wearing a billowing shirt and occasionally a white rabbit mask, he guides his audience through the web of stories that weaves in, out, and around Sunderland's roots.

- *The Pilgrim*, dressed in a black dress shirt, provides more factual information about the subjects. While not without emotional interest, he is decidedly more reserved than the Performer. Although he is ostensibly being projected onto a screen behind the Performer, the two in fact share narrative duties, sometimes seamlessly switching back and forth as the subject changes.

- *Bryan Talbot* appears periodically throughout the book as himself, in a metatextual context, to comment on his creative process; he even has an existential crisis about it midway through. All of the main characters are simply extensions of Talbot and could be said to loosely represent his id, ego, and superego. Throughout the book, the characters melt from one to another, sometimes making it difficult to determine which character is speaking. Given the monologic nature of the narrative, however, this does not pose any real problems for the reader.

Artistic Style

Talbot employs a great many styles throughout the single volume. The main story is told using black-and-white figures and is drawn in his elegant, fairly traditional comic book style. As the Performer begins his story, Talbot works in collage elements, depicting photographs of persons and locations the character is discussing. Effects filters are frequently used on the photos, which vary widely in quality and style, to give the images a more unified feel. As the book goes into discussions of other artists, such as Tenniel or Scott McCloud, Talbot occasionally adopts those artists' individual styles for short periods to emphasize his points about their work. Though the illustration style changes repeatedly, it does so in a way that serves the story and still allows for a smooth progression throughout the book.

Occasionally, Talbot also places comic book stories within the context of the narrative, and then presents them to the reader. Here, again, he adopts an artistic style appropriate to the subject. For example, when referencing a castle that is allegedly haunted by a ghost, he includes a four-page sequence that tells how the castle came to be haunted in a style reminiscent of the

Alice in Sunderland. (Courtesy of Dark Horse Comics)

1950's horror books published by Entertaining Comics (better known as EC Comics).

Themes

The primary theme throughout *Alice in Sunderland* is storytelling. There is little discussion of the craft of storytelling; rather, the narrative uses repeated examples to illustrate how stories can be generated and passed along. Talbot is deliberately broad with his definition of storytelling and does not confine himself to the typical narratives of books, plays, and comics; though he certainly speaks to them, he also points out how individuals tell their own stories in how they live their lives. He looks forward and back, as people are able to influence both their past (by presenting it differently) and their future (by their direct actions).

Talbot also touches on the notion of cycles and renewal through storytelling. The same elements in storytelling can be used repeatedly by different creators, which in part is how the Alice stories can be told again and again in multiple media and with alternate takes on the same ideas. In addition, many of the ideas presented in the stories can wind their way into all sorts of seemingly unrelated and unexpected places, in some cases impacting the very language itself.

Talbot repeatedly uses both Sunderland and Carroll to illustrate his points. By referencing all of the stories he can find that are even slightly related to them, he is able to showcase a wide variety of examples of both storytelling and cycles, while still anchoring the reader with the Alice books as a common touchstone.

Impact

Alice in Sunderland is perhaps one of the broadest attempts at chronicling the life of Carroll and his most popular works. While other authors have delved into Carroll's life in more detail, Talbot views his subject within a much larger macrocosm. He is less concerned with the intricacies of the man and more interested in his place within the much broader context of storytelling.

In that vein, Talbot tries to weave in as many references to Carroll and the Alice books as possible. He cites not only retellings and reinterpretations but also parodies and loosely derivative works, including *Adolf in Blunderland* (1939) and *Night of the Jabberwock* (1977), and even more oblique references, such as the image of Carroll on the album cover of the Beatles' *Sgt. Pepper's Lonely Hearts Club Band* and the brief discussion of the "Walrus and the Carpenter" poem in Kevin Smith's film *Dogma* (1999). Many of the works Talbot does not mention by name show up in background collages.

Not surprisingly, given the medium, Talbot pays close attention to comics-related work. The influence of McCloud is apparent, especially in Talbot's look at the Bayeux Tapestry, which McCloud similarly discussed in *Understanding Comics*, and of course when McCloud makes a cameo appearance to reenergize Talbot's conviction to the work. Talbot seems to follow McCloud's definition of comics, specifically pointing to many of the fine-art installations currently in Sunderland, such as Craig Knowles's sculpture *Taking Flight*, as a form of comics.

Sean Kleefeld

Further Reading

Carroll, Lewis, Leah Moore, John Reppion, and Erica Awano. *The Complete Alice in Wonderland* (2010).

Gaiman, Neil. *The Sandman: Fables and Reflections* (1993).

Talbot, Bryan. *Grandville* (2009).

Bibliography

Brooker, Will. *Alice's Adventures: Lewis Carroll in Popular Culture*. New York: Continuum, 2004.

Carroll, Lewis, John Tenniel, and Martin Gardner. *The Annotated Alice: "Alice's Adventures in Wonderland" and "Through the Looking-Glass."* New York: Norton, 2000.

McCloud, Scott. *Understanding Comics*. Northampton, Mass.: Kitchen Sink Press, 1993.

See also: *Lost Girls*

ALIENS

Author: Byrne, John; Guinan, Paul; Verheiden, Mark

Artist: Sergio Aragones (illustrator); Peter Bagge (illustrator); Steve Bissette (illustrator); John Byrne (illustrator); Richard Corben (illustrator); Ronnie Del Carmen (illustrator); Paul Guinan (illustrator); Paul Johnson (illustrator); Kelley Jones (illustrator); Moebius (illustrator); Mark A. Nelson (illustrator); Doug Wheatley (illustrator); Bernie Wrightson (illustrator); Tim Hamilton (penciller); Flint Henry (penciller); Mike Mignola (penciller); Doug Mahnke (penciller and inker)

Publisher: Dark Horse Comics

First serial publication: 1988-1999

First book publication: 2007-2009

Publication History

Building upon the world established in the films *Alien* (1979) and *Aliens* (1986), Dark Horse Comic began to publish various miniseries and one-issue comics in 1988, initially with the title *Aliens* and then with specific subtitles. Shorter pieces ran in *Dark Horse Presents* and *Dark Horse Comics*, regular anthology titles, and in special single-issue anthologies from Dark Horse, often to celebrate the company's anniversary. Dark Horse also published some miniseries, such as *Aliens: Earth War* (1991) and *Aliens: Tribes* (1992), in trade paperback, hardback, and signed, numbered collector's editions. For the most part, these publications are superseded by the six-volume omnibus edition published between 2007 and 2009, although the omnibus does not include *Tribes*, for example. This omnibus edition includes works by more than thirty writers and more than fifty illustrators.

The first *Aliens* miniseries and some other comics were originally published in black and white, but they were colored for the omnibus edition. Volume six contains some work in black and white, as well as Bernie Wrightson's uninked pencils. Also, the series initially featured the characters Hicks and Newt, major characters in the film *Aliens*. However, Hicks and Newt die in *Alien 3* (1992), so the characters are renamed Wilks and Billie in later printings.

Plot

Ten years after the events of the movie *Aliens*, Billie is in a mental hospital and Wilks is struggling as a marine; both suffer trauma from their experiences with the violent, almost unstoppable aliens. When aliens invade a spaceship, Colonel Orona assigns Wilks to accompany a mission to capture a specimen. Wilks rescues Billie, about to be lobotomized, and takes her with him. Meanwhile on Earth, a cult has grown up around the aliens, and volunteers gestate aliens in their own bodies.

Despite efforts to control them, the aliens take over Earth. Orona is in favor of the aliens wiping out the unfit, while the human leaders leave Earth. A member of the other extraterrestrial species from the film *Alien*—seen in the original film as the huge skeleton of

A terrified Ellen Ripley (Sigourney Weaver) comes face to face with an alien in David Fincher's 1992 science fiction horror film, *Alien 3*. (© Bureau L.A. Collection/Corbis)

the "space jockey" near the breeding chamber—comes to Earth, but it does not aid the humans.

After time at General Thomas Spears's secret base, Wilks and Billie encounter Ellen Ripley, hero of the films but a minor character in the comics. Ripley knows where the aliens' home world is and that it contains an "überqueen." The three capture the queen, hoping to lure all the aliens into one place and then kill them in an explosion. This endeavor succeeds, but the space jockey's alien species has manipulated Ripley to purge the Earth of the invaders only so that it can eventually take over Earth. Ripley and Wilks take revenge, and Billie rescues Amy, a girl on Earth.

After this narrative arc in the first two volumes of the omnibus, the three characters from the film *Aliens* do not reappear in the comics; the next volumes continue the story with imaginative extrapolation. Earth has somewhat rebuilt, and alien royal jelly has become a much-valued drug. A billionaire mounts an expedition to obtain more from the aliens' home planet and finds that lacking an überqueen, red and black aliens fight in a manner similar to ants. Dr. Stan Mayakovsky, a brilliant scientist addicted to royal jelly, creates a synthetic alien to infiltrate the hive.

"Colonial Marines" depicts soldiers fighting aliens and alien/human hybrids, called Bug-Men, in space and on non-Earth planets. In one fight, the soldiers are aided by obsolete and abandoned maintenance robots. New weapons include acid-resistant armor and a pheromone band to disguise humans from alien senses.

The remainder of the series consists of separate stories, all with different characters and often on different worlds. "Earth Angel" takes place on Earth in the 1950's and "Stalker" among the Vikings. Some stories—such as "Labyrinth," "Frenzy," and "Stronghold"—are connected to the earlier stories, with plots featuring the Colonial Marines or attempts to exploit the aliens by the corrupt company Weyland-Yutani or its successor, the Grant Corporation. Some stories, such as "Sacrifice" and "Wraith," explore how humans living in off-world colonies might respond to invasion by one alien or a small group. "Alchemy" features the passengers of a ship long cut off from Earth who now believe they are a separate species.

"Alien," "Taste," and "Incubation" show new intelligent extraterrestrial species interacting with the aliens; in the first, the pretechnological protagonist thinks that human beings in space suits are dangerous, and he kills one for a trophy.

Volumes

- *Aliens Omnibus* Volume 1 (2007). Collects "Outbreak" (*Aliens*, issues 1-6; 1988-1989), "Nightmare Asylum" (*Aliens* series 2, issues 1-4; 1989-1990), "Female War" (*Aliens: Earth War*, issues 1-4; 1990), "Theory of Alien Propagation" (*Dark Horse Presents,* issue 24; 1988), and "The Alien" (*DHP*, issue 56; 1991). Follows one narrative, a continuation of the film *Aliens*, and features Wilks and Billie (formerly named Hicks and Newt) and Ripley.
- *Aliens Omnibus* Volume 2 (2007). Collects "Genocide" (*Aliens: Genocide*, issues 1-4; 1991-1992), "Harvest" (*Aliens: Hive*, issues 1-4; 1992), and "Colonial Marines" (*Aliens: Colonial Marines*, issues 1-10; 1993-1994). Continues and concludes the story of Wilks, Billie, and Ripley.
- *Aliens Omnibus* Volume 3 (2008). Collects "Rogue" (*Aliens: Rogue*, issues 1-4; 1993), "Sacrifice" (*Aliens: Sacrifice*; 1993), "Labyrinth" (*Aliens: Labyrinth*, issues 1-4; 1993-1994), "Salvation" (*Aliens: Salvation*; 1993), "Advent/Terminus" (*DHP*, issues 42-43; 1990), "Reapers" (*Dark Horse Presents Fifth Anniversary Special*; 1991), and "Horror Show" (*Dark Horse Comics*, issues 3-5; 1992). Expands beyond the movies, introducing new characters but primarily retaining the basic theme of someone battling the aliens while someone else tries to experiment on, train, or otherwise use them.
- *Aliens Omnibus* Volume 4 (2008). Collects "Music of the Spears" (*Aliens: Music of the Spears*, issues 1-4; 1994), "Stronghold" (*Aliens: Stronghold*; 1994), "Frenzy" (*Aliens Berserker*, issues 1-4; 1995), "Taste" (*DHC*, issue 11; 1993), "Mondo Pest" (*Aliens: Mondo Pest*; 1995), and "Mondo Heat" (*Aliens: Mondo Heat*; 1996). Explores new ideas and experiments with genres other than suspense and adventure.

- *Aliens Omnibus* Volume 5 (2008). Collects "Alchemy" (*Aliens: Alchemy*, issues 1-3; 1997), "Kidnapped" (*Aliens: Kidnapped*, issues 1-3; 1997-1998), "Survival" (*Aliens: Survival*; 1998), "Cargo" (*DHC*, issues 15-16; 1993), "Alien" (*DHC*, issues 17-19; 1994), "Earth Angel" (*Aliens: Earth Angel*; 1994), "Incubation" (*DHP*, issues 101-102; 1995), "Havoc" (*Aliens: Havoc*; 1997), "Lovesick" (*Aliens: Lovesick*; 1996), and "Lucky" (*Decade of Dark Horse*, issue 3; 1996). Expands upon the ideas behind the films *Alien* and *Aliens*, taking them in new directions and into new settings.

- *Aliens Omnibus* Volume 6 (2009). Collects "Apocalypse" (*Aliens: Apocalypse—The Destroying Angels*, issues 1-4; 1999), "Once in a Lifetime" (*DHP*, issue 140; 1999), "Xenogenesis" (*Aliens: Xenogenesis*, issues 1-4; 1999), "Headhunters" (*DHP*, issue 117; 1997), "Tourist Season" (*Dark Horse Presents Annual 1997*; 1998), "Pig" (*Aliens: Pig*; 1997), "Border Lines" (*DHP*, issue 121; 1997), "45 Seconds" and "Elder Gods" (*Aliens: Special*; 1997), "Purge" (*Aliens: Purge*; 1997), "Glass Corridor" (*Aliens: Glass Corridor*; 1998), "Stalker" (*Aliens: Stalker*; 1998), and "Wraith" (*Aliens: Wraith*; 1998). Offers some humor and compelling human characters.

Characters

- *Wilks* (*Hicks* in the original publication) is a belligerent, frequently drunk marine who had a traumatic encounter with the aliens ten years before. While being manipulated by the government and fighting an alien invasion, he teams up with Ripley again, but he does not seem to soften. His face is scarred in "Outbreak" and "Female War" but not in "Nightmare Asylum," the second story of that three-story arc.

- *Billie* (*Newt* in the original publication) is an unhappy young woman who was institutionalized after her encounter with the aliens. She is bitter about being abandoned by Ripley, but they are reunited. Billie falls in love with Beuller, an android marine, neither of them knowing he is synthetic.

She almost envies the aliens' ruthlessness, but she eventually realizes that love is an essential component of humanity and that her love for Beuller is real. She rescues Amy, a girl who reminds her of her younger self.

- *General Thomas A. W. Spears* is one of the many ruthless, monomaniacal agents of government and business trying to breed, train, or otherwise use the aliens. Spears was raised in an artificial womb and has served in the Colonial Marines all his life. He is willing to sacrifice even his own men in pursuit of his goals. Finally, his own aliens kill him.

- *Colonel Doctor Church* is one of many evil scientists to appear in *Aliens*. He survives capture in an alien hive by cutting the alien embryo out of his own body and goes on to cruelly experiment on human beings and captured aliens alike.

- *Norbert* and *Jeri* are synthetic, human-produced "xenomorphs" that can infiltrate the alien nests but are friendly to humans and have human abilities, such as speech, weapons usage, and even

---

Stephen Bissette

A key figure in the revival of interest in horror comics in the 1980's and 1990's, Stephen Bissette rose to prominence as the illustrator (with Rick Veitch) of the Alan Moore-written revival of *Saga of the Swamp Thing* from 1983 to 1987. In 1988, he launched the horror anthology *Taboo*, which notably began the serialization of *From Hell* by Moore and Eddie Campbell, and *Lost Girls* by Moore and Melinda Gebbie. In 1993, he collaborated with Moore and artists John Totleben and Rick Veitch on the limited series *1963*, which offered a retro take on superheroes that parodied Silver Age Marvel comics. In 1994, he launched a comic series about a Tyrannosaurus rex, *Tyrant*, which lasted only four issues. Bissette's art is characterized by its fine lines and careful compositions. His work on *Swamp Thing* often privileged the development of mood over action, and his sense of realism contributed to the earthy tones of that work.

proper manners. They represent the series' ongoing theme about the definition of human.

- *Alien King* is created by scientist Professor Ernst Kleist using alien queen and human DNA. He is supposed to mate with a queen alien but is killed by her, after which Kleist destroys both of them and himself.
- *Herk Mondo* is an independent exterminator of aliens. He is capable of killing multiple aliens at once, yet he is oddly endearing. His stories demonstrate a charming humor, partly through the exaggeration or even parody of heroism.
- *Damon Eddington* is an avant-garde musician who has an alien captured so he can record its sounds and use them in his compositions.
- *Ivy Derringer* is a gorgeous and incredibly rich celebrity. Her "terraformed" asteroid spa, Celeste, is invaded by an alien.
- *Victor Thompson* is a geologist who is secretly experimented upon with alien DNA. His hallucinations resulting from the experiment combine with his feelings of guilt for failing to save his family.
- *Gropius Lysenko* is a scientist for Weyland-Yutani. His experiments with royal jelly have separated his consciousness from his body, and when a team salvages the ship in which he conducted research, Lysenko controls various members to warn the team and help it fight the aliens.
- *Alecto Throop* is the head of Throop Rescue and Recovery, which is hired to retrieve survivors of a Weyland-Yutani mission. She is clever, and in addition to fighting aliens, she discovers interesting history about them.

Artistic Style

More than fifty artists contributed to the stories collected in the omnibus, not counting the forty-three who created single pages for the story "Havoc." Contributors include many artists famous for other work. Richard Corben, first active in underground comics in the 1960's, and French artist Moebius also contributed to the magazine *Heavy Metal*, while Sergio Aragones became well-known in *MAD* magazine. John Byrne primarily worked for Marvel Comics and DC Comics, while Mike Mignola (*Hellboy*, 1994-   ) and Peter Bagge (*Hate*, 1990-1998) are known for their independent comics. Few of the artists are known primarily for work on horror comics.

Generally, the art strikes a good balance between realistic representation and expression of tone or stylistic experiment. Paradoxically, science-fiction stories often need to be more realistic than other stories, because readers do not have the touchstones they do in a story about ordinary life. Mark A. Nelson's art shows recognition of this, setting the standard for the artists who followed.

Within these parameters, the art is individual, usually fitting the story well. "Harvest," a character-oriented story, is well served by Kelley Jones's close-ups and expressive faces, while Paul Guinan, in "Colonial Marines," and Doug Mahnke, in "Stronghold," excel in creating action sequences and "starscapes." Tim Hamilton depicts magnificent gore in "Music of the Spears." Ronnie Del Carmen, in the "Mondo" stories, notably blends humorous exaggeration and dark, brooding shadows to capture the appropriate tone, and Flint Henry does the same in "Pig." Paul Johnson's "Sacrifice," Den Beauvais's "Nightmare Asylum," and, to some extent, Doug Wheatley's "Apocalypse" offer lush, painted appearances, while Mignola's "Salvation" and Phil Hester's "Purge" effectively use blocks of inked shadows to convey menace and strangeness.

Themes

Like the *Alien* movies, the comic book stories exhibit a basic distrust of corporations and highlight the greed and hubris that make the aliens attractive as soldiers or as the source of other products. Unlike in the film *Aliens*, this distrust often extends to the government, which may work hand in hand with corporations. In the comics, the Colonial Marines are often, but not always, the "good guys." As one marine says in "Outbreak," "There are no sides anymore—just money—and we're expendable." Many of the stories depict various types of manipulation, deceit, and betrayal.

The first two volumes of the omnibus, "Stronghold," and other stories continue the thematic discussion from the movie *Aliens* about what it means to be human; the answer seems to be that human beings without compassion are worse than synthetic beings. This definition of "human" may be influenced by the fiction of Philip K. Dick and the movie *Bladerunner* (1982), based on Dick's book *Do Androids Dream of Electric Sheep?* (1968).

The comics also explore issues of gender, as do the films. Ripley appears as a significant minor character, and the stories feature many strong, intelligent, and independent women. Men can often be judged by their treatment of women; for example, the mad scientist Dr. Nordling sexually abuses his female android, with whom the female protagonist, Dr. Strunk, sympathizes. The first two volumes continue the theme of motherhood from the movie *Aliens*, placing Ripley, Billie, and then Amy in opposition to the alien queen and her brood.

Many of the stories depict Earth and, thus, extrapolate more cultural trends than the films do. The impact of television on society increases, and not for the better, as seen in "Outbreak" and "Kidnapped." Given that every known society has developed some kind of consciousness-altering substance, the manufacture of drugs from alien royal jelly is original yet natural. The first two volumes of the omnibus and stories such as "Sacrifice," "Alchemy," "Apocalypse," and "Elder Gods" all feature religions that are at worst malevolent and at best a source of morality but prone to misuse.

Impact

From the beginning, writer Mark Verheiden said that he did not want to adapt but to continue the movie *Aliens*. Although the practice of basing comics on successful television shows and films extends back to the 1960's, with comics based on *Star Trek* and various Disney characters, the *Aliens* comics go farther in adding new material to an established fictional universe.

In fact, the expanded universe of the comics may have influenced the subsequent *Aliens* films, since human/alien hybrids and other experiments with alien DNA appear in comics published before the release of *Alien 3* and *Alien Resurrection* (1997). Dark Horse Comics also published stories pitting these aliens against the predator from the film *Predator* (1987) long before the release of *AVP: Alien vs. Predator* (2004).

Indisputably, the success of the *Aliens* comics proved that licensing a television show or film franchise on which to base a comic book series could be highly profitable. In addition to *Aliens* and *Predator*, Dark Horse bought the *Star Wars* license in 1991. Other companies followed Dark Horse's lead, basing comics on licensed characters and films.

Bernadette Bosky

Further Reading

Claremont, Chris, Dave Cockrum, and Paul Smith. *Essential X-Men*, Volumes 3 and 4 (1981-1984).

Mignola, Mike. *Hellboy* (1994-   ).

Moore, Alan. *Saga of the Swamp Thing* (1984-1987).

Bibliography

Gordon, Ian, Mark Jancovich, and Matthew P. McAllister. *Film and Comic Books*. Jackson: University Press of Mississippi, 2007.

McIntee, David. *Beautiful Monsters: The Unofficial and Unauthorized Guide to the Alien and Predator Films*. Surrey, England: Telos, 2005.

Verheiden, Mark, and Mark Nelson. "Writer and Artist: Mark Verheiden and Mark Nelson." Interview by David Anthony Kraft. *Aliens: Comics Interview Special Edition*, 1988, 3-27.

See also: *Hate; Predator; Robot Dreams; Walking Dead*

AMERICAN BORN CHINESE

Author: Yang, Gene Luen
Artist: Gene Luen Yang (illustrator); Lark Pien (colorist)
Publisher: First Second Books
First book publication: 2006

Publication History

Gene Luen Yang began creating installments of *American Born Chinese* in 2000, disseminating photocopied pages to friends, family, and other independent comic writers and creators. However, some elements of *American Born Chinese* originated long before 2000; Yang first drew the stereotypical Asian character Chin-Kee, based on a mixture of negative stereotypes and clichés found in historical and contemporary political cartoons and popular culture, in his fifth-grade notebook. Yang's friend and later collaborator on *The Eternal Smile* (2009), Derek Kirk Kim, sent pages from *American Born Chinese* to Mark Siegel of First Second Books. After reading the story, Siegel called Kim and asked him to arrange a meeting with the author, leading to the book's publication. Yang collaborated on the book with colorist Lark Pien, with whom he also worked on *The Rosary Comic Book* (2003).

Plot

American Born Chinese is a trilogy of seemingly unconnected stories about a Chinese American childhood. It begins when the shoeless Monkey King is denied entrance to the heavenly gods' dinner party. He uses his prowess in kung fu to pummel the gods, who then appeal to the creator god, Tze-Yo-Tzuh, for assistance. The Monkey King shuns his creator and pays for his impudence by being imprisoned under a mountain. After a few eons, a monk is chosen by Tze-Yo-Tzuh to journey to the west and deliver three packages, but first he must gather his disciples, including the Monkey King. The Monkey King retrieves his soul and escapes his prison by returning to his true form; he discovers that a monkey has no need for shoes.

The central story begins when Jin Wang arrives at his new home in suburbia. He misses Chinatown and

recalls his mother's weekly visits to the herbalist, whose sage wife tells him, "It's easy to become anything you wish . . . so long as you're willing to forfeit your soul."

Jin's first day at Mayflower Elementary is marked by a stunning array of prejudice, with students and even Jin's teacher making assumptions based on Jin's Chinese heritage. Even so, Jin just wants to fit in. When a new student, Wei-Chen Sun, arrives from Taiwan, Jin wants nothing to do with the "fresh off the boat" geek; he soon changes his mind, and they become best friends.

In junior high, Jin discovers girls, but he misses his opportunity to befriend his crush, Amelia Harris, by refusing to care for the class pets. When Wei-Chen and Amelia get locked in the pet-food closet, Jin rescues the pair, giving him the confidence to ask Amelia to the movies. Amelia agrees to go on the date; however, Jin is not allowed to date, so he asks Wei-Chen to lie to his parents regarding his whereabouts.

Greg, an all-American classmate, warns Jin to stay away from Amelia, since she is not "right" for him. Shortly afterward, Jin's Japanese classmate, Suzy Nakamura, breaks down in tears after being called a "Chink." Jin responds by kissing her, which angers Wei-Chen, her boyfriend. When Wei-Chen confronts Jin, Jin remarks that Suzy is not "right" for someone "fresh off the boat." Wei-Chen punches Jin, ending their friendship. Jin dreams of the herbalist's wife that night and awakes as Danny.

The final thread in the trilogy is presented as a television sitcom titled "Everyone Ruvs Chin-Kee," costarring Danny, a typical American teenager. Danny has a problem: the arrival of his Chinese cousin, Chin-Kee, whose yearly visits always lead to trouble. During this visit, Chin-Kee embarrasses Danny by showing off in class, harassing female students, and holding a personal talent show in the school library. Angry, Danny hits his cousin, causing his head to pop off and reveal that Chin-Kee is truly the Monkey King. Danny returns to his true form, that of Jin Wang, thus merging the sitcom with the central story.

The retransformed Jin discovers that his onetime best friend, Wei-Chen, is the Monkey King's son and was sent to Earth to test his virtue. However, after Jin asked his best friend to lie, Wei-Chen resigned as an emissary for the gods and instead decided to remain mortal and use the world for pleasure. The Monkey King resolves the action, leaving Jin with his advice: "I would have saved myself from five hundred years' imprisonment . . . had I only realized how good it is to be a monkey." Jin finds Wei-Chen and apologizes, a reconciliation that leads Jin to accept himself as a Chinese American.

Characters

- *Jin Wang*, the protagonist, is a second-generation American of Chinese descent. He has short, straight black hair—except when he gets a "perm" in an attempt to look Caucasian—and wears typical teenage clothing. After moving from San Francisco's Chinatown to suburbia, he faces not only prejudice but also the challenges

faced by every teen, such as new love and embarrassment. Eventually, he overcomes his own internalized prejudice and shame and accepts himself as both Chinese and American.

- *Monkey King of Flower Fruit Mountain* is an earthbound deity in the body of a monkey. After much study he transforms into the "Great Sage Equal of Heaven" and challenges the heavenly deities, causing his imprisonment under a mountain. On Earth, he is disguised as the Asian stereotype Chin-Kee but reveals himself to Danny.

- *Tze-Yo-Tzuh* is the creator god and the only deity who can put the Monkey King in his place. He wears a floor-length robe, carries a staff, and has a long white beard and hair reminiscent of a Chinese monk. His love of humanity closely resembles that of the Christian god.

- *Wei-Chen Sun* is a stereotypical geeky immigrant from Taiwan who arrives in the United States wearing large round glasses and secondhand clothes. He speaks with a heavy accent and often reverts to Mandarin. He is the disguised son of the Monkey King, but after Jin betrays him, he becomes a rebellious teenager who smokes cigarettes, drinks pearl tea, and drives a "rice rocket."

- *Suzy Nakamura* is one of three Asian students at Mayflower Elementary. She has short black hair with bangs. Like Jin Wang, she is stuck between two worlds: she wants to escape her parents' Japanese culture, but the other children and their teachers are prejudiced and unwelcoming. In middle school, she begins to date Wei-Chen.

- *Danny* is a typical blond-haired, blue-eyed American teenager who plays basketball and is popular with his classmates. He is forced to change schools every year after his Chinese cousin, Chin-Kee, visits and embarrasses him. After encountering the Monkey King, Danny transforms back into Jin.

- *Chin-Kee* is a grotesquely stereotypical Chinese teenager with yellow skin, buckteeth, and slits for eyes. He wears old-fashioned Chinese clothing and cannot pronounce *l* or *r*. His unbridled libido leaves him drooling over every female at

Oliphant High, and he constantly embarrasses his cousin, Danny. Chin-Kee is revealed to be the Monkey King and helps Jin Wang reconcile his conscience.

- *Amelia Harris* is a blond-haired, blue-eyed teenager and Jin Wang's love interest. She goes on a date with Jin, but when told Jin is not right for her, she decides she just wants to be friends.
- *Greg* is an all-American boy with wavy blond hair and many female admirers. He tells Jin to stop dating Amelia and hints that Jin would be better off dating an Asian girl, thus revealing his racism.
- *Wong Lao-Tsu* is a bald monk who helps the poor, wears the brown robe of service, and is recruited by Tze-Yo-Tzuh to go on a long journey. He is accompanied on his journey by his new disciple, the Monkey King. The monk helps the Monkey King finally realize that on his journey of self-discovery, he just needs to be himself.

Artistic Style

Yang's sunshine-yellow cover art with its orange outline of the imprisoned Monkey King serves as a backdrop for the full-color image of young Jin Wang, who holds his Transformers toy. A stylized wood-block print announces the book's title.

Between the covers, the panels are carefully laid out in tight squares within generous white space, tempting readers to linger and giving the book an uncluttered feel. A small, red wood-block print is centered above each gallery, while single wood-block prints representing the book's characters mark the chapter breaks. Yang's solid black outlines serve as a border for Pien's strong yet muted colors that work across cultures and heavenly orbits, giving the whole work a clean feel. The scenes taking place in the Monkey King's heaven have a distinctly Asian feel to them, with curlicues adorning clouds, mountains, clothing, and hairstyles. The gods, especially the nonhuman deities, are particularly detailed. The scenes in Yang's mundane world, whether in Chinatown or suburbia, have a distinctly American feel, but the panels flow smoothly together regardless of the scenes depicted.

Chinese pictographs are sprinkled throughout the text, giving the work an Asian authenticity. Text boxes have frill work that resembles Chinese screens. Occasionally, Yang encloses Chinese pictographic language in speech bubbles, such as when the Monkey King argues with Tze-Yo-Tzuh. Speech in Mandarin is rendered as bracketed English text. Sound effects and laugh and applause tracks add to rather than detract or distract from the story line.

Themes

Yang's autobiographical response to multicultural ignorance is shame and alienation. Like Yang, the novel's Jin Wang does not fit in either the world of his first-generation immigrant parents or the world of the white suburban mainstream. Instead, Jin must make his own way, letting his conscience, as represented by Wei-Chen, be his guide. Yang's art must similarly make its own way through the comic genre, and it does so by fusing a Disneyesque style with Asian overtones in an unexpected, yet familiar, way. Yang additionally reconciles Eastern and Western religion as the Monkey King recovers his identity. A devout Catholic, Yang depicts the Monkey King giving offerings to baby Jesus after completing his journey to the west, thus blending religious traditions.

Jin is a typical teenage boy, and Yang treats his young-adult readers as such, indulging in many low-brow gags and relatable cultural references. While Jin's Transformers toys serve as a recognizable symbol of childhood and pop culture for the book's readers, there is also an obvious symbolic connection between such toys and Jin as he dreams of his own physical transformation. Yang's slapstick delivers comic relief as he delves into the darker themes of alienation, shame, and prejudice while exploring cultural identity. *American Born Chinese* juxtaposes American teenage angst against a backdrop of anti-Asian prejudice, both by society at large and by Asian Americans trying to escape their roots. It is this humorous treatment of a serious subject that makes *American Born Chinese* accessible to its young-adult audience while making it stand apart from other graphic novels. The book offers a coming-of-age story that takes an honorable path, while not being overly moralistic.

Impact

With the publication of *American Born Chinese*, Yang became one of a number of rising stars in the Asian independent comics community of the San Francisco Bay Area, which also includes Kim and Pien. The work introduced Yang's art style, an updated Asian fusion of sorts, to a wide audience. The popularity and positive critical reception of the work allowed Yang to publish a number of additional graphic novels. As an accessible yet meaningful examination of multicultural identity, *American Born Chinese* has been incorporated into the curriculum of various high schools and universities, contributing to the increasing perception of the graphic novel as a relevant and legitimate form of literature.

Doré Ripley

Further Reading

Love, Jeremy. *Bayou* (2009).

Satrapi, Marjane. *Persepolis* (2003).

Yang, Gene Luen. *Gordon Yamamoto and the King of the Geeks* (2004).

Bibliography

Beeler, Monique. "A Born Storyteller. The ABCs of Graphic Novelist and National Book Award Finalist Gene Yang '03." *Cal State East Bay Magazine*, Spring/Summer, 2009, 11-17.

Boatwright, Michael D. "Graphic Journeys: Graphic Novels' Representation of Immigrant Experiences." *Journal of Adolescent and Adult Literacy* 53, no. 6 (March, 2010): 468-476.

Song, Hyoung Song. "'How Good It Is to Be a Monkey': Comics, Racial Formation, and American Born Chinese." *Mosaic: A Journal for the Interdisciplinary Study of Literature* 43, no. 1 (March, 2010): 73-92.

Yang, Gene Luen. "Printz Award Winner Speech." *Young Adult Library Services* 6, no. 1 (Fall, 2007): 11-13.

See also: *Persepolis; The Arrival*

AMERICAN SPLENDOR: FROM OFF THE STREETS OF CLEVELAND

Author: Pekar, Harvey

Artist: Greg Budgett (illustrator); Robert Crumb (illustrator); Gary G. Dumm (illustrator); Spain Rodriguez (illustrator); Joe Sacco (illustrator); Gerry Shamray (illustrator); Frank Stack (illustrator); Joe Zabel (illustrator); Mark Zingarelli (illustrator)

Publisher: Harvey Pekar; Dark Horse Comics; DC Comics

First serial publication: 1976-1991; 1993-2008

First book publication: 1987

Publication History

Harvey Pekar self-published the first fifteen issues of his autobiographical *American Splendor* from 1976 to 1991. He began recording his personal experiences in his thirties. Pekar could not draw, but he found willing underground comics publishers and illustrators, although it was not easy to tap into these resources from Cleveland. A further difficulty Pekar faced was the fact that comic artists found it difficult to draw in the "novo realism" style Pekar requested for his stories. Then, in the mid-1970's, Pekar's comics lost their main outlets when the head shops that sold underground comics became widely outlawed for selling drug paraphernalia.

Such complexities motivated Pekar to self-publish and led to the birth of *American Splendor* in 1976. Pekar also handled distribution during this time and kept back issues in print. A panel in *American Splendor* shows an exasperated Pekar sitting on undistributed bundles of issue 7 around the time he met actor Wallace Shawn, star of the film *My Dinner with André* (1981), hoping to make connections to buyers.

American Splendor's publishing history after 1990 is sporadic. Pekar contracted lymphoma and became involved with multiple publishing companies including Tundra Publishing, Dark Horse Comics, and DC Comics. Dark Horse published several *American Splendor* one-shots: *Comic-Con Comics* (1996); *Odds and Ends*, *Music Comics*, and *On the Job* (1997); *Transatlantic Comics* (1998); *Terminal* (1999); *Portrait of the Author in His Declining Years* (2001). Dark Horse also released themed issues or miniseries, such as *American Splendor: Windfall* (1995), containing two issues covering six months from 1993 to 1994 that center on Pekar's concerns about hip replacement, and *American Splendor: Unsung Hero* (2002), about an African American war hero. DC Comics published one issue, *Bedtime Stories*, in 2000, which was the last limited series of *American Splendor* (four issues in 2006 and five issues in 2007), and *American Splendor Season Two* (2008).

Pekar had numerous collaborators, such as Robert Crumb, who illustrated the first *American Splendor* in 1976. Throughout the years, stories in *American Splendor* were gathered into trade paperbacks. Pekar died nine months before his last book was scheduled for release.

Plot

Story lines in *American Splendor* emerge from the daily minutiae of real life in Cleveland, notably the author's own life, including episodes from his job as a clerk for the Cleveland Veterans Administration hospital, and are developed for adult readers as aesthetic representations of his mundane encounters. Important story lines involve some of Pekar's significant relationships, such as those with his wives and, particularly, Crumb, whom he met in 1962 when Crumb lived in Cleveland and worked for the American Greeting Corporation. Crumb's friendship significantly influenced the direction of Pekar's life and work. Crumb's edgy comic drafts, his overnight success as a greeting-card artist, and his later stardom in underground comics in San Francisco provided significant motivation for Pekar in the inception of *American Splendor*, as told in "The Young Robert Crumb Story."

Story lines follow Pekar's march through time. They involve the hero's confrontations with mundane experiences or fellow workers, his interactions with wives and girlfriends, and his own thoughts expressed in philosophical monologues. Important turns of plot follow the events in the author's real life, such as his contracting lymphoma in 1990. Pekar's need for the security of his government job gave consistency to his stories and provided an overall story arc until his retirement from civil service in October, 2001.

Drawings by diverse illustrators of the central character have tended to destabilize the visual identity and, thus, plot stability. In addition, Pekar sometimes narrated his experiences through Jack the Bellboy, the "sides hustler," or collector jazz records, or through Herschel, the intellectual author, both of whom look like Harvey. Just as Jack collects jazz "sides," readers of *American Splendor* collect Harvey "sides" in the multiple perspectives offered through the different lenses of the many illustrators.

Although Pekar was the most powerful unifying force, another element that lends stability is the setting of Cleveland, a microcosm of the United States that one panel advertises on the side of a bus: "The best things in life are right here in Cleveland." The sign goes unnoticed by a depressed hero as he climbs onto the bus and is characteristic of Pekar's narrative style in his use of irony and social commentary.

Volumes

- *The Comics Journal: Special Harvey Pekar Issue* (1985). *American Splendor* panels from various issues are included in a twenty-page script of a phone interview with Pekar and Gary Groth titled, "Harvey Pekar: In This Interview: Stories About Honesty, Money, and Misogyny."
- *From off the Streets of Cleveland Comes . . . American Splendor—The Life and Times of Harvey Pekar* (1987). Collects issues 1-9. This collection of comics from 1976 to 1984 features an introduction by Crumb. Pekar is listed along with Crumb as a cover artist.
- *The New American Splendor Anthology: From off the Streets of Cleveland* (1991). Collects a mix of stories from *American Splendor* and other stories from Pekar.
- *American Splendor Presents Bob and Harv's Comics* (1996). Collects issues 1-9, 12, and *The People's Comics*, issue 1. This collection of comics from 1972 to 1984 includes Pekar's first comic, "Brilliant American Maniacs Series, No.

1: Crazy Ed," first published in 1972 in Crumb's *The People's Comics*. Pekar is listed along with Crumb as a cover artist.
- *American Splendor: Unsung Hero* (2003). Collects issues 1-3 of *American Splendor: Unsung Hero*. A three-issue biography of Robert McNeill, an African American veteran of the Vietnam War.
- *American Splendor: The Life and Times of Harvey Pekar* (2003). Collects trade paperbacks *American Splendor: The Life and Times of Harvey Pekar* and *More American Splendor: The Life and Times of Harvey Pekar*.
- *American Splendor: Our Movie Year* (2004). Recounts the making of the 2003 film *American Splendor*.
- *Best of American Splendor* (2005). Collects *American Splendor* essays from the 1990's and 2000's.
- *American Splendor: Another Day* (2007). Collects issues 1-4 of 2006-2007 series. Numerous artists collaborate with Pekar on more stories of everyday life.
- *American Splendor: Another Dollar* (2009). Collects issues 1-4 of 2008 series. Stories look at the process of creating comics; others follow Pekar through the aging process.

Characters

- *Harvey Pekar*, the eponymous hero based on the author. The character is both the protagonist and his own antagonist. He is generally described as irascible, fidgety, and never satisfied. The character also has a philosophical nature and a tendency to examine the morality of acts that are often overlooked or considered insignificant.
- *Jack the Bellboy* is a "sides hustler," a collector of jazz and other musical recordings that he tries to sell to fellow employees. The narrator describes him as an "obsessive-compulsive jazz record collector," or a "demon record hustler." He is drawn as Harvey's visual doppelgänger. A facile reading identifies him with the author, since Pekar was known as a jazz record collector.
- *Herschel* is another split image of Harvey. The narrator describes him as a man who knows what

he wants. He works as a file clerk in a government job, but writing is the most important thing in his life. He has been writing and publishing on many aspects of popular culture since he was nineteen, and he wants public recognition for his work.

- *Robert Crumb* is an avant-garde artist and writer of 1960's underground comics, such as *Zap Comix* (1968-2005) and *Fritz the Cat* (1965-1972). The character, a reticent, educated, and talented young man who hits the San Francisco scene, provides a stable thread based on his long friendship with Pekar.

- *Toby Radloff* is perhaps the most famous of *American Splendor* characters since the character's namesake, real-life Toby, became "Genuine Nerd" for MTV. Radloff was hired at the Cleveland Veteran's Administration as a file clerk in 1980. The character is featured in issue 9, "Lent and Lentils," in 1984.

- *Mr. Boats* is Harvey's wise supervisor who quotes poetry and homilies. He gives free violin lessons at a community center and worries about the degeneration of youth and music.

- *Joyce Brabner* is based on Pekar's third wife. All of his wives figure significantly as characters in his stories and in his life. Brabner's character vacillates between depression and being controlling.

- *Danielle* is Pekar's and Brabner's adopted daughter.

- *David Letterman* is a character based on the NBC talk-show celebrity; his appearance marks important turning points in Pekar's life and stories. For a year, Pekar had become a regular on Letterman's show. Although his appearances bring needed publicity, the relationship ends when, as represented in the story, Pekar's wife becomes dissatisfied with his relationship with Letterman and Harvey aggressively challenges Letterman on air to condemn General Electric, the parent company of NBC.

Artistic Style

Pekar storyboarded his scripts with stick figures and sometimes collaborated as the artist on covers. He viewed his stories as play scripts that gave stage direction to the illustrator. Pekar came to know what to expect from the many illustrators who, in their own way, helped visualize and actualize his stories, such as Crumb's drawings in the "Maggies" story, which actualized and intensified the humor. Pekar could count on the intense physical responses that Crumb gave to characters, whereas for other illustrations, Gary Dumm's, for example, Pekar knew that the dialogue or narration would receive greater prominence.

The monochromatic stories are depicted in black and white, and the imposition of the mental in thought bubbles and narration add to the intellectual tone that Pekar sought in his stories. The use of bubbles also emphasizes the importance of individual life in each of the panels. Pekar also captures individuality with his keen ear for a character's speech dialect. When it occurs, narration is generally straight across at the top or bottom of the panel. In first-person narration, the narrator and Harvey sometimes compete for space. This happens, for example, in "The Young Crumb Story" drawn by Crumb, where, in the end, narration disappears in the struggle and an embarrassed cartoon-Harvey apologetically takes over the black space of the last panels as the only character in the black void of fiction, as if neither fiction nor reality can exist independent of the other.

Most artistically significant is the graphic construction of Harvey, the central character. Artistic input was especially important in the aesthetic creation of Harvey, because the stories revolve around the author's personal experience. Through the medium of pictures, Pekar and his illustrators are able to re-create the tension in personal identity between, paradoxically, the fragmentation and the coherence of disparate aspects of a self. By drawing other characters, such as Jack the Bellboy and Herschel, to resemble Harvey visually, the illustrators re-create the interior tension in the interplay between fragmentation and coherence of the self. Adding to the weirdness of this interplay and tension is a more focused attempt to imitate the visual reality of Pekar. For example, Pekar had said that Gerry Shamray took photographs of him in various positions and traced the photographs, and that Crumb began drawing Pekar from Shamray's renderings. These attempts to trap reality within the space of comics add to the author's insertion of his mundane world in the fictive world of representation, an important theme of *American Splendor* that the film adaptation captures more graphically.

Themes

American Splendor involves the everyday struggles, aspirations, or moral dilemmas that challenge the characters in the comic. Pekar saw *American Splendor* as his ongoing autobiography, and his belief in the intimacy of art and life, the interplay of the fictive and the real, the mental and the physical in the daily life of an individual were major thematic concerns in his life and work.

The author's interest in capturing reality in comics, combined with artistic and narrative techniques, works to develop this fundamental theme of the displacement of personal experience into an artistic space for an ultimately greater understanding of the small things that play a big role in the daily life of a regular, working guy. The characters are depicted as trying to understand their predicaments or feelings through rational thought and language.

Illustrations and characters express Pekar's philosophy of the intimacy between life and art. Harvey ultimately realizes that he "sublimates" things that bother him by writing stories about them.

Impact

American Splendor pushed the edges of the potential of comics as a storytelling medium. Pekar became an advocate for the comics medium in the early 1970's. His stories about the daily lives of ordinary characters drawn from his everyday life blazed a new path for comics, which had previously focused on fantasy themes or talking animals. Although Crumb had been instrumental in the underground comics scene in San Francisco, evading censorship and the Comics Code Authority and taking comics into new political and sexual territory. Pekar's idea was that comics had the resilience and flexibility of prose as a storytelling medium. Pekar's "novo realism," as he called his style, influenced comics published in the wake of American

Splendor, such as Joe Sacco's *Palestine* (2001) and Gilbert Hernandez's *Love and Rockets* (1981-1996).

The series gave minor celebrity to several of the characters' eponyms, such as Toby Radloff, who became the "Genuine Nerd" roving reporter for MTV in the 1980's and gained more fame after the movie adaptation in 2003. Joyce Brabner, Pekar's third wife, began writing comics and was coauthor of *Our Cancer Year* (1994).

For many years, commercial success eluded the author until after the film adaptation and his retirement as a civil servant. But *American Splendor* gained critical acclaim early on from respected reviewers. Although *Our Cancer Year*, which lacked the *American Splendor* logo, was the weakest selling of all of his books, it won the 1995 Harvey Award for Best Graphic Album of Original Work and its stories were included in the film adaptation.

Films

American Splendor. Directed by Shari Springer Berman and Robert Pulcini. Good Machine/HBO Films (2003). This film adaptation stars Paul Giamatti as Harvey Pekar, Earl Billings as Mr. Boats, and Hope Davis as Joyce Brabner. The film stirs up fiction and reality more graphically than the comics and won the 2003 Sundance Film Festival Grand Jury Prize for Dramatic Film.

Cristine Soliz

Further Reading

Campbell, Eddie. *Alec* (1981-   ).

Crumb, Robert. *The Complete Fritz the Cat* (1965-1972).

Pekar, Harvey, and Joyce Brabner. *Our Cancer Year* (1994).

Thompson, Craig. *Blankets* (2003).

Bibliography

O'English, Lorena, J. Gregory Matthews, and Elizabeth Blakesley Lindsay. "Graphic Novels in Academic Libraries: From *Maus* to Manga and Beyond." *The Journal of Academic Librarianship* 32, no. 2 (March, 2006): 173-182.

Pekar, Harvey. "*Maus* and Other Topics." *The Comics Journal* 113 (December, 1986): 54-57.

Sperb, Jason. "Removing the Experience: Simulacrum as an Autobiographical Act in *American Splendor*." *Biography* 29, no. 1 (Winter, 2006): 123-139.

Witek, Joseph. *Comic Books as History: The Narrative Art of Jack Jackson, Art Spiegelman, and Harvey Pekar*. Jackson: Mississippi University Press, 1989.

_____. "From Genre to Medium: Comics and Contemporary American Culture." In *Rejuvenating the Humanities*, edited by Ray B. Browne and Marshall W. Fishwick. Bowling Green, Ohio: Bowling Green State University Popular Press, 1992.

See also: *Alec: The Years Have Pants; Blankets; Our Cancer Year; The Complete Fritz the Cat*

ARRIVAL, THE

Author: Tan, Shaun
Artist: Shaun Tan (illustrator)
Publisher: Lothian Books
First book publication: 2006

Publication History

Like all of Shaun Tan's previous titles, *The Arrival* was first published by Lothian Books, an imprint of Hachette Australia. In the publishing industry, Lothian is known for its high-quality titles for children, especially innovative picture books that regularly win prestigious awards. In October, 2007, Arthur A. Levine Books, an imprint of Scholastic, produced the first American edition.

In response to the enormous success of *The Arrival*, Lothian treated fans to a special slipcase edition in September, 2010, which contains not only the original graphic novel but also *Sketches from a Nameless Land*, a companion volume that explores the creative process behind the book. This oversized box set boasts a high production value in terms of the two volumes' covers and binding.

Two months later, the Deluxe Limited Collector's Edition followed, of which only fifteen hundred copies were produced, containing both books and a first-release print of an illustration taken from *The Arrival*, individually numbered and signed by Tan. All this came packed in a box made to look like a worn leather suitcase, featuring an actual handle and strap. These editions are clearly targeted at adult readers, and comics connoisseurs in particular, indicating a new sales strategy of marketing *The Arrival* as a premium-quality art book.

Plot

The Arrival, a wordless graphic novel about immigration and its attendant hardships, achieves three things with remarkable aplomb. First, it transcends its humble beginnings as a picture book without losing sight of the simple story at its heart, holding as much fascination for a young reader as it would for a more literary-minded adult. Second, it strikes the right

(Getty Images)

Shaun Tan

Shaun Tan, an Australian painter, writer, and muralist is best known in the United States for illustrated books that deal with social, political, and historical subjects with dreamlike images. His long picture books and graphic novels are visually complex compositions of symbols, fantastical creatures, and emotive settings and situations. Haunting and mysterious, his work interprets mature themes like alienation, depression, and relocation in a way that is clever, fresh, and thought-provoking. His use of visual metaphors and references and his uncanny mix of the familiar with the surreal are best appreciated by sophisticated readers.

balance between a universal tale and the specific tale of one family, compromising neither its allegorical nature nor its heartfelt sympathy for the main protagonist. Third, the book ingeniously places the reader in the role of the immigrant, confronting its audience with situations that they do not really know how to read. Since Tan does not provide any verbal clues and frequently narrates through surreal images and symbols, readers need the full power of their imagination to navigate the fantastic landscapes of this new world.

The Arrival is divided into six chapters. The first reveals that the family's country of origin is afflicted by an unknown danger, symbolized by enormous black serpents winding through the empty streets. The nameless protagonist packs his suitcase and walks to the railway station with his wife and daughter, where he leaves them in search of a better life abroad.

The next chapter introduces the enormous ocean liner that will take the protagonist across the sea to the land of promise and hope. After many weeks confined in a small cabin or huddled on deck, he arrives in the harbor of a metropolis, where he is processed along with dozens of others by the local authorities. His physical condition is checked, he is asked countless questions in a foreign language, and his clothes are marked with strange symbols. In the end, he manages to obtain a work permit, and a hot-air balloon takes him to a residential area, where another immigrant assists him in finding a place to stay. There he encounters a strange, tadpole-like creature, which he eventually adopts as his pet.

Parts three and four are concerned with life in the new city. The immigrant struggles with the most mundane activities, such as operating a ticket machine or buying food at the market; however, his real challenge is finding a job. In all of these instances, he is helped by other immigrants, three of whom narrate their own dramatic life stories in flashbacks. The protagonist also befriends a man and his young son, who assist him and even invite him to their own home.

In the fifth chapter, the immigrant writes a letter home, enclosing money so that his wife and daughter can join him eventually. However, many months pass before they are finally reunited.

In the final chapter, we see the family firmly established in their new home. What used to be strange and unfamiliar is now part of everyday life, and the book ends with the daughter helping another immigrant find her way. The family has finally "arrived" in their new country—not just physically, but emotionally.

Characters

The *unnamed protagonist* is the only major character, and he serves as a stand-in for the reader to explore a unique world that is both alien and strangely familiar. It is to this end that the endpapers show sixty tiny portraits of various immigrants from all over the world, including one of Tan's father at the time he came to Australia from Malaysia in 1960. While the book aspires to tell a universal tale of immigration, Tan also acknowledges his own family history and endows the protagonist with enough dignity and character to sustain readers' interest in his fate. The immigrant bears a striking resemblance to the artist himself, for Tan based all of the characters on digital photographs and videos of himself and his friends, which he specifically took to use as reference material.

The protagonist is of Eurasian descent, is in his early thirties, and consistently wears his best suit and hat, possibly the only items of clothing he has left. The rest of his possessions fit into a small suitcase. He is a cautious, reliable, and diligent man, whose friendships are marked by quiet appreciation rather than boisterous shows of affection. A master in the art of origami, he can instantly produce a paper replica of any animal he encounters. Since the overall design of the book is based on old photo albums and archival material, the characters look slightly old-fashioned, as if they belong to a bygone age of steam power and early industry.

Artistic Style

It took Tan almost five years to complete *The Arrival*, from 2001 to 2006, partly because he was working on several other projects at the same time. Tan had to prepare himself for the daunting transition from drawing a thirty-two-page picture book, his usual format, to creating a full-fledged graphic novel. He found an ideal model for such a transition in Raymond Briggs's *The Snowman* (1978); the most important influence, however, came from the "language" of pictorial archives (Ellis Island Immigration Museum) and old photo albums, which have the documentary clarity of evidence, yet remain mysterious and resistant to easy interpretation due to their lack of explanatory text.

The Arrival is a hybrid between picture book and graphic novel. Tan repeatedly arrests the narrative flow to focus the reader's attention on silent, often very detailed drawings, spread across one or two pages and seemingly frozen in time, which invite contemplation rather than a quick transition to the next panel. Otherwise, he shows great variety and ingenuity in the page layouts, the result of a long and arduous research process involving the use of three "dummy" books in different stages of abstraction to test the narrative flow of the work.

Tan used only graphite pencils (H to 2B) on cartridge paper, achieving the photorealism of the illustrations through extensive pencil shading. He then digitally added colors (a reduced palette of sepia tones, grays, and yellows) and texturing (mostly creases, stains, and blotches) in Photoshop in order to re-create the worn, yellowish look of old and frequently perused albums.

The Arrival includes several visual references to well-known paintings, such as Tom Roberts's *Coming South* (1886) and Gustave Doré's *Over London by Rail* (c. 1870), and photographs from the Ellis Island photo archive. These allusions contextualize the book in terms of industrial history and some of the major immigration waves in the history of Australia and the United States.

Themes

The most obvious thematic concerns in *The Arrival* are migration, displacement, and the questions of identity and belonging. Since Tan envisions his new world as a utopian society in which everyone seems to be exceptionally kind and helpful, the harsher aspects of immigration, such as tyranny and exploitation, are exclusively associated with the characters' homelands.

The book is also about traveling, leaving behind the safety and familiarity of a culture in which everything and everyone is accounted for, and engaging with a new environment that has many surprises in store for the willing adventurer. This fresh look requires an open mind, such as a child's or an artist's point of view, that can bring out the extraordinary in everyday life.

Like the main character, the readers are temporarily impaired in the full exercise of their abilities; they become illiterate, overwhelmed by the experience of strangeness that Tan creates through his surreal and densely symbolic images. Even the most careful reader will not be able to rationally understand every single panel, resulting in an interesting exercise in imagination and humility.

As the book depicts life with a major impairment that can be overcome through perseverance and social contacts, it may also be encouraging to disadvantaged readers, not only those who are immigrants themselves but also readers who have to live with disability, illiteracy, or a lack of certain skills. This particularly includes the deaf or mute, since the wordlessness of the novel mirrors the immigrant's inability to understand the dominant language of his new home or make himself understood.

Impact

The Arrival has been extremely well received across the whole range of publication formats with which it can be associated—picture book, children's literature, young-adult fiction, graphic novel, art book—gaining recognition and winning several awards in these categories around the world. It calls attention to the picture book as a literary form and firmly establishes the wordless graphic novel as a viable option for tackling serious subject matter; Eric Drooker's *Blood Song* (2002) and Peter Kuper's *Sticks and Stones* (2004) are two important forerunners of this genre, but Tan takes the concept to a new level. Since he does not see himself as a comics artist, preferring to work as an illustrator, *The Arrival* is likely to remain his only graphic novel.

Within the narrower field of picture books for young adults, Tan may be the most prominent artist, but there is a noticeable trend developing, of which *The Arrival* is just the tip of the iceberg. Like animated films, picture books are gradually finding a new audience of adults who are willing to keep an open mind and enjoy the astounding complexities of these narratives, even if the basic story is geared toward children. This noticeable shift in readership is also evidenced by the latest editions of the book, which clearly target a different audience. The same can be said about the two stage productions based on the novel.

Stage Adaptations

The Arrival developed simultaneously as a graphic novel and a stage play, using puppetry, pantomime, music, and digitally animated illustrations. Tan was involved in the initial creative development phase, providing sketches and finished illustrations, but left the actual dramatization to director Philip Mitchell, scriptwriter Michael Barlow, and designer Jiri Zmitko of the Spare Parts Puppet Theatre company. Despite plans to present both book and stage adaptation simultaneously to the public, Tan was late in finishing his own project, which meant that the play came out three months before (June, 2006) and deviated in several points from the finished book. The play was generally well received and won the 2006 Western Australian Equity Guild Award for Best Production of the Year.

The Arrival was also adapted for the stage by Kate Parker and Julie Nolan for the Red Leap Theatre company, based in Auckland, New Zealand, where it was first staged during the Auckland Festival of March 12-15, 2009, under the direction of Nolan. It used pantomime, puppetry, dance, movable set pieces, and various props to imaginatively re-create the visual impact of the book. The play was highly acclaimed, winning six Chapman Tripp Theatre Awards in 2010.

Markus Oppolzer

Further Reading

Briggs, Raymond. *The Snowman* (1978).

Drooker, Eric. *Blood Song: A Silent Ballad* (2002).

_____. *Flood! A Novel in Pictures* (1992).

Kuper, Peter. *Sticks and Stones* (2004).

Satrapi, Marjane. *Persepolis* (2003).

Bibliography

Tan, Shaun. "A Conversation with Illustrator Shaun Tan." Interview by Chuan-Yao Ling. *World Literature Today* 82, no. 5 (September/October, 2008): 44-47.

_____. "Silent Voices: Illustration and Visual Narrative." The 2009 Colin Simpson Memorial Lecture, March 28, 2009. http://www.asauthors.org/scripts/cgiip.exe/WService=ASP0016/ccms.r?PageId=10216.

_____. *Sketches from a Nameless Land: The Art of "The Arrival."* Melbourne: Lothian, 2010.

Yang, Gene Luen. Review of *The Arrival*, by Shaun Tan. *The New York Times*, November 11, 2007. http://www.nytimes.com/2007/11/11/books/review/Yang-t.html.

See also: *American Born Chinese*

ASTERIOS POLYP

Author: Mazzucchelli, David
Artist: David Mazzucchelli (illustrator)
Publisher: Pantheon Books
First book publication: 2009

Publication History

After an early career working for Marvel and DC Comics, David Mazzucchelli left the world of superhero comics and turned to more experimental projects. Most notably, comics creator Art Spiegelman encouraged him to collaborate with cartoonist Paul Karasik on an adaptation of *City of Glass* (1994), the acclaimed Paul Auster novella. Its critical success raised expectations about Mazzucchelli's next book, his first as the sole author and artist. *Asterios Polyp* was published in the summer of 2009 by Pantheon Books, which has been a major force in graphic novels since the 1980's. Pantheon has handled the work of such comics luminaries as Raymond Briggs, Marjane Satrapi, Spiegelman, and Chris Ware. Mazzucchelli submitted a preview of about half of the material in the book in November, 2007.

Since the mid-1990's, Mazzucchelli has been teaching, notably at Manhattan's School of Visual Arts. As a participant in the U.S./Japan Creative Artists Program, he lived and worked in Japan from August, 2000, to January, 2001. These experiences presumably influenced *Asterios Polyp*, which tells of a professor's relationship with a Japanese American sculptor.

Plot

Asterios Polyp starts with a thunderstorm, a lightning strike, and a fire in Manhattan. The date is June 22, 2000, Asterios Polyp's fiftieth birthday. Living alone and in a state of disarray, he must flee his burning apartment. However, he manages to gather three objects: a cigarette lighter, a watch, and a penknife. The significance of each is revealed later. Although the fire occurs at the beginning of the book, it falls in the middle of Asterios's larger story. The book's twenty-two chapters alternate between ones set before and after the fire, forming a lengthy "abab" pattern.

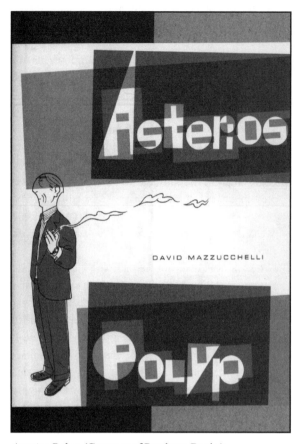

Asterios Polyp. (Courtesy of Pantheon Books)

Ignazio, Asterios's deceased twin, claims to narrate those chapters dealing with events preceding the fire. He tells of the life and career of Asterios, a brilliant but egotistical professor of architecture. After a string of casual affairs (often with students), Asterios meets and marries Hana Sonnenschein, a colleague and sculptor. Later, Hana accepts a commission to make set designs for a dance production, *Orpheus (Underground)*, based on the Greek myth of Orpheus and Eurydice, and she increasingly spends her time with its director, Willy Ilium. Soon life echoes myth, and Asterios finds Hana slipping away from his grasp. In December, 1993, after seven years of marriage, she files for divorce.

The chapters of the book set after the fire are no longer narrated by Ignazio, who nevertheless reappears in five of Asterios's dreams. Leaving his apartment and Manhattan behind him, Asterios takes a Greyhound bus as far as he can, to an unfamiliar town called Apogee. Here, Asterios sets about making a modest life for himself. Finding a job as an auto mechanic, he lodges with his boss, Stiffly Major, and socializes with Stiffly's friends and family. He helps Stiffly construct a tree house for his son, Jackson—it is the first structure the architect has ever built—and sees his friends' band play in a bar. While there, a near stranger hits Asterios with a bottle and blinds his left eye. Asterios resolves to leave Apogee. He does so in an improbable manner, fixing Stiffly's solar-powered car and driving it to the house of his former wife. Upon arriving, Hana and Asterios talk of their past together and about life since their divorce. The atmosphere becomes increasingly convivial and reconciliation seems possible.

Events then take a cosmic turn. A meteor or asteroid suddenly plunges toward Hana's house, leaving her and Asterios's future uncertain. Back in his Apogee tree house, Jackson spots a shooting star in the sky.

Characters

- *Asterios Polyp*, the protagonist, is the son of Greek and Italian immigrants and a middle-aged professor of architecture at a university in Ithaca, New York. He is a successful author and theoretician, but he is only a "paper architect" since none of his designs has been constructed. He is brilliant but rather unlikable, and his egotism is tempered by a sense of incompleteness. He is searching for something beyond himself, some complementary person or point of view. Usually depicted in strict profile, Asterios's most unusual

Asterios Polyp. (Courtesy of Pantheon Books)

physical attribute is his head, which resembles the blade of an upturned ax.

- *Ignazio Polyp* is Asterios's stillborn identical twin brother. Although the narrator of the book claims to be Ignazio, the dead twin may persist only in Asterios's complicated psyche. Thus, he appears in several of Asterios's dreams, which reveal Asterios's complicated feelings of rivalry, guilt, aggression, and anger. In the last of these, Asterios sees his twin as an impostor and attacks him with a wrench. The two are sometimes difficult to tell apart; however, Ignazio is right-handed, while Asterios is left-handed.

- *Hana Sonnenschein* (whose last name means "sunshine" in German), Asterios's wife between 1986 and 1993, is a Japanese American sculptor and an art professor with long hair and large eyes. She is inspired by nature, and her art stresses organic, curvilinear forms; her aesthetic influences Asterios's writing and thinking, but it also stands in sharp contrast to them.

- *Willy Ilium*, a squat man with dark hair and a double chin, is an avant-garde choreographer whose work makes extensive use of quotations from existing dance compositions. He hires Hana as the art designer for his "new" and ill-fated work, *Orpheus (Underground)*. While Hana and Asterios's relationship begins to falter, Willy flatters her with his attention.

- *Stiffly Major* is the large, mustachioed Apogee mechanic who offers Asterios a job in his repair shop and lodging in his house.

- *Ursula Major* is Stiffly's wife and Jackson's mother. Blond and buxom, she is confident of her ability to attract men, but her relationship with Asterios remains platonic. Ursula is drawn to Native American traditions, astrology, and other manifestations of New Age culture. Like Hana, she offers a distinctive counterpoint to Asterios's worldview.

Artistic Style

Asterios Polyp requires its reader to consider how visual elements contribute to the story's possible meanings. Notably, Mazzucchelli employs a number of different representational styles and makes innovative use of color, experimenting to aid organizational clarity, for thematic ends, and to suggest important differences among characters.

Thus, each main character is associated with a specific color, drawn using an appropriate style, and given a particular type of speech balloon and font. Asterios is associated with blue and rendered in sparse and geometric lines. His speech bubbles are rectangular and enclose all-caps lettering. In a number of scenes between Asterios and Hana, their contrasting design elements blend harmoniously when they are getting along, but suddenly separate when conflict arises.

The book's page layouts are notably varied. Conventional panels are used extensively but are interspersed with borderless panels, bleeds, splash pages, and near the center of the book, a double spread. The author helps the reader to navigate the complicated architecture of his unpaginated book by breaking the material into twenty-two chapters, each preceded by a blank leaf and a single illustration in the middle of the opposite (recto) page.

Through calculated use of the "printer's primaries" (cyan, magenta, and yellow), color also plays a crucial organizational role. Cyans, purples, and reds are used for the pre-fire chapters of the book, while the scenes set in Apogee are rendered using yellows and purples. Found in both palettes, purple, not black, serves for most of the line work and for most of the retelling of the Orpheus myth, which links the two major sections of the book. Late in the story, after Asterios is partially blinded, Mazzucchelli introduces a more varied color scheme. The reader encounters oranges, greens, and browns for the first time. This more naturalistic palette hints that Asterios is leaving the stark divisions of his past behind him.

Themes

Asterios Polyp is a book about doubles, divisions, dualism, and the relationship among these things. Its eponymous character is a twin who has been separated from his stillborn brother and whose dualistic worldview seems to emerge from this primary trauma. "Duality is rooted in nature," Asterios informs a skeptical colleague. Events test and soften Asterios's philosophical convictions, while the characters he meets advance alternative and less rigid worldviews.

Accordingly, Asterios maintains that the important thing about the World Trade Center's Twin Towers is simply "that there are two of them." During a sculpture class, Hana echoes their arrangement by placing two bricks on end. She asks her students, "How many do you see?" and, on the grounds that the space between the bricks "is the same size and shape of a brick," welcomes the answer "three." The choice of the Twin Towers is hardly casual: This, after all, is a book set largely in 2000 (not long before the September 11, 2001, terrorist attacks that destroyed both towers) and about the untimely destruction of twins. Through this imagery, Mazzucchelli teaches the reader about negative space, about how absent things can be evoked merely by the things surrounding them.

Just as James Joyce's novel *Ulysses* (1922) and the Coen brothers' film *O Brother, Where Art Thou?* (2000), this book retells and modernizes the Greek classics. Like the divided twins mentioned in Plato's *Symposium*, Asterios is driven by a desire to find wholeness and companionship. Further parallels are made between Asterios's life and the mythical lives of the poet Orpheus and the wandering warrior Odysseus: Asterios also experiences trauma and loss, is compelled to wander far from home, and will eventually return, except that his destination will not be Ithaca but the person he met there, Hana.

Asterios Polyp explores how loss and suffering may also allow for personal reinvention. Asterios starts out an inflexible egotist, but he gradually becomes a sympathetic character—generous, companionable, helpful, and vulnerable. The paper architect is now substantial, having moved from believing in a world of two dimensions to living in one of three.

Impact

Upon publication, *Asterios Polyp* was greeted with widespread critical acclaim. A book with evident crossover appeal, it was reviewed positively both in publications devoted to comics and in several major daily papers, including *The Guardian*, *Los Angeles Times*, and *The New York Times*. In 2010, French and German translations of the book appeared, thus broadening its

---

David Mazzucchelli

David Mazzucchelli began his career as a superhero artist and then slowly transformed himself into one of the most respected creators of literary comics. In the superhero genre, Mazzucchelli is best remembered for his collaborations with Frank Miller: *Daredevil: Born Again* for Marvel and *Batman: Year One* for DC. The latter, in particular, is grounded in a starkly minimalist style, filled with shadows and grit. Mazzucchelli's Batman appeared more like a real-life person in costume than a superhuman caped crusader. Abandoning the field of superhero comics, Mazzucchelli self-published three volumes of an anthology titled *Rubber Blanket* and adapted Paul Auster's postmodern detective novel, *City of Glass*, into comics form. In 2009, after a near-fifteen-year hiatus from comics publishing, he released *Asterios Polyp*, a graphic novel about an architect that uses several different cartooning styles to delineate different characters.

---

readership and realm of influence. Positive reviews stressed the book's appeal as a beautifully designed object, applauded Mazzucchelli's ability to integrate formal experimentation and philosophical themes into his story, and observed that the book repays multiple readings.

More skeptical voices countered that the artist's visual inventiveness merely masks a routine story. Some critics found the book's secondary characters underdeveloped and stereotyped rather than humorous, taking particular issue with the characterization of Willy Ilium and the Majors. The book's dense web of literary, artistic, and astronomical references also had the power to either enchant or irritate. Scholars, critics, and fans alike will undoubtedly continue debating its merits.

Benjamin Harvey

Further Reading

Madden, Matt. *Ninety-Nine Ways to Tell a Story: Exercises in Style* (2005).

McCloud, Scott. *Understanding Comics: The Invisible Art* (1993).

Spiegelman, Art. *In the Shadow of No Towers* (2004).

Bibliography
Mazzucchelli, David. Interview by Frank Young. *Comics Journal* 152 (August, 1992): 114-119.
"TCJ 300 Conversations: David Mazzucchelli and Dash Shaw." *Comics Journal*, December, 16, 2009. http://classic.tcj.com/tcj-300/tcj-300-conversations-david-mazzucchelli-dash-shaw/

Wolk, Douglas. "Shades of Meaning." Review of *Asterios Polyp* by David Mazzucchelli. *The New York Times Book Review*, July 26, 2009, p. 11.

See also: *Maus: A Survivor's Tale; The Arrival; Persepolis*

ASTERIX

Author: Goscinny, René; Uderzo, Albert

Artist: Albert Uderzo (illustrator)

Publisher: Editions Dargaud; Editions Albert-René; Hachette

First serial publication: 1961-1979 (English translation, 1969-1975)

First book publication: 1961 (English translation, 1969)

Publication History

Asterix was created during an afternoon-long brainstorming session in the summer of 1959 by writer René Goscinny and cartoonist Albert Uderzo as one of the flagship series for the weekly anthology comic *Pilote*. The character appeared in the magazine's premiere issue on October 29, 1959. The first volume, *Astérix le Gaulois*, a 44-page graphic novel, was published in France as a hardback in 1961 as part of a bid by new *Pilote* owner Georges Dargaud to market several of the weekly's most popular series in regular bookstores.

After a slow start, the series became a publishing phenomenon within its first four years. Twenty-four volumes co-created by Goscinny and Uderzo were released from 1961 to 1979. Brockhampton Press's English translations (beginning with *Asterix the Gaul* in 1969) were subsequently picked up by William Morrow in the United States. After Goscinny's premature death in 1977, Uderzo single-handedly produced ten more volumes from 1980 to 2009 under his own imprint, Editions Albert-René. Since 2011, Asterix has belonged to the publishing consortium Hachette.

Except for five volumes translated into American English by Robert Caron for Dargaud International in the late 1980's, all *Asterix* books available in North America are Anthea Bell and Derek Hockridge's British translations.

Plot

All thirty-four *Asterix* volumes take place in Roman-occupied Gaul in 50 B.C.E., two years after Julius Caesar's troops defeated the Gaulish leader Vercingetorix at Alesia. Each volume opens on a map of France with

Albert Uderzo and René Goscinny (Gamma-Keystone via Getty Images)

René Goscinny

Arguably the greatest writer of humor comics in the history of France, René Goscinny's legacy is so great that the Angoulême comics festival presents an award named for him. Best known in the English-reading world as the writer of the *Asterix* series (with artist Albert Uderzo), Goscinny is equally known in Europe as the author of *Lucky Luke* (with Morris) and *Iznogoud* (with Jean Tabary). Goscinny was one of the most prolific writers of the 1950's and 1960's in France, producing dozens of albums and series, and a number of short works that have not been collected. In 1960 he became the editor-in-chief of the hugely influential comics magazine *Pilote*, and an entire generation of artists and writers came of age under his tutelage. Goscinny's stories are marked by their clever humor and creative wordplay. His adventure work featured elaborate worlds and truly memorable characters, many of whom remain household names in France.

a Roman standard stuck on the approximate spot of the previous battle of Gergovia (in the present-day Auvergne region), the last Gaulish victory against Rome.

In Brittany, one unnamed village of indomitable Gauls holds out against the invaders thanks to druid

Getafix's secret mistletoe-based magic potion that gives the drinker temporary superhuman strength. Under the benevolent leadership of chieftain Vitalstatistix, the villagers, who fear nothing except that the sky might fall on their heads, live a peaceful daily life interrupted by occasional attacks against one of the four Roman camps surrounding the village.

Asterix stories unfold in the perpetual present. There is little continuity from one volume to the next except in the setting (the village, the surrounding forest, and the nearby seashore); consistent characterization of the recurring figures; and repeated jokes about the pirates, whose boat sinks in practically every book, or the bard tied and gagged during the final feast.

Each story focuses on an adventure, most often a quest or rescue, featuring Asterix and Obelix. The action takes place either around the village, elsewhere in Gaul, in Rome, or in foreign lands, such as Great Britain, Spain, Switzerland, and Belgium.

Volumes

- *Astérix le Gaulois* (1961; *Asterix the Gaul*, 1969).
- *La Serpe d'or* (1962; *Asterix and the Golden Sickle*, 1975).
- *Astérix et les Goths* (1963; *Asterix and the Goths*, 1975).
- *Astérix Gladiateur* (1964; *Asterix the Gladiator*, 1969).
- *Le Tour de Gaule* (1965; *Asterix and the Banquet*, 1979).
- *Astérix et Cléopâtre* (1965; *Asterix and Cleopatra*, 1969).
- *Le Combat des Chefs* (1966; *Asterix and the Big Fight*, 1971).
- *Astérix chez les Bretons* (1966; *Asterix in Britain*, 1970).
- *Astérix et les Normands* (1967; *Asterix and the Normans*, 1978).
- *Astérix Légionnaire* (1967; *Asterix the Legionary*, 1970).
- *Le Bouclier Arverne* (1968; *Asterix and the Chieftain's Shield*, 1977).
- *Astérix aux Jeux Olympiques* (1968; *Asterix at the Olympic Games*, 1972).

- *Astérix et le Chaudron* (1969; *Asterix and the Cauldron*, 1976).
- *Astérix en Hispanie* (1969; *Asterix in Spain*, 1971).
- *La Zizanie* (1970; *Asterix and the Roman Agent*, 1972).
- *Astérix chez les Helvètes* (1970; *Asterix in Switzerland*, 1973).
- *Le Domaine des Dieux* (1971; *The Mansions of the Gods*, 1973).
- *Les Lauriers de César* (1972; *Asterix and the Laurel Wreath*, 1974).
- *Le Devin* (1972; *Asterix and the Soothsayer*, 1975).
- *Astérix en Corse* (1973; *Asterix in Corsica*, 1975).
- *Le Cadeau de César* (1974; *Asterix and Caesar's Gift*, 1977).
- *La Grande Traversée* (1975; *Asterix and the Great Crossing*, 1977).
- *Obélix et Compagnie* (1976; *Obelix and Co.*, 1978).
- *Astérix chez les Belges* (1979; *Asterix in Belgium*, 1980).
- *Le Grand Fossé* (1980; *Asterix and the Great Divide*, 1981).
- *L'Odyssée d'Astérix* (1981; *Asterix and the Black Gold*, 1982).
- *Le Fils d'Astérix* (1983; *Asterix and Son*, 1983).
- *Astérix chez Rahazade* (1987; *Asterix and the Magic Carpet*, 1988).
- *La Rose et le Glaive* (1991; *Asterix and the Secret Weapon*, 1991).
- *La Galère d'Obélix* (1996; *Asterix and Obelix All at Sea*, 1996).
- *Astérix et Latraviata* (2001; *Asterix and the Actress*, 2001).
- *Astérix et la rentrée gauloise* (2003; *Asterix and the Class Act*, 2003).
- *Le Ciel lui tombe sur la tête* (2005; *Asterix and the Falling Sky*, 2005).
- *L'Anniversaire d'Astérix et Obélix: Le Livre d'or* (2009; *Asterix and Obelix's Birthday: The Golden Book*, 2010).

Characters

- *Asterix*, a.k.a. *Astérix*, is the series' unlikely hero. A diminutive mustachioed Gaulish warrior with a huge nose and a winged helmet, he is essentially a no-nonsense fellow that the village leader relies on for secret missions or to solve various problems. He and Getafix are essentially the only levelheaded villagers capable of foresight. He regularly uses the druid's magic potion.

- *Obelix*, a.k.a. *Obélix*, a maker and carrier of monoliths, is Asterix's devoted and likeable best friend and sidekick. He is redheaded and obese, wears characteristic side braids, and sports white-and-blue breeches. While childish, immature, and occasionally jealous of Asterix, he uses his permanent superhuman strength (the result of a childhood fall into the cauldron of magic potion) to beat up Roman soldiers and to get himself and Asterix out of trouble.

- *Getafix*, a.k.a. *Panoramix*, a druid, is the creator and sole maker of the magic potion; he is also the village doctor and schoolteacher. Unlike the other villagers, he rarely loses his temper and proves a reliable advisor in even the most difficult circumstances. He is a key character in the village's balance and survival.

- *Vitalstatistix*, a.k.a. *Abraracourcix*, is the village chieftain. A veteran of the Alesia battle, in which Julius Caesar defeated Gaulish leader Vercingetorix, he is a sometimes grouchy but always courageous middle-aged man, except around his wife, Belladonna (a.k.a. *Impedimenta*).

- *Cacofonix*, a.k.a. *Assurancetourix*, the bard, is a terrible singer and musician with affected body language and a high opinion of himself. He is usually bound and gagged to prevent him from singing during the final feast. He is most often a supporting character but is sometimes a central element, as in the stories *Asterix and the Magic Carpet* and *Asterix and the Secret Weapon*.

- *Dogmatix*, a.k.a. *Idéfix*, is Obelix's pet dog and the series' only recurring animal character. Originally an off-the-radar character present in nearly every panel of *Asterix and the Banquet*, he was noticed by the protagonists only at the end of the story and became a central character in the next volume. Dogmatix is both a stereotypically mute and faithful dog and a comic foil capable of showing human feelings such as disapproval, grief, and jealousy.

- *Julius Caesar*, a.k.a. *Jules César*, is the authoritarian leader of the Roman troops trying to conquer Gaul and the sole recurring Roman character in the series.

Artistic Style

From the start, *Asterix* was the product of a highly successful collaboration between co-creators and long-time friends Goscinny and Uderzo. Goscinny's storytelling skills and witty, multilayered dialogue make *Asterix* an enjoyable comic for readers of all ages. The co-creators complement each other's strengths: Goscinny crafted ultratight synopses and Uderzo turned them into pictures, inside which he deftly added secondary visual gags such as the changing positions of the wings on Asterix's helmet and the background antics of Dogmatix. Another key aspect to the series' success was the exceptional cartooning ability of its largely self-taught illustrator, Uderzo. By the 1950's, he had become a consummate penciller and brush inker, whose drawing style combined stylized cartoony characters and fairly realistic backgrounds.

While the first volume was still rough on plot and characterization and its artwork was relatively unpolished, the following ones quickly demonstrated the co-creators' increasing command of their respective crafts. The heyday of the series corresponds to the 1965-1973 period: the fourteen titles published from *Asterix and Cleopatra* to *Asterix in Corsica* (books 6 to 20) combined Goscinny's best writing and Uderzo's best artwork.

Ranging from slapstick comedy to light social satire, each of Goscinny's stories should be construed more as amused commentary on French society in the 1960's and 1970's than as a historically accurate re-creation. Goscinny's consistent reliance on puns, witticisms, Latin quotations, allusions to French history and contemporary popular culture, and the jokes on regional or national stereotypes—while admittedly difficult for translators to handle and sometimes misunderstood by foreign critics—made *Asterix* a uniquely literate instance of comic-strip entertainment driven primarily by plot and dialogue.

Uderzo refined the series' artistic style over the years. He incorporated sophisticated page and panel layouts (as in the Satyricon-like orgy scene in *Asterix in Switzerland*) as well as detailed architectural compositions (as in the opening pages of *The Mansions of the Gods* and *Asterix and the Laurel Wreath*). He also spoofed famous paintings (Théodore Géricault's *Raft of the Medusa* in *Asterix the Legionary* and Rembrandt's *Anatomy Lesson of Dr. Tulp* in *Asterix and the Soothsayer*), and occasionally included unusual speech balloon designs, as for foreigners speaking in Greek or Gothic type or for the tax collector's administrative form-like balloons in *Asterix and the Cauldron*.

The original synergy between writer and illustrator largely accounts for the creative and critical break that followed Goscinny's death. Except for *The Class Act* (a collection of older, mostly Goscinny-scripted short pieces), the books written and drawn by Uderzo after 1980 were consistent with the previous installments as far as the artwork is concerned, and sales remained high. However, the storytelling and humor (particularly when Uderzo heavy-handedly satirizes contemporary issues, such as feminism in *Asterix and the Secret Weapon* and cultural globalization in *Asterix and the Falling Sky*) have been excoriated by critics for being subpar.

Themes

The creators of *Asterix* never intended to create a historically accurate series; rather, they sought to mix humor and adventure with light touches of social satire in stories based on the clichés of primary and secondary school ancient history classes and on the still relatively widespread familiarity of French readers with Latin. Whether intentional or not, the series also reflects contemporary political concerns.

Asterix's historical backdrop is ironically inconsistent with Gaul of 50 B.C.E.: While the battles at Gergovia and Alesia took place within months of each other, the Gauls' frequent allusions to the then two-year-old Roman conquest actually echo post-World War II French collective representations of their country's early twentieth-century military rivalry with Germany. For example, Vitalstatistix is depicted as a veteran of a not-so-distant war

in *Asterix and the Chieftain's Shield* and the village elder, Geriatrix, is implicitly referred to as a World War I veteran. While this longtime military rivalry was addressed directly only in *Asterix and the Goths*, some have read the resistance to Roman subjugation as a transposition of President Charles de Gaulle's policy to make France a first-tier world power in the post-World War II context of global U.S. hegemony. However, Goscinny and Uderzo, both born in the mid-1920's, belonged to an older generation, less liberal by inclination, who did not think of comics as a vehicle for ideological messages; hence, the early assessments of the series as a Gaullist-inspired blend of chauvinism, sexism, and conservatism should be read primarily as reflections of the post-1968 critique of contemporary popular culture. If anything, such accusations seem more justified in relation to the books written by Uderzo after 1979.

Several political themes typical of the Gaullist 1960's can nevertheless be found in the Goscinny-era *Asterix* corpus. The worship of resistance as a shared national value is particularly apparent in *Asterix and the Banquet*, *Asterix and the Big Fight*, and volumes set in foreign lands under Roman sway. Other volumes have overtones of anti-imperialism—often echoing anti-Americanism and anticolonialism—reflecting De Gaulle's policy of Algerian decolonization, his praise of national identities, and his reluctance toward long-term European integration. Increasing tensions between local power and Parisian centralization following World War II are embodied in the critique of central government bureaucrats in *Asterix and the Cauldron*'s tax collector, *Asterix in Switzerland*'s and *Asterix in Corsica*'s corrupt Roman governors. Finally, *The Mansions of the Gods* and *Obelix and Co.* provide a critique of capitalism, and *Asterix and the Golden Sickle*, *Asterix and the Banquet*, and *Asterix and the Laurel Wreath* critique modern urban life.

Impact

With over 300 million books sold in more than a hundred languages, *Asterix* is a publishing phenomenon, although not a global success.

The French strip became a national sensation as early as 1965 due both to the books themselves and to a comprehensive marketing strategy based on radio broadcasts, record adaptations, and animated movies. Not only did Asterix and the series cast become household names, but some of its one-liners also entered everyday language. By 1967, the French media interpreted the series' popularity as the sign of France's newfound cultural respect for the comic medium.

In the rest of the world, *Asterix* has enjoyed a mixed reception. If sales figures may be considered reliable cultural indicators, the series struck a responsive chord among Western European countries, especially Germany and Austria, during the post-World War II decades when those countries were simultaneously recovering from the war and initiating European construction against a background of reluctant admiration toward the United States. However, its attempted importation to Japan in the 1970's was a fiasco for marketing and cultural reasons. In North America, *Asterix* has never broken into mainstream comics reading but has remained an upscale cultural product most frequently appreciated by upper-middlebrow readers with some proximity to European culture.

Films

Asterix and Cleopatra. Directed by René Goscinny, Lee Payant, and Albert Uderzo. Dargaud Films/Belvision, 1968. This animation was based on the eponymous book.

Asterix and Obelix Meet Cleopatra. Directed by Alain Chabat. Canal Plus et al., 2002. Clavier returns as Asterix and Depardieu as Obelix in this live-action adaptation based on *Asterix and Cleopatra*.

Asterix and Obelix Take on Caesar. Directed by Claude Zidi. AMLF et al., 1999. This live-action adaptation starring Christian Clavier as Asterix and Gérard Depardieu as Obelix combines plot elements from seven books.

Asterix and the Vikings. Directed by Stefan Fjeldmark and Jesper Møller. M6 Films/Mandarin SAS/2d3D Animations, 2006. This Franco-Danish co-production is based on *Asterix and the Normans*, with elements from a few other books.

Asterix at the Olympic Games. Directed by Frédéric Forestier and Thomas Langmann. Pathé Renn Productions et al., 2008. This film adaptation starring Clovis Cornillac as Asterix, Depardieu as Obelix, and Alain

Delon as Julius Caesar is loosely based on *Asterix at the Olympic Games* and *Asterix and Son*.

Asterix Conquers America. Directed by Gerhard Hahn. Extrafilm/Jurgen Wohlrabe/Gerhard Hahn Film, 1994. This film is a German-produced animation loosely based on *Asterix and the Great Crossing*.

Asterix in Britain. Directed by Pino van Lamsweerde. Gaumont/Dargaud Films, 1986. This animation is based on the eponymous book.

Asterix the Gaul. Directed by Ray Goossens. Dargaud Films/Belvision, 1967. This animation was based on the eponymous book.

Asterix versus Caesar. Directed by Gaëtan Brizzi and Paul Brizzi. Gaumont/Dargaud Films/Productions René Goscinny, 1985. The screenplay of this animation combines elements from *Asterix the Legionary* and *Asterix the Gladiator*.

Operation Getafix. Directed by Philippe Grimont. Gaumont/Extrafilm, 1989. The screenplay of this animation combines elements from *Asterix and the Big Fight* and *Asterix and the Soothsayer*.

The Twelve Tasks of Asterix. Directed by René Goscinny, Henri Gruel, Albert Uderzo, and Pierre Watrin. Dargaud Films/Productions René Goscinny/Studios Idefix, 1976. This animation follows an original screenplay.

Jean-Paul Gabilliet

Further Reading

Goscinny, René, and Albert Uderzo. *Ompa-pa* (1977-1978).

Hergé. *The Adventures of Tintin* (1930-1976).

Morris, and René Goscinny. *Lucky Luke* (1949-1967).

Bibliography

Decker, Dwight R. "*Asterix*: 'These Frenchmen Are Crazy!'" *Comics Journal* 38 (February, 1978): 22-33.

Kessler, Peter. *The Complete Guide to Asterix*. London: Hodder Children's Books, 1995.

Nye, Russell B. "*Asterix* Revisited." *Comics Journal* 72 (May, 1982): 59-65.

See also: *The Adventures of Tintin; Blueberry; Airtight Garage of Jerry Cornelius*

AYA OF YOPOUGON

Author: Abouet, Marguerite

Artist: Clément Oubrerie (illustrator); Mario Bruno (colorist); Philippe Bruno (colorist); Tom Devlin (letterer)

Publisher: Gallimard (French); Drawn and Quarterly (English)

First serial publication: 2005-2010 (English translation, 2007-2009)

First book publication: 2007

Publication History

While working as a legal assistant in Paris, Marguerite Abouet began writing children's stories. Encouraged by friends to write about growing up in the Ivory Coast (which she left at age twelve when she went to Paris to live with relatives), she conceived a lighthearted story about the everyday lives of a group of Ivorian teenagers. When Clément Oubrerie, an established artist, animator, and children's book illustrator, expressed interest, the project became a graphic novel, the first for both of them.

Aya was published in France in 2005 as part of Joann Sfar's Bayou collection of juvenile graphic novels for Gallimard Jeunesse. Following the critical success of *Aya de Yopougon 1*, Abouet and Oubrerie collaborated on five more volumes, producing one each year, bringing the series to a satisfying close with the publication of the sixth volume in 2010. The first three volumes in English were published by Drawn and Quarterly as *Aya*, translated by Helge Dascher (2007); *Aya of Yop City*, translated by Dag Dascher (2008); and *Aya: The Secrets Come Out*, translated by Helge Dascher (2010). The series enjoyed great popularity in Africa, especially in Abouet's native Ivory Coast, where Gallimard made the books more affordable by issuing less expensive paperback versions.

Plot

Aya consists of multiple interwoven stories about a group of families living in the working-class neighborhood of Yopougon in Abidjan, Ivory Coast, in the late 1970's and early 1980's. In order to emphasize the

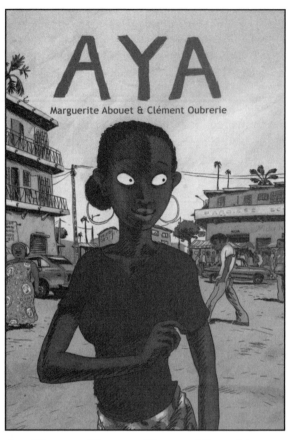

Aya of Yopougon. (Courtesy of Drawn and Quarterly)

commonality between her Ivorian characters and their non-African counterparts, Abouet adopted the structure of a soap opera. The series began as a comedy of manners, but over time, introduced more serious story lines involving rape, racism, and homophobic violence.

Broadly speaking, the story arcs center on Aya, Bonaventure Sissoko, and Innocent. Aya, a nineteen-year-old student studying to be a doctor, is a serious and responsible girl who is the moral center of the novel. She listens to her friends, Bintou and Adjoua, discussing their love lives; Bintou throws herself at Grégoire because he has been to Paris, and Adjoua dates Moussa Sissoko because he is rich. When Adjoua gets pregnant, she first claims that Moussa is the father but finally admits that it is Mamadou, a lazy young man with no money.

Aya helps her friends rehearse for the Miss Yopougon contest and sets up the shy family maid, Féli, with Bintou's equally shy cousin, Hervé. Sometimes she meddles where she is not wanted, scolding Mamadou for being a gigolo or warning Hervé that his new girlfriend, Rita, is after his money. When her father's mistress shows up with two illegitimate children, it is Aya who tries to reconcile her parents. When Féli, the surprise winner of the Miss Yopougon contest, is abducted by her greedy father, Zékinan, Aya plots to rescue her.

Ultimately, Aya faces a crisis of her own when a professor tries to rape her and then gives her low grades. She subsequently stops going to school and becomes depressed. She begins dating Didier, a handsome young lawyer, but when he invites her to a party at his home, she is shocked to learn that his godfather is her professor. After the professor lies to Didier about her, a mortified Aya becomes seriously ill and is taken to the hospital. Aya's indignant girlfriends confront Didier with the truth about Aya and enlist his support to arrest the professor.

Bonaventure Sissoko, the wealthy head of Solibra Beer (where Aya's father works), is an overbearing bully who physically and verbally abuses his son, Moussa, whom he despises. When Moussa robs his father's safe and disappears, Sissoko and his wife embark on a military-style expedition to find him and the money. Eventually they locate him in a village, where he is celebrated as a hero, having donated his father's money to build maternity hospitals. Sissoko insists on seeing his son imprisoned as punishment, only to learn that he is receiving a presidential award for his philanthropy. He realizes that his son's cell mate, Grégoire, in jail for fraud, is his illegitimate son and offers him a job.

Innocent is the third major character in the series. A stylish Yopougon hairdresser, he first falls in love with Adjoua's brother, Albert, but moves to Paris rather than continue seeing Albert secretly and in disguise. Afraid to tell his parents, Albert plans to marry a woman he does not love until he accidentally lets slip that he is gay. In Paris, Innocent struggles to find work and to fit into the Ivorian immigrant community. He alienates the men when he gives their wives makeovers because the men prefer their wives to look and act like traditional African women. He then befriends Sébastien, a gay white man

Aya of Yopougon. (Courtesy of Drawn and Quarterly)

and a victim of homophobic violence, who offers him a place to live; gradually the two men fall in love. Although Sébastien's father wants nothing to do with his son and Innocent once he finds out they are together, Sébastien's mother treats Innocent like a son.

Volumes

- *Aya de Yopougon* 1 (2005). Aya's father, Ignace, wants her to get married. Aya's friend Adjoua gets pregnant.
- *Aya de Yopougon* 2 (2006). The paternity of Adjoua's baby is a mystery. Ignace's mistress turns up with two children.
- *Aya de Yopougon* 3 (2007). The Miss Yopougon contest takes place. The women of the neighborhood intervene to stop Bintou's father from taking a second wife. Innocent leaves for Paris.
- *Aya de Yopougon* 4 (2008). Innocent moves to Paris and meets Sébastien. Aya's professor tries to rape her. Féli's father claims her money. Mamadou finds a rich older mistress. Moussa Sissoko robs the family safe and leaves home.
- *Aya de Yopougon* 5 (2009). Grégoire becomes a faith healer. The Sissokos search for Moussa.
- *Aya de Yopougon* 6 (2010). Moussa and Grégoire meet in prison. The professor is arrested. Mamadou reunites with Adjoua. Sébastien's parents learn that he is gay. Moussa is honored for his philanthropy. Bintou starts a music career.

Characters

- *Aya*, the heroine, is a nineteen-year-old girl studying to become a doctor. Tall, thin, and pretty, she wears her braided hair in a bun and favors large hoop earrings. Responsible and unselfish, she is the one on whom everyone relies.
- *Ignace*, Aya's father, is a short, overweight, bald, middle-aged man who works for Bonaventure Sissoko. His home life is complicated when his mistress shows up with his two illegitimate children.
- *Fanta* is Aya's mother, a kindly woman shown in traditional dress. She is unafraid of standing up to her husband, his friends, or the village chief. She works in an office and as a traditional healer.
- *Adjoua*, a close friend of Aya, wears her short hair

in thick ringlets. A single mother, she is ambitious and hardworking, running her own restaurant.
- *Bintou*, another friend of Aya, wears her long braids with beads. She makes her living as a relationship counselor but dreams of finding a rich husband and moving to Paris.
- *Bonaventure Sissoko* is wealthy, egotistical, and rude. Overweight and bald, he verbally and physically harasses his son, Moussa.
- *Moussa Sissoko* is a spoiled, lazy young man with a small, round head, which is bald except for one large tuft of hair. Aya rejects his attentions, but Bintou and Adjoua fight over him. Fed up with his overbearing father, he raids his father's safe and leaves home.
- *Mamadou*, a tall, handsome man with an Afro and goatee, is the father of Adjoua's son. He finally abandons his rich, older mistress to be with Adjoua and their son.
- *Grégoire*, a stocky young man with a shaved head, likes women, money, and expensive clothes. He dates Bintou until she realizes that he is two-timing her. He is arrested for posing as a faith healer, but Sissoko eventually recognizes him as his illegitimate son.
- *Félicité*, a.k.a. *Féli*, a maid in Aya's home, is thin and gawky with short hair and extremely shy. In love with Hervé, she is abducted by her father, Zékinan, who plots to marry her off and take her money.
- *Hervé*, Bintou's cousin, is a shy, gawky car mechanic who owns a garage. In love with Féli, he is distracted by the seductive Rita, who wants his money.
- *Innocent*, a.k.a. *Inno*, is a young Michael Jackson look-alike, with a red jacket, black pants, and a white T-shirt. He is a hairdresser who prides himself on his stylishness. He moves to Paris to live as an openly gay man but encounters racism and homophobia there. He is fond of speaking in proverbs.
- *Albert*, Adjoua's brother, has a flattop haircut and wears glasses. Afraid to tell his family that he is gay, he gets engaged to an ugly woman he does not love.

- *Zékinan*, Féli's father, a wiry, bad-tempered old man, lives in the village with several wives and many children. He sold his daughter as a child and now, persuaded that she is rich, plots to have her married against her will and take her money.
- *Sébastien* is a young white Parisian with a long nose and shaggy brown hair. Hiding the fact that he is gay from his parents, he befriends Innocent and offers him a room. Eventually he becomes Innocent's lover.

Artistic Style

A children's book illustrator and a television and film animator, Oubrerie employs a cartoonish style in *Aya* that depends on highly exaggerated facial expressions, sometimes verging on caricature, to convey characters' emotions. However, the backgrounds of his panels are full of carefully observed details that reward the close reader. Through these details, Oubrerie satirizes the characters, offers insights into them, and provides social commentary. Much of the humor in the text emerges from the drawings. Bonaventure Sissoko's monstrous pink house, for example, towers over the houses of his neighbors, as if to devour them, aptly capturing the greedy personality of its owner.

One striking feature of *Aya* is Oubrerie's use of bold, flat colors, especially red, yellow, orange, and turquoise, achieved by applying gouache over his pen-and-ink drawings. Oubrerie's pages make the reader feel the heat, the brightness, and the dust of Abidjan. For the Paris scenes, however, he chooses a gray, relatively dark palette; the rainy weather reflects Innocent's gloomy outlook. Oubrerie increasingly incorporates transparent watercolors in muted shades for special effects, such as Bintou's daydream sequence.

Oubrerie also plays with the story's format. Some panels resemble screen shots, a testament to his experience as an animator; he also playfully re-creates two pages as a photo-novel. He also introduces song lyrics into his panels, which sometimes act as ironic counterpoint to the action or act as accompaniment and give *Aya* a virtual sound track.

An initial criticism of the graphic novel was that Aya, Bintou, Adjoua, and Féli were nearly indistinguishable apart from their hairstyles. In later volumes, Oubrerie

---

Marguerite Abouet

Born in the Ivory Coast, Marguerite Abouet has become a well-known figure in contemporary French comics as the writer of the six volumes of *Aya de Yopougon* (three volumes of which have been translated by Drawn and Quarterly as *Aya*). An aspiring author of fiction for young adults, Abouet turned to writing graphic novels with her husband, illustrator Clément Oubrerie, after becoming frustrated with the limitations of the young adult fiction market. Inspired by the success of Marjane Satrapi, Abouet has created a series that focuses on the quotidian nature of life in Africa. Breaking with the traditional representations of African life—civil war and famine, or an exotic place for adventures for European boy reporters—Abouet has crafted a series in which life is presented in all of its tremendous complexity. Abouet has denied suggestions that the *Aya* series is autobiographical, but does admit that it is strongly based on people that she knew growing up in the Ivory Coast.

---

more clearly accentuates differences in the characters' facial features and skin color.

Themes

The primary theme of *Aya* is the importance of relationships. The strongest and most positive relationships depicted in *Aya* are those among women, whether between female friends or mothers and daughters. Women are presented as the social conscience of the community. Major story lines involve women supporting one another by confronting the village chief to plead for Féli, setting a trap to expose Aya's lecherous professor, and stopping Bintou's father from taking a second wife.

The impact of urbanization and modernity is another recurring theme throughout *Aya*. The clash between traditional village life ruled by the patriarchal figure of the chief and the modern city, with its Western cultural influences, materialism, and greater independence for women, drives many of the conflicts in the series. The men in *Aya*, defining themselves as the chiefs of their families, appeal to this traditional past to justify mistreatment of wives and daughters. The disparity in living standards and job opportunities between the villages and the city also creates resentment and tension within families.

The series also addresses the complex postcolonial relationship between the Ivory Coast and France. The idealized image of France circulated in the popular culture available to the characters, through music and film, is at odds with Innocent's experiences of racial discrimination as an African immigrant in Paris. Innocent also becomes a vehicle through which French society is satirized from the standpoint of an "innocent" visitor.

Finally, *Aya* tackles sexual politics in Ivory Coast. Abouet touches on the community's homophobia through the plotlines involving Innocent, Albert, and Sébastien, as each man goes to great lengths to hide his homosexual identity, from dressing as a woman to getting engaged. Furthermore, *Aya* exposes the double standard in the community that tolerates adultery and child abuse but stigmatizes homosexuality. Abouet also implicitly criticizes the pressure placed on fathers and sons to live up to a stereotypical masculinity and the way that it can drive a wedge between them.

Impact

Aya's roots lie not only in the French-language graphic novel but also in the Ivorian comics tradition, exemplified by the popular Ivorian humor magazine *Gbich!*, and in Ivorian literature, such as Bernard Binlin Dadié's satiric novel *Un Nègre à Paris* (1959; *An African in Paris*, 1994). Abouet's focus on telling stories of everyday life with humor gave Western readers a dramatically different view of Africa from the tragic images that they were accustomed to seeing in television news reports and documentaries. In subverting the negative stereotypes that linked Ivory Coast with civil war, poverty, and AIDS, Abouet and Oubrerie sought to offer their audience a more balanced, and in some ways, more realistic picture of Ivorian life.

Another unusual aspect of the series concerned Abouet's linguistic choices. Rather than standard French, Abouet's dialogue in *Aya* incorporated an Abidjan French slang that includes loan words from African languages, repurposed French words, and a liberal

sprinkling of colorful Ivorian proverbs. In addition, *Aya*'s depiction of a wide variety of African girls and women, of varying size, shape, age, and skin color, was an important corrective to the relative absence of black girls and women from graphic novels. Finally, *Aya* was notable for being a graphic novel series written by an African woman, still a rarity.

Films

Aya de Yopougon. Directed by Marguerite Abouet and Clément Oubrerie. Autochenille Production, 2011. The script for this animated feature film was written by Abouet and roughly follows the series' original plot.

Marla Harris

Further Reading

Abel, Jessica. *La Perdida* (2006).
Corman, Leela. *Subway Series* (2002).
Satrapi, Marjane. *Embroideries* (2005).
_____. *Persepolis* (2003).

Bibliography

Abouet, Marguerite. "Drawing on the Universal in Africa: An Interview with Marguerite Abouet." Interview by Angela Ajayi. *Wild River Review*, February 9, 2011. http://www.wildriverreview.com/interview/drawing-universal-africa/marguerite-abouet/ajayi-angela.

Harris, Marla. "Sex and the City: The Graphic Novel Series *Aya* as West African Comedy of Manners." *International Journal of Comic Art* 11, no. 2 (Fall, 2009): 119-135.

Lent, John A. "Out of Africa: The Saga of Exiled Cartoonists in Europe." *Scan: Journal of Media Arts Culture* 5, no. 2 (September, 2008).

Repetti, Massimo. "African Wave: Specificity and Cosmopolitanism in African Comics." *African Arts* 40, no. 2 (June, 2007): 16-35.

See also: *La Perdida; The Arrival; Embroideries; Persepolis*

B

BACCHUS

Author: Campbell, Eddie; Campbell, Mark; Kublick, Wes; Moore, Marcus; White, Daren

Artist: Eddie Campbell (illustrator); Ed Hillyer (illustrator); Dylan Horrocks (illustrator); Teddie Kristiansen (illustrator); Wes Kublick (illustrator); Marcus Moore (illustrator); Peter Mullins (illustrator); April Post (illustrator); Steve Stamatiadis (illustrator)

Publisher: Harrier Comics; Dark Horse Comics; Eddie Campbell Comics

First serial publication: 1987-2001

First book publication: 1995-2010

Publication History

In 1984, British publisher Harrier Comics, wanting to take advantage of the increasing popularity of black-and-white comics, consulted with Eddie Campbell and others about a line of "new wave" comics. The first issue of *Deadface*, introducing Campbell's character Bacchus, appeared in April, 1987. Harrier folded in late 1988, after publishing eight issues of *Deadface* and two of the spin-off series *Bacchus*.

Campbell took the *Bacchus* series to Dark Horse Comics, which published the new four-issue miniseries *Deadface: Earth, Water, Air and Fire*, written with Wes Kublick, in 1992. Stories featuring another *Deadface* character appeared in the anthology comic *Cheval Noir* from November, 1989, to May, 1991, illustrated by Ed Hillyer; these stories were reprinted by Dark Horse as a three-issue miniseries, *The Eyeball Kid*, in 1992. *The 1,001 Nights of Bacchus* was released in 1993.

Many of the *Bacchus* stories first appeared in Dark Horse's main anthology title, *Dark Horse Presents* (*DHP*). In 1991, these stories, including several written by or with Kublick, were reprinted in the three-issue miniseries *Deadface: Doing the Islands with Bacchus*. *DHP* also published "Afterdeath," written with

Bacchus. (Courtesy of Top Shelf Productions)

Kublick, in 1991, and the story arcs *Hermes Versus the Eyeball Kid* and *The Picture of Doreen Grey* in 1993-1994 and 1995, respectively. Dark Horse republished *Hermes Versus the Eyeball Kid* as a three-issue miniseries in 1994-1995. In 1995, the company published a one-issue color story, *The Ghost in the Glass*, that is not reprinted in the books.

Stories featuring Bacchus also appeared in *A1*, a black-and-white anthology comic published by the

British company Atomeka Press, in 1989, and *Trident*, the anthology of Trident Comics (also British), in 1990.

In 1995, with the encouragement of Dave Sim, Campbell began to self-publish as Eddie Campbell Comics (ECC). Campbell states that he was happy with his creative freedom at Dark Horse and that the move was purely for financial reasons. For six years, ECC re-issued the *Bacchus* stories in comic book format, added new material to the series, and began to produce the trade paperbacks, for which Campbell reworked earlier material, sometimes substantially.

Plot

The series presents a genre-bending combination of myth, adventure, crime, near-superheroic battles, romance, tender character study, and philosophy. The first story arc, in Volumes 1 and 2, alternates between present-day stories and explanations of the characters' pasts. Because the gods are not truly immortal, they fight over what power is left and try to settle old scores while they can.

In the United States, Joe Theseus's hit men ambush Bacchus in a bar, killing Bacchus's acolytes. Theseus leaves town, but is found on his departing plane by the Eyeball Kid. Theseus and the Eyeball Kid fight, their plane crashes in Belize, and they become guards and attendants for a rich widow in Guatemala. Theseus then returns to the United States, where the police are investigating the bar shoot-out. When enemies of Theseus set him up for a hit, the Kid, who has accompanied Theseus, destroys them.

Meanwhile, the Telchines plan to use a leech from the river Styx to steal Zeus's thunderbolt power from the Kid, who previously stole it from Zeus himself. They kidnap the Kid and the leech takes the power, but the Telchines do not know how to access it. The Telchines are also involved in the death of Theseus's child and the suicide of his wife. In remorse, Theseus leaves everything behind, tears out his eyes, and lives under the sea.

The third volume leaves the plot of the previous two to follow Bacchus on a trip around the Greek islands, accompanied by Hermes and Simpson. He gains short-term acolytes and tells stories from mythology and history, many of them about himself or wine. Bacchus also encounters Tam O'Shanter and goes to see a Greek showing of the film *Close Encounters of the Third Kind* (1977).

The main story returns in Volumes 4 and 5, the former of which focuses on the Kid. He seems to find a spiritual mentor, but in fact she leads him back to the Telchines. The Telchines have an Old West-style showdown with the Kid until they are interrupted by Hermes, who fights using an enormous glove. The Kid escapes with the leech and becomes entrapped within it, but manages to regain the power of Zeus. When the Kid attacks the Telchines, Chalcon dies and Chryson escapes.

Earth, Air, Water and Fire connects Greek mythology to crime and politics in modern-day Sicily. Still underwater, Theseus meets and falls in love with a water-breathing woman who turns out to be one of his daughters, sent to him by the Kabeiroi. This volume also introduces the Eye of Past Futurity and the Eye of Fate, powerful false eyes made by Hephaestus for Bacchus and the Kid. The Kid kills the Kabeiroi, and then he and Theseus literally crash into Bacchus and Simpson. During an escape from jail, Simpson dies for the final time.

1,001 Nights of Bacchus is a collection of stories unrelated to the main plot. The framing conceit is that patrons of a pub, the Traveller's Joy, must tell stories to keep Bacchus awake so the owner will stay open and serve drinks after hours. The end introduces the Castle and Frog, which will reappear in Volume 9.

The final volumes concentrate on the main plot, though not necessarily on Bacchus. In Volume 7/8, the Eyeball Kid and Hermes engage in an epic fight, while Chryson and Eva, the niece and heir of Don Skylla from Volume 5, watch the fight from a blimp. The ending of this story implies that the battle between the Kid and Hermes is eternal and irresolvable. Though blind, Theseus gains the ability to see the patterns of fate, which are apparently drawn with a Spirograph. Big Ginny, Queen of the Amazons, is destined to become Theseus's thirty-fifth wife, but a fading actress named Doreen Grey wants Ginny's face to replace the transplanted one her body is rejecting. In the end, Doreen lives in Ginny's body, and in the realm of fate, Theseus meets God (drawn by

Campbell's grade-school-age daughter), becomes God, and lives happily ever after with Ginny's soul.

With Theseus's story resolved and that of Hermes and the Kid in eternal balance, the two final volumes concentrate on Bacchus. The Castle and Frog declares itself an independent state, governed by Bacchus, but it is beset by both the British police and eternal enemies of drink: the small, demonlike Screaming Habdabs, Bacchus's archenemy Delirium Tremens, and the abstemious Mr. Dry. Bacchus is pursued through various pictures, in which he meets the new love of his life, Collage. Life in the pub is joyful and chaotic; along the way, Campbell satirizes the police, political collectives, and, above all, comics. Finally, an explosion destroys the pub and hurls into space a giant wood phallus, a carved likeness of Bacchus's own.

This exhibitionism by proxy leads to *Banged Up,* a more somber and somewhat more coherent story

Bacchus. (Courtesy of Top Shelf Productions)

of Bacchus in jail. His cell mate declares himself an acolyte but only makes Bacchus's life difficult. Collage visits, showing Bacchus their baby. Instead of the mythic interpolations of most previous stories or the narratives of *1,001 Nights*, this volume primarily presents the histories of the various inmates. In the conclusion, Bacchus meets Theseus, who is now God, before ending up living happily with Collage; the Eyeball Kid is robbing banks with Eva; and Hermes takes a well-earned rest.

Volumes

- *Eddie Campbell's Bacchus,* Book 1: *Immortality Isn't Forever* (1995). Collects *Deadface*, issues 1-4. With the second volume, forms the indispensable core of the series. Introduces Bacchus and other important characters while retelling certain Greek myths through the eyes of the protagonist.
- *Eddie Campbell's Bacchus,* Book 2: *The Gods of Business* (1996). Collects *Deadface*, issues 5-8. Provides more action than Volume 1 and introduces the Telchines.
- *Eddie Campbell's Bacchus,* Book 3: *Doing the Islands with Bacchus* (1997). Collects material from *DHP*, issues 32, 37, 40, 42, 46, 52, 71; *A1*, issues 1-3; *Trident*, issues 1, 2, 4, 5; and Harrier's *Bacchus*, issues 1-2. Leaves the main plot to accompany Bacchus on a present-day trip around the Greek islands.
- *Eddie Campbell's Bacchus,* Book 4: *The Eyeball Kid—One Man Show* (1998). Collects material from *Cheval Noir*, issues 3, 5, 7, 9, 12, 15, 17, 18, and *Dark Horse Insider*, Volume 2, issue 3. More linear than many later volumes, but still strikingly creative. Focuses on the Eyeball Kid.
- *Eddie Campbell's Bacchus,* Book 5: *Earth, Water, Air and Fire* (1998). Collects the Dark Horse miniseries of the same name. Connects ancient Greek mythology to crime and politics in modern-day Sicily. Features Joe Theseus as a main character.
- *Eddie Campbell's Bacchus,* Book 6: *The 1,001 Nights of Bacchus* (2000). Collects material from *Trident*, issues 6-8; Dark Horse's story arc

The 1,001 Nights of Bacchus; and material from ECC's *Bacchus*, issues 15, 32, 33, 35-38, 40, 42, and 43. Unrelated to the main plot, apart from introducing the Castle and Frog. Features various amusing mythical stories told in a dazzling variety of ways.
- *Eddie Campbell's Bacchus,* Book 7/8: *The Eyeball Kid Double Bill* (2002). Collects the *Hermes Versus the Eyeball Kid* story arc from *DHP*, issues 76-84, and the *Picture of Doreen Grey* story arc from *DHP*, issues 94-99. Resolves the main story line of Theseus, Hermes, and the Eyeball Kid, while implying that their stories can never truly be resolved.
- *Eddie Campbell's Bacchus,* Book 9: *King Bacchus* (1996). Collects material from ECC's *Bacchus*, issues 2-15. Comprises a single story in which Bacchus rules over a tavern that declares itself an independent country. More metafictional than most story lines in the series.
- *Eddie Campbell's Bacchus,* Book 10: *Banged Up* (2001). Collects material from ECC's *Bacchus*, issues 16-31. A relatively somber story of Bacchus in jail, featuring many interesting and minor characters.

Characters

- *Bacchus*, the protagonist but not always the focus, is the Greek god of wine and ecstasy. In the comic book, he looks like an old, rough sailor with one eye, and occasionally has horns. He is down-to-earth, preferring to drink wine in a pub rather than pursue world-shaking intrigue, and his sardonic views expose the follies of gods and human beings alike.
- *Joe Theseus* is the legendary slayer of the Minotaur. He is also the son of Poseidon, the god of the sea. He drinks seawater from his divine father's skull in order to remain young and handsome. He has become the head of a crime cartel and is an incorrigible womanizer, with former lovers and illegitimate descendants around the globe.
- *The Eyeball Kid*, the series' most original and engaging character, is the grandson of Argus, the hundred-eyed guardian who was slain by

Hermes. The Eyeball Kid has nineteen eyes, having lost one via an arrow of Athena. When Zeus catches him with Hera, he gains Zeus's power by trickery, then kills Zeus and most of the gods, largely by accident. He speaks in a fractured slang full of telling malapropisms.

- *Hermes* is the other remaining Olympian, aging but much younger in both looks and physical strength than Bacchus. His major goal is to retrieve the dead souls that escaped when the Telchines killed Hades and fled to the land of the living, leaving the afterlife in chaos. He and the Kid are archenemies because Hermes slew Argus.

- *The Telchines* are lesser-known figures from Greek mythology, probably based on the original gods of Rhodes. Originally, they were skilled metallurgists, killed by the gods for malevolent magic; in this series, they have established themselves in the present as rich businessmen and consider themselves gods of capitalism. Clever Chryson is accompanied by musclemen Chalcon and Argyron.

- *The Kabeiroi*, lesser-known figures of Greek myth, were underworld gods worshiped in a mystery cult associated with Hephaestus. In the series, they begin as apprentices to the god of smiths and become an inbred, greedy, and unpleasantly fat secret society seeking Theseus's protection.

- *Simpson* is Bacchus's assistant and friend, a modern American professor of literature who was taken to Hades's hell by mistake and escaped when Hades was killed. Simpson's relationship with Bacchus is understated but moving, and he provides a chilling perspective on death and life.

- *Collage* is Bacchus's wife and the mother of his child. She is absurd looking but attractive, wears outrageous outfits or nothing at all, and has a surrealistic way of speaking.

Artistic Style

Credit for specific jobs on the books is not always clear, because Campbell began a studio in which various people contributed various work as needed. This is

---

Eddie Campbell

Best known as the artist on Alan Moore's seminal Jack the Ripper graphic novel *From Hell*, Scottish cartoonist Eddie Campbell also enjoys an international reputation for his self-published adult works, such as the semi-autobiographical *Alec* series and *Bacchus*, a modernized take on the classic Greek gods. Campbell's scratchy, impressionistic style features stark black-and-white imagery, shaky handwritten lettering, and close renditions of real-world figures and objects, combined with a wry sense of humor.

---

especially true of the art; sometimes Campbell would draw a face while someone else would illustrate the rest of the figure. Even Campbell often does not recall who did what. However, the *Bacchus* books do show an overall consistent approach.

The two most-mentioned characteristics of the style of *Bacchus* are its extreme energy and its great flexibility. While some panels seem relatively static, others surge with action. Close-ups are intercut with long views, and the juxtaposition of various viewpoints and perspectives creates a high level of energy.

Campbell's art has been described in terms ranging from scratchy to luxurious, with a variety of approaches that includes photocollage. The *Bacchus* books deliberately explore various established styles, such as that of 1980's superhero comics, 1960's and 1970's pinup girls, and minimalistic caricature. The style also varies by mood, from light and airy to dark, blocky, and somber. The series' art is as eclectic as its characterization, mythology, and plotting, while still evincing the control of one experimental yet targeted sensibility.

Themes

The most basic concern in *Bacchus* is stories: how they are shaped by the teller, how they change over time, and how they are used to codify and explore human existence. Bacchus and many other characters both tell and listen to stories, a kind of currency that is subject to myriad uses but is not easily abused. Related to this is the characters' witty and moving dialogue, demonstrating a love of language.

Power is another major theme. Bacchus is a lord of misrule, governing ungovernable situations and populations, whether in a pub or a prison. The work provides overt political commentary via Chryson's praise of rapacious capitalism, the police in *King Bacchus*, and the hierarchies of both guards and prisoners in *Banged Up*, among other examples. Those who seek power rarely do well, whether it is Zeus being killed by the Eyeball Kid or the Kid and Hermes forever locked in battle. The work implies that instead of seeking power and control, it is better to relax with some nice wine and a good spouse. Some of the plots and many of the stories within the series concern dynasties of fathers and sons, such as the Titans and the Olympians or Bacchus and his child. Women are weaker figures in the earlier volumes, but this is counteracted by later characters such as Collage and Eva.

Violence is not so much a theme as an always-available device to advance the stories. The gouged-out eyes of Bacchus, the Kid, and Theseus may have more to do with a theme of perceptiveness, or the lack thereof, than a theme of violence.

Impact

While Marvel Comics had long used mythology as a basis for superheroes, *Bacchus* used it in a new way. Campbell's take is momentous yet wry and self-aware, firmly historical but wildly innovative. Preceding Neil Gaiman's *The Sandman* (1989-1996) by almost two years, it might have been either an inspiration or a result of the same creative zeitgeist.

The style of the work is inimitable but nonetheless influenced others to take the genre seriously, to take it in unexpected directions, and to develop their own styles. Campbell encouraged others at Trident, such as Phil Hester, who much later explored the cosmic and comic in *Golly!* (2008-2009), and Paul Grist, creator of *Jack Staff* (2003-2009) and the comedic crime series *Burglar Bill* (2003). *Bacchus* specifically and ECC in general both played pivotal roles in the black-and-white comics revolution of the 1980's and the self-publishing movement of the 1990's, helping to reestablish an experimental sensibility that had begun with the underground comics of the 1960's.

Bernadette Bosky

Further Reading

Hester, Phil, and Brook Turner. *Golly!* (2008-2009).
Shanower, Eric. *Age of Bronze* (1998-   ).
Templeton, Ty. *Stig's Inferno* (1984-1986).

Bibliography

Campbell, Eddie. "Eddie Campbell." Interview by Dirk Deppey. *The Comics Journal* 273 (January, 2006): 66-114. Excerpt available at http://archives.tcj.com/273/i_campbell.html.
Kreiner, Rich. "Lust for Life, Man! Twenty-Five Years of Eddie Campbell." *The Comics Journal* 220 (February, 2000): 45-56.
Vollmar, Rob. "The Importance of Being Bacchus." *The Comics Journal* 273 (January, 2006): 62-65.

See also: *From Hell; Age of Bronze*

BALLAD OF DOCTOR RICHARDSON, THE

Author: Pope, Paul
Artist: Paul Pope (illustrator)
Publisher: Horse Press
First book publication: 1994

Publication History

The Ballad of Doctor Richardson was self-published by its creator Paul Pope in late 1993, though the original edition has a 1994 copyright. The year before, Pope had started his own publishing imprint, Horse Press, from his working base in Columbus, Ohio, with the exclusive intention of releasing his work free from outside influence. Pope had released his debut solo project, *Sin Titulo* (1993), under the Horse Press imprint.

In addition to publishing *The Ballad of Doctor Richardson*, Pope wrote, penciled, inked, and lettered the work, collaborating only with editor Robin Snyder. Though the work garnered a respectable amount of critical attention in the year it was published, including a 1995 Eisner Award nomination in the category of "Best New Graphic Novel," it remained out of print for five years.

In 1998, Pope rereleased the title, again through Horse Press, in a "Fifth Year Edition." Among the changes in the second edition was a new cover, endorsement blurbs from Will Eisner and Dave McKean, a sketch of Pope on the inside of the back cover by artist Batton Lash, and additional material by Pope, including commentary on some of his inspiration for the book and a page of reflections on the book.

Plot

The Ballad of Doctor Richardson follows a middle-aged art history professor through one extraordinary and life-changing night in a slightly futuristic city. As the story opens, Dr. Jefferson Richardson is administering an end-of-term Renaissance art history exam. Following the exam, he retreats to the university's faculty lounge, where he overhears several of the department faculty members disparaging him. They comment that his recent manuscript has been rejected by another publisher, most likely because of his radical

---

Paul Pope

Paul Pope is one of the most acclaimed comics creators to have crossed over from independent comics to the mainstream. Beginning his career with self-published graphic novels *Sin Titulo* and *The Ballad of Dr. Richardson*, Pope rose to fame with his work on *THB*, a manic and sporadically published science-fiction story about a young woman on Mars. This work was followed by a number of popular limited series, including *Heavy Liquid*, *Batman: Year 100*, and *100%*. Pope is celebrated for his striking visuals, and his illustrations have been collected into art books. His work features heavy, inky blacks with strong erotic undercurrents that have made him a favorite among the style-conscious and with advertisers. His stories tend to focus on independent heroes and heroines who implicitly promote Pope's libertarian political philosophy.

---

and unpopular views and his refusal to accept editorial alterations. They further iterate that Richardson has not published or presented in nearly a decade and that his credibility is nearly exhausted. Richardson listens in, unbeknownst to all his colleagues, save for the sympathetic Anne, who tells him in private that he could easily be published if he would align himself with the perspective of the academic majority. He responds that to do so would be tantamount to killing himself.

Returning to an empty home, save for his cat James, Richardson broods on his professional failures and loneliness. He reflects on his passions for poetry, music, and his own indelible ideas, but regrets that he has little to show for his life. Deciding to clear his head, Richardson goes walking through the snow-covered city, passing through crowds of faceless people. He makes his way to the subway, stopping before getting on a train to listen to a busking trumpeter.

On the train, Richardson is approached by Noel, one of his former students, whom he has forgotten, who dropped out four years earlier. She awkwardly tries to explain that she was inspired by his opinions on artists who rejected tradition in favor of rendering the real, and shows him a small print of one of Caravaggio's paintings, one of the few things she always carries with her. Richardson accepts Noel's invitation to dinner at the last moment, and the two leave the underground together.

Over dinner, Noel tells Richardson about her experiments in music and about an instrument she has built to be capable of playing the chaotic sounds she hears in her own mind. Richardson is inspired and impressed by her passion and drive, and the two are beginning to connect when several of Noel's friends arrive to drag her away to the Vanguard, the bar where they all work. Realizing Noel has left behind her Caravaggio print, Richardson follows them at a distance to the Vanguard, only to be refused entry.

Undeterred, Richardson sneaks through a bathroom window, only to find that Noel has already left. At this point, Richardson meets the subway busker again, who he learns is King Kush, the front man for the house band at the Vanguard. Kush recognizes the Caravaggio print and immediately identifies Richardson, hinting that Noel may have feelings for the professor. Using T.S. Eliot's poem "The Lovesong of J. Alfred Prufrock" (1915) as a metaphor, Richardson asserts that he does not want to let fear stop him from trying to forge a bond with Noel.

Kush directs Richardson to Café Armageddon, where he looks for Noel in a dressing room. Richardson hides, eavesdropping as Noel reclaims a Les Paul guitar of hers, speaks lovingly to the instrument, and plays a beautiful tune. Noel catches Richardson spying but seems unfazed. She leads him to the main floor and asks him to wait while she explains to Taro, her apparent former boyfriend, that she is taking back her Les Paul. After a short but nervous wait, Richardson follows Taro and Noel outside and finds them struggling over the guitar. Richardson jumps to Noel's aid, and the two manage to drive Taro away.

In the dark snowy night, Richardson bares his soul to Noel, saying that he could probably go the rest of his life without knowing her, but he does not care to try. The two return to the Vanguard, listen to King Kush play, and at the story's end make their way to Noel's spartan apartment, where they have their first embrace. In an epilogue, the story cuts to King Kush in his home, transcribing a piece he has composed for the lovers, to which he has given the same title as the book.

Characters

- *Dr. Jefferson Richardson*, the titular character of the book, is a middle-aged academic whose career is declining because of his unpopular views on Italian Renaissance art. He finds himself depressed after the latest rejection of his book and mourns that he has no one with whom to share life. Richardson is stirred from his torpor after reconnecting with Noel and finds his loneliness quelled with the discovery of someone with passions equal to his own.

- *Noel* is an attractive young woman who dropped out of university to pursue a musical career after coming to view the academic system as a homogenizing factory environment. While still a student, however, she studied briefly under Richardson and became infatuated with him. She has recently left her boyfriend, Taro, and his band, Huron, to build an instrument with the versatility necessary to play the music she hears in her mind. Noel encounters Richardson again, four years after being his student, and the two form a profound bond.

- *King Kush* is a trumpeter who fronts his own band, the King Kush Experience, the regular headliner at the Vanguard bar. He also moonlights as a subway busker, returning there often for sentimental reasons. Kush is seemingly close enough to Noel to know about her love for Richardson and is instrumental in bringing the couple together.

- *Taro*, a.k.a. *Huron*, is Noel's former boyfriend and the front man for the band Huron. He advertises himself as a Native American, although in truth, he has no such heritage. Taro is portrayed as petty and egotistical, displaying bitterness over his breakup with Noel and insecurity over being exposed as ethnically inauthentic. In the story's climax, Taro gets into an altercation with Noel and Richardson after refusing to return Noel's Les Paul guitar. Eventually, he relinquishes both the instrument and his imagined claim on his former girlfriend.

Artistic Style

In the back of *The Ballad of Doctor Richardson*, Pope notes that the book was produced using an 18 x 24 inch hot press Bristol board, FW opaque acrylic inks, Morilla and Winsor Newton brushes, Design artgum, and Gaebel graphic Design tools. The edition was published as an undersized volume, measuring 6.5 x 9 inches rather than the usual 6.5 x 10 inches. This contrasts sharply with Pope's first self-published book, *Sin Titulo*, which measured 8 x 10.5 inches. For *The Ballad of Doctor Richardson*, Pope utilized only black acrylic inks, giving the book a somewhat grainy, black-and-white appearance. The small size of the book, combined with Pope's heavy use of ink, which often melds foreground and background, gives the book a hushed and intimate feel that supports the story's romantic themes.

In the collected edition of his later work, *100%*, Pope comments that he finds inking to be the most satisfying aspect of making comics. This observation offers insight into *The Ballad of Doctor Richardson*'s style, although Pope's early effort lacks the refinement that he later developed. Pope's indulgence in ink sometimes contrasts with his tendency to render his characters' faces in thin, sharp lines with few shadows and little shading. The result is an occasional contradiction of styles, in which a character looks somewhat out of place in the surrounding panel. In the story's key emotional moments, however, Pope lights scenes intricately, merging his distinct line work with abundant soft brushstrokes.

Overall, *The Ballad of Doctor Richardson* seems to be an effort to merge European techniques with a neonoir sensibility in the heavy use of black. However, Pope's tendency to overink at times leaves the work looking crude and unpolished, which indicates the book was published early in Pope's career. Generally, the piece can be regarded as an effort by the young artist to cultivate a working method for his craft and hone his raw talent.

Themes

Primarily, *The Ballad of Doctor Richardson* is a romance, but it is infused throughout with various treatises on themes such as age and youth, poetry, art history, both self-imposed and socially imposed ostracism, artistic freedom and artists' goals, and desire. Beyond Richardson's occupation as a professor of art history and Noel's as a musician, the book reveals, through dialogue and narration, the importance both characters place on art, whether it be their own or someone else's. Richardson feels that poetry and art are his lifeblood, and he values them over personal relationships and professional advancement. Noel seems to feel the same way, expressing disdain for music that places image above artistic expression. However, both wrestle with loneliness, an emotion that could be blamed on their respective artistic devotions. This struggle, and the question of whether or not it must exist, is a key theme in the novel, as both Noel and Richardson come to realize that perhaps they can have both art and love.

The book also addresses the notion of release from both fears and inhibitions. Both the central characters of the story have repressed themselves to their detriment: Noel by stifling her years-long ardor for Richardson, and Richardson by limiting himself through propriety and passivity. In Richardson's positivist affirmation of pursuing the possible and embracing opportunity, and in the story's climactic confession by both characters of their feelings for each other, *The Ballad of Doctor Richardson* delivers a message about the dual passions of art and love.

Impact

In the year following its publication, *The Ballad of Doctor Richardson* gained a degree of positive critical attention but little press attention. The book was nominated for a 1995 Eisner Award, making it Pope's first "hit." In crafting the work, Pope was clearly influenced by the European comics of the late 1980's and early 1990's, and he mixed these sensibilities with influences from American pop artists such as Jack Kirby and Roy Crane. The narrative and thematic contents were influenced by Arthur Rimbaud's poem "The Triumph of Hunger" and Eliot's poem "The Lovesong of J. Alfred Prufrock," the art of the northern Renaissance, specifically that of Caravaggio, and the music of Johann Sebastian Bach.

However, *The Ballad of Doctor Richardson* has had little lasting impact on anything besides Pope's career. Until the publication of *The Ballad of Doctor Richardson*, Pope's work had mainly gone unnoticed in the Western world; most of his work was produced for Japanese manga publisher Kodansha. The praise garnered by *The Ballad of Doctor Richardson* may have opened more publishing avenues for Pope in the United States. Even this claim is debatable, though, as Pope began his pop science-fiction series *THB* (1994-1995) in the year following the first publication of *The Ballad of Doctor Richardson*, and of the two, *THB* is more widely known. The book may be of most interest to fans of Pope's later work, as it speaks volumes about the evolution of the artist's skill and style. As it stands, *The Ballad of Doctor Richardson* has faded into obscurity, and as Pope has announced no plans to publish another edition, the book will likely remain little known.

Kalervo A. Sinervo

Further Reading

Malès, Marc. *Different Ugliness, Different Madness* (2005).

Pope, Paul. *100%* (2002-2003).

_____. *Sin Titulo* (1993).

Thompson, Craig. *Blankets* (2003).

Bibliography

Attaboy. "Paul Pope: Ball in Play." *Hi-Fructose Magazine* 7 (2008): 54-61.

Pope, Paul. *100%*. New York: DC Comics, 2005.

_____. "Paul Pope Interview, Part 1." Interview by Ray Mescallado. *The Comics Journal* 191 (November, 1996): 98-118.

_____. *Pulphope: The Art of Paul Pope*. Richmond, Va.: AdHouse Books, 2007.

See also: *Blankets; The Playboy; Scott Pilgrim*

BERLIN: CITY OF STONES

Author: Lutes, Jason
Artist: Jason Lutes (illustrator)
Publisher: Drawn and Quarterly
First serial publication: 1996-2000
First book publication: 2000

Publication History

Jason Lutes began his comics career working for Fantagraphics Books and drawing a comic strip for *The Stranger*, a Seattle newspaper for which he later served as art director. The strip was collected as *Jar of Fools* (1994) and published by Canadian publisher Black Eyes Productions.

   Berlin: City of Stones is a collection of the first eight issues of Lutes's comic book series *Berlin*. The series began its run in 1996 with Black Eyes Productions, and publication was taken over by Drawn and Quarterly in 1998. Lutes embarked on the creation of the *Berlin* series with a plan to produce a total of twenty-four chapters with twenty-four pages each. Having set out this plan, he then decided to split the chapters into three volumes, each with a unifying theme and made up of eight chapters. The first book in the trilogy, *Berlin: City of Stones*, collects issues 1-8 of the series, and it was followed in 2008 by *Berlin: City of Smoke*, which collects issues 9-16. The third and final installment in the series, *Berlin: City of Light*, collects volumes 17-24 and has an anticipated publication date of 2013. While writing *Berlin*, Lutes has continued to produce other works, including *The Fall* (2001) with Ed Brubaker and *Houdini: The Handcuff King* (2007) with Nick Bertozzi.

Plot

A work of historical fiction, the *Berlin* trilogy is anchored by three major events in German history: the May Day massacre of 1929, the Reichstag elections of 1930, and Adolf Hitler's assumption of the chancellorship in 1933. Using these events as guideposts, Lutes constructs a story of interpersonal relationships and the impact that the social and political climate in Berlin have on them. Written for an adult audience,

Berlin: City of Stones. (Courtesy of Drawn and Quarterly)

Berlin provides a realistic look at the way people function, both alone and with others, and includes nudity and sexual situations. Throughout the trilogy, Lutes explores the lives of the citizens of Berlin, including workers, artists, writers, musicians, public-service employees, and children. He also delves into the homosexual culture of the city as well as the influx of American jazz music that was taking place at the time. While each volume centers on a different set of relationships, all three focus ultimately on the city of Berlin as the main "character" of the trilogy.

   The first volume in the series, *Berlin: City of Stones*, spans the period between September, 1928, and the May Day massacre of May 1, 1929. The book opens with the chance meeting of Marthe Mueller and Kurt

Severing as they travel by train to Berlin. Marthe is a privileged young art student traveling to Berlin for the first time, and Kurt is a somewhat disenchanted journalist returning to the city. The reader is quickly plunged into the hustle and bustle of the city as experienced through Marthe's eyes and private journal entries. As she attends art classes and befriends a group of fellow students, Marthe struggles with her lost passion for art and her desire to find a place among the many inhabitants of the city.

A parallel plotline involves a working-class family splintered by political differences. As the husband, Otto, turns toward the Nazi Party, his wife, Gudrun, begins to entertain thoughts of aligning with the Communist Party. When challenged by Otto about her views, Gudrun decides to leave him and find a more suitable place to explore her sociopolitical ideas. Otto allows her to take their two daughters but insists that their young son, Heinz, remain behind with him. Upon departing her home, she is forced to find refuge in a Salvation Army shelter and struggles to eke out a living. As time passes, Gudrun learns more about communism, and Otto and Heinz become more involved with the Nazi Party.

A third plotline delves into the life of a young Jewish radical, David Schwartz, who idolizes both famed magician Harry Houdini and Marxist thinker Rosa Luxemburg. When traveling through the streets of Berlin, David is persecuted by some for being a Jew, his plight evoking the growing anti-Semitic atmosphere of the city. At home, David witnesses the struggles that his parents and grandfather endure as they attempt to come to terms with the fact that they must identify themselves more as Germans than as Jews.

At first glance, these characters' stories may seem to show unrelated, disparate lives. However, the people of Berlin are ultimately all connected by the social and political upheaval of which they are a part.

Characters
- *Marthe Mueller*, the protagonist, is a young woman of privilege traveling to Berlin to attend art school. Plain but not unattractive, she spends much of her time sketching or writing in her journal. She is the embodiment of small-town naïveté and seems tentative in her interactions with those whom she meets in Berlin. She flounders in Berlin until she begins a love affair with Kurt Servering.
- *Kurt Severing* is Marthe's love interest. He is bespectacled, often wears a hat and overcoat, and smokes almost constantly. A freelance journalist, Kurt represents the intellectual elite in Berlin.
- *Franz Wolzendorf* is Marthe's landlord. He is a large, unpleasant-looking man. He served under Marthe's father during World War I and harbors contempt for both Marthe and her father.
- *Anna*, a young lesbian whom Marthe meets in art school, appears pointedly masculine in the book. She becomes a close friend to Marthe and eventually develops romantic feelings for her.
- *David Schwartz*, the protagonist in a second plotline, is a Jewish youth. Handsome and clean cut, he lives with his mother, father, and grandfather. He works selling issues of a communist newspaper and spends his free time obsessing over Houdini.
- *Gudrun Braun*, the protagonist in a third plotline, is a textile worker and mother. She appears strong but tired; years of hard work have marred her looks. She eventually becomes a member of the Communist Party.
- *Otto Braun* is Gudrun's husband. He is clean cut and frequently looks angry. He joins the Nazis.
- *Silvia* and *Elga Braun* are Gudrun and Otto's daughters. When Gudrun leaves Otto, she takes them with her.
- *Heinz Braun* is Gudrun and Otto's son. When Gudrun leaves Otto, Heinz is left behind at Otto's request. He also becomes involved with the Nazis.
- *Otto Schmidt* is a kind, nondescript looking man whom Gudrun meets upon leaving her husband. With his guidance, Gudrun finds work and becomes involved in the Communist Party.

Artistic Style

The *Berlin* series is drawn and written entirely by Lutes. His black-and-white illustration style is decidedly realistic, with clean lines that reflect the influence of artists such as *The Adventures of Tintin*'s Hergé and *Louis Riel*'s Chester Brown. Lutes's characters are drawn accurately, complete with depictions of excess fat, sagging breasts, and body hair.

Within panels, there is a liberal use of white space, allowing readers to complete the scene mentally with their own emotional interpretations. Lutes employs this technique to engage readers in constructing meaning from the story in lieu of presenting everything explicitly and offering little room for interpretation. In contrast to this, Lutes also includes greatly detailed images that clearly show human emotions, architectural detail, and the devastation evident in certain parts of the city. This combination of stark white and vivid detail creates a work that actively engages the reader and brings the characters' stories to life.

Transitions among story lines are virtually seamless as Lutes creates visual connections between the first panel in a chapter and the one immediately preceding

it. Lutes's art has a cinematic quality that uses unusual angles to emphasize points and allows readers to feel as if they are viewing a scene through the eyes of a specific character, rather than as a detached viewer. When Lutes does employ a more stylized approach to drawing, the contrast is marked and noticeable, and this serves to accentuate the drawing style that permeates the book.

Themes

Berlin focuses primarily on the connection between individuals' interpersonal relationships and the broader social and political fabric of their lives. Lutes's readers become deeply involved in the lives of his characters as they attempt to navigate the upheaval that is taking place around them. For instance, the romance between Marthe and Kurt offers a glimpse into the elite class in Berlin and the way in which they go about their lives.

Berlin: City of Stones. (Courtesy of Drawn and Quarterly)

Their reality is in marked contrast to that of the other characters, all of whom inhabit lower social strata.

In the characters of Gudrun and Otto Braun, the reader sees a working-class family influenced just as deeply by the poverty in which its members live as they are by the political allegiances that they develop. Compelled to leave her husband because of their conflicting political views, the impoverished Gudrun eventually finds her place in the Communist Party, while her husband and son become increasingly involved in the activities of the Nazi Party.

David Schwartz's struggles with identity as a Jew in Berlin play out through a variety of interactions: among his family, in relation to his boss, and with the other young men with whom he comes in contact. At the same time as David's parents and grandfather are struggling to become more "German" and less "Jewish," and he himself is experiencing anti-Semitic persecution on the streets, David is learning about Luxemburg and her importance as both a Jew and a communist.

Through all of these story lines, Lutes's *Berlin* presents readers with vivid personal stories that serve to deepen understanding of German politics and society in this time period.

Impact

Berlin: City of Stones is widely recognized as an outstanding work of historical fiction produced in the sequential art medium. Epic in scope, the *Berlin* trilogy explores a period in history that is underrepresented in both graphic and prose literature. Although it is a work of fiction, *Berlin* is frequently referred to in relation to such award-winning nonfiction memoirs as Art Spiegelman's *Maus* and Marjane Satrapi's *Persepolis*.

Lutes pays specific attention to the architecture of the page and historical detail, and praise abounds for both his ability to render realistic figures and his technical precision. Frequently cited as an outstanding example of the way in which words and pictures can work together to bring a story to life, *Berlin: City of Stones* was recognized by *Time* magazine as representative of high-quality and impactful graphic novel work.

Britt White

Further Reading

Lutes, Jason. *Berlin: City of Smoke* (2009).

Lutes, Jason, and Nick Bertozzi. *Houdini: The Handcuff King* (2007).

Sacco, Joe. *Palestine* (2001).

Satrapi, Marjane. *Persepolis* (2003).

Taniguchi, Jirō. *A Distant Neighborhood* (2009).

Bibliography

Buhle, Paul. "History and Comics." *Reviews in American History* 35, no. 2 (June, 2007): 315-323.

Lutes, Jason. "Back to the City: Jason Lutes on Berlin 2." Interview by Michael C. Lorah. *Newsarama*, October 1, 2008. http://www.newsarama.com/comics/100801-Berlin2.html

Mikkonen, Kai. "Presenting Minds in Graphic Narratives." *Partial Answers: Journal of Literature and the History of Ideas* 6, no. 2 (June, 2008): 301-321.

See also: *Maus: A Survivor's Tale; Persepolis; Houdini; The Adventures of Tintin; Palestine*

BINKY BROWN SAMPLER

Author: Green, Justin
Artist: Justin Green (illustrator)
Publisher: Last Gasp
First serial publication: 1968-1995
First book publication: 1995

Publication History

Inspired by the burgeoning underground comics scene and artist Robert Crumb, Justin Green began to create comics while still in art school. His first strip, "Confessions of a Mad School Boy," was published by a periodical in Providence, Rhode Island, thanks to the mentorship of the Mad Peck, another underground cartoonist. The titular religion-plagued character was later named Binky Brown, based on a childhood nickname given to Green by an uncle, in "Binky Brown Makes up His Own Puberty Rites," in *Yellow Dog*, issue 17, published by the Print Mint in 1969. In 1970, Green created "The Agony of Binky Brown," published in 1971 in *Laugh in the Dark*, issue 1, from Last Gasp Eco Funnies.

Binky Brown Meets the Holy Virgin Mary, a single-issue, mostly autobiographical story produced completely by Green, was published by Last Gasp in 1972 to continuing acclaim. By 1998, Last Gasp had sold fifty thousand copies of the comic. The only difference between the first and second editions is that a drawing of the Virgin Mary overlays a piece of text in the first edition but not in the second.

In addition to reproducing *Binky Brown Meets the Holy Virgin Mary*, the *Binky Brown Sampler* contains some material from Green's other major Binky Brown work, *Sacred and Profane*, originally published by Last Gasp in 1976. That volume primarily consisted of "We Fellow Traveleers," a more mythic recasting of the autobiographical struggle of Binky Brown, which the sampler does not reprint. The sampler does include such material from *Sacred and Profane* as "Sweet Void of Youth" and a sketch of how purgatory works, as well as the covers of that publication and of Green's *Show and Tell Comics*, published by the Print Mint in 1973.

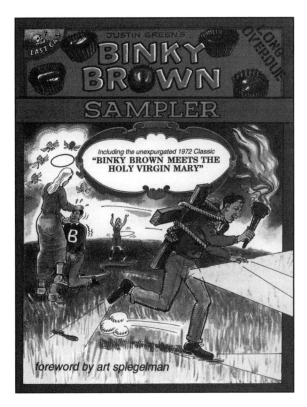

Binky Brown Sampler. (Courtesy of Last Gasp)

By the early 1980's, Green had almost entirely left the field of comics to make a living as a sign painter. However, he continued to work on two comics: *The Sign Game*, in *Signs of the Times*, and *Musical Legends*, in *Pulse* magazine. He also published material in *Raw*, edited by Art Spiegelman and Françoise Mouly, and *Weirdo*, edited by Robert Crumb. Some of the material in the *Binky Brown Sampler* may have come from these sources, although the sampler gives no information about the original publication of the comic work. A prose piece in the sampler began as an essay in *The Sun* magazine.

Plot

Binky Brown Meets the Holy Virgin Mary is a thinly veiled autobiography concerning Green's lifelong struggle with his Catholic upbringing and, although the diagnosis was made long after the 1972 publication of the comic, obsessive-compulsive disorder. Green explores these issues through his fictionalized avatar, the adolescent Binky Brown. After Binky enters puberty, his religious guilt over his sexual thoughts and feelings becomes a major focus of obsession. He comes to believe that sexual rays are emitted from his body—at first from his penis, then his fingers and toes as well— and, eventually, any tube-shaped or even rectangular object; if these rays intersect with any church or holy statue, he will be guilty of sin.

However, while these sexual issues are the most obvious of Binky Brown's problems, in some ways, they are the least important. Perhaps because adolescence is frequently a time of obsession and neurosis, these problems interweave seamlessly with problems with which many underground comics readers could identify: intimidation by older and more physically developed boys, helpless adoration of girls of higher social status mixed with a growing misogyny, and desires to be admired by parents for being good and by girls for being tough.

Deciding he is inevitably damned, Binky rejects the Catholic Church, but he is still haunted by guilt. A page depicts "various avenues of experiment" undergone between 1959 and 1971, including "Beer," "Speed," "Crime," "Hesse Novels," "Yoga," "Pot," "Mysticism," "Psychiatry," "Painting," "The Blues," and "Acid." One turning point occurs at the end of an acid trip in 1971, when a statue of the Virgin Mary tags Binky, saying "You're it!" "She finally talked," Binky says, "and turned out to be the bogeyman. Haw haw. The bogeyman who is really that l'il ol' ventriloquist, me!" With that insight, Binky buys dozens of cheap statues of the Virgin Mary and smashes most of them, after which the rays disappear.

In reality, as the prose piece at the end of the sampler shows, Green's problems, the result of brain chemistry and an inability to socialize, were not that easily resolved. However, the symbolic ending of *Binky Brown Meets the Holy Virgin Mary* is in many ways justified, as Green notes that he has since learned to manage his obsessive-compulsive disorder and overcome many of the specific issues stemming from his Catholic childhood.

Other pieces in the *Binky Brown Sampler* expand upon this story. "Bathos Playhouse: Right Field" features Sister Virginia from *Binky Brown Meets the Holy Virgin Mary*, and "Binky Brown in the Taboo Gown" shows his distress over the fact that his "lucky shirt" is the same color as Christ's gown in the film *The Robe* (1953). Other short features focus more on typical adolescent heartache and embarrassment, such as enduring physical-education classes. "Sweet Void of Youth" depicts Green's development as a cartoonist and artist, using the same mostly literal yet highly symbolic approach as *Binky Brown Meets the Holy Virgin Mary*.

Characters

- *Binky Brown* is an adolescent whose undiagnosed obsessive-compulsive disorder and complicated relationship with the Catholic Church cause him a great deal of mental and emotional distress. He serves as a reflection of his time and place, the Midwest of the 1950's and after. A sympathetic character obviously based on Green, Binky is the effective opposite of a superhero; his greatest accomplishment is to become more or less normal.

- *Other characters* are all minor, important only insofar as they affect Binky's life. These include his father and mother, his family's African American maid, the nuns and priests, the girl he has a crush on, the tough boy for whom he does artwork when they are both in grade school, and his school principal. The reader is told only bits about each. For instance, all that is said about Binky's mother is that she reads and sings sad songs while cleaning. A one-page panel about his father is titled "Great Moments in Alcoholism," but nothing about his drinking is brought up in *Binky Brown Meets the Holy Virgin Mary*, as relevant as the topic might seem. Sometimes, the artwork provides the most information, such as in the case of Father Runkem, the demented-looking priest in *Binky Brown Meets the Holy Virgin Mary* who exacerbates Binky's guilt. Some of the more striking characters are symbolic; "Sweet Surrender," a short piece in the sampler, features Binky's dog, Nostalgia, who wears a theater usher's costume, imprisons Binky in a shoe, and constantly shows him movies based on embarrassing moments from his childhood.

Artistic Style

Green's artwork is idiosyncratic, expressive, eclectic, and experimental. His skill advances with experience, as the juxtaposition of earlier and later works in the sampler demonstrates, though it does not change radically. Throughout the sampler, Green uses a quintessential comic book style that features exaggerated figures with simplified but amazingly individual and communicative faces. The work is well designed for black-and-white publication, using drawn textures and blocks of black or white to give depth and detail. Green's panels are not packed like those of the early *MAD* magazine or his underground compatriots such as S. Clay Wilson, but they always provide an important background, either realistic or symbolic, rather than a stark stage for the characters. The layout of the panels ranges from traditional to highly inventive.

The back cover of *Binky Brown Meets the Holy Virgin Mary*, reprinted in the sampler, makes clear Green's artistic influences in popular culture, cartoons, and historical works of art. The devil, masquerading as the Virgin Mary, has a snout with a bulbous nose, similar to that of a cartoon canine, and wears 1950's-style men's socks with garters; a background city street is dominated by an advertising billboard and fast-food franchises; and the devil is being bitten on the calf by a lion that resembles the green lion of alchemical imagery. These incongruous approaches work together throughout *Binky Brown Meets the Holy Virgin Mary* and the other pieces in the *Binky Brown Sampler* to create Green's own iconography. For instance, in one panel, in which Binky considers the atom bomb and God's Last Judgment, the skeleton with an hourglass

Binky Brown Sampler. (Courtesy of Last Gasp)

pictured over his head would not be out of place in a medieval or Renaissance woodcut. One panel in "Sweet Void of Youth" presents a coherent allegory, with "Fame," an angel somewhat like that in Albrecht Dürer's *Melencolia I* (1514), and "Oblivion Way" depicted in the background.

Themes

The most obvious theme of *Binky Brown Meets the Holy Virgin Mary* and the *Binky Brown Sampler* as a whole is the conflict between sexuality and the Catholic Church. In interviews from the 1980's and 1990's, Green states that he no longer considers Catholicism the enemy, both because it has changed and because he feels that hatred and fear of sexuality is not inherent to the doctrine. Yet, *Binky Brown* continues to speak to the widespread conflict between sexuality and religion.

Other themes are deserving of attention as well. As an autobiography, the *Binky Brown Sampler* constantly investigates the role of social and personal history in the development of identity. In addition to *Binky Brown Meets the Holy Virgin Mary*, other stories in the sampler explore this theme. For instance, "Scribe" is a history of lettering that begins with prehistoric pictographs, forming a diptych with the more personal "Sweet Void of Youth."

Another theme is the paradoxical way in which myths help humans understand their lives but also mislead them. For instance, "Binky Brown Meets Olympic Legends" concerns the mother of a friend, a one-time Olympic runner, and the sad contrast between her life as Binky imagines it, based on an Olympic Legends trading card, and as he finds it in reality. The general themes of finding one's purpose in life and the place of art in life intersect in this autobiographical work.

Although the works in the sampler depict sex only once and barely refer to drugs, they consistently support counterculture values of truth, freedom, rebellion, introspection, and experimentation, in life and in art. They are also almost never explicitly political, although the end of "Scribe" depicts concerns about war.

Justin Green

A key figure in the development of autobiographical and semi-autobiographical comics stemming from the American underground comics movement, Justin Green is best known for his work on the 1972 comic book *Binky Brown Meets the Holy Virgin Mary*. Binky Brown is the alter ego of the artist himself, and the book tells the story of his personal obsession with the idea that he might contaminate religious sites with sexual thoughts. The book was a landmark event in the development of the American "comix" underground, and it offered a profound influence on an entire generation of cartoonists who would follow his lead. In the 1980's, Green retreated from comics and took up work as a commercial sign painter, a subject that is addressed in his 1994 book *Justin Green's Sign Game*. Since the 1990's Green has returned to comics, but his total output remains small but highly influential.

Impact

Both Crumb and Spiegelman credit Green with initiating the genre of autobiographical comics, one that has become almost as entrenched as the superhero genre. Although many taboos in comics had already been broken by 1972, no one had yet put the result into a coherent personal story. Green paved the way for Spiegelman's *Maus* (1986) by using the comic form to provide both intimacy and distance in autobiography. Just as Spiegelman uses animal characters to make the Holocaust visible yet bearable, Green uses cartooning and imagery from various sources to force readers into Binky's head while still maintaining a necessary perspective. One of the few underground artists trained in fine art, Green may also have been influential in his artistic use of a range of sources and iconography, from 1950's middle-American signage to Renaissance art. Green further anticipated and preceded the mix of myth and mundane life, later prominent in the work of Neil Gaiman, Grant Morrison, and others.

Bernadette Bosky

Further Reading

Brown, Chester. *I Never Liked You* (1994).

Green, Justin. *Sacred and Profane* (1976).

Gregory, Roberta. *Naughty Bits* (1991-2004).

Kominsky, Aline, Robert Crumb, and Sophie Crumb. *The Complete Dirty Laundry Comics* (1993).

Spiegelman, Art. *Maus: A Survivor's Tale* (1986).

Bibliography

Green, Justin. "Comics and Catholics: Mark Burbey Interviews Justin Green." Interview by Mark Burbey. *The Comics Journal* 104 (January, 1986): 37-49.

Levin, Bob. "Rice, Beans, and Justin Greens." *The Comics Journal* 203 (April, 1998): 101-107.

Manning, Shaun. "Justin Green on *Binky Brown*." *Comic Book Resources*, January 22, 2010. http://www.comicbookresources.com/?page=article&id=24518.

Von Busak, Richard. "Memoirs of a Catholic Boyhood: Birth of the Comic Book Autobiography." *Metroactive*, 1995. http://www.metroactive.com/papers/metro/10.12.95/comics-9541.html.

See also: *American Splendor; Maus: A Survivor's Tale; The Complete Fritz the Cat; I Never Liked You*

BLACK HOLE

Author: Burns, Charles
Artist: Charles Burns (illustrator)
Publisher: Kitchen Sink Press; Pantheon Books
First serial publication: 1995-2004
First book publication: 2005

Publication History

In 1988, as part of what would become his *Big Baby* cycle, Charles Burns created a story entitled "Teen Plague," which was first serialized in a number of weekly papers and then compiled and published as a complete work in *RAW* magazine, Volume 2, issue 1, in 1989. In addition to the work's slowly unfolding appearance, key aspects of its verbal elements—including the use of crosscutting narrative voices and the intertwining themes of adolescence, escape, dream, and illness—along with the stark visual architecture and imagery—suggest that "Teen Plague" served as the primitive precursor to *Black Hole*.

Burns stripped away the absurdist humor and overt use of classic horror comic and film tropes from his original experiment and refined a more serious vision in *Black Hole*, which originally appeared in limited-series comic books between 1995 and 2005. Kitchen Sink Press published the four original issues; after Kitchen Sink Press folded, Fantagraphics Books republished the earlier volumes and released another eight volumes.

Pantheon Books gained rights to the work, and in 2005, released a hardcover edition, with a compelling jacket designed by Chip Kidd. The book version, including the trade paperback edition that followed in 2008, does not include some key panels from the original comic books that provided rapid pictorial insight into the characters and implied a potentially significant story line regarding how fear of the other often results in violence.

Plot

Black Hole is a multiple-perspective, coming-of-age novel that unfolds in an alternative and geographically significant Pacific Northwest coast suburb of Seattle

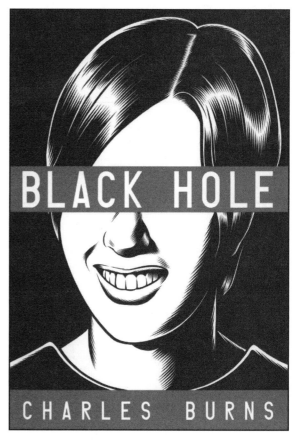

Black Hole. (Courtesy of Pantheon Books)

during the era of David Bowie's *Diamond Dogs* (1974), when promiscuous and unprotected sex, while perhaps not necessarily wise, was not considered deadly. The book examines the relationships, psyches, dreams, and psychological terrors of several white, mainstream teens during their closing years of high school.

Eschewing a linear narrative structure, the story is both propelled and halted along the course of nineteen interlaced sections primarily by the layered, alternating viewpoints of Keith Pearson, Chris Rhodes, and Rob Facincani. A fourth, less vocal yet crucial, perspective emanates from Eliza, an artist whose paintings and sculptures lead viewers in subconscious narrative tendrils, including that of her own rape by dope-dealing college burnouts. While most of the narrative tension is generated by the desires of the major characters, significant additional interest is established through mysterious disappearances and murders of and by key secondary figures.

A dark prologue establishes the disturbed, disconcerting tone of the ensuing narrative. While dissecting a frog during biology class, Keith falls into a swoon and is assaulted by grotesque visions that portend future events. Shortly thereafter, he learns that Rob has contracted "the bug," a virus that infects young people through sexual contact and manifests itself in a bizarre array of physical maladies, including boils, necrosis, webbed fingers, a regenerative tail, and in Rob's case, an increasingly sentient mouth.

Keith is obsessed with Chris, who becomes infected as a result of having sex with Rob in a graveyard. Initially unaware of her condition, Chris attends a keg party, where she goes for a swim, the first of her several symbolic immersions into water. Here, the other teens learn that her manifestation of the virus is a gash along the spine, a precursor to the literal shedding of her entire skin. After leaving her parents a good-bye note, she runs away with Rob to live in a tent in a deep, dark part of the woods known as "The Pit," where growing numbers of the infected gather in a colony of the alienated. Amid hunger and deformity, the adolescents' needs, jealousies, and lusts still run rampant and eventually culminate in murder and suicide.

Meanwhile, during a marijuana pickup, Keith encounters Eliza, who, frightened by the sinister events occurring in the colony, has been living and making art in the basement of the dealers' house. Still trying to be Chris's "knight in shining armor," Keith finds himself drawn to Eliza, an attraction that culminates in the loss of his virginity during an intense, drug-enhanced encounter, during which Eliza's tail snaps off and Keith contracts the virus.

Eventually, Keith and Eliza flee the sordid world of their past, seeking hope in the arid desert of the Southwest. The members of the other major dyad do not fare as well: Rob is savagely beaten to death, and Chris hitchhikes to the coast, where she is last seen floating naked in the ocean, staring up at the constellations.

Characters

- *Keith Pearson* is a typical, long-haired high school student primarily concerned with drugs and sex. For most of the book, his callow infatuation with Chris blinds him to other possibilities and leads him to inadvertently create the arena where the mass murder of the infected occurs. His physical appearance changes partway through the narrative as the virus eventually manifests itself as a series of tadpole-like growths along his ribs.

- *Chris Rhodes* is a shy, quiet girl who, before the spread of the virus, never skipped a day of class. One of the more complex and developed characters, she reveals her initial attraction to Rob and the consequences of their ensuing relationship through a series of journal entries and conversations with her friends. She seeks to escape the constraints of her life, particularly after becoming infected, and contemplates suicide at several points.

- *Rob Facincani* is a cigarette-smoking protagonist with long hair and a small goatee. While still involved in a relationship with a secondary character named Lisa, he becomes involved with Chris, and his indiscretion, along with suggestions of his eventual remorse and demise, are revealed by a voice issuing from his deformity, a mouth at the base of his throat. While he is attentive to other members of the colony, his primary concern for Chris eventually leads to his murder.

- *Eliza*, a pale, dark-haired, blue-eyed beauty with a tail, is slightly older than the other students. She is somehow able to tap into subconscious depths, and her artwork reveals the dark mysteries and dreams that haunt the other characters. After being raped and marked with graffiti by the drug dealers, who label her "the Lizard Queen," Eliza destroys her artwork, seduces Keith, and eventually flees with him toward the desert.

- *Dave Barnes*, an antagonist, was a friendly sophomore whom the virus transformed into a dog-faced, bitter stalker. A leader among the infected, he helps Chris and Rob establish their tent at the colony and offers newcomers advice on where to get food and, ostensibly, how to avoid danger. He later murders his old friend Rick as well as the infected who have taken refuge in the temporary comforts of a house. After killing Rick, he commits suicide.

- *Rick Holstrum*, a.k.a. *Rick the Dick*, an antagonist, appears in his yearbook photo as a clean-cut, short-haired young man wearing a tie, but the virus has transmogrified him. Always lurking in the woods, he is a shuffling, cadaverous ogre who commits extreme acts of violence. He is killed by his former friend Dave.

Artistic Style

In spite of some familiar adolescent tropes and clichés, *Black Hole* presents readers with a dark and singular vision. Renouncing the use of color, pagination, and direct verbal cues, Burns skillfully manipulates and layers the passages and collisions of time and shifting points of view through the rhythmic movement of stark black backgrounds, clean lines, various types of white-panel borders, and repetitive imagery. While traditional narrative boxes depict internal monologue and speech balloons present conversation, the absence of thought balloons and the interplay of light and darkness combine to create an overall effect of witnessing a collective, waking dream.

Readers enter the book through the woods, passing by a femur lashed to one tree while another nearby tree sprouts bulbous, pestilential growths. Turning the page, they descend visually into the first of many gashes, ultimately finding themselves ensnared in depictions of archetypal terrors.

Burns juxtaposes familiar objects to achieve an increasingly eerie and disturbing mood, creating effects similar to those achieved in the "exquisite corpse" games of the Surrealists. Renditions of memory and dream soon begin overpowering those of the fictional reality. Talismans abound (decapitated dolls, splintered bones, human-faced worms, half-eaten food, broken beer bottles, tadpoles) with meanings that invert the rationality of the verbal text. Appearances are deceptive and fluid.

Double splash pages that precede each section offer carefully designed pairings that further emphasize a

Black Hole. (Courtesy of Pantheon Books)

world of shifting desires and colliding fears. A marijuana bud becomes a hand cupped against pudenda; a broken Popsicle duplicates the angle of a bound and naked Keith; a microscopic close-up of a germinating seed appears beside Eliza's taut breast; and an orange becomes a mountain that promises hope.

Burns depicts his characters in an exaggerated, realistic style that allows for distortion and emphasizes the face as the visual component most essential for transmitting emotion. Grimaces suggest variants of pain, smiles are toothy and forced, and glances speak of longing and remorse. Burns captures the adolescent fascination with the body through careful layouts, some of which include bisected panels that paradoxically separate two characters while fusing them into one being.

Themes

Considered in reductive, purely verbal terms, *Black Hole* sometimes reads like a deranged teenage soap opera, and any traditional literary analysis falls short of capturing how the visual elements alter and distort potential meanings. Because of its psychological complexities and ambiguities, the work has been interpreted through several critical lenses.

Given its gradual appearance over a decade, and although set during the 1970's, it has been seen as a reflective, metaphorical exploration regarding the increasing spread of AIDS and its attendant fears of invisible penetration into mainstream American society during the 1980's. However, *Black Hole* reminds readers that the physical symptoms of older sexually transmitted diseases, such as gonorrhea, herpes, and syphilis, often appeared in the mucous membranes, and became blatant, physical markers upon the bodies of those who transgressed against the prevailing cultural narrative.

Since teachers, parents, and other adult authority figures are nearly absent—appearing, at most, as minimal presences in any of the novel's intertwining worlds—*Black Hole* can also be read as an exploration of the intensely subjective, often narcissistic world of late adolescence, and how social pairings and larger groupings develop and often hinder and distort liminal identities.

The book's intense portrayals of sexuality invite a variety of gender analyses. Some critics see Burns's portrayals, both verbal and visual, of the female characters as furthering the medium's long-running objectification of women. Others have explored the book's images of bondage, sadomasochism, and castration.

Links between the fictional acts of violence and real-life mass shootings such as those that occurred at Columbine, Colorado, in 1999, have also been suggested. Nonetheless, like any worthwhile literary work, *Black Hole* defies any singular, comprehensive thematic summation.

Impact

Like a lot of sequential art that began appearing in the late twentieth century, particularly in the pages of *RAW*, *Black Hole* demonstrates the medium's capacity to tell intelligent, complex stories. What sets Burns's masterpiece apart is its creator's relentlessness in forging the medium into forms that might better express primordial levels of human consciousness.

Black Hole strikes a resounding, resonating chord with readers who are just learning or still willing to admit that sexual awakening is fun, sometimes dirty, and often dangerous; that drugs and alcohol can transport human consciousness; and that the struggle to render images of those ancient impulses in any medium takes hours of concentrated work, craft, and courage to sustain. The book sets a high benchmark for any creators working within the medium.

Black Hole inevitably influenced subsequent alternative graphic novels; however, the primary impact of its completion and ensuing popular and critical reception was to allow Burns to create his next major work: The first volume of *X'ed Out* appeared in October, 2010. The new series promises to be a further disturbing expression of Burns's essential truth: There are aspects to humanity that the rationality of words alone will never be able to express.

Film rights to *Black Hole* were optioned by Plan B, MTV Films, and producer Kevin Messick in 2005. Further interest was generated when Neil Gaiman and Richard Avery signed on in 2006 to write the screenplay adaptation. After the original director, Alexandre Aja, was replaced by David Fincher in 2008, the writers abandoned the project. Independent filmmaker Rupert Sanders created a short adaptation that

---

Charles Burns

Charles Burns uses a wickedly effective combination of words and pictures in his horror graphic novels. At the best of times, the stories are unsettling; more often they are grotesque, gruesome, or terrifying, with artwork that vividly illustrates the supernatural afflictions plaguing the characters (though in fairness, many of those characters are unlikeable and deserve to be plagued). The haunting imagery and creepy events will keep readers up at night.

circulated for a brief time in 2010 before it was pulled from most Web sites for nudity or sexual-content violations.

David Sims

Further Reading

Burns, Charles. *Big Baby* (1999).

_____. *El Borrah* (1984-2005).

_____. *X'ed Out* (2010).

Gaiman, Neil. *The Sandman* (1989-1996).

Bibliography

Burns, Charles. "Charles Burns, Chip Kidd, Seth, and Chris Ware Panel." Interview by Jeet Heer. *Comics Journal*, March 31, 2010. http://classic.tcj.com/alternative/charles-burns-chip-kidd-seth-and-chris-ware-panel-part-one-of-three/.

_____. "Charles Burns is *X'ed Out*." Interview by Alex Dueben. *Comic* Book *Resources*, October 18, 2010. http://www.comicbookresources.com/?page=article&id=28938.

Raney, Vanessa. "Review of Charles Burns' *Black Hole*." *ImageTexT: Interdisciplinary Comics Studies* 2, no. 1 (2005).

Wolk, Douglas. *Reading Comics: How Graphic Novels Work and What They Mean*. Cambridge, Mass.: Da Capo Press, 2008.

Zeigler, James. "Too Cruel: The Diseased Teens and Mean Bodies of Charles Burns's *Black Hole*." *Scan: Journal of Media Arts Culture* 5, no. 2 (September, 2008).

See also: *Maus: A Survivor's Tale*

BLACKMARK

Author: Goodwin, Archie; Kane, Gil
Artist: Gil Kane (illustrator)
Publisher: Bantam Books; Fantagraphics Books
First serial publication: 1974 (Volume 1); 1979 (Volume 2)
First book publication: 1971 (Volume 1); 2002 (Volumes 1 and 2)

Publication History

Gil Kane began working as a comic book artist in the late 1940's and by the mid-1960's had grown restless with the traditional format. He sought to expand the reach of graphic storytelling, making his first attempt to do so with a black-and-white magazine titled *His Name Is . . . Savage!* (1968), a crime story that failed to find a place on newsstands. At the same time, Kane pitched *Blackmark*, a sword-and-sorcery series with some science-fiction elements, to Bantam Books' chief executive officer, Oscar Distel.

Distel liked the concept, and Kane later claimed that he was contracted for an eight-volume series. Kane produced the first volume within several months and completed the second prior to the January, 1971, release of the first book. He worked a torturous schedule, producing as many as thirty pages of *Blackmark* in a week while also working for DC Comics and Marvel Comics.

Each volume of *Blackmark* paid a mere thirty-five hundred dollars, a rate of less than thirty dollars per page for story and art, far below industry standards. Kane struggled with the schedule and received layout help for some pages from Harvey Kurtzman and art assistance on other pages from Neal Adams. As Kane completed the first volume, typesetting and Zip-A-Tone pasteups were handled by Howard Chaykin. Kane enlisted Archie Goodwin to help him polish the plots and provide the text and dialogue late in the process. The initial plan was to release two volumes back-to-back, followed a month later by the third volume, in order to gain attention and secure shelf space.

Bantam soured on the series as the first volume sold poorly. The second volume had been printed but was canceled before it could be bound and shipped. The

Blackmark. (Courtesy of Fantagraphics Books)

first volume was reformatted and serialized in Marvel Comics' black-and-white magazine *The Savage Sword of Conan*, issues 1-4 (August, 1974, to February, 1975). The second novel, *The Mind Demons*, finally saw print as the winter 1979 issue of *Marvel Preview*.

Kane claimed that layouts were completed for Volume 3 and were mostly penciled by the time the series was canceled, although no artwork was released. The two complete volumes were collected in an oversized trade edition in 2002 by Fantagraphics Books, restoring the illustrations to their original proportions.

Plot

In the first book, Marnie, a young woman married to Old Zeph, is approached by the dying King Amarix of the Westlands, who asks her to preserve his knowledge of the old science in order to help the world rebuild. The high-tech device he uses subtly alters her physiology, allowing the barren woman to conceive a child, an heir who will possess Amarix's knowledge. She agrees, and soon after, the king dies, leading Zeph to beat her for even thinking about the forbidden science. In time, she bears a son Zeph names Blackmark, a reminder of her misdeed. The infant softens Zeph's hard heart, and they eventually form an important bond.

When the boy is six, a warrior comes seeking the fealty of the family's village, but Zeph refuses to bow to the sword and is killed for his defiance. When Marnie fights back, she is also slain, and Blackmark is left alone. He vows revenge and uses the knowledge that haunts his dreams to survive and lead his people until he is captured and enslaved by King Kargon.

At the age of twenty-one, Blackmark has become a successful gladiator in Kargon's cruel games and is also the object of Kargon's daughter Lyllith's lustful desire. After spurning her, Blackmark must battle the king's favored Fire Lizard in the company of Balzamo, King Amarix's aid who had awaited the coming of the people's savior.

After dispatching the beast, Blackmark dares to enter the silver cylinder that is said to be unmovable by all save the man who is destined to be king. Blackmark's hidden knowledge allows him to activate the engines; the spaceship shudders and then flies. Aboard, he finds Amarix's sword, which is outfitted with sonic control, enhancing its power.

Kargon refuses to submit to the will of the people and tries to flee, only to be killed during the ensuing riot. Lyllith also attempts to escape but is brought to heel by the throng. Blackmark is chagrined to learn that a visiting warlord, the man who killed his parents, has managed to escape.

In the second book, *The Mind Demons*, Blackmark takes control of Kargon's castle and uses it as a base to help unite the various societies, asking the leaders to pledge their support to the people. All agree save Reynard, who schemes to topple Blackmark. In the meantime, Blackmark is tortured by recurring nightmares and visions that Balzamo cannot interpret. Instead,

Blackmark. (Courtesy of Fantagraphics Books)

Balzamo studies the spaceship, trying to learn its secrets. Shanflux, lord of the Icewastes, sends a runner to ask for Blackmark's help, as his keep is under attack by the Psi-Lords, mutants who live in the forbidden north. Blackmark and his group arrive to fight these enemies, but Shanflux is already dead.

Blackmark meets and falls in love with Shandra, the dead lord's daughter. His nightmares keep him preoccupied, and in time, the gap between Blackmark and Shandra grows, and she succumbs to Reynard's attentions. She leaves Blackmark just before he decides the time has come to battle the Psi-Lords.

The bulk of the freemen travel north with Blackmark, but the psionic powers of the Psi-Lords are great, causing massive sea squalls that sink all but three of the vessels. Along the way, the group finds a small boat carrying a mortally wounded Shandra, who has been betrayed by Reynard. A vengeful Blackmark takes the battle to the mountains, where Reynard is revealed to have murdered not only Shandra but also Blackmark's parents. Their fight is fierce, but Blackmark is victorious. As Reynard dies, so too does the Psi-Lords' control over the mutated men, giving the freemen a chance for victory. The price for this victory seems unusually steep to Blackmark, and he sails into uncharted waters.

Characters

- *Blackmark*, the protagonist, is the man who is destined to restore science to a world that fears it. He unites disparate societies under his sword as he opposes threats from the far corner of a war-ravaged world. He rarely finds pleasure, though, as he is haunted by both his parents' deaths and his visions of a future he does not understand.
- *Balzamo* is the science adviser to King Amarix and, two decades later, to Blackmark. He does not fear science and attempts to understand it to further help humankind reclaim its place in the world. His unflappable counsel proves invaluable to Blackmark.
- *Reynard* is a tight-fisted warlord who kills those who oppose him. He kills Old Zeph and Marnie, beginning a feud with Blackmark that is resolved decades later.

- *Marnie* is Blackmark's mother, the woman to whom King Amarix bequeaths his accumulated scientific knowledge. His technology allows her to bear children. She possesses a unique birthmark that is also passed on to her son.
- *Old Zeph* is a tinker who married Marnie to have a companion. When she suddenly becomes pregnant, he is angered by the seeming betrayal. In time, he softens and accepts the boy, whom he names Blackmark. Moving the family to the island of Longsound, he turns to farming before being killed by Reynard.
- *Shandra* is the daughter of Shanflux, lord of the Icewastes. She falls in love with Blackmark but betrays him, becoming involved with Reynard when Blackmark grows too distant. She pays for her betrayal with her life.
- *Lyllith* is the daughter of King Kargon. Her lustful attitude toward Blackmark ultimately prolongs his life, allowing him to fulfill his destiny.

Artistic Style

As a youth, Kane read pulp magazines and watched pulp films, developing a taste for the epic, and these influences are evident in the story and art of *Blackmark*. The skillful rendering of anatomy allows Kane's characters to move in a fluid, almost balletic style, which he refers to as "primitive lyricism."

The page design of *Blackmark* displays Kane's first true experimentation in this area. Citing the periodical *House Beautiful* as inspiration, he sets the narrative text and dialogue apart from the illustrations in a style similar to that employed by the *Prince Valiant* comic strip. Kane uses Zip-A-Tone patterns to add texture to the black-and-white illustrations, while Archie Goodwin's script conveys additional detail. The result is a wide variety of page designs that are easy to follow and ideal for publication in the paperback format, with no more than three panels appearing on a page.

While Kurtzman's involvement in the artistic process is easily masked by Kane's distinctive art style, Adams's inking is clearly his own. Though the styles blend nicely, Adams's inking in the latter pages of the first volume can be distracting.

Themes

Blackmark is set on a postapocalyptic Earth where enough time has passed that society has begun to rebuild itself on the remnants of the previous world. The apparent cataclysmic event is never addressed, but the publication date of *Blackmark* indicates that the work plays on the fears of the Cold War era. Both humans and animals have been mutated by nuclear radiation, with psionically powered men living in the north and lizardlike creatures existing in the sea and on land. Society has degraded to a feudal European model complete with gladiatorial games. Technology and science are often feared, a common theme in postapocalyptic science fiction of the time. Blackmark's climactic use of the spaceship at the end of Book 1 mirrors the sword-in-the-stone motif of Arthurian legend. Blackmark is a man of destiny, is tortured by the loss of his parents, and is filled with visions of a brighter future, all of which are hallmarks of the genre.

Impact

Kane showed prescience in 1968 when he addressed a comics convention and declared that sword and sorcery would be the next genre to gain a following. This occurred two years before Marvel Comics acquired the rights to *Conan the Barbarian*, which officially launched the genre in comics. Although the term "graphic novel" had been in use since 1964, *Blackmark*'s initial release described it as "a new fusion of images and words in an action book—the next step forward in pictorial fiction." Not until 1978's simultaneous release of Marvel's *Silver Surfer* and Will Eisner's *A Contract with God* did the graphic novel concept take hold in mainstream book publishing. Kane's contribution has been largely overlooked by general readers and historians despite its significant role in connecting longer-form comic books and magazines with mainstream book publishing.

Robert Greenberger

Further Reading

DeMatteis, J. M., et al. *The Chronicles of Conan, Volume 17: The Creation Quest and Other Stories* (2009).

Grell, Mike, et al. *The Warlord: The Saga* (2010).

Kane, Gil, and Jan Strnad. *Sword of the Atom* (2007).

Bibliography

Eisner, Will. *Will Eisner's Shop Talk*. Milwaukie, Ore.: Dark Horse Comics, 2001.

Groth, Gary. Afterword to *Blackmark Thirtieth Anniversary Edition*. Milwaukie, Ore.: Fantagraphics Books, 2002.

_____. "Preface to Mid-Life Creative Imperatives (Part 1 of 3)." *The Comics Journal*, February 24, 2010. http://www.tcj.com/history/preface-to-independent-spirits-a-comics-perspective-part-1-of-3.

Herman, Daniel. *Gil Kane: Art and Interviews*. Neshannock, Pa.: Hermes Press, 2002.

Jones, Gerard, and Will Jacobs. *The Comic Book Heroes*. Rocklin, Calif.: Prima Books, 1997.

Kane, Gil. "Interview with Gil Kane, Part 1." *The Comics Journal* 186 (April, 1996): 88

Schumer, Arlen. *The Silver Age of Comic Book Art*. Portland, Ore.: Collectors Press, 2003.

Stiles, Steve. "His Name Is Kane: A Master of the Comics Field." *stevestiles.com*. http://stevestiles.com/kane2.htm.

See also: *A Contract with God, and Other Tenement Stories; Asterix; Far Arden*

BLANKETS: AN ILLUSTRATED NOVEL

Author: Thompson, Craig
Artist: Craig Thompson (illustrator)
Publisher: Top Shelf Comics
First book publication: 2003

Publication History

Craig Thompson's first graphic novel, *Goodbye, Chunky Rice* (1999), recounted the adventures of a pet turtle on the run. In terms of inspiration and subject matter, the author and illustrator stayed closer to home for his second graphic novel, the largely autobiographical *Blankets*.

Thompson's story about a developing artist's midwestern childhood is based on events in his life growing up in rural Wisconsin, as the eldest son in a devoutly religious family. First published as a hardcover edition in 2003, the expansive *Blankets* was subsequently reprinted in best-selling paperback editions. At 582 pages, it is among the longest graphic novels published as a single volume. As the book's sole author and illustrator, Thompson has received numerous awards in categories that honor both his storytelling skills and his artistry. In 2004, *Blankets* was one of *Library Journal*'s Top Ten Young Adult Books; a year later, it appeared on *Time* magazine's list of Ten Best Graphic Novels.

Plot

Blankets is a *Künstlerroman*, a literary work that traces the development of an artist from childhood through adolescence to young adulthood. Thompson shares his first name with his protagonist, Craig, and depicts him in various scenes from his formative years. Events play out against a backdrop of institutions—church, school, and family—that thwart the budding artist's creativity. Various authority figures deem Craig's talents sinful and wasteful. Craig must overcome numerous obstacles, both external and internal, that impede his development as an artist; above all, he must remain true to his calling. Ultimately, his story is a testimonial about human endurance, the balm of love, and the power of artistic expression.

Blankets: An Illustrated Novel. (Courtesy of Top Shelf Productions)

The story of Craig's childhood, maturation, and emergence as an artist unfolds in nine chapters. The central event in chapter 1, titled "Cubby Hole," results from a fight between brothers over bedcovers. As a punishment, the younger brother, Phil, is locked overnight in a dark cubbyhole by their strict father. Craig, now the sole occupant of the bed, hears Phil's cries but is unable to rescue him. Interspersed in this episode are memories of other scenes of bullying that Craig experiences at the hands of teachers, classmates, and parents. When a teenage babysitter molests the young brothers, Craig's guilt derives again from his inability to protect Phil. In response to these traumas, Craig finds solace in art, nature, and religion. Among the few joyful scenes of childhood presented in *Blankets* are those that show the brothers drawing together or playing outside in the snow. Art offers Craig an escape from reality through the exercise of his imagination; the natural world provides him an escape from human institutions; and for a time, religion offers him the promise of a happy afterlife.

The second chapter, titled "Stirring Furnace," refers literally to the insufficient heating unit in the farmhouse in which Craig is reared. Metaphorically, the title alludes to his developing sexuality and to the origins of his relationship with Raina, a girl he meets at winter Bible camp. While playing hooky from scheduled activities—the skiing they cannot afford financially and the revival sessions they cannot embrace intellectually—the two form a bond. The divisions among high school cliques are heightened in this setting. Craig and Raina recognize the hypocrisy of young Christians who exclude others even as they sing about fellowship. Following their experience at camp, Craig and Raina, who live in different states, continue their relationship through the exchange of letters, drawings, and poems.

Chapters 3 through 7 chronicle Craig and Raina's developing friendship and love. When Craig visits Raina in Michigan for two weeks, he encounters a different family structure, one more welcoming but also fraught with complications. Her parents' separation places much of the burden and joys of caring for two older Down syndrome children upon the young teen's shoulders. Raina's older married sister, Julie, also depends on her for babysitting. These responsibilities keep Raina from attending high school regularly. On a rare visit to her school, the outsider Craig is surprised by Raina's popularity. His jealousy increases when her behavior at a party conflicts with his own values: Craig does not smoke or drink. During the day, Craig assists Raina with her family responsibilities, and at night, when others are out of sight, the teens engage in intimate, but mostly innocent, physical encounters. Raina presents Craig with a quilt, a gift she made by hand, and eventually the two make love in its folds.

Chapter 8, titled "Vanishing Cave," finds Craig returning home to the same circumstances he left: critical adults and ostracizing peers. Touched by Raina's genuine love for her siblings, Craig reengages with Phil

by expressing interest in his drawings, a pastime they had shared as younger children. Although Craig tries to sustain his love for Raina, the distances between them, geographic and emotional, eventually prove insurmountable, and they break up.

The final chapter, titled "Foot Notes," provides a glimpse of Craig's life after his relationship with Raina. He has left his rural home to work in the city and to enroll in art classes. A visit home at Christmas affords him the opportunity to reflect upon his early life. With magnanimity, Craig accepts the comforts of family rituals, the joy recalled in memories of his first love, and the possibilities afforded by young adulthood. The final scenes depict him joyfully planting footsteps in blankets of fresh fallen snow.

Characters

- *Craig*, the protagonist, is an aspiring artist who narrates and illustrates his life from childhood through young adulthood.
- *Raina*, an aspiring poet, is Craig's first love.
- *Phil* is Craig's younger brother.
- *Craig's parents* are devout Fundamentalist Christians and authoritarian in their parenting.
- *Raina's parents* are separated, which intensifies the stress of Raina's home life.
- *Ben* and *Laura* are Raina's adopted brother and sister. Both have Down syndrome.
- *Julie* is Raina's older sister, who has escaped home by marrying young. She is Sarah's mother.
- *Dave*, a dentist, is Julie's husband and Sarah's father.
- *Sarah* is Julie and Dave's baby, for whom Raina frequently provides care.

Artistic Style

Thompson illustrates his life in a series of fluid, black-and-white drawings, most of which are contained in squares in semitraditional comic-strip format. While the drawings are realistic, occasional deviations represent Craig's dreamscapes, nightmares, and fantasies. Drawings that depict the childhood artistic endeavors of Thompson's main character are juvenile in execution, distinguishing them from more mature illustrations. In certain sections, Thompson utilizes black space to evoke emotional voids; in others, he exceeds frame boundaries to depict the emotional overload of a character. In some scenes, frames are abandoned entirely, and the illustrations are spread outward, suggesting that the story cannot be contained at that point.

Thompson's black-and-white technique works well in depicting the snow-covered terrains and dark skies of midwestern winters. On a symbolic level, the illustrations reflect the truisms of Craig's Fundamentalist upbringing, providing clear demarcations between good and evil, salvation and damnation, which his parents and church community insist are indelibly black and white. In a clever nod both to the comic-strip format and to the main symbol of his novel (blankets), Raina's quilt is spread out upon one page by Craig's hands; on the accompanying page, the characters themselves appear in various quilt squares, engaged in a conversation

Blankets: An Illustrated Novel. (Courtesy of Top Shelf Productions)

about the patches that unite both the covering and the young lovers.

Themes

In *Blankets*, Thompson creates an intimate story inspired by events in his own youth, one marked by rejection, loneliness, and despair as well as acceptance, connection, and joy. For older readers, Craig's story may recall their own adolescent angst. Younger readers may be experiencing their own painful adolescences even as they read Thompson's account. In either case, Blankets offers a message of hope for the future. However painful childhood and adolescence may appear in actuality or in retrospect, Thompson suggests that adulthood offers a fresh start. Like an untouched blanket of snow or a blank sheet in a sketchbook, two images that appear in the novel, adulthood affords the opportunity to make a new mark. In contrast to many novels for young adults that idealize childhood, Thompson offers the reverse. For any child who has ever felt or been made to feel like a social outcast, this tale of survival is full of promise for a better adulthood.

The chief motif in the novel is drawn from its title. Blankets in the story are both literal and metaphorical. They are coverings that unite young brothers in adventurous play and ensnare them in battles, real and imaginary. Blankets are also fragments of cloth pieced together by hand that unite young lovers. When Craig destroys the artifacts of his relationship with Raina, he burns letters, photographs, cassette recordings, and drawings. The one item he cannot discard—though it too is a painful reminder of what he has lost—is the quilt Raina gave him, under which they comforted each other and explored their nascent sexualities.

Like the fabric scraps that contain Raina's early memories, Craig's drawings capture his imaginative escape from childhood woes and form another type of protective blanket. Additionally, blankets of snow alter the winter landscape; they cover the roughness of the terrain and create a canvas upon which first the brothers and then the young lovers create snow angels. As Craig philosophically observes, "How satisfying it is to leave a mark on a blank surface," whether that surface be snow or craft paper or the page of memory. While these blankets certainly entertain and comfort,

Thompson reminds readers that they can also entangle and suffocate. For these reasons, a heartbroken Craig places Raina's quilt in a box for safekeeping. When the emotional wounds of his lost first love have healed sufficiently, he is able to revisit the memories the quilt's squares contain.

Blankets also recounts Craig's struggles with faith and doubt. As Craig develops a mature understanding of his own spirituality, he questions the narrow perspectives of his Fundamentalist upbringing. In one poignant scene in a Sunday school classroom, Craig announces he will honor God in heaven by drawing pictures of His creations, and the teacher dismissively ridicules his vision of the afterlife. The inquisitive artist forges ahead in his faith journey nonetheless. As a teenager, Craig interrogates his minister on the problems posed by literal interpretations of the Bible, a scene reminiscent of an adolescent Jesus debating with rabbis in the temple. The underprepared minister suggests that Craig, whom he feels has a calling for the ministry, attend a Bible college to seek the answers. Instead, Craig leaves both his church and his Bible. Abandoning his childhood religion allows Craig, now a young adult, the freedom to reflect upon rituals of faith and family from a distance. Returning home for a holiday visit, he appreciates the solaces such practices afford. His spiritual journey suggests that one can lose one's religion but gain one's faith.

Impact

Since its publication in 2003, minor controversy has surrounded *Blankets*. Complaints about Thompson's depictions of adolescent sexuality and Fundamentalist Christianity have caused some libraries to remove the work from their young-adult sections. Nonetheless, *Blankets*' overall positive message about surviving a difficult childhood, its expression of the joys and heartaches that accompany a first love, and its compelling illustrations have contributed to the book's increasing popularity and regard. Efforts to keep the book out of the hands of young-adult readers have not been successful. *Blankets* appears on recommended reading lists for high school and college students, and its appeal for both young-adult and adult readers endures.

Dorothy Dodge Robbins

Further Reading

Bechdel, Alison. *Fun Home: A Family Tragicomic* (2006).

Clowes, Daniel. *Ghost World* (2001).

David B. *Epileptic* (2006).

Van Lente, Fred, and Ryan Dunlavey. *The More Than Complete Action Philosophers!* (2009).

Bibliography

Chenowith, Emily, and Jeff Zaleski. "*Blankets*." Review of *Blankets*, by Craig Thompson. *Publishers Weekly* 250, no. 33 (August 18, 2003): 60-61.

Fiske, Amy. "*Blankets*." Review of *Blankets*, by Craig Thompson. *Journal of Adolescent and Adult Literacy* 48, no. 2 (October, 2004): 178-179.

Flagg, Gordon. "*Blankets*." Review of *Blankets*, by Craig Thompson. *Booklist*, June 1, 2003, p. 1724.

See also: *Fun Home; Ghost World; Epileptic*

BLUEBERRY

Author: Charlier, Jean-Michel; Corteggiani, François; Moebius (pseudonym of Jean Giraud); Wilson, Colin

Artist: Moebius (illustrator); Michel Blanc-Dumont (illustrator); François Corteggiani (illustrator); René Follet (illustrator); Michel Rouge (illustrator); William Vance (pseudonym of William van Cutsem, illustrator); Florence Breton (colorist); Jannick Dionnet (colorist); Fraysic (colorist); Janet Gale (colorist); Claudine Giraud (colorist); Petra Scotese (colorist); Scarlett Smulkowski (colorist); Evelyne Tran-Le (colorist); Phil Felix (letterer); Michael Heisler (letterer); Jijé (pseudonym of Joseph Gillain) (letterer); Kenny Lopez (letterer); Jim Novak (letterer); Bill Oakley (letterer); Gaspar Saladino (letterer)

Publisher: Editions Dargaud

First serial publication: 1963- (English translation, 1977-1993)

First book publication: 1965- (English translation, 1977-1993)

Publication History

Blueberry debuted as *Fort Navajo* in 1963, in the weekly Belgian comics anthology *Pilote*. The long-running series was the brainchild of French artist and writer Jean Giraud, who later worked under the pseudonym "Moebius." As a teenager, Giraud created several Western strips, and in the early 1960's, he contributed to the established Western series *Jerry Spring* in another Belgian anthology, *Spirou*. Giraud proposed a new Western series to Belgian writer and artist Jean-Michel Charlier, a *Pilote* editor, who agreed to the idea after seeing Death Valley firsthand.

In *Fort Navajo*, Blueberry was one of several lead characters. The series ran in brief installments over more than twenty consecutive issues of *Pilote*. Five chapters comprising a single story cycle were printed under the *Fort Navajo* title through 1965. Blueberry became the title character in 1966 and afterward became a regular feature in *Pilote*. Between 1968 and 1970, nine separate *Blueberry* Super Pocket format

Blueberry. (Courtesy of Dargaud)

(14-to-16-page) comics were also published. Editions Dargaud, publisher of *Pilote* and the Super Pocket books, began releasing albums of collected strips in the mid-1960's.

Since 1974, *Blueberry* has not appeared in *Pilote*, except for special teasers published in 2003 and 2004. Instead, Charlier and Giraud completed a series of *Blueberry* albums, beginning in 1975. Eleven books, containing parts of story arcs, were released before 1990, published by Dargaud. The publisher has since reprinted the complete *Blueberry* epic, with supplemental materials and new covers.

Charlier and Giraud also collected prequel Super Pockets into the *Young Blueberry* series. These comprised three full-length titles, released in album form between 1975 and 1979. Charlier and Colin Wilson added to *Young Blueberry*, contributing series extensions between 1985 and 1987. Following Charlier's death, François Corteggiani and Wilson continued *Young Blueberry* (1992-1994), and Corteggiani and Michel Blanc-Dumont teamed to create ten additional albums between 1998 and 2010. Giraud, meanwhile, spun off *Marshal Blueberry*, writing stories for William Vance (1991-1993) and Michel Rouge (2000) to illustrate. Between 1995 and 2005, Giraud also wrote and drew a five-volume story under the *Mister Blueberry* title.

In all its incarnations, *Blueberry* has been popular throughout continental Europe. The series has been translated from the original French into more than a dozen languages. Only selected titles of the complete *Blueberry* oeuvre, mostly from the 1970's and 1980's, have thus far been translated into English. These began appearing in the late 1970's, after Giraud, as "Moebius," became internationally renowned for his association (as co-founder and frequent contributor) with the groundbreaking magazine *Métal Hurlant* (*Heavy Metal*). English-language versions from a number of publishers have been released, featuring different combinations of stories. Numerous reprints exist in a variety of formats, from inexpensive comic-book-sized black-and-white abridgements on pulp, to high quality, full-color bound volumes on slick paper in signed, limited first editions.

Plot

A sweeping chronicle of the American Old West, *Blueberry* depicts the adventures of fictional character Mike Blueberry against a historical backdrop. Spanning two decades of the late nineteenth century and traversing the United States, the series dramatically thrusts Blueberry into a succession of exciting, endlessly complicated, and life-threatening situations. Meticulously researched storylines are based on documented fact: hidden Confederate gold, the Lost Dutchman Mine, the Transcontinental Railroad, American Indian wars, and celebrated gunfights. Actual persons, such as Ulysses S. Grant, Cochise, Sitting Bull, General George A. Custer, Sam Bass, the Earp brothers, and Wild Bill Hickok, coexist alongside venerable character types.

Soldiers, gunmen, barmaids, half-breeds, scoundrels, and drifters have been borrowed from Western movies then filtered through the fertile imagination of Charlier and Giraud. The result is a fresh retelling of familiar events, presented from a unique perspective.

The central figure throughout the series is Blueberry. A young, handsome Southerner (originally modeled after French movie star Jean-Paul Belmondo), he serves as a Union army soldier during the Civil War. His physical prowess and mental agility allow him to rise to the rank of cavalry lieutenant. Blueberry's strategic skills in unraveling tangled knots of trouble attract the attention of superior officers, and he is invariably chosen for the most challenging assignments. The *Blueberry* tales are grouped in four periods. *Blueberry* (twenty-three volumes, some initially published under the title *Lieutenant Blueberry*) deals with the years 1868-1881. *Young Blueberry* (nineteen volumes) primarily concerns the Civil War years, with flashbacks to earlier times. *Marshall Blueberry* (three volumes) focuses on the late 1860's, while *Mister Blueberry* (five volumes) goes forward and backward in time.

Blueberry often works in concert with grizzled former prospector and inveterate drunk Jimmy MacClure and laconic former letter carrier Red Wooley, two undependable but ultimately loyal friends who usually arrive in the nick of time to help extricate the hero from dire straits. Many characters recur from volume to volume, particularly in the *Blueberry* and *Young Blueberry* series. Villains who oppose Blueberry typically wind up dead or disgraced.

Volumes

- *Fort Navajo* (1965; *Fort Navajo*, 1977). Collects *Pilote*, issues 210-232.
- *Tonnere à l'ouest* (1966; *Fort Navajo: Thunder in the West*, 1977). Collects *Pilote*, issues 236-258.
- *L'aigle solitaire* (1967; *Fort Navajo: The Lone Eagle*, 1978). Collects *Pilote*, issues 261-285.
- *Le cavalier perdu* (1968; *Fort Navajo: The Lost Rider*, 1978). Collects *Pilote*, issues 288-311.
- *La piste des Navajos* (1968; the trail of the Navajos). Collects *Pilote*, issues 313-335. This five-part, 240-page story introduces Mike Blueberry. Sent to Arizona, he becomes enmeshed in

Blueberry. (Courtesy of Dargaud)

intrigue between Indian-hating Major Bascom and white-hating renegade Quanah, each bent on fomenting war.

- *L'homme à l'étoile d'argent* (1969; *The Man with the Silver Star*, 1983). Collects *Pilote*, issues 337-360. A self-contained single volume, inspired by the movies *High Noon* (1952) and *Rio Bravo* (1959). Blueberry is sheriff of Silver Creek, Arizona, and comes into conflict with bandit Sam Bass and his gang.
- *Le cheval de fer* (1970; *The Iron Horse* (1991). Collects *Pilote*, issues 370-392.
- *L'homme au poing d'acier* (1970; *Steel Fingers*, 1991). Collects *Pilote*, issues 397-419.
- *La piste des Sioux* (1971; *The Trail of the Sioux*; 1991). Collects *Pilote*, issues 427-449. Published in English as a chapter in *General Golden Mane*.

- *Général tête jaune* (1971; *General Golden Mane*, 1991). Collects *Pilote*, issues 453-476. Blueberry negotiates with Indians for Union Pacific rights-of-way in advance of the Transcontinental Railroad. He runs afoul of Indian hunter General "Yellow Mane" Allister and opposes Jethro Steelfingers, working for rival Central Pacific.
- *La mine de l'Allemand perdu* (1972; *The Lost Dutchman Mine*, 1991). Collects *Pilote*, issues 497-519.
- *Le spectre aux balles d'or* (1972; *The Ghost with the Golden Bullets,* 1991). Collects *Pilote*, issues 532-557. Published in English as a chapter in *The Lost Dutchman Mine*. This was partially inspired by the 1969 movie *Mackenna's Gold*. Now sheriff of Palomito, Blueberry battles bounty

hunters, Indians, and the unforgiving desert, chasing a gold-hungry fugitive.

- *Chihuahua Pearl* (1973; *The Chihuahua Pearl*, 1989). Collects *Pilote*, issues 566-588.
- *L'homme qui valait 500.000$* (1973; *The Half-Million-Dollar Man*, 1989). Collects *Pilote*, issues 605-627. Published in English as a chapter in *The Chihuahua Pearl*.
- *Ballade pour un cercueil* (1974; *Ballad for a Coffin*, 1989). Collects *Pilote*, issues 647-679. Drummed out of the cavalry, Blueberry goes undercover to trace the whereabouts of $500,000 in Confederate gold intended to finance another Civil War—only to learn the bullion has been used to buy arms for the Mexican Revolution.
- *La hors la loi* (1974; *The Outlaw*, 1989). Collects *Pilote*, issues 700-720. Published in English as a chapter in *Ballad for a Coffin*.
- *Angel Face* (1975; *Angel Face*, 1989). Falsely accused of stealing the Confederate gold, Blueberry is a fugitive with a price on his head. He learns of a plot to kill President Grant and foils the attempt, but he is mistakenly believed to be the assassin. Escaping pursuers, he appears to die in a fiery locomotive crash.
- *La jeunesse de Blueberry* (1975; *Blueberry's Secret*, 1989). Collects Dargaud Super Pockets "The Secret of Blueberry" (1968), "The Chattanooga Bridge" (1969), and "3000 Mustangs" (1969). Young Mike Donovan squires girlfriend Harriet before being falsely accused of murdering her father. Donovan flees northward, joins the Union army as a bugler, and assumes the pseudonym Blueberry. He participates heroically in two dangerous missions.
- *Un yankee nommé Blueberry* (1979; *A Yankee Named Blueberry*, 1990). Collects Dargaud Super Pockets "Ride Towards Death" (1969), "Hunt the Man" (1969), and "Private M.S. Blueberry" (1970). Captured by Confederates, Blueberry escapes with information detailing Southern battle strategy. Returning to Northern lines, he is thought to be a spy and condemned. Freed, he blows up a Southern ammunition train and is severely wounded.
- *Cavalier bleu* (1979; *The Blue Coats*, 1990). Collects Dargaud Super Pockets "Thunder Over the Sierra" (1968), "Hunt the Man," part 2 (1970), and "Double Game" (1970). Former girlfriend Harriet helps Blueberry escape military prison but is killed in the process. The Rebels rescue Blueberry, and he plays double agent. He receives a broken nose freeing captured Union general Grenville M. Dodge.
- *Nez cassé* (1980; *Broken Nose*, 1989). Published in English as a chapter in *Angel Face*.
- *La longue marche* (1980; *The Long March*, 1990). Published in English as a chapter in *The Ghost Tribe*.
- *La tribu fantôme* (1982; *The Ghost Tribe*, 1990). Blueberry resurfaces as a refugee with Apaches led by Cochise and Victorio. Known as Tsi-Na-Pah ("Broken Nose"), he assists in foiling the U.S. Army's attempts to relocate the tribe to a barren reservation and helps them escape to Mexico.
- *La dernière carte* (1983; *The Last Card*, 1990). Published in English as a chapter in *The End of the Trail*.
- *Les démons du Missouri* (1985; *The Missouri Demons*).
- *Le bout de la piste* (1986; *The End of the Trail*, 1990). Blueberry journeys with companions McClure and Wooley into Mexico to find the one man who can prove Blueberry is innocent of charges against him. He learns of another assassination plot and works to thwart it.
- *Terreur sur le Kansas* (1987; *Terror Over Kansas*). Blueberry leads a troop of soldiers to the border states of Missouri and Kansas, ordered to put an end to the depredations of raider William C. Quantrill.
- *Le raid infernal* (1987; *The Train From Hell*).
- *Arizona Love* (1990; *Arizona Love*, 1993). Smitten by beautiful Lily Calloway, the feisty entertainer known as the "Chihuahua Pearl," Blueberry locates, woos, and wins her affection.
- *Sur ordre de Washington* (1991; *Under Orders From Washington*). Part of the *Marshal Blueberry* series.

- *La Poursuite impitoyable* (1992; *Pitiless Pursuit*). Blueberry volunteers to go undercover with a group of condemned soldiers into Southern territory. His mission: to find and destroy a cache of Confederate arms and ammunition.
- *Mission Sherman* (1993; *Mission Sherman*). Part of the *Marshal Blueberry* series.
- *Trois hommes pour Atlanta* (1993; *Three Men for Atlanta*).
- *Le prix du sang* (1994; *The Price of Blood*). Blueberry and another Northern soldier volunteer to go undercover in Atlanta. With the help of a slave, they observe the city's defenses in preparation for a Union assault.
- *Mister Blueberry* (1995; *Mister Blueberry*).
- *Ombres sur Tombstone* (1997; *Shadows Over Tombstone*).
- *La solution Pinkerton* (1998; *The Pinkerton Solution*).
- *Geronimo l'Apache* (1999; *Geronimo the Apache*).
- *Frontière sanglante* (2000; *Bloody Frontier*). Returning to the southwest, Blueberry is installed as marshal and ordered to halt the raids of Chato and his band of Apaches and to stop illegal traffic in firearms. Part of the *Marshal Blueberry* series.
- *La Piste des maudits* (2000; *The Track of The Cursed*).
- *Dernier train pour Washington* (2001; *Last Train for Washington*).
- *Dust* (2003). As writer and artist, Girard projects the series forward into the future and backward into the past. Blueberry, now an aging alcoholic, reminisces to a reporter about meeting Geronimo and being present at the fight at the O.K. Corral.
- *Il faut tuer Lincoln* (2003; *Lincoln Must be Killed*). This cycle follows several threads involving Blueberry in undercover work to soften the South for invasion and to prevent an early attempt to assassinate President Abraham Lincoln.
- *OK Corral* (2003).
- *Le boucher de Cincinnati* (2005; *The Butcher of Cincinnati*).
- *La sirène de Vera-Cruz* (2006; *The Mermaid of Vera Cruz*). A Civil War mission takes Blueberry and several companions from Washington, D.C.,

to Mexico, while working to prevent the South from securing the use of the Gatling gun.
- *100 dollars pour mourir* (2007; *100 Dollars to Die*).
- *Le sentier des larmes* (2008; *The Trail of Tears*). Blueberry becomes involved in the disappearance of a Rothschild's bank representative kidnapped to extort a trainload of gold to assist the Southern cause.
- *1276 Âmes* (2009; *1,276 Souls*).
- *Rédemption* (2010; *Redemption*). Blueberry is sent on a mission to rescue the daughter of General Philip H. Sheridan, held captive by a sect led by a madman.

Characters

- *Blueberry*, a.k.a. *Michael Steven Donovan* and *Tsi-Nah-Pah* (*Broken Nose*), is the central figure throughout the series. A dashing hero/antihero combining brains and brawn, he is a formidable fighter, a skilled poker player, and a ladies' man. Though raised in the South, he turns his back on slavery, later extending his egalitarian attitudes toward other oppressed minorities, particularly the American Indians. Outwardly confident, he internally questions his motives and actions even as he develops creative ways to solve problems. A man with a finely tuned sense of honor, a well-developed instinct for survival, and fierce determination, he has little respect for authority or discipline.
- *Jimmy McClure* is a bearded, balding prospector introduced in *Fort Navajo*. Often a sidekick in Blueberry's adventures, he is a faithful companion, but not always reliable because of his fondness for alcohol. A chubby character that often provides comic relief, he uses colorful expressions.
- *Red Wooley*, a.k.a. *Red Neck*, introduced in *The Iron Horse*, is a former courier. Another frequent companion and friend of Blueberry, he has a penchant for strong drink. Red, tall, and slender, he is often seen wearing a fringed buckskin jacket.
- *Sergeant Grayson* is a brave American Indian fighting for the North in *Young Blueberry*. He

often accompanies Blueberry on risky missions either as a soldier or as Pinkerton agent.

- *Homer*, from *Young Blueberry*, is a former slave in Atlanta who assists Blueberry on several missions and is later hired by Pinkerton.
- *Allan Pinkerton*, the real head of the investigative and presidential protective agency, figures in several *Young Blueberry* stories.
- *Baumhoffer* is a Pinkerton agent who is a key contributor to the success of several missions in *Young Blueberry*.
- *Angel Face*, a.k.a. *Marmaduke O'Shaughnessy*, is a handsome, young contract killer who becomes horribly disfigured during a fight with Blueberry. He is involved in two separate attempts to assassinate President Grant.
- *Lily Calloway*, a.k.a. *Chihuahua Pearl*, is one of several strong female characters in the series. Blueberry's ultimate love interest, she is a beautiful, blond Southern showgirl first encountered in Mexico.
- *Duke Stanton* is Blueberry's rival for the Chihuahua Pearl's affections.
- *Kelly* is the sadistic commander of a federal prison where Blueberry is confined for a time, and a co-conspirator in the Grant assassination attempts.
- *Blake*, a genial but treacherous holdup artist, is another component of the complicated assassination plot.
- *Guffie Palmer*, a female dancehall entertainer, is encountered several times over the course of the series. A love interest of Grant in his youth, she gains considerable weight but plays a heroic role in preventing a presidential assassination.
- *Ulysses S. Grant*, U.S. president, appears several times in the series.
- *Cochise*, the Apache chief, is a key figure both early and late in the series.
- *Victorio*, an Apache warrior, is Cochise's apparent heir and Blueberry's rival for the affections of Chini.
- *Chini* is a beautiful young Apache woman and an object of affection to both Victorio and Blueberry.

- *Wild Bill Hickok*, a famous frontiersman, is seen as an Indian fighter in the series.
- *Jedediah*, a.k.a. *Eggskull*, is a bloodthirsty tracker and frontiersman who survived scalping. With his ferocious mastiffs Gog and Magog, he relentlessly hunts, kills, and scalps Indians.
- *General "Golden Mane" Allister* is a figure that appears several times throughout the narrative and is revealed to be the lead conspirator in the presidential assassination plot.

Artistic Style

As a plot-heavy, character-laden, history-based series, *Blueberry* crowds an abundance of text into each story, by means of speech and thought balloons, explanatory introductions, boxes and labels, and sound effects. There are few spreads without any verbiage. Charlier's terse dialogue and sharp wit make the amount of information palatable. Giraud's detailed, realistic renderings and creative layouts, plus a judicious use of luscious colors, add dimension and clarity, bringing the narrative to life. Other contributing scenarists, illustrators, and colorists have remained faithful to the look, feel, and intent of the strip's creators, though later story cycles, particularly in *Young Blueberry*, have grown shorter, with fewer complications.

Blueberry began as a standard European-flavored Western that only got better with age. The initial offerings in *Fort Navajo* were verbose, and storylines were cliché. Visuals were stiff and formal. The look and pacing of the series significantly improved as writer and artist became comfortable with the material and played to each other's strengths. Charlier grew skilled in telling extremely complex stories and in juggling dozens of different real and imaginary characters, while remaining within the boundaries of historicity. Giraud, meanwhile, kept experimenting with his sequential techniques. Whether in his epic Western strip or in other more far-ranging works, he has the uncanny knack of choosing the correct panel shape, the perfect angle of perspective, and the right amount of detailing needed both to keep the story flowing and to provide visual interest. While Giraud is not quite as verbally skilled as his late collaborator, he has more than made up for any deficiency as a storyteller with his superb abilities to show character, emotion, and action.

Themes

The *Blueberry* series celebrates the grandeur of the United States and the glory of nineteenth-century American history. The stories, which simultaneously uphold and explode clichés of Western mythology, are underscored by the uniquely Gallic ideals of liberty, equality, and brotherhood.

Blueberry symbolizes the ultimate free spirit. A man of flexible morality, he rejects his Southern heritage to fight for the North, and this action sets the tone for his attitude throughout the saga. He is not bound to any region, but roams the wide-open spaces of North America at will, going where his adventures take him, and doing what is necessary to accomplish goals. Blueberry does not follow orders unless objectives match his own and he does not have to sacrifice his free agency.

During the nineteenth century, women, African Americans, American Indians, Hispanic Americans, and other ethnic groups were considered inferior in the mostly Caucasian and male-dominated United States. Though the roles of such people are treated realistically in *Blueberry*, there is a conscious effort to illustrate the deleterious effects of discrimination. The main character is color-blind and treats everyone as equal. Blueberry is more concerned with basic good versus evil than with the relative worth of characters along racial or gender lines, so characters of all types are presented as both heroic and villainous.

Finally, though Blueberry is the essence of freedom, he is still just one human in the vastness of the American landscape. As such, he must always work with others to achieve his ends. Even as Blueberry steadfastly maintains his individuality, his adventures consistently illustrate the principle of strength through unity.

Impact

Blueberry is an institution in Europe, just as *Batman* and *Superman* are in the United States. Europeans have a long-time fascination for the United States of yesteryear. In the nineteenth century, they eagerly read the translated novels of such authors as James Fenimore

---

Jean-Michel Charlier

One of the most important writers in the history of French mainstream comics creation, Jean-Michel Charlier began working for *Spirou* after World War II as an artist, and, in 1947, created (with Victor Hubinon) the adventure strip *Buck Danny*. In the 1950's, he gave up drawing comics to focus exclusively on writing. Over the course of the next three decades he would create many of the best-loved stories in the Franco-Belgian comics tradition, including *Valhardi*, *La Parrouille des Castors* (with Mitacq), *Tanguy et Laverdure* (with Albert Uderzo), and *Barbe-Rouge* (with Victor Hubinon). It was in 1965 that Charlier created the series for which he is best known, *Blueberry* (with artist Jean Giraud), a revisionist Western for which he wrote twenty-three volumes. Charlier's work is well regarded for its commitment to craft. In the 1970's he became increasingly interested in telling sophisticated stories and was an instrumental figure in creating the movement for comics for adults both as a writer and, later, as an editor at *Pilote* and *Tintin*.

Cooper. Later, they flocked to Buffalo Bill Cody's traveling shows.

In the twentieth century, Europeans began devouring numerous homegrown Western-flavored strips, many inspired by American comics, movies, and television. French-language comics such as *Lucky Luke*, *Tex*, *Jerry Spring*, *The Adventures of Chick Bill*, *Durango*, *Sergeant Kirk*, *Comanche*, *The Adventures of Jim Cutlass*, *Priest*, and *Buddy Longway* sustained interest in the American Old West. None, however, have had the lasting influence of *Blueberry*. Part of this longevity is the result of Charlier's ability to blend fact and fiction to present exciting, ambitiously convoluted stories founded upon real incidents. The stories, however, would be merely mildly interesting melodramatic pulp without the superb illustrations that juxtapose a larger-than-life main character against the panorama of the United States. Through his vision and imagination Giraud has, over the course of four decades, taken an ordinary comic strip and elevated it to fine art.

Films

Renegade. Directed by Jan Kounen. A.J.O.Z. Films/La Petite Reine/Union Générale Cinématographique (2004). Originally released in France as *Blueberry: L'Expérience secrete* (The Secret Experience), this film loosely based on the comic book series stars Vincent Cassel as Blueberry and Colm Meany as McClure and features a cameo by Giraud. The confused, existential plot includes a number of disparate story lines from the graphic novels involving lost gold and American Indians. Much of the good-looking but slow-moving and unfocused movie surrounds the Native American ritual use of psychedelics.

Jack Ewing

Further Reading

Hergé. *The Adventures of Tintin* (1929-1976).
Moebius. *Airtight Garage* (1976-1980).
Moebius, and Alejandro Jodorowsky. *The Incal: Classic Collection* (2011).

Bibliography

Grove, Lawrence. *Comics in French: The European Bande Dessinée in Context*. New York: Berghahn Books, 2010.

McKinney, Mark, ed. *History and Politics in French-Language Comics and Graphic Novels*. Jackson: University Press of Mississippi, 2008.

Vessels, Joel E. *Drawing France: French Comics and the Republic*. Jackson: University Press of Mississippi, 2010.

See also: *The Adventures of Tintin; Asterix; Airtight Garage of Jerry Cornelius*

BONE

Author: Smith, Jeff
Artist: Jeff Smith
Publisher: Cartoon Books; Image Comics
First serial publication: 1991-2004
First book publication: 1993

Publication History

Published beginning in 1991 as a bimonthly, black-and-white, twenty-four-page comic book by Jeff Smith's own imprint, Cartoon Books, *Bone* ran for fifty-five issues, finishing in 2004. Issues 21-27 (December, 1995, to April, 1997) were published by Image Comics. Cartoon Books resumed publishing *Bone* with issue 28. *Bone* was also published as a complete nine-volume graphic novel series beginning as *The Complete Bone Adventures,* Volume 1, in 1993. The nine volumes were collected in one book called *Bone: One Volume* in 2004. The nine *Bone* graphic novels were republished in color on a biannual schedule by Scholastic Press under the Graphix imprint beginning in 2005 and finishing in 2009.

The Complete Bone Adventures*, Volume 1 (later renamed *Out from Boneville*), was serialized in *Disney Adventures* during 1997-1998. *Disney Adventures* published an original eight-page *Bone* story, "The Powers That Be," in August, 1994.

Bone. (Courtesy of Cartoon Books)

Plot

The plot centers on the three Bone cousins, Fone Bone, Phoney Bone, and Smiley Bone, who have been banished from Boneville and into an unknown valley. The cousins find a map, which Fone Bone hopes will lead them back to Boneville. While escaping a swarm of locusts, they become separated, and Fone Bone falls off a cliff. Stumbling around, he chances upon the cave inhabited by Red Dragon, the only member of the dragon race who has not gone underground. Fone Bone is immediately chased by two rat creatures and is saved by Red Dragon.

Fone Bone continues his quest to find the others, but he cannot get out of the forest before winter begins. He spends the winter with a friendly possum family and

has several scrapes with rat creatures. As winter begins to thaw, he meets Thorn, a teenage girl with whom he is smitten. Thorn befriends Fone Bone, and he moves into her house with her grandmother, Gran'ma Ben.

Thorn and Gran'ma Ben attend a town festival; Phoney Bone goes before them, hoping to exploit the townspeople. Before Fone Bone, Thorn, and Gran'ma Ben leave, rat creatures attack their farmhouse. While Gran'ma holds off the rat creatures, Thorn and Fone Bone escape. They are trapped by more rat creatures and then rescued by Red Dragon.

Phoney Bone makes it to the town, Barrelhaven. In a bar owned by Lucius Downs, he finds his cousin Smiley. Phoney convinces Smiley to masquerade as a cow so they can enter the annual cow race. During the cow race, the rat creatures invade Barrelhaven. A fight ensues, and the villagers hold off the rat creatures. As the story closes, readers learn that the rat creatures follow a being named the Hooded One, who is looking for Phoney Bone.

Next, Phoney, still hatching plots to make money, convinces the townspeople that he can protect them from dragons, and he temporarily catches Red Dragon. This leaves the townspeople unprepared when the rat creatures attack again. As this is happening, Thorn experiences "the turning," something that happens to members of the royal family as they come into their power. This is the climactic moment in the *Bone* story; the war for control of the valley has begun, and everyone must be ready to join the battle, even a teenage princess.

Next, Fone Bone and Smiley embark on an adventure of their own while escaping some dangerous rat creatures. The rats want the Bones, and a giant lion, Rock Jaw, master of the same mountain range that the Bones travel, intends to deliver them to the leader of the rat creatures, Kingdok. As he is about to turn over Smiley and Fone Bone, Kingdok and Rock Jaw fight, allowing the Bone cousins to escape.

The war escalates. The Hooded One, who is also Briar Harvestar (Gran'ma Ben's sister), visits Lucius Downs as the townspeople intend to make a stand at Old Man's Cave and Thorn rescues Smiley and Fone Bone from a troop of rat creatures. Meanwhile, Phoney Bone has run away. Gran'ma finds Phoney; at the same time, Rock Jaw finds them and leaves, intending to deliver Phoney and Thorn to the Hooded One. In an attempt to save Thorn and Phoney, Gran'ma, Smiley, and Fone Bone follow Rock Jaw to temple ruins where the Hooded One intends to sacrifice Phoney Bone. There is an earthquake, and Gran'ma, Thorn, and the Bone cousins escape once again.

The Hooded One has released deadly "ghost circles" across the valley, and only Thorn is safe. She attempts to lead Gran'ma and the Bone cousins through the circles as the rat creatures attack, including Bartleby, a cub raised by Smiley Bone. Bartleby changes sides and helps the Bones, Thorn, and Gran'ma evade the rat creatures. Meanwhile, more rat creature troops attack Old Man's Cave, and the Veni Yan (an association

of hooded warrior monks) leave the cave headed to Atheia, the ancient city.

Thorn has been instructed by a voice to seek out the "Crown of Horns." The companions reach Atheia, where Thorn falls under the spell of the Hooded One. A wise man brings Thorn out of her trance, and she reveals that she is looking for the Crown of Horns. The wise man knows that if Thorn touches it, all life will be erased. Thorn and Fone Bone are arrested while the city is attacked by rat creatures and their allies.

As Thorn and the Bones are imprisoned, the rat creatures, led by the Hooded One, attack Atheia. Meanwhile, Phoney and Smiley have found the treasure of Atheia, and Phoney intends to bring it back with him to Boneville. Thorn realizes only by touching the magical Crown of Horns will order be restored, and that she must do it. Followed by Fone Bone, Thorn leaves the city, believing that the Crown of Horns must be in the dragon burial ground. After several scrapes with the rat creatures, Thorn finds the Crown of Horns, which is guarded by Kingdok. Thorn kills him but cannot reach the crown because the dead Kingdok holds onto her leg. Fone Bone arrives, and together they are able to touch the Crown of Horns. This wakes all the dragons, who have been sleeping underground. Red Dragon rescues Thorn and Fone Bone and an energy bolt emitted from the crown kills the Hooded One. The war is over, and now Thorn is queen. The Bone cousins, with Bartleby in tow, return empty-handed to Boneville.

Volumes

- *Out from Boneville* (1996). Collects issues 1-6. Describes how the Bone cousins come to the valley.
- *The Great Cow Race* (1996). Collects issues 7-12. Introduces the villagers, as Thorn begins to awaken to her destiny.
- *The Eyes of the Storm* (1996). Collects issues 3-19. The war with the rat creatures intensifies.
- *The Dragonslayer* (1997). Collects issues 20-27. Phoney manipulates the villagers to hire him to protect them from dragons.
- *Rock Jaw: Master of the Eastern Border* (1998). Collects issues 28-32. Fone Bone and Smiley go

on an adventure and run into Rock Jaw, a giant mountain lion.

- *Old Man's Cave* (1999). Collects issues 33-37. As the war intensifies, Thorn and the Bone cousins seek shelter in Old Man's Cave.
- *Ghost Circles* (2001). Collects issues 38-43. While trying to get to the old city, Thorn must lead her party through deadly "ghost circles."
- *Treasure Hunters* (2002). Collects issues 44-49. As the war rages, Phoney Bone finds the hidden treasure beneath the old city.
- *Crown of Horns* (2004). Collects issues 50-55. Thorn and Fone Bone reach the Crown of Horns, defeating the enemy.

Characters

- *Fone Bone* is the hero of the *Bone* series. He is good-natured and helpful. He left Boneville because he was concerned about his cousin Phoney Bone. He has a fondness for *Moby Dick: Or, The Whale* (1851) and is often found reading the novel. When he meets Thorn, he is completely smitten with her. As the adventure progresses, he helps Thorn win back the kingdom of Atheia for the Harvestar family.
- *Smiley Bone* is the tallest of the cousins and is a happy-go-lucky character who moves from one experience to another without reflection or insight. Smiley wants to help people, but his simplemindedness usually ends up irritating them. Smiley is willing to go along with any of Phoney Bone's schemes, but he is also capable of strength of character when it is completely necessary.
- *Phonciple "Phoney" Bone* is a greedy, self-centered character. He was run out of Boneville after campaigning for mayor. He is always scheming ways to cheat people out of money and he makes enemies easily. At times, he is deeply concerned for the welfare of his cousins. This was evident when they were children when he plotted ways to steal food.
- *Thorn* appears to be a farm girl but is soon revealed to be heir to the valley, something she does not know as the story unfolds. She is also the "awakened one" or the "Veni-Yan Cari," and

a member of the royal Harvestar family. As she learns of her destiny, she becomes very powerful; she is able to fly on occasion, possesses great strength, and has tremendous courage. Her only real confidant is Fone Bone.

- *Rose Harvestar*, a.k.a. *Gran'ma Ben*, is the dethroned queen of Atheia. She is living in the country to keep her granddaughter Thorn hidden until Thorn is ready to assume a leadership position. She is incredibly strong and strong-willed.
- *Lucius Downs* was Captain of the Guards before the war. Even though he is old, he is still strong and athletic. He is an innkeeper, living in the country, doing his best to protect Thorn until it is time for her to assume power.
- *The Red Dragon* is centuries old and is the son of Mim, the queen of dragons. While all the other dragons have gone underground, only Red Dragon is left to help the Harvestar family. Red Dragon often arrives just in time to rescue Fone Bone.
- *Bartleby*, a baby rat creature whom Smiley adopts, chooses to stay with the Bone cousins after Thorn has been made queen rather than returning to the rat creatures.
- *Briar Harvestar*, a.k.a. *The Hooded One*, is Rose's sister. As a beautiful young girl, Briar fell under the spell of the Lord of the Locusts. Now, as an adult, her devotion to the Locusts has made her deformed and hideous. She intends to deliver the valley to the Lord of the Locusts.
- *The rat creatures*, originally afraid of humans, now run freely through the valley and pose a threat to humans. They are especially fascinated by the Bone cousins.

Artistic Style

The artistic style of *Bone* is one of its greatest contributions to the comics world. Using deceptively simple line drawings, Smith conveyed a number of contrasts. The Bone cousins are small, while the rat creatures are large; therefore, pitting the two groups against each other is visually humorous, particularly during rapid scene changes in which the hero suddenly experiences a life-and-death situation. It is also accomplished because the Bone cousins are odd-looking and vaguely resemble small animals. Smith put great effort toward facial expressions and body language, and many responses one character gives to another are humorous. The realistic representation of human characters and landscapes further reveal the comedic aspect of *Bone*. The sparse narration made readers focus on the drawings, leading them to read entire pages quickly, giving the full page more impact than a single panel. It is worth noting that there are few full-page illustrations in the entire *Bone* series.

Although the style Smith employed was consistent throughout the series, one occasion on which he used specific techniques in order to more deeply involve the reader was the chapter "Double or Nothing" in the book *Eyes of the Storm*. In this story, the characters are caught in a heavy rainstorm. Smith physically moves the characters through the storm in about ten minutes, the same time it takes the reader to read the issue of *Bone*. The result is that the reader is not detached from the story but, because of the frantic pacing, feels like a participant.

The original *Bone* series was produced in black and white. The color contrasts further developed the humorous and dramatic aspects of *Bone*, as the book became in part a series of visual contrasts: The Bone cousins were small, the rat creatures large, and the Hooded One always dark surrounded by light. When the series was reproduced in color, the contrasts were more subtle, particularly the backgrounds, which mirrored the emotional state of the protagonists. By introducing color, not only was the reading experience deepened visually, but also the colored version presented a more complicated story.

Themes

There are several themes that run throughout *Bone*. One is control, specifically of the valley where Fone, Phoney, and Smiley have found each other. The royal family is in hiding after a war with the rat creatures fifteen years earlier. The Bone cousins are taken in by the royal family and help them win back control of the valley after Thorn Harvestar (the princess) discovers her power when she becomes sixteen. Once Thorn

realizes her power, she is able to win back the kingdom for her family.

Other themes of *Bone* are self-discovery and change. Fone Bone begins the story as a reluctant hero. Although he is loyal to his cousins, he has yet to give himself to another person. After Fone grows to love Thorn, he takes on her mission to regain control of the valley and stands up to his cousins when they ask him to return to Boneville. The other main character who experiences change is Smiley Bone, Fone Bone's happy-go-lucky cousin. As Smiley cares for Bartelby, the orphaned rat creature, he discovers mature qualities within himself.

Impact

Bone became one of the most influential of the alternative comic books of the 1990's. It set a new standard for self-published comic books because Smith held himself to professional standards in terms of quality printing and distribution as well as issue delivery dates. *Bone* was one of the early adopters of the graphic novel format. *The Complete Bone Adventures,* Volume 1,

Jeff Smith

Serialized from 1991 through 2004, Jeff Smith's *Bone* is one of the best-loved children's graphic novels published in the past quarter century and ranks as one of the most important comic book series for children published in the American comics market. Smith's mixture of fantasy elements with slapstick humor established *Bone* as an all-ages work that is likely to attract readers for generations. His art work mixes two registers: the Bones are drawn with bold, cartoony strokes that recall animation traditions, while other characters and backgrounds are depicted with thinner and more static lines and greater degrees of texture. The tension between cartoons and naturalism is reflective of the overall storytelling in the series as a whole. Since finishing *Bone*, Smith has worked on a variety of series, including *Shazam! The Monster Society of Evil* for DC Comics and the self-published *RASL*, a science-fiction story about an art thief.

sold more than fifty thousand copies in 1993, and the Cartoon Books motto, "always in print, always available," helped comic book publishers see the viability of the graphic novel format. As graphic novels blossomed out of the traditional comic book marketplace, *Bone* was one of the first to be collected by public librarians. *Bone* also broke new ground for the graphic novel format in 2005 when Scholastic Books colorized it and made it the cornerstone of its own graphic novel publishing imprint, Graphix.

Stephen Weiner

Further Reading

Smith, Jeff. *Shazam! The Monster Society of Evil* (2007).

Smith, Jeff, with Tom Sniegoski. *Bone: Tall Tales* (2010).

Smith, Jeff, and Charles Vess. *Rose* (2009).

Bibliography

Smith, Jeff. *The Art of Bone*. Milwaukie, Ore.: Dark Horse Comics, 2007.

_____. *Bone Handbook*. New York: Graphix, 2010.

Weiner, Stephen. *Faster Than a Speeding Bullet: The Rise of the Graphic Novel*. New York: NBM, 2003.

See also: *Rose*

BOOK OF GENESIS, THE

Author: Crumb, Robert
Artist: Robert Crumb (illustrator)
Publisher: W. W. Norton
First book publication: 2009

Publication History

Robert Crumb's *The Book of Genesis* began as a satirical story about Adam and Eve; however, noting the compelling nature of the biblical text, Crumb decided to create a respectful, mostly literal depiction of the Genesis narratives. To accomplish this goal, Crumb relies primarily on Robert Alter's *Genesis: Translation and Commentary* (1996) and occasionally on the King James Version of the Bible. Crumb also notes that though many comic book versions of stories from Genesis exist, these works invariably add extratextual dialogue. Crumb believes that the texts translate well into graphic form and need no inventive dialogue to make them more readable.

After working on the project for more than four years, often in seclusion, Crumb published *Genesis* with W. W. Norton as a hardcover edition in October, 2009. The 11 x 9-inch book has a dust jacket designed to suggest *Comics Illustrated*, with its title resting upon a solid yellow rectangle and a significant scene from the work: God casting Adam and Eve out of the Garden of Eden. The dust jacket includes the warning "adult supervision recommended for minors."

Plot

In the Bible, Genesis is a large collection of highly compact, self-contained narratives that span from Creation to Joseph's death in Egypt. These narratives are often linked through recurring themes and motifs. Many of these narratives have been interpreted typologically, in essence prefiguring or foreshadowing later events in other books in the Old Testament and the New Testament, as certain narrative elements are subtly repeated and expanded.

Crumb's *Genesis* follows the stories of the biblical book, beginning with Creation and the Fall of Man (Adam and Eve disobeying God by eating from

(AP Photo)

Robert Crumb

Arguably the most important figure in the history of American underground and independent comics, Robert Crumb's publication of *Zap Comix* #1 in 1968 is widely regarded as one of the defining moments in the history of comics production. Crumb was a key figure in the underground comix movement, publishing in a number of anthologies, counterculture magazines and newspapers, and in titles dedicated to his own work. The vast majority of his work has taken the form of short stories, often autobiographical, and has been collected in *The Complete Crumb* from Fantagraphics Books. He produced one of the earliest graphic novels, *The Yum Yum Book*, a work that also introduced his Fritz the Cat character. He is well known for his collaborations with writer Harvey Pekar and with his wife Aline Kominsky-Crumb. His collaboration with David Zane Mairowitz on *Introducing Kafka* and his adaptation of the *Book of Genesis* are among his best-known long-form works. His visual style is heavily cartoony, and he uses a great deal of cross-hatching in the construction of his images.

the Tree of the Knowledge of Good and Evil). First-born Cain's sacrifice is rejected by God while younger brother Abel's is accepted, and Cain murders Abel. Generations later, God commands Noah and his three sons to build an ark and gather animals into it; floods the entire world, leaving only Noah, his family, and the animals in the ark; and promises never to destroy the earth again with water.

God tells Noah's descendant Abraham to leave his hometown, Ur, and establishes a covenant with him. In an effort to continue the family line, Abraham's childless wife, Sarah, sends her to Abraham to impregnate, and Hagar gives birth to Ishmael. When Sarah gives birth to Isaac, her only son, at the age of ninety, Ishmael and Hagar are expelled from the family. When God decides to destroy the cities of Sodom and Gomorrah, Abraham pleads with God to save Sodom, but only his nephew Lot's family is saved just before God destroys the cities. Lot's wife is turned into a pillar of salt for looking back on the destruction. Lot commits incest with his two daughters after they force him to become drunk. Following a directive from God, Abraham takes Isaac to Mount Moriah to be sacrificed, only to be stopped at the last minute by God's messenger.

Abraham's servant providentially finds Rebekah, Isaac's future wife. Their elder son Esau sells his birthright to younger twin Jacob, who steals their father's blessing. Jacob flees home and dreams of a ramp (Jacob's ladder) reaching up to heaven, with God's messengers ascending and descending it. Jacob meets future wife Rachel at a well and begins working for her brother Laban. Laban deceives Jacob, giving him older sister Leah as a wife instead of Rachel and makes him work longer to win Rachel. Jacob and family flee Laban. He successfully wrestles with a heavenly being and demands a blessing. His daughter Dinah is raped, and his sons Simeon and Levi kill the men of Shechem in retaliation.

Jacob gives his youngest son Joseph an elaborate tunic (coat of many colors). Joseph has a dream of honor and glory. His brothers throw him into a pit and sell him into slavery. He becomes a slave to an Egyptian official, Potiphar, whose wife attempts to seduce Joseph and has him imprisoned.

Meanwhile, Judah's son Er dies, and following ancient Hebrew custom, Er's widow, Tamar, marries his brother Onan. When Onan dies, her father-in-law Judah wrongfully prohibits Tamar from marrying another of his sons to continue her husband's line. She disguises herself as a prostitute and becomes pregnant by tricking Judah, who then sees the error of his ways.

In jail, Joseph interprets the dreams of the royal cupbearer and the chief baker. He later interprets Pharaoh's dreams about the coming seven years of plenty and the seven years of famine and becomes regent. When a famine strikes the region, Joseph's brothers come to Egypt for grain and unknowingly bow before his feet. He forgives them, and the family is reconciled and settles in Egypt.

Characters

- *God*, the primary protagonist, is drawn as a large man with a long white beard, flowing white hair, and a wrinkled brow modeled on Crumb's own father. God appears about a foot taller than Adam and Eve. God creates the world, makes covenants with those whom he chooses, passes judgment on the wicked, and provides blessings to those he chooses.
- *Adam* is physically well-proportioned with long dark hair. He names the animals, eats the forbidden fruit along with Eve, and fathers Cain and Abel.
- *Eve* is presented as an idealized woman with full breasts, wide hips, a full bottom, and thick thighs and calves. She is tempted by the serpent, eats the forbidden fruit along with Adam, and gives birth to Cain and Abel.
- *The Serpent*, the first antagonist, is a foot shorter than Adam and Eve and appears as a large lizard standing upright on two legs. He tempts Eve to eat the forbidden fruit and is consequently cursed by God to slither on his belly.
- *Cain* is a strong man with a thick beard and full head of hair. He murders his younger brother Abel.
- *Abel* appears as a young man with soft features and no facial hair. He is murdered by Cain.
- *Noah* is an old man with receding white hair and a full white beard. Noah, his family, and

the animals in the ark are the only survivors after the Flood.

- *Abraham*, a.k.a. *Abram*, is an older man shown with wild white hair (later bald) and a scraggy beard. He obeys God's commands and is even willing to sacrifice Isaac, though he is ultimately stopped.
- *Sarah*, a.k.a. *Sarai*, is Abraham's wife and Isaac's mother. Although she is about ninety, Crumb depicts her with the familiar body type of his idealized female physique.
- *Lot*, Abraham's nephew, appears initially as a young man with dark hair and a beard. He is forcefully dragged out of Sodom shortly before Sodom and Gomorrah are destroyed.
- *Hagar*, a younger woman with short stringy hair, is Sarah's servant and Ishmael's mother.
- *Ishmael*, a wild, rugged young man, is the son of Hagar and Abraham. After being expelled from Abraham's family, he prospers with twelve sons who become chieftains of their own clans.
- *Isaac*, born when his mother is ninety, marries Rebekah and fathers the twins Jacob and Esau. He favors Esau but mistakenly gives his dying blessing to Jacob.
- *Rebekah*, the beautiful wife of Isaac, favors Jacob and directs him in deceiving Isaac into giving his blessing to Jacob rather than Esau.
- *Esau*, a hairy, redheaded, rugged hunter favored by his father, sells his birthright to his younger twin brother and loses his father's blessing to Jacob.
- *Jacob*, a.k.a. *Israel*, a mild man who prefers to stay in tents, is favored by his mother. He successfully bargains with Esau for his birthright and misleads their father into giving him Esau's blessing.
- *Leah*, the older and less beautiful sister of Rachel, marries Jacob through the trickery of her brother, Laban. She gives birth to many children.
- *Rachel*, the beautiful, favored wife of Jacob, gives birth to Joseph but dies giving birth to Benjamin.
- *Joseph*, the favored son of Jacob, is sold into slavery by his older brothers but later gains power

when he interprets Pharaoh's dream. Eventually, Joseph brings his family to live in Egypt.

- *Tamar* is the widow of Isaac's grandsons Er and Onan. When prevented from marrying their younger brother, she tricks her father-in-law, Judah, into impregnating her, thereby taking through sexual politics what was hers by right under ancient Hebrew custom.

Artistic Style

Crumb uses his typical black-and-white crosshatch drawing technique but avoids wildly exaggerated caricatures found in much of his other work in favor of more realistic body types. *Genesis* uses boxes for exposition, word balloons for dialogue, and the rare thought balloon. The panels are clearly defined, and their number varies from page to page, with as few as one per page (as in illustrating God's creation of the world) to as many as eighteen (illustrating each of Esau's named descendants).

Crumb avoids using sound effects of any kind, preferring to rely solely on the images. For example, on one three-paneled page, Crumb depicts the fiery destruction of Sodom and Gomorrah. In the first panel, as the flaming hailstones fall on the cities, no sound is represented other than the images of panicked people attempting to escape. The second panel presents a street-level view of bodies and buildings burning, but again, without relying on overt sound effects. The final panel presents a long-range view of both cities being consumed by fire, smoke rising to the sky.

Crumb does occasionally use speed lines, as when Jacob's sons Simeon and Levi swing their swords to kill Shechem and Hamor. He also indicates a character's surprise using various techniques, such as a question mark in a speech bubble, drops of sweat, or lines encircling a character's face. The panel borders appear freehand, as they are slightly wavy.

Themes

The narrative of Genesis presents a large inventory of themes, including the nature of God, the relationship between God and humanity, and humanity's relationship with itself and Creation. Genesis presents God as the source of all life and the controller of Creation. The creation account describes a highly structured but unnatural event as God simply speaks into existence light, air, water, land, plants, sun, moon, stars, and animals, suggesting both the power and the orderliness of God.

One important theme concerning God's relationship with humanity in Genesis is that God favors the disfavored. Throughout Genesis, the favored position of firstborn is consistently diminished, as the latter born is honored: God accepts Abel's offering but rejects Cain's; God favors Isaac over Ishmael; God chooses Jacob over Esau to establish the Israelite nation; God elevates Joseph over his older brothers. This theme is also echoed in Jacob's favoring of Rachel over her older sister Leah and in Jacob crossing his arms so that his right hand rests upon Joseph's younger son, Ephraim, instead of the firstborn, Manasseh, when Jacob speaks his blessing.

Genesis also deals with some purely human themes, as humanity is shown at both its heights and its depths. These issues include temptation, immoral choices, sibling rivalry, the significance of the spoken word, the uniqueness of humanity, sexual politics, deceit, hatred, jealousy, murder, revenge, family politics, doubt, redemption, mercy, love, and forgiveness. Many of these themes have been richly and consciously reproduced throughout much of Western literature and beyond by Edmund Spenser, John Milton, Søren Kierkegaard, Flannery O'Connor, and many other writers.

Impact

The response to Crumb's *Genesis* has been mixed. Initial reports concerning the work led some to believe that Crumb was going to create a satirical and salacious send-up of Genesis. Indeed, Crumb's reputation and earlier body of work gave credence to these concerns. In the introduction of the work, Crumb acknowledges that he expected some readers would be outraged. A number of critics suggested that Christians would be scandalized when they discovered the sordid details contained in Genesis.

Upon publication, however, that anticipated outrage never materialized. In fact, reviews varied from mild praise to mild disappointment. Those hoping for a sardonic treatment of Genesis were disappointed in Crumb's straightforward presentation, while reviews

in *Christian Century*, *Commonweal*, and *First Things* offered guarded praise and *Christianity Today* and its more cerebral counterpart, *Books and Culture*, did not bother to review it. The sharpest criticism came from Albert Mohler, president of the Southern Baptist Theological Seminary, who restated a long-standing view within Christianity that visual representations of God are forbidden.

While praising much of Crumb's *Genesis*, Alter, whose translation makes up almost the entirety of the text, notes the difficulties of visually representing the text's rich ambiguity. He at once faults the work for limiting the range of possible readings while recognizing this inherent characteristic of the medium.

Daniel D. Clark

Further Reading

Lee, Young Shin, and Jung Sun Hwang. *Manga Bible: Names, Games, and the Long Road Trip—Genesis-Exodus* (2007).

Siku. *The Manga Bible, from Genesis to Revelation* (2008).

Wolverton, Basil. *The Wolverton Bible: The Old Testament and Book of Revelation Through the Pen of Basil Wolverton* (2009).

Bibliography

Alter, Robert. *The Art of Biblical Narrative*. New York: Basic Books, 1981.

_____. "Scripture Picture." Review of *The Book of Genesis*, by Robert Crumb. *New Republic* 240, no. 19 (October 21, 2009): 44-48.

Alter, Robert, and Frank Kermode. *The Literary Guide to the Bible*. Cambridge, Mass.: Belknap Press, 1999.

Bloom, Harold. "Yahweh Meets R. Crumb." Review of *The Book of Genesis*, by Robert Crumb. *New York Review of Books* 56, no. 19 (December 3, 2009): 24-25.

Crumb, Robert. "R. Crumb, The Art of Comics No. 1." Interview by Ted Widmer. *Paris Review* 193 (Summer, 2010): 19-57.

Frye, Northrop, and Alvin A. Lee. *The Great Code: The Bible and Literature*. Toronto: University of Toronto Press, 2006.

Jeffrey, David Lyle, ed. *A Dictionary of Biblical Tradition in English Literature.* Grand Rapids, Mich.: W. B. Eerdmans, 2009.

Ryken, Leland. *The Literature of the Bible.* Grand Rapids, Mich.: Zondervan, 1981.

Ryken, Leland, and Trempor Longman III, eds. *A Complete Literary Guide to the Bible.* Grand Rapids, Mich.: Zondervan, 2010.

Ryken, Leland, James C. Wilhoit, and Trempor Longman III, eds. *Dictionary of Biblical Imagery.* Downers Grove, Ill.: InterVarsity Press, 1998.

See also: *The Complete Fritz the Cat*

BOULEVARD OF BROKEN DREAMS, THE

Author: Deitch, Kim; Deitch, Simon
Artist: Kim Deitch (illustrator)
Publisher: Pantheon Books; Fantagraphics Books
First serial publication: 1993 (*The Boulevard of Broken Dreams* and *The Mishkin File*) and 1994 (*Waldo World*)
First book publication: 2002

Publication History

The Boulevard of Broken Dreams, a roman à clef that laments the gradual decline of American animation in the twentieth century, brings together three titles originally published in the early 1990's. *The Boulevard of Broken Dreams*, which looks at the early years of cartooning and the tension between individual creativity and the emerging industry of animation, appeared in the last issue of Art Spiegelman's *RAW* magazine; "The Mishkin File," which looks as the pivotal decade of the 1950's and the pernicious influence of Walt Disney Studios and commercial television syndication, and "Waldo World," which looks at postmodern culture and the sordid commercialization of animation through kitschy toys and as the vehicle of the theme park, were both published by Fantagraphics Books.

The novel reflects three decades of evolution. Kim Deitch drew on childhood experiences and recollections as the son of Gene Deitch, a successful animator in his own right and, during the 1950's, the creative director of Terrytoons, which in its heyday was responsible for iconic series such as *Heckle and Jeckle*, *Mighty Mouse*, and *Mr. Magoo*. The central animated character in Deitch's novel, the blue anthropomorphic cat named Waldo, who becomes the muse and tormentor of his tragic fictional animator, had been a staple in Deitch's alternative underground comics since the mid-1960's.

Plot

The first book details the early years at Fontaine Fables Studio. In 1927, Ted Mishkin, a young idealistic cartoonist, comes under the spell of Winsor Newton, whose vaudeville extravaganzas had long experimented with animation and live action. (Newton would

The Boulevard of Broken Dreams. (Courtesy of Pantheon Books)

appear to interact with the cartoons in meticulously timed performances.) Wary of the expense, the animation industry began to move away from such creative, individualistic efforts.

Studio boss Fred Fontaine hires Ted on the recommendation of Ted's brother, Al, who runs the business end of Fontaine studios under conditions that the anachronistic Newton decries as assembly-line work that destroys creativity. At Fontaine studios, Ted pitches the character of Waldo the Cat. Growing up in a community home (his mother could afford to raise only one child), Ted invented the blue cat as his imaginary friend. The combination of charm and deviltry makes Waldo a studio bonanza. During this time, Ted is captivated by a fellow animator, the beautiful, free-spirited Lillian Freer.

To compete with the emerging Walt Disney Studios brand of syrupy cartoons with melodramatic plots, one-dimensional characters, and tidy homespun lessons, Fontaine studios redesigns Waldo. Ted is upset. (Waldo, Ted's constant companion, taunts him, feeling the studio has turned Ted into a pansy.) Ted is fired when he takes a swing at the former Disney executive in charge of revitalizing the studio. Upset and drunk, he goes to his brother's house, only to find Lillian there in his brother's bed. He suffers a nervous breakdown and ends up committed to Berndale Acres Sanitarium.

While institutionalized, Ted meets Newton, and the two develop a friendship in which, over several years, they share a vision of the grand possibilities of animation. Ted is released in 1933. Newton dies suddenly, and Ted and Lillian attend a Christmas party where the wife of the studio boss mysteriously falls to her death from a window. (Ted blames Waldo.)

Over the following decade, Ted is in and out of Berndale; in between his stays at the institution, he secures menial work as a comic book illustrator. Al chances to see one of the comic books and brings his brother back to the studio. Waldo the Cat has been morphed into a one-dimensional sidekick for the studio's big moneymaker, Rocket Rat. Although not happy with the changes, Ted works for the studio and is reunited with Lillian. He also meets his troubled nephew, Nathan, who is being treated at Berndale, diagnosed as delusional—like his uncle, he sees Waldo the Cat.

The third book takes place in 1993. Classic Fontaine characters are now cheap toys that appeal to baby boomers nostalgic for the Rocket Rat cartoons. The studio negotiates with Disney to introduce both Waldo and Rocket Rat as strolling characters in Disneyland.

The new line of Waldo toys is to be unveiled at a mall store. Ted attends in a wheelchair—doctors had used electroshock therapy to affect a "cure." Lillian has become his caregiver. In an awkward conversation at the mall, Al reveals to Lillian that in the early 1950's, Fred Fontaine had envisioned a vast theme park that would bring animation to life, an idea dismissed because Fontaine was seen as deranged after his wife's death. Al then drops dead in the mall.

Afterwards, Nathan, who was invited to the premiere, visits his uncle and is accompanied by Waldo. Waldo leads Ted to a hidden room where he finds visionary designs for a theme park that actually date to Newton. In the closing scene, Ted and Lillian, holding hands, find a quiet refuge watching an old Waldo cartoon with Waldo himself.

Characters

- *Ted Mishkin* is a gifted animator whose career spans nearly fifty years. He is the creator of the character Waldo the Cat, who is both his muse and tormentor.

- *Al Mishkin* is Ted's pragmatic brother, who, as an executive with Fontaine Fables Studio, has little interest in the creative processes of animation.

- *Fred Fontaine* is a studio executive (a composite of Paul Terry and Max Fleischer) whose talent pool of gifted animators produces increasingly sentimental cartoons geared for wide market acceptance. He never recovers emotionally from the death of his wife.

- *Lillian Freer* is a talented animator in Fontaine's studios in the late 1920's and the woman Ted loves from afar. Disenchanted with the artistic direction of Fontaine studios, she heads west and produces avant-garde animation until her involvement with the Communist Party ends her career there. She returns to New York and helps in the resurgence of Fontaine studios in the 1950's.

- *Winsor Newton* is a visionary, if temperamental, pioneer in animation (based on the iconic Winsor McCay); he tutors a young Ted and shares his sweeping perception of animation as an art form whose compelling theme is the triumph of the artistic endeavor over the tackiness of ordinary life.

- *Nathan Mishkin* is Al's emotionally damaged and alcoholic son, who apparently shares his uncle's awareness of Waldo the Cat as a real entity. He fits the tragic outsider archetype reserved for sensitive misfits.

Artistic Style

Appropriate to a work that chronicles the evolution of animation, the pages of Deitch's novel teem with barely contained motion and elaborate and crowded panels with irregular borders. Scenes such as the hapless Ted catching his beloved Lillian in bed with his brother, Fontaine's wife falling from the window, or Winsor Newton taking Lillian on a tour of his animation studio recall the feverish densities of Hieronymus Bosch. Deitch's pages are broad and inviting, suggesting the vision of Winsor Newton himself, sumptuously imagined "inkscapes" where the eye can linger, explore, and engage.

Deitch uses intricate variations of tight parallel lines to create his most vivid visual effects—shadings, facial expressions, motion, and even perspective are generated by parallel lines that give the black-and-white panels the depth and immediacy of classic animation, at once an homage to and an extension of the medium's possibility for creating nuance. Interspersed amid such riotous and grandly conceived panels, however, given the novel's interest in the often twisted psychologies of the characters, Deitch uses the film technique of the

The Boulevard of Broken Dreams. (Courtesy of Pantheon Books)

close-up to allow a character's facial expressions to reveal layers of conflict. Reflecting Deitch's own signature work in the underground comics of the 1960's, the visual style often reflects the willingness to bend the clean, hard lines of mimetic realism, a visual texture that suggests drug-induced and/or alcoholic hallucinations, which underscores the novel's thematic interest in the uncertain boundary between fact and fantasy and reality and the fabulous.

Themes

Most pointedly, Deitch indicts the commercialization of the American animation industry, embodied here by Disney and its vision of animation as tame, low-brow entertainment with cutesy characters that affirm middle brow platitudes, all produced by teams of animators rather than artisans. More than pop-culture criticism, however, the novel explores the tangled relationship between Ted Mishkin and his alter ego, Waldo the Cat, one that tests the boundary between the fantastic and the real. Waldo, the novel's principle of anarchy and creativity, maintains his own integrity and regularly defies the confines of the drawing board. He is both Ted's inspiration and private demon. As such, Deitch's work is a Künstlerroman, albeit an unconventional one.

Deitch investigates the genesis of inspiration, the energy of creativity, and, ultimately, the tragic isolation of the truly original artist in the United States who must contend with a marketplace culture that cannot respond to the audacity of the full-throttle imagination. The industry's abandonment of Winsor McKay's sweeping vision—that animation, like all art, can redeem the tawdry stuff of the everyday by conjuring grand worlds of pen lines that can provide temporary (and entirely symbolic) refuge from the crushing oppression of everyday life—is Deitch's tragic theme.

Impact

Given the breadth and the sophisticated narrative lines of Deitch's novel and that Deitch so deftly and confidently defies genre, *The Boulevard of Broken Dreams* is sui generis. In an era when graphic novels centered on either nerdy, angst-ridden adolescent antiheros or

grand superheroes in alternative universes, Deitch's novel turned the genre to broader concerns.

The Boulevard of Broken Dreams is at once a cutting satire, howlingly funny in its indictment of the "Disney-fication" of cartoons, and a bittersweet, even romantic, tragedy of the lonely tormented artist. If the novel succeeds as historic realism, it also wildly defies the boundaries of realism in riotous fantasies that sweep the reader into dimensions of psychedelic daring. If it succeeds as a conservative work of psychological realism, *The Boulevard of Broken Dreams* is also an edgy, postmodern exercise in self-reflexive metafiction that foregrounds its creation with its author serving as the framing authority. Few graphic novels have aspired to such accomplished construction.

The impact of *The Boulevard of Broken Dreams*, thus, is not so much measured by its impact on its era or by any coterie of imitators it inspired as by its impact on Deitch's career. At the time of the story's publication, Deitch was a "cartoonist's cartoonist," a minority

---

Kim Deitch

One of the most important figures in the American underground comics movement of the 1960's, Kim Deitch has been serializing the adventures of Waldo the Cat for decades, creating a highly personalized mythology that ties many of his works together. A contributor to the New York-based underground paper the *East Village Other* in the 1960's, Deitch was the son of animator Gene Deitch. His work often involves the fields of popular culture, particularly in its earliest days. *Boulevard of Broken Dreams*, his best-known work, focused on the origins of the American animation industry and features his signature character, Waldo. The graphic novel *Alias the Cat*, which includes a metafictional version of Deitch, deals with the history of comic strips. *Shadowland* addresses movie serials, and *The Search for Smilin' Ed*, originally serialized in *Zero Zero*, deals with children's television shows. Deitch's art work is decidedly retro, with characters derived from early animation and comic strip influences, coupled with a high degree of cross-hatching in his images.

enthusiast among knowing pop-culture critics. An established figure in the late 1960's New York City underground comics movement, Deitch, nearly sixty, broke through at last to mainstream interest. Just three years after its publication, the novel appeared on *Time* magazine's list of the ten most influential graphic novels of all time. Deitch—and his work—garnered wide media attention, which led to follow-up works that received similar reception.

Joseph Dewey

Further Reading

Crumb, Robert. *R. Crumb's America* (1995).
Culhane, Shamus. *Talking Animals and Other People* (1998).
Spiegelman, Art. *The Complete Maus* (2003).

Bibliography

Deitch, Kim. "An Interview with Kim Deitch." Interview by Jeffrey Ford. *Fantastic Metropolis* (October 9, 2002).

_____. "An Interview with Kim Deitch." Interview by Joshua Glenn. *Hilobrow* (August 3, 2010).

_____. "Underground Comix Come of Age: An Interview with Kim Deitch." Interview by Steven Heller. *AIGA: Journal of Graphic Design* 27 (March, 2007).

Hatfield, Charles. "The Presence of the Artist: Kim Deitch's *The Boulevard of Broken Dreams* Vis-à-Vis the Animated Cartoons." *ImageTexT: Interdisciplinary Comics Studies* 1, no. 1 (2004).

Irving, Christopher. "Kim Deitch: A Novel Approach." *NYC Graphic*, January 5, 2010.

See also: *Maus: A Survivor's Tale; The Complete Fritz the Cat; The Book of Genesis; The Rabbi's Cat; Tales of the Beanworld*

BOX OFFICE POISON

Author: Robinson, Alex
Artist: Alex Robinson (illustrator)
Publisher: Antarctic Press; Top Shelf Productions
First serial publication: 1996-2000
First book publication: 2001

Publication History

Box Office Poison was originally published in twenty-one installments of about thirty pages each at Antarctic Press, an independent comic book publisher founded in San Antonio, Texas, specializing in the style known as American manga. *Box Office Poison* was the first major work to be published by New York author, artist, and School of Visual Arts graduate Alex Robinson. The content of the black-and-white series is loosely based on events and acquaintances from the creator's life. The episodic format was inspired by the work of Dave Sim in his *Cerebus* (1977-2004) series, of which Robinson is an avowed admirer.

After initial publication, *Box Office Poison* was collected into a graphic novel of more than six hundred pages and published by Top Shelf Productions, a comics publisher founded in 1997 in Marietta, Georgia. Since its release, *Box Office Poison* has been translated into a number of foreign languages, including French, Spanish, Italian, Portuguese, Polish, and German, under a variety of titles.

Plot

The plot of *Box Office Poison* revolves around the lives, loves, and aspirations of a group of interconnected characters in New York City and its environs during the mid-1990's. The stories are loosely based on Robinson's experiences as a bookstore employee and hopeful cartoonist struggling to get his work accepted. Most of the major characters are young adults, like the intended audience for the work, and the plot hinges on their typical concerns.

One of the primary plot threads deals with the difficulties of living arrangements. At the beginning of the story, Sherman is looking for an inexpensive dwelling so he can save more of his meager salary. He becomes a

Box Office Poison. (Courtesy of Top Shelf Productions)

roommate in the apartment of lovers Stephen and Jane, which brings him into contact with the irascible, foreign landlady Mrs. Sora Tweed. Sherman also comes in conflict with noisy neighbors who play loud music or have crying babies and barking dogs, and he causes occasional embarrassing complications when romance is in the air.

Meanwhile, Sherman's best friend, Ed, still lives with his parents and suffers under their control. Sherman's girlfriend, Dorothy, who sometimes stays with Sherman at his place, maintains her own apartment because when she formerly roomed with Jane and Stephen, Jane grew to hate her for a variety of reasons. Dorothy is reluctant to let Sherman into her apartment because she never does housekeeping chores or cleans up after her untrained dog.

Another plot thread involves the woes of employment. Sherman hates his job at the bookstore, where he has worked for several years. Though he dislikes having to cut his hair and wear a tie and complains constantly about his unfeeling boss and low salary, his main objection is to the people he must serve. There are hilarious examples throughout of the inane questions customers ask: "Do you have books on how to hypnotize girls?" (from a creepy, furtive man); "Are these all the books you have on Norwegian tree frogs?" (from a professorial type).

Sherman, who halfheartedly sends out written pieces and receives rejections, is too insecure to quit, unlike his colleague, James, who abruptly resigns and, without even trying, lands a higher paying position, much to Sherman's chagrin. On the other hand, Ed works to escape from his stifling job at his father's store and to improve his opportunities. He interviews with a comic book publisher before becoming an assistant with Golden Age cartoonist Irving Flavor, whom he encourages to seek fair compensation from the publishers profiting from his early creations.

Characters

- *Sherman Davies* is tall, thin, and blond. A major viewpoint character, he has a tendency to convert amounts of money into the cost of musical compact discs (for example, fifty-six dollars equals five CDs).
- *Beatrice Dorothy Lestrade* is Sherman's flaky, needy girlfriend. She goes by her middle name. A short, dark-haired young woman who smokes and drinks too much, she is a writer and assistant editor for *Metro-Chic* magazine.
- *Jane Pekar* is slender; has long, dark hair; and wears glasses. A cartoonist, she struggles to get her work published and suffers through numerous rejections. She has been Stephen's girlfriend for four years and initially turns him down when he asks her to marry him.
- *Stephen Gaedel* is large, hairy, and menacing, with a full beard and long hair. In his late twenties, he teaches college-level history in the city.

Stephen has a secret: As a boy, he was spokesperson for a popular children's cereal called Brown-e-os.

- *Ed Velasquez* is a short, flabby, and genial man sporting a goatee and close-cropped hair. He is Sherman's best friend and former classmate at Hunter. Born in Costa Rica, he has aspirations of becoming a cartoonist and finding a girlfriend.
- *Irving Flavor* is an old-time cartoonist. He wears toupees and large glasses and is generally cranky. Creator of a popular and profitable cartoon character, the rights of which he sold for a pittance, Irving is relegated to rendering cartoon characters for cereal boxes.
- *Greg Davies* is Sherman's father, whom his son will come to resemble, both physically and mentally.
- *Hildy Kierkegaard* is a large, young, buxom, blond woman who usually wears her hair braided. She and Ed, both painfully shy, are attracted to one another.

Artistic Style

The predominant style of *Box Office Poison* is loose and "cartoony," closer to caricature than realistic portraiture. Characters, more "types" than actual people, are always recognizable, even when their features are distorted or exaggerated to suggest strong emotions. Robinson uses simple line drawings (with crosshatching in close-ups to create dimensionality) enhanced by areas of solid black to set off figures or gestures; he also uses sufficient detail to lend visual interest to objects and backgrounds.

Layouts are founded upon two different grid patterns. One, consisting of a series of vertical panels, periodically presents individual characters as though they were responding to particular questions, such as "If you could have brunch with any fictional character, who would it be?" or "If you could change one aspect of your appearance what would it be?" The other regular pattern is of six panels in two columns per page, though Robinson frequently diverges from this form to emphasize particular action, to speed up or slow down time, or simply to explode preconceived expectations. Illustrations range throughout, from full-page spreads to multiple small frames to odd-shaped panels surrounded by white space. For variety, there are pages of typewritten prose so readers can view the type of material the hero is trying to get published.

One interesting technique occasionally employed is overlapping speech balloons during conversations among characters, which reproduces the often fragmentary, interrupted nature of face-to-face human verbal encounters. This technique, while confusing the issue of who is speaking, also rewards patient readers with bits of illuminating dialogue that reveal character.

Themes

One major theme among many in *Box Office Poison* is the agony of establishing and maintaining relationships among friends, relatives, lovers, and colleagues in a world fraught with issues of trust and betrayal, where the borders between illusion and reality blur. In addition to the major characters, dozens of minor characters are introduced, who are followed for a time then disappear or reappear at the whim of fate, just as in real life. Each has an effect—sometimes large and permanent, sometimes small and temporary—upon those with whom they intersect.

A second significant theme is the author's recognition of and reverence for the influences of the past. A massive and continuous homage to cultural icons real and imaginary, *Box Office Poison* contains numerous references to fictional and factual figures. The name of Sherman's girlfriend, for example, Dorothy Lestrade, suggests both the real Dorothy Parker and the fictional Inspector Lestrade, the foil for Sherlock Holmes; Dorothy also resembles cartoon character Betty Boop. Jane Pekar's name is an obvious salute to cartoonist Harvey Pekar. Sherman and Stephen watch and call out questions during an episode of *Jeopardy!* Members of a nightclub band look just like the Beatles. Some of the annoying bookstore customers with whom Sherman must deal are identifiable: a man built along the lines of Sir Arthur Conan Doyle asks

Box Office Poison. (Courtesy of Top Shelf Productions)

about the whereabouts of Sherlock Holmes novels and a character from the Scooby-Doo cartoons panics when she learns a textbook is sold out. Incidental bystanders, passersby, street people, or subway passengers are often suspiciously familiar.

Impact

An excellent example of the modern, angst-ridden comic that blends fantasy and reality, *Box Office Poison* owes much to Sim's *Cerebus*, which demonstrated the power of black-and-white illustrations in detailing lengthy, complicated story lines that are simultaneously serious and humorous. The publication of the graphic novel jump-started the author's career. In 2003, Robinson produced a sequel for Top Shelf Productions: *BOP! More Box Office Poison*. In turn, this led to the publication of *Tricked* (2005), a sophisticated graphic novel that concerns the lives of six unrelated characters whom fate brings together, and which won Harvey and Ignatz awards.

Further works published by Top Shelf have included the superhero fantasy *Alex Robinson's Lower Regions* (2007) and the Harvey Award-winning fantasy *Too Cool to Be Forgotten* (2008). Since mid-2009 Robinson has become extremely influential, particularly among aspiring cartoonists, thanks not only to his outstanding work but also to *The Ink Panthers Show*. A weekly half-hour humorous podcast featuring Robinson and fellow cartoonist Mike Dawson (and guests such as Tony Consiglio, John Kerschbaum, and Josh Flanagan), *The Ink Panthers* dispenses useful advice about the craft of comics.

Jack Ewing

Further Reading

Robinson, Alex. *Bop! More Box Office Poison* (2003).

_____. *Tricked* (2005).

_____. *Too Cool to Be Forgotten* (2008)

Bibliography

Frey, Nancy, and Douglas Fisher. *Teaching Visual Literacy: Using Comic Books, Graphic Novels, Anime, Cartoons, and More to Develop Comprehension and Thinking Skills*. Thousand Oaks, Calif.: Corwin Press, 2008.

Sabin, Roger. *Comics, Comix, and Graphic Novels: A History of Comic Art*. London: Phaidon Press, 2001.

Tabachnick, Stephen E. *Teaching the Graphic Novel*. New York: Modern Language Association of America, 2009.

Weiner, Stephen. *Faster Than a Speeding Bullet: The Rise of the Graphic Novel*. New York: Nantier Beall Minoustchine, 2003.

See also: *American Splendor; It's a Good Life, If You Don't Weaken; Why I Hate Saturn; Jimmy Corrigan*

BURMA CHRONICLES

Author: Delisle, Guy

Artist: Guy Delisle (illustrator)

Publishers: Delcourt (French); Drawn and Quarterly (English)

First book publication: 2007 (English translation, 2008)

Burma Chronicles. (Courtesy of Drawn and Quarterly)

Publication History

Upon arriving in Burma with his wife, cartoonist and animator Guy Delisle did not intend to write a travel memoir about his experiences there. The author of two previous travel memoirs—*Shenzhen* (2006), about living in China, and *Pyongyang* (2005), about working as an animator in North Korea—Delisle was working on another book, which he never finished. He has not written books on all of his travels; he has also lived in Vietnam and Ethiopia, though neither inspired a full-length work. However, in Burma, he looked at his notes halfway through his yearlong stay and found that he had enough material and interest to write the book. *Burma Chronicles* was originally published in French as *Chroniques birmanes* (2007) and translated to English by Helge Dascher for a 2008 Drawn and Quarterly publication.

Plot

Burma Chronicles opens with Delisle at home in Canada, preparing to travel with wife Nadège and infant son Louis to Guatemala, where Nadège is being sent for a year to practice humanitarian medicine for Médecins sans Frontières (MSF), or Doctors Without Borders. Delisle prepares for their trek to Central America by watching *Star Trek* with Spanish subtitles. A moment later, in the sort of comic twist emblematic of their journey, they learn MSF has decided to send them to Myanmar (Burma), a Southeast Asian country unfamiliar to Delisle and one that, to his chagrin, uses a language not available on the *Star Trek* DVD. Thus, Delisle begins his journey to a nation U.S. president George W. Bush labeled an "Outpost of Tyranny," totally unprepared for what he will find, as an affable, curious, but culturally ignorant accidental tourist.

When they arrive, however, Delisle's concerns are not grand, nor political; instead, he is preoccupied with the everyday trials and travails of being a new father. Louis has been crying the entire flight, and when the family arrives in the capital city of Yangon, jet-lagged and exhausted, they find that MSF has not set up a permanent house for them. In his first few days in a guesthouse that MSF has lent them temporarily, Delisle is more concerned with protecting Louis from open wall sockets and figuring out how to give him a bath than with going out adventuring.

However, before he even has the chance to leave the house, Delisle is reminded that he is living in a dictatorship: He reads a *Time* magazine left by the previous tenants, in which pages are missing; they have been cut out by the censorship bureau, which intercepts all press before it arrives in Burma and clips out unflattering articles. Even in his everyday life, Delisle finds, he cannot escape the reach of the totalitarian government.

The Delisle family begins to settle into Burma with their permanent house and their guard, Maung Aye, whom Delisle likes but never quite understands. Nadège begins her medical work at MSF, which often takes her to remote areas of the countryside. At home, Delisle works hard on finishing a children's book and starts an animation group for local Burmese graphic artists while taking care of Louis. He often walks Louis around his neighborhood and finds the Burmese flocking around them whenever Louis is around. In their social life, Guy and Nadège attend events in the expatriate community, with MSF doctors and members of other humanitarian organizations, who tend to discuss the great medical problems in Burma—malaria, rampant AIDS, and heroin abuse—and how the Burmese government makes it so difficult for them to perform their jobs helping with these problems.

During this time, Delisle becomes increasingly aware of the complex plight of the Burmese people and the difficulties in helping them. Early on, Delisle speaks freely about his disdain for Burmese censorship and dictatorship. Throughout his stay, Delisle wants to see Nobel Peace Prize-winner Aung San Suu Kyi, a political prisoner of the Burmese government, who had been under house arrest for the previous fifteen years. He walks by her walled property with Louis and is turned away; ultimately, the closest he ever comes to seeing her is by briefly driving by her compound, which is guarded by the military and laced with barbed wire. He momentarily imagines forming a nonviolent protest to save her but plays with Louis instead.

Later, Delisle critiques the Burmese government to a visiting journalist, which he promptly forgets about until the article is published. When Delisle shows this article to his animation students, they become fearful that they will become associated with his negative comments and be taken away. Frightened that the government will find the article and come after his students, Delisle frantically collects all editions he has distributed. The next session, one of the students who worked for the government does not show up.

With increasing resistance from the Burmese government, MSF closes its mission in Burma, and as a result, Delisle's trip comes to an end. He is doubtful about what sort of impact MSF or he can have on the many serious problems the Burmese face. As his stay ends, Delisle visits a Buddhist retreat for three days, where he must remain silent and meditate standing and sitting. After initially finding the experience remarkably difficult, he leaves the retreat feeling immensely peaceful, though this proves a fleeting sense. In the final panel of the book, Delisle stares upward in puzzled amazement at a fast-whirling hand-pulled Ferris wheel, showing him as puzzled, curious, and relatively ignorant about life in Burma as when he arrived.

Characters

- *Guy Delisle* is the author and protagonist. This friendly, self-deprecating French Canadian cartoonist and animator is perpetually clad in a frumpy T-shirt and shorts. He is a sensitive observer of life, a trait that drives his childlike curiosity, compulsion to cartoon, passion for the plight of the Burmese people, and nearly paranoid love for his son. While he may want to overthrow the oppressive Burmese government, he is more interested in his personal relationships and never sacrifices them for his politics.

- *Nadège Delisle* is Guy's wife. She is a lithe, active, and courageous doctor for MSF, and her humanitarian work is the reason for their move to Burma. A working mom, she balances travel to dangerous, remote, war-torn regions of the country with caring for both her new baby and her Burmese co-workers.

- *Louis Delisle* is Guy and Nadège's pear-headed baby boy and Guy's silent companion as he wanders through the streets of Yangon. Louis is a gateway to the Burmese people for Delisle: The locals swarm Louis and Guy to play with the little Caucasian baby, a rare novelty. Also, Guy connects with the expatriate community when he takes Louis to day care. Most of all, Louis is Guy's muse and keeps him ever vigilant against Burma's hidden dangers, from open light sockets to poisonous snakes and rebel bombings.

- *Maung Aye* is a young, exuberant, rail-thin Burmese man who guards the Delisle house in Burma. He always greets Delisle with an enthusiastic smile, which happens to be bright red from his nearly constant betel-nut consumption. He is Delisle's closest link to the Burmese culture, often translating for him perplexing events and surroundings.

- *Aung San Suu Kyi*, a.k.a. "the Lady," is the Nobel Peace Prize-winning leader of the Burmese

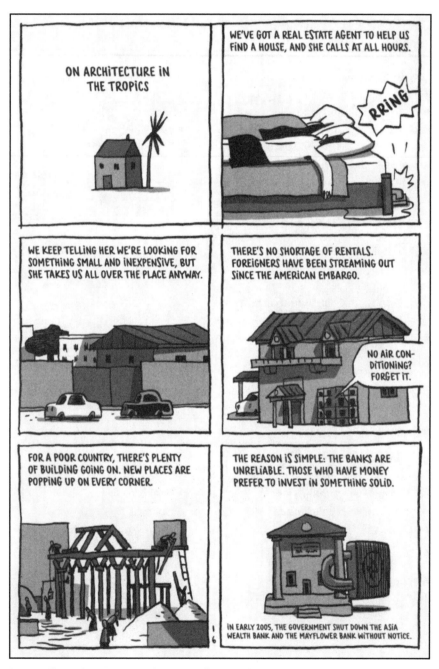

Burma Chronicles. (Courtesy of Drawn and Quarterly)

resistance and the absent heroine of Delisle's journey. A political prisoner, she is allowed to leave the country but not her home, where she has stayed for the previous fifteen years, essentially cut off from the outside world.

- *The Burmese dictatorship* is the collective antagonist of the story, represented by nearly indistinguishable generals and soldiers in ornately decorated military fatigues. While Delisle occasionally sees members of the dictatorship in person, such as the guards in front of Aung San Suu Kyi's house, the dictatorship comprises a largely unseen force, represented more in its influence than in its physical presence, such as in the missing, censored pages of *Time* magazine.

Artistic Style

Delisle said that he wanted *Burma Chronicles* to be a "postcard" home, one that might inspire more people to become interested in Burma and the situation of the Burmese people. In this way, *Burma Chronicles* is not unlike a stylized educational comic and, thus, is graphically readable: It includes spacious, uncrowded panels and simple iconography that helps the reader move through Delisle's observations with ease. These observations are not linked together in comprehensive chapters but, rather, are depicted in short episodes (sometimes only a page) that are self-contained strips, each like an entry in a diary.

In the tradition of French memoirists who have worked with the publisher L'Association, such as Marjane Satrapi in *Persepolis* (2000) and David B. in *Epileptic* (1996-2003), Delisle does not make much effort to realistically depict what he sees and remembers. Rather, he presents the reader with images in a stripped-down, though highly expressive, cartoon style, one that no doubt owes itself to his experience as an animator. Delisle's hand-drawn, sketchy panels suggest that what the reader is seeing is a subjective, impressionistic rendering of his experience, rather than an authoritative, objective account of reality. This is best seen in one panel in which he attempts to draw with his left hand after his right arm is sore; the product is a messy, inept cartoon, one that in its sloppiness captures his difficulty in drawing with the wrong hand.

Using sparse, highly appropriate details, Delisle creates distinguishable, emotionally vivid caricatures of the people he meets and of himself, using only black, white, and gray. Delisle depicts himself simply, though with iconic detail: His fire-hydrant-shaped head, with wing-tipped black hair, is exceptionally simple, almost childlike. With this characteristic look, he is able to deftly capture his reactions and moods, essential to a story that is fundamentally about his impressions.

In depicting the unique architecture, engineering, and nature of Burma, however, Delisle breaks from this cartooning style and takes pains to render accurately what he sees in all its complexity, drawing with fine, precise lines, often contained in expansive panels. Conversely, when depicting a travel sequence, he strips the cartooning down to exceptionally simple iconography, breaking out the action into a crowd of thumbnail panels.

Themes

The most important theme in *Burma Chronicles* is oppression, which is best illustrated on the cover. Two guards posted outside the fenced-off compound of Nobel laureate Aung San Suu Kyi stare warily back as Guy pushes Louis's stroller past them. "The Lady," who was elected president by the population while under house arrest, represents the oppression of the dictatorship, which does not listen to its people. The reader also hears about, but never actually sees, the government that makes it difficult for MSF to carry out its humanitarian mission, thus leaving many Burmese to die of diseases such as malaria and AIDS. While these are the most blatant examples, most of the oppression is seen in the everyday aspects of life: in the missing pages in magazines and in a slowly loading Internet being monitored carefully by the government.

Censorship is another theme connected with Delisle's journey. A major reason that Delisle never sees government oppression firsthand is that the dictatorship guards him and the Burmese people from seeing it, through their immense censorship and propaganda efforts. The real news, which cannot be found in the state-owned newspaper *The New Light of Myanmar*, is passed through whispered rumors. The problem with the rumors is that nobody really knows whether they are true, distorted, or false.

Guy, Nadège, and the MSF workers want to help the people of Burma but find that it is difficult as outsiders to help make this change. Thus, another important theme is altruism: How do people actually help those who are victims of oppression? When Delisle speaks out against the regime, he puts his Burmese friends in danger. Similarly, after MSF has decided to leave, Delisle speaks with an MSF doctor who points out that if they stay in Burma and continue to provide medical care, they will actually aid the regime rather than force the Burmese government to take care of its own citizens. Thus, *Burma Chronicles* demonstrates how thin the line between hurting and helping victims of an oppressive government can be for outsiders to that culture.

Impact

Delisle's *Burma Chronicles* is firmly within the tradition of nonfiction comics: Harvey Pekar, Art Spiegelman, and Joe Sacco were publishing, and earning acclaim, with comics that dealt in reality decades before the *Burma Chronicles*. Comics depictions of life under an oppressive regime also began about sixty years earlier: In the late 1940's and early 1950's, Danzig Baldaev was using cartoons to create exceptionally detailed and truly graphic factual recordings of torture in the Russian gulags. More recently, L'Association alumna Satrapi earned acclaim for showing life under the Iranian dictatorship in *Persepolis*, also illustrated in an animated cartoon style similar to that employed by Delisle.

Delisle, however, is one of the first comic travel memoirists, a subgenre of nonfiction. Whereas Pekar recorded his life at home, Spiegelman and Satrapi composed autobiographies, and Sacco and Baldaev were interested in factually recording their observations, Delisle uses comics to explore his subjective impressions abroad. While travel memoir is a popular genre in print text, Delisle is the first to make his career and popular mark as a comics travel writer. However, *Burma Chronicles* may not be his defining work, as his earlier work *Pyongyang: A Journey in North Korea* (2005) presents a rare glimpse into a country that few journalists can report on and, as a result, has garnered greater attention.

Adam Bessie

Further Reading

Delisle, Guy. *Pyongyang: A Journey in North Korea* (2005).

_____. *Shenzhen: A Travelogue from China* (2006).

Sacco, Joe. *Palestine* (2002).

Satrapi, Marjane. *Persepolis* (2003).

Bibliography

Baldaev, Danzig. *Drawings from the Gulag*. London: FUEL, 2010.

Pekar, Harvey. Introduction to *The Best American Comics 2006*. Boston: Houghton Mifflin Harcourt, 2006.

Versaci, Rocco. "Creating a 'Special Reality': Comic Books Versus Memoir." In *This Book Contains Graphic Language: Comics as Literature*. New York: Continuum, 2007.

See also: *Persepolis; Maus: A Survivor's Tale; Shenzhen; Pyongyang; Palestine*

C

CAGES

Author: McKean, Dave
Artist: Dave McKean (illustrator)
Publishers: Tundra; Kitchen Sink Press; NBM; Dark Horse Comics
First serial publication: 1990-1996
First book publication: 1998

Publication History

Dave McKean initially began serializing *Cages* in 1990, publishing a total of ten issues between 1990 and 1996. The early volumes were released by Tundra Publishing. After Tundra folded, Kitchen Sink Press took over the project and printed the final issues. This first phase of *Cages'* publication history is notable for the erratic release schedule of the initial issues, especially for the three-year gap that separates the release of the eighth issue from that of the ninth. While these original issues attracted considerable attention, the project as a whole remained incomplete until 1998, when Kitchen Sink issued the first complete collection of the book. *Cages* lapsed out of print after Kitchen Sink Press shut down the following year and did not return to print until 2002, when NBM issued a new edition. Dark Horse Comics released a version of the book in 2010.

Prior to the publication of *Cages*, McKean was best known for his collaborations with other comics creators, especially Neil Gaiman, for whom he illustrated the books *Violent Cases* (1997), *Black Orchid* (1988-1989), *Signal to Noise* (1989), and *The Tragical Comedy or Comical Tragedy of Mr. Punch: A Romance* (1994), as well as several books for children and other illustrated texts. McKean also contributed covers to all seventy-five issues of Gaiman's *The Sandman* series (1989-1996) over a period roughly contemporaneous with the creation of *Cages*. Another important and widely read collaboration paired McKean and Grant

Cages. (Courtesy of Dark Horse Comics)

Morrison on the Batman story *Arkham Asylum: A Serious House on Serious Earth* (1990).

Plot

Stylistically diffuse and often nonlinear in its narrative style, *Cages* is a volume that rewards careful attention and regular rereading. Although McKean originally conceived of *Cages* as a series of entangled short stories, the finished novel does have a clear narrative line. After a lengthy opening prose sequence in which McKean relates four original creation myths, *Cages* introduces the reader to Meru House, the mysterious apartment building at the center of the novel's labyrinthine plot. Throughout much of the book's first chapter, a black cat prowls from window to window, pausing briefly to study the building's various residents and visitors. Developments in later chapters suggest that this sequence is temporally disjointed, many of the events taking place out of the order in which the text ultimately presents them. As such, the cat's perambulations function as a sort of overture to the book as a whole, offering brief, literal windows into the discrete lives of Meru House's various residents.

The first few chapters of *Cages*' true narrative follow Leo Sabarsky, a frustrated painter who takes a room in Meru House in the hope of kick-starting his artistic process. Through Leo, the reader gradually comes to know of the building's other residents, first glimpsed through the black cat's eyes. Among them is Jonathan Rush, a once acclaimed novelist who has been in hiding since his most recent book, also titled *Cages*, sparked riots. As McKean eventually reveals, Rush is now at the mercy of a pair of thuggish men in bowler hats who provide for his needs but take away everything that he loves. Leo also befriends Angel, a brilliant jazz musician who lives upstairs. Through Angel's machinations, Leo later comes to know Karen, a botanist who has somehow grown a forest in her own apartment. Karen repeatedly sits for Leo, allowing him to draw her, and the two gradually fall in love.

After Jonathan's tormentors remove and murder the black cat—for which Jonathan has been caring—Leo learns of his friend's predicament. With the help of Karen and Angel, Leo helps Jonathan and his wife, Ellen, escape from Meru House. As the book comes to a close, Karen and Leo consummate their relationship, recommitting themselves to the value and promise of human creativity.

A number of other stories intercut these events, including a lengthy monologue delivered by Edie Featherskill to her parrot in which she ruminates on what to cook and reflects on her past, eventually revealing that her husband Bill abandoned her years before. Near the close of the novel, the reader learns that Bill was somehow transformed into a cat years before, only to return to his own form upon the black cat's death.

Elsewhere, Angel delivers a parable about the origins of music and an unnamed mother tells her child a story about a tower that a king built in order to make his kingdom greater only to learn that it would undo all his past accomplishments. Other interwoven elements include a small handful of fantastical wordless sequences seemingly run through with allegorical import but not obviously connected to the central story.

Characters

- *Leo Sabarsky* is a visual artist who moves into Meru House near the beginning of the narrative. Observant and sincere, he strikes up friendships with several of the building's residents, as well as with a handful of other neighborhood characters. Although his own work tends to frustrate him, he gradually comes into a new contentment with the help of Karen.
- *Jonathan Rush* is a novelist and essayist whose most recent work, the inflammatory *Cages*, sparked outrage. Now in hiding with his wife, Jonathan begins the novel as little more than a shell of a man, beaten down by past disappointments and the torments of his ostensible keepers. He is loosely based on the novelist Salman Rushdie.
- *Angel* is an uncommonly talented jazz musician who tends to speak in the form of suggestive parables. Seemingly capable of drawing music from everything, Angel crafts stories that can be made to sing.
- *Karen* is a botanist who lives across the way from Leo in an apartment where she has somehow grown a forest. Though she is initially an object of distant fascination for Leo, the two soon grow romantically entangled.
- *Edie Featherskill* is an older woman who lives by herself in Meru House. Though she has apparently been abandoned by her husband, Bill, she generally operates under the delusion that he is merely late for dinner.
- *Ellen* is Jonathan's wife. Though she sometimes seems to rage at her husband's melancholic powerlessness, she remains largely undefined in her own right.
- *The gallerist* is a small, peculiar man who speaks by way of note cards printed with words and

Cages. (Courtesy of Dark Horse Comics)

phrases that he rearranges to form sentences and questions, frequently resulting in malapropisms.
- *Doris* is the landlady of Meru House. Because of her comical tendency to mishear what others say, Leo occasionally refers to her as "Mrs. What."

Artistic Style

Prior to beginning work on *Cages*, McKean was best known for maximalist multimedia images of the sort seen in his contributions to *The Sandman* and in books such as *Arkham Asylum*. *Cages* marks a pointed departure from this less restrained style; the majority of its innumerable panels are drawn in spare pen and ink accented only by limited shading done in grays and blacks. McKean largely refuses realist forms of representation, and the bodies and faces of his characters are often distorted and distended, as if the lines themselves are striving to escape the shapes that hold them together. This sketchy approach has the effect of suggesting that the lives of the book's characters are very much in progress; they are beautiful drafts of things yet to come.

At numerous points throughout, McKean embraces altogether different artistic techniques. In the opening chapter, for example, as the black cat peers into the different windows of Meru House, McKean intermittently adopts a more fully realized style, introducing painterly panels that resemble underdeveloped

black-and-white photographs. Other sections find him making use of photo manipulation during fantasies and dreams and even deploying brief bursts of color during some of the book's most vivid depictions of its characters' troubled psyches. When questioned about these shifts of style, McKean tends to suggest that he simply took on whatever form seemed most appropriate to the narrative. While this willingness to play and experiment can make *Cages* difficult to parse at certain junctures, it contributes to the book's rich narrative climate in which allegories are piled atop one another.

Cages also contains a number of moments of virtuosic cartooning. Most famous among these is a sequence near the middle of the novel in which a conversation between Karen and Leo bleeds into a musical performance by Angel. As the sequence descends into abstraction, the couple's dialogue bubbles take on a pictographic character, suggesting those conversations in which the overall emotional tenor is far more important than anything actually said. In a few scant pages, McKean is able to suggest hours of rich and deeply felt discourse without actually telling the reader anything specific that his characters have said or done.

Themes

Taken as a whole, *Cages* works as a study of various creative processes and the frustrations thereof.

Virtually all of McKean's major characters are artists of one kind or another, from the novelist Jonathan Rush to the painter Leo Sabarsky and the musician Angel. Indeed, even Mrs. Featherskill, who spends much of her section of the text fussing over her cabinet of recipes, might be understood as a practitioner of the culinary arts. Struggling—and often failing—to realize their dreams and desires, these characters speak to the promises and pains of art. Approaching the book in these terms also helps explain the presence of its most controversial element, the four prose creation myths that appear at the beginning. What is at stake here and throughout *Cages* is a celebration of acts of creation as such, regardless of their products or consequences.

Cages is also deeply concerned with romances and relationships. Throughout the book, a number of different interpersonal bonds are shown at a range of different points in their respective arcs. Whereas the bond between Leo and Karen only grows over the course of the narrative, Jonathan's marriage is in a heightened state of dissolution. Worn down by years of creative and interpersonal disappointment, Jonathan and his wife seem all but incapable of communicating with one another. Elsewhere on the spectrum, Mrs. Featherskill has long been separated from her husband, Bill, of whom she speaks incessantly. These and other couplings are deeply intertwined with the questions of creativity that are at the heart of the novel. As the text repeatedly suggests, humans are at their best when they are able to make things with others.

Finally, *Cages* can be read as a meditation on the nature of allegory. The novel is replete with stories and other elements that seem to stand in for something else, though what they purport to illuminate or otherwise explain is rarely self-evident. Many characters—especially Angel—comment on and call attention to this tendency in the text, making allegory itself as much a subject as a technique. *Cages'* continual slippage in and out of allegorical forms of representation may be frustrating for some readers, as it can be difficult to distinguish what is really happening from that which merely comments on the narrative.

Impact

Cages emerged on the scene at a critical juncture for independent comics in the English-speaking world. In the wake of Art Spiegelman's 1992 Pulitzer Prize for *Maus*, the medium seemed primed for broader mass-market acceptance, but its future direction was still uncertain. Eschewing the more narrowly personal narratives of many independent comics of its day, *Cages* aspired to offer a story of far-reaching import. The book's real impact, however, may have been more material: Originally printed on high-quality paper in an expensive hardback edition, *Cages* helped pave the way for more elaborately produced independent comics. Today, the book is memorable in significant part for its desire to push the "artiness" of comics art to its limits. Though McKean's style has influenced some younger artists, his often dizzying formal aspirations in *Cages* remain largely unmatched.

While he has continued to work in comics, publishing works such as the short-story collection *Pictures That Tick* (2001), McKean has focused much of his energy on other art forms in the years since *Cages* was published. *Cages* remains in high regard with most critics, and its various reissues have garnered generally favorable reviews.

Jacob Brogan

Further Reading

Barry, Lynda. *What It Is* (2008).
Campbell, Eddie. *Alec: The Years Have Pants* (2009).
Pope, Paul. *100%* (2005).

Bibliography

Feltman, Matthew. "Phantom Towers: Crypto-Towers Haunting Dave McKean's *Cages* and *Mirrormask*." *ImageTexT: Interdisciplinary Comics Studies* 4, no. 1 (2008). http://www.english.ufl.edu/imagetext/archives/v4_1/feltman.

_____. "The Art of Dave McKean." Interview by Dan Epstein. *Underground Online*. http://www.ugo.com/channels/freestyle/features/davemckean/default.asp.

McKean, Dave. "Dave McKean on *Arkham Asylum* and *Cages*." Interview. *Comics Career* 2, no. 1 (1990). http://www.comicscareer.com/?page_id=55.

McKean, Dave, and Neil Gaiman. *Dustcovers: The Collected Sandman Covers, 1989-1997*. New York: Vertigo, 1998.

See also: *What It Is; Alec: The Years Have Pants; Violent Cases; Signal to Noise; The Tragical Comedy or Comical Tragedy of Mr. Punch*

CANCER VIXEN: A TRUE STORY

Author: Marchetto, Marisa Acocella
Artist: Marisa Acocella Marchetto (illustrator); Dennis Bicksler (colorist); Jason Zamajtuk (colorist)
Publisher: Alfred A. Knopf
First book publication: 2006

Publication History

By the time Marisa Acocella Marchetto was diagnosed with breast cancer in 2004, at the age of forty-three, she was a successful artist whose cartoons had appeared in a variety of publications, including *Mirabella*, *Elle*, *The New Yorker*, *Talk*, and *Glamour*. She had also published her debut graphic novel, *Just Who the Hell Is She Anyway?* (1994), through Harmony Books. When her editors at *Glamour*, Cindi Leive and Lauren Smith-Brody, heard the news about her cancer, they encouraged the cartoonist and graphic novelist to write about her experiences for the magazine.

The May, 2005 issue of *Glamour* included a six-page version of *Cancer Vixen*. Alfred A. Knopf published the full graphic novel version in September, 2006. A digitally archived copy of the former is available on the *Glamour* Web site; by comparing the earlier draft to the finished book, one can see the evolution from a condensed but witty narrative with rather one-dimensional characters to a poignant and intimate retelling of the events, in which even the minor characters are imbued with subtle and memorable details.

Plot

On the first page of the book, which takes place in April, 2004, the protagonist notices a lump in her breast while swimming. Rather than dramatizing this moment, though, Marchetto includes an X ray alongside the text and cartoon with the black mass of the tumor clearly labeled. At her initial examination, she knows immediately that something is wrong since the doctors and hospital staff flash multiple "100,000-watt smiles" at her, even as they tell her it could be nothing.

Marchetto sees a specialist, Dr. Christopher Mills, who takes a sample from the tumor; one day (and

Cancer Vixen: A True Story. (Courtesy of Pantheon Books)

fifty-seven conversations between Marchetto and her concerned friends, family, and fiancé) later, the doctor calls to confirm that there is an abnormality in the test results. Marchetto represents this singular event in her life as akin to being sucked up into outer space by a gigantic vacuum cleaner and into a freezing black hole. She calls her parents in New Jersey to tell them the news, but she fears her fiancé's reaction. After an hour-long shower and the application of "Brave" lipstick by M.A.C., she phones him at the Italian restaurant he owns, and he dashes across the street to their shared apartment where she waits, apprehensively.

At this point, the story flashes back three years to August, 2001, and details Marchetto's work at *Talk* magazine, including a piece on New Yorkers' reactions in the immediate aftermath of the terrorist attacks of September 11, 2001, and a feature article on "how to be an 'it' girl," which leads to her meeting her future husband and restaurateur Silvano Marchetto. Their romance is an old-fashioned one (he asks her to go steady on their first date) mixed with contemporary New York City sensibilities (he admits that he thought she was a lesbian since she always came to the restaurant accompanied by girlfriends). They move in together after dating for two months and are soon engaged to be married.

Shifting back to the present, on May 15, 2004, at 10:12 A.M. (shown literally ingrained in the author's gray matter), only three weeks before her wedding, Marchetto learns that she has breast cancer. She tearfully breaks this news to her fiancé as well as the fact that she has allowed her health insurance to lapse, fearing that the financial burden of the latter might be enough to destroy their relationship. Silvano reassures her and tells her not to worry before returning to the restaurant. Unable to work, Marchetto revisits her old apartment; in a surreal, existentialist scene, she destroys a vanity mirror inherited from her grandmother and is visited by Mary Poppins and the Virgin Mary, who urge her to overcome her self-pity.

Marchetto's friends and family begin offering a wide range of advice: Her friend Lisa insists that she come to the Kabbalah center for a healing service; her mother argues that rather than merely getting a second opinion, she may want to get a seventh or eighth; and her friend Bob suggests that she stop moping around in sweatpants and sneakers and take care of herself. On the negative side, gossip of Marchetto's illness spreads to strangers, and in a pivotal scene at the restaurant, a woman approaches Silvano with her card, telling him that she is available and cancer-free if he wants a "healthy relationship."

After her lumpectomy, Marchetto wrestles with insecurity when her fiancé neglects to call her that evening at her parent's home in New Jersey where she is recovering. The following day, he arrives in his Maserati with a trunk full of gourmet ingredients, and the couple immediately goes upstairs to the bedroom, erasing any earlier doubts about their love for each other. They marry on June 11, 2004, and afterward, the newlyweds take a weekend trip to Montreal to watch the Grand Prix Montreal. After consulting with the oncologist, Marchetto and Silvano decide to take a three-week honeymoon in Italy before beginning her chemotherapy.

The final section of the book details the protagonist's eight sessions of chemotherapy. The three-week cycles are represented via a red bar graph tracing Marchetto's energy level from an initial euphoric high of one to three days to the lethargic low of day ten—during which she requires a cappuccino to get out of bed—and a gradual return to normalcy over the course of days eleven to twenty-one (at which point the cycle starts over again). During the process, Marchetto celebrates her forty-fourth birthday and New Year's 2005. Following her chemotherapy, she starts a regimen of radiation therapy five days a week for six and a half weeks.

At the conclusion of her treatment, Marchetto emerges a changed person: When Jennifer, "the rival cartoon girl," confronts her at a party, Marchetto asks her for forgiveness rather than lashing out in anger. At Silvano's restaurant, where she once saw only petty, jealous women vying for her husband's attention, she now meets more and more breast-cancer survivors who want to share their stories with her.

Characters

- *Marisa Acocella Marchetto*, the protagonist, is a blond, fashion-conscious, Italian American cartoonist who discovers she has breast cancer three weeks before her wedding. She copes with her diagnosis and treatment through the support of friends and family (particularly her mother) and by documenting each stage of the process with photographs and tape recordings, which she later uses as source material for her art.

- *Silvano Marchetto*, Marchetto's fiancé and later husband, is a restaurant owner and proprietor who exudes the easy charm and romantic sensibilities of an older Italian man. He drives a Maserati sports car, always wears brightly colored shirts, and is an eternal optimist even in the face of Marchetto's cancer.

- *Bob Morris*, one of Marchetto's best friends, is a mildly misanthropic writer for *The New York Times'* Fashion and Style section. He inspires his friend to stop dressing like a victim and more like a vixen, which marks a turning point in Marchetto's approach to her diagnosis.

- *Jennifer*, a.k.a. *Rival Cartoon Girl*, is a fellow cartoonist who picks a fight with Marchetto at a party after she spots her boyfriend Mitch dancing with the protagonist. The two women meet, hosted by *The New Yorker*, three years later, and Marchetto's newfound perspective allows them to forgive each other.
- *(S)mother*, Marchetto's mother, affectionately nicknamed by her daughter because of her extremely supportive but slightly overbearing nature, is almost always shown wearing purple with multiple pieces of gold jewelry and sunglasses. She is also a bit of a hypochondriac who alternates between claiming to suffer from sciatica, carpal tunnel syndrome, or bad knees.
- *Sam*, one of Marchetto's best friends, is a fellow cartoonist who is sometimes pictured as an anthropomorphic street rat, since he inspires Marchetto to do whatever it takes to survive as an artist in New York.

Artistic Style

Cancer Vixen's art favors emotional expression over realism. Often the most dramatic scenes verge into surrealism: When the protagonist first learns that there is an anomaly in her test results, a giant vacuum cleaner descends from the purplish black of outer space and sucks the character up into its hose; in another scene, her fellow cartoonist friend, Sam, suddenly transforms into a giant rat as he explains how to survive as an artist in New York. In instances of extreme emotion (such as when Marchetto first tells Silvano about her diagnosis) the protagonist's face is replaced with a smiley

Cancer Vixen: A True Story (Courtesy of Pantheon Books)

face and then an exaggerated sad face as the character moves through a spectrum of different feelings.

Marchetto also incorporates various photographic media within the graphic novel format, such as an X ray of her tumor, a black-and-white photo of her great-grandfather, a photocopied medical form, and a picture from the couple's wedding day. Rather than distracting from the narrative, the photos lend a journalistic quality to what might otherwise be considered highly personal and subjective events, and this objective element provides contrast to the more surreal and whimsical moments of the story.

The overall drawing style utilizes thick, black outlines and a vibrant color palette tending toward bright oranges, blues, and pinks. A majority of the pages employ a traditional panel layout, but in several instances, the author has opted for one-page or two-page spreads or for a panel surrounded by typewriter-style text.

Themes

Halfway through the narrative, the protagonist meets with her friend Bob Morris along the Hudson River, and he urges her to focus less on her mind-set and negative thoughts and more on her outward appearance, telling her to stop dressing like a victim and more like a vixen. In a 2006 interview with *New York Magazine*, Marchetto revealed that this conversation inspired her to change the title of her book from *Breast Case Scenario* to *Cancer Vixen*. This theme, that the relatively superficial or ephemeral aspects of life (such as fashion or comics) and the deep or existential elements (such as spirituality or cancer) need not be thought of as mutually exclusive, resonates throughout the narrative. For each session of chemotherapy, the author illustrates both the IV needle (along with a running tally) and the Giuseppe Zanotti or Emilio Pucci designer shoes she wears to her appointment. By the end of the story, the protagonist's internal struggles with cancer and her concerns with her external appearance reach a parallel resolution: As she blows out the candles for her forty-fourth birthday, she realizes that she no longer dreads old age, but actually welcomes it.

A second theme one can trace throughout *Cancer Vixen* is the ability of the individual to effect changes

---

Marisa Acocella Marchetto

A cartoonist whose work has appeared in *The New Yorker*, *Glamour*, and *Modern Bride*, Marisa Acocella Marchetto is best known in the comics world as the author of two graphic novels: *Just Who the Hell Is She, Anyway?* (1994) and *Cancer Vixen* (2006). *Cancer Vixen*, which was a crossover success that sold well beyond the traditional confines of the comics world, tells the autobiographical story of Marchetto as she undergoes treatment for cancer after having allowed her health insurance to lapse. Marchetto's art is notable for its sketchy quality, in which she uses an unpolished line in order to convey a sense of immediacy and directness, and her pages are extremely text-heavy, with cartoonish figures largely dwarfed by dialogue. A portion of all sales of *Cancer Vixen* go to the Breast Cancer Research Foundation and Marchetto is the founder of the Cancer Vixen Fund at Saint Vincent's Comprehensive Cancer Center in New York.

---

in his or her social environment. Over the course of the narrative, Silvano is constantly assaulted by seductive women who attempt to sit on his lap, demand rides in his Maserati, and generally ignore Marchetto's presence. However, after her experiences with breast cancer, Marchetto finds that something has shifted in how she carries herself and that women now ask Silvano to meet her, since many of them are also cancer survivors.

In the most telling moment of Marchetto's change in attitude, Jennifer, "the rival cartoon girl," approaches Marchetto at a party and demands that the protagonist apologize for dancing with the former's boyfriend, Mitch, at an event three years previous. Marchetto's initial response of incredulous anger turns to empathy as she recalls the parade of jealous women who have attempted to entice Silvano over the years. She apologizes; Jennifer's mood suddenly softens, and she asks how Marchetto is feeling. In the bottom margin, the author asks if this resolution of a petty, but all-consuming, rivalry might indicate that there is some hope in the world.

Impact

Marchetto's *Cancer Vixen: A True Story* belongs to the subgenre of graphic novel memoir, which includes such notable autobiographical titles as Art Spiegelman's *Maus: A Survivor's Tale* (1986-1991), Harvey Pekar and Joyce Brabner's *Our Cancer Year* (1994), Marjane Satrapi's *Persepolis* (2000), and Craig Thompson's *Blankets* (2003). Since *Cancer Vixen*'s 2006 publication, several more graphic novel memoirs specifically dealing with the authors' personal experiences with cancer have been published: Miriam Engelberg's *Cancer Made Me a Shallower Person: A Memoir in Comics* (2006), Brian Fies's *Mom's Cancer* (2006), and Ross Mackintosh's *Seeds* (2011). Notably, of all these works, only Pekar and Brabner's and Engelberg's address cancer from a first-person perspective, aligning them with Marchetto's work.

Thomas Knowlton

Further Reading

B., David. *Epileptic* (2005).

Engelberg, Miriam. *Cancer Made Me a Shallower Person: A Memoir in Comics* (2006).

Fies, Brian. *Mom's Cancer* (2006).

Mack, Stan. *Janet & Me: An Illustrated Story of Love and Loss* (2004).

Bibliography

Chute, Hillary. "*Our Cancer Year, Janet and Me: An Illustrated Story of Love and Loss, Cancer Vixen: A True Story, Mom's Cancer, Blue Pills: A Positive Love Story, Epileptic,* and *Black Hole.*" Review of *Cancer Vixen*, by Marisa Acocella Marchetto. *Literature and Medicine* 26, no. 2 (2008): 413-429.

Levy, Ariel. "*Cancer Vixen: A True Story.*" Review of *Cancer Vixen: A True Story*, Marisa Acocella Marchetto. *The New York Times Book Review*, October 22, 2006, 30.

Marchetto, Marisa Acocella. *Cancer Vixen. Glamour*, August, 2006. http://www.glamour.com/health-fitness/2006/08/cancer-vixen-cartoon.

See also: *Epileptic; Our Cancer Year; Black Hole; Blankets*

CARTOON HISTORY OF THE UNIVERSE, THE

Author: Gonick, Larry
Artist: Larry Gonick (illustrator)
Publisher: Rip Off Press; Kitchen Sink Press; Doubleday; HarperCollins
First serial publication: 1979-1992
First book publication: 1990-2009

Publication History

The *Cartoon History* series started as nine individual issues published by Rip Off Press from 1978 until the late 1980's. Larry Gonick worked with Jacqueline Kennedy Onassis, the former First Lady, at Doubleday to publish them as collected editions beginning with *The Cartoon History of the Universe I* in 1990 and *The Cartoon History of the Universe II* in 1994, while in 2002 W. W. Norton published the last three books in the series, *The Cartoon History of the Universe III*.

Gonick changed the title of the next book to *The Cartoon History of the Modern World,* Part 1 to align with the historical tradition of recognizing the sixteenth century as a period that ushered in the modern world. This was published in 2007 with HarperCollins and was followed up with the final book in the series, *The Cartoon History of the Modern World,* Part 2 in 2009. HarperCollins had published many other "Cartoon Guides" with Gonick, beginning with *The Cartoon Guide to Genetics* in 1981.

Plot

The *Cartoon History* series covers history from the Big Bang to the Iraq War (2003-2010) and is composed of five books with each book being five to seven volumes long, and each of these "subvolumes" is about fifty pages in length. Each book covers less time than the previous, which is similar to many standard world history books. For example, *The Cartoon History of the Universe* I covers more than ten billion years (mostly in the first two volumes), whereas *The Cartoon History of the Modern World,* Part 2 covers roughly 220 years. Overall, Gonick's history focuses on the West, but he does provide volumes concerned with the histories

The Cartoon History of the Universe. (Courtesy of Three Rivers Press)

of non-Western countries and regions, such as India, China, and pre-Columbian America.

In the first volume, *The Cartoon History of the Universe* I, Gonick traces history from the beginning of the universe (he maintains the Big Bang theory) to the dawn of primates. The following two volumes focus on the evolution of man from primate to farmer and on early civilizations. The remaining four volumes explore mostly Middle Eastern and Mediterranean history.

In *The Cartoon History of the Universe* II, Gonick focuses on Indian and Chinese history. The rest of the book returns to the West to explain the rise and fall of the Roman Empire.

Moving into the modern era with *The Cartoon History of the Universe* III, Gonick still uses each volume to focus on one geographic location with the first volume looking at the rise of Islam, which leads into the next volume and a focus on Africa. With Africa, Gonick provides a brief history of the continent, since it has largely gone unaddressed until this point (with the exception of northern Africa). The third volume considers China, India, and central Eurasia during the first millennium of the Common Era.

The last three volumes focus on European history with major influences from Asia, including the Mongol Empire and the Black Death. The final two books explore Europe and the United States as dominant powers in the world. They also cover globalization and the increasing interdependence of nations.

Volumes

- *The Cartoon History of the Universe* I (1979). Collects Volumes 1-7, covering the origin of the universe, evolution of man, and early civilizations to the rise and dominance of Greek culture.
- *The Cartoon History of the Universe* II (1994). Collects Volumes 8-13, covering the origins of Buddhism to the fall of the western Roman Empire.
- *The Cartoon History of the Universe* III (2002). Collects Volumes 14-19, covering the growth of Islam through the Renaissance (fourteenth to seventeenth century).
- *The Cartoon History of the Modern World,* Part 1 (2007). Collects Volumes 1-5, covering Europe's encounter with the Americas to the American Revolution (1775-1783).
- *The Cartoon History of the Modern World,* Part 2 (2009). Collects Volumes 6-10, covering the French Revolution (1789-1799) to the Iraq War.

Characters

Unnamed guide, who appears to be a stand-in for Gonick himself, is a caricature of Albert Einstein. He has wild hair and wears a suit and a tie. The guide provides a page of introduction prior to each volume and every few pages after that in which he talks directly to the reader or with historical figures or nameless characters.

Artistic Style

The black-and-white comics are hand-drawn in a cartoon manner in which caricature dominates. Gonick

portrays himself as an Einstein-like guide, visually mocking the concept of a historian while using an authoritarian voice to dictate how it transpired. Historical characters are given specific traits, but the nameless people featured throughout the series are not distinguishable. Gonick keeps the art simple, occasionally using cross-hatching but mostly sticking to black-and-white depictions and avoiding excessive detail, which would distract from the history. Gonick drew the entire series with no significant shifts in the style, and he plays with the visual representations of footnotes and maps. He provides bottom-row panels that give footnotes to the ongoing history. Footnotes are indicated by a drawn foot holding a pen or brush next to musical notes or squiggles, resulting in the visual pun ("foot" plus "note"). Maps usually include a mixture of factual layout and humor. Gonick employs symbolic icons to represent people, places, and resources. Unlike standard maps, which might use coloring, borders, or simple representative icons, Gonick uses iconic images that fall between stereotype and representation, such as camels for Saharan Africa, a building (presumably the Taj Mahal) for Delhi, and a bearded priest holding a cross for Russia. These maps also can include text addressed to specific spaces. For example, in a spread-page map in *The Cartoon History of the Modern World,* Part 1, Gonick displays Europe with a mixture of icons and short blurbs for each country. The summaries provide both information and location.

The word and image interplay challenges some readers. Comic histories offer additional challenges to keeping track of names, dates, and events. For this series, the challenge comes from the interplay among history, commentary, and imagery. On a given page, the narrative box provides the straightforward history and the image provides some means of representing it. However, characters in those panels often speak in ways that humorously reinforce, contradict, or challenge what was said in the narrative box. This mixture between history and commentary is hard to differentiate at times.

Gonick uses the cartoon style, along with the humor, purposely to undermine the history being told. He is relaying history while also challenging cultural assumptions about history. His points are not groundbreaking.

However, Gonick turns the historiography and the history into an accessible and amusing narrative for the layperson. While written books have tried to make history accessible, Gonick's series does it well since he can employ a range of methods not traditionally used in standard writing, particularly the continued interplay between written words and images.

Themes

The *Cartoon History* series provides a basic understanding of historical events and their influence while also challenging the standard concept of history. Gonick illustrates major events but also critiques historians and leading figures in history. Power players are scrutinized throughout the series, whether they are institutional, cultural, or individual. The series informs the reader of the events but often avoids the straight and clear answers. Few figures make it through his retelling without some criticism.

Gonick's overall work indicates that while there are answers, they are subject to scrutiny, since much of what is known of history is not always reliable. He delivers this criticism through a range of comedic practices including hyperbole, irony, puns, sarcasm, and slapstick.

This theme reveals itself at almost all levels of the series. His drawings soften the serious tone of most history books while many of the asides by the guide and other random characters further undermine and challenge what is being presented. This running commentary allows readers to receive the history while also being skeptical of the information.

Gonick creatively mocks standard practices of historians with maps, footnotes, and even the bibliography. His maps include a mixture of text and sometimes amusing iconic cultural representations. His footnotes often discuss particular historians and historical theory while simultaneously challenging or undermining them. His annotated bibliographies are often filled with amusing quips and comments, such as those from *The Cartoon History of the Modern World,* Part 2, which include comments such as "confusing, detailed, but convincing portrait of Bolivar's character," "flawed biography," and "the life of a principled, hard-working, farsighted, insufferable tyrant."

The Cartoon History of the Universe. (Courtesy of Three Rivers Press)

The other major theme throughout the series is making history accessible through a modern cultural frame. Many times Gonick invokes events of the late twentieth century and early twentieth-first century to explain or compare to the historical event he is discussing. Often, he does this by using political buzzwords that would otherwise be anachronistic. In *The Cartoon History of the Modern World,* Part 1, one nameless Aztec says to another, "Our national security is at risk, even though it's our own fault." Later in the book, a nameless French soldier remarks to another about France's invasion of Naples, "Is it possible we skimped on the post-conflict analysis?" In both of these instances, it is clear Gonick is drawing comparisons with the tragedy of September 11, 2001, and the invasion of Iraq, both of which were hot-button concerns when he was composing the book.

Impact

Though the series started as an independent title from a small press, the popularity of Gonick's "Cartoon Guides" nudged it into the mainstream. This not only

Larry Gonick

Arguably the best-known creator of educational comics in the world, Larry Gonick began releasing *The Cartoon History of the Universe* in 1977, a title that he continued for decades. Based on the success of that title, Gonick has produced a wide range of *Cartoon Guides*, including the *Cartoon Guide to Physics*, *to the Environment*, and *to Sex*. He has also published *Cartoon Histories of the United States* and *of the Modern World*. In the 1990's he published a two-page strip about recent scientific discoveries in every issue of *Discover*. For *Common Ground* he published an anti-corporate humor strip, "The Commoners." Gonick's art is notable for its extremely cartoony style. His pages tend to be conservatively structured and individual panels generally include a great deal of text—often in captions—with the images frequently supplementing the words as in a textbook.

helped its popularity within the comics realm but also within mainstream publishing, which placed the series in bookstores well before many big comic publishers had found their niche.

The *Cartoon History* series has been a major influence on the history genre within comics, which became more substantial in the late twentieth and early twenty-first centuries. While classic works such as Art Spiegelman's *Maus* (1972-1991) or Harvey Pekar's *American Splendor* (1976-) have popularized the autobiographic and nonfiction narratives, Gonick's series has been influential on the more removed history series such as Rick Geary's *Treasury of Victorian Murder* (1987-) and *Treasury of XXth Century Murder* (2008-); Hill and Wang's Novel Graphics imprint, which features biographies on Malcolm X, Ronald Reagan, Che Guevara, and J. Edgar Hoover; and historical pieces such as *The 9/11 Report: A Graphic Adaptation* (2006), *Students for a Democratic Society* (2008), and *The Vietnam War* (2009). Two additional books that are

clearly derived from Gonick are *Still I Rise: A Cartoon History of African Americans* (1997), by Roland O. Laird and others, and *Latino U.S.A.: A Cartoon History* (2000), by Ilan Stavans and Alcaraz Lalo. In both cases, the tone, style, and imagery are similar to Gonick's work.

Overall, the *Cartoon History* series has been well received and influential, though Gonick has been criticized at times for his use of caricature, which results in utilizing stereotypes to some degree. This has created some concern from various groups; however, given that all his characters are reduced to stereotypes, regardless of race, gender, or religious affiliation, the criticism seems slightly irrelevant.

Lance V. Eaton

Further Reading

Gonick, Larry. *The Cartoon History of the United States* (1991).

Laird, Roland O., Taneshia N. Laird, and Elihu Bey. *Still I Rise: A Cartoon History of African Americans* (1997).

Stavans, Ilan, and Lalo Alcaraz. *Latino U.S.A: A Cartoon History* (2000).

Zinn, Howard, Mike Konopacki, and Paul Buhle. *A People's History of American Empire: A Graphic Adaptation* (2008).

Bibliography

Gonick, Larry. "Cartoon Larry Gonick—Curriculum Vitae." http://www.larrygonick.com/html/cv/cv.html.

_____. Interview by Matthew Surridge. *The Comics Journal* 224 (June, 2000): 34-68.

Witek, Joseph. *Comic Books as History: The Narrative Art of Jack Jackson, Art Spiegelman, and Harvey Pekar*. Jackson: University Press of Mississippi, 1989.

See also: *American Splendor; A Treasury of Victorian Murder; The 9/11 Report*

CASTLE WAITING

Author: Medley, Linda
Artist: Linda Medley (illustrator); Todd Klein (letterer)
Publisher: Olio; Cartoon Books; Fantagraphics Books
First serial publication: 1996-2010
First book publication: 2006

Publication History

With a grant from the Xeric Foundation, Linda Medley self-published (under the name Olio Press) the first *Castle Waiting* publication, *Castle Waiting: The Curse of Brambly Hedge*, in 1996. That initial publication, a prologue to the series, was followed by seven additional issues and a hiatus issue, all self-published from 1997 to 1999.

In 2000, Cartoon Books published the first four issues of Volume 2 (numbers 8-11 of the 1997-1999 series). In 2001, Medley returned to self-publishing, releasing five more issues of *Castle Waiting* (Volume 2, numbers 5-9).

In 2006, Fantagraphics Books published a hardback collection, *Castle Waiting:* Volume I, which included previously published issues and a new epilogue produced specifically for the volume, and relaunched the continuing series in July of that year. Fifteen new issues were published and collected in a second hardcover book, *Castle Waiting:* Volume II. Fantagraphics also published an expensive, hand-assembled edition of Volume 1.

Critics and readers of Volume 1 have noted the abrupt switch in the story line from the castle setting to the lengthy tale of Sister Peace and the Solicitine Order. In interviews, Medley has revealed that the bearded ladies stories were to come much later in the series, but that Cartoon Books insisted that she change the story line to settings outside the castle. When the second volume of the hardcover edition of *Castle Waiting* was published in 2010, Medley had her name removed from the spine, cover, and title page. Only a removable sticker next to the bar code on the back cover mentions Medley as the author and artist. The dispute between Medley and Fantagraphics Books has not been identified, but Fantagraphics has stated that the removal of

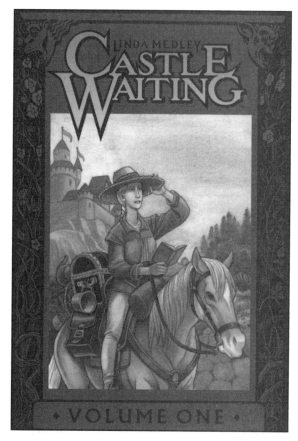

Castle Waiting. (Courtesy of Fantagraphics Books)

Medley's name from the second volume was done at her request. Fantagraphics Books has also announced that the series is on hiatus, which has left many story lines unresolved.

Plot

A set of linked tales, *Castle Waiting* opens with a humorous retelling of the Brothers Grimm classic fairy tale "Briar Rose" (Sleeping Beauty). At a christening for the newborn daughter of the king and queen of Putney, twelve wise witches bestow special gifts upon the infant. Suddenly, an evil witch named Mald, angry at not having been invited to the ceremony, enters and bestows a death curse upon the princess, declaring that on her fifteenth birthday she will prick her finger on a spindle and die. The last good witch, who had yet to give her gift, lifts the death curse by declaring that the princess will instead fall into a deep sleep, protected for one hundred years, to be eventually awakened by a prince. The princess is tricked on her fifteenth birthday into pricking her finger on a spindle, and she and all the inhabitants of the castle fall fast asleep. Townspeople flee the once prosperous and bustling medieval kingdom, and woods claim the castle. After one hundred years, a brave prince passes through the thorns and awakens the sleeping princess; the two immediately leave the castle for his realm.

Years pass, and the abandoned and isolated castle, renamed Castle Waiting, becomes a legendary sanctuary for those who have no other place to reside. The remaining former denizens (Patience, Prudence, and Plenty, the now elderly handmaidens to the princess) along with an eccentric crew of humans and magical beings run the castle.

Escaping an abusive husband, the pregnant Lady Jain flees her home for the refuge of Castle Waiting. After a series of adventures, she arrives at the castle. Jain quickly settles in as the librarian; she teaches Simon, the half-giant, how to read and bears a son named Pindar, who mysteriously appears to be only partly human. As Jain adjusts to the community, the everyday lives of the eccentric characters are explained. Like the participants in Geoffrey Chaucer's *The Canterbury Tales* (first transcribed, 1387-1400), the characters tell their stories to one another, often in flashbacks or in stories within stories.

The final third of the graphic novel (seven chapters and the epilogue) focuses on the story of Peaceful Warren as she moves from a pub to a circus to a convent, finally stopping at Castle Waiting. Having developed a beard as a teenager, Warren runs off to join a circus. When she finally finds one, she discovers there already is a beautiful bearded lady known as Mabel or Clytemnestra, Queen of the Nile, serving as the star attraction, and she accepts a position as barmaid.

Clytemnestra and Warren become fast friends. When Mabel discovers that her abusive husband, Lint, is having an affair, the two friends flee to seek refuge at the Abbey at St. Wilgeforte, a convent for bearded women. After fending off Lint and his henchmen, the nuns welcome the two women into the convent. Mabel eventually remarries a farmer, but Warren joins the Solicitine Order, changes her name to Sister Peace, and then has a series of adventures before joining the inhabitants of Castle Waiting.

As Mable and Warren settle into the convent, Abbess Clarice tells them the story of the founding of the Solicitine Order, which is based on the story of St. Wilgefortis. Nejmah, a beautiful Middle Eastern princess who has converted to Christianity, is forced by her father to

Castle Waiting. (Courtesy of Fantagraphics Books)

marry a pagan prince. The night before her wedding, Nejmah, who has taken a vow of chastity, prays that she will be made repulsive; in answer to her prayers, she sprouts a beard. In anger, Nejmah's father has her crucified. Nejmah's remaining six sisters then spread the story of their martyred sister throughout the world and establish the order named Wilgeforte (holy fire).

Abbess Clarice also tells her own remarkable story. Repulsed that their daughter has been born with a beard, Clarice's parents sell her to Luther and Anna Munrab, owners of a traveling circus. A timid teenager, Clarice is coaxed out of her shyness by a gypsy lion tamer named Nilo, who teaches her to tell fortunes. Clarice and Nilo eventually marry and inherit the circus, and upon Nilo's death, Clarice enters the convent.

Volume 2 continues the tale of the castle's odd inhabitants, filling in, with flashbacks, the life stories of Jain, Iron Henry, Dinah Cully, and Dr. Fell. Mrs. Cully tells the story of how she met and married her husband, a gentle giant named Tom. Rackham reveals the horrible events leading up to Dr. Fell's arrival at Castle Waiting.

A brilliant Venetian surgeon, Dr. Fell had volunteered to assist victims of the Black Death sent to the small island of Poveglia, a lazaretto, during a plague outbreak. A Poveglia native, Dr. Fell believed that he could find a cure that would then lead the doge of Venice to return Poveglia to its rightful people. When Dr. Fell's friends visit the island months later, they find everyone dead but Dr. Fell, who has gone mad with grief. Transported to Castle Waiting by his friends, Dr. Fell spends his time in search of a cure for the plague.

Tolliver and Dayne, two dwarves, arrive at Castle Waiting seeking clothes for a human fosterling (implied to be Snow White). Jain reveals that she owns a magic trunk that will produce anything she desires and offers to create an entire new wardrobe. Tolliver and Dayne make needed repairs to the castle, discover more hidden passageways, participate in a magical bowling tournament, and try to determine the real identity of Pindar.

Volumes

- *Castle Waiting:* Volume I (2006). Collects issues from Volumes 1-2 published by Cartoon Books and self-published by Medley from 1996 to 2001.

- *Castle Waiting:* Volume II (2010). Collects the fifteen issues published by Fantagraphics Books from 2006 to 2009.

Characters

- *Jain Solander*, posing as the countess of Carbas, is the daughter of a wealthy merchant. She has fled from her abusive husband to seek refuge at Castle Waiting, where she gives birth to Pindar. Her arrival at the castle sets in motion the narrative after the prologue.

- *Patience*, *Prudence*, and *Plenty* are the now elderly former ladies-in-waiting to the princess. The three handmaidens have stayed on at Castle Waiting because they have no other place to go.

- *Rackham Adjutant* is the kindly "storkman" steward of Castle Waiting. He is named for Arthur Rackham, a children's book illustrator and one of Medley's major artistic influences.

- *Sir Chess* is a horse-headed champion swordsman who stops at Castle Waiting between tournaments.

- *Dinah Lucina Cully* is the warmhearted and outspoken cook and housekeeper of the castle. A widower, she is the mother of Simon Cully, a slow-witted but sweet half-giant.

- *Iron Henry*, a devoted friend of the dwarves, is a taciturn blacksmith. He was brought to Castle Waiting dying of a broken heart and is kept alive by three forged iron rings that protect his heart.

- *Dr. Hieronymous Fell* is a formerly brilliant, but now mentally disturbed, Venetian physician who was driven mad during a Black Death outbreak. He wears a long beak mask adopted by surgeons treating plague victims.

- *Peaceful Warren* is a former barmaid who joins the Order of Solicitine and takes the name of Sister Peace.

- *Clytemnestra, Queen of the Nile*, a.k.a. *Mabel*, is the bearded star attraction of a traveling circus. She and Peaceful Warren, who are close friends, flee the circus to escape Mabel's abusive husband and seek refuge at the Abbey of St. Wilgeforte.

- *Abbess Clarice* is a former bearded fortune-teller who heads the Solicitine Order at the Abbey of St. Wilgeforte.
- *Tolliver* and *Dayne*, friends of Iron Henry, are dwarves who visit Castle Waiting unexpectedly. Their arrival in Volume 2 sets offs a series of events and adventures within the castle.

Artistic Style

In the afterword to the first issue of *Castle Waiting*, Medley reveals that while studying children's book illustration at college, she had wanted to illustrate the fairy tales of the Brothers Grimm, but she abandoned the idea when she discovered that what really interested her were "the background characters—their unexplained pasts, and their unresolved tales." *Castle Waiting* is her attempt to create a fairyland world of characters left behind after Sleeping Beauty and Prince Charming have abandoned the castle. To create her fantastical world, Medley blends storytelling elements—fairy tales, nursery rhymes, fables, folklore, mythology, and chivalric tales—while evoking a visual style reminiscent of classical fairy tales.

The two hardcover volumes of *Castle Waiting* physically look like collections of fairy tales, similar to Andrew Lang's colored fairy tale books. The volumes recall the artwork of such classical children's book authors as Rackham and William Heath Robinson, two of Medley's major influences. Her exquisitely detailed black-and-white art evokes medieval-style woodcuts, but with a much more charming and playful approach.

Medley's strong line work is clear and crisp and particularly suited to creating detailed backgrounds and the expressive faces of her eccentric characters. The tales within *Castle Waiting* are character-driven, and Medley takes the time to make each figure distinct and instantly identifiable. She did historical research on the medieval period, and all of the finely drawn details help to create a fully realized world. To force readers to reflect upon something that has happened within the story, on occasion, Medley will repeat identical panels, such as the four-panel sequence at the end of the prologue in which the characters slowly realize that the prince and princess have really left and will not be returning.

Themes

Although Linda Medley's setting and characters arise from fairy tales and fantasy, her themes are hearth-centered and leave no room for the dark uncanny. The story revolves around a group of eccentric societal misfits with troubled pasts who seek refuge in Sleeping Beauty's deserted castle, which takes on a new identity as their haven. At the castle, they live comfortable, everyday lives, and the theme of communal living prevails. The reader sees the characters eating dinner together, doing the dishes and other mundane tasks. Themes of acceptance come into play. Though Jain's son is born green with a snout and tail, everyone loves and accepts the infant without question.

Gender roles are often reversed or spoofed, and the theme of strong, independent women who have overcome oppression is stressed. A large portion of the first volume is devoted to the story of Sister Peace, who formerly belonged to an order of bearded nuns called the Solicitines. These beautiful bearded women joined this order to escape the misogynistic culture of their time. While both the female and male characters have harrowing adventures, it is the women who prevail, while the men crumble.

The theme of domestic violence against women runs through the work. Jain comes to the castle to flee her abusive husband's wrath. (She is pregnant, and the child is not his.) Mable escapes her equally abusive husband. While the interlinked stories take place in a medieval fantasy world, the individual story lines have a modern feminist point of view. Her female-oriented

Linda Medley

Graphic novelist Linda Medley is the antidote to the stereotypical comics fare of scantily clad women and wanton violence. With a refreshing feminist perspective, she uses her savvy prose and enchanting black-and-white images to tell stories about the people living in an abandoned castle (formerly home to Sleeping Beauty). Medley has a light touch, but the topics are deep: domestic violence, human rights, and religious freedom are par for the course. Her invented fairytales are deceptively simple yet extremely moving.

themes, which stress relationships over adventures, give the tales a modern feel.

Medley's themes are highlighted by her graphic art, featuring strong but simple drawings with much attention to detail. Her themes are best communicated in her large graphic panels where she omits words and delineates character through detailed facial expressions alone. The graphics are sometimes quite light and humorous even when the story line is serious.

Impact

When the *Castle Waiting* series began publication in 1996, it quickly developed a small but devoted following, especially with women readers, and went on to win prestigious Eisner and Harvey awards. Medley promoted her series at comic conventions, but because the issues were self-published and often difficult to obtain, her work remained largely unrecognized and underappreciated. All of that changed in 2006 when the first hardcover collection of the tales was published by Fantagraphics Books. Volume 1 was nominated for an Eisner Award for Best Graphic Novel, and the two hardback volumes received uniformly glowing reviews from such mainstream sources as *Fantasy and Science Fiction*, *Time*, *Kirkus Reviews*, *School Library Journal*, and *Library Journal*.

A writer, colorist, penciller, and children's book illustrator, Medley is a successful female graphic novelist in a field dominated by male authors and artists. Her work is often singled out for its women-centered narratives. While the adaptation of classic fairy tales to a graphic novel format is common, Medley's tales are unique in that they reimage or reinvent the traditional stories with a feminist slant.

Debora J. Richey and Mona Y. Kratzert

Further Reading

Shannon, Hale, Dean Hale, and Nathan Hale. *Rapunzel's Revenge* (2008).

Spiegelman, Art, and Françoise Mouly. *Big Fat Little Lit* (2006).

Willingham, Bill. *Fables* (2002-   ).

Bibliography

Coale, Mark. *Breaking the Panels: Over Seventy-Five Short Interviews from Around the Comics Industry.* Colora, Md.: O-Ghoshi Studios, 1998.

Furey, Emmett. "CCI Xtra: Spotlight on Linda Medley." *Comic Book Resources*, July 25, 2006. http://www.comicbookresources.com/?page=article&id=7689.

Medley, Linda. "Linda Medley Interview." Interview by Eric Evans. *The Comics Journal* 218 (December, 1999): 93-105.

Robins, Trina. *From Girls to Grrrlz: A History of [Women's] Comics from Teens to Zines*. San Francisco: Chronicle Books, 1999.

_____. *The Great Women Cartoonists*. New York: Watson-Guptill, 2001.

See also: *Mouse Guard; Journey into Mohawk Country; Age of Reptiles; The Adventures of Tintin*

CHICKEN WITH PLUMS

Author: Satrapi, Marjane

Artist: Marjane Satrapi (illustrator)

Publisher: L'Association (French); Pantheon Books (English)

First book publication: *Poulet aux prunes*, 2004 (English translation, 2006)

Publication History

Following the success of Marjane Satrapi's autobiographical *Persepolis: The Story of a Childhood* (2003) and *Persepolis 2: The Story of a Return* (2004) and *Embroideries* (2005), which tells the stories of the women in Satrapi's life, Satrapi decided to relate the tale of her great-uncle, one of Iran's most famous musicians. His story, *Chicken with Plums*, was originally published in French in 2004 as *Poulet aux prunes* by L'Association. The book was translated into English by Anjali Singh in 2006 and published by Pantheon Books. It was reprinted by Pantheon in 2009.

Plot

Chicken with Plums is the story of the last eight days of Nasser Ali Khan, one of Iran's most revered players of the *tar* (an Iranian lute). After his *tar* is broken, he cannot find a replacement and decides to go to bed and wait to die. Following the introduction of Nasser's situation, the narrative is structured as Nasser's final eight days. During these days, Nasser rests in bed, and the story flashes back, telling of his life and lost love, Irane, then flashes forward, showing the lives of his children and relatives in the future.

As it unfolds, the narrative reveals that, as a young adult, Nasser was in love with a wealthy beauty, Irane, but was forbidden from marrying her because of his dubious career as a musician. Desolate after losing Irane, he pours his love into his music, eventually marrying an adoring neighborhood girl, Nahid, at the urging of his mother, even though he does not love her.

Over the years, he becomes more and more selfish, doing little for his wife and family. Eventually, Nahid breaks his *tar*, angry at his lack of family

Chicken with Plums. (Courtesy of Pantheon Books)

responsibility. After Nasser's lapse into depression, Nahid makes chicken with plums, Nasser's favorite dish, in hopes of reconciling with her husband and lifting his spirits. He cannot forgive her and reiterates that he never loved her.

As he is walking to find a replacement instrument, Nasser happens upon Irane in the street. She claims she does not know him, and Nasser is heartbroken again. Depressed by Irane's rejection and his inability to replace his *tar*, Nasser decides life is not worth living, and he eventually passes away on the eighth day. The final images in the book are of Nasser's funeral and of the angel of death, Azrael.

Characters

- *Nasser Ali Khan* is Satrapi's uncle and an exceptional musician. A handsome man with dark hair and a moustache, he is moody and selfish.
- *Irane* is the daughter of a prosperous merchant and is Nasser's true love. She is particularly beautiful, with deep, almond-shaped eyes; a bob haircut; and a beauty mark on her cheek. She wears a stylish white hat and a fur coat. She returns Nasser's affection, but her father forbids them to marry. In Tehran, many years later (1958), she encounters Nasser on the street. She is still fashionably dressed, with high-heeled boots and a scarf, and looks much the same but for a few wrinkles.
- *Nahid*, Nasser's wife, is a teacher. She wears glasses and severe, shapeless dark dresses. She is depicted as stern and angry. She has been in love with Nasser since she was eight, when she acted as a messenger for him, delivering letters to a girl he admired. After Irane breaks Nasser's heart, Nahid visits him frequently, bringing small gifts. Nasser's mother encourages him to marry Nahid. After four children and many years of taking care of all the needs of the household, Nahid breaks Nasser's *tar* in a fit of rage after Nasser forgets to take their son to the doctor.
- *Azrael,* a.k.a. *the Angel of Death*, visits Nasser on the sixth day and on the eighth and final day. He is a shadowy, dark figure with horns—all black except for the white outline of his nose, eyes, and mouth. He is surprisingly jovial, laughing with Nasser, despite his mission. He also appears at the funeral scene, gazing in Irane's direction.
- *Abdi*, Nasser's younger brother, tries to lift his brother out of his depression by encouraging him to go see the film *Woman of the River* (also known as *The River Girl*, 1954), starring Sophia Loren. He has short hair, glasses, and a concerned expression. A flashback reveals that he excelled in school, while his brother failed. Nasser chastises him for becoming a communist and going to jail, leaving his family behind.
- *Farzaneh* is Nasser's favorite child. She resembles her father, and Nasser takes this as an indication of their special bond. She is a sweet-looking child, with pigtails and a round face. In a flashback, Nasser laments that his gift to her of pink sandals was not appropriate for the season, and Nahid chides him for his frivolous purchase. On the fifth day of his time in bed, Nasser assumes it is Farzaneh who is praying for him and keeping him alive. As an adult, she marries and divorces an actor and smokes profusely. She greets Satrapi and her mother while playing cards, smoking furiously. As an adult woman, she has a sleek bob haircut and wears a low-cut blouse. She dies shortly after Satrapi and her mother visit.
- *Mozaffar* is the youngest of Nasser's children and his least favorite. He is loquacious, overweight, and uninterested in art and music and does not look at all like his father. He is depicted with a round face and eyes and a wide smile. He is the only child to pray for his father. A flash-forward reveals that he married a woman named Gila in 1975 and had three children. In 1979, he worked as a manager in the army, but after the war broke out in 1980, the family settled in the United States.
- *Mina*, one of the oldest of Nasser's children, has a long nose and a bobbed haircut. She assists her mother when asked.
- *Reza*, another of Nasser's children, rarely appears.
- *Nasser's mother* favors her younger son, Abdi. In old age, she asks Nasser to stop praying for her so that she might die. She smoked continuously leading up to her death, and there is an enormous cloud of smoke around her body when she dies.
- *Marjane Satrapi* is the great-niece of Nasser and is the narrator of the story. However, she only makes a brief appearance in the actual narrative, when she goes with her mother to visit her aunt Farzaneh. Satrapi is pictured with long black hair and a small beauty mark on her nose.
- *Taji*, Satrapi's mother, goes to visit her cousin Farzaneh in 1998. She has close-cropped white hair and wrinkles. She scolds Farzaneh for smoking.

- *Mirza* owns a music store and tries to sell Nasser a new *tar* on numerous occasions. However, Nasser is never satisfied with any of the instruments and calls Mirza a charlatan. He is a kindly, solid man, depicted with a round face, short hair, a mustache, and glasses, and patiently tries to please the irritated Nasser until the latter insults his father.
- *Housang* sells *tars*, among other things, including opium. He sells Nasser a new *tar* at an outrageous price and gives Nasser and Mozaffar opium. Housang has a long nose and deep, dark circles under his eyes.

- *Parvine*, Nasser's sister, appears only as a silhouette at the door to Nasser's room. She thanks Nasser for his support during her divorce and pledges her love and gratitude.

Artistic Style

Satrapi is well known for her stark, black-and-white color scheme and the thick, dark lines of her drawing style, as popularized in her memoirs *Persepolis: A Story of a Childhood* and *Persepolis 2: A Story of Return*. Although her drawing technique has advanced somewhat over her career, her style has changed very little. Her figures are simply drawn, with few background

Chicken with Plums. (Courtesy of Pantheon Books)

details; the scenes are reminiscent of woodcuts or block prints. The figures are bold and minimally rendered with thick lines, bringing each character's facial expressions into sharp focus. Backgrounds are generally sparse, drawing attention to individual figures.

Satrapi sometimes uses traditional borders between panels but occasionally abandons the borders altogether. The strips generally follow a fairly traditional format of three panels per each of the three rows on a page. At times, Satrapi deviates from this format to emphasize a particular scene or moment.

The narrative text, written from Satrapi's point of view, and text within speech balloons are lettered in straightforward capital letters. Panels and words are spaced evenly, without being overcrowded or packed too much into any one frame or page. Satrapi's simple, unadorned style of drawing and lettering and her black-and-white color scheme reinforce the dualistic themes of good and bad, guilt and innocence, love and hate, and life and death that permeate the text. Satrapi's blunt style also reflects her childlike point of view as she narrates the story, looking back and forward through time.

Themes

While Satrapi is known primarily for her autobiographical memoirs, in *Chicken with Plums* she moves beyond her own personal story to consider the life story and development of another family member. *Chicken with Plums* has many themes. It is a story of lost love, family relationships, and resignation and loss. It also echoes the form of the *Künstlerroman*, the story of an artist's development, as the plot chronicles not only Nasser's personal life but also his career as a musician.

The book also functions in the form of a mystery; while Nasser's death is clear from the outset, the source of his sadness and exactly how the *tar* was broken are only revealed as the story progresses. The text explores the value of one man's life and the reasoning behind his decision to end it. *Chicken with Plums* asks the reader to consider both what aspects of life make it worth living and what one might do in the face of lost love.

Nasser's story resonates for those who have lost love, and the black-and-white colors, coupled with the unadorned figures, emphasize that this is a story of life-and-death decisions. Nasser refuses to dwell in the

margins or in the grayness of a life half-lived, choosing to die when he loses his music and his great love. The book serves to universalize and humanize the experience of love gone wrong, setting an archetypal story within Iran during the 1950's.

Impact

Chicken with Plums, along with Satrapi's other works, joins the growing trend of personal autobiographical and biographical narratives being told through the form of comic art, which includes Art Spiegelman's *Maus* (1986), Alison Bechdel's *Fun Home* (2006), and Lynda Barry's *One Hundred Demons* (2000-2001). Like many autobiographical comic-art endeavors, its realism is emphasized through the flaws of each character, by citing specific dates and historical events, and by introducing elements of storytelling into the plot of the narrative. Satrapi's work continues to draw readers to the genre of graphic memoir, and as the result of its appealing style and the intriguing moral issues that it addresses, *Chicken with Plums* garnered good reviews.

While *Chicken with Plums* did not make as much of an impact commercially or critically as *Persepolis* or *Persepolis 2*, the book was well received and expanded Satrapi's oeuvre, looking beyond her personal autobiography. It also introduces Satrapi's interest in a narrative with a male protagonist, whereas her earlier efforts focused on female experience.

Marjane Satrapi

Marjane Satrapi's graphic novel memoirs directly address American misconceptions and misunderstandings about the Iranian people and their history. Her vivid characters, universal storylines, and engaging drawings capture our hearts. Her graphic novels, set mainly in Iran, portray the everyday lives of Iranians, capturing both the emotional and the political with simple but eloquent drawings and just enough text to get her point across. The coming-of-age aspect of her stories will appeal to teen readers as well as adults.

Films

Chicken with Plums. Directed by Vincent Paronnaud and Marjane Satrapi. uFilm/Celluloid Dreams Productions/Studio Babelsberg, 2011. A live-action film version of *Chicken with Plums*, starring Isabella Rossellini and Mathieu Amalric. Satrapi wrote the screenplay and co-directed with Vincent Paronnaud.

Susan Kirtley

Further Reading

Barry, Lynda. *One Hundred Demons* (2000-2001).

Bechdel, Alison. *Fun Home: A Family Tragicomic* (2006).

Satrapi, Marjane. *Persepolis: The Story of a Childhood* (2003).

_____. *Persepolis 2: A Story of Return* (2004).

Bibliography

Davis, Rocio. "A Graphic Self: Comics as Autobiography in Marjane Satrapi's *Persepolis*." *Prose Studies* 27, no. 3 (2007): 264-279.

Naghibi, Nimi, and Andrew O'Malley. "Estranging the Familiar: 'East' and 'West' in Satrapi's *Persepolis*." *English Studies in Canada* 31, nos. 2-3 (June/September, 2005): 223-247.

Satrapi, Marjane. "Interview with Marjane Satrapi." Interview by Robert L. Root. *Fourth Genre: Explorations in Nonfiction* 9, no. 2 (Fall, 2007): 147-157.

Tensuan, Theresa. "Comic Visions and Revisions in the Work of Lynda Barry and Marjane Satrapi." *Modern Fiction Studies* 52, no. 4 (Winter, 2006): 948-964.

See also: *Embroideries; Persepolis; Maus: A Survivor's Tale; Fun Home; One Hundred Demons*

CITY OF GLASS

Author: Auster, Paul; Karasik, Paul; Mazzucchelli, David
Artist: David Mazzucchelli (illustrator)
Publisher: Avon Books
First book publication: 1994

Publication History

In the early 1990's, Avon Books editor Bob Callahan launching Neon Lit, a series of comics adaptations of noir literature, and brought in well-known comics creator Art Spiegelman as co-editor. Spiegelman had a personal connection with Paul Auster, a poet, playwright, and critic who had become an acclaimed novelist with the publication of his 1985 novella *City of Glass* (collected as part of his *New York Trilogy* in 1987). Spiegelman had previously invited Auster to contribute to a putative series of comics scripted by literary novelists, but Auster ultimately suggested someone adapt one of his existing novels instead. When the Neon Lit project came up, *City of Glass* seemed an ideal candidate.

Spiegelman passed the challenge on to David Mazzucchelli, who had risen to prominence with art for *Daredevil* (starting in 1985) and *Batman: Year One* (1987), before moving into the independent sector with work for Fantagraphics Books and Drawn and Quarterly. However, Mazzucchelli became frustrated with his attempts to restructure the text, feeling that he was only managing a superficial telling of the story. Spiegelman then contacted Paul Karasik, a former Fantagraphics editor, for assistance. By coincidence, Karasik had tried some rough layouts for an adaptation of *City of Glass* after first reading the book in 1987. He produced a new set of breakdowns that were more successful and Mazzucchelli remained on the project to develop Karasik's breakdowns. The two artists also met with Auster to seek his input. As a result, the final piece was a collaborative effort.

Plot

Daniel Quinn, a writer of detective fiction, receives two telephone calls asking for Paul Auster of the Auster Detective Agency. On the second call, he claims that he

(AP Photo)

Paul Auster

Paul Auster is the award-winning postmodern novelist best known for his ability to blend absurdism and existentialism within the generic tropes of the crime novel. His *New York Trilogy*, comprised of the sequentially published novellas *City of Glass* (1985), *Ghosts* (1986), and *The Locked Room* (1986), was the inspiration for the graphic novel version of *City of Glass*, adapted in 1994 by Paul Karasik and drawn by David Mazzucchelli. The book tells the story of a private investigator who descends into madness as he is drawn deeper into a case. Auster's complex language and extremely minimalistic plot made the process of adaptation extremely challenging, though Karasik and Mazzucchelli worked diligently to produce a work that was faithful to the source novella and that fully utilized the attributes of the comics form.

is Auster and agrees to meet and discuss a case. Quinn is hired by a traumatized young man named Peter Stillman, Jr., who fears that his father, just released from prison, is coming to kill him. Peter's wife, Virginia, pays Quinn five hundred dollars to find Peter's father, follow him, and warn Peter of any danger.

Quinn researches the case. He reads the elder Stillman's book, which concerns the Fall of Man. A seventeenth-century pastor named Henry Dark believed that humans had forgotten the language they had spoken in the Garden of Eden and that relearning this language could restore paradise. Stillman, Sr., tried to discover this language by conducting cruel experiments on his son, forcing him to grow up without human contact. This is the reason Stillman, Sr., was imprisoned.

Quinn sees Stillman, Sr., arrive in New York and follows him. When the two finally converse, Stillman, Sr., admits that he invented Henry Dark and that those deranged beliefs were his own. Stillman, Sr., seems insane but harmless, collecting discarded objects and giving them new names.

Quinn loses the trail and then loses contact with his employers. Out of ideas, Quinn goes to find the real Paul Auster, but he knows nothing of the Stillmans or detective work. Eventually Quinn decides to watch the Stillmans' apartment around the clock, living in the alleyway opposite. After months, he gives up and goes home, but he finds his apartment has been let to someone else. Auster tells him Stillman, Sr., committed suicide. Quinn returns to the Stillmans' apartment, finding it empty. Staying there, he fills the rest of his notebook on the case.

The narrator, a friend of Auster, returns from abroad. The narrator hears the story from Auster and castigates him for not doing more to help. The two of them search for Quinn but find only his notebook.

Characters

- *Daniel Quinn*, the protagonist, is a thirty-five-year-old man. He was a poet, playwright, and literary critic but gave up those endeavors after his wife and son died. He now writes mystery novels under the name William Wilson, and his mental state appears to be declining. When he receives

calls intended for "The Paul Auster Detective Agency," he poses as Auster and accepts the case.

- *Peter Stillman, Jr.*, is a young man damaged by his father's language experiments. He was locked in a darkened room as a child, was permitted no contact with the outside world, and was beaten if he used adult language. He struggles to speak coherently. He hires Quinn to seek out his father.

- *Virginia Stillman*, an attractive young woman, is Peter's wife. Formerly his speech therapist, she married him to get him out of a psychiatric hospital. Because Peter struggles to communicate clearly, she fills in important details for Quinn.

- *Peter Stillman, Sr.*, is an elderly man, disheveled and disordered. He was an academic: After the death of his wife, he gave up work to look after their son. When his experiments were discovered, his son was taken into custody, and he was sent to prison. In the present, his sentence is over, and he returns to New York.

- *Paul Auster* is a thirty-eight-year-old writer entirely based on the real-life Auster but is not the narrator of *City of Glass*, who is a separate character. When Quinn goes to meet him, Auster says he knows nothing of the Stillmans or why anyone should think he runs a detective agency.

Artistic Style

Appropriately, Auster's clear, stripped-down prose is accompanied by a simple, uncluttered visual style, in black and white. This was partly dictated by the small panel size, but it was also a choice Mazzucchelli made to facilitate Karasik's intention that some sections of the book should use iconic imagery. Hence, characters' neutral expressions are sometimes rendered with no mouth, and the background is often left unoccupied as in cartoons. The flexibility of this style allows for playfulness that connects with the themes of Auster's original story. The completed art bears more resemblance to Mazzucchelli's style than Karasik's, but the drafts passed between each of them. The art style uses heavy lines and is largely clean and orderly but not quite slick; the figures are slightly angular, and some rough edges are present.

The book uses a nine-panel grid: Karasik initially planned to adhere more strictly to this structure, but Mazzucchelli opened it out, merging some panels to accommodate Neon Lit's small page size. The regimented style is appropriate to Auster's prose but also reflects the streets of New York. The regular intervals often serve to add punch to prose that has been drawn from the novella and broken down into captions. Mazzucchelli's first attempt, from before Karasik came aboard, incorporates longer chunks of the text in captions, and this rhythm is lacking.

The style breaks down toward the end in two ways. First, the artwork becomes less orderly after Quinn begins to "lose his grip." The lines become rougher and sketchier, in tune with Quinn's deterioration. Finally, the panel structure also breaks down: first with broadening gutters, then with panel layouts drawn freehand, before the panels seem to finally break loose and drift away from the page. Once Quinn's story is over, another style is adopted for the entrance of the narrator. There are no panel borders, and the bold chiaroscuro lines of the main text are replaced by a softer gray wash. Quinn's world has vanished, and the way the world looked, which gave the reader such insights, has vanished with it.

Themes

The novella's major themes concern language and the naming of things. When Stillman, Sr., says that when things are broken they need new names, he is unwittingly talking about Quinn, who was broken by the deaths of his wife and child and became William Wilson. Throughout, the reader encounters shifting identities, names lost and replicated, and the confusion of one thing for another. The comics adaptation adds its own angle on this subject.

After the blackout of the first page, the first images include a slow zoom away from a telephone. By panel four, the zoom seems complete, but it continues, revealing that the "telephone" is actually an image in the corner of a notepad, on which rests a telephone. The reality of what the reader sees is immediately brought into question, but more important, the reader has been led to mistake a symbol for the thing itself.

Stillman, Sr., believes that words and the objects they described were once interchangeable. This is illustrated when Adam invents the word "shadow," and his shadow is shaped like the word. In a comic, text and images coexist and are able to interact in a way that would be contrived onscreen. The comic also draws the readers' attention to different typographical approaches: The disordered speech of Stillman, Jr., features a mixture of upper- and lower-case letters, while the biblical delusions of grandeur Stillman, Sr., holds are suggested by the use of initiums (the large, elaborate initials in an illuminated manuscript) in his speech balloons.

In flashbacks and exposition of abstract ideas, the book draws on other types of imagery, which, as Mazzucchelli observes, allow "the style of drawing to act as another layer of information in this already dense presentation." Virginia's narration of her husband's traumatic past renders everything in iconic imagery, in the minimal style of universal symbols, which has the effect of depersonalizing the narrative. At the other extreme, the artists sometimes import images, using something far more detailed than their normal style. For instance, they reproduce a 1563 painting of the Tower of Babel by Pieter Bruegel the Elder. (This is in sharp contrast to the rest of the page, which uses a piece of commercial art to make a visual pun regarding New York being the "big apple" and the new paradise.) Yet another type of image is imported when Quinn is placed against a street map of New York. The spectrum this creates is reminiscent of Scott McCloud's scale of pictures and words in *Understanding Comics* (1993), running from "received" information to "perceived" information.

Much of the artwork in *City of Glass* suggests pictures becoming more like words. If *City of Glass* is primarily a novella about language, its comics adaptation expands its range to encompass the language of images.

Impact

The Neon Lit series produced only one more book, Barry Gifford's *Perdita Durango* (1995). According to a contemporary review of *City of Glass* in *The New York Times*, William Gresham's *Nightmare Alley* was to have been the third in the series but this never materialized. In his introduction to Picador's 2004 reprint, Spiegelman called *City of Glass* a "breakthrough" in the field and so it was. Karasik made this seemingly impossible project work, and his approach to the adaptation is instructive to anyone looking to undertake a similar project.

Some reviewers have even suggested that the adaptation is a worthy equal to the novella, a rare accolade for this type of book. However, few works like it have been published since. Turning novels into comics still carries the stigma of illustrated classics for readers unwilling to read the so-called proper book. Additionally, most comics adaptations of literature are of out-of-copyright works, for understandable financial reasons, and so postmodern fiction is not considered. However, the U.K. publisher SelfMadeHero has led the way in adapting some of the more challenging classics, including adaptations of Franz Kafka's *The Trial* (2008), by David Zane Mairowitz; Laurence Sterne's *Tristram Shandy* (1996), by Martin Rowson; and Miguel de Cervantes's *Don Quixote* (2011), by Rob Davis.

Eddie Robson

Further Reading

Mazzucchelli, David. *Asterios Polyp* (2009).

Karasik, Paul, and Judy Karasik. *The Ride Together: A Brother and Sister's Memoir of Autism in the Family* (2004).

Rowson, Martin, and Laurence Sterne. *The Life and Opinions of Tristram Shandy, Gentleman* (2010).

Bibliography

Coughlan, David. "Paul Auster's *City of Glass*: The Graphic Novel." *Modern Fiction Studies* 52, no. 4 (2006): 832-854.

Karasik, Paul. "Coffee with Paul Karasik." Interview by Bill Kartalopoulos. *Indy Magazine*, Spring, 2004. http://www.indyworld.com/indy/spring_2004/karasik_interview/index.html.

Mazzucchelli, David. "Three Questions for David Mazzucchelli." Interview by Bill Kartalopoulos. *Indy Magazine*, Spring, 2004. http://www.indyworld.com/indy/spring_2004/mazzucchelli_interview/index.html.

See also: *Asterios Polyp*

CLUMSY

Author: Brown, Jeffrey
Artist: Jeffrey Brown (illustrator)
Publisher: Top Shelf Comics
First book publication: 2002

Publication History

In 2000, Jeffrey Brown left Grand Rapids, Michigan, at age twenty-five to pursue an M.F.A. at the School of the Art Institute of Chicago. Although a lifelong comic book enthusiast, Brown came to Chicago with ambitions to be a serious, commercially viable painter. At the same time, he kept carefully bound volumes of diary-like sketchbooks in which he recorded his emotional life. A year into the program, Brown began to feel as if his studio paintings did not reflect his best work and were not generating enthusiasm among his teachers. He met Chris Ware, only five years his senior, whose groundbreaking graphic novel *Jimmy Corrigan: The Smartest Kid on Earth* (2000) had just been released. With Ware's encouragement, Brown decided to develop his sketchbooks.

As Brown was in the midst of a catastrophic breakup of a year-long relationship, the material that came most readily to him was the raw elements of that relationship. He shaped the experience into a manuscript that related the breakup in a nonlinear narrative of more than 100 one- and two-page vignettes, accompanied by his own deliberately crude, childlike drawings. The work became his M.F.A. thesis. It was initially rejected by publishers, most notably Top Shelf Comics and Fantagraphics Books. At Ware's suggestion, Brown photocopied one hundred copies at a Kinko's and circulated them himself in small comic book outlets around Chicago. A producer for *This American Life*, an influential syndicated talk show on National Public Radio, happened on a copy and pursued Brown for a segment. The exposure caused an upsurge in demand, as did Internet buzz about the book's originality and its frank treatment of adult relationships. Brown was subsequently signed by Top Shelf Comics, which released *Clumsy* in 2002.

Clumsy. (Courtesy of Top Shelf Publications)

Plot

Clumsy chronicles a one-year, largely long-distance relationship between Jeff, a hypersensitive graduate student in art and design who suffers from Crohn's disease (periodic inflammations of the digestive system), and Theresa, a freelance ceramist. The plotline frustrates retelling, as Brown mirrors the fragmented logic of recollection by using a nonlinear narrative. Events during the relationship are recounted in apparently random order, although later editions of the book provide a time line. Thus, reading the novel mimics Jeff's own memory, itself clumsy and inefficient, as readers move through emotional highlights, both wonderful and painful.

Jeff and Theresa meet during a summer road trip with two mutual friends. Jeff is just four months past a long-term relationship and is initially put off by Theresa, who looks to him like a renegade hippie. However, during the course of the trip, in the close confines of his friend's camper, Jeff and Theresa find their attraction irresistible. When they make love for the first time, they only know each other's first names.

The vignettes reveal tender moments. They huddle close in a steady rain to watch airplanes land, comb a beach for shells, and doodle on placemats in Arby's. Theresa gives Jeff a haircut. They exchange Valentine's Day gifts. She poses nude while he sketches her. They go on a series of increasingly competitive dates that include air hockey, bowling, go-carts, foosball, and miniature golf.

There are also moments that recount with unflinching candor the couple's quickly escalating sexual life, including mutual oral sex in Jeff's bedroom at his home while his parents are in the other room, making love during Theresa's period, Jeff's inability to enjoy sex while wearing a condom (and the subsequent pregnancy scare), Theresa's gratitude following a tectonic orgasm, and phone sex (as most of their relationship is long distance). There are also petty fights over her smoking, his neediness, her fantasies about sleeping with female comic book heroes, his inclination to pout, and her obsession with the imperfections of her body. If there is a narrative center, it is the revelation late in the story that Theresa, too, has been diagnosed with Crohn's disease.

The breakup, in the closing pages, is executed over the phone, appropriate for a relationship that has been long distance. Jeff calls Theresa at her Florida home. Her mother summons her to the phone, saying that "John" is calling. Paranoid, Jeff asks anxiously about John, and discovers that he is a friend who has been calling Theresa recently. This leads to a conversation in which Theresa ends their relationship, saying that she is tired of the pain that she and Jeff cause each other. The closing vignette is an earlier phone conversation during which Jeff and Theresa joked lightly about getting married, and the last frame shows Jeff alone on his single bed, the phone at his feet.

Jeff is portrayed as overly sensitive and needy, a depiction that some critics have found to be melodramatic. Partially in response to this criticism, Brown published a kind of parody of *Clumsy* in 2004. Titled *Be a Man*, it offered a much different take on Jeff, using the same experiences but portraying him as something of a chauvinist who will say anything to get Theresa into bed.

Characters

- *Jeff*, the protagonist, is a twentysomething art student living in Chicago. His face is shadowed by a "retrogrunge" stubble, and he carries an unflattering paunch. Socially clumsy and introspective, Jeff is given to sweet gestures rather than earnest communication, often communicating his emotions via his sketches or with long, meaningful stares. In his first serious relationship, the sensitive Jeff evinces his radical neediness, a smothering attachment that masks the emptiness of his larger life and creates inevitable friction in his relationship.

- *Theresa*, Jeff's love interest, is a twentysomething ceramist who specializes in freelance pottery work. Seen objectively—that is, not through the lens of Jeff's obsession—Theresa is something of a whiner with significant self-esteem issues; she harps on the fact that she did not finish high school and is uncomfortable with her body, seeing herself as fat and considering her body hair to be unsightly. Despite this, she is quick to use sex as a substitute for intimacy. Against the spongy and effeminate Jeff, she is cool, less enamored with the romantic. Nothing about her is typically feminine. She is fiercely competitive on their dates and in bed, is forthright about sex and frank about her orgasms, and is drawn to female superheroes such as Jet Girl and Xena. When Theresa learns that she has Crohn's disease, she does not indulge in self-pity, but rather is matter-of-fact about the diagnosis.

Artistic Style

Brown creates a visual format that reflects the naïveté and vulnerability of his fictional persona. The artwork consists of rough black-and-white pen sketches that mimic the slapdash composition style of an adolescent, resembling more the immediacy and untutored honesty of study-hall doodling than the work of an M.F.A. candidate. The handwritten dialogue, rendered in clumsy bubbles, is irregular, cramped, and difficult to read at times, as Brown uses the visual text to impede communication with the reader and thereby underscore the growing emotional distance between his two characters. Some dialogue is actually scratched out, or inserted into the text with a caret. Lines carelessly violate the frame, perspective within the frame is skewered, and everyday objects such as telephones, tables, and windows are rendered without realistic detailing.

The bodies, critical given the frank sexual content, are decidedly nonerotic. Leg hair looks like lesions, Jeff's facial hair resembles runaway acne, and Theresa's pubic hair is a shocking, even angry, crosshatching of scribbled lines. Visually, each page creates a sense of absence and isolation. The six tight panels on each page underscore the loneliness at the thematic center of the work: Each frame maintains its own integrity, never touching another, and each page is latticed with overly generous white space.

Themes

As a "perzine," that is, an autobiographical work (a "personal zine"), *Clumsy* does not aspire to grand themes. Rather, much like a talk show that is earnestly invested in revealing the joy and agony of relationships and the risks of intimacy, *Clumsy* finds its deepest rapport with readers who share Brown's disarmingly honest perspective on the realities of a young person's first serious relationship. The *Seinfeld*-esque vignettes record the entire arc of such a relationship, revealing ordinary elements with wrenching realism: the small gestures of caring, the thrill of discovering sexual intimacy, the squabbles over trivia, the settled routine of dating, and the special tensions of relationships maintained across distance.

Honesty, then, is perhaps Brown's most compelling theme. He neither pretties up his persona's character nor distorts his former girlfriend into a convenient villain. At one point, Jeff and Theresa attend a Chicago taping of *The Jerry Springer Show*, in its day

---

Jeffrey Brown

Jeffrey Brown's deceptively simple illustrative style examines relationships under a microscope—most frequently, his own. In a series of adult collections, Brown chronicles, often in nonchronological order, moments from his day-to-day life, usually focusing on the minutiae of small interactions and specific moments, including several romantic relationships and his own evolution as a cartoonist. His heavily caricaturized characters capture surprisingly subtle emotions and much of his work has an observational quality. He has also parodied his own style and his love of popular culture in several works, including the Transformers spoof *Incredible Change-Bots*.

---

the epitome of trashy talk shows, in which cartoonish guests offered the most lurid and extreme examples of relationship nightmares. Although they join the audience in shouting at the guests, both Jeff and Theresa are disappointed, finding the show to be dishonest and silly. In this way, Brown underscores his own decision to maintain an honest account of a relationship and to resist the cartoonish, an ironic gesture given his medium. Like viewers of more sophisticated talk shows, readers of Brown's novel can certainly gain some insight (be less possessive, more considerate, and more patient, for example), but Brown does not insist on such themes. The theme here is broader: Brown's assertion that the most personal stories of love are significant in and of themselves.

Impact

That Brown grew up enthralled by the superheroes of classic Marvel Comics and the *Transformers* series is a reminder of the dimension of his impact on the graphic novel. *Clumsy* counters the assumption that graphic novels must indulge in extravagant fantasy or escape into grandiose conceptions of alternative realities animated by high-tech innovations and peopled by caricatural superheroes and supervillains. Rather, it introduced into the graphic novels of its era the concept of an intimacy between the writer and the reader. *Clumsy* is a novel created by the writer's decision to use the format to share the most intimate details of his personal life, details that would find resonance at the most intimate levels of readers. Despite its disarmingly childlike drawings, *Clumsy* required a mature appreciation.

Although it was hardly the first such autobiographical effort, *Clumsy* created a receptive audience for low-key graphic novels about the complex relationship issues experienced by the adolescent readers who comprise the genre's main demographic. Much like the minimalist short fiction of a generation earlier, in which writers pared down the presentation of character and plot to reveal the hard realities of intimacy with often-uncomfortable directness, Brown's novel suggests that the graphic novel genre could tackle thorny coming-of-age experiences without relying on splashy, colorful sheets. *Clumsy* is a forthright treatment of sex, which had long been the province of traditional novels.

Brown returned to the genre to finish publishing what has come to be described as his "girlfriend trilogy," which includes *Clumsy*; *Unlikely* (2003), a prequel about Jeff losing his virginity a year before he meets Theresa; and *AEIOU: Any Easy Intimacy* (2005), a sequel about another relationship, this one with a video-store clerk named Sophia. These are not happy narratives. Brown created for Generation X a subgenre of the graphic novel that follows a circumscribed arc

in which relationships apparently cannot resist the centripetal pull toward disappointment. The books thus generate an oppressive sensibility in which Brown's readers are left to return to a grown-up world, one that diminishes rather than rewards expectations and leaves sensitive hearts profoundly alone.

Joseph Dewey

Further Reading

Brown, Chester. *I Never Liked You* (1994).
Clowes, Daniel. *Ghost World* (1997).
Doucet, Julie. *My New York Diary* (2004).

Bibliography

Brown, Jeffrey. "When Jeffrey Was Brown: An Interview." Interview by Ian Brill. *Comic Book Galaxy*, 2010. http://www.comicbookgalaxy.com/jbrown.html.

Montero, Patrick. "Comic Book Artist Jeffrey Brown: More Than Meets the Eye." *New York Daily News*, November 1, 2007. http://articles.nydailynews.com/2007-11-01/entertainment/17905837_1_comics-fantagraphics-graphic-novel.

See also: *I Never Liked You; Ghost World; Black Hole; Blankets*

COLOR TRILOGY, THE

Author: Kim Dong Hwa

Artist: Kim Dong Hwa (illustrator)

Publisher: Daewon Culture Industry (Korean); First Second Books (English)

First serial publication: *The Story of Life on the Golden Fields*, 1992-1995 (English translation, 2009)

First book publication: 1995-1996 (English translation, 2009)

Publication History

While observing his ill, aged mother sleeping, South Korean *manhwa*, or comics, writer and artist Kim Dong Hwa realized that his mother had once been a young, attractive girl. Kim began to imagine what his mother's early years must have been like and later investigated her childhood more formally. These efforts resulted in the creation of *The Color of Earth*, *The Color of Water*, and *The Color of Heaven*, or the Color trilogy, as it is sometimes known, which is loosely based on some of his mother's childhood experiences.

The Color trilogy, originally titled *The Story of Life on the Golden Fields*, was first serialized in the *manhwa* magazine *Twenty Seven* beginning in 1992. The series concluded three years later. Between August, 1995, and April, 1996, Daewon Culture Industry published the work in five volumes. Kim noted that he had wanted to publish the work as a trilogy, but regulations at that time limited *manhwa* to no more than 180 pages. Eventually this standard was lifted, and in 2003 a three-volume set of the work was published in South Korea.

The trilogy was translated into French and published by Franco-Belgian publisher Casterman as *Histoire couleur terre* in 2006 and 2007. In November, 2007, Casterman released a boxed set containing all three volumes. In 2008, Planeta DeAgostini published a three-volume Spanish edition titled *Historias color tierra: Los pequeños cuentos di mi madre*. In 2009, First Second Books published the trilogy in English with each volume titled individually: *The Color of Earth*, *The Color of Water*, and *The Color of Heaven*.

Kim Dong Hwa

One of the best-known names in Korean manwha since the 1970's, Kim Dong Hwa has had three books translated into English by First Second Books. The Color trilogy—comprised of *The Color of Earth*, *The Color of Water*, and *The Color of Heaven*—tells the story of Ehwa, a sweet-faced young girl in the provinces of Korea who cares for her mother. The books are keenly nostalgic for a simpler time in Korean life, but are also inflected by Freudian themes surrounding the sexual awakening of a young woman. Kim's art is deliberately flat, with thin lines and occasionally florid imagery. Like many manwha, the work shifts between extremely cartoonish figures and elaborately detailed backgrounds. Among his other titles are *The Story of Kiaseng*, *Bug Boy*, *Ugly*, and *The Yellow Story*.

Plot

Kim's trilogy, set in rural pre-Korean War (1950-1953) Korea, presents a linear coming-of-age narrative that follows Ehwa from age seven to seventeen. The only daughter of a young widow who runs the village tavern, Ehwa is bright and energetic, but she has remained innocent and naïve. As the narrative progresses, she learns about the physical differences between the sexes. She also experiences her first crush, along with the confusion it brings; unrequited love; recognition of her emotional and sexual longings; a painful separation from her love; marriage; and, finally, her first sexual experience.

Much of what Ehwa learns about sex originates from her interactions with Bongsoon, her more worldly and adventurous friend. Bongsoon teaches Ehwa about the sex act, genitalia, and masturbation. Much of what Ehwa learns about romance originates from conversations with her mother, who uses euphemistic flower, insect, and bird metaphors to describe women's hearts and their relationships with men.

As Ehwa matures, she experiences three loves. At nine, she encounters Chung-Myung, a boy monk, on a narrow footbridge. Though they have few additional encounters, the two maintain an infatuation with each other for several years. Chung-Myung considers renouncing his Buddhist vows for Ehwa, but the physical and spiritual distances between them are too great to overcome.

At fifteen, Ehwa, following Bongsoon's advice, tosses a dried flower into the reflecting pool, hoping to see the face of her true love appear. As Ehwa stares at the water, the face of Sunoo, the orchard farmer's son, materializes. Turning around, Ehwa sees Sunoo and becomes infatuated with him. Although Sunoo is kind to Ehwa, he does not return her affections. Ehwa is confused and brokenhearted when he returns to school, leaving her behind.

Finally, Ehwa falls in love with Duksam, a farmhand from a neighboring village. As the relationship between the two intensifies, Duksam's elderly employer, Master Cho, meets Ehwa and is aroused by her beauty. He sends Duksam on an extended trip and attempts to convince Ehwa's mother to sell Ehwa to him. Ehwa's mother sees through the ruse and refuses the offer. Upon returning and learning of his master's deceit, Duksam destroys some of Master Cho's property, but then he must flee for his life. He promises Ehwa that he will return for her and joins a fishing vessel in a distant coastal city. Ehwa dutifully waits for Duksam's return. Upon his homecoming, the two marry and experience their first conjugal union.

A secondary narrative presents Ehwa's mother's romance with a traveling pictograph painter. The first evening he comes through the village, he asks Ehwa's mother for a place to sleep for the night. He leaves a paint brush behind, promising to return for it. Ehwa's mother tacks the brush to the wall and spends much of her leisure time pining for him to return. As his visits increase, she eventually displays seven brushes on the wall. The narrative ends after Ehwa's wedding night, with Ehwa's mother sitting outside her home. She tells the picture man that it is a woman's fate to wait, but that she had never thought she would be waiting for her daughter.

Volumes

- *The Color of Earth* (2009). Follows Ehwa from seven to fifteen and presents her first two relationships, with Chung-Myung and Sunoo.
- *The Color of Water* (2009). Follows Ehwa from fifteen to sixteen and presents her relationship with Duksam and his flight from the village.
- *The Color of Heaven* (2009). Follows Ehwa from sixteen to seventeen and presents Duksam's return and their subsequent marriage.

Characters

- *Ehwa*, the protagonist, is a young, beautiful girl who is energetic, bright, and curious, though rather sheltered. She is presented between the ages of seven and seventeen and slowly comes of age; the story culminates in her marriage and first sexual experience.
- *Ehwa's mother*, a secondary protagonist, is a beautiful young widow who believes in highly romantic notions of love. She artfully fends off the sexual advances of some of her male customers. She also teaches Ehwa about women's hearts, speaking euphemistically. She develops a passionate relationship with a traveling pictograph artist.
- *The Picture Man* is a traveling pictograph artist who sells small paintings and calligraphy. After spending the night at Ehwa's mother's house, he intermittently returns unannounced but leaves a paint brush behind after each visit. He develops an intimate relationship with Ehwa's mother.
- *Dongchul* is a childhood friend of Ehwa. He is sexually preoccupied, asking to see under Ehwa's skirt, often fondling his penis inside his pants while in public, and talking incessantly about sexual matters. He and Bongsoon develop a relationship and appear to experiment sexually with each other.
- *Bongsoon* is a childhood friend of Ehwa and her chief instructor in sexual matters. She convinces Ehwa to "play wedding" and wrestles Ehwa to the ground to demonstrate how a man and a woman "become one." She later convinces Ehwa to "play adults," telling Ehwa to lie down and

imagine a man she likes as Bongsoon fondles her. Ehwa protests, after which Bongsoon teaches her how to masturbate.

- *Chung-Myung* is Ehwa's first love. He is an eight-year-old monk when he first meets her. Over the following seven years, he is conflicted by his deep longing for Ehwa and his Buddhist vows of celibacy.

- *Sunoo* is Ehwa's second, though unrequited, love. He is a slight, handsome boy and the son of a relatively wealthy orchard farmer. Ehwa first meets him after seeing his reflection in the reflecting pool. He is kind to Ehwa but does not return her feelings. Upon his recuperation from an injury, he returns to school, leaving Ehwa brokenhearted.

- *Duksam* is a large, ruggedly built farmhand from another village who eventually falls in love with Ehwa. He desires to have the financial means to care for Ehwa before marrying her. He flees his village after destroying his master's property because his master had attempted to claim Ehwa for himself. Duksam tells Ehwa he will work on fishing vessels, save sufficient money, and return to marry her. He finds the separation too painful and returns earlier than expected to marry Ehwa.

- *Master Cho* is the master of the house where Duksam works and lives. He is old and decrepit, but upon seeing Ehwa, he becomes aroused and grows obsessed with possessing her. He sends Duksam out of town and makes multiple futile attempts at securing Ehwa for himself. He tries to kill Duksam after Duksam destroys some of his property.

Artistic Style

The Color trilogy is printed in black and white, although some international editions include a few pages of color. Kim's drawings of landscapes, structures, and clothing are highly detailed, while facial features are quite simple. The characters are fairly typical of *manhwa*, as they are drawn with realistic features, clothing, and hair.

The covers of each volume illustrate Ehwa's maturation. The cover of *The Color of Earth* depicts Ehwa as a seven-year-old, awkwardly holding her right elbow while looking over her right shoulder. *The Color of Water* presents Ehwa sitting with a bouquet of flowers in her left hand as she looks coquettishly to her left. *The Color of Heaven* displays a confident Ehwa holding a red flower in her right hand and wearing traditional wedding garb.

Kim uses distinct gutters to separate panels while varying the number of panels per page. Most pages contain three to five panels, but a few contain six or seven. Kim also includes single-panel pages as well as two-page panels. A few full-page panels bleed off the page.

Kim's art contains a great many visual symbols. Most notable are the recurring images of butterflies, a traditional Korean symbol of happiness and love freely chosen. Kim's narrative associates butterflies with potential suitors as well as personality types. Other notable symbols in the trilogy are shoes, indicating the status of a relationship; brushes on the wall, suggesting the promise of a return; rain, signifying life transitions; and more than thirty varieties of flowers, representing the multiplicity of human characteristics, emotions, and relationships. Adding to the authenticity of the setting, Kim presents lush images common in rural prewar Korea. He draws the female characters in traditional dress (*hanbok*) and includes images of small structures used by farmers for shaded rest breaks (*wondoomak*), small village temples containing guardian deities (*seonghwangdang*), small oil lamps (*horongbool*), wooden drums struck by Buddhist priests (*moktak*), and large jars used to store soy sauce, soybean paste, and red-pepper paste (*jangdok*).

Kim's drawings of Ehwa and Duksam consummating their marriage are rather minimalist, as genitalia are obscured and Ehwa is drawn without nipples. The scene is, however, juxtaposed with many symbolic images: a droplet forming a ripple, which transforms into a ring of flowers hovering over their bed; flowers streaming down around the lovers; two hearts slowly converging; paper lanterns swaying; a wave transforming into two cloud-like bodies intertwined; rain pouring; the sun blazing; Duksam running among sand dunes and splashing in a puddle; gongs striking loudly; a pestle vigorously grinding inside a mortar; dandelion seeds floating toward the sky, transforming into kites; a tall waterfall crashing; and, finally, two butterflies frolicking in flight.

Themes

One pervasive theme throughout Kim's trilogy is the highly romanticized view that freely chosen love supersedes all other concerns for women. Ehwa's mother ruminates on love and romance throughout the work, reinforcing the view of women as primarily passive parties in love. Ehwa's mother sits nightly on her front stoop, facing the village entrance and waiting for the picture man to return. She views women as lovesick creatures who must faithfully wait for their men to return. Ehwa and her mother appear to think of little else but romance, which is repeatedly expressed in their euphemistic discussions about the characteristics of flowers.

Though presenting highly patriarchal notions of women's inner lives, Kim's work does offer pointed criticism of the suffering women endure in arranged marriages, noting that new wives experience years of agonizing subservience to their in-laws. Ehwa's mother's privileging of freely chosen love would have run counter to the culture of her day, and she rebuffs two offers for Ehwa, allowing Ehwa to experience the happiness of love freely chosen.

The importance of feminine beauty in capturing the heart of a man is another prevalent theme. Ehwa's mother often gives Ehwa beauty tips. Bongsoon and Ehwa discuss the marks of feminine beauty by making lists of threes, determining that to be considered beautiful, women must have clear skin, straight teeth, and delicate hands; black eyes, eyebrows, and eyelashes; red lips, cheeks, and nails; soft bodies, hair, and hands; short teeth, ears, and legs; thin lips, waists, and ankles; voluptuous arms, bottoms, and thighs; and small nipples, noses, and heads.

Impact

Although Kim's work has been lauded by some as an example of *manhwa* that deals with mature content, many critics and readers have objected to its uncritical handling and seeming endorsement of traditional patriarchal views of gender roles. Ehwa and her mother seem to accept traditional gender roles and stereotypes. The importance of feminine beauty, women's obsession with romance and state of perpetual lovesickness, the undesirability of daughters, women's tolerance of men's sexual harassment, women's fate to endure, double standards for men and women, narrowly defined boundaries for women, the necessity of cooking well to make husbands happy, the misery of unmarried women, and women's contentment with simple pleasures are all presented with little to no disapproval in the trilogy.

Some critics of the work have also called attention to the negative portrayal of Bongsoon's licentiousness as compared to Ehwa's chasteness, noting that Bongsoon's features are piglike; however, Ehwa repeatedly notes that she wishes she could be as bold as Bongsoon even though she is often scandalized by Bongsoon's behavior. In some ways, the narrative challenges traditional views of women's roles. Ehwa's mother is a young widow who owns and operates the village tavern, which would have been considered a fairly disreputable occupation for a woman of that era. In addition, while Ehwa adheres to societal expectations of chastity, her mother, in her relationship with the picture man, does not. However, she maintains sufficient income to support Ehwa, cleverly fends off the sexual advances of her male customers, and does not compromise her personal values for gain.

Daniel D. Clark

Further Reading

Hagio, Moto. *A Drunken Dream and Other Stories* (2010).

Kouno, Fumiyo. *Town of Evening Calm, Country of Cherry Blossoms* (2009).

Bibliography

Kim, Dong Hwa. "The Colors of Kim Dong Hwa: The 'Color' Trilogy." Interview by Michael C. Lorah. *Newsarama*, April 16, 2009. http://www.newsarama.com/comics/040916-Colors-First-SecondA.html.

Korea Culture and Content Agency. *Manhwa: Another Discovery in Asian Comics*. Seoul: Communication Books, 2007.

_____. *Manhwa 100: A New Era for Korean Comics*. Seoul: C&C Revolution, 2008.

See also: *Aya of Yapougon; Blankets; Persepolis; Pyongyang*

COMPLETE ESSEX COUNTY, THE

Author: Lemire, Jeff
Artist: Jeff Lemire (illustrator)
Publisher: Top Shelf Productions
First book publication: 2007-2008

Publication History

Published in three volumes from 2007 to 2008—*Essex County,* Volume I: *Tales from the Farm*; *Essex County,* Volume II: *Ghost Stories*; and *Essex County,* Volume III: *The Country Nurse*—Jeff Lemire's *Essex County* trilogy was collected as *The Complete Essex County* in 2009. The collected volume includes an introduction by cartoonist Darwyn Cooke and two previously uncollected stories from *Essex County*: "The Essex County Boxing Club" and "The Sad and Lonely Life of Eddie Elephant-Ears." The 2009 collection also includes early drawings of the *Essex County* characters as well as some promotional materials.

Plot

The Complete Essex County tells the stories of four generations of the LeBeuf family, settled in Essex County, Ontario, Canada. In this book, interdependent and interlocking stories from four generations are told through memories and present-day action. *Tales from the Farm* focuses on Lester Papineau, living with his Uncle Ken after the death of his mother from cancer. Lester does not know who his father is and withdraws into a fantasy world, reading comics and often wearing a cape and a mask. His uncle admonishes Lester and orders him to take off the mask and cape, but Lester refuses. Against his uncle's wishes, Lester befriends Jimmy LeBeuf, who owns the local gas station.

Jimmy briefly played hockey for the Toronto Maple Leafs but retired early because of an injury. Lester and Jimmy run into each other at the creek owned by Ken, and Lester lets Jimmy in on his fantasy: He is watching for an alien invasion. Jimmy actively engages in Lester's play world and offers to help him build a lookout tower. Lester's relationship with his uncle is rocky. He continues to be drawn to Jimmy. The two meet at the creek regularly, and Lester shows Jimmy a superhero

The Complete Essex County. (Courtesy of Top Shelf Productions)

comic book that he drew himself. Jimmy appreciates Lester's work and then lets Lester in on his fantasy: He is still a professional hockey player. Lester plays the part of Jimmy's opponent, while Jimmy skates around him.

Uncle Ken learns that Lester and Jimmy are meeting and refuses to allow Lester to see Jimmy. He also confronts Jimmy one night at the gas station. Jimmy denies having anything to do with Lester. Lester runs away, and, unable to find Jimmy at the creek, goes to the gas station. Jimmy is curt with Lester, and Lester leaves, spending the winter night in an unheated barn.

Spring arrives. Lester remembers seeing Jimmy crying from a distance at his mother's funeral and realizes that Jimmy is his father. He runs into Jimmy in the fields and asks Jimmy to tell him what it was like to play professional hockey. Jimmy starts to answer, but the aliens for which Lester has been watching finally arrive and shoot Jimmy in the chest, mirroring his hockey injury. Lester is suddenly empowered with flight and destroys the alien ship in the air.

Jimmy gives Lester his most prized possession, a hockey card of himself, and both Jimmy and Lester acknowledge that they are father and son. Lester goes home, able to make peace with his life with his uncle, and takes off his mask and cape.

In Volume II, *Ghost Stories* concerns characters related to Lester and Jimmy. The volume opens as deaf seventy-year-old Lou LeBeuf (Jimmy's great-uncle) returns to the family farm, reliving his life through memories. Lou is cared for by his nurse, Anne Quenneville.

As young men, Lou and his brother Vince played hockey for the Grizzlies, a semiprofessional hockey team in Toronto. Lou was a good player, while Vince was the team star.

As a result of the LeBeuf boys' play, the Grizzlies perform well and make the playoffs, but are defeated by Brampton. After the season, Vince marries Beth, retires from hockey, and returns to the family farm. Unbeknownst to Vince, Lou and Beth have a one-night stand.

With Vince gone, Lou stays in Toronto and plays a few more seasons; a knee injury eventually ends his career. Following his time as a hockey player, Lou becomes a streetcar driver, drinks too much, and does not return to the family farm until his mother dies, twenty-five years later. At the funeral, he is reunited with Vince and Beth and meets Mary, a child who may be the result of his one-night stand with Beth years before. After the funeral, Lou returns to Toronto and retires. When he learns that Vince is critically injured in a car accident that kills Beth and Mary, he returns to the family farm to care for Vince. Vince and Lou make amends; Vince dies, leaving Lou alone on the family farm.

In Volume III, *The Country Nurse*, the story of Vince and his nurse Anne continues. On her rounds, Anne checks on Jimmy, retired from the Maple Leafs and running the gas station. Anne reminds Jimmy to visit his uncle Lou, and then she stops to see Lester, while seeing how Lester's uncle Ken's arm is healing. Lester is now a hockey player also.

Lou dies, and Anne is overcome with memories of her grandmother, Sister Margaret Byrne, who ran an orphanage in which Lester's grandfather, Lawrence Papineau, lived. Sister Margaret has an affair with the handyman, Charles Gerrard, and orders him to sleep in the barn. When the church catches fire, Charles dies while saving one of the orphans. Sister Margaret bears a child, Catherine, who becomes Anne Quenneville's mother.

Anne Byrne's memories are prompted by her involvement with her patients; she questions whether or not her work has value. When she informs Jimmy that Lou has died, Jimmy takes the opportunity to make amends with Ken and Lester and make a fresh start as a family.

Volumes

- *Essex County*, Volume I: *Tales from the Farm* (2007). Tells the story of Lester Papineau; he lives with his uncle after the death of his mother and forms a relationship with his father, Jimmy LeBeuf.
- *Essex County*, Volume II: *Ghost Stories* (2007). Tells the stories of brothers Vince and Lou LeBeuf, who set out to play professional hockey. After one season, Vince retires and moves back to the farm. Lou stays in the city.
- *Essex County*, Volume III: *The Country Nurse* (2008). Focuses on Anne Quenneville. As a nurse, she checks on patients Lou LeBeuf, Ken Papineau, and Jimmy LeBeuf.
- *The Complete Essex County* (2009). Contains Volumes I-III and includes additional Essex County stories "The Essex County Boxing Club" and "The Sad Lonely Life of Eddie Elephant-Ears," along with other material.

Characters

- *Lester Papineau* is the ten-year-old child of Claire Papineau and Jimmy LeBeuf; however Lester initially does not know that Jimmy is his father. When Claire dies of cancer, he goes to live with his uncle Ken. He is an imaginative boy who dresses in a mask and cape and draws and writes comics.

- *Ken Papineau* is the brother of Claire Papineau. When Claire dies, he takes her son Lester into his home. Ken refuses to allow Lester to interact with Jimmy LeBeuf.

- *Jimmy LeBeuf* is a onetime star of the Toronto Maple Leafs. After a blow to the head, he retires and buys an Esso gas station in Essex County. He is Lester's father. Jimmy befriends Lester, plays imaginary games with him, and supports his interest in comic books. After Lou LeBeuf dies, Jimmy is welcomed into Ken Papineau's home.

- *Lou LeBeuf* played hockey for the Toronto Grizzlies. After a knee injury ended his career, he drove a Toronto streetcar. He has a one-night stand with Beth Morgan and may be the father of her child. After Beth is killed in a car accident and his brother Vince is critically injured, he returns to the family farm to care for Vince. After Vince dies, he spends his days reminiscing.

- *Vince LeBeuf* was the star of the Toronto Grizzlies, but after playing only one season, he marries Beth Morgan and returns to the family farm, where he helps raise Beth's daughter, Mary. Mary and Beth are killed in a car accident in which Vince suffers debilitating injuries; afterward, he is cared for by Lou until his death.

- *Beth Morgan* is the wife of Vince LeBeuf. Beth had a one-night liaison with Lou, and Lou may be the father of her daughter, Mary. Beth and Mary die in a car accident.

- *Mary LeBeuf* is the daughter of Beth Morgan. It is unclear who her father is; it may be her "uncle" Lou. When Mary meets Lou for the first time as a young woman, she expresses great interest in him and wants to visit him in Toronto. A few years after meeting Lou, Mary dies in a car accident that also kills her mother and seriously injures Vince, her mother's husband.

- *Anne Quenneville*, the granddaughter of Sister Margaret Byrne, is a country nurse. She has cared for Claire Papineau, Jimmy LeBeuf, and Lou LeBeuf. Anne's husband has died, and her son is a problem for her. Her satisfaction in life is derived from caring for the residents of Essex County.

- *Sister Margaret Byrne* is Anne Quenneville's grandmother and directs an orphanage. She bears Catherine Byrne, the illegitimate child of the orphanage's handyman, Charles Gerrard. Catherine is Anne Quenneville's grandmother. Gerrard dies in the orphanage fire, and Sister Margaret leads the children across a several days' trek to Essex County.

- *Lawrence LeBeuf* is the oldest child in the orphanage run by Sister Margaret. When a fire destroys the orphanage, he helps lead the orphans across Canada, where they settle in Essex County. Lawrence is the father of Lou and Vince LeBeuf, the grandfather of Mary LeBeuf, and the great-grandfather of Lester Papineau.

Artistic Style

Lemire's artistic style is deceptively simple. Generally, pages are divided into a series of small, active panels that focus on interaction between characters. The characters vary in size; if Lemire is making an emotional

---

Jeff Lemire

After self-publishing *Lost Dogs* in 2005, Jeff Lemire gained attention for the *Essex County Trilogy* of books published by Top Shelf: *Tales from the Farm*, *Ghost Stories*, and *The Country Nurse*. These works were acclaimed for their ability to evoke the quietly somber life in southwestern Ontario. Lemire's work on this series used stark, black-and-white images composed of thick black lines. Based on the success of these independent works, Lemire began working for DC Comics' Vertigo imprint, producing *Sweet Tooth*, a post-apocalyptic story featuring a world where some characters are human-animal hybrids. For this series, Lemire loosened his artistic style somewhat, bringing it more in line with the aesthetic conventions of the contemporary mainstream while still maintaining his own idiosyncratic character designs and page layouts. Lemire is also the writer of a number of series for DC Comics, including *Superboy*, *Animal Man*, and *Frankenstein: Agent of SHADE*.

point, the character crowds into the panel. If the purpose of the panel is to move the story along, the characters are smaller and more casual. When Lemire wants to focus on a single character, he positions that character toward the reader. In moments of isolation, characters occupy a one-page panel alone. If the isolated moment is transformational, the character faces the reader. If it is a sad moment, the character faces away from the reader.

The book is done completely in black and white, which mirrors its somber tone. The backgrounds are mixed; most panels have realized backgrounds where the drawings are representational, but many panels have only white space for background, allowing readers to focus on the character in the panel. Lemire is also a master of cartoon timing; he is able to slow the pace down long enough to allow the reader to linger over a character when necessitated by the story.

Themes

Several themes run through *Essex County*. One is how the human race is perpetuated in part by illicit sexual liaisons. In the context of the story, in each generation there is one child born out of wedlock: Catherine Byrne, Mary LeBeuf (probably), and Lester Papineau. Another theme is the dual nature of passion, for which hockey stands as a metaphor. Through three generations, LeBeuf family members have a relationship with hockey: Superstar Vince is indifferent to it, while Lou, a lesser talent, finds life meaningless without the sport. For Jimmy, who scores a goal in the same game in which he suffers a career-ending injury, getting injured is worth the thrill of scoring a goal. As Lester begins to recover from his mother's death, he joins a hockey team.

The characters survive, rather than thrive, and they either come or return to Essex County for sustenance. When Lawrence leads orphans to safety, they walk until they reach Essex County. When Vince wants to live a full life, he stops playing professional hockey and returns to Essex County to farm. When Lou wants to make peace with his brother, he does not bring him to Toronto; instead, he returns to Essex County. After Jimmy's accident, he, too, returns to Essex County.

Nurse Anne, who has no family except her son, tends to the sick and wounded, and she personifies the healing properties of Essex County. Her caring nature appears to come from the county itself, as she drives from patient to patient dispensing advice as well as medicine. When one member of Essex County dies, the loss is palpable to Anne.

Like the LeBeuf family, Anne takes sustenance from the crows of Essex County, who have watched over both the Byrne and LeBeuf families for generations: Lawrence and Sister Margaret follow a crow to Essex County; when Lou returns to Essex County as an old man, a crow befriends him; and as Lester slowly recovers from his mother's death, a crow flies overhead.

Impact

Before writing and drawing *The Complete Essex County*, Lemire was a relative newcomer to graphic novels, producing only a few short pieces. One of them, *Lost Dogs* (2005), earned a Xeric Award. With the publication of *Essex County*, Lemire was thrust into the upper tier of cartoonists. *Essex County* was recognized by the American Library Association. With its recognition as one of the Essential Canadian Novels of the Decade by the Canadian Broadcasting Corporation, *Essex County* helped elevate the status of Canadian cartoonists.

Stephen Weiner

Further Reading

Lemire, Jeff. *Sweet Tooth: Out of the Deep Woods* (2010).

Powell, Nate. *Swallow Me Whole* (2008).

Smith, Jeff. *Bone* (1991-2004).

Bibliography

Newman, Lee. "Trading Up: The Complete Essex County." *Broken Frontier*, January 13, 2010. http://www.brokenfrontier.com/lowdown/p/detail/trading-up-the-complete-essex-county.

Sanders, Joe Sutliff. "*Essex County*." Review of *Essex County*. *Teacher Librarian* 36, no. 3 (2009): 25.

Weiner, Stephen. "Dreams Deferred in a Harsh Landscape: Essex County, Volume 2: Ghost Stories." *Boston Globe*, March 8, 2008.

See also: *Scott Pilgrim*; *Good-Bye, Chunky Rice*; *Ethel and Ernest*

COMPLETE FRITZ THE CAT, THE

Author: Crumb, Robert
Artist: Robert Crumb (illustrator)
Publisher: Bélier Press
First serial publication: 1965-1972
First book publication: 1978

Publication History

The publication history of *Fritz the Cat* is a complex one. The first published story appeared in Harvey Kurtzman's *Help!* magazine in January, 1965. Further strips appeared in *Help!* and *Cavalier* magazine between 1965 and 1968, and individual panels and sketches can be found in Robert Crumb's *Sketchbook 1966-1967*, which was published in Germany by Zweitausendeins in 1981. Further major stories were then published in *Head Comix* in 1968 and *R. Crumb's Fritz the Cat: Three Big Stories* in 1969.

After his disillusionment with the animated film version of the character, Crumb killed off the character in the final Fritz story in *The People's Comics* in 1972. The majority of these stories were then reprinted in *The Complete Fritz the Cat* in 1978. Although this compilation was not conceived as a graphic novel when Crumb began working on the character in 1965, it nevertheless represents an episodic telling of the character's development through the 1960's and 1970's.

The collection includes a series of single drawings from Crumb's sketchbooks and other sources and the following strips: *Cat Life* (1959-1960) an unpublished pencil strip of Crumb's cat Fred, who morphed into Fritz; "Fritz Comes on Strong" (from *Help!*, issue 22, January, 1965); "Fred, the Teen-Age Girl Pigeon" (from *Help!*, issue 34, May, 1965); "Fritz the Cat" (from *R. Crumb's Head Comix*, 1968); "Fritz Bugs Out," "Fritz Special Agent for the CIA," and "Fritz the No-Good" (all from *R. Crumb's Fritz the Cat: Three Big Stories*, 1969); "Fritz the Cat: Magician" (from *Promethean Enterprises* 3, 1971); "Fritz the Cat: Superstar" (from *The People's Comics*, 1972); and a number of one-page strips, mainly from *Cavalier* in 1968.

An animated still from *Fritz the Cat*, directed by Ralph Bakshi, 1972. Despite the fact that Crumb disowned the film, it continues to be widely praised and captures Crumb's style effectively. (Getty Images)

Plot

There are fourteen stories in the anthology, varying from short, six-panel strips to a twenty-three-page story. The first appearance of Fritz is in "Fritz Comes on Strong," a three-page strip with six borderless panels on each page. Against minimal or nonexistent backgrounds, Fritz and a female cat enter a room wearing winter clothing. Fritz gradually undresses the female, but when she is naked he confounds the reader's expectations by crouching over her as he announces, "Now be patient, my sweet . . . them little fleas are hard t' get hold of!"

Fritz's status in the stories varies hugely. In some he is a vagrant and in others, such as "Fred, the Teen-Age

Girl Pigeon," he is a superstar rock musician. Arriving at an airport, Fritz is mobbed by crowds, including the girl pigeon of the title. Accompanied by a disapproving literal (and figurative) fat cat manager figure, Fritz enters a limousine. The pigeon jumps on the car, but when the police try to remove her, Fritz invites her inside, where a flutter of tiny hearts above her head indicates her devotion to him. Arriving in his hotel room, Fritz is now leering, and she has become nervous and is sweating. The final two panels show Fritz yawning in bed with the pigeon's clothing strewn over him, and then him burping (the only piece of dialogue in the whole story) with a contented smile on his face.

"Fritz Special Agent for the CIA" is different from most of the stories in the book. Although Fritz is still recognizable for his arrogance and his libido, the narrative is a fairly straightforward parody of the James Bond spy craze, and as such, reveals little about his character and makes few comments on contemporary society.

"Fritz the Cat" identifies Fritz as a college student who lives in "supercity." It begins with Fritz and two friends in a park, moaning about being surrounded by phonies. Fritz and his friends argue about which of them has the most sensitive soul, but they are distracted by three girls (actually another cat and two doglike animals), whom they fail to impress with an energetic but incompetent musical performance. Fritz notices that the girls are impressed by a crow, and he dupes the crow into leaving to look for some nonexistent cheap drugs. He then impresses the girls with a bravura performance about his tormented soul. Persuading them that they can save each other's souls, he lures them to an apartment where they all cavort naked in a bath. Despite protesting that he and the girls are "seekin' after truth!" they are joined by the other occupants of the apartment in a pot-fueled orgy in the bathroom. Two policemen burst in, but Fritz shoots the toilet, and in the ensuing confusion he escapes. On the final page he obtains a top hat and suit from a drunken chicken, and by the next day, the park is full of imitators of Fritz's "new look."

The final Fritz story is "Fritz the Cat, Superstar." Fritz is a film star, living in a mansion, where he treats a voluptuous crocodile, Abigail, with disdain. He explains to Mr. Bear, an expert who is helping him with his tax problems, that he likes his women, "tall 'n' proud . . . [I]t's more fun to cut 'em down ta size!!" His attempts to have sex with Abigail are interrupted by a phone call from his producers. He goes to a meeting with his producers, and they try to persuade him to read the script for the latest in what is clearly a series of poor films. Killing time before appearing on the Johnny Giraffe show, Fritz picks up a cute bunny and has rough sex with her. After dumping her, Fritz appears on the show, plugging his latest film and making condescending comments about the "counter culture." Later, he bumps into an old girlfriend, Andrea Ostrich. Despite criticizing his attitude on the show, she begs him to have sex with her. However, once in her apartment he is distracted by watching his appearance on television and becomes aroused only when she hides her head under a chair. She refuses to move from that position so Fritz kicks her and leaves, muttering to himself, "Ha ha, foolish female." She then kills him with an ice pick and stands over him exclaiming, "Ha yourself, smart ass!!" A small sign points to Fritz's prone body with the attached phrase, "Violence in the media."

Characters

- *Fritz* is the only regular character in the stories. Occasionally troubled by guilt and thoughts of bettering himself, Fritz is mainly driven by selfish desires, mostly for sexual satisfaction. He has little compunction about this and will say or do almost anything to achieve his ends. In short, he has the morals of an alley cat. His occupations vary hugely in the stories and include being merely a vagrant, then a rock musician, a college student, a college dropout, a revolutionary, a secret agent, and a Hollywood star.

- *Winston* is a female fox who is one of the few recurring characters in Fritz's love life (other "old girlfriends," such as Angela Ostrich, in fact appear only once). She is lucky in that she is not eaten, as Fred the pigeon girl was, but Fritz does treat her badly and falls out with her in the stories "Fritz Bugs Out" and "Fritz the Cat Doubts His Masculinity." Fritz's selfish treatment of both females and colleagues tends to mean that they appear for a short time and are then discarded.

- *Charlene* is another girlfriend (a cat) who is seduced by Fritz at the start of "Fritz Bugs Out." She appears to have deep feelings for Fritz, but he regards her as "a good lay." She makes a brief appearance later in the same story, and she is physically similar to characters (including Fritz's wife) in "Fritz Comes on Strong," "Fritz the Cat," and "Fritz the No-Good," but in these she is never identified by name and may not be the same character.

Artistic Style

Crumb was influenced by the "funny animal" comic books that he and his brother Charles read during their childhood, such as *Little Lulu* by John Stanley; *Donald Duck* by Carl Barks; and *Pogo* by Walt Kelly. His drawing style in early *Fritz the Cat* episodes is a combination of these styles and a loose free line seen in the work of classic American newspaper strip artists such as George Herriman, Milt Gross, and Rube Goldberg. The meandering spidery line of Crumb's early work is partially due to the fact that he was drawing with a rapidograph pen, whereas the comic book artists he admired often used brushes, and the comic-strip artists mainly used dip pens.

The stories in the anthology clearly demonstrate the development of Crumb's drawing style. The earlier strips are linear, with minimal cross-hatching, and are similar to the work Crumb did for the American Greetings card company in the early 1960's. Gradually, the style changes, and by the final story, the drawings have heavier lines and, at times, dense and heavy crosshatching. This gives the figures and settings a solid, almost plastic, depth, reflecting not only early American newspaper artists but also earlier graphic artists Crumb admired such as William Hogarth and Thomas Rowlandson. The effect is to create a sense of light falling across the figures that sets them in a solid, albeit surreal, world.

Crumb's panel borders, always drawn by hand and with thin gutters, also show changes. In the earlier strips the lines are loose and quite thin. The panels may be distorted, but by the later stories, they are darker,

much tighter, and more controlled. The strength of Crumb's mature drawing style, for all its "cartoony" feel, is that it is, underneath, solid traditional draftsmanship. Crumb's sketchbooks demonstrate his talent for observational drawings, but close examination of the later *Fritz the Cat* strips in particular reveals a sure handling and graphic sophistication that is unrivaled in underground or in many mainstream comics and graphic novels.

Themes

In *Fritz the Cat*, Crumb deals with sexual issues via his anthropomorphic characters; through them, he comments on the nature of both the counterculture and mainstream society. During the 1960's and 1970's, the idea of sexual freedom could be seen as part of a wider political set of ideas that stemmed from disenchantment with the mores of mainstream society.

Crumb's work occupies a strange and ambivalent position within the counterculture. While he entered into the general spirit of the underground and remains its most famous cartoonist, much of his work is actually highly critical of the counterculture. Fritz is a classic example of this, in that in order to satisfy his own (mainly sexual) desires, he will pay lip service to anything he sees as part of a trendy new set of ideas. Although he may be seen as "cool" by other characters, Crumb shows him to be, in fact, a shallow faker. He cannot be trusted or believed at any stage in his career, and if lies and duplicity will not suffice, he will resort to violence, as in his unprovoked attack in the one-page story "I Hates Ol' Ladies."

Crumb also plays with the nature of anthropomorphism. Fritz's rampant sexual desires can be seen as entirely catlike, and for all his humanlike foibles, he can resort to feline behavior, as he does at the end of "Fred, the Teen-Age Girl Pigeon."

"Fritz the Cat, Superstar," seems to be somewhat autobiographical in that Fritz appears to reflect Crumb's disillusionment with the entertainment industry and the idea of stardom. The film producers in the story are parodies of producer Steve Krantz and director Ralph Bakshi, and the titles of the series of films Fritz stars in show the desperation and redundancy of Hollywood—in the context of the story the Bakshi character is making *Fritz the Cat, Ski Bum* and is moving on to *Fritz Goes to India*.

Impact

Despite the comparatively short publication life, *Fritz the Cat* became one of the iconic figures of the underground, along with Crumb's Mr. Natural and Gilbert Shelton's Fabulous Furry Freak Brothers. Two animated films helped to increase Fritz's fame in mainstream society, but they perhaps also fixed his image more simplistically as a symbol of a new sexual freedom. Financial success was seen by some in the underground as part of a process of "selling out," and the fame of Fritz was not welcomed by Crumb or others in the alternative media. In January, 1972, Michael O'Donoghue and Randall Enos produced a parody of Fritz in *National Lampoon*'s "Is Nothing Sacred?" issue. Their two-page strip is similar to Crumb's own debunking of the character in the same year, and even includes Fritz plugging his latest film on a talk show, while being condescending about the counterculture.

Crumb's work on Fritz also helped to fuel an ongoing debate about whether his depiction of sexual acts was part of this new freedom or an abuse of license bordering on pornography. Opinion has varied: Art critic Robert Hughes described Crumb as "an American Hogarth"; underground cartoonist Trina Robbins described his work as "heavily misogynistic." A rape scene in "Fritz the No Good" is reminiscent of some of Crumb's later work and these kinds of images still divide critics. Crumb has also been criticized for his portrayal of black characters as crows. In 1968, Viking Press censored his work and even rejected some *Fritz the Cat* stories, which were then published by Ballantine Books in 1969.

Crumb's work on *Fritz the Cat* and his early *Zap* comics was also hugely influential on a wide range of cartoonists, both in terms of style and in demonstrating the range of issues that could effectively be dealt with in the medium of comic books. Artists as varied as Dan Clowes, Steve Bell, and Matt Groening have specifically acknowledged their debt to Crumb.

Films

Fritz the Cat. Directed by Ralph Bakshi. American International, 1972. The animated feature film, publicized as the first X-rated animation, played an unusually significant part in the history of the character. Crumb loathed the film and felt cheated by its producer, Krantz, although accounts of the way Crumb lost control of his character are contradictory. The film persuaded Crumb to kill off Fritz, which he duly did in 1972. The film begins with a sequence taken directly from Crumb's Fritz story from *Head Comix* from 1965, in which after failing to impress three girls with his singing, Fritz fakes existential angst in order to have sex with them; later a sequence from "Fritz Bugs Out" is used. Much of the film, however, moved away from the original stories, and as soon as that happened, Crumb felt that the film lost its way and lost its grip on the nature of the character. Despite the fact that Crumb disowned the film and wanted his name removed from the titles, Bakshi and his animators did catch Crumb's style effectively. The film still has many fans and has been featured on lists of the top one hundred animated films.

The Nine Lives of Fritz the Cat. Directed by Robert Taylor. Cinemation Industries, 1974. Krantz produced this animation after the success of the first film. If Crumb was isolated in his disdain for the first film, he had the company of many critics and audiences in his dislike of this one.

David Huxley

Further Reading

Crumb, Robert. *The Complete Crumb Comics* (1986-).

_____. *Sketchbook, 1966-'67* (1981).

Donahue, Don, and Susan Goodrick, eds. *The Apex Treasury of Underground Comics* (1981).

Shelton, Gilbert. *The Adventures of Fat Freddy's Cat* (1977).

Bibliography

Beauchamp, Monte, ed. *The Life and Times of R. Crumb: Comments from Contemporaries.* New York: St. Martin's Griffin, 1998.

Crumb, Robert, and Peter Poplaski. *The R. Crumb Handbook*. London: MQ Publications, 2005.

Feine, Donald. R., and Robert Crumb. *Crumb Checklist of Work and Criticism, with a Biographical Supplement and a Full Set of Indexes*. Cambridge, Mass.: Boatner Norton Press, 1981.

George, Milo, ed. R. *Crumb*. Seattle, Wash.: Fantagraphics Books, 2004.

Poplaski, Peter, ed. *The R. Crumb Coffee Table Art Book*. Boston: Little, Brown, 1997.

See also: *The Book of Genesis*

CONTRACT WITH GOD, AND OTHER TENEMENT STORIES, A

Author: Eisner, Will
Artist: Will Eisner (illustrator)
Publisher: Baronet Books; Kitchen Sink Press
First book publication: 1978

Publication History

Will Eisner spent two years working on the four stories that make up *A Contract with God, and Other Tenement Stories*. Hoping to create a more mature form of "sequential art," Eisner's career was rejuvenated by the work, which indicated a new potential for comic books. The book was first published by Baronet Press in October of 1978, with an initial run of fifteen hundred hardcover copies. DC Comics acquired the rights to the work in 2001 and reissued it as part of the Will Eisner Library imprint. The book also forms the first part of *The Contract with God Trilogy: Life on Dropsie Avenue*, a collection published by W. W. Norton in 2006.

The other two novels in the collection, *A Life Force* and *Dropsie Avenue*, were published later and separately. *A Life Force* was first serialized from 1983 to 1985 in *Will Eisner Quarterly* and eventually collected and published in book form by Kitchen Sink Press in 1988. Eisner considered *A Life Force*, along with *A Contract with God*, to be his most accomplished work because it demonstrated the full potential of graphic novels. The final installation in the trilogy was *Dropsie Avenue*, which was first published by Kitchen Sink Press in 1995 as *Dropsie Avenue: The Neighborhood*.

Plot

A Contract with God, and Other Tenement Stories, consists of four stories, "A Contract with God," "The Street Singer," "The Super," and "Cookalein," related by their common setting of a single tenement in the Bronx neighborhood of New York City. "A Contract with God" follows the life of Frimme Hersh, who makes a contract with God as a young boy, escaping the pogroms of czarist Russia. Although the reader never learns the details of the contract, Hersh strives to live a holy life, helping those in need in

(© Alberto Estevez/epa/Corbis)

Will Eisner

One of the most innovative visual stylists in the history of comics, Will Eisner literally wrote the book on expressivity in comics art. The creator of *The Spirit* in 1940, Eisner was celebrated for his unusual sense of layout and design, often incorporating the title of his strip into the splash pages in innovative ways. Eisner was a master of pacing and character design, relying on decades of experience to create highly memorable comics pages. He was also an innovator in the area of graphic novels, and his 1978 book *A Contract with God, and Other Tenement Stories* is widely regarded as pioneering this concept. In 1985, he authored *Comics & Sequential Art*, an influential textbook outlining a general theory of comics creation. In 1988, in tribute to his remarkable influence on comic aesthetics, the Eisner Awards were created. They continue to be awarded each summer at Comic-Con International: San Diego.

his new home in the United States. Hersh eventually adopts an orphan child, Rachele, who dies while still a young girl. Devastated, Hersh claims that God has violated his end of the contract; he rejects his faith and becomes a greedy slumlord. Eventually, he repents and has three rabbis write up a new contract with God, only to be struck dead by a heart attack as he reads it.

"The Street Singer," set during the Great Depression, focuses on a day in the life of Eddie, a destitute man with a golden voice who sings for pennies in alleyways in the Bronx. Eddie is discovered by a former opera singer, Marta Maria, who renames him "Ronald Barry" and becomes both his manager and his lover. However, at one point, Eddie realizes that he cannot remember where Marta lives, which dooms him to a life of ignominy and poverty.

"The Super" follows the manager of 55 Dropsie Avenue, Mr. Scruggs, on the day of his death. A German immigrant, Scruggs is constantly irritated by the demands and disrespect of the tenants in his building. His only comforts are his dog, Hugo, and the countless photos of naked women covering his basement room. However, these both prove to be his downfall, as the ten-year-old niece of a tenant sneaks down to Scruggs's room, offering to give him a glimpse of her genitals for a nickel. Scruggs agrees, but the young girl poisons his dog and steals the rest of his money while he is distracted. With the police on their way and his beloved dog dead, Scruggs stokes the furnace one last time, locks himself in his room, and shoots himself in the head.

The final portion of the original volume, "Cookalein," presents a broader perspective by illustrating several narratives rather than just one story line. It takes place at the farms in the mountains of upstate New York where vacationers from the crowded city spend their summers. The story follows three different groups of characters as they explore their sexuality outside the confining city.

A Life Force, the second novel, documents the survival instinct of the Shtarkah family during the Great Depression. Through an extended simile comparing humanity and cockroaches, the plot interweaves a historical account of the Great Depression with the family's attempt to live and prosper amid the economic hardship in America during the 1930's.

Dropsie Avenue, the final novel in the trilogy, is a history of a fictional street in the Bronx, from the 1870's to the modern day. It depicts the cycle of urban decay and renewal through the ethnic divisions, individual exploitation, and daily life of the tenement apartment building at 55 Dropsie Avenue.

Characters

• *Frimme Hersh*, the protagonist of the first story, is a short, portly, rabbinical-looking man in traditional Jewish religious dress. Once his adopted daughter dies, he shaves his beard, discards his religious attire, and becomes a slumlord, complete with suit, tie, and a cigar clamped between his fat lips. His callous disregard for the community following this transformation provides a thematic foundation for the entire collection.

• *Eddie*, the street singer, is an athletic-looking man in his mid-thirties. He dresses shabbily and drinks heavily, which causes his appearance to vary drastically throughout the story. His familial- and self-abuse contribute to his downfall.

• *Mr. Scruggs*, the superintendent, is a short, fat, bald German who looks similar to his beloved dog, Hugo. He desires respect and authority yet receives only derision and demands from the tenants. His lust proves ruinous: Humiliated and shamed after falling for the seductions of a young girl, he shoots himself while holding the corpse of his poisoned dog in his arms.

• *Goldie* is a beautiful young secretary at a fur shop. She goes away to the country on vacation, intent to find a rich husband. She puts on airs to appear wealthy and refuses the attentions of men she deems below her station. She falls for Benny, who attempts to rape her in the woods when he finds out that she is not wealthy. She is rescued by Herbie, who marries her.

• *Benny* attempts to find a wealthy spouse by going to the country and pretending to be wealthy. Initially attracted to Goldie, whom he believes is from a prosperous family, he attacks her when she reveals that she is poor. He is dashing and handsome and ends up seducing a diamond heiress.

- *Jacob Shtarkah*, the protagonist of *A Life Force*, is an aging Jewish carpenter most often pictured wearing a hat and overcoat. Downtrodden and distraught at losing work, he is pessimistic and continually questions the nature of the human experience and the existence of God.
- *Elton Shaftsbury*, a well-educated, wealthy, young white man, loses his inheritance during the stock market crash and nearly kills himself. He finds work as a runner in a brokerage firm, where he eventually becomes partner by suggesting shrewd investments that benefit both the firm and the Shtarkah family. He eventually

marries Jacob's daughter, Rebecca Shtarkah, who is pregnant with his child.
- *Izzy Cash* is a ragpicker and clothes seller who eventually saves enough money to buy the tenement at 55 Dropsie Avenue. Dirty and disheveled, with a coarse beard and vest that highlights his short stature, he is self-interested and contributes to the urban decay of his neighborhood until prompted toward philanthropy by Abie Gold.
- *Abie Gold* is a young skinny Jewish boy with curly hair and glasses living on Dropsie Avenue who grows up to be a powerful lawyer and politician in the Bronx. As a lawyer, he attaches

"Protest against eviction of a family from a tenement in the Bronx neighborhood of New York City in 1932. The four stories of *A Contract with God, and Other Tenement Stories*, are related by their common setting of a single tenement in the Bronx neighborhood in the 1930's. (NY Daily News via Getty Images)

himself to powerful men but continually tries to help those in the Dropsie Avenue neighborhood.

Artistic Style

Eisner has called comic art a type of impressionism, and his own work is an attempt to depict life realistically. He was greatly influenced by European experimental woodcut graphic artists; in the preface to the trilogy, he claims to have aspired to a similar form in writing *A Contract with God*. This emulation is evident in the single-line shading he uses throughout the trilogy, reminiscent of woodcut art. The roughness of the shading contributes to Eisner's vaunted realistic style, because his landscapes, buildings, and even people are less sharply defined and contrasted, just as in real life. His ability to make ordinary characters memorable became a hallmark of his realism. Even so, he also occasionally employs stock characters, such as short, obese men with predatory, squinting eyes for the "bad guys."

All three novels in *The Contract with God Trilogy* are produced solely in black-and-white ink, which simultaneously enhances their realistic, gritty feel and pays homage to the woodcut art that inspired them. The world of the tenements they depict is one of alleyways, shadow, dirt, and grime, and Eisner does not artificially brighten the events by employing color. Eisner is generally known for an easy-reading style of uncluttered squares of dialogue, expressive lettering, and figures that seem to be drawn like the cartoon strips of his early career.

Even though *The Contract with God Trilogy* took more than sixteen years to complete, there is remarkably little difference in the artistic style Eisner employs for the three novels. Nevertheless, there are minor exceptions. For example, *A Life Force* introduces entire pages of outside text, usually newspaper accounts of the Great Depression, in order to place the struggles of the Shtarkah family into historical context.

Themes

The primary thematic concerns of *A Contract with God* are existential. *A Contract with God* and *A Life Force* both contain protagonists who wrestle with both the existence of God and the significance of their actions in a seemingly arbitrary world. Eisner felt that in writing about the human relationship with God, he could explore a subject that had never been dealt with in comics. Furthermore, by addressing a fundamental question of the human experience, the novel had the potential to be taken more seriously than a mere comic book.

Frimme Hersh's contract with God questions the validity of religious faith, and the theme receives even more treatment in *A Life Force*, in which Jacob Shtarkah repeatedly reflects upon the will to live that animates the human experience. Some readers find Eisner to be fatalistic in his approach to spirituality, noting the lack of human agency and the indifference of the universe to the plight of individuals throughout the work.

Nearly all of the stories that comprise *The Contract with God Trilogy* contain some depiction of human sexuality, which is another important theme in Eisner's graphic novels. Nudity and sexual relationships drive the plot of stories such as "The Super" and "Cookalein," and Jacob Shtarkah's rekindled affair with the love of his youth influences the plot of *A Life Force*. For all of the nudity and sex acts presented within *A Contract with God*, Eisner does not present the sexual behavior of his characters in a way that promotes condemnation. Rather, his depiction of sexuality implies that it is an animating and natural part of the human experience.

Much of Eisner's later work explores his Jewish identity. *A Contract with God* is primarily concerned with Jewish characters and their interaction with other ethnic and racial groups. With the exception of "The Super," all of the stories contain Jewish protagonists. Eisner claimed to have patterned the characters in *A Contract with God* after real figures from his own life growing up as a young boy in a Bronx tenement. Consequently, the novels establish autobiography, Jewish history, and ethnic experiences in general as important themes in the collection.

Impact

Produced during the Bronze Age (1970's-1980's) and Modern Age (late 1980's-   ) of comics, *A Contract with God* is somewhat reminiscent of comics from earlier periods. In fact, had Eisner ended his career during the 1960's, he would still be regarded as a major figure in comics. However, his most influential and important works were produced in the final part of his long career, and, in large part, it is because of his efforts that graphic novels receive widespread recognition today.

A Contract with God remains the work most often credited with establishing graphic novels as a literary medium worthy of serious artistic and philosophical study. Eisner claimed that he came up with the term "graphic novel" as a way to avoid pitching a publisher a comic book. He later realized that he was not the first to use the phrase (although he is often credited with inventing it).

In a 2002 speech, he acknowledged that his lifelong dream was for sequential art to be recognized as a form of literature by the academic community. Eisner was, more than any other American comic artist, responsible for bringing about that level of recognition. His graphic novels, while foundational and accomplished in their own right, inspired most of the premier American graphic novelists, including Robert Crumb, Art Spiegelman, Frank Miller, and Neil Gaiman. Many of Eisner's works have been analyzed in premier literary journals, and academic conferences, awards, and journals that discuss graphic novels have been named in his honor.

Ryan D. Stryffeler

Further Reading

Eisner, Will. *Life, in Pictures: Autobiographical Stories* (2007).

_____. *The Plot: The Secret Story of the Protocols of the Elders of Zion* (2005).

_____. *The Spirit Archives* (2000-2009).

Bibliography

Andelman, Bob. *Will Eisner: A Spirited Life*. Milwaukie, Ore.: M Press, 2005.

Beronä, David A. "Breaking Taboos: Sexuality in the Work of Will Eisner and the Early Wordless Novels." *International Journal of Comic Art* 1, no. 1 (Spring/Summer, 1999): 90-103.

Couch, N. C. Christopher, and Stephen Weiner. *The Will Eisner Companion: The Pioneering Spirit of the Father of the Graphic Novel*. New York: DC Comics, 2004.

Dauber, Jeremy. "Comic Books, Tragic Stories: Will Eisner's American Jewish History." In *The Jewish Graphic Novel: Critical Approaches*, edited by Samantha Baskind and Ranen Omer-Sherman. Piscataway, N.J.: Rutgers University Press, 2010.

Eisner, Will. "Comic and the New Literary: An Essay." *Inks: Cartoon and Comic Art Studies* 1, no. 2 (May, 1994): 2-5.

Schumacher, Michael. *Will Eisner: A Dreamer's Life in Comics*. New York: Bloomsbury, 2010.

See also: *Maus: A Survivor's Tale; Dropsie Avenue; The Jew of New York*

CURIOUS CASE OF BENJAMIN BUTTON, THE

Author: Fitzgerald, F. Scott; DeFilippis, Nunzio; Weir, Christina

Artist: Kevin Cornell (illustrator); Bryn Ashburn (letterer)

Publisher: Quirk Books

First book publication: 2008

Publication History

"The Curious Case of Benjamin Button" began as a satirical work of fantasy written by American novelist F. Scott Fitzgerald in the early 1920's. Although he was proud of it, Fitzgerald struggled to find a willing publisher because the story departed so dramatically from his more popular flapper stories. Nevertheless, *Colliers* magazine accepted "Benjamin Button" for its May 27, 1922, issue, and the story also appeared in the "Fantasies" section of Fitzgerald's anthology *Tales of the Jazz Age* (1922).

The work largely disappeared into obscurity after the 1920's, but once David Fincher's intentions to adapt the tale for film became known, readers and scholars alike developed new interest in the strange piece. In 2007, Quirk Books opted to revitalize the story as a richly illustrated graphic novel, and editorial director Jason Rekulak contracted Nunzio DeFilippis and Christina Weir to adapt Fitzgerald's text, Kevin Cornell to create the illustrations, and Bryn Ashburn to handle the typesetting and design. The book's release was coordinated to occur just two months before the release of Fincher's movie in December, 2008. As of 2011, the graphic novel version of Fitzgerald's story had yet to be released in a paperback edition.

Plot

The graphic novel adaptation of Fitzgerald's short story faithfully re-creates the tale of Benjamin Button, a man born in 1860 with the body and mind of a seventy-year-old man. The most important things in the world to Roger Button, Benjamin's father, are family and social standing, so the anomalous appearance of his son shocks and offends him. As a result, young Benjamin's parents force him to live the first fourteen

The Curious Case of Benjamin Button. (Courtesy of Quirk Books)

years of his life in disguise, playing the role of a youth, with regular shaves, dyed hair, and ludicrous outfits, despite his adult vocabulary and penchant for cigars.

Benjamin's unnatural appearance is just part of his abnormality: The man actually ages in reverse. As the story progresses, his health improves, his stoop disappears, and his hair grows gradually darker. Anxious to leave home and to curry favor with his distant father, Benjamin travels to Yale as a freshman, but he is kicked out for being too old. Instead, he begins working at his father's hardware store and gradually enters the high-society life of upper-class Baltimore.

At a lavish party, Benjamin meets Hildegarde Moncrief, a wealthy socialite. Although the two are roughly the same age, Benjamin falls for her physical youth and beauty, and Hildegarde is enamored by the maturity of a man she assumes is fifty. The two soon marry, and their perceived age difference causes a scandal. Unfortunately, because the couple married for superficial reasons, the romance quickly dies, as Hildegarde begins to age visibly and as Benjamin enjoys physical invigoration as his body continues to grow younger.

Bored with his wife and having no real relationship with his son, Roscoe, Benjamin enlists in the army to fight in the Spanish-American War. As a soldier, he excels, rising quickly through the ranks and receiving a medal. Once back in Baltimore, the dashing war hero finds opportunity to golf, dance, and cavort with younger women, much to the disgust of his son, as the two now look roughly the same age. Finally, Benjamin is able to attend college, but this time he chooses Harvard. As a star football player, the seemingly young man enacts his revenge on Yale by defeating their football team almost single-handedly.

Tragically, however, Benjamin's body continues to grow younger. He is forced to leave college without graduating, and his youthful appearance prevents him from reenlisting to fight in World War I. Before long, he must live with his son Roscoe, who tells everyone he is Benjamin's uncle. As he ages younger and younger, Benjamin is soon at the mercy of his nurse, a caring woman who treats him with love and compassion. The reverse aging fails to stop, and eventually the infant Benjamin simply fades from existence.

Characters

- *Roger Button*, Benjamin's father, is a prim and proper Baltimore business owner who consistently appears in a dark suit and tie and who sports long whiskers and a mustache. Although he is the first developed character to appear in the novel, he ends up playing an adversarial role, particularly in his refusal to acknowledge Benjamin's curious condition or to accommodate his special needs.
- *Benjamin Button*, the protagonist, is a tall man with a long, gaunt face, but his physical appearance changes drastically over the course of the novel as he gradually grows younger. Initially, the white-haired Benjamin has a long beard; later, he

Nunzio DeFilippis

A television writer with his wife, Christina Weir, Nunzio DeFilippis is best known in the comics industry for the independent comics that he produced for Oni Press. In 2003 the duo produced *Skinwalker* (with artist Brian Hurtt), a crime story set on a Navajo reservation. *Three Strikes* (also with Hurtt) tells the story of a petty thief on the run from a bounty hunter after being sentenced to twenty years in prison because of California's controversial "three strikes" rule. Other graphic novels include *Maria's Wedding* (with Jose Garibaldi), *The Tomb* (with Christopher Mitten), and *Once in a Blue Moon* (with Jennifer Quick). In 2004, DeFilippis and Weir began writing for Marvel Comics, producing *The New X-Men: Academy X*, a comic series about a group of new mutants being trained at Professor Xavier's school. DeFilippis and Weir are known for well-constructed genre works and have worked extensively in a range of media and genres.

sports thick black hair and a pencil-thin mustache; and finally, he takes on the appearance of a young boy, a toddler, and a baby. The entire plot revolves around Benjamin, whose strange appearance and reverse aging constitute the essence of the story.

- *Hildegarde Moncrief*, Benjamin's wife, is initially depicted as a young, beautiful blond woman. As the story progresses, she ages noticeably, becoming heavier with deep lines about her face. She represents the shallow, superficial perspective of society, as she loves Benjamin only when he appears to be old, and he loves her only when she appears young.
- *Roscoe Button*, Benjamin's son, looks exactly like his father, although aging in reverse. Roscoe rejects his father because of his condition and only reluctantly cares for Benjamin when he grows too young to care for himself.

Artistic Style

Because *The Curious Case of Benjamin Button* is a period piece, illustrator Kevin Cornell strives for historical accuracy and a sense of realism. He painstakingly reproduces clothing, accessories, hairstyles, architecture, and famous landmarks with precise, if sometimes impressionistic, detail.

Cornell's illustrations are primarily red-and-black sepia-toned watercolors that replicate the monochromatic look of early photographs and daguerreotypes. This approach not only gives the work a dated feel but also underscores the book's themes of time, age, and aging. Many of the panels, especially the portraits, are overtly framed to resemble photographs, with wide, rectilinear spacing and gutters, making the book seem like a scrapbook or family album. In fact, each of the eleven chapter title pages consists of just such a formalized portrait—almost always of Benjamin depicted at the age he will be in the following chapter—with no text or written title; these progressively younger images offer visual cues regarding each chapter's focus and content. In addition, Cornell's trademark loose, easy style and the washed-out quality of the watercolors give the entire book a dreamlike quality, as if the images are faint memories or even hearsay. Near the end of the work, the illustrations become increasingly less defined, symbolizing and re-creating Benjamin's own fading existence.

As the story relies exclusively on the verbatim words of Fitzgerald's short story, designer Ashburn chooses to present the graphic novel's printed text in formal, blocked paragraphs in a serif typographical font, and these blocks are often offset from the illustrations by rectangular, colored frames. Although dialogue appears in traditional conversation bubbles, it too is rendered typographically, albeit in an almost maroon color. The formal approach to reproducing the source material underscores the literary origins of the written text.

Themes

Despite the story's rather sad ending, *The Curious Case of Benjamin Button* is actually a fanciful satire condemning selfishness, vanity, and superficiality. As an aristocratic businessman with a refined family tree, Roger Button's chief concern is his appearance to others, and his family must adhere to rigid codes of social propriety. Ironically, however, he stubbornly refuses to address Benjamin's physical appearance, focusing instead on maintaining a superficial facade.

Thus, another, related theme in Fitzgerald's tale is the difference between appearance and reality. For example, Hildegarde focuses on surface alone, misreading who Benjamin is on the inside because of how he looks on the outside. Benjamin is hardly any better; his initial interest in Hildegarde is similarly based on her looks, and he throws her aside when she begins to age visibly. Later in the story, the military, Harvard officials, and even Benjamin's own son treat him as nothing more than a child, despite his many years of wisdom and experience. In the end, Benjamin must become a child because he looks like one.

Finally, *The Curious Case of Benjamin Button* addresses the bittersweet realities of aging and mortality. Benjamin may begin his life a seasoned, intelligent man, but he cannot take care of himself because of his infirmities. At the end of his life, Benjamin is back to being helpless, now a physical infant who needs a nurse to look after him, feed him, and change his diapers. Most of Benjamin's life is prosperous, however: He marries, has a child, survives war, and becomes successful in business and football.

Impact

As adapters, DeFilippis and Weir were obviously influenced by Fitzgerald's original short story; in fact, all the written text in *The Curious Case of Benjamin Button: A Graphic Novel* comes directly from that literary antecedent. However, Fitzgerald also drew upon preexisting source material, an idea created offhandedly by renowned novelist Mark Twain. In the table of contents from *Tales of the Jazz Age*, Fitzgerald wrote that the concept for Benjamin Button was "inspired by a remark of Mark Twain's to the effect that it was a pity that the best part of life came at the beginning and the worst part at the end."

This curious idea of a man aging backward has been echoed and imitated, if not outright stolen, by a number of other writers, including Gabriel Brownstein (the 2002 story *The Curious Case of Benjamin Button, Apt. 3W*), Andrew Sean Greer (the 2004 novel *The Confessions of Max Tivoli*), and Fincher (the 2008 film *The Curious Case of Benjamin Button*).

Since the publication of the graphic novel version of Fitzgerald's classic literary text, a number of other such books have appeared on the market, in particular, graphic novel adaptations of Shakespearean plays, Jane Austen novels, and classic gothic fiction. Although the proliferation of such "literary" graphic novels likely has no direct connection to DeFilippis and Weir's adaptation of Fitzgerald's story, a new trend in graphic novels has nonetheless emerged.

Films

The Curious Case of Benjamin Button. Directed by David Fincher. Warner Bros. Pictures/Paramount Pictures, 2008. This film adaptation stars Brad Pitt as Benjamin Button and Cate Blanchett as Daisy. The film differs from the novel dramatically: In addition to shifting the time period about fifty years into the future, almost all crucial plot points and characters were changed. In fact, the name of the title character and the conceit of his aging backward are the only plot elements retained from the original Fitzgerald story.

Kyle William Bishop

Further Reading

Austen, Jane, Nancy Butler, and Sonny Liew. *Sense and Sensibility* (2011).

Cornell, Kevin, and Matthew Sutter. *The Superest: Who Is the Superest Hero of Them All?* (2010).

Shakespeare, William, et al. *Romeo and Juliet, the Graphic Novel: Original Text* (2009).

Bibliography

Cornell, Kevin. "The Curious Job of Kevin Cornell." *Bearskinrug*, August 13, 2008. http://www.bearskinrug.co.uk/_articles/2008/08/13/curious_job.

Publishers Weekly. Review of *The Curious Case of Benjamin Button: A Graphic Novel*, by Nunzio DeFilippis and Christina Weir. 255, no. 39 (2008): 65.

Russell, Benjamin. Review of *The Curious Case of Benjamin Button: A Graphic Novel*, by Nunzio DeFilippis and Christina Weir. *School Library Journal* 55, no. 1 (2009): 135.

Sheehy, Donald G. Afterword to *The Curious Case of Benjamin Button: A Graphic Novel*, by Nunzio DeFilippis and Christina Weir. Philadelphia: Quirk Books, 2008.

See also: *City of Glass; Alice in Sunderland*

D

DAVID BORING

Author: Clowes, Daniel
Artist: Daniel Clowes (illustrator); John Kuramoto (illustrator)
Publisher: Pantheon Books
First serial publication: 1998-2000
First book publication: 2000

Publication History

David Boring first appeared in three acts, or chapters, in Daniel Clowes's comic book series *Eightball* (1989-2004), published by Fantagraphics Books. Act 1 of *David Boring* appeared in issue 19 (May, 1998) of *Eightball*, while Act 2 was published in issue 20 (February, 1999) and Act 3 in issue 21 (February, 2000). In 2000, a hardcover collected edition was published by Pantheon Books, with a paperback volume released in 2002.

Clowes served as the author, book designer, and illustrator of *David Boring*, while John Kuramoto provided the art featured within the novel as panels from *The Yellow Streak*, a comic created by the title character's missing father; the back cover of the collected novel features such images. He is further credited for his technical supervision of the graphic novel.

The cinematic structure of the graphic novel seems to indicate that Clowes may have worked on *David Boring* during the development of the feature film *Ghost World* (2001), an adaptation of his previous graphic novel (1993-1997). For example, Clowes calls the chapters in *David Boring* "acts," and the characters in the graphic novel appear as "credits" at the end of the volume. Some panels give "previews" of an upcoming act.

Plot

The plot of *David Boring* presents the reader with many problems in need of resolution, keeping the

David Boring. (Courtesy of Pantheon Books)

reader actively engaged. In rapid order, Act 1 introduces the reader to some of the varied conflicts in *David Boring*. The narrator and protagonist, David Boring, seeks to avoid his domineering mother; discover what happened to his cartoonist father, creator of *The Yellow Streak*; identify the murderer of his friend Whitey Whitman; find his "perfect woman"; enter his ideal profession; and survive both his assailant, who has already shot him once in the head, and the predicted apocalypse.

The setting of Act 2 is Hulligan's Wharf, where David's mother takes her wounded son to recuperate. David's great-grandfather had purchased this island property after the remaining houses sank into the sea. The servants allow the Boring family members to visit whenever they wish in exchange for living rent-free in the large house. A montage of characters assembles there.

Act 2 introduces additional unanswered issues: the result of David's affair with Mrs. Capon, the identity of Mrs. Capon's killer, the meaning of David's father's comic panels, the outcome of the Iris's marital difficulties, Dot's next unpredictable action, David's selection of his life's work, and the result of Mr. Hulligan and David's attempted escape from Hulligan's Wharf.

Act 3 answers some of the unsettled questions presented in the first two acts. As the chapter opens, both Mr. Hulligan and David wash ashore in Southern New Lapland County. David finds an ideal job in the film industry and still has free time to write his own films. The act reveals that Professor Ferdinand Karkes has plagiarized David's work and was responsible for shooting

David Boring. (Courtesy of Pantheon Books)

David in the first act, as they were both attracted to the same woman, Wanda.

Dot rescues David from two attackers, and they return to Hulligan's Wharf, where they find David's cousin, Pamela. David, Dot, Pamela, and Pamela's baby remain on the island. David decides not to try to predict the immediacy of the apocalypse or to pursue the unsolved mysteries. The love triangles, David's family issues, and other conflicts remain unresolved at the end of the narrative.

Characters

- *David Boring*, the protagonist, is the narrator of the graphic novel. He is twenty years old and a skinny, quiet, passive security guard. He searches for the "perfect woman" throughout the graphic novel, desiring a woman with measurements of 36-32-48; these numbers also correspond to the number of pages in each act in the paperback. Most of his searches—for the murderers, for his father, for the meaning behind the comic book clues—remain incomplete at the end of the novel.

- *Dot Paar* is David's roommate, best friend, and filmmaking partner. A lesbian, she woos a number of the other female characters. Dot wields a gun expertly to protect David against two attackers. While other female characters are generally depicted as sex objects, Dot is a well-rounded character; she displays competence, emotions, and a genuine concern for David.

- *Whitey Whitman* is a friend of David whom he describes as "cynical." Whitey is murdered after he goes home with a girl, and David attempts to find his murderer.

- *Wanda Kraml* is a woman with whom both David and Professor Karkes become infatuated. She is a passenger on the bus in which David travels to Whitey's funeral.

- *Professor Ferdinand Karkes* is an older, distinguished man who becomes infatuated with Wanda. He admits to shooting and wounding David out of jealousy. He locates the missing Wanda in a religious commune.

Artistic Style

Clowes's art is equally effective in the original comics and the hardcover and paperback editions. Within the large paperback format of 10.5 x 7.5 inches, Clowes is able to present several panels on each page without crowding and print the text within the panels in a large, readable size. Clowes's scenes, figures, and printed words are bold and appear uncomplicated. Heavy black lines are placed against a stark white background; such sharp, clear lines lend some clarity to the story line, which is often disordered. Clowes uses both thought and dialogue balloons for the characters in *David Boring*, and the captions on some of the panels further clarify the plot.

The colored panels from the fictional comic *The Yellow Streak* serve artistic as well as narrative functions, adding variety to the pages while also breaking up the action and helping to present the subplot. Kuramoto's art features a classic style, often incorporating cross-hatching, and enhances Clowes's black-and-white artwork.

Clowes has a particular talent for stopping the action in his illustrations at nontraditional moments, showing a bullet in mid-flight, for example. He also conceals clues in the panels; he includes sketches of a car ("Kar") and keys ("kes") near the introduction of the character Karkes.

Themes

David Boring focuses on several themes. The theme of survival of the unfittest is especially evident when skinny, passive David survives a shot to the head by an unknown assailant, recovers, and continues trying to resolve some of the issues surrounding him. David's departure from home, his travels to Hulligan's Wharf, and even his ventures to the big city serve to express the theme of the journey. The theme of family is evident as well. David searches for his missing father and seeks to avoid his domineering mother, who cares for him after his gunshot injury. Clowes weaves this dysfunctional family theme throughout the novel.

Relationships between men and women are important in *David Boring*. Love triangles abound: Karkes, David, and Wanda form one important triangle, while David, Pamela, and Dot suggest another. David and

Professor Karkes typically view women as sex objects, and David's "perfect woman" has prescribed physical dimensions. His relationships with women do not always involve love; he often does not note anything other than their appearance. *David Boring*, therefore, includes many undeveloped characters. Plot is paramount to characterization in the novel.

Reversal of fortune is also a significant theme. By the end of the novel, David becomes interested in a woman for reasons other than her appearance, and this reversal is emphasized by his decision to remain on the island with Pamela and Dot.

Impact

David Boring found its niche among adult fans of crime comic books, a genre that lost much of its popularity after the 1940's. The graphic novel helped renew interest in the genre of crime comics.

The fact that *David Boring* was collected in both hardback and paperback volumes is significant, as it suggests not only a demand for the book but also its acceptance in bookstores as a serious work. Discovering that graphic novels are not just for children, new readers may remain actively engaged with resolving the many overlapping, yet varied, conflicts within the narrative. *David Boring* cannot be read rapidly and superficially; it requires careful scrutiny.

Anita Price Davis

Further Reading

Clowes, Daniel. *Art School Confidential* (2006).
_____. *Ghost World* (2007).
_____. *Mister Wonderful: A Love Story* (2011).

Bibliography

Arnold, Andrew D. "*Boring*'s Exciting Ride: A Comic-Book Saga Comes to a Resonant End." *Time* 155, no. 16 (April 24, 2000): 81. Available at http://www.time.com/time/magazine/article/0,9171,996711,00.html.

Clowes, Daniel. "And Here's the Kicker: Daniel Clowes Interview." Interview by Mike Sacks. *And Here's the Kicker*. http://www.andheresthekicker.com/ex_daniel_clowes.php.

Parille, Ken. "What's This One About? A Re-Reader's Guide to Daniel Clowes's *David Boring*." In *Best American Comics Criticism*, edited by Ken Schwartz. Seattle, Wash.: Fantagraphics Books, 2010.

See also: *Ghost World; Love and Rockets*

DEAD MEMORY

Author: Mathieu, Marc-Antoine

Artist: Marc-Antoine Mathieu (illustrator); Dirk Rehm (letterer)

Publisher: Delcourt (French); Dark Horse Comics (English)

First book publication: *Mémoire morte*, 2000 (English translation, 2003)

Publication History

Dead Memory is the English translation (by Helge Dascher) of *Mémoire morte* by Marc-Antoine Mathieu. It was published by Dark Horse Comics in 2003. *Dead Memory* is the first of Mathieu's books to be translated into English. As of 2011, the only other graphic novel by Mathieu available in English was his *Les Sous-sols du révolu: Extraits du journal d'un expert* (*The Museum Vaults: Excerpts from the Journal of an Expert*) which is the second of four graphic novels commissioned by the Louvre Museum and copublished by the Louvre and Futuropolis. The English edition was released by NBM ComicsLit in 2007.

Mathieu is a highly successful and admired graphic artist in France. His first graphic novel, *Julius Corentin Acquefacques 1. L'Origine*, won the Alph'art Coup de Coeur Prize for best first book at the Angoulême International Comics Festival in 1991, and his third book in the series, *Julius Corentin Acquefacques 3. Le Processus*, received the Alph'art award for best story in 1994.

In addition to writing graphic novels, Mathieu is involved in a graphic-design business, Lucie Lom, which he founded in 1985 with Philippe Leduc. The firm is one of the major creators of expositions throughout France, including the *Forêt suspendue* (suspended forest) exhibit in Lille in 2004. After publishing the fourth volume of the *Acquefacques* series, *Le Debut de la fin*, Mathieu devoted himself to the projects of Lucie Lom and did not write and publish another graphic novel until *Dead Memory*.

Mémoire morte, the original work in French, was published by Delcourt in 2000. Mathieu's first volume of his *Julius Corentin Acquefacques* series

(© David Lefranc/Kipa/Corbis)

Marc-Antoine Mathieu

One of the most innovative experimenters in mainstream French comics, Marc-Antoine Mathieu is best known as the creator of the *Julius Corentin Acquefacques* series, whose adventures he wrote and drew between 1990 and 2004. The *Acquefacques* adventures interrogated the formal limits of the comics form, with the mysteries revolving around the role of formal elements including panel placement and the use of color in black-and-white comics. Stand-alone graphic novels have included *Mémoire morte*, *Le Dessin*, and *Dieu en personne*. In 2006 he produced a book in conjunction with the Louvre Museum in Paris, *Les Sous-sols du révolu* (translated as *The Museum Vaults*), in which he returned to the formal concerns about the construction of images that shaped his earlier Acquefacques work. Mathieu's art is defined by its stark contrasts between black and white and his round, cartoony figures. He creates elaborate, dreamlike worlds in his comics.

was published by Delcourt in 1990. This experimental graphic novel, the first to be drawn without delineated panels, launched Delcourt as a publisher of experimental and alternative graphic novels, and it is the major publisher of Mathieu's work in France.

Plot

Dead Memory is a philosophical science-fiction graphic novel that targets an adult audience. It addresses issues of human existence and elements, such as language, that define and delimit human beings. In *Dead Memory*, Mathieu portrays a city of the future that is organized and controlled by a computer "ROM." Each citizen has a black box, a communication device through which he or she receives real-time information. The black boxes also serve as a means of verifying the identity of each individual. The city is infinite, yet it is organized in every detail. Everything from its physical plan to the events that happen there is recorded, analyzed, evaluated, and preserved in ROM. Stability, order, and conformity reign in the city.

A twofold crisis is occurring in the city; mysterious walls dividing neighborhoods and sections of the city are appearing overnight, and the residents are losing their memories. The city administration is at a loss as to how to handle the crisis. Firmin Huff, an employee in the Land Registry, is assigned to investigate the problem. Huff begins his investigation at the Land Registry, where the staff is attempting to map the locations of the walls; however, walls are appearing so quickly that the registry cannot keep up. ROM is strangely quiet and unresponsive about the problem.

Next, Huff heads to the observatory. On the way, he is detained; a neighborhood is blocked off to let a Grinder demolish a building to make a new street. Huff suggests that the Grinder could be used to knock down the walls. His colleague Menilmont is appalled at the utopian character of such an idea. At the observatory, Huff learns that only the past is observed and hypotheses about the present and future are proposed. Huff proceeds to the Department of Communication, where he learns that ROM is still not speaking. He is given an enormous file containing all the dimensions of the walls and told that he has been appointed director of the "Incident Observation and Preliminary Investigation Commission."

With the walls proliferating at an overwhelming rate, Huff turns his attention to the problem of memory loss. He counts all of the words that he still knows and disconnects his black box. Later when he confronts ROM, the computer will mock Huff for this daring act. That night he dreams. In the dream, he enters ROM's complex and finds the entire city existing in a virtual world that has replaced the other "real" world. Upon waking, Huff searches through libraries and books to see if words are still there; he observes people leaving the city and decides to visit ROM. The confrontation between ROM and Huff ends with Huff unplugging ROM. Huff leaves and receives a message prerecorded by ROM on his black box. It is an account of ROM's last dream. The city is shut down and silent. Letters begin to rain down; words are returning, and walls are being knocked down. The novel ends with ROM explaining that systems are living forms that die; ROM proposes that his story exists or does not depending upon whether or not the residents have relearned words and understand the story. The novel begins with ROM repeating Huff's question about "who he is" and rephrasing it to "who are you?" It ends with another question, asking if there is reality without language.

Characters

- *Firmin Huff*, the protagonist, is a management-level employee in the Land Registry. He is assigned the task of finding out why walls are suddenly appearing throughout the city. Physically, he is more a caricature of a human being than an actual realistic person. He is short; has a large, round head; and has a large moustache. He wears large glasses that obscure his eyes. He is the only human character who has a significant role in the graphic novel. He moves about in the infinite city, consults various departments, and finally interacts with ROM as he attempts to solve the mystery of the walls and the residents' memory loss.
- *ROM* is a computer that collects and stores all facts about the city, the events that take place there, and all of the actions and words of the

residents, so they have no need to remember anything. ROM is both antagonist and friend to Huff. He identifies himself as having become all of the residents of the infinite city. Without him, Huff could solve nothing, yet he must cease to exist for the residents to reclaim their identities.

- *The Infinite City* is an overpopulated city without limits or borders that is controlled by ROM. It is organized and cataloged, with everything about it recorded. Ironically, however, the city administration has no idea of its size.

- *Black Boxes* resembling early mobile phones are devices that continuously transmit real-time information to the city's residents. The residents are totally dependent on the boxes and must consult them to know what they are to do and where they are to go. The residents are required to always have their boxes with them because, in addition to providing controlling information about daily life, the boxes verify the identity of each resident and are a technological replacement for the required French *carte d'identité* (identification card).

Artistic Style

Mathieu avoids the use of color throughout his graphic novels. In his opinion, color tells too much and restricts the creative participation of the reader in the story. Mathieu's complex use of black and white is the most striking feature of *Dead Memory*. It delineates and controls the story line and, at the same time, frees the reader to imaginatively elaborate the story at certain points.

The story is narrated by ROM. All of ROM's narration appears as white words on a black background; by contrast, the dialogue of the various characters is presented in black words on white background. The story is divided into a prologue, eight chapters, and an epilogue, similar to a traditional novel. Each part is introduced by a title in a framed white box and is concluded with a frameless black panel. In this way, Mathieu introduces the section's story and then opens the story's end to the imagination of the reader. The final black panel represents the failure of the characters to find answers and also invites the reader to find the answers. However, the use of final black panels at the end of each section also adds a dimension of irony; there may be hidden answers, or the blackness may simply represent a void. Interestingly, only once in the novel does Mathieu use an image within an image. In the last chapter, a vague image that is difficult to identify appears in the shadow of a man knocking down a wall.

The use of black and white only is also an important element of character portrayal. The characters have really no distinguishing qualities. They are the crowd, the amorphous overpopulation of the city. They are the physical shells of human beings, whose thoughts, emotions, and memories have been stored in ROM. Only Huff, with his round head, his enormous glasses that hide his eyes, his large mustache, and his round white hat, stands out at all. Even Huff shares almost all of his physical features with various other characters. The reader has the impression that Huff has been made more visible in order for him to serve as a guide through the congested, confusing complexity of the city in crisis and to provide access to ROM.

Geometrical shapes are also a significant element of Mathieu's graphic novel. They reflect the order and stability of the city. The use of vertical and perpendicular lines gives a sense of the infinite quality of the city. Many of the panels and drawings of the city resemble blueprints or diagrams of machines. Geometrical shapes also reaffirm the themes of the story: The prologue is entitled "Rectilinear Ruins"; the epilogue is "Circular Foundations." One of the unanswerable questions considered by the characters is whether the city is round or square, which, by extension, is a question about infinity.

Themes

Dead Memory examines the relationship between human beings and the technology that they have produced. Mathieu questions how much of human activity and existence can be relegated to technology without reducing the human being to a creature who lacks the ability to remember, reason, create, and use language. The residents of the infinite city have lost control of their lives and their individuality and eventually lose their ability to remember and to use language. They live only in the present and are totally dependent on their black boxes for information and for direction for their daily activities.

Mathieu also satirizes the modern bureaucratic tendency to survey, analyze, evaluate, and record without taking effective action. The various city departments create large, useless files that provide no solution to either the appearance of the walls or the loss of memory. The observers see the past but are not really aware of its connection to the present or the future. They lack any sense of continuity in human existence. Mathieu also portrays how the human need for conformity and avoidance of change restricts human existence. These themes lighten the tone of *Dead Memory* and permeate the work with an ironic humor, as what may have appeared beneficial becomes an obstacle.

The importance of language is also an integral theme in Mathieu's graphic novel. Language that enables communication between human beings, the expression of individuality, and the intellectual realization of the past play major roles in the story. For reality to exist, language must exist, be understood, and used. Without language, nothing is understood or remembered, and, thus, there is no reality.

Impact

For Mathieu, the graphic novel is a medium in which he can give full freedom to his imagination and creativity. His stories are compilations of influences from his intellectual interests and experiences, both artistic and scientific, which he has reworked and filtered through his creative genius. *Dead Memory* presents a world that reflects the influence of his mathematical investigations, his readings of Franz Kafka and Jose Luis Borges, and his interest in the Surrealists and *le nouveau roman*.

From the earliest volume of his *Julius Corentin Acquefacques* series, Mathieu has taken the graphic novel in the direction of serious literature and significantly contributed to it being considered art. He uses it to investigate philosophical questions about human existence and the existence of reality. Mathieu also enlarges the creative possibility of the graphic novel as he explores the use of images within images and stories within stories and challenges the reader to look beyond what is presented. Mathieu's graphic novels have been successful in France, but their effect on the graphic novel on a global scale has been restricted by lack of translated versions, particularly translations to English. None of the five *Julius Corentin Acquefacques* volumes have been translated into English. The two graphic novels that have appeared in English have enjoyed a good reception.

Shawncey Jay Webb

Further Reading

Mathieu, Marc-Antoine. *The Museum Vaults: Excerpts from the Journal of an Expert* (2007).
Schuiten, François, and Benoît Peeters. *The Great Walls of Samaris* (1987).
_____. *The Tower* (1993).

Bibliography

Dauncey, Hugh, ed. *French Popular Culture: An Introduction*. London: Arnold, 2003.
Fosdick, Charles, Laurence Groves, and Libbie McQuilan, eds. *The Francophone Bande Dessinée*. New York: Rodopi, 2005.
Groensteen, Thierry. *The System of Comics*. Translated by Bart Beaty and Nick Nguyen. Jackson: University Press of Mississippi, 2007

See also: *Glacial Period; Give It Up; City of Glass; The Rabbi's Cat*

DEAR JULIA

Author: Biggs, Brian
Artist: Brian Biggs (illustrator)
Publisher: Black Eye Productions; Top Shelf Comics
First serial publication: 1996-1997
First book publication: 2000

Dear Julia,. (Courtesy of Top Shelf Productions)

Publication History

Dear Julia, was originally published in four parts by Black Eye Productions of Montreal, between 1996 and 1997. After Black Eye went out of business, the series was published in a single volume by Top Shelf Comics in 2000. The Top Shelf edition does not reproduce the four full-color cover illustrations that Brian Biggs created for the series, which, according to the author, are the closest thing to "actual traditional painting" that he has done. A French translation of the work, hand-lettered by Biggs, was published by Montreal-based La Pastèque in 2002.

Plot

On a trip to Arizona, Boyd Soloman and his girl-friend, Julia, come across a dead man along the road. Two years later, a man named Leo Legyscapo seeks out Boyd to question him about the dead man. Leo first approaches Boyd on the bus, but then he visits Boyd's apartment. He shows Boyd a photograph of a man flying with wings strapped to his back; it is the man Boyd and Julia found in the desert. Leo questions Boyd about the dead man and what Julia saw, but Boyd is more interested in the huge pair of wings that Leo presumably used to enter the apartment via the window. When Leo threatens Julia, Boyd grabs for the wings.

In the struggle that follows, Boyd falls to the floor and is knocked out. Leo exits the apartment quickly, leaving the wings behind in his haste. When he comes to, Boyd writes a letter to Julia, telling her what happened and warning her. As Leo enters the apartment building, by the front door this time, and rings the doorbell to Boyd's apartment, Boyd straps on the wings. He puts the letter in his pocket and jumps out of his eighth-floor window. He had written that he wants to deliver the letter to Julia himself.

Several weeks later, Leo is sitting on a park bench with a woman who lives across the hall from Boyd. Leo looks dejected and asks her if she has seen any wings. When she points out an extraordinarily large and odd-looking bird, Leo breaks into a smile.

Biggs's *Dear Julia,* is narrated in fits and starts, jumping between the present and the past as Boyd is writing his letter to Julia. Certain important plot points are established only obliquely, such as whether Leo actually flies into Boyd's apartment using the wings or what happens to Boyd after he leaps from his window, while others are never addressed at all, such as what exactly happened to the man in the desert. The story is a puzzle of sorts and engages readers by inviting them to connect the fragments and pay attention to all the minute details in the pictures to find out what is happening.

Volumes

- *Dear Julia,:* Part One (1996). The first install-ment starts at the end of the story: Leo is walking up to Boyd's apartment. As Boyd's letter begins in the captions, *"August 17, Dear Julia,"* the im-ages show the apartment in disarray but empty, and Boyd is poised to jump off his windowsill. Subsequent scenes show how Boyd and Leo met, then switch to Boyd writing his letter, and finally show a flashback of the trip to Arizona and a po-liceman talking to Boyd next to the body.

- *Dear Julia,:* Part Two (1996). The second part fills in Boyd's background, as his letter to Julia continues. He relates his childhood, how he lost his parents in a car accident, and how he was al-ways fascinated with flying, to the point of ob-session. The final page shows Leo gazing up at Boyd's window, taking notes.

- *Dear Julia,:* Part Three (1997). This volume is completely devoted to the confrontation between Boyd and Leo in Boyd's apartment. By the final pages, Boyd is unconscious on the floor of his kitchen, and Leo is in the corridor outside the apartment, locked out and realizing he has left his wings behind.

- *Dear Julia,:* Part Four (1997). Part Four begins where Part Three ends. Boyd regains conscious-ness and starts writing the letter the reader has been reading all the while. Leo is keeping an eye on the apartment and trying to get back into the building. Finally, the narrative catches up to where the story started in Part One and then con-cludes with Leo watching the sky.

Characters

- *Boyd Soloman,* the protagonist, is a man prob-ably in his late twenties with perpetually raised eyebrows, freckles, and deep grooves in his face. He suffers from mountain fever, the "over-whelming urge to leap from high places," which he inherited from his father, who drove his car off a cliff seventeen years earlier, killing himself and Boyd's mother. Boyd has always been fas-cinated by birds and flying insects, wanting to know how they are able to fly, and he becomes

alienated from the people around him as a result. After he attempts to jump off the Golden Gate Bridge with homemade wings, his insect and bird collections are taken away. Over time, he be-lieves he has recovered from his mountain fever and his life takes on normality; he even has a girlfriend, Julia. Boyd Soloman's name is a pun, with "Boyd" sounding slightly like "bird" and "Soloman" referring to Boyd's life as a loner.

- *Leopold Legyscapo,* a.k.a. *Leo,* is a tiny balding man who likes to wear ties and basketball sneakers. He befriends Boyd at the bus stop, but it turns out he has an ulterior motive, wanting to find out what Boyd knows about a dead body in the Arizona desert. Throughout the story, it is unclear whether or not Leo is an antagonist: He seems to stalk Boyd, appearing in his apartment uninvited and making threatening comments about Julia. On the other hand, he seems to be happy when Boyd takes off with his wings. The ambiguity about Leo's motives adds to the ten-sion of the narrative.

- *Julia* was once Boyd's girlfriend. They went to a wedding in Tucson, Arizona, together two years ago, but they have broken up since then. She is never actually shown in the comic: Her face only appears in a series of photographs that depict the trip to Arizona, and her face has been scratched or crossed out in all of these, presumably by Boyd. However, Boyd still has strong feelings for her, wanting to protect her; the entire narrative is a letter to Julia, telling her about what is happening and warning her.

Artistic Style

The artwork on *Dear Julia,* is done in black ink, with a wash for grays. Biggs's drawings include a lot of detail, in lines and patterns such as wood grain, making the overall effect deeply textured. Over the course of the four parts, Biggs's line becomes bolder and clearer, as he develops a style that relies more on thick outlines, which has become the typical style of his children's book illustrations. The human figures in *Dear Julia,* are caricatural, with great attention paid to wrinkles, folds, and spots. However, the backgrounds, in terms of perspective and detail, are quite realistic. The detail in the representational style supports the attention to detail in the settings, and together, they capture Boyd's obsession with flight and his compulsion to find a way to take to the air: The pages are populated with pigeons with meticulously rendered feathers, and in the background, many of the panels reveal Boyd's obsession through glimpses of rockets, bird cages, and paper airplanes.

With the exception of Part One, which keeps a relative distance, the panels include a striking amount of close-up points of view, as well as views from odd angles, giving a claustrophobic sense of tightness. This dominant point of view reflects Boyd's paranoid feelings of being trapped. The tightness is emphasized by the grid layout of the panels: Each page contains four panels that are arranged in a square, without any blank gutters between them. This "squeezed" layout is completely regular and applied throughout, with the exception of the end of Part One, where for several pages the grid layout is replaced by four drawn photographs arranged loosely on each page, sometimes slightly overlapping, with shadows rendered underneath them.

Captions, which start on page 5, play an important role in this work, since they represent the letter to Julia. Biggs created the lettering for the captions as well as the dialogue. While there is not a huge amount of dialogue in this narrative (conversations are usually a halting, fragmented back-and-forth), the spoken words are made to reflect the characters uttering them, as Biggs uses different font styles and word balloons for each individual character. Thus, the policeman at the end of Part One speaks in clear block capitals, and Boyd's speech is represented by a spidery cursive not unlike his handwriting depicted in the captions.

Themes

The main theme of *Dear Julia,* is obsession. This theme appears in several forms, the most important and prominent of which is Boyd Soloman's obsession with flying. This obsession is explained in *Part Two* as he tells of mountain fever, his collections of birds and insects and experiments with them, his construction of huge wings, and his attempt at flight by jumping off a bridge. The book also shows other obsessions:

Brian Biggs

Now working primarily as the author of children's books, Brian Biggs established a name for himself in comics with his mid-1990's graphic novels *Dear Julia* and *Frederick and Eloise*. Strongly influenced by graphic novels from the time he spent in France as a student, Biggs adds a European flavor to his illustrations and often depicts his characters with exaggeratedly cartoonish features. In the area of children's books he is particularly well known as the illustrator of the *Shredderman* series, written by Wendelin Van Draanen, which was developed into a television series for Nickelodeon, and for the *Everything Goes* series, which he both writes and draws. A former instructor of illustration, Biggs's work is defined by its playful sensibility, vibrant colors, and rejection of classical three-point perspective. His images tend to be overloaded with visual information, and his comics and children's books are notable for their reliance on puns and sight gags.

Leo's obsession is expressed in his dogged determination to find answers, stalking Boyd and breaking into his home. A final form of obsession is Boyd's single-minded commitment to warning Julia, to the point that he jumps out of his eighth-floor window to get a letter to her.

Boyd's fascination with flying also provides the comic's second theme, namely, flight. This theme is brought to the foreground in countless details throughout the comic's images, from clouds on wallpaper, birds on stamps, and Boyd's books to the names of Boyd's neighbors (Lindbergh and Earhart, among others). The paper planes, windup birds, and pigeons in Boyd's apartment bind together the themes of obsession and flight.

The connection between flight and obsession is made explicit when pigeons start speaking to Boyd in Part Four. They utter phrases that were previously spoken to Boyd in Part Three by Leo, and the pigeons' voices cast doubt on Boyd's sanity. The lines between flights of fancy and reality have become blurred. When Boyd jumps out of his window, the pigeons follow him, and Boyd is last seen in their park, where Leo is feeding pigeons with Boyd's neighbor; the implication is that Boyd and the pigeons have joined forces.

Impact

Dear Julia, is illustrative of the difficulty of pursuing a career in alternative comics, a scene in which cartoonists try to release their work through small publishers (or by self-publishing), hoping to be picked up by larger publishers. Biggs studied at Parsons The New School for Design in New York City and created a number of comics after his education. His first comic, *Frederick and Eloise*, was published by Fantagraphics in 1993. He then published the four parts of *Dear Julia,* after which he self-published *Nineteen Weird Guys and a Portrait of the Artist* and *Interim* in 1997. Black Eye Productions was in business for only six years, but *Dear Julia,* was acquired by Top Shelf Comics, a young company at the time. The collected edition did not lead to new comics projects for Biggs. Biggs has stated that making comics is time-consuming work with little monetary reward. After having had some success in comics, including an Eisner Award nomination, Biggs decided to give up cartooning and turn to children's book illustration.

Films

Dear Julia. Directed by Alistair Banks Griffin. Self-produced, 2002. This film was Griffin's thesis project for the Rhode Island School of Design. The nineteen-minute film was shot in Providence, Rhode Island, and starred Christian de Rezendes as Boyd and John Los as Leo.

Dear Julia. Directed by Isaac E. Gozin. Self-produced, 2003. Gozin directed *Dear Julia* as an art-school project in Belgium. This short was twelve minutes long, with Ted Fletcher as Boyd and David B. Lobb as Leopold. The adaptation, written by Bert van Dael, is faithful to Biggs's comic, using much of the dialogue verbatim and following the panels almost like a storyboard. This version condenses the story of Biggs's comic and clears up some of its ambiguities. The main difference with the comic is that instead of being a little man, Leo is quite large in the film.

Barbara Postema

Further Reading

Berry, Hannah. *Britten and Brülightly* (2009).

Huizinga, Kevin. *Curses: Glenn Ganges Stories* (2006).

Lutes, Jason. *Jar of Fools* (1994-1995).

Bibliography

Postema, Barbara. "Mind the Gap: Absence as Signifying Function in Comics" (doctoral dissertation, Michigan State University, 2010).

Salisbury, Martin. "Brian Biggs." In *Play Pen: New Children's Book Illustration*. London: Laurence King, 2007.

Steinberg, Sybil S. Review of *Dear Julia,*, by Brian Biggs." *Publishers Weekly*, March 6, 2000: 84.

See also: *Jar of Fools; It's a Good Life If You Don't Weaken*

DEOGRATIAS: A TALE OF RWANDA

Author: Stassen, Jean-Philippe
Artist: Jean-Philippe Stassen (illustrator)
Publishers: Dupuis (French); First Second Books (English)
First book publication: 2000 (English translation, 2006)

Publication History

Jean-Paul Stassen developed the graphic novel *Deogratias* based partly on the coverage of the Rwandan genocide and partly on his own love of the country, where he eventually settled with his family. *Déogratias* was published in French and Dutch by Dupuis and Uitgeverij Dupuis, in 2000. It was later translated to Portuguese, Italian, and Spanish, and the first English publication appeared in 2006. The English version features an introduction by translator Alexis Siegel, who gives an account of the events leading up to the genocide and discusses the shortcomings of the international response. Siegel also includes background information on the political climate and international relations that influenced the development of some of the characters.

Plot

Deogratias was inspired both by the events of 1994 and 1995 that later became known as the Rwandan genocide and the lack of response from the international community, as scenes of ethnic cleansing unfolded on television and in other media. While the horrific images that came out of the area during the genocide were well publicized, world leaders were reluctant to intervene or even to use the term "genocide." An essentially powerless U.N. peacekeeping force was the only help available for victims.

The graphic novel represents Stassen's attempt to depict both the victims and the perpetrators of the genocide as fully developed individuals, a response to the images of large-scale suffering disseminated by the media. *Deogratias* is among a number of graphic novels that examine large-scale violence and genocide and is meant to stand alongside other works about historical events that address young-adult or adult

(AP Photo)

Jean-Philippe Stassen

Born in Liège, Belgium, Jean-Philippe Stassen began contributing to *L'Écho des savanes* when he was only seventeen years old. Having traveled extensively in Africa at a young age, Stassen began producing comics about that continent with the two volumes of *Le Bar du Vieux Français* (written by Denis Lapière) in 1992, which won several awards. In the late-1990's he began writing his own stories with *Louis le Portugais* and *Thérèse*. His best-known work was published in 2000, *Déogratias*, a story that depicts the Rwandan genocide in a series of flashbacks from the point of view of a young Hutu teenager. The book won several industry awards in France and was translated into English by First Second Books in 2006. Stassen is known for images that feature thick, clean, black lines with very little shading. Depth is created by the use of gradiated color. His page designs are very classical, lending his stories an easy flow.

audiences. *Deogratias* was originally written in French, which is significant partly because of the French government's tacit involvement in the genocide depicted in the graphic novel. Rwanda was initially colonized by Germany (beginning in the late nineteenth century) and later controlled by Belgium, but France made extensive arms shipments to Rwanda prior to its civil war.

Deogratias depicts the experiences of one man during the aftermath of the Rwandan genocide. The main character, Deogratias, is a member of the Hutu majority and is among those Hutu that carried out extensive mass killings of the Tutsi minority during the genocide. The plot oscillates between Deogratias's experiences in the present and his memories of the time before the genocide. In the present, he is an alcoholic who becomes insane when he cannot find enough to drink to obliterate his memories. Prior to the genocide, he is depicted as an average young man trying to win the affections of two local Tutsi sisters, Benina and Apollinaria, whose mother is forced to prostitute herself so that Benina has the opportunity to go to college. Apollinaria prefers to work at the local church, where Father Prior Stanislaus ministers to the local population. Father Prior Stanislaus and Brother Philip are both committed Catholics who are attempting to do ministry work in the region, but when the genocide begins, they are forced to flee. Whether or not they are able to save any of the local Tutsis as they flee is treated ambiguously in the text. Benina and Deogratias date briefly, and at the beginning of the genocide, he attempts to hide her in his room until she escapes to find her sister and her mother. He ultimately joins the Hutu militia and assists in the rape and slaughter of his neighbors. At the end, he tells Brother Philip, who has returned to Rwanda, that he has murdered all of the other complicit parties through the use of poison.

Characters

- *Deogratias*, the main character, is a Hutu man and an alcoholic who uses Urwagwa, a liquor, to forget about crimes he perpetrated during the Rwandan genocide. When he cannot get drunk, he is depicted as turning into a dog, remembering moments during the genocide. His flashbacks form the bulk of the dramatic action in the comic.

- *Venetia*, the mother of Benina and Apollinaria, is a Tutsi woman who fled Rwanda during an earlier period of ethnic strife, hiding in Zaire. She returned to Rwanda and is attempting to get her daughters into college in spite of the ethnic quotas, which limit the number of Tutsi allowed into schools. She works at least partly as a prostitute.

- *Apollinaria* is Tutsi, the daughter of Venetia and, rumor has it, Father Prior Stanislas. Deogratias is in love with her, but she denies him because he goes to taverns and he is forward with her. She prefers her work in the local church, hoping to gain the opportunity to go to college.

- *Benina*, the half sister of Apollinaria, is a Tutsi and in love with Deogratias. She works as a translator for the French. Her mother, Venetia, is attempting to send her to college, which is difficult because of ethnic quotas, but she eventually manages it. She becomes involved in politics and is easily angered by the ethnic slurs directed at Tutsis.

- *Brother Philip* is a heavyset young white priest who works at the church. He arrives in Rwanda at the beginning of the narrative.

- *Father Prior Stanislas* is the primary caretaker of the church. He previously helped Venetia flee Rwanda during an earlier attack on the Tutsi and apparently had a sexual relationship with her, during which he fathered Apollinaria.

- *Augustine*, a Twa, has been a friend of Venetia's since childhood. He is a groundskeeper for the white residents. He is bitter about his circumstances because he trained at a university, but professors' salaries are lower than those in the service industry.

- *Bosco* is an acquaintance of Deogratias in the aftermath of the genocide. He provides him with Urwagwa and mythologizes the political climate of Rwanda prior to white colonization.

- *Sergeant*, a.k.a. *the Frenchman*, is a white man from France serving as a member of the French postcolonial military contingent tasked with keeping peace in Rwanda. However, he is more interested in promoting the brewing ethnic strife, having sexual relationships with as many Tutsi women as possible, and calling the people of Rwanda "savages."

- *Julius* is one of the leaders of the Hutu militia that massacres Tutsi citizens.

Artistic Style

Stassen uses a realistic style. The primary transitions are those between day and night, for which he uses different color palettes: The daytime colors are warm, while the nighttime and interior palettes are cool. Characters and objects are depicted using heavily inked outlines. Individual characters are differentiated partly through facial structure and body type and through skin tone. Deogratias is depicted as a dark-skinned and muscular young man. Benina and Apollinaria are drawn similarly, but Benina is depicted with darker skin than Apollinaria, which is meant to call into question the ethnic divisions around which the plot revolves.

Panels are densely packed on the page, but the minimal color shading lends a sense of spaciousness within panels. Action-to-action and scene-to-scene panel transitions dominate and are particularly effective in smoothly transitioning between present-day scenes and flashbacks. Temporal transitions are marked by visual cues within similarly structured panels, including panels depicting Deogratias as a clean-cut young man followed by panels depicting him as a ragged alcoholic beggar, standing in the same position.

Unlike many autobiographical graphic novels that deal with large-scale violence, *Deogratias* is careful to avoid fully collapsing the reader into the perspective of any particular character. This is partly because of the historical context of the work—the Rwandan genocide was well publicized as it occurred, but the world stood by and watched. The structure of the artwork is an implicit indictment of the readers' attempt to access this experience vicariously and to find catharsis through fictionalized works of art based on an actual historical situation.

The artistic style is important partly for its response to the widely disseminated photographs of the genocide, many of which lent the sensation of witness to the viewer but failed to produce an adequate international outcry to stop the violence. *Deogratias* works partly because it maintains distance between viewer and subject, and, while vicarious access to the experiences depicted is limited, it uses this distance to implicitly indict the viewer.

Themes

The primary thematic elements of *Deogratias* concern what human beings are capable of becoming. While the flashbacks in the narrative develop a fairly familiar coming-of-age story, this bildungsroman is disrupted by the genocide and Deogratias's complicity in it. During his development into an adult, Deogratias is concerned with girls and drinking, making him quite recognizable to the average Western reader. However, at the cusp of his adulthood, rather than becoming a man, he becomes a dog; his involvement in the genocide, in terms of both what he has witnessed and what he has done, damage his self-image. This is important not only in its subversion of the coming-of-age narrative but also in its allusion to Art Spiegelman's *Maus: A Survivor's Tale* (1972-1991) and other graphic novels in which human characters are depicted as animals. *Deogratias* modifies this familiar trope, however, by depicting a physical transformation that takes place during the incursion of traumatic memories—that is, Deogratias becomes a dog only when he cannot find enough alcohol to dull his senses.

Additionally, both the visual and the textual elements of *Deogratias* question to what extent imaginatively accessing the experiences of victims of genocide is ethical. The connection between the passive reader and the text is made partly through the sympathy the reader develops for the Deogratias character, who is ultimately revealed to be among the perpetrators and not the victims. In addition, the artwork, while rendering violent scenes, never positions the reader within the perspective of victims, effectively closing the reader off from vicarious access. This can be read as an indictment of the international community that watched these events unfold in Rwanda but did nothing about them.

Impact

Deogratias represents a broadening of the politically themed autographs of the late 1990's and early 2000's.

Works such as Marjane Satrapi's autobiographical *Persepolis* (2003) and Spiegelman's biographical *Maus* used individual experiences to contextualize broader historical events, the Iranian Revolution in the former and the Holocaust in the latter. Both *Persepolis* and *Maus* have been used extensively in classrooms and have been widely lauded for their impact on the way readers view distant historical events. By fictionalizing characters and certain events, *Deogratias* contributes something new to this framework. It resembles much of the earlier works' political motivations but, as a fictional work, is given significantly more latitude in terms of artistic invention. It draws on but alters the conventions of earlier autographic works. For example, as in *Maus*, it depicts a human character as an animal, but instead of depicting the character based on national or ethnic identity, Stassen chooses to have Deogratias transform into a dog to represent his complicity and guilt. Additionally, while many autographs position the reader within the viewpoints of their characters, *Deogratias* remains largely closed off from the perspectives of its characters, implicitly arguing against the way many people teach about genocides. Genocide is conceptualized as something that can be avoided if one feels for the victims, as this will reduce the likelihood that one will engage in violence, but the Rwandan genocide in particular demonstrates the limits of this assumption.

Deogratias won several awards after its publication and met generally positive reviews, though some reviewers predicted that the story would not be widely read given its emotionally demanding content and lack of catharsis.

Katharine Polak

Further Reading

Abouet, Marguerite. *Aya* (2007-2009).

Kannemeyer, Anton, and Conrad Botes. *The Big Bad Bitterkomix Handbook* (2008).

Spiegelman, Art. *Maus: A Survivor's Tale* (1987).

Vaughan, Brian K., and Niko Henrichon. *Pride of Baghdad* (2008).

Bibliography

Chute, Hillary, and Marie DeKoven. "Introduction: Graphic Narrative." *Modern Fiction Studies* 52, no. 4 (2006): 767-782.

Groensteen, Thierry. *The System of Comics*. Translated by Bart Beaty and Nick Nyugen. Jackson: University of Mississippi Press, 2007.

McCloud, Scott. *Understanding Comics: The Invisible Art*. New York: Harper, 1994.

Repetti, Massimo. "African Wave: Specificity and Cosmopolitanism in African Comics." *African Arts* 40, no. 2 (Summer, 2007): 16-35.

See also: *Maus: A Survivor's Tale; Persepolis; Aya of Yopougon; Pyongyang*

DIARY OF A MOSQUITO ABATEMENT MAN

Author: Porcellino, John
Artist: John Porcellino (illustrator)
Publisher: La Mano
First serial publication: 1989-1999
First book publication: 2005

Publication History

Each of the individual stories in *Diary of a Mosquito Abatement Man* come from an issue of John Porcellino's self-produced minicomic *King-Cat Comics*, which began in 1989. The chapters "Asparagus" (2004), "Chemical Plant/Another World" (2004), and "Death of a Mosquito Abatement Man" (2003-2004) were previously unpublished. The stories from *King-Cat Comics* are "The Forest" (issue 3, published in June, 1989); "Hellhole," "Scott," and "Sex on the Beach" (issue 6, August, 1989); "Inhuman Bastards of the Deep" and "Attacked by Wasps" (issue 7, October, 1989); "Twenty-Four Hours" (issue 22, October, 1990); "Channahon" and "Untitled Drunk Comic" (issue 23, November, 1990); "f——k" (issue 46, October, 1994); "Waukegan" (issue 48, May, 1995); "Mountain Song" (issue 49, October, 1995); and "The Owl" (issue 55, June, 1999).

Plot

Porcellino's *King-Cat Comics* has been at the forefront of independent autobiography. Initially produced as a series of "minis" (small, stapled and photocopied booklets, measuring about 2 x 4 inches), they read as unprocessed memoirs, disingenuous in their effect.

The dedication to *Diary of a Mosquito Abatement Man* is indicative of Porcellino's Zen mind-set. It is reminiscent of the Native American belief in the living consciousness of the natural world. "This book is dedicated, with love, to mosquitoes, men, women, and all beings; grasses, rocks, fences and sky." Porcellino places mosquitoes on the top of the list, above humans and other sentient beings. In the lines that follow, "fences," a product of humanity, are juxtaposed with grasses and rocks, natural elements that Native Americans feel possess a life-force.

The book traces Porcellino's would-be career as a pest exterminator. As he begins his first season on the job, he is intoxicated with the freedom to explore the marginal wooded spaces that demarcate and abut suburban housing developments, as he did in his footloose youth. As an adult, he is officially sanctioned to root around. As a new "mosquito man," Porcellino is also charged with a mission. Nature is full of thorns and snares as well as mosquito larvae that carry disease. The two-page sequence at the top of the book illustrates the pitfalls of the forest for the defenseless worker; soaking rain, pointy branches at eye level, and tripping vines. In this sequence, only a cemetery is considered beautiful, as an example of nature with a "makeover," improved by man.

Porcellino likes the extermination work. He is paid to make the world a safer place by forcibly changing "things that should not be." At this point, the narrator considers nature something to master, a "festering mosquito paradise." Using his dipper, a long-handled, spoonlike sampling tool that becomes a distinctive icon of the abatement profession, he evaluates the swarm in the stagnant puddle. Having demonstrated the presence of mosquito larvae and pupae, he returns to Site 19-01 and bombs the bugs with a half pound of pesticide.

Porcellino displays a level of formality that seems excessive for someone who spends his day hanging out in ditches in the borderlands beyond tract-house developments. The text does not initially justify the eradication of known pests. However, "Hellhole" demonstrates the extent to which humanity, abstracted, perceives threats and distances itself from the natural world.

In the next two segments, Porcellino encounters people while on his rounds. The first, a vagabond named Scott, hitches a ride. Glad for the companionship of even a misfit, Porcellino details their dialogue at length. Next, he spies on an unappealing disheveled couple, parked at the beach in Waukegan, Illinois, having sex.

In the one-page "Inhuman Bastards of the Deep," with a logo rendered in a mock horror-film font, Porcellino composes a visual list with captions of various insect nuisances, but with a sense of humor and even affection. The next chapter, "Attacked by Wasps," returns the narrative to nature as tormentor.

Porcellino's second season as an exterminator begins with a lengthy assignment, driving a route at twelve miles per hour while emitting a fine spray of pesticide. Although his supervisor has conjectured that the pesticide powder was harmless to the point that it can be ingested on a peanut butter sandwich, somewhat suspiciously, the stuff is airborne and now distributed wholesale. However, doing so is Porcellino's assignment, and he struggles to stay awake for the entire shift. This phase is marked by extreme negativity and fear; a night ride becomes a visit to an alien, terrifically uncool habitation. A key sequence follows in which Porcellino endlessly drives his route through a vast, surreal, industrial factory zone, with "belching steam," and "unearthly light."

Porcellino relocates to Denver, Colorado, a comfortable place within his world. However, he is still struggling with his work in pest control. He confronts and mingles with the fauna and flora; this passage features a quizzical encounter with a squirrel and an essay on wild asparagus. After some whimsy involving a lemonade stand and a bull with its head stuck in a fence, Porcellino's health begins to decline. He develops a disabling ear condition that turns him inward, away from his hard-partying ways, and toward religion, thanks to a chance encounter with a book. He makes it through another extermination season while suffering extreme discomfort. Medical attentions are inconclusive, but, evidently, exposure to the mosquito spray is either responsible for his problem or is making a bad situation worse.

At this juncture in the novel, Porcellino's medical problems, the Boulder County area's progressive politics, and his own religious convictions begin to dovetail, causing him to reexamine his place in the world and his treatment of the environment. It is at this point that he renounces his former life as a mosquito abatement man.

Character

John Porcellino, the author's persona, is the only main character in this first-person, confessional autobiography.

Artistic Style

Simplicity of expression has been Porcellino's benchmark, but this volume is particularly interesting in that it reprints some of his earliest minicomic efforts, and the simplification and refinement of his artwork is laid out during the progression of the pages. The book includes some of his rawest punk expressions, with that movement's "do-it-yourself" directive to create lines eschewing either premeditation or revision.

At first, the marks are clotted, rushed, and childlike. While Porcellino's signature style has always come across as deceptively simple, even at its crudest beginnings, he has a basic consideration of placement, angle variation to enhance emphasis, and other fundamentals of composition in the service of effective storytelling.

As the episodes advance, a sense of spatial control can be observed via the line work, as the contours contain and describe the forms in an increasingly economic manner. This particular compilation of *King-Cat Comics* reveals the artist's evolution as a visual designer, as it progresses from Gary Panter-esque ratty markings, to mature, essentialist shorthand.

The open quality of the artwork is what reinforces the normally meditative, calming effect of much of Porcellino's comics work. The lettering is handwritten and lowercase, a style sometimes associated with poetry, and it can be taken as a sign of directness or sincerity. The poetic association of Porcellino's minimalist work can fail to engage its audience at first, because it is too "quiet" to compete with more typical, flashy media. Once focus is attained, however, Porcellino is able to slow down the reader's attention to evoke a sense of quietude. Porcellino's work is similar to that of eighteenth- and nineteenth-century Japanese printmaker Katsushika Hokusai and lesser-known Asian calligraphers, who were in vogue among twentieth-century Western artists for their elegant, gestural minimalism.

Themes

Environmental awareness, and, by extension, a celebration of the sanctity and wonder of life, is the major theme of *Diary of a Mosquito Abatement Man*. This is a notable theme to have emerged from a work featuring so many tawdry, demeaning, and painful episodes. A subtheme of self-discovery, or of a "vision quest," appropriately played out in natural settings, can also be observed. Overall, this is a story of a person who began by believing he could control nature but, in the end, is under nature's influence.

Impact

In terms of direct influence, *King-Cat Comics*, in its idiosyncrasy, is difficult to pin down. Porcellino is a unique creator and his position within even the alternative scene is too tenuous to support such a study. However, there are convergences that make it possible to see him as part of a broad artistic movement, rather than as a lone eccentric, copying his pamphlets for an indeterminate audience. His emergence on the scene was timed to coincide with the latter end of the 1980's autobiographical comic book school and can be linked within the continuum of underground music or art "zine" production beginning in the 1960's and running for several decades. There are a few creators whose work carries on the almost morbidly confessional tone Porcellino brings to autobiography; Jeffrey Brown is one such example.

Harvey Pekar's *American Splendor* defined what autobiography, even among much younger creators, would look like. In essence, he boilerplated what should be a highly personalized mode of working. While a "warts-and-all" ethic has become the norm, attention to precise literary expression and a degree of polished visual production values still predominate.

Porcellino is a pioneer in the extreme low-tech method of minicomic production, and that form has had many exponents, though it remains an under-the-radar aesthetic. Porcellino is one of a few creators who has done enough work of consistent quality to have his work reprinted.

Lawrence Howard Rodman

Further Reading

Pekar, Harvey. *American Splendor: The Life and Times of Harvey Pekar* (2003).

Porcellino, John. *Map of My Heart* (2009).

Thoreau, Henry David, and John Porcellino. *Thoreau at Walden* (2008).

Bibliography

McCloud, Scott. *Understanding Comics*. Northampton, Mass.: Kitchen Sink Press, 1993.

Moore, Anne Elizabeth, ed. *The Best American Comics 2007*. Boston: Houghton Mifflin, 2007.

Porcellino, John. "A Comic Strip Interview with Comic Artist John Porcellino." Interview by Noah Van Sciver. *The Comics Journal* 299 (August, 2009): 14-16.

Ware, Chris, ed. "King Cat." In *McSweeney's Quarterly 13*. San Francisco: McSweeney's Quarterly, 2004.

See also: *American Splendor; Our Cancer Year; Clumsy*

DROPSIE AVENUE: THE NEIGHBORHOOD

Author: Eisner, Will
Artist: Will Eisner (illustrator)
Publisher: Kitchen Sink Press
First book publication: 1995, 2006 (*The Contract with God Trilogy*)

Publication History

As the third in the trilogy of Will Eisner's narratives centered on a neighborhood in the south Bronx, *Dropsie Avenue* was originally published in 1995 by underground comics pioneer Denis Kitchen, under his Kitchen Sink Press. *A Contract with God* (1978) and *A Life Force* (1988) complete the trilogy. When Kitchen's company went out of business in 1999, DC Comics bought the rights to Eisner's catalog, including not only his graphic novels but also *The Spirit* reprints.

DC republished *Dropsie Avenue* in 2000 as part of its Will Eisner Library series. Like the 1995 original, the reprint was issued in both hardcover and paperback formats. In 2006, when W. W. Norton acquired Eisner's catalog, *Dropsie Avenue* was reissued once again, this time as part of the hardcover single-volume *The Contract with God Trilogy: Life on Dropsie Avenue*, which also included *A Contract with God* and *A Life Force*. This was only the second Eisner title released under his new publisher, the first being an original graphic novel, *The Plot: The Secret Story of the Protocols of the Elders of Zion*. The following year, Norton reissued *Dropsie Avenue*, along with the other two graphic novels in the trilogy, as a separate paperback edition.

Plot

Eisner began his Dropsie Avenue trilogy with the 1978 publication of *A Contract with God, and Other Tenement Stories*, a work that is, mistakenly, considered by many to be the first "graphic novel." He returned to the same setting ten years later with *A Life Force*.

It is appropriate that Eisner ended his trilogy with *Dropsie Avenue*, because it has an epic scope and functions as a kind of summation. While the previous two works focus on the lives of just a few Dropsie residents, *Dropsie Avenue* is a multifaceted, composite

work in which the main protagonist is arguably the neighborhood itself. While several major characters recur throughout the narrative, no one figure commands the spotlight. Instead, each shares the stage with a large cast of minor or walk-on actors, and together they reveal the dynamic life force underlying the neighborhood.

Dropsie Avenue can be read as an example of American realism, adhering to verisimilitude and emphasizing growth through the various choices individuals make. A more accurate analysis would place it in the naturalist tradition, in that the book's many characters (and the neighborhood itself) seem at the mercy of forces beyond their control. At different times throughout the graphic novel, individuals note the cyclical and inevitable nature of the events.

The events begin in 1870, at a time when the area was farmed by Dutch immigrants. The Van Dropsie family notices how the English are beginning to settle in the region, realizing that the neighborhood is changing. In order to stave off the impact of the new arrivals, the drunken Dirk van Dropsie sets fire to the English crops, inadvertently killing his niece; he is then shot by his brother-in-law. These events set the stage for what follows: an episodic and cyclical series of ethnic entrenchments, followed by efforts to resist newer arrivals from other ethnic communities, leading inevitably to bigotry, classism, violence, and destruction.

As the narrative unfolds, the Dutch are supplanted by the English, who become upset at the arrival of the Irish, who hound out German immigrants and eventually find themselves competing against the Italians. The Italians then contend with an emerging Jewish presence and eventually confront an influx of Puerto Rican families, who ridicule the arrival of a Hassidic sect and then find themselves living among a growing African American population.

Along with its racial strife and class warfare, the Dropsie Avenue neighborhood undergoes suburbanization, transit modernization, tenement housing, gang violence, urban decay, conflagration, and, finally, gentrification. The graphic novel ends with black and white neighbors, apparently living harmoniously, discussing the "foreigners" who have moved onto the block and who decorate their houses with "weird colors [and] dinky ornaments." In the final panel, a "For Sale" sign is planted outside one of the new homes.

Characters

Given the ensemble nature of *Dropsie Avenue* and its focus on the evolution of an area in the south Bronx, one could argue that the neighborhood itself functions as the main figure in this graphic novel and that its multiple facets and the many changes it undergoes are analogous to a rounded and dynamic character.

- *The Van Dropsie family*, whose name comes to mark the neighborhood, is made up of Dutch farmers who lament the encroachments of the English in the 1870's. Dirk van Dropsie's disgruntlement and drunken rampage not only bring ruin to the family but also serve as a thematic blueprint for the events that follow.

- *Sean O'Brien* is a nouveau riche Irish immigrant in the construction business. His rivalry with the O'Leary family introduces class antagonism into the narrative, and the turmoil of his children, Neil and Coleen, comes to represent the prejudice the Irish experience at the hands of their English neighbors.

- *Danny Smith* functions as an all-American everyman. He is a hero in World War I and brings a French bride back from Europe. He gets a job as a Bronx city planner, and although wanting to be a selfless public servant, he is eventually corrupted by Big Ed Casey. Big Ed manipulates Danny into building a train station near his tenement property, thereby enriching him, and it is this action that brings rapid urbanization to Dropsie Avenue.

- *Rowena Shepard* is a wheelchair-bound idealist with a passion for gardens. With the help of her deaf-mute husband, Prince, she builds a successful flower business and leaves Dropsie Avenue. Late in the graphic novel, she returns as a millionaire to finance the redevelopment of the burned-out neighborhood, creating Dropsie Gardens as a residential community.

- *Izzy Cash*, a Jewish ragman with a pushcart, accumulates enough money to purchase a Dropsie Avenue tenement building during the Great Depression; he amasses a fortune in the real estate business. His initial resistance, and then acceptance, of housing integration ignites many of the ethnic conflicts throughout the narrative.

- *Polo Palermo*, a boxer who defeats Irish Mike, becomes the hero of the neighborhood's growing Italian community. He eventually becomes a public leader whose political club oversees the development of Dropsie Avenue. His efforts with Abie Gold to clean up drug trafficking in the neighborhood lead to his murder.

- *Abie Gold* and his parents, fleeing the growing Nazi presence in 1930's Europe, are one of the earliest Jewish families to move onto Dropsie Avenue. His gifts for argument and conflict resolution, as well as his love of the neighborhood, make him not only a successful lawyer but also a city council member. Of all the figures in the graphic novel, he comes closest to being a central character.

- *Father Gianelli* and *Rabbi Goldstein* are the primary religious leaders of the neighborhood. Their teamwork mirrors that of the Leone and Gold families and they are two of the few interethnic relationships built on cooperation and mutual respect.

- *Sven Svenson* is a Swedish-born superintendent who wins the lottery and uses the money to buy the tenement building where he works. His property eventually becomes a central location for racial conflict, symbolically represented by a boiler explosion that nearly destroys the building.

- *Ruby Brown* is one of the first African American residents on Dropsie Avenue. Her father works for Sven Svenson until the latter has to sell his building. Years later, she becomes the deputy mayor for city planning and works with both Abie Gold and Rowena Shepard to create Dropsie Gardens.

- *"Crazy" Bones* is a pusher who buys Svenson's building and uses it as a central house for his drug running. He orchestrates the murder of Polo

Palermo and, along with Red (a Vietnam veteran and paraplegic), brings decay to the neighborhood through his illegal enterprise.

Artistic Style

Like Eisner's other graphic novels, *Dropsie Avenue* is presented in black and white. His drawings are highly realistic, underscoring the kind of style he laid out in his theoretical and instructional texts, *Comics and Sequential Art* (1985), *Graphic Storytelling and Visual Narrative* (1996), and *Expressive Anatomy for Comics and Narrative* (2008). His lines are primarily clean when representing characters, and he makes substantial use of shading to capture the nuances of lighting. Along with this, Eisner often relies on a bold, heavy inking (especially of backgrounds, but also in terms of silhouettes) to accentuate the dilemmas in which characters find themselves. This stark black-and-white contrast is analogous to the moral conflicts that constantly arise in the narrative, suggesting that characters find themselves trapped by extreme forces over which they have little control.

The art of *Dropsie Avenue* is also defined through another hallmark of Eisner's style: his unconventional use of panels and framing. While there are many pages of the book that adhere to a more traditional use of paneling, more numerous are the instances of panel rupture. Here, as in most of Eisner's other comics, the integrity paneled segments are compromised by the intrusion of word balloons, a part of characters' anatomies, or elements of the background from another panel on the page. The result is a "bleeding" of one narrative segment into another. Similarly, Eisner often forgoes symmetrical, angled panels altogether. Instead of containing an event within a traditional straight-lined perimeter, he uses detail from the panel's background, or even elements from an adjacent segment, to frame a portion of the page's story. For example, the fire of a burning building, a window casing, the smoke of a cigarette, or even the streets of the neighborhood serve as borders that separate one narrative event from another.

On some pages, there is a complete absence of any sort of panel, and events on one part of the page blend seamlessly with others. Eisner's distinctive style of framing and paneling, while not unique to *Dropsie Avenue*, is nonetheless part and parcel of the book's themes. Just as one panel intrudes upon another, the individual lives on Dropsie Avenue are in constant conflict with those living around them. The visual clash between panels suggests the ever-present tensions underlying the neighborhood's many constituents. Furthermore, the breakdown or the absence of solid frames gives the narrative a greater sense of flow, where one event follows naturally from another. This stylistic effect not only drives the narrative forward, but it suggests a causal link between events that creates a sense of inevitability.

Themes

The overriding theme of *Dropsie Avenue* concerns ethnoracial conflict. Not only does the clash among the many segments of the neighborhood reveal the darker side of the American Dream, but also the interethnic struggles generate almost perpetual action, and this propels the plot forward. These constant conflicts are symbolized through icons of barriers and destruction. Windows, fire, and "for sale" signs proliferate and are woven throughout the story.

If the graphic novel is read within the tradition of literary naturalism, then Eisner's message about ethnic relations is a bleak one. It exposes the myth of the American melting pot as a useless fiction, and it questions multicultural idealism. While there are pockets of hopefulness in the narrative (such as the philanthropy of Rowena Shepard, the dogged determinism of Abie Gold, and the civic-minded efforts of Polo Palmero and Ruby Brown), the final tone is one of somber inevitability. As such, Eisner broaches a larger philosophical theme regarding human destructiveness and ongoing civil discord.

Impact

While nowhere near as groundbreaking as *A Contract with God*, *Dropsie Avenue* is nonetheless significant in that it completes a larger graphic cycle that, for many, best defines the final stage of Eisner's career. When W. W. Norton acquired the rights to Eisner's non-*The Spirit* catalog in 2005, *The Contract with God Trilogy* was the first volume of material the publisher chose to reissue.

Dropsie Avenue is also important in that it mitigates the charges of sentimentality in Eisner's comics. In graphic novels such as *The Dreamer* (1986), *Minor Miracles* (2000), *Fagin the Jew* (2003), and even the other works in *The Contract with God Trilogy*, there is a slight strain of melodrama that, at times, threatens to undermine the socially critical edge of Eisner's narratives. In concluding the multifaceted portrait of Eisner's south Bronx setting, *Dropsie Avenue* throws into question any easy or unequivocal interpretation of Eisner's text and, as such, adds to a grittier, hard-edged, and more realistic reading of the landmark trilogy. While scholarship on Eisner's comics is still relatively sparse, what does exist focuses primarily on the texts that compose *The Contract with God Trilogy*.

Derek Parker Royal

Further Reading

Eisner, Will. *Life, in Pictures: Autobiographical Stories* (2007).

_____. *New York: Life in the Big City* (2006).

Pekar, Harvey. *The Best of American Splendor* (2005).

Bibliography

Andelman, Bob. *Will Eisner: A Spirited Life*. Milwaukie: M Press, 2005.

Dauber, Jeremy. "Comic Books, Tragic Stories: Will Eisner's American Jewish History." In *The Jewish Graphic Novel: Critical Approaches*, edited by Samantha Baskind and Ranen Omer-Sherman. New Brunswick, N.J.: Rutgers University Press, 2008.

Roth, Laurence. "Drawing Contracts: Will Eisner's Legacy." *The Jewish Quarterly Review* 97, no. 3 (Summer, 2007): 463-484.

Royal, Derek Parker. "Sequential Sketches of Ethnic Identity: Will Eisner's *A Contract with God* as Graphic Cycle." *College Literature* 38, no. 3 (Summer, 2011): 150-167.

_____. "There Goes the Neighborhood: Cycling Ethnoracial Tension in Will Eisner's *Dropsie Avenue*." *Shofar* 29, no. 2 (Winter, 2011): 120-145.

Schumacher, Michael. *Will Eisner: A Dreamer's Life in Comics*. New York: Bloomsbury, 2010.

See also: *American Splendor; A Contract with God, and Other Tenement Stories; The Spirit*

DYKES TO WATCH OUT FOR

Author: Bechdel, Alison
Artist: Alison Bechdel (illustrator)
Publisher: Firebrand Books; Houghton Mifflin
First serial publication: 1983-2008
First book publication: 1986-2008

Publication History

Alison Bechdel first used the title "Dykes to Watch Out For" on an early 1980's drawing of a naked woman. She was encouraged to publish her humorous drawings in a feminist newspaper, and her work first appeared in June, 1983; she soon expanded the series to include multipanel comics. *Dykes to Watch Out For* was picked up by a growing number of alternative and gay-and-lesbian newspapers as well as *Funny Times*, and the first collection of comics was published in 1986.

At first, the series consisted of isolated strips. In 1987, Bechdel changed direction, beginning episode 1 as a full-page comic, with character Mo complaining about her love life to Lois. From that point, Mo and Lois would be two major characters in an ongoing narrative chronicling the lives of many others, mostly lesbians. The numbered episodes continued until 2008, when Bechdel announced with episode 527 that she was taking a break.

In addition to republishing the newspaper strips, most of the collections include graphic novellas related to plot developments in that volume, often featuring sex scenes more graphic than those depicted in regular episodes. *Dykes to Watch Out For: The Sequel* (1992) includes an autobiographical piece titled "Serial Monogamy."

The last of the sequential collections, *Invasion of the Dykes to Watch Out For* (2005), ends with episode 457; the remaining episodes are included in *The Essential Dykes to Watch Out For* (2008), which also includes the majority of the prior individual episodes but none of the graphic novellas. Bechdel has also published selected strips on her Web site.

Plot

The intersecting stories of *Dykes to Watch Out For* occur mostly in an unnamed northern city. When the numbered episodes begin, Mo is single and works at

Dykes to Watch Out For. (Courtesy of Houghton Mifflin Harcourt)

Madwimmen Books, as does Lois, who lives with Ginger and Sparrow. Their mutual friends Clarice and Toni are in a committed relationship. Ginger is in graduate school, Clarice is in law school, Toni is an accountant, and Sparrow works at a women's shelter.

Most episodes focus on the women's friendships and romantic relationships, as well as their professional aspirations and frustrations. They discuss politics and current events at length, and the series satirizes political figures, the media, and American consumerism from the late 1980's to the late 2000's. Characters address the reader in some episodes, commenting on the story and characters as well as their creator.

Bechdel has described the series as "half op-ed column and half endless, serialized Victorian novel," and the plot is somewhat similar to that of a soap opera. However, major plot developments do occur throughout the series. Even though most of the characters maintain their liberal politics, these changes mirror a cultural shift from the radical days of their youth to an increasingly mainstream middle age.

Volumes

- *Dykes to Watch Out For* (1986). Collects the earliest individual strips.
- *More Dykes to Watch Out For* (1988). Completes the collection of individual strips and collects episodes 1-23. Mo and her friends, among them Lois, are introduced.
- *New, Improved! Dykes to Watch Out For* (1990). Collects episodes 24-77. The cast is expanded to include Mo and Lois's boss, Jezanna, and Lois's housemates, Ginger and Sparrow.
- *Dykes to Watch Out For: The Sequel* (1992). Collects episodes 78-126. Mo's relationship with Harriet becomes troubled, and Clarice and Toni consider having a baby.
- *Spawn of Dykes to Watch Out For* (1993). Collects episodes 127-170. Clarice and Toni's baby, Raffi, is born.
- *Unnatural Dykes to Watch Out For* (1995). Collects episodes 171-221. The characters transition from youth to middle age, and a flashback depicts how they met.
- *Hot, Throbbing Dykes to Watch Out For* (1997). Collects episodes 222-263. Clarice and Toni adapt to parenthood, and Mo meets Sydney.
- *Split-Level Dykes to Watch Out For* (1998). Collects episodes 264-297. Clarice and Toni move to the suburbs.
- *Post-Dykes to Watch Out For* (2000). Collects episodes 298-337. Stuart moves in with Sparrow and her housemates.
- *Dykes and Sundry Other Carbon-Based Life-Forms to Watch Out For* (2003). Collects episodes 338-397. Jezanna's bookstore is in jeopardy, and Lois experiments with drag.
- *Invasion of the Dykes to Watch Out For* (2005).

Collects episodes 398-457. Mo attends library school, Sydney is diagnosed with cancer, and Stuart and Sparrow expect a baby.

- *Essential Dykes to Watch Out For* (2008). Collects 390 of the 527 episodes, including 60 episodes not collected in the previous volumes.

Characters

- *Mo* is a bespectacled white woman who is high strung and often critical. Early in the story she begins a relationship with Harriet, who later breaks it off. She eventually enters a long-term relationship with Sydney. She works as a clerk at Madwimmen Books and later decides to attend library school.
- *Lois* is a white woman who begins the series with a short haircut and later experiments with a masculine look. She prefers multiple affairs to a long-term relationship. Although less educated than many of her friends, she often provides a critical voice of common sense, and despite her exterior toughness, she has a good heart. After her job at Madwimmen Books ends when the store closes, she works at a large chain bookstore.
- *Ginger* is an African American woman with a short Afro. She wants a steady relationship but finds having one challenging; her affair with Clarice and their mutual attraction also create tensions. She is often critical of her friends. After earning her Ph.D. in English and teaching part time, she reluctantly takes a position at a college two hours away.
- *Sparrow* is a woman of mixed white and Asian descent who lives with Ginger and Lois and at first is obsessed with therapy and spirituality. She works at a women's shelter and eventually is made director. Although she considers herself a lesbian, she begins dating Stuart and has a daughter with him.
- *Clarice* is an African American woman who, after finishing law school, works to promote environmental justice. She lives with her partner, Toni, and is also attracted to Ginger, with whom she has a brief affair. She and Toni eventually have a commitment ceremony and move to the

suburbs, where they have a child through artificial insemination.

- *Toni* is a Latina accountant whose Catholic parents are at first unaware and later disapproving of her relationship with Clarice. She is generally calm but can be passionate during emotional situations. She is committed to Clarice despite Clarice's affair and her own attraction to another woman. She is the birth mother of their son and spends more time with him while Clarice focuses on her career. Eventually the tensions escalate, and they separate.

- *Raffi*, a.k.a. *Rafael*, is the son of Toni and Clarice. Despite his unconventional family, he grows—with the help of Carlos, a gay African American man Clarice and Toni hire as a masculine role model—from an adorable toddler to a boy obsessed with video games to a typically surly teenager absorbed in music and other forms of electronic entertainment.

- *Jezanna*, a.k.a. *Alberta*, is a middle-aged African American woman. She owns Madwimmin Books and reluctantly leaves her employees in charge when she returns home during family emergencies. This is where she meets her lover, whom she convinces to relocate when Jezanna's mother dies and her father moves in with her. Jezanna is a gruff and no-nonsense person but can present a pleasant face to the public.

- *Thea* is a white, bespectacled woman with red hair. She has multiple sclerosis and uses crutches or a wheelchair. She joins the staff at Madwimmin Books, and Mo develops a crush on her. She has a strong sense of humor but is angry when Sydney moves to the city. They were a couple, but Sydney abandoned Thea upon learning of her diagnosis.

- *Sydney*, a slightly built white woman with glasses and short hair, is an English professor new to the city and Thea's former lover. Mo initially finds her arrogance distasteful, but they later become a couple. Sydney is often sarcastic but equally often speaks truth to pretention. Although she loves Mo and even proposes to her

unsuccessfully, she finds fidelity a challenge, along with controlling her spending.

- *Stuart* is a balding, bearded, middle-aged white man. He and Sparrow begin dating when she begins to question her exclusive attraction to women, and eventually, he moves in with Sparrow, Ginger, and Lois. After Sparrow gives birth to their daughter, he quits his job to raise her. He is a political radical, a Jewish freethinker, and a loving father and partner, but he is firm in his views even as his daughter desires a more typical childhood.

- *Jasmine* is an African American woman with glasses and a single mother to Jonas, who is transgendered. She struggles with Jonas's wish to change his gender, but she allows him to transition to Janis. She briefly dates Ginger but later becomes Lois's first long-term relationship.

- *Samia* is an Arab woman with frizzy hair who describes herself as a lapsed Westernized Muslim. Although she has a husband, she married him so that he could stay in the United States. She becomes involved with Ginger, and they buy a house in the suburbs.

- *Cynthia* is a bespectacled, red-haired student at Ginger's college. An evangelical Christian, she spars with Ginger in class but later confesses to confusion about her sexual identity. She eventually comes out but struggles to reconcile her desires with her religious belief in chastity.

Artistic Style

Bechdel has worked consistently in black-and-white inked images. However, the earliest individual cartoons and narrative episodes of *Dykes to Watch Out For* dramatically differ from the later episodes. Initially she employs thin lines for every image, and the quality of the early artwork is crude compared to her mature style, which emerged between the late 1980's and early 1990's. This style features lines of varying thicknesses and a greater degree of realism, even while maintaining a cartoonish quality. Bechdel cites Belgian artist Hergé as an influence, and the uncluttered clarity and specific detail of his clear-line style is evident in her work.

Bechdel employs panels of a consistent height but variable width. Despite the story's lack of action and abundant dialogue, Bechdel's artwork is enlivened by her satirical news headlines and parodies of brand-name merchandise and especially by her expressive faces. Although the content is largely progressive, the cartooning is traditional, employing speech and thought balloons, verbalized sound effects, movement lines, and exaggerated sweat drops. The lettering is also traditional, with all words in capital letters and emphasized words in boldface.

Themes

Since *Dykes to Watch Out For* is a character-based strip combining comedy and drama, it is unsurprising that its central themes include love, friendship, work, parenthood, and aging. Romantic love and sexual desire are usually intertwined, but sometimes characters engage in purely physical affairs. Generally, though, the quest for the ideal partner motivates almost all of the characters, and Bechdel presents this as a constant challenge.

Personality clashes result in breakups, and even long-standing relationships are tested by daily stresses and temptations. On a related note, some characters critique monogamy as a patriarchal construction and consider nonmonogamous relationships, while Lois enjoys multiple partners yet finds herself in an exclusive relationship in later episodes.

Sexual identity and gender identity also are significant themes in *Dykes to Watch Out For*. Most characters are lesbians; some are active advocates for women's and lesbian issues, while others focus more on their personal and professional lives. As the series progresses, Bechdel also introduces other considerations. Lois, for instance, participates in "drag king" competitions and is attracted to Jerry, a transgendered individual. Sparrow becomes attracted to a man and has a child with him, and Jasmine struggles with her son's desire to be a girl. Cynthia also struggles with her sexual identity because of her evangelical Christian beliefs and conservative politics.

Politics, in fact, play a central role in the story. Almost all characters are politically liberal, and their discussions often revolve around their responses to contemporary events. Also, some characters aspire to collectivist ideals, even while finding themselves increasingly surrounded by an individualistic consumerism. Some characters also struggle with their desires for success and possessions.

In addition to romantic and sexual relationships, other relationships are important in *Dykes to Watch Out For*. The intertwining story lines repeatedly address issues such as friendship, getting along with co-workers, being an adult child of one's parents, and becoming a parent oneself. Related to these themes is that of aging. The story progresses in real time, moving the main characters from youth to middle age. Problems relating to each of these themes arise, and characters struggle to cope with them.

Impact

Dykes to Watch Out For became better known to the general public following the critical success of Bechdel's graphic memoir, *Fun Home* (2006), but before that, it was widely known and admired in gay and lesbian communities. Its success, however limited, would have been impossible without certain social and publishing developments. It could not have been widely published prior to the gay-rights movement, and second-wave feminism also contributed to creating a receptive environment for such a strip. In addition, the emergence of politically liberal independent newspapers helped create a forum for comics such as *Dykes to Watch Out For* that could not have been published in mainstream newspapers.

Darren Harris-Fain

Further Reading

Bechdel, Alison. *Fun Home: A Family Tragicomic* (2006).

Camper, Jennifer. *Rude Girls and Dangerous Women* (1994).

Hernandez, Gilbert, Jaime Hernandez, and Mario Hernandez. *Love and Rockets* (1982-1996).

Bibliography

Bechdel, Alison. *The Indelible Alison Bechdel: Confessions, Comix, and Miscellaneous Dykes to Watch Out For*. Ithaca, N.Y.: Firebrand Books, 1998.

Beirne, Rebecca. "*Dykes to Watch Out For* and the Lesbian Landscape." In *Lesbians in Television and Text After the Millennium*. New York: Palgrave Macmillan, 2008.

Martindale, Kathleen. "Back to the Future with *Dykes to Watch Out For* and *Hothead Paisan*." In *Un/popular Culture: Lesbian Writing After the Sex Wars*. Albany: State University of New York, 1997.

Warren, Rosalind. "Alison Bechdel." In *Dyke Strippers: Lesbian Cartoonists A to Z*. Pittsburgh: Cleis Press, 1995.

See also: *Fun Home; Love and Rockets; Ghost World*

E

ED THE HAPPY CLOWN: THE DEFINITIVE ED BOOK

Author: Brown, Chester
Artist: Chester Brown (illustrator)
Publishers: Drawn and Quarterly; Vortex Comics
First serial publication: 1983-1989
First book publication: 1989

Publication History

Few graphic novels have a publication history as tangled as *Ed the Happy Clown*. The first *Ed* stories were drawn before Chester Brown even began publishing his minicomic *Yummy Fur* in 1983, but the character did not appear until the second issue of *Yummy Fur*. The 1992 collected edition's "introductory pieces," as well as chapter 1, appeared in the seven-issue run of the *Yummy Fur* minicomic. *Yummy Fur* was picked up by Toronto-based publisher Vortex Comics in 1986, and the first three bimonthly issues reprinted material from the minicomic, including all of the *Ed* stories.

The story line of *Ed the Happy Clown* continued until 1989, culminating in issue 18 of *Yummy Fur*. However, the first Vortex paperback edition of the comic, released in 1989, collects only selected material from issues 1 through 12. As Brown continued *Ed the Happy Clown* through issue 18, he came to believe that the story should have ended with the installment published in *Yummy Fur*, issue 12. Consequently, the "definitive" 1992 edition excludes all material from issues 13 through 16 and 18. It does, however, incorporate a chapter from issue 17 as well as a dark, four-page coda created specifically for the definitive edition and a few new or redrawn images. From 2005 to 2006, the story line of the 1992 edition was serialized by Brown's new publisher, Drawn and Quarterly, in nine quarterly issues featuring new covers and extensive notes. In these, Brown revealed his plans to eventually reissue the book with another new ending and with largely redrawn art.

© Rick Eglinton/Zuma Press/Corbis

Chester Brown

Chester Brown began publishing his minicomic *Yummy Fur* in 1983 and the title was picked up as a series by Vortex Comics in 1986. His *Ed the Happy Clown* storyline was one of the surrealist masterpieces of 1980's cartooning and made him a star in the post-underground scene. His autobiographical comics, begun in later issues of *Yummy Fur*, and collected as *The Playboy* and *I Never Liked You*, trace the effects of a strict religious upbringing in Quebec on Brown and his obsessions with sex and pornography. *Louis Riel: A Comic-Strip Biography* (2006) marked a major turning point after the abortive late-1990's serial *Underwater*. The biography of the Métis leader and visionary cemented Brown's reputation as a leading figure not only in Canadian comics, but in contemporary Canadian arts generally. Brown's 2011 memoir, *Paying for It*, details his experiences with prostitutes and marks a turn toward didacticism and the expression of his libertarian politics in his work. Brown's visual style is extremely influenced by *Little Orphan Annie* creator Harold Gray.

Plot

The plot of *Ed the Happy Clown* unfolds in two parallel dimensions, linked by the anal opening of the Man Who Couldn't Stop, who cannot stop defecating. In one dimension, Americans consume so much food that fecal-matter production is getting out of control; therefore, a newly discovered portal into another dimension is used as a depository. Inspecting the plant, President Ronald Reagan falls into the giant funnel leading into the other dimension, but only his head fits into the opening. On the other side, Reagan's head mysteriously attaches itself to the penis of Ed the Happy Clown.

Before all this occurs, however, Ed is imprisoned after being wrongfully accused of stealing a detached hand. He escapes when the Man Who Couldn't Stop, who is in the next cell, breaks the prison walls by producing large amounts of feces. Next, an anarchist who mistakenly thinks Ed has had an affair with his girlfriend beats him unconscious, and while in that state, he is carried into the sewers by a band of pygmies. Ed awakes next to Josie, who has been killed in a religious act by her boyfriend, Chet, and discovers that the head of Reagan is attached to his penis. Ed and a reanimated Josie escape, but Josie is soon shot by pygmy hunters and later turns into a vampire.

Captured by scientists from the television show *Adventures in Science*, who are concerned that everyone from the other dimension is homosexual and will infect their world, Ed and Josie nevertheless manage to escape once again. The scientists catch up with Ed, but only after he has been mistaken for a man undergoing a penis transplant. After Reagan's head has been replaced with a regular penis, Ed is free to drive away with the man's wife, who does not notice the switch. Josie, meanwhile, kills Chet in an act of revenge but is consequently damned. The story ends with Josie and Chet burning in Hell.

Characters

- *Ed the Happy Clown*, the protagonist, is a childlike, passive, and miserable figure around whom the story revolves. His clown makeup and wig are removed before he is sent to jail, and for the remainder of the narrative, he is neither happy nor clownlike. After his encounter with the Man Who Couldn't Stop, the head of Ronald Reagan becomes mysteriously attached to his penis.

- *Chet Doodley* is a cleaner at a hospital who enters the story just as his hand has inexplicably fallen off. When it is later found and reattached, it remains floppy and lifeless. After reading that Saint Justin cut off his own hand to prevent it from sinning, he kills Josie, with whom he was having an extramarital affair. The hand is then miraculously healed, but Josie later exacts revenge by killing him after she becomes a vampire. The final chapter depicts him burning in Hell.

- *The Man Who Couldn't Stop* is a man who cannot stop defecating. Introduced while sitting on the toilet, he is later jailed after fighting with a man who believes the bulge of feces in his pants to be a sign that he is turning into a werewolf. Soon, his jail cell fills up with feces, which eventually breaks the walls. This allows Ed to escape from a neighboring cell. It is later revealed that his anus is the gateway to another dimension, in which the inhabitants are solving their sewage problem by disposing of feces through the portal.

- *Josie* is a petite and often naked young woman with large black curls. She is in a sexual relationship with the married Chet, who kills her in order to heal his hand. Despite first becoming a ghost, she is able to drift back into her body and reanimate it. Shortly after, she is shot by a pygmy-hunting grandmother. Because she originally died while engaged in the sin of fornication, she then becomes a vampire. Josie finds and kills Chet, but his redetached hand exposes her to sunlight. The act of revenge dooms her to Hell, where she burns alongside Chet at the story's end.

- *Ronald Reagan* is a small man from an alternate dimension who bears no resemblance to the actual U.S. president. While inspecting the sewage-disposal plant, he falls into the feces funnel leading into the portal and enters the other dimension. As only his head fits through the opening, it alone makes it to the other side, where it becomes attached to Ed's penis in the chaos surrounding the prison break. Subjected to various humiliations associated with being attached to a penis, he nevertheless believes that his status as president of the United States grants him authority over the other characters.

Artistic Style

The style of *Ed the Happy Clown* varies somewhat from chapter to chapter, as Brown uses a mixture of brushed inks, markers, and photocopied pencils to create the art. The collected volume of black-and-white drawings appears as a whole despite the stylistic variations, but it is obvious throughout that Brown was still developing his style and experimenting with different techniques and approaches during the artistic process. The improvisational nature of the style serves to underscore the spontaneous quality of the narrative and gives the book a freewheeling, anything-goes sensibility.

Brown typically uses a regular grid of either six or eight panels per page, and his relatively spare yet surprisingly detailed drawings bring a sense of narrative order and visual coherence to a thoroughly disordered and anarchic world. The simplicity of the drawings serves the flow of the story well, and Brown's sense of pacing and composition becomes increasingly impressive as the originally serialized narrative develops.

Characters and backgrounds are for the most part drawn in a cartoonlike yet realistic manner, befitting a classic adventure story, but the style also exhibits an eager willingness to portray the ugly, revolting, and extremely violent. The book includes graphic depictions of murder, disfiguration, excrement, and various bodily fluids, and the austere black-and-white images perform the difficult double task of placing the work within an underground tradition of cheaply produced and often offensive comic books while also rendering the thematic excesses visually palatable. Eschewing sensationalism, Brown depicts most events objectively as everyday occurrences, an approach that is underscored by the regularity of the page layouts and supports the thematic concerns about an inherently unfair universe.

Themes

Brown was inspired by surrealism in his approach to writing and drawing *Ed the Happy Clown*; therefore, the story was conceived as he went along, adhering to principles of automatic and spontaneous creation. Despite being created over the better part of a decade and published in installments without a clear knowledge of where the story would go next, the comic nevertheless features a few recurring themes. The most dominant of these is a quasi-religious view of the universe as a chaotic and inherently unfair place in which bad things can and will happen to good people. Despite his largely passive role in the story, Ed often finds himself in humiliating and highly unfortunate circumstances; his innocence and childlike demeanor do not exempt him from being repeatedly beaten, stabbed, and disfigured. Much of the story line surrounding Chet and Josie is informed by religious allusions and references to the mysticism of early Christian cults, and Brown has said that he sees the finished book as a meditation on how unfair a world run by the Christian god would be.

This skepticism toward organized religion is part of a larger distrust of authorities based in Brown's developing political views as first an anarchist and later a libertarian. In the course of the story, a dark undercurrent dealing with the abuse of power by authorities gradually appears, as virulently homophobic scientists shoot to kill, doctors perform irresponsible surgeries, and fascist police officers wear masks and require women to hold permits for wearing pants. In the world of *Ed the Happy Clown*, human justice is as arbitrary and indifferent as that administered by religious authorities, and the irreverent use of scatological humor and intense body horror serves to underline the unpredictable nature of an anarchic and perversely unjust universe.

Impact

Inspired equally by surrealism and the underground "comix" of the 1960's and 1970's, *Ed the Happy Clown* appeared in the middle of the 1980's minicomic revival. Its iconoclastic humor, bizarre story line, and basic black-and-white style were early influences on such cartoonists as Joe Matt, Seth, and Julie Doucet. Doucet, in particular, employs a similarly irreverent approach to both storytelling and the depiction of bodily functions, and her black-and-white "art brut" style owes a clear debt to Brown's earliest work in

Yummy Fur, including *Ed the Happy Clown*. Brown, in turn, was later inspired by Doucet and Matt, as he turned to autobiography with *The Playboy* (1992) and *I Never Liked You* (1994).

Ed the Happy Clown is routinely considered a highlight of the fertile 1980's alternative comics scene, and affinities in style and theme can be found with the work of such creators as Daniel Clowes and Charles Burns. Clowes's *Like a Velvet Glove Cast in Iron* (1989-1993) and Burns's *Black Hole* (1995-2005) share with Brown a reliance on black-and-white visuals and an interest in exploring surrealism and nightmarish dream logic. Additionally, works such as *Canvas* (2004) by Alex Fellows and *Lost at Sea* (2003) and the Scott Pilgrim series (2004-2010) by Bryan Lee O'Malley display the lasting influence of *Ed*'s surreal and unpredictable universe on the world of indie comics.

Frederik Byrn Køhlert

Further Reading

Burns, Charles. *X'ed Out* (2010).

Clowes, Daniel. *Like a Velvet Glove Cast in Iron* (1993).

Doucet, Julie. *My Most Secret Desire* (2006).

Bibliography

Grammel, Scott. "Chester Brown: From the Sacred to the Scatological." *The Comics Journal* 135 (1990): 66-90.

Juno, Andrea. "Chester Brown." In *Dangerous Drawings: Interviews with Comix and Graphix Artists.* New York: Juno Books, 1997.

Levin, Bob. "Good Ol' Chester Brown: A Psycho-Literary Exploration of Yummy Fur." *The Comics Journal* 162 (1993): 45-49.

Wolk, Douglas. "Chester Brown: The Outsider." In *Reading Comics: How Graphic Novels Work and What They Mean.* Philadelphia: Da Capo Press, 2007.

See also: *Like a Velvet Glove Cast in Iron; Black Hole; Louis Riel; It's a Good Life, If You Don't Weaken*

ELK'S RUN

Author: Fialkov, Joshua Hale

Artist: Noel Tuazon (illustrator); Scott A. Keating (colorist); Jason Hanley (letterer)

Publisher: Villard

First serial publication: 2005

First book publication: 2007

Publication History

The first four chapters of *Elk's Run* were originally published as four 24- to 26-page, full-color comic book issues (eight issues had been planned). Beginning in March, 2005, issues 1-3 of *Elk's Run* were self-published by Joshua Hale Fialkov's Hoarse and Buggy Productions. Although the series was lauded by several comics industry professionals and received critical acclaim from *Variety* and *Entertainment Weekly*, *Elk's Run* sold well below expectations, prompting its creators to move the series to an outside publisher, the short-lived Speakeasy Comics.

In September 2005, Speakeasy published a bumper edition of *Elk's Run*, collecting and reprinting the first three issues with a new cover illustration by Darwyn Cooke, an introduction by Steve Niles, and behind-the-scenes back matter such as character design sketches, the initial proposal for the series, and a coloring tutorial. In November 2005, two months before going out of business, Speakeasy released the fourth and, as it turned out, final published issue of *Elk's Run*.

In June 2006, the incomplete *Elk's Run* series was nominated for Harvey Awards in seven categories: Best Writer, Best Artist, Best Letterer, Best Cover Artist, Best New Talent, Best Continuing or Limited Series, and Best Single Issue. The series was also popular in the Los Angeles offices of Random House. The Villard division of Random House took over as publisher soon after Speakeasy's demise, and *Elk's Run* was completed and published as a single graphic novel.

Plot

Elk's Run is the story of fifteen-year-old John Kohler, Jr.; his parents, John and Sara; and their town's descent into chaos. The town, Elk's Ridge, West Virginia, is a

"[*Elk's Run*] manages to tell the same tale from different points of view, yet make each as compelling as the last. [Grade:] A." —*Entertainment Weekly*

elk's run

JOSHUA HALE FIALKOV • NOEL TUAZON • SCOTT A. KEATING

Introduction by Charlie Huston, author of *Already Dead*

Elk's Run. (Courtesy of Villard)

separatist utopian militia community built atop a defunct mine by a group of Vietnam War (1965-1975) veterans and their wives, connected to the outside world only through the Elk's Run Tunnel, which is closed at night.

John Jr. and his friends Matt Jones, Adam Smith, and Mike Taylor are playing there around 11 P.M. when the Kohlers' neighbor, Arnold Huld, drives through the tunnel in a drunken attempt to flee Elk's Ridge and reunite with his estranged wife. Huld runs into Mike, killing him. After Mike's funeral, John Jr. witnesses his father leading the men of Elk's Ridge as they hold Huld down while someone backs a car over him.

Two days later, Sara Kohler defends Huld's murder to the other wives while preparing for a monthly delivery of supplies. Two policemen arrive looking for Huld, whose wife has reported him missing. When the police officers discover crates of assault rifles in the delivery truck, John Sr. shoots the police officers, tells truck driver Jim Miller he is now a resident of Elk's Ridge, and orders John Jr., Jones, and Smith to bury the two bodies.

The three boys and the only young woman in town, Alysha, abandon grave digging to attempt an escape from the town. Smith spots two armed townsmen, Nick Silvas and Steve Jaeger, searching for them. The teens ambush the pair and wrest away their guns. Enraged, John Jr. beats Nick to death; Smith is shot in the gut during the struggle. The teenagers hide in the mine below the town, where they find John Sr.'s plans for bombing government buildings and, as a contingency, Elk's Ridge.

John Jr. sneaks to the delivery truck, where Jim Miller gives him a CB radio. Jones radios the police for help and tells the operator his location. Upon hearing Jones's transmission, John Sr. kills Shane, the man tasked with searching the delivery truck. John Sr. leads a group into the mine in pursuit of the teenagers.

A gunfight erupts between the teenagers and the adults. A stray bullet sets off the napalm John Sr. had rigged to the town's gas lines as the contingency plan. The first explosion caves in the mine and buries Smith. More explosions set Elk's Ridge ablaze. Sara unsuccessfully orders people at gunpoint to stay in town. She finds her husband and tells him the townspeople are fleeing through the tunnel. John Sr. tells his wife that the tunnel is closed and locked and that anyone in the tunnel will burn to death. Sara suggests saving the people, then recoils when her husband alludes to killing their son; John Sr. then savagely beats his wife. The beating is stopped when John Sr. spots John Jr. and Jones with guns raised.

John Sr. shoots his son in the shoulder, disarming him. The father and son fight until another group of townspeople restrain the father, and John Jr. then persuades the group to leave his father and rescue their friends and family trapped in the tunnel. Jones, John Jr., and Alysha also run into the tunnel and force open the tunnel door. Police and rescue vehicles waiting outside the tunnel assist with the evacuation. John Jr. runs

back into the town, returns with his mother, and tells police Elk's Ridge is empty, leaving his father to the encroaching flames.

Characters

- *John Kohler, Jr.*, the protagonist, is the restless, rebellious fifteen-year-old son of a leading voice in Elk's Ridge. He hates his father but shares his father's leadership abilities and capacity for violence, albeit with a stronger moral compass. He leads his friends against his father to escape the town.

- *John Kohler, Sr.*, the antagonist, is a middle-aged Vietnam War veteran, husband, father, and a leader in the Elk's Ridge militia. He killed an entire Vietnamese family, and his willingness to destroy repeats in his efforts to preserve Elk's Ridge through escalating acts of violence.

- *Sara Kohler*, wife of John Sr. and mother of John Jr., is quick to slap John Jr.; officious and hostile to the other women in Elk's Ridge; and, above all, subservient to her husband. She loves him for his quick decisive actions until he talks about killing their son.

- *Matt Jones* is one of the teenagers who rebels against the town. He is friends with John Jr. but is closer to their mutual friend Adam Smith. He initially blames John Jr. for Smith's death but later apologizes.

- *Adam Smith*, Jones's best friend, is the one teen reticent to join John Jr. in his escape from Elk's Ridge, going so far as suggesting they bury the bodies of the policemen.

- *Arnold Huld*, the Kohler's next-door neighbor, kills teenager Mike Taylor while drunk driving out of Elk's Ridge in search of the wife that left him and the separatist community. The men of the town execute Huld, inciting events that end with Elk's Ridge exploding.

- *Alysha* is a teenager and friends with John Jr.

Artistic Style

Noel Tuazon's rough-edged, curvilinear brushwork, with lines used sparingly and that do not often connect, hovers between realistic and cartoony in ways comparable to comics artists such as Matt Kindt and Eddie Campbell. As colorist Scott A. Keating has said, Tuazon's line work is "flowing and naturalistic," suggesting form rather than dictating it.

Tuazon sometimes varies the thickness of his lines for compositional effect (with backgrounds drawn in thin lines differentiated from thick-lined foreground objects) and, occasionally, as a narrative technique. The heaviest lines are saved for drawings of flashbacks to John Sr. killing people in Vietnam, while flashbacks to John Jr., Smith, and Jones becoming friends over a contraband issue of *Rolling Stone* are rendered with

Elk's Run. (Courtesy of Villard)

thin lines only. Variations in line thickness are used to differentiate past from present, and to contrast the blunt violence of one generation with the fragile innocence of another. Overall, the rough-edged sketchiness of Tuazon's lines and his dynamic placements of solid black give his images and page composition a propulsive, restrained frenzy that amplifies the creeping dread, ratcheting tension, and snowballing violence of the narrative.

Keating uses a digital coloring process to evoke a painterly aesthetic compatible with the naturalism of Tuazon's ink lines. He overlays textures from hand-drawn watercolors in every image except those depicting flashbacks to distinguish the messiness of the present from the fixed nostalgia of the past. In early chapters a muted palette and diffuse lighting evoke the claustrophobia and uncertainty of the story. Later, as the story reaches its fiery, bloody climax, bright dramatic lights pierce deep dark reds. Jason Hanley's digital lettering is equally subtle, incorporating sound effects only occasionally and thus to greater impact.

Panel layouts take full advantage of the medium to create precise, controlled pacing. Standard rectangular panel grids stop and start with dramatic pauses created through omitted panel borders and backgrounds. Emotionally intense scenes are stretched out in horizontal panels across two-page spreads. The high drama of a rare splash page is always complicated by small panels superimposed on the larger image, depicting close-ups of uncomfortable details invisible in the bigger picture.

Themes

Elk's Run was inspired by a year of Fialkov's youth spent living with his family in an isolated small town, so it is unsurprising that themes related to the inescapable connections of family pervade the work. John Jr. fights John Sr. with lessons John Sr. taught him. John Jr. returns for his mother, despite her support for John Sr. throughout the events of the novel. Traditional elements of a coming-of-age story about teenagers defying their parents' authority, leaving home, and becoming adults are distorted in an echo chamber of post-September 11, 2001, paranoia. Additionally, the book's references to the Vietnam War and antigovern-

ment militias also imply a historically based critique of American militarism.

The book achieves much of its character development and world building by visualizing the inextricability of past and present. Panels showing John Sr. killing a family in Vietnam are interwoven with the murder of Arnold Huld. The scenes in which John Jr. decides to escape and kills Nick Silvas are paralleled by scenes in which John Sr. teaches his son how to shoot a bear. Jim Miller gives Smith and Jones contraband magazines in a flashback, and he later gives John Jr. a contraband CB radio. Jones and Smith affirming their friendship in the past is juxtaposed with Jones watching Smith die in the present. History and family give events meaning, but those meanings are portrayed as emotionally conflicted, tragic, murky, and complex.

Impact

The fraught publication history of *Elk's Run* was viewed as a commentary on the state of the American comic book specialty-shop direct market. The attention the initial issues received from well-known comics professionals like Warren Ellis, Brian Michael Bendis, Brian K. Vaughn, and Steve Niles and from mass-

---

Joshua Hale Fialkov

Since breaking into the comic book industry in the 2000's as a writer, Joshua Hale Fialkov has produced a number of series that have received critical acclaim and been nominated for significant awards. Best known for his work on *Elk's Run*, an adventure comic that sets the young inhabitants of a fictional American town in a struggle for freedom from their parents, Fialkov is also the writer of the crime-fiction graphic novel *Tumor*, which was produced for Amazon's Kindle before being collected in print form. His series *Echoes*, with artist Rashan Ekedal, tells the story of a man who learns that his father may have been a serial killer. In the 2010's he began to take on an increasing amount of work in the superhero genre, working with DC Comics on *I, Vampire* and *Superman/Batman*. Fialkov is known for a dark and independent sensibility where action is filtered through a crime novel aesthetic.

---

market magazines like *Variety* and *Entertainment Weekly* was extremely rare for a self-published comic book. The lackluster sales that followed were seen as a signal that the comic-shop market had become effectively closed to independent small-press creators making innovative work outside of the two dominant comics publishers, Marvel and DC. In reaction, several online comics communities rallied around the series.

When Speakeasy Comics went bankrupt, the lack of sales on *Elk's Run* was again discussed as symptomatic, not of the failure of the industry as a whole, but of the failure of Speakeasy to properly promote its titles. The final move of *Elk's Run* to a graphic novel format marketed to general-interest bookstores seemed to confirm that the comic-shop market could no longer sustain small-press comic books, a view echoed by Fialkov when he and Tuazon created *Tumor*, their follow-up to *Elk's Run*, for the electronic-book reader, the Amazon Kindle.

Damian Duffy

Further Reading

Aaron, Jason, and Cameron Stewart. *The Other Side* (2007).

Fialkov, Joshua Hale, and Noel Tuazon. *Tumor* (2010).

Urasawa, Naoki. *Monster* (2006-2008).

Bibliography

Fialkov, Joshua. "Bug Talks *Tumor* with Joshua Hale Fialkov!" Interview by Mike L. Miller. *Ain't It Cool News*, November 9, 2009. http://www.aintitcool.com/node/43012.

Fialkov, Joshua, Noel Tuazon, and Scott A. Keating. *Elk's Run Bumper Edition*. Toronto: Speakeasy Comics, 2005.

Watson, Sasha. "Sons Against Fathers in *Elk's Run*." *Publisher's Weekly*, March 13, 2007. http://www.publishersweekly.com/pw/by-topic/new-titles/adult-announcements/article/14188-sons-against-fathers-in-elk-s-run-.html.

Weiland, Jonah. "Catching Up on *Elk's Run* with Johsua Fialkov." *Comic Book Resources*, September 20, 2005. http://www.comicbookresources.com/?page=article&id=5689.

_____. "The Horror of It All: Fialkov Talks *Western Tales of Terror* and *Elk's Run*." *Comic Book Resources*, December 21, 2004. http://www.comicbookresources.com/?page=article&old=1&id=4579.

See also: *30 Days of Night; A History of Violence; Last Day in Vietnam*

EMBROIDERIES

Author: Satrapi, Marjane
Artist: Marjane Satrapi (illustrator)
Publishers: L'Association (French); Pantheon Books (English)
First book publication: 2003 (English translation, 2005)

Publication History

While working on *Persepolis*, Marjane Satrapi wrote and drew a memoir entitled *Embroideries*, which was released in France as the one-volume *Broderies* in 2003 by L'Association, the publisher that also released *Persepolis* and *Poulet aux prunes* (2004; *Chicken with Plums*, 2006). L'Association had a history of publishing successful comics titles during the 1990's; this success continued into the twenty-first century with Satrapi's work. Featured as part of L'Association's "Collection Côtelette" of small-format graphic narratives, *Broderies* enjoyed multiple editions in the years following its first release.

Like *Persepolis*, the text of *Broderies* was translated and published in a variety of languages. The Italian version, *Taglia e cuci*, was also released the same year. In 2004, the Spanish publisher Norma Editorial released Castillian and Catalan editions, *Bordados* and *Brodats* (translated by Marta Marfany) as part of their Cómic Europeo collection. The following year, *Broderies* was translated into both English and German. Anjali Singh translated the English-language edition, *Embroideries*, which was distributed by Pantheon Books in the United States and Canada and by Jonathan Cape in the United Kingdom. Martin Budde translated the German *Sticheleien*, published in Zurich by Édition Moderne. In 2006, the novel was released in five more languages: Danish, Dutch, Indonesian, Japanese, and Swedish. In 2008, Satrapi's text reached farther across Europe, being published in Czech, Greek, and Polish. In 2010, Hungarian, Finnish, and Portuguese editions were published.

Plot

Following the success of Satrapi's *Persepolis*, an autobiographical bildungsroman relating the story of a

Embroideries. (Courtesy of Pantheon Books)

young Iranian girl living through the Iranian Revolution and its aftermath, *Embroideries* intervenes in a specific moment near the end of the time span covered in *Persepolis*. The year is 1991, and a twenty-something Marji is taking part in the tradition of *samovar* (afternoon tea) in a living room full of Iranian women linked by familial and affective ties. In this space, bookended by the men's departure after the midday meal and return after their naps, Marji's grandmother dominates, entreating the other women to engage in gossip-laden discussion, "the ventilator of the heart."

This particular long session covers matters of sex and sexuality, as the women tell their own stories and share those of other friends. The women, who range in age and experience, tell of their problems with virginity, weddings, unfaithful and inadequate husbands, divorces, affairs, and plastic surgery, among other issues. One story prompts another in this narrative, which is very much *Sex in the City* (1998-2004) meets Geoffrey Chaucer's *The Canterbury Tales* (1387-1400). In fact, as one critic has pointed out, one story echoes Chaucer's "The Miller's Tale," as a woman reveals her plastic surgery transformation, which reduced her buttocks and increased her breast size by transferring fat from the former to the latter area. The woman jokes, "Of course this idiot [my husband] doesn't know that every time he kisses my breasts, it's actually my a--s he's kissing."

This coupling of humor and revelation pervades the narrative and explains the title, *Embroideries*, which itself contains both a hidden meaning and a punch line. Pictured on the title page, embroidery, a traditionally female art, is the kind of activity expected of such a gathering. Instead, the women weave explicit stories, in which "a full embroidery," what Grandmother jokingly asks for as a gift from Marji, euphemistically refers to the surgery that restores the vagina to its virginal state. This climactic moment near the novel's end displays the open and friendly camaraderie among the three generations of women that fills this entire story, which serves as a vignette that opens onto a larger world of female relationships.

Characters

- *Marjane*, a.k.a. *Marji*, the protagonist and narrator, is a slender twenty-something woman pictured with shoulder-length dark hair and clad in collared top and pants. As the author's autobiographical avatar, Marji relates the importance of the samovar tradition and the story of her grandmother's life, thereby centralizing Grandmother in the tale. She also participates in the women's gossip, sharing the story of her friend Shideh.

- *Grandmother*, Marji's unnamed grandmother, is an elderly woman with cropped hair and still-pert breasts, whose dress and pearl necklace are respectable yet fashionable. An opium addict who began taking the drug in her youth to attract men, she now must "dissolve a small bit of burnt opium" in her morning tea to "regain her sense

Embroideries. (Courtesy of Pantheon Books)

of humor and her natural kindness." This thrice-married woman directs the gossip session, wherein she relates the story of her friend Nahid and discloses her desire for a full embroidery, showing herself in these instances to be worldly, cosmopolitan, and ever youthful.

- *Satrapi*, Grandmother's third husband, is a bespectacled elderly man who is deferential to his wife. He appears at the novel's beginning and end, framing the gossip session. He is unable to penetrate the women's interior world.

- *Parvine* is Marji's chatty middle-aged aunt, who, with her long, wavy hair, full makeup, and revealing v-neck dress, comes across as the most sexually liberal woman of the group. Much of her life story is revealed as she liberally interjects in others' narratives, spreading her advice and experience. After surviving her first marriage to General Mafakherolmolouk, who was fifty-six years her senior, she moved to Europe to become a painter. There, it is suggested, she experienced the pleasures of sexuality, which inform her opinions about penises. She believes that being a mistress is "the better role," since husbands mistreat their wives, not their mistresses.

- *Amineh Arshadian*, a participant in the samovar discussion, has chin-length hair and wears a dress. Her contributions to the discussion revolve around the fidelity of the men in her life. Married first for love, she discovered that her husband Houshang was cheating on her when she moved in with him in Germany. In response, she left him and took her married dance partner, Herbert, as her lover. Eventually, she returned to Iran because Herbert would not leave his wife. She believes that her new husband, Hossein, is unfaithful too.

- *Taji*, Marji's mother, has a pixie haircut and wears a long-sleeve shirt and pants. Near the story's end, she recounts the tale of Bahar, the daughter of her cousin Pavaneh. The story concerns Bahar's marital troubles that arise because she weds an unfamiliar man. Throughout the story, Taji presents herself as one with a more modern and enlightened idea of marriage than her relatives, whose old-fashioned notions land them in trouble.

- *Azzi*, a discreet neighbor, who appears similar in dress and age to Marji, remains silent for most of the discussion. Upon hearing of Bahar's troubles, she relates her own marital ordeal, in which her former husband ran off with her jewels and then demanded a divorce.

- *Two unnamed women* also participate in the discussion. One with a shorter hairdo is relatively ignorant about the penis despite being a wife and mother, but she knows what "a full embroidery" is. The other, who wears her long hair in a bun, lauds the wonders of plastic surgery for improving her figure and helping to keep her husband faithful.

Artistic Style

As in *Persepolis*, Satrapi drew *Embroideries* in black and white, but the artistic style in *Embroideries* departs from that in *Persepolis*. Most obviously, no strict panels exist to separate moments, and the unnumbered pages further complicate attempts to demarcate and isolate instances. Rather, one experience flows into another, as the women spin tales of their personal experience and others'. This narrative style, which incorporates a large amount of dialogue, has been described as a "comic play" and "graphic drama." Satrapi arranges the women on the page in a manner that visualizes this mode of exchange. When sharing a story, the speaker is present as a talking head (often at the top of the page), which illustrates the process of gossip, since the one who has intervened in someone else's private affairs is pictured on the same page as the other person's actions. Moreover, this visual voice-over moves out of dialogue boxes, such that each woman's voice slinks through the events she relates.

These stories begin and end in discussions among the larger group, which is pictured in various configurations, both as seated figures and as disembodied heads. This profusion of representation demonstrates that the women are active in the discussion; they are not just passively reclining and sniping behind others' backs but are sharing and learning from this exchange with one another. All of these elements reflect the fact that these women weave stories rather than garments.

In the original French and in many translations, the font is a cursive script, which echoes the interweaving and interpenetrating experiences that touch each woman and tease out her inner concerns. In the North American translation, the text is rendered in plain print; the letters do not connect to each other and thus do not show the movement of ideas through the words themselves. Rather, the presence of the cursive is preserved only in the title cards that introduce *Embroideries* on an embroidered surface, detracting from the textual and visual representation of the gossip and wrongly implying a confinement of this type of experience. By contrast, in the French version, the cursive text flows out of the living room and into the framing moments, representing the persistence of this unifying energy even after the tea is finished.

Themes

By limiting the space and time of *Embroideries* to afternoon tea, Satrapi is able to present concerns that not only are particular to the women in the room but also are more generally applicable to women around the world. In this living room, Satrapi represents family and friends of various ages, allowing the exploration of generational issues and camaraderie among women. Moreover, the flow, intent, and engagement in discussion revise a negative notion of gossip. Here, gossip is productive and unveils a number of matters important to all the women, which is shown by how the stories overlap, as one often provokes another.

Sex and sexuality permeate every thread of discussion, as the women talk about the problematic dimensions of male-female relationships, fidelity to a sense of self or tradition, bodily alterations and beauty, negotiating the concerns of Iran versus those of Europe, and the cycle of marriage and divorce. Through these concerns rooted in the personal, the women reach outward in trying to express a stable notion of modernity. Their many viewpoints and beliefs prevent such an articulation, but the use of humor in their tales creates a unified womanhood toward which feminism continually strives. Their world is one that deals in hybridity, as each woman holds a different view but integrates these other views into her understanding of the world. The image of embroidery encapsulates this entire experience, as all these singular threads of existence are woven into a cohesive yet multifaceted whole.

Impact

Unlike the much acclaimed *Persepolis* and *Chicken with Plums*, *Embroideries* experienced a mixed reception among critics. While Satrapi's other works were awarded prizes at the annual Angoulême International Comics Festival, *Embroideries* lost the 2004 prize for best album to the first portion of Emmanuel Larcenet's *Le Combat ordinaire* (2003; *Ordinary Victories*, 2005). Even so, *Embroideries* went on to be translated into numerous languages.

Arguably more so than the other texts, *Embroideries* fits into a Western cultural moment obsessed with the Middle Eastern woman's experience in general and the Iranian woman's memoir in particular. This fact is echoed in the critical discourse surrounding the text; *Embroideries* is often reviewed alongside or compared with memoirs such as Azar Nafisi's *Reading Lolita in Tehran* (2003) and Azadeh Moaveni's *Lipstick Jihad* (2005). These texts allow people to see through the "axis of evil" and beyond the veil to understand these women not as others but as people. *Embroideries* is especially pertinent in this regard, as Satrapi visually ushers the reader into a private space in which women speak to one another without the bother of *chadors*, *hijabs*, or the men who necessitate them. The candor found in this private space is not unlike the bare honesty that pervades many other graphic memoirs, a genre that has become an increasingly popular form following the success of Art Spiegelman's *Maus* (1972-1991) and Satrapi's own *Persepolis*.

Margaret Galvan

Further Reading

Dabaie, Marguerite. *The Hookah Girl and Other True Stories: Growing up Christian Palestinian in America* (2007).

Davis, Vanessa. *Make Me a Woman* (2010).

Glidden, Sarah. *How to Understand Israel in Sixty Days or Less* (2010).

Satrapi, Marjane. *Chicken with Plums* (2006).

_____. *Persepolis* (2003).

Bibliography

Chute, Hillary L. "Graphic Narrative as Witness: Marjane Satrapi and the Texture of Retracing." In *Graphic Women: Life Narrative and Contemporary Comics*. New York: Columbia University Press, 2010.

Jansen, Sharon L. *Reading Women's Worlds from Christine de Pizan to Doris Lessing: A Guide to Six Centuries of Women Imagining Rooms of Their Own*. New York: Palgrave Macmillan, 2011.

Mozaffari, Nahid. Review of *Journey from the Land of No*, *Lipstick Jihad*, and *Embroideries*. *Women's Studies Quarterly* 34, nos. 1/2 (Spring/Summer, 2006): 516-527.

Pulda, Molly. "The Grandmother Paradox: Mary McCarthy, Michael Ondaatje, and Marjane Satrapi."

A/B: Auto/Biography Studies 22, no. 2 (Winter, 2007): 230-249.

Satrapi, Marjane. "Interview with Marjane Satrapi." Interview by Robert Root. *Fourth Genre: Explorations in Nonfiction* 9, no. 2 (Fall, 2007): 147-157.

Whitlock, Gillian. "From Tehran to Tehrangeles: The Generic Fix of Iranian Exilic Memoirs." *Ariel: A Review of International English Literature* 39, no. 1/2 (2008): 7-27.

See also: *Persepolis; Maus: A Survivor's Tale; Chicken with Plums*

EPILEPTIC

Author: B., David (pseudonym of Pierre-François Beauchard)

Artist: David B. (illustrator); Eve Deluze (letterer); Fanny Dalle-Rive (letterer); Jean-Christophe Menu (cover artist)

Publishers: L'Association (French); Pantheon Books (English)

First serial publication: *L'Ascension du Haut Mal*, 1996-2003 (English translation, 2005)

First book publication: 2005 (English)

Publication History

David B.'s (Pierre-François Beauchard's) *Epileptic* was first published in France as the award-winning *L'Ascension du Haut Mal* (*The Rise of the High Evil*) by L'Association, of which Beauchard was a founding member. Beauchard began drawing *Epileptic* from the first day his brother was struck by epilepsy, and *Epileptic* provides some early examples (real or re-created) of Beauchard's childhood artwork. In 2000, he won the French Angoulême International Comics Festival Prize for Best Script for *L'Ascension du Haut Mal*'s fourth volume. In 2002, an English translation gathered the first three volumes into *Epileptic* 1, followed by the complete *Epileptic* in 2005, which won the Ignatz Award for Outstanding Artist. For the English volume, Beauchard's black-and-white drawings are accompanied by Kim Thompson's translations.

Epileptic is David B.'s way of visually verbalizing the profound affect epilepsy had on his family. It took him twenty years to discover how to translate his dreams and feelings into pictures that display the intricacies of the war going on inside his brother, himself, and his family. The family history is portrayed as a battle of struggles over poverty, wars, and, finally, epilepsy. Beauchard's fascination with the occult is clearly present in the work because, as he says, "it alludes to another dimension, another possibility . . . a hidden dimension. And that's exactly what was going on with my brother's illness."

Epileptic. (Courtesy of Pantheon Books)

Plot

Epileptic opens on the idyllic childhood of Beauchard; his older brother, Jean-Christophe; and younger sister, Florence, in 1970's France. Beauchard relishes stories of epic battles, and his art-teacher parents encourage his love of drawing, in spite of his subject matter.

Beauchard's childhood innocence is cut short by his brother's first epileptic seizure, which begins the family's medical odyssey to find a cure. Beauchard lets Genghis Khan lead the charge in his rage-filled battle drawings, as his brother's medication fails to stop his terrifying seizures. Beauchard's mother and father turn to the Psycho Pedagogical Institute and then contemplate surgery, but Jean-Christophe seeks out a disciple of Zen macrobiotics, and his seizures stop miraculously. The whole family moves into a macrobiotic commune until the petty ego trips of the adults begin—and summer vacation comes to an end. The family then moves to a country estate while maintaining their commitment to the macrobiotic diet and acupuncture, but Jean-Christophe's seizures eventually return.

Beauchard soon realizes that his brother's epilepsy has wormed its way into everyone's lives. Jean-Christophe begins a regimen of medication, but the family soon seeks out another macrobiotic commune filled with backbreaking work and guilt. Eventually, Jean-Christophe relapses into seizures and the family experiences ignorance and intolerance, causing Beauchard to sharpen his pencil against such attacks. As a teenager, Jean-Christophe finally rebels against treatment and begins school at a center for the handicapped, where he gives up on the idea of being cured.

The family never gives up, however. Alternative therapies are tested through psychics peddling past-life regression and Ouija boards. Meanwhile, Beauchard draws his own guardian angels, demons, and monsters while his birdlike grandfather haunts him. His mother takes up Swedenborgian philosophy and talking to the dead. At the end of 1970, having fully sealed himself into the intricate armor of his drawings, Beauchard changes his name from Pierre-François to David. When Jean-Christophe returns from boarding school, he has completely escaped into his own disease.

As a teenager, Beauchard gives up children's books for fantastic realism and esoteric works, as they seem to best represent his life. Jean-Christophe, on the other hand, escapes into his childhood fantasies about Nazis, while his disease consumes the entire family. The family soon begins a new regimen of healers: a magnetizer, followed by a homeopath/psychiatrist, mediums, gurus, Rosicrucians, alchemy, voodoo, anthroposophy, astrology, and transactional analysis. Nothing works, but guilt keeps them seeking new cures.

Eventually, Jean-Christophe becomes violent and is sent to a handicapped school in Paris. Beauchard also goes to Paris as a student at the Applied Arts School, drawing his way past his brother's disease and furiously walking the streets. He flunks out of school, is drafted into the army, and is eventually discharged into

the streets of Paris. He and a few friends start L'Association comics publishing collective. The final pages of *Epileptic* record Beauchard's dreams before returning to the present day, in which readers see Jean-Christophe bloated, scarred, and delusional. In the concluding panels, Beauchard dreams of following his brother into his epilepsy while riding a white horse to fight his way through the armies of disease.

Volumes

- *Epileptic* 1 (2002). Collects Volumes 1 through 3 and depicts the first half of the family's struggle against their son's epilepsy.
- *Epileptic* (2005). Collects all issues, reflecting the Beauchard family's battle against epilepsy.

Characters

- *Pierre-François Beauchard* (*David B.*), the protagonist, has black hair and often wears glasses. His brother's epilepsy haunts him and forms his imagination as he escapes the demon disease in a world of fantasy, storytelling, and illustration. He feels guilty about being healthy and resenting his brother's strain on the family resources. As an adolescent, he changes his name to David B. to wall himself off from epilepsy and its manifestations.
- *Jean-Christophe Beauchard* is the oldest of the Beauchard children. He has black hair, a long nose, and protruding lips and wears glasses. At the age of eleven, he is struck with epilepsy, and as he grows older, he retreats into the twisted world of his disease, often becoming violent, paranoid, and delusional.
- *Florence Beauchard* is the author's sister. She has long black hair and is the youngest of the family. She is caught in the web of the family disease, ignored by her parents, and abused by her brothers. At one point, she tries to take her life, but, eventually, she comes to terms with her family, her brother's disease, and her place in the universe. She provides *Epileptic*'s foreword and conclusion.
- *Marie-Claire Beauchard* (*Mom*), is a slim, blond-haired art teacher and mother of three. Her quest

to heal her son's epilepsy leads the family through communes, quack cures, and alternative schools. Her great-grandmother introduced her to the occult, white magic, and fairies, one of the worlds she consults in search of a cure.

- *Father Beauchard* (*Dad*), has black hair that, over the course of his family's ordeal, goes from long to short to thinning. He is severe looking with bushy eyebrows. An art teacher and army veteran, he has his own ideas about treating epi-

lepsy, including Rosicrucianism and Catholicism.
- *Grandfather Gabriel* is Beauchard's maternal grandfather and a military veteran. He likes poetry, opera, viticulture, and women. When he dies, he haunts Beauchard's imagination in the form of a long-beaked bird.
- *Grandmother Fernande*, Beauchard's maternal grandmother, wears her dark hair parted on the side, and her glasses denote her schoolteacher's

Epileptic. (Courtesy of Pantheon Books)

intellectualism and love for poetry. She comes from a poor family, but that did not matter to Grandfather Gabriel, who loved her at first sight.

- *Grandfather André*, Beauchard's paternal grandfather, is a military veteran. He is a large man who likes to eat and has far-right political leanings. When the young Beauchard learns he was not named David because his grandfather thought it sounded too Jewish, he promptly changes his name to David.

Artistic Style

An oval of yellow surrounding the red title is the only color to be found in this black-and-white graphic memoir. The invasion of epilepsy into the family's life is portrayed in intricately drawn panels, featuring mythological iconography from medieval Europe to Gothic illuminated texts and Mesoamerican calendar stones to Buddhist, Christian, Babylonian, and Norse traditions. It is often hard to separate artful depictions from reality, as the slithering snake of illness, sometimes resembling the dragon figurehead of a Viking ship, moves in and around Jean-Christophe and the rest of the Beauchards. Even in the smallest panel, intense battles are fought among numerous combatants, with devils, monsters, ghosts, and knights fighting alongside Babylonians, Spartans, Assyrians, hoplites, and Mongols, all vying for victory over the demon Epilepsy. Portrayals are sharply drawn in this cartoonish world of high contrast black and white, with backgrounds ranging from common scenery to flat black or stark white and dense mazes of symbolic iconography.

The reader is encouraged to loiter over these scenes to wonder at the sheer overwhelming determination of Beauchard's parents as they navigate their way toward a cure, one that they never find. Often portrayed as mad scientists, doctors hook elaborate machinery to Jean-Christophe's brain to no avail. Many panels contain drawings accompanied by only text boxes. Speech bubbles often repeat what has been posited in a text box, and while this may be for emphasis, it can be distracting.

Themes

Epileptic can be considered a coming-of-age memoir of disease, as the author grows up while his family seeks a cure for his brother's epilepsy. Beauchard's dark pages are more than just a Hieronymus Bosch nightmare of despair; his black rage flows onto the pages as he fights back using his weapon of choice: the pen. As an adult, he realizes he coped with the family's malady by escaping into esoteric works, his backyard, and drawing; his escape created the artist.

David B. draws epilepsy as a snake slithering through his brother, a Norse dragon that twists around his body like the snake found curling up the tree of knowledge of good and evil in the Garden of Eden. The grandfather's ghost takes on the guise of a thirteenth-century physician, wearing the long beaklike mask meant to hold the herbs and medicines that will ward off the plague, but modern medicine will not save Beauchard's grandfather or his brother. Full-panel eso-

---

David B.

Best known for his graphic novel *Epileptic*, David B. (Pierre-François Beauchard) was one of the founding members of the influential French comics publishing house L'Association in 1990. After producing a number of short works, including *Le Cheval blême*, a collection of short stories based on his dreams, David B. began serializing the autobiographical *Epileptic* in France as *L'Ascension du Haut Mal* in six volumes, three of which were nominated for prizes at the Angoulême Festival. In the late-1990's he began to produce highly ironized genre work for the major French comics publishers, including two volumes of the *Hiram Lowatt and Placido* western series (with art by Christophe Blain), *La Ville des mauvais rêves* (with Joann Sfar), and *Capitaine écarlate* (with Emmanuel Guibert), among others. After breaking with L'Association, he continued to produce highly personal works for other publishers, including *Babel* (Coconino Press) and *Les Complots nocturnes* (Futuropolis). His style is marked by his extremely idiosyncratic use of imagery, innovative page designs, and use of solid blacks.

teric symbolism is intricately drawn, giving the reader a child's impression of intellectual overload, while cat-like Asians practice exotic therapies from the East.

David B. juxtaposes epilepsy with his family's historical struggles to escape poverty, but with each commune the family inhabits comes a new round of toil and intolerance. He creates articulated knights to protect him as he escapes into his moonlit backyard to wander among the friendly ghosts awaiting him. Skeletons, ghosts, and images of the long dead fight through the battle scenes as representations of his brother's illness, in which two warring factions jerk his brother this way and that and eventually entangle the whole family in an epileptic imbroglio.

Impact

David B. wrote his childhood in a surreal way that, as he says, "ruptures reality" by moving between flashbacks, family stories, and dreams while exploring fantasy and symbolic elements, thereby creating breaks in the linear narrative. The tone is different from other comic books because, as he puts it, he is "trying to shatter" the traditional comic format. Most of his works have a rebellious theme, and in *Epileptic*, nature rebels against the body.

Beauchard's comics publishing history began soon after art school. He is a founding member of L'Association comics publishing collective and has collaborated on and drawn many graphic works, including *Babel* (2004, 2006), an autobiographical dream journal in which the artist escapes from know-nothing parents and do-nothing doctors, to *La Lecture de ruines* (*Reading Ruins*, 2001), featuring a mad scientist who is driven crazy by war. *Les Complots nocturnes: Dix-neuf rêves, de décembre 1979 à septembre 1994* (*Nocturnal Conspiracies: Nineteen Dreams from December 1979 to September 1994*, 2005) reflects nightmare conspiracies, while *Les Ogres* (2000), which was published as part of *Hiram Lowatt et Placido*, is another battle-laden work and gives in to the cravings of cannibals.

David B.'s artistic influences range from the caricatural works of George Grosz to the collages of Max Ernst. Comic artists such as Jacques Tardi and Hugo

Pratt inspired his striking black-and-white style. Another artistic force in his life is *L'Planête*, a heavily illustrated esoteric magazine he discovered as a child, which "depicted feelings, sensations, symbols, and it delighted me." The family's many cultural outings to Paris museums seem to have been absorbed on a molecular level, as Beauchard's work reflects early woodcuts, engravings, illuminated Gothic manuscripts, pre-Columbian art, socialist art, medieval paintings, and Assyrian temple facades. What is fascinating is that this mishmash of stylistic renderings makes complete sense under Beauchard's tutelage. *Epileptic* is a graphic memoir that David B. says helped "forge the weapons that allow me to become more than a sick man's brother."

Doré Ripley

Further Reading

B., David. *Babel* (2004, 2008).

Miller, Frank, and Lynn Varley. *300* (1998).

Satrapi, Marjane. *Persepolis* (2003).

Small, David. *Stitches: A Memoir* (2009).

Bibliography

Moody, Rick. "*Epileptic*: Disorder in the House." *The Best American Comics Criticism*. Edited by Ben Schwartz. Seattle, Wash.: Fantagraphics Books, 2010.

Squier, Susan M. "So Long as They Grow Out of It: Comics, The Discourse of Developmental Normalcy and Disability." *Journal of Medical Humanities* 29, no. 2 (June, 2008): 71-88.

Wivel, Matthias. "David B. Interview." *The Comics Journal* 275 (March, 2006). http://archives.tcj.com/275/i_davidb.html.

Wolk, Douglas. "This Sweet Sickness: David B.'s *Epileptic* Lays Bare the Author's Tortured Muse—and Transfigures the Graphic Novel." *The New York Magazine*, May 2005. http://nymag.com/nymetro/arts/books/reviews/10851.

See also: *300; Stitches; Persepolis*

ETHEL AND ERNEST: A TRUE STORY

Author: Briggs, Raymond
Artist: Raymond Briggs (illustrator); Carol Devine (cover artist)
Publisher: Jonathan Cape
First book publication: 1998

Publication History

Ethel and Ernest was published after Raymond Briggs had become a celebrated creator of children's, young-adult, and adult books. It evolved from his creative development and adaptation of experiences, people, and places. As he develops his art, Briggs draws on his family and home and on world events. His father, a milkman, grumpily but dutifully going about his work, models grumpy, dutiful Saint Nick in *Father Christmas* (1973). *The Snowman* (1978) depicts Briggs's own house, the house that is the home of Ethel and Ernest. Briggs begins to utilize a comic-book-style format to tell more serious, even satiric stories. Cartoonlike *Fungus the Bogeyman* (1977) depicts the filthy world of bogeys who scare human beings. *When the Wind Blows* (1982) presents the life of a couple living before, during, and after a nuclear war. Characters and places in these books draw on Briggs's own experience. After experimenting with serious themes and comic book style, Briggs dramatized the story of his parents' life in *Ethel and Ernest*, a work categorized as a graphic novel. Using bubbles for dialogue and panels for characters, he presents his parents and working-class England during a period of change and trauma between 1920 and 1970, the years of the married life of Ethel and Ernest.

Plot

Ethel and Ernest renders the life and historical circumstances of two ordinary but representative people who lived through the ever-changing, sometimes traumatic events of the middle years of the twentieth century. Describing his parents, the author tells a love story that resonates with all who have experienced social changes and all who have worked to keep a marriage joyful.

Ethel and Ernest: A True Story. (Courtesy of Pantheon Books)

The novel begins with the courtship of Ethel and Ernest, a story that has become family lore for this small and close family. Ethel initiated the meeting when, while working as a ladies' maid, she saw out the window the handsome Ernest approaching on his bicycle. Boldly, she waved her dusting cloth at him. He, charmed, waved back. After they greeted each other like this for a few days, Ernest appeared at the front door with flowers and an invitation to dinner and a film. They both felt their love was meant to be. Though they had distinct backgrounds and differing political opinions, they nourished first and foremost their loving relationship, which was enhanced by the arrival, after a few anxious years, of a child, Raymond, born when Ethel was thirty-seven. Raymond was doted on.

Their life then revolves around making their home, meeting the challenges of the Battle of Britain (1940), adapting to a changing society, and marveling at new inventions. They follow the complicated discussions about war while listening to the radio, one of the first technical advances from which they would benefit. Their responses to impending war, the speeches of Winston Churchill, and the postwar shift in political power present the individuality of the two people who reflect differing political and class philosophies. Their actions and their quiet courage demonstrate the suffering, strength, and cheerfulness the British people exhibited during these years.

Postwar years bring challenges and surprises. Ethel and Ernest acquire a washing machine, a television, and a telephone. They experience the Cold War; they learn of the explosion of the atom bomb; and on the television, they watch a man walk on the moon. Their son becomes an artist, a disappointing career choice in their minds. They grow old and die, and their son contemplates selling the family home. *Ethel and Ernest* is a straightforward story of an ordinary life that projects simple beauty.

Characters

- *Ernest Briggs* recognizes the honor and the opportunity of Ethel's special greeting from the window and responds, creating the fortuitous turning point of their lives. A versatile, handy man, he enhances their home and thrives on his work, delivering milk, refusing to be persuaded by his wife to seek advancement. He embraces the politics of the Labor Party and advocates socialization. Though he expresses his views with gusto, he knows when to hold his tongue.
- *Ethel Briggs* initiates the relationship with Ernest. Her simple act of spontaneity and courage typifies the woman who has her own opinions about politics and class structure, views that are different from her husband's. While she does not hesitate to assert them, she, like her husband, values their family bonds above their political disagreements.
- *Raymond*, the artist son, pursues his talents even when his choice causes his parents some consternation. He depicts clearly the beauty of

their ordinary life and reflects on it as he deals with their deaths.
- *Julie Briggs*, Raymond's wife, because she suffers from schizophrenia, chooses, with her husband, to limit their family to themselves.

Artistic Style

The graphics of this novel reflect the artist's skill and training. Briggs draws with accurate and realistic detail, including each check on Ethel's apron, each brick on the facade of their home, and each repeated pattern of the paper on the walls. The characters express joy, sadness, anger, and delight in face and body. Through the artwork, daily life is conveyed, as, for example, Ernest taps replacement nails into the soles of his worn boots with his special hammer. This is the work of an artist/illustrator accustomed to writing wordless picture books in which each emotion and activity is fully

Ethel and Ernest: A True Story. (Courtesy of Pantheon Books)

represented through picture. There is nothing car-toonish about the artwork.

Briggs also uses color to convey mood. While the work as a whole is colorful, the palate is muted. Within this palate are variations. Dark colors for the jackets and boots present the somber mood when, for example, Ethel helps Ernest off with his boots after he returns from fourteen hours of putting out fires and picking up bodies of children following a particularly devastating bombardment during World War II. Bright colors present the birthday party for two when they celebrate Ethel's pregnancy.

Generally, speech is conveyed in traditional comic-strip bubbles; sustained conversation appears in boxes of text with speakers alternating in order on opposite halves of the text boxes. The picture panels vary in size. At times they are small, depicting a face or two. At other times, they fill half a page to display the culmina-tion of a process, as when Ethel washes clothes in the old (but "new") washing machine and then hangs them on the line in their little back yard where they blow in the breeze. Drawn in pencil and filled in with color, the pictures present an intimate look at two lives.

Themes

A hardworking ladies' maid, no longer young, who feels life may soon pass her by, waves flirtatiously at a young man cycling by. The young man, no fool, seizes the op-portunity and soon presents himself with flowers in hand. Thus begins Ethel and Ernest's tale of love. The rest of the story shows that married life includes much to try the spirit. However, despite economic depression, war, life in the nuclear world, and social changes (from the introduction of radio to the atomic bomb and then a man walking on the moon), the love of these two people, committed to marriage and each other, endures and deepens. The challenges to their marital happiness un-fold in their dialogue and individual responses to polit-ical and social changes. While bluster and disagreement reflect on their faces and in their words, in their hearts the two clearly value their relationship with each other and their son above all. In the end, both get old, then get sick, and then die. The lonely husband follows the wife. When the husband dies, the once faithful cat, who wrapped himself around the husband's neck while he

read the paper, is pictured walking away, seeking a new home. Their son, reflecting on their lives while noting the blossoming of a pear tree he planted during the war, moves ahead, as he must; he sells the family home and recycles their possessions. Their gentle world has come to an end, and yet it has been dramatized and celebrated.

Impact

Ethel and Ernest depicts vividly the reality of "happily ever after." The romantic story of how Ethel met Ernest is followed by what life brings to this ordinary, working-class couple. The novel expresses a natural evolution of the artistry of Briggs, renowned first as a children's book artist, whose wordless picture books present characters, even snowmen, so expressively that words are not necessary.

In *Ethel and Ernest*, though, the bubbles of dialogue create context, especially when the words are quotes or summaries of the news. In many ways this graphic novel is similar to others of the Modern Age (the late 1980's to the present) of graphic novels. Like *Maus* (1986-1991) by Art Spiegelman, it explores the re-sponse of a son to his parents' life. Like *Persepolis* (2003) by Marjane Satrapi, it explores the lives of people caught in a particular historical moment.

The artistic style makes this graphic novel different, however. The highly detailed, careful drawings set it apart from other acclaimed graphic novels to which it might be compared. In the mode of a children's book, it presents a realization, a clear theme, and an affirming, though adult, resolution. The artwork is so descriptive that it could almost stand alone and is the work of a practiced artist, who, through painstaking detail, ex-presses subtle differences in mood and personality. In its appearance, which is more like a children's book than a graphic novel, *Ethel and Ernest* melds word, picture, and dialogue so that the total effect is like the experience of delight produced by music or poetry.

Bernadette Flynn Low

Further Reading

Briggs, Raymond. *The Man* (1992).
Katchor, Ben. *The Jew of New York* (1998).
Satrapi, Marjane. *Persepolis* (2003).
Spiegelman, Art. *Maus: A Survivor's Tale* (1986).

Bibliography

Lehmann-Haupt, Christopher. "Mum, Dad, and Not Always So Merry Old England." *The New York Times*, September 23, 1999.

Murray, Mike. "Which Was More Important Sir, Ordinary People Getting Electricity or the Rise of Hitler? Using *Ethel and Ernest* with Year Nine." *Teaching History* 107 (June, 2002): 20-25.

Tabachnick, Stephen E. "A Comic-Book World." *World Literature Today* 81, no. 2 (March/April, 2007): 24.

"The Way I See It: Raymond Briggs—Artists Tackle Ten Existential Questions." *New Statesman* 136 (December 17, 2007): 72.

See also: *Maus: A Survivor's Tale; Persepolis; The Jew of New York*

EXIT WOUNDS

Author: Modan, Rutu

Artist: Rutu Modan (illustrator)

Publisher: Coconino Press (Italian); Drawn and Quarterly (English); Am Oved (Hebrew)

First book publication: *Unknown/Sconosciuto*, 2006 (English translation, 2007)

Publication History

Rutu Modan's first graphic novel was an international phenomenon and garnered a positive critical reception. *Exit Wounds* first appeared in 2006 in an Italian translation published by Bologna comics publisher Coconino Press under the title *Unknown/Sconosciuto*. In 2007, Canadian comics publisher and distributor Drawn and Quarterly published a hardback, English-language edition of this work for the North American market, while the British publisher Jonathan Cape released this version of the book for the European market. The English edition was translated by Noah Stollman, who also provided the English title.

Before publishing *Exit Wounds*, Modan was renowned in Israel as a prize-winning illustrator and comics artist who had edited the Israeli edition of *MAD* magazine and who was a founding member of the comics art collective Actus Tragicus. She also published several illustrated versions of her short stories. *Exit Wounds* has been translated into Danish and French, and an edition of the graphic novel in Modan's native Hebrew was published by the leading Israeli publisher Am Oved in 2008. Drawn and Quarterly published softcover editions of the book in 2008 and 2010, which include influential comics journalist Joe Sacco's 2008 interview with Modan that originally appeared in *The Comics Journal*. *Exit Wounds* received the 2008 Eisner Award for Best New Graphic Album.

Plot

In several interviews, Modan claimed that two unrelated historical events provided the background stories treated in *Exit Wounds*. The first was a terrorist bombing of a bus traveling from Tel Aviv to Tiberias in June, 2002. Of the seventeen casualties, one

Exit Wounds. (Courtesy of Drawn and Quarterly)

victim remained unidentified. Israeli filmmaker David Ofek documented the case of this unidentified victim in his 2003 film *No. 17*, a tale that fascinated Modan. The other event was rooted in Modan's personal experience. Having gone on a few dates with a new boyfriend, Modan did not hear from the man for several days and assumed that he had died or been killed. She, like Numi in *Exit Wounds*, was mistaken.

Koby Franco works as a taxi driver in Tel Aviv. His mother is dead, and his sister lives in New York. Estranged from his father, he works with his elderly aunt. He responds to a fare request at an army checkpoint, where he meets a female soldier who tells him an unidentified victim of a terrorist bombing in Hadera may be his father. For reasons that remain mysterious, the anonymous young woman asks Koby to get a blood test to verify the identity of the unknown bombing victim.

Though Koby angrily rejects the young woman's suggestion, he does attempt to locate his father, who appears to have disappeared. Discovering a love note signed with the letter N, Koby tracks down Numi, the soldier who first contacted him. They embark on a quest to confirm that the unidentified bombing victim is Gabriel Franco, Koby's father

Exit Wounds. (Courtesy of Drawn and Quarterly)

and Numi's lover. Finding the scarf Numi had knitted for the elder Franco as a birthday present (which was recovered from the scene of the attack) they conclude that the unknown victim is the elder Franco. Koby agrees to get a blood test to confirm the relationship.

A series of misleading clues and administrative bungles eventually leads Koby and Numi to an elderly woman who was Gabriel's former lover both in his youth and since Numi last saw him. Both emotionally worn down by Gabriel's deceptions and betrayals, Koby and Numi begin to fall in love. After an awkward sexual encounter, the two depart on bad terms. Koby eventually receives proof that his father is not only alive, but recently married to a widow. Koby travels to their home in hopes of confronting his father, but Gabriel never shows up. Abandoned once again, Koby reconsiders his relationship with Numi. *Exit Wounds* closes with Koby attempting to reconcile with Numi.

Characters

- *Koby Franco* is a taxi driver in Tel Aviv. He looks average, chain smokes, and harbors a grudge against his father. He demonstrates a reluctance to make friends or date and seems to move from one shallow relationship to the next. He is quick to take offense.

- *Numi Herman* is recently discharged from the Israeli army and lives with her wealthy family in an opulent Tel Aviv mansion, where her worldly mother and vain sister constantly harass her for her plain appearance and romantic failures. She is nicknamed "the giraffe" because of her height, and her last lover was Koby Franco's father. Like Koby, she is defensive and insecure. Unlike him, however, she is idealistic.

- *Gabriel Franco* appears only once in *Exit Wounds*, in a snapshot belonging to his estranged son Koby. He is a portly version of his son. He is a serial adulterer, and his former lovers suggest that he is charming and romantic.
- *Orly* lives in New York City and encourages her brother Koby to get over his animosity toward their father. She appears either in a bathrobe or putting on makeup.
- *Aunt Ruthie* works with Koby. She is his mother's good-natured twin sister and may have had an affair with his father.
- *Uncle Aryeh* is Aunt Ruthie's elderly husband. In poor health, he spends most of his time watching television and complaining about Aunt Ruthie's cooking.

Artistic Style

In *Exit Wounds*, Modan's characteristically strong line and gifts for color and composition are evident on every page. Comparing this book to her previous work, which typically treated shorter story lines, Modan's style here is sparer and subtler and seems better suited to supporting a longer narrative. Her use of gutters and panels, for example, suggests a careful consideration of how each page relates to the ones before and after, and it especially suggests how readers experience facing pages. Though Modan does not adhere to a consistent size and arrangement of gutters and panels in *Exit Wounds*, illustrations remain within the parameters of each panel frame, and Modan's striking use of color and shape both advances the plot and enriches the emotional texture of what her characters are thinking and feeling.

By and large, primary colors appear in panel foregrounds and on characters' clothing and personal effects, while backgrounds tend to feature secondary and tertiary colors. In addition, though she utilizes strong, flat colors and a bold, simple line throughout, Modan skillfully suggests depth and dimensionality through her use of perspective, which she further emphasizes by reserving line drawing in black for foreground figures. Backgrounds, settings, and interiors, in contrast, are often rendered in soft colored lines.

Modan's illustration calls to mind the clear-line style

Rutu Modan

After graduating from art school, Israeli cartoonist Rutu Modan edited the Hebrew-language version of *MAD* magazine with Yirmi Pinkus. In 1995, the two were involved with the founding of the independent Israeli comics group, Actus Tragicus. With Actus, Modan published a number of short works in collective anthologies (many of which are collected in *Jamilti and Other Stories*). In 2007, Modan published her first long-form graphic novel, *Exit Wounds*. Inspired by the clear-line visual style of Hergé, but with a decidedly modern twist, *Exit Wounds* tells the story of a young Israeli cab driver whose life is upended when he learns that his estranged father may have been the victim of an attack by a suicide bomber. The book won prizes at both the Angoulême Festival and at the Eisner Awards. Modan has also published comics in the *New York Times*, including "Mixed Emotions," a visual blog in 2007, and *The Murder of the Terminal Patient*, serialized in 2008.

of cartooning pioneered by Hergé, the Belgian creator of the seminal comics series *The Adventures of Tintin* (1929-1976). Characters in *Exit Wounds* even feature Hergé's instantly recognizable pinpoint eyes. In previous work, Modan would sometimes combine this distinctive use of strong line with other techniques such as cross-hatching, shading, and dramatic contrasts between dark and light spaces. In *Exit Wounds*, however, she capitalizes on the economy of Hergé's innovation and avoids combining these techniques. The result is stunning, especially in wordless sequences where characters' emotional and mental states are revealed or dramatically altered over the course of a few panels.

Themes

Exit Wounds contains a mystery story and therefore revolves around the themes of discovery and the quest for knowledge. While both Koby and Numi seek answers to what has really happened to Gabriel Franco, they are also searching for clues as to who they are. In many ways, the elder Franco has defined each of them by abandoning them, and it is up to Koby and Numi to make sense of this absence in their lives. Modan has suggested in interviews that the theme of identity is central in *Exit Wounds*, and she has attempted to treat it in ways that resist potentially misleading social and political contexts.

While the characters in *Exit Wounds* live with the Israeli-Palestinian conflict (indeed, this ongoing reality and the terror it has sponsored provides the occasion for Koby's connection with Numi), it is not otherwise addressed in the book. Instead, Modan implies that the basic human struggle to understand oneself persists even against the backdrop of terrorist threats and political instability. This prospect is further complicated by the idea that these personal negotiations inhibit people coming together in love and mutual interest. Numi and Koby's romance, though ambiguous even at the book's end, implies the possibility of cultivating hope with another in the wake of tremendous personal pain. It is ironic that the full disclosure of Gabriel Franco's personal betrayals, always motivated by his infidelities, ultimately brings Koby and Numi together.

Impact

Exit Wounds has exposed Israeli comics and graphic novels to a worldwide audience. Before the novel's publication, comics in Israel had been a minor industry dominated by a small group of writers and artists, with Modan's comics collective, Actus Tragics, providing its core.

Unlike Joe Sacco's *Palestine* (2001) and Ari Folman and David Polonsky's *Waltz with Bashir* (2008), *Exit Wounds* does not directly address the political realities of Israel. While she has endured some criticism for not doing so, Modan has argued that her book is an accurate portrayal of the day-to-day lives of urban Israelis. As such, her work offers a compelling counterpoint to other graphic novels, both fiction and nonfiction, that address this region and its problems.

Some recent criticism of *Exit Wounds* does not exhibit the enthusiasm expressed by some of its early readers, citing Modan's apparently limited facility with characterization as a significant weakness in this work. On the other hand, *Exit Wounds* frequently appears on higher-education reading lists in a variety of curricula, especially literature and political-sciences courses. In addition, research about this book and Modan's work in general has begun to appear in scholarly books and journals, suggesting its growing cultural and artistic relevance to the academy.

Greg Matthews

Further Reading

Al-Ali, Naji. *A Child in Palestine: The Cartoons of Naji al-Ali* (2009).

Folman, Ari, and David Polonsky. *Waltz with Bashir: A Lebanon War Story* (2008).

Sacco, Joe. *Palestine* (2001).

Bibliography

Juneau, Thomas, and Mira Sucharov. "Narratives in Pencil: Using Graphic Novels to Teach Israeli-Palestinian Relations." *International Studies Perspectives* 11, no. 2 (May, 2010): 172-183.

Kahn, Ariel. "Between Eros and Thanatos: Death and Desire in the Short Fiction of Koren Shadmi and Rutu Modan." *International Journal of Comic Art* 12, no. 1 (Spring, 2010): 157-182.

_____. "From Darkness into Light: Reframing Notions of Self and Other in Contemporary Israeli Graphic Narratives." In *The Jewish Graphic Novel: Critical Approaches*, edited by Samantha Baskind and Ranen Omer-Sherman. New Brunswick, N.J.: Rutgers University Press, 2008.

Modan, Rutu. "An Interview with Rutu Modan." Interview by Joe Sacco. *The Comics Journal,* no. 288 (February, 2008): 29-38.

Morris, Janice. "Suspended Animation." Review of *Exit Wounds*, by Rutu Modan. *Canadian Literature* 197 (Summer, 2008): 166-167.

See also: *Palestine; Waltz with Bashir; Footnotes in Gaza*

F

FAR ARDEN

Author: Cannon, Kevin
Artist: Kevin Cannon (illustrator)
Publisher: Top Shelf Productions
First serial publication: 2006-2008
First book publication: 2008 (self-published edition);
    2009

Publication History

Far Arden began as a dare between Kevin Cannon and fellow Minneapolis cartoonist Steve Stwalley. Cartoonists in Minneapolis, Minnesota, Cannon's birthplace and home, annually celebrate 24-Hour Comics Day, an event started by Scott McCloud in which creators write and draw a twenty-four-page comic in only twenty-four hours. After the event, Stwalley challenged Cannon to do a twenty-four-hour comic once a month for an entire year, which resulted in a 288-page graphic novel.

Under the guidelines of the twenty-four-hour comic, creators cannot work on the project before the event begins; they are not even supposed to think about plot or characters. Cannon mostly obeyed these rules, starting the comic without a clear plot, but he decided on certain elements beforehand. As Cannon described in a short comic explaining the origin of the book, he had a vague preliminary idea of the story: "A crusty sea dog named Army Shanks searches for a mythical tropical island in the middle of the Canadian High Arctic." For the first four months he followed the terms of the bet exactly, producing twenty-four pages in a twenty-four-hour period once a month. After this point, Cannon started writing and drawing at a more regular pace, creating chapters longer than twenty-four pages. Cannon serialized the chapters online as he finished them. He completed *Far Arden* in the spring of 2008 and printed one hundred copies, selling them through his Web site and at conventions. (This first, self-published edition

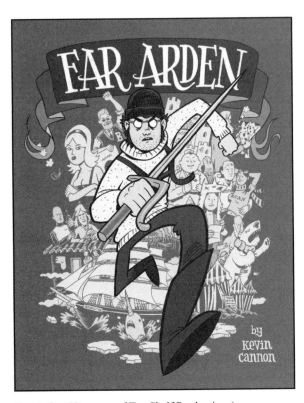

Far Arden. (Courtesy of Top Shelf Productions)

features an introduction by Stwalley.) Top Shelf Productions picked up the book and published its edition in 2009.

Plot

Although *Far Arden* is meant to be a single-volume graphic novel, it was originally created and serialized online as individual chapters. Because of the circumstances of the story's creation, much of the plot was developed spontaneously, with characters and plot points introduced almost at random, sometimes making the story difficult to follow. The basic plot involves the search for the mythical Far Arden, a tropical island somewhere in the Canadian high Arctic.

The story begins with Armitage (Army) Shanks and his partner, Hafley, attempting to steal back their ship, the *Areopagitica*. They make their way to the ship, only to confront Fortuna and her partner, Pinho, who capture Hafley. Army is forced to flee, along with Alistair Cavendish, a young orphan who appears on the dock. While they escape, Army and Alistair reveal their goals to one another: Army hopes to find Far Arden with the help of something on board the *Areopagitica*, while Alistair wants to get revenge on the man who killed his father. The two are soon joined by college students David and Amber.

Afterward, the plot takes rapid twists and turns, as characters join and separate, forming temporary alliances only to split up again. Eventually the backstory is revealed: Army, Barty, Pinho, and Emile Bessehl were all college students together under professor Simon Arctavius. The five of them formed a club dedicated to finding Far Arden. Arctavius eventually devised a map to the island, but only shared it with Army, who carved it into the wood of the *Areopagitica*. Arctavius sailed to the island alone and never returned. Army was supposed to follow, but he was distracted by his romance with Fortuna and never left. David is revealed to have been working for Bessehl, who is still obsessed with finding the island. Bessehl eventually kidnaps Army and tries to use a "Death MRI" to read the map from Army's brain. David saves Army, though Amber dies as the machine's first test.

Finally, David, Fortuna, Alistair, and Army join together. The *Areopagitica* is destroyed, along with the map, but by sheer chance, the four happen to see the fabled gold-colored narwhal that leads the way to Far Arden. Upon reaching the island, David, Fortuna, and Alistair leave Army to recuperate in the boat while they travel to the crater at the top. There they discover a lush tropical paradise and are reunited with friends they believed lost. Meanwhile, Army is finally reunited with Arctavius, who appears on the boat out of nowhere. However, when Army puts on his oxygen mask, Arctavius disappears. Army goes up to the crater where he sees a barren wasteland with corpses surrounding a fuming vent. Army drags his companions back to the

boat—discovering along the way the mummified corpse of Arctavius.

In the epilogue, it is revealed that Far Arden is actually a myth: The island naturally produces hallucinogenic vapors that make it seem like a tropical jungle. Army survived thanks to his oxygen mask, but the rest have all died. Ultimately, Army has fulfilled his mentor's dream and found Far Arden but at the cost of many lives. He is left friendless, alone, and with nothing to show for his efforts.

Characters

- *Armitage Shanks*, a.k.a. *Army Shanks*, the protagonist, is a crusty sea captain with permanent stubble and opaque glasses (which he never removes). His clothes are based on those worn by explorers of the late nineteenth and early twentieth centuries, in particular Sir Ernest Henry Shackleton. Though Shanks is shown to be misanthropic and cynical, he is loyal to those he considers his friends. Cannon deliberately left much of Army's backstory vague so that he could explore it in further stories.

- *Emile Bessehl*, Army's former classmate, is the closest the book has to an antagonist. A bearded, cigarette-smoking professor at (fictional) Boothia College, Bessehl is obsessed with discovering Far Arden and was enraged when Arctavius preferred Army as a protégé. He is based on Emil Bessels, a ship's physician on a nineteenth-century polar expedition who poisoned and killed his captain.

- *Hafley* is Army's closest friend and confidant. At the beginning of the book, the two are working together to take back the *Areopagitica*. How Hafley and Army became friends and partners is not shown in the course of *Far Arden*, as Cannon hopes to cover this in a later story.

- *David* is a student at Boothia College and the boyfriend of Amber. Although he appears to have been dragged along on the search for Far Arden by Amber, he is actually working for Bessehl.

- *Amber* is another Boothia College student. She has been fed stories of Army's bravery and David's heroism (working for Bessehl). When she is given a letter from Arctavius for Army—really a forgery crafted by Bessehl—she sets off to find Army.

- *Fortuna* is a former lover of Army, a thin blond femme fatale who seems to be coldly using Army in order to find Far Arden but who secretly still loves him. She is revealed to be Alistair's long-absent biological mother.
- *Alistair Cavendish* is an orphan who gets pulled into Army's adventures and the search for Far Arden. He is searching for the man who killed his father three years previously. At first he is told that Army killed his father, but he later discovers the truth: Army is his biological father's brother. Alistair's biological father was murdered by his foster father, whom Army killed in revenge.

Artistic Style

Cannon's style is cartoony: Facial features are simple and clear, and backgrounds are drawn with just enough detail to identify the location. This is especially notable in action sequences: When characters throw punches, their arms often turn into elongated curves and arcs. Cannon specifically credits Peter Bagge's style for this noodle-limbed aspect of his own art. The simplicity of figures and backgrounds is partly because pages had to be completed quickly, according to the rules of 24-Hour Comics Day, but even after Cannon stopped producing chapters in twenty-four-hour periods, his style remained largely consistent.

Far Arden is illustrated in black-and-white pen. Rather than use grayscale, all shading is done with cross-hatching. There are also no digital effects, nor was any part of the book produced using a computer; even the lettering is hand-done. Again, this is partly because of Cannon's original time constraints, which did not give him time to go back over his work with a computer. This hand-drawn style gives an antique feeling to the book, similar to wood-block prints or old newspaper illustrations.

The sound effects in *Far Arden* are a notable feature of the book. Rather than being onomatopoetic—trying to imitate the sound of an action—they are often just literal descriptions of an action. Someone tossing aside an object is accompanied by the sound effect "cast aside"; punching through a window produces the sound "breakthrough"; and two people shaking hands is illustrated with "handshake!" These overly literal sound effects are used humorously throughout the book.

Themes

Far Arden is largely a story about exploration. In interviews, Cannon has described his interest in the age of polar exploration and how this influenced the book. The search for Far Arden is similar in many ways to these expeditions: the journey into unexplored territory, the struggle to survive in harsh conditions, the desire to discover the unknown. Some of these allusions are more specific. For example, Fortuna's last words to Shanks are the last words of Titus Oates, a member of the doomed British Antarctic Expedition of 1910, who sacrificed himself in the hope that the other members of the party would live.

In alluding to this period, Cannon is also making a point about the dangers of exploration—not just the physical dangers of extreme weather and rough terrain but also the mental danger of self-delusion. The explorers who mapped the Antarctic went out in search of

---

Kevin Cannon

Kevin Cannon broke into the comics industry working as an assistant to artist Zander Cannon (no relation) on the *Smax* miniseries with writer Alan Moore. Cannon was subsequently asked to write the sequel to Moore's *Top Ten*. He is best known as the creator of the lengthy adventure graphic novel *Far Arden*, which was originally serialized online and later collected in book form by Top Shelf. *Far Arden* tells a humorous tale of seafaring adventurers and talking animals. It is drawn in a black-and-white cartoony style with extremely exaggerated characters. Pages shift between heavily crosshatched images and panels with considerable white spaces. In addition to his work as a comic book artist, Cannon has worked as the creator of children's books, including *Pond Hockey*. He has also published a nonfiction graphic novel, *Evolution: The Story of Life on Earth*.

glory; they found only a barren, inhospitable waste-land, and many died in the process. Similarly, characters search for Far Arden in the belief that it will bring them happiness: Bessehl is obsessed with finding the last remaining blank spot on the map; Barty wants to exploit Far Arden for the Canadian government; even Alistair hopes to finally find happiness and love in this mystical island. Ironically, Shanks is the only person not actually searching for Far Arden—he is only looking for his mentor, Simon Arctavius—yet he is the only one who sees the island and lives.

The name of the island comes from a song by Jim Morrison, lead singer of The Doors: "I'll always be true / Never go out, sneaking out on you, babe / If you'll only show me Far Arden again." In searching for Far Arden, characters end up losing their friends, their careers, even their lives. In the end, the island itself is a deathtrap with nothing of value. The ultimate theme of *Far Arden*, then, is that exploration can be a self-destructive process in which people find the thing they seek but end up losing everything else that they value.

Impact

Far Arden is a strong debut work that has received high critical acclaim. In 2010, it was nominated for an Eisner Award in the Best Publication for Teens category, though it lost to Evan Dorkin and Jill Thompson's *Beasts of Burden*. *Far Arden* is not Cannon's first solo work; he created several strips for his college newspaper, one of which, *Johnny Cavalier*, has been collected. However, since then, most of Cannon's work has been either as a commercial, work-for-hire artist or as an assistant to his business partner Zander Cannon (no relation) as part of their studio Big Time Attic.

Far Arden is notable for the unique nature of its creation. As a multichapter work made up of twenty-hour comics, it was made both spontaneously and gradually over the course of eighteen months. Also, the book is one of the first to be made available for free online while still being sold in print, and it has had strong sales. It may become a model for future graphic novel distribution.

Ted Anderson

Further Reading

O'Malley, Bryan Lee. *Scott Pilgrim* (2004-2010).
Renier, Aaron. *The Unsinkable Walker Bean* (2010).
Weing, Drew. *Set to Sea* (2010).

Bibliography

Aamodt, Britt. *Superheroes, Strip Artists, and Talking Animals: Minnesota's Contemporary Cartoonists.* St. Paul: Minnesota Historical Society Press, 2011.

Cannon, Kevin. "CR Sunday Interview: Kevin Cannon." Interview with Tom Spurgeon. *The Comics Reporter*, June 21, 2009. http://www.comicsreporter.com/index.php/cr_sunday_interview_kevin_cannon.

_____. "Kevin Cannon Talks *T-Minus* and *Far Arden*." Interview with Alex Dueben. *Comic Book Resources*, June 9, 2009. http://www.comicbookresources.com/?page=article&id=21527.

Hogan, John. "Cannon Fodder." *Graphic Novel Reporter.* http://graphicnovelreporter.com/content/cannon-fodder-interview.

See also: *Scott Pilgrim*

Fax from Sarajevo: A Story of Survival

Author: Kubert, Joe
Artist: Joe Kubert (illustrator)
Publisher: Dark Horse Comics
First book publication: 1996

Publication History

Ervin Rustemagić founded Strip Art Features in 1972 at the age of twenty, naming the venture after the comics magazine he had started the previous year. He worked diligently to secure artists' publishing rights with a variety of European publishers; by the 1980's, he had become the European agent for comics creators Hermann Huppen, Warren Tufts, Joe Kubert, Martin Lodewijk, and others, and he was regularly working with over five hundred comics publishers worldwide.

Rustemagić was a native of Sarajevo and established the city (then part of Yugoslavia) as his business headquarters. Years after the company's founding, however, Bosnia and Herzegovina declared independence from Yugoslavia in early 1992. On April 6, open warfare began, and Serbs were soon marching through Sarajevo, shelling the city during the night, while snipers fired at people in the streets during the day. Rustemagić and his family were trapped in the city and sent intermittent faxes to Kubert and Lodewijk.

Once Rustemagić and his family were safe, Kubert asked permission to tell Rustemagić's story in an attempt to highlight what life was like in Sarajevo during that period. He worked with Rustemagić to get the facts and emotions as accurate as possible, and the resulting book, *Fax from Sarajevo*, was published in hardcover by Dark Horse Comics in 1996. Through Strip Art Features, Rustemagić later helped to get the story translated and published in Germany, Spain, France, and Italy. Dark Horse Comics released an English-language paperback version in 1998.

Plot

In early 1992, Ervin Rustemagić returns to Sarajevo from a business trip to the Netherlands, despite some underlying concerns and confusion about the state of affairs in Bosnia. The city appears the same as when he

(Getty Images)

Joe Kubert

Born in Poland, artist Joe Kubert began working in the American comic book industry in the early 1940's in Harry Chesler's sweatshops. In the mid-1960's he began producing the work for which he is best remembered, a long run on DC Comics' *Sgt. Rock*. Kubert was a well-regarded adventure comic illustrator during this period, with a classical sensibility and figure drawing that was much better than the industry's norm. In 1976 he founded the Kubert School in New Jersey, teaching the skills of cartooning and comics art to a new generation of cartoonists, including Steve Bissette, Rick Veitch, Dave Dorman, Eric Shanower, and his sons, Adam and Andy Kubert. In 1996 Kubert published the graphic novel *Fax from Sarajevo*, a depiction of the civil war in the former Yugoslavia based on the writings of his friend Ervin Rustemagić. In 2003 he published *Yossel: April 19, 1943*, an alternate family history that imagines what might have become of his life had his family not immigrated to the United States in 1927.

left, except it is unusually quiet. He enjoys a happy reunion with his wife, Edina, and their two children, Edvin and Maja.

That night, however, a shell explodes just outside their house. They briefly discuss fleeing, but a neighbor warns them that Serbs are killing anyone who tries to leave the city limits. Within a few days, the frequency of bombings has the entire family huddled and trembling together in their basement.

Ervin tries to continue his business in as usual a manner as possible, but the continued attacks make this difficult. Food and cigarettes have become increasingly hard to come by, and Ervin finds himself becoming more of a caretaker, providing first aid to those wounded by shell fire and tending to his feverish son. Still, he is able to continue sending faxes to his friends and contacts in the outside world, explaining his situation to them.

Before long, however, the Rustemagić home is destroyed, sending the family to seek shelter in an abandoned building. Witnessing a man caught in another blast, Ervin manages to drive the man to the local hospital. Seeing the deplorable situation there, he offers his car to the hospital as a makeshift ambulance. Ervin then begins to make overtures to the ministry in Sarajevo to get his family out; they move into a hotel to remain close to the building. Mortar and rifle fire continue to keep them on edge, becoming a near daily occurrence.

After repeated meetings at the ministry, which all come to no avail because of seemingly endless and ever-changing bureaucratic regulations, Ervin eventually realizes he will need as much outside assistance as he can get. Over the ensuing months, friends and co-workers make as many phone calls as they can on his behalf and continue to deposit funds in his bank account to pay for his family's hotel lodgings.

Taking matters more directly into his own hands, Ervin takes his family on a midnight dash across a protected airfield. They are shot at and forced back into the city. The quasi-legal contacts of Ervin and his friends, who have promised to aid the family's escape, disappear. Eventually, Ervin's friends are able to acquire journalistic accreditation for him, which allows him to

travel more freely. He is finally able to fly out with the U.S. Air Force but cannot take his family with him.

Once outside the country, Ervin makes his way to Poreč, Croatia, where he connects with a friend. Using Poreč as a base of operations, Ervin makes as many contacts as he can, both by fax and in person, with various ministries and consulates in an effort to find a way to get his family out of Sarajevo. He works tirelessly, deeply worried about his family's well-being. After nearly two months of work, Ervin is able to secure Slovenian citizenship for himself, which, in turn, confers citizenship on his wife and children as well, meaning they will be granted permission to leave Sarajevo. Although the departure of the Rustemagić family takes another several months of preparations, in late September, 1993, Ervin finally meets his family members as they step off a U.S. Air Force plane in Croatia.

Characters

- *Ervin Rustemagić*, the protagonist, is an agent for comic book creators. A proud and practical businessman, he has great love for his family. Throughout the story, he is primarily driven by the need to provide for his family and keep them as safe as he can under the circumstances. That impetus gives him the courage and compassion to help as many people as he can.

- *Edina Rustemagić* is Ervin's wife and the mother of their two children. She is largely portrayed as having a traditionally supportive role opposite her husband, taking care of the cooking and looking after the children while he is away. Like her husband, she is also concerned for her family's safety, though she tends to express her fears more openly. She can see through the brave front her husband displays and tries to hold herself up to his example, though she is not always as successful as he is.

- *Butzo*, a chain-smoking co-worker of Ervin, remains cheerful and optimistic despite the fighting. He is last seen heading off to find his family just before the Rustemagić home is destroyed.

- *Joe and Muriel Kubert* are seen only briefly in the book, but it is clear from the faxes exchanged throughout the book that their relationship with Ervin extends beyond business and has become a solid friendship between both families. The Kuberts provide what assistance and encouragement they can from New Jersey.

- *Martin Lodewijk* is Ervin's Dutch business associate and friend, who tries to help the Rustemagić family from his home in the Netherlands and passes along updates to many of their friends. Ultimately, he is the one who secures the journalistic accreditation for Ervin.

Artistic Style

Kubert uses a rougher, almost sketchier illustration style than most mainstream comic book artists. This style has made his work well-suited to dark and gritty stories and helped his success on comics such as *Our Army at War* (1952-1977), *G.I. Combat* (1952-1956, 1957-1987), *Tales of the Green Beret* (1967-1969), and, most notably, *Sgt. Rock* (first appearing in 1959). This distinctive style in war comics was especially appreciated as combat became less and less glamorous in the public's opinion. Kubert's somewhat harsh depictions of soldiers and military vehicles reflected a broader attitude shift toward armed combat.

While *Fax from Sarajevo* is not a war comic in the same sense as the works for which Kubert was previously known, the Bosnian War (1992-1995) is ever-present throughout the story. The rough-hewn faces and ragged clothing, while not generally depicting soldiers in this case, are entirely appropriate for those caught in the crossfire. Indeed, Ervin's last fax shown in the book notes that his wife and daughter had been wearing the same clothes for nearly a year.

The coloring, too, serves to emphasize the story. The novel has a somewhat dark and musty feel, with lots of browns and muted greens and blues. Though local color is generally used throughout the book, limited light sources provide ample opportunities for creating darker moods and focusing the reader's attention on the emotional elements of the story.

Interspersed with the comic narrative are replicas of the faxes that were exchanged. They provide a time line for the story and represent the knowledge to which Ervin Rustemagić himself had access. Few portions of the story depict events that Ervin does not witness firsthand, and the faxes serve to establish his perspective more firmly by largely eliminating an omniscient narrative approach.

Themes

The primary theme in *Fax from Sarajevo* is the importance of the love of friends and family. From the outset of the book, the characters express a desire to be with and support the ones they love. The focus on the Rustemagić family and Ervin Rustemagić's constant concern for their safety is an obvious indication of this, but it extends through nearly all of the secondary characters and events as well. Early on, Ervin notes that the family has remained in Sarajevo to be near Edina's father and brother. On the occasions when Butzo is not making jokes, he talks about family. Even a brief interlude in the Kubert household shows their extended family celebrating Passover together, with Muriel expressly citing her pleasure in having everyone visiting. This theme extends to friendships as well. Ervin's business associates all seem to be comfortable and friendly with the entire Rustemagić family. Butzo makes jokes with Ervin; some of the faxes to Huppen, Lodewijk, and the Kuberts are signed by the entire Rustemagić family; most of the faxes to New Jersey are addressed to both Joe and Muriel. Ultimately, those able to help Ervin are his friends, not any of the politicians, bureaucrats, or government officials who continually make idle promises and insincere gestures of goodwill.

The second theme, no less significant than the first, is the atrocious effect war has on those who are caught between fighting factions. Many civilians are senselessly killed throughout the book, and Ervin's only goal is to remove his family from the war zone. Sarajevo is all but leveled, largely by unseen attackers, and nearly everyone is forced to run from place to place to avoid the shelling. Kubert clearly wants to make a point about what happened to the everyday people who were not being showcased by the media.

Impact

Fax from Sarajevo is one of three significant comics focusing on the Bosnian War; the other two (*Safe Area Goražde: The War in Eastern Bosnia 1992-1995*, 2000;

The Fixer: A Story from Sarajevo, 2003) were written by Joe Sacco, who visited the area as a journalist in 1994. Together, the three books paint a vivid picture of the Bosnian War that was largely absent from popular American mass media beforehand. Sacco had visited Sarajevo and was working on *Safe Area Goražde* before Kubert's book was published, so the works did not directly influence one another.

While working independently of one another, Kubert and Sacco used different approaches to depict the war. Thus, there is little overlap between their works. Though their books are decidedly personal in nature, Kubert's story shows the war through a decidedly more apolitical perspective. Framed within the context of the Bosnian War, his book provides the backdrop for a larger statement about war in general. There is no real discussion about the politics behind the decisions to attack, and none of the characters express any political opinions themselves. Even the government officials act in a politically neutral manner, expressing basic sympathy for Ervin Rustemagić's situation but little else.

Prior to *Fax from Sarajevo*, Kubert had been viewed as a master storyteller, so the book was well received from the outset. It quickly earned praise for both the subject matter and the expert care Kubert provided it, and it remains a hallmark work in his career.

Sean Kleefeld

Further Reading

Kubert, Joe. *Dong Xoai, Vietnam 1965* (2010).
_____. *Yossel: April 19, 1943* (2003).
Sacco, Joe. *The Fixer: A Story from Sarajevo* (2003).
_____. *Safe Area Goražde: The War in Eastern Bosnia 1992-1995* (2000).

Bibliography

Burg, Steven L., and Paul S. Shoup. *The War in Bosnia-Herzegovina: Ethnic Conflict and International Intervention*. London: M. E. Sharpe, 2000.

Sacco, Joe. *Safe Area Goražde: The War in Eastern Bosnia 1992-1995*. Seattle, Wash.: Fantagraphics Books, 2000.

Schelly, Bill. *Man of Rock: A Biography of Joe Kubert*. Seattle, Wash.: Fantagraphics Books, 2008.

See also: *Yossel; The Fixer; Safe Area Goražde; Photographer; Pyongyang*

THE FIXER: A STORY FROM SARAJEVO

Author: Sacco, Joe
Artist: Joe Sacco (illustrator)
Publisher: Drawn and Quarterly
First book publication: 2003, 2005

Publication History

Joe Sacco went to Sarajevo in 1995 and 2001 (with help from a Guggenheim grant the second time) to do research for his *Stories of Bosnia* series with Drawn and Quarterly. To date, this series comprises *The Fixer: A Story from Sarajevo* (2003) and *War's End: Profiles from Bosnia, 1995-1996* (2005), each published initially as separate books; they have been combined in the paperback *The Fixer, and Other Stories* (2009). Like *Footnotes in Gaza* (2009), also by Sacco, *The Fixer* incorporates into the story the process of doing research for the book. In it, the difficulty of relying on witnesses for accuracy, the recording of conversations, and the general business behind journalistic production are all prominently featured. In fact, this work goes further than others by Sacco in emphasizing that the process is unreliable by centering on one fascinating figure and by faithfully reporting that what he hears is at best prone to exaggeration or, at worst, to lying. The ambiguous quality of the narrative seems highly appropriate to the conditions in which Sacco researched his book: a city under siege in which multiple factions struggle and corruption is the norm.

Plot

Using his 2001 trip to Sarajevo as a framing device, Sacco flashes back to 1995 to tell his story about Neven (the fixer), who can procure, arrange, translate for, and guide touring journalists in Sarajevo. The reader is repeatedly asked to view situations from Neven's perspective; Sacco details Neven's experiences in a second-person narrative. Neven's story is developed through a series of episodes that are framed by his narrative. In the episodes, Neven makes Sacco feel perpetually guilty or obligated, such as when Neven comically wrestles money from him with professional skill. The reader learns about Neven's past association with

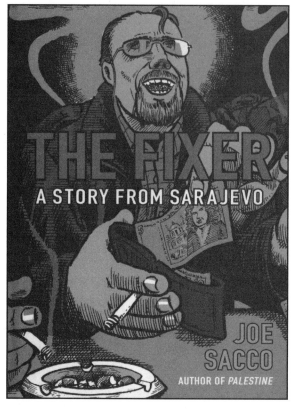

The Fixer: A Story from Sarajevo. (Courtesy of Drawn and Quarterly)

one of Sarajevo's paramilitary warlords, Ramiz Delalac, under whom a special wing of soldiers called the "Green Berets" was formed with support from the Stranka Demokratske Akcije (SDA, the Party of Democratic Action), the Muslim nationalist party. Something of a mercenary group, the SDA is suspicious of Neven's loyalties, eventually asking him to leave the group. Ultimately, some of Neven's stories are revealed to be tall tales, and Sacco comes to understand that his guide is not the most reliable narrator. Nonetheless, by the end of the story, Neven's years of paramilitary service (or crimes) appear to be confirmed.

The Fixer relates the chaotic and desperate conditions of those living in Sarajevo during the siege, which took place from April 5, 1992, to February 25, 1996.

The earliest images in the book focus on the abandonment of public spaces and the desperate attempts by the public to live life as usual. Eventually, though, Sacco shows the wealthy being harassed, people being brutalized and executed, rape being referred to as merely a sexual act, and desensitized soldiers looting and "living large." Thus, the state of affairs is far from normal by nearly anyone's standards.

Characters

- *Joe Sacco*, the author and narrator, has prominent round eyeglasses, which are used as a masking device that allows readers to see events from the author's perspective. He is portrayed as a comically bumbling character, a humble exaggeration of Sacco himself.
- *Neven*, a.k.a. *The Fixer*, is the primary character and Sacco's most important source for the material in the book. He was born to a Muslim mother and a Serbian father and is a former sniper for the Yugoslav People's Army. He is active in informal gangs and paramilitary groups associated with the SDA. Though fighting alongside those with Muslim loyalties, as a Serb he is conflicted and insists that his "enemies" be referred to by the derogatory term "chetniks," which allows him to dehumanize them and, thus, commit acts of violence against them. In the present tense of the book, he is working as a fixer for journalists and diplomats visiting Sarajevo.
- *Ismet Bajramovic*, a.k.a. *Celo*, is a charismatic leader of one of the Green Beret's cells in Sarajevo. He did prison time for murder and has been involved with organized crime.
- *Jusuf Prazina*, a.k.a. *Juka*, is an egotistical thug and warlord. He is a "patriot" who views himself as the future salvation of Sarajevo.
- *Vildania Selimbegovic* is a writer for the reputable *Dani* magazine and an important and reliable source for Sacco.
- *Musan Topalovic*, a.k.a. *Caco*, is a folk musician before the Bosnian War. He becomes a criminal and warlord, leading a Green Beret unit called Bosna 10.

- *Ramiz Delalic*, a.k.a. *Celo*, is the central warlord in most of Neven's war stories and the leader of his unit. He has a criminal background but manages to get more followers than the other warlords. Sacco consistently uses his last name to avoid confusion with Bajramovic, who is also nicknamed Celo.
- *Jovan Divjak* is a general in the Bosnian army during the siege of Sarajevo.
- *Alija Izetbegovic* is the first president of Bosnia and Herzegovina, serving from 1990 to 1996.
- *Munir Alibabic* is the chief of intelligence services in Sarajevo during the siege.

Artistic Style

Sacco has garnered much acclaim for his journalistic rigor and realism, as well as for his commitment to authenticity, immersing himself in the areas he researches. His excellent eye for character and ear for dialogue often go unmentioned, though. However, these are the qualities that make *The Fixer* a remarkable (if overlooked) text. In Neven, Sacco found not only someone with great war stories but also a soldier of fortune and con man who could provide the horrific, heroic, and humorous anecdotes that make for great war reporting and storytelling, the nuances of which Sacco captures so well. Using characters like Neven, for example, creates not only comic relief, making serious matters more palatable and accessible, but also human interest stories that work like war diaries, such as Zlata Filipovic's *Zlata's Diary* (1994), by enabling readers unfamiliar with life under occupation to comprehend the everyday trauma and oppression of such situations.

Two techniques that help Sacco achieve this effect are the use of second-person narration, which allows the reader to see from Neven's perspective, and a masking effect, in which Sacco's eyes are hidden behind blank glasses. The latter technique is used to reflect the general reader's perspective. In the background, however, unpleasant details are unmasked. Considering that Sacco employs such a method, it is no surprise to discover that he admires the work of Pieter Bruegel, the Elder, whose work also documents peripheral or obscured everyday details. Shadows are meticulously crosshatched, and the black-and-white pen work seems appropriate to Sacco's subject matter. Granting levity to heavy content, Sacco draws himself in caricature: His self-representation is consistently of a self-deprecating and Robert Crumb-influenced curmudgeonly fellow who is much more naïve than the actual author/artist. This depiction also helps readers to reflect on their own political privilege or complicity in world events. (Sacco has admitted to having an American audience, in particular, in mind for his work.)

Themes

The Fixer is unique among Sacco's works in that it is as much, or more, a character study as it is an engrossing and realistic war comic. The story is Neven's story. Most of the other players in the plot are revealed through Neven's episodic narrations.

Sacco never really followed superhero comics, finding them too predictable, and *The Fixer* offers much evidence for why he did not. Not only is the title character an original antiheroic figure, but also the book provides a multilayered critique of the

The Fixer: A Story from Sarajevo. (Courtesy of Drawn and Quarterly)

hypermasculine world of superhero comics. In an interview with Mark Binelli of *Rolling Stone*, Sacco commented, "I can't tell if Neven is the baddest-ass in Bosnia or if he read the same comics as me." The character of Neven allows Sacco to develop an ongoing critique of the treatment of war in the American media and in pop culture in particular.

At every turn, Neven reveals himself to be antiheroic. He tells quintessentially formulaic heroic war stories, but the motivations for his "actions," as he calls the missions, are never altruistic or heroic. He is a soldier of fortune unable to recall why he chose to fight with Bosnian forces. Even his patriotism is available for purchase. His military skills were honed in gang warfare, on the streets, and in criminal acts—not out of some sense of honor or duty.

Set in sharp contrast to Neven are the iconic warlords of the text: Bajramovic, Prazina, Topalovic, and Delalic. Most of the warlords have their reputations bolstered with legends that inspired, though not usually for good reason, the support of fighting men. Bajramovic is famous for local stories, such as the one in which he pulls a gun on two men who are beating another at a café. Prazina has been seriously wounded in an early conflict and is known to beat followers severely with his crutch if they are insubordinate. Delalic is said to have been involved with the beginning of "enmity between Serbs and Muslims," while Prazina claimed he would resolve the conflict single-handedly and on a snow-white steed. Topalovic refuses to adhere to the hierarchy among military and police, putting "himself further and further above the law." Later, he is ousted and arrested in what is described as a "showdown" with Delalic. The language of spaghetti Westerns is used in the legends surrounding all four warlords, but the relatively formal accounts from reliable sources at the end of the book read more brutally.

One critic, Michel Faber of *The Guardian*, seems to peremptorily apologize in his review for all of Sacco's macho-infused madness, claiming that female readers might feel alienated or disgusted. However, Sacco constantly re-centers each narrative neutrally. In contrast to Neven and the warlords, Sacco is free of pretense, is

innocent, and is the perfect amoral but humanist cipher to convey such inhumane happenings. Some have even commented on the homoeroticism in the text. However, Sacco seems to be completely asexually innocent and the ideal reporter, bringing the reader the facts as transparently as possible. He acknowledges honestly any spin he provides, which is a common thread running through all of Sacco's work.

Impact

Although Sacco has denied that he set out to form a new genre (he is not the first to write war comics, graphic nonfiction, or political cartoons), his critical success—which includes the 1996 National Book Award for *Palestine*, a 2001 Eisner Award for *Safe Area Goražde*, and 2010 Ridenhour Prize for *Footnotes in Gaza*—has allowed him to cross over to a wider audience than many similar publications have enjoyed. Both Edward Said and Christopher Hitchens have written his prefatory material. He has been called the "best" and even the "only" comics journalist. His primary influences also cross over genre and medium: George Orwell, Noam Chomsky, Michael Herr, and Hunter S. Thompson. Like the New Journalists, he utilizes the full expressive potential of reporting, but in addition, he is able to use his "hobby" of illustrating to create a subtler text, combining more comprehensive and simultaneously diverse perspectives. When he was younger, Sacco read war comics such as those produced under Harvey Kurtzman, and it is likely that his impact will be just as strong on future generations as Kurtzman's was on him.

Susan Honeyman

Further Reading

Delisle, Guy. *Burma Chronicles* (20).

_____. *Pyongyang: A Journey in North Korea* (2009).

Guibert, Emmanuel. *The Photographer: Into War-Torn Afghanistan with Doctors Without Borders* (2010).

Kubert, Joe. *Fax from Sarajevo* (1998).

Sacco, Joe. *Safe Area Goražde: The War in Eastern Bosnia, 1992-1995* (2011).

Bibliography

Binelli, Mark. "Joe Sacco's Cartoon Violence." *Rolling Stone* 940 (January 22, 2004): 40-41.

Bowe, Marisa. "No Laughing Matter: Marisa Bowe on Joe Sacco." *Bookforum* (Summer, 2005): 26-57.

Hajdu, David. "Joe Sacco and Daniel Clowes." In *Heroes and Villains: Essays on Music, Movies, Comics, and Culture*. Cambridge, Mass.: Da Capo Press, 2009.

Venezia, Antonio. "New New (Graphic) Journalism." *Radical Philosophy* 161 (May/June, 2010): 58-60.

See also: *Burma Chronicles; Fax from Sarajevo; Pyongyang; Photographer; Safe Area Goražde*

FLAMING CARROT COMICS

Author: Burden, Bob
Artist: Bob Burden (illustrator); Roxanne Starr (letterer)
Publisher: Dark Horse Comics
First serial publication: 1979-1987, 1988-1994
First book publication: 1997-2006

Publication History

The publication history of *Flaming Carrot Comics* is almost as bizarre and convoluted as the series itself. The series began as a drunken joke. In 1979, Bob Burden was living with a comic book fan who was determined to create what he hoped would be the next great independent comic book series: *Visions*. Burden watched as his roommate spent a week tweaking a single page. While they were drinking one night, Burden boasted that he could write and illustrate an eight-page comic book in a single night, and if he did, his friend should publish it in *Visions*. Burden delivered on his own dare, penning the first *Flaming Carrot* installment; it was published in *Visions*, issue 1, by the Atlanta Fantasy Fair in 1979. *Flaming Carrot* appeared in all subsequent yearly issues of *Visions* until 1987.

In 1981, Burden self-published *Flaming Carrot Comics*, issue 1, using the publisher title Killian Barracks Press. A year later, a four-page *Flaming Carrot* comic in *Visions*, issue 4, caught the attention of Dave Sim, creator of the self-published series *Cerebus* (1977-2004), also initially a spoof comic. Sim first incorporated the Flaming Carrot character into the pages of *Cerebus* and later published *Flaming Carrot* as a regular series under the Aardvark-Vanaheim imprint. The first issue was published in May, 1984. It ran for five issues until January, 1985, even appearing once in 3-D.

Twelve more issues of the comic were published by Renegade Press between March, 1985, and July, 1987. Then, the series was picked up by Dark Horse Comics, which published fourteen more issues of *Flaming Carrot* from June, 1988, to October, 1994; a *Flaming Carrot Stories* special in 1994; and *Flaming Carrot Comics Collected Album* in 1997. The last *Flaming*

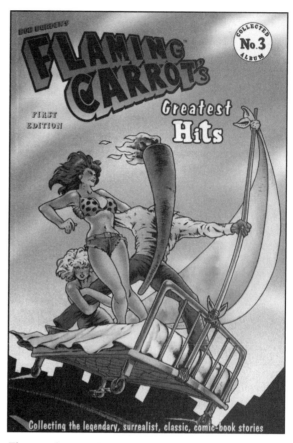

Flaming Carrot's Greatest Hits. (Courtesy of Dark Horse Comics)

Carrot comic published by Dark Horse was the crossover special *Flaming Carrot and Reid Fleming, the World's Toughest Milkman*, which appeared in 2002.

Over the years, the Flaming Carrot continued to appear in numerous crossover comics, including *Cerebus, Teenage Mutant Ninja Turtles*, and *Normalman-Megaton Man*. In 2006, the series was relaunched by Image Comics with *Bob Burden's Flaming Carrot Comics*, Volume 6: *Unacceptable Behavior*.

Plot

The series revolves around Flaming Carrot, a crime-fighting superhero without superpowers who wears a large carrot mask with a flame on top. As described in several exposés throughout the series, the Flaming Carrot is brave, ruthless, and incredibly dumb. His stupidity is rumored to have been brought on by reading five thousand comic books in a single sitting. The Carrot speaks in incomplete sentences that often lack verbs. He is a heavy drinker and a tireless womanizer, often sleeping with inappropriately young women. Despite his poor judgment and imbecilic behavior, he manages to avert catastrophe by sheer dumb luck. For example, he inadvertently deactivates a bomb by putting a quarter into it, thinking that it is a soda machine.

The Flaming Carrot bounces around using a nuclear-powered pogo stick. His flaming mask, pogo stick, and various other weapons and technological devices are designed by Dr. Heller, an elusive mad scientist and the Flaming Carrot's right-hand man. The Flaming Carrot lives in the unfashionable Palookaville section of Iron City, a working-class town, where he is widely lauded as a "blue collar" superhero.

After a few years of fighting crime, the Flaming Carrot indulges in alcohol, womanizing, and other vices. He burns out, spends all his money, and ends up in Shanty Town, dropping from the public eye until journalist Radzak Zokey reads about him in a comic book and seeks him out for an interview. The Flaming Carrot refuses to talk to the journalist until the latter gets a haircut. When aliens begin taking over Iron City, Zokey gets a haircut and returns to the Carrot, persuading him to save them all from the scourge. The Flaming Carrot agrees, emerging from obscurity to become the people's superhero again.

Most of the issues are self-contained stories that can be easily understood out of the context of the rest of the series. The majority of the stories follow a similar template: A villain wreaks havoc on Iron City, causing catastrophic death and destruction. Flaming Carrot manages to save the day using an obscure weapon or random, nonsensical tactic. For example, in "Road Hogs from Outer Space," the Flaming Carrot saves the world from mass-murdering aliens by telling them about income tax; the aliens are so outraged by the concept that they leave Earth by themselves. Typically, the Flaming Carrot is honored by the city in a highly publicized event or makes an appearance at a press conference at the end of the story. He is frequently given awards for bravery, which are often presented to him by buxom women, typically dressed in bikinis.

The Flaming Carrot fights a variety of bizarre and quirky villains, including the Artless Dodger, who massacres several people in order to steal a box of vanilla wafers; a vampire dog with blood dripping from its canine teeth; and the Chair, whose only superpower is to turn into a chair. The Carrot stops several alien invasions and even battles Death himself.

Some of the stories are highly experimental, such as "Adventures in Limbo," wherein circus workers discuss how to dispose of the body of an elephant that one of them killed. Afraid that the elephant's death will bring bad press, they try to dispose of the elephant's corpse by marrying it off to a jilted bride. When this does not work, they try to lose the elephant in a poker game and finally end up sending the elephant to film producer Dino De Laurentiis's studio in Hollywood.

The Mystery Men first appear in *Flaming Carrot*, issues 16 and 17, and play a prominent role throughout the rest of the series. The Mystery Men occupy the lowest rung of the superhero ladder. These misfits either lack superpowers altogether or possess uncontrollable, unremarkable, or useless powers. However, they do all possess impressive names, flashy costumes, and unshakable zeal. Since most of them are just ordinary people with more chutzpah than talent or competence, the group has a high casualty rate.

Volumes

- *Flaming Carrot Comics Presents Flaming Carrot, Man of Mystery* (1997). Collects issues 1-3. Flaming Carrot stops an alien invasion by telling the aliens to go home, and he battles Death.
- *Flaming Carrot Comics Presents, the Wild Shall Wild Remain* (1997). Collects issues 4-11 and adds a new five-page story. The Flaming Carrot lifts his mask.
- *Flaming Carrot's Greatest Hits* (1998). Collects issues 12-18. The Mystery Men make their first appearance.
- *Flaming Carrot Comics, Fortune Favors the Bold* (1998). Collects issues 19-24. Flaming Carrot stops yet another alien invasion, this time with the help of a bubble pipe.

- *Bob Burden's Flaming Carrot Comics,* Volume 6: *Unacceptable Behavior* (2006). Relaunch of the series with Image Comics.

Characters

- *Flaming Carrot*, the protagonist, is an unintelligent superhero with no superpowers who wears a

large carrot mask that is almost as long as his body. On top of the mask, and above his head, is a flame created by an infernal device designed by Dr. Heller. The flame can be used as a weapon. The Flaming Carrot always wears flippers on the off-chance that he might someday have to swim. He carries a nuclear-powered pogo stick and a

Flaming Carrot's Greatest Hits. (Courtesy of Dark Horse Comics)

pair of plungers, which he uses to climb walls. What he lacks in superpowers, he makes up for in daring and dumb luck.

- *Dr. Heller* is a scientist who designs most of the Flaming Carrot's regalia and equipment and helps him fight crime. He is a workaholic who does not halt scientific experiments for interviews with reporters. He takes his work and himself extremely seriously and has a sign on the wall that says, "I am always right," which he cites as scientific evidence.

- *Death* is one of the Flaming Carrot's more notable adversaries, appearing in the issue *Death Gets Drunk*. Death wears a trench coat and dark, triangular sunglasses and has a long, razor-thin mustache. In addition to taking lives, Death has the power to turn people into bugs and make wild bulls appear out of thin air. Although alcohol has no effect on him, a large dose of strychnine can make him tipsy.

- *Mr. Furious* is one of the Mystery Men. He is so furious about crime that he is impervious to bullets, although he loves to shoot them at other people. He wears a black and yellow costume and uses a machine gun. When not in his superhero costume, he works as a car repossessor.

- *The Shoveler* is another of the Mystery Men. He is a blue-collar ditchdigger, quarryman, and superhero who wields a lethal shovel that once belonged to King Arthur of Camelot. The Shoveler's costume consists of a pair of purple overalls with a large "S" on the bib and a black mask worn over the eyes.

- *Sponge Boy* is one of Flaming Carrot's good friends. He is stick-figured, diminutive, and made completely of sponge. Virtually helpless because of his body size and lack of solidity, he is kidnapped by the bandit moons in a 1984 issue and is finally rescued over the course of several crossover issues with *Cerebus* in 1987. Cartoon artist Stephen Hillenburg had originally wanted to name SpongeBob SquarePants "SpongeBoy,"

but when Hillenburg learned that Burden had trademarked the name "Sponge Boy," he renamed his character SpongeBob, in honor of Burden.

Artistic Style

Burden's line drawings are clean, well-defined, and surprisingly realistic for a comic as experimental as *Flaming Carrot*. The characters' facial features are caricatured but not wildly exaggerated. However, the female characters are consistently drawn with grotesquely large hips and busts.

Burden adds random objects here and there in the illustrations, lending to the comic's surrealistic aesthetic. For example, the Oddity Exhibit in "The Artless Dodger" features Mr. Potato Head's telephone bills, a glass hat, and Stalin's mustache. Burden is also fond of written sound effects and incorporates onomatopoeic words such as "bzzzz," "boosh," and "splat" into the artwork, often emphasizing them with bold letters, shadows, and jagged lines.

The characters in *Flaming Carrot* take themselves seriously, which contributes to the series' comedy. There are many furrowed brows, piercing eyes, and gesticulating arms. The Flaming Carrot himself is frequently drawn with his arms out from his sides, his knees bent, and his head slightly hunched, as if he is getting ready to spring to action.

Burden's backgrounds frequently portray Shanty Town and working-class urban landscapes. Many of the frames depict factories, boarded warehouses, and greasy-spoon restaurants. Burden does not want readers to forget that Flaming Carrot is the people's hero. The mundaneness of the scenery also reminds readers that even in this fantastical world of the deluded "superhero," the "real world" still remains in the background.

Burden is playful and creative with the panels. In one instance, a character shoots through a panel, killing a character inside its frame. In another, the bottom of the Flaming Carrot's mask pierces one of the panels below him.

Themes

The Flaming Carrot is inspired by the title character of *Don Quixote de la Mancha* (1605, 1615; English translation, 1612-1620). In Miguel de Cervantes's classic work, Don Quixote's mind becomes addled by reading too many books of chivalry; the Flaming Carrot is reduced to stupidity by reading more than five thousand comics. Like *Don Quixote,* the *Flaming Carrot* series is a cautionary tale about the dangers of getting too absorbed in a fictional world. This is a contradictory message for a comic book, and Burden plays with this paradox throughout the series.

In the world of *Flaming Carrot Comics*, life imitates art and not vice versa. Comics addict and journalist Radzak Zokey begins writing a story about the Flaming Carrot and alien invaders after reading about the Flaming Carrot in a comic book. His editor refuses to print his story; however, a few days later, when aliens begin taking over Iron City, the irate editor yells at Zokey, "These aliens are all over now! See what you started with your silly comic-book stories!" The narrative implies that by writing something, one can will it to happen. At times, the characters are aware that they are in a comic book and frequently mention the writer's name. When the Flaming Carrot muses about the identity of the Artless Dodger, he conjectures that the character came out of the mind of Burden. Thus, the series has a self-reflexive quality that could be described as postmodern.

The Flaming Carrot is the ultimate antisuperhero. Burden subverts nearly every superhero cliché in creating the character. Like Batman, the Flaming Carrot carries a utility belt, but unlike Batman, the Carrot's belt is full of useless sundry items such as PEZ dispensers, Silly Putty, and stink bombs that he somehow manages to turn into weapons. Unlike more conventional superheroes, the Carrot is not gentlemanly or a fair fighter, and he does not hesitate to shoot or otherwise injure his foes.

Impact

Flaming Carrot Comics is credited as the first surrealist comic book series. It is distinctly postmodern in the way it critiques its own message. Surrealism and postmodernism are relatively rare in comic books, and

Burden is one of the few creators to venture into this territory. He helped make surrealism accessible, even popular. Despite its experimental nature, *Flaming Carrot* is mainstream enough that it appeared as the answer to a *Jeopardy!* question.

Flaming Carrot Comics is also one of the most popular comic book parodies. The Flaming Carrot is on equal footing with other favorite spoof characters such as Cerebus and the Teenage Mutant Ninja Turtles, with whom he has appeared in numerous crossovers. *Flaming Carrot Comics* has been nominated for several Eisner Awards, including Best Continuing Series and Best Humor Publication, which it won in 2007.

Flaming Carrot has a significant cult following, and there are many fan Web sites dedicated to the character, including some with instructions on how to make a Flaming Carrot costume. The Mystery Men have also made cameo appearances in several comics, including *Teenage Mutant Ninja Turtles*, and been featured in their own series, *Bob Burden's Original Mysterymen* (1999), published by Dark Horse.

Films

Mystery Men. Directed by Kinka Usher. Universal Pictures, 1999. This comedy film is based on a feature in *Flaming Carrot*, although the Flaming Carrot himself does not appear as a character. The film stars Ben Stiller, Eddie Izzard, Janeane Garofalo, and Tom Waits and features a screenplay written by Neil Cuthbert. Although the film performed poorly at the box office, it eventually garnered a cult following, much like the comic series upon which it is based.

Bettina Grassmann

Further Reading

Gerber, Steve, et al. *Howard the Duck* (1973-1978).

Laird, Peter, and Kevin Eastman. *Teenage Mutant Ninja Turtles* (1984-1993).

Sim, Dave. *Cerebus* (1977-2004).

Bibliography

Davisson, Zack. "This Flame, This Carrot." *Comics Bulletin.* December 1, 2010. http://www.comics bulletin.com/grind/129126934663262.htm.

Rabin, Nathan. "My Year of Flops Case File 24 *Mystery Men*." *A.V. Club*, April 17, 2007. http://www.avclub.com/articles/my-year-of-flops-case-file-24-mystery-men,15144.
Sim, Dave. Introduction to *Flaming Carrot Comics Presents Flaming Carrot, Man of Mystery*! Milwaukie, Ore.: Dark Horse Comics, 2008.

See also: *The Complete Fritz the Cat; Ed the Happy Clown; The Frank Book; Tales of the Beanworld*

Flood! A Novel in Pictures

Author: Drooker, Eric
Artist: Eric Drooker (illustrator)
Publishers: Four Walls Eight Windows; Dark Horse Comics
First serial publication: 1986; 1990
First book publication: 1992

Publication History

Flood! A Novel in Pictures was first published in book form by Four Walls Eight Windows in 1992. Chapter 1 ("Home") and chapter 2 ("L") had appeared in limited self-published editions in 1986 and 1990, respectively. The book was subsequently reprinted by Dark Horse Comics in 2002 and again in 2007. The 2007 edition includes an introduction by author and book reviewer Luc Sante, an interview with author Eric Drooker by comics creator Chris Lanier, and a "Sketchbook," featuring "Preliminary Drawings, Thumbnail Sketches, and Rough Ideas."

Plot

Flood! A Novel in Pictures is divided into three sections: "Home," "L," and "Flood." In each, readers follow a nameless male character's travels through New York City. "Home" follows events of the character's life over the course of two days. At first, readers observe his path to his job at a factory, only to discover the factory has been shut down. Thus begins the first of several journeys. After passing by common sights such as a storefront full of television screens, street peddlers, and pizza restaurants, the character goes to a bar, where he meets a woman, whom he seduces. He learns she is a junkie prostitute with an angry pimp, who beats him and throws him out on the street. The character continually encounters and escapes from difficulties and threats, such as poverty and eviction. After picking someone's pocket, he ends up in jail but is subsequently released. At the end of "Home," the character fades into nothingness, dissolving, literally and psychologically, into a stick figure.

In "L," the man goes underground and falls asleep on the subway, a mode of transportation that, for

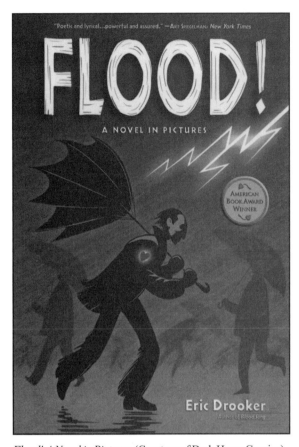

Flood! A Novel in Pictures. (Courtesy of Dark Horse Comics)

Drooker, symbolizes "the unconscious state of the masses." In the man's dream, the tunnels are transformed into mystical caves inhabited by mysterious, fantastic, subterranean, subaquatic, and fearsome but ecstatic beings. Rather than going across town or to Brooklyn, the character, before being awakened by a police officer with a vicious dog, is taken somewhere new. In this place, historical art is depicted, including archetypal cave paintings and the Roman goddess Venus. The character encounters tribes of people and animals for whom tribal consciousness is vital. Locating his own underground tribe, he receives a drum and an invitation to join in. The character finds an intensely stimulating, Edenic landscape and community before being exiled to the street again.

In "Flood," the character emerges from the subway to find rain pouring on everything, including his dilapidated studio. With a cat on his shoulder, he draws nonetheless. "Flood" alternates between the artist's drawing and the scene in which he is drawing. A sequence of passages appears, containing a continuous verbal message; an Eskimo hunter sings a hopeful song that includes the lines: "There is nothing but ice around me, that is good! / Aya, I am joyful, that is good! / My country is nothing but slush . . . that is good!" More tribalism is reflected, as water begins to accumulate on the studio floor. The artist draws a man with an umbrella walking through sheets of rain, and then he becomes that man. He goes out, is carried away through the storm by a gust of wind that snares his umbrella, sees the city through clouds, and lands on a Coney Island roller coaster.

The character roams amid the amusement park's freak shows. A cultural history is depicted, initiated by a tattoo appearing on a performer's arm. Christopher Columbus, Indian genocide, slave ships, and battleships are recalled. Disillusioned by seeing his body distorted by funhouse mirrors, the character emerges from a building, regaining his human features to begin the book's final journey.

Returning to the city, he encounters a forceful woman who leads an uprising. She is brutalized by police, and a riot ensues. Scenes of passionate fighting, including one depicting slingshots fighting against tanks, continue until the flood overtakes everything. The artist returns home and continues to draw while underwater. Then he and his cat float away on the umbrella. He is overcome by a wave; the cat boards a ship containing pairs of other animals and a Noah figure, who float away from circling sharks, leaving tops of skyscrapers behind.

Characters

- *An unnamed man* is a contemporary, imaginary Everyman and serves as the central figure and dramatic focus throughout *Flood! A Novel in Pictures*. This character's appearance changes between the first and second section, as if the stories are portraying any individual for whom

Flood! A Novel in Pictures. (Courtesy of Dark Horse Comics)

urban circumstances are challenging and solitary. In "Home" and "L," the character is rendered as outgoing, if downtrodden; the artist who is portrayed in "Flood" is much more energetic.

- *An unnamed woman*, highlighted for several pages in "Home," forms a brief relationship with the male character. She is a prostitute, whose pimp also appears.
- *Police or soldiers* are presented as antagonists in each section of the book.
- *A man and woman*, amid the many beings the character encounters in "L," they are the only ones to emerge from the crowd. They are shown coupling in a jungle.
- *An Eskimo hunter*, featured in "Flood," sings and is rescued by tribesmen.

- *A second unnamed woman* appears and dominates the segment depicting the uprising and riot. This particular character became a prototype for Drooker: She also appears in his *Blood Song: A Silent Ballad* (2002).
- *Cat*, predominantly featured in "Flood," is the main character's steady companion and ultimately emerges as the flood's sole survivor.
- *Noah-like character* is introduced at the end of the narrative. He is clearly modeled after popular depictions of the biblical character, wearing a tunic and sporting a long white beard.

Artistic Style

Using scratchboard technique, Drooker's art mirrors woodcut designs. His powerful, stark imagery suggests the graphics and aesthetics of woodcut artists Lynd Ward and Frans Masereel, whom Drooker acknowledges as influences in his interview with Lanier. In the first two sections, his drawings appear to be black on white; in "Flood," many are white on black.

Words appear in one section, enabling Drooker to situate *Flood! A Novel in Pictures* as a primitive, tribal celebration. Discussing the absence of language in his novels, Drooker explains that dozens of languages were spoken in the Lower East Side, the New York City neighborhood in which he grew up. "My wordless approach is an attempt at communication," he states. "Pictures are a means of communicating with people when words feel inadequate."

Drooker subtly yet powerfully captures how many events are always simultaneously occurring in the urban environment. As the character walks through city streets, something else is happening; these concurrences are transmitted poetically throughout the book. To be urban is to be nonsingular, which has its consequences, particularly in difficult or desperate times.

In the sequence following the character's encounter with the pimp, the number of panels appearing per page multiplies, at first numbering sixteen and then sixty-four. Some of the minuscule panels are indecipherable; others are roughly intimate, passing through urban scenarios. Drooker explains these segments as "a reflection of a feeling of claustrophobia," symbolizing an individual's smallness in relation to the overall human scale of the city and abstraction within its experience. In the final scene of "Home," the character becomes a small blue blur on a page containing 256 panels. Use of the color blue is then pervasive in "Flood," strategically animating the presence of water, energy, and emotion.

Themes

Flood! A Novel in Pictures portrays a character's tumultuous confrontations with and escape from authority in a decaying New York City. "Personal experience was my starting point," states Drooker; living in the Lower East Side of Manhattan, he regularly witnessed cultural encounters. Turmoil and subcultures are effectively rendered. Television and commercial iconography are frequently present, as he recognizes their impact on landscape and culture. New York City is unmistakable as the visual setting. Iconic structures as well as street-level symbols, such as Keith Haring graffiti and the logo of the band Missing Foundation, predominate. These figures are often rudimentarily accompanied by international commercial iconography, such as the golden arches of fast food giant McDonald's. Through these cultural indicators, Drooker conveys multiple stories at once.

Pages at the beginning and end feature sheet music, credited as "traditional," with new lyrics by Drooker. The second verse begins, "Lord gave Noah the rainbow sign. No more water but fire next time!" Drooker rewrites lyrics of a hymn to fit his context. A poetic transformation occurs in this artistic gesture: The deluge becomes purposeful—keeping the fire of biblical prophecy from consuming Earth. As Sante suggests in the introduction, the flood may be part of a cycle of larger events, possibly with particular religious connotations, but it is also rooted in science. By the 1990's, Drooker would have heard speculation regarding the effect of global warming on sea levels, which would have strongly propelled his imagination.

Flood! A Novel in Pictures is passionate, visionary, dystopic, and relevant. There is a prevailing sense that greed and commerce wear everything down. Sexual scenarios, indicative of human needs or desires, are present, but this motif is only one of many subtexts. In the dream sequence of "L," Drooker imagines and

---

Eric Drooker

Best known for his wordless comics and graphic novels produced as woodprints, Eric Drooker is a politically active artist who got his start as a poster artist and contributor to leftwing magazines and underground publications. A former editor of *World War 3 Illustrated*, Drooker achieved some mainstream notoriety for his short story "L" in *Heavy Metal*, which was later included in his most famous work, *Flood! A Novel in Pictures*, which won an American Book Award. In the 1990's, Drooker collaborated with poet Allen Ginsberg on *Illuminated Poems*. After Ginsberg's death, Drooker completed the animation to the 2010 film *Howl*. A tenant organizer in New York's Lower East Side, Drooker published *Street Posters and Ballads*, a collection of work inspired by his experiences in the area. Drooker's images, which frequently grace the covers of *The New Yorker*, are notable for their use of scratchboard, which gives them a stark, dramatic feeling.

---

while reviewing Drooker's "hefty" work, Spiegelman writes, "Each drawing in the sequence must work not only as a self-contained composition but also as a kind of hieroglyphic picture-writing." Drooker presents tangible examples of how this is accomplished; as Spiegelman writes, he has "discovered the magic of pulling light and life out of an inky sea of darkness." The images presented by Drooker not only garnered critical acclaim, but also the book's historical significance was recognized when the Library of Congress acquired the original artwork for its prints and photographs division. Further, since the appearance of *Flood! A Novel in Pictures*, Drooker's images have been featured many times on the cover of *The New Yorker* literary magazine.

Christopher Funkhouser

Further Reading

Drooker, Eric. *Blood Song: A Silent Ballad* (2002).

Drooker, Eric, and Allen Ginsberg. *Illuminated Poems* (1996).

Masereel, Frans. *Passionate Journey: A Vision in Woodcuts* (2007).

Ward, Lynd. *Six Novels in Woodcuts* (2010).

Bibliography

Drooker, Eric. *Street Posters and Ballads: A Selection of Poems, Songs, and Graphics*. New York: Seven Stories Press, 1998.

Speigelman, Art. "Gloomy Toons." Review of *Flood! A Novel in Pictures* by Eric Drooker. *The New York Times Book Review*, December 27, 1992.

Varnum, Robin, and Christina T. Gibbons. *The Language of Comics: Word and Image*. Jackson: University Press of Mississippi, 2007.

See also: *Cages; City of Glass; The Arrival*

projects visions of humanity within calamitous times. One of the clouds floating above the multitudinous, monolithic city buildings at the opening of "Flood" takes shape as a fish, suggesting the deluge to come has animated, organic, mythic properties.

Impact

While comics creator Art Spiegelman's *Maus* received the Pulitzer Prize Special Award the same year that *Flood! A Novel in Pictures* was published, the graphic novel genre had not yet blossomed. Drooker's book is among those that helped advance the wordless novels genre. Recalling the demands of the graphic novel

FOOTNOTES IN GAZA: A GRAPHIC NOVEL

Author: Sacco, Joe
Artist: Joe Sacco (illustrator)
Publisher: Metropolitan Books
First book publication: 2009

Publication History

First conceived in 2001 during Joe Sacco's research with journalist Chris Hedges for a *Harper's Magazine* piece that was never printed, *Footnotes in Gaza* was specifically inspired by the lack of coverage given in the American media to two Israeli mass killings of Palestinians in Gaza in November of 1956. Wanting to research the massacres more deeply, Sacco returned in November of 2002, then again in March of 2003, to gather and record the testimonies of eyewitnesses. As Sacco explains in his foreword, the events of 1956 "hardly deserved to be thrown back on the pile of obscurity. But there it lay, like innumerable historical tragedies over the ages that barely rate footnote status in the broad sweep of history—even though they often contain the seeds of the grief and anger that shape present-day events."

In *Footnotes in Gaza*, the massacres at Khan Younis and Rafah are brought from the periphery of history and turned into an award-winning exposé. As is noted in introductory matter to the special edition of *Palestine* (1996) and again in his foreword to *Footnotes in Gaza*, Sacco gathered all of his data before drafting his illustrations, eventually working carefully from detailed notes and photographs.

Metropolitan Books published the initial hardcover edition of *Footnotes in Gaza* in December of 2009 and released a paperback version the following year.

Plot

Footnotes in Gaza develops episodically through numerous testimonials of witnesses and family members directly affected by the massacres. In November of 1956, during the Suez Canal Crisis, Israel Defense Forces (IDF) rounded up and massacred Palestinians in Khan Younis and Rafah. Sacco shows the unfolding events in a complicated but highly rewarding manner,

(Getty Images)

Joe Sacco

The best-known cartoonist working primarily in the field of journalism, Joe Sacco broke into comics as an autobiographer, but rose to fame for his tough-minded reporting from some of the world's most dangerous locales. From 1988 to 1992 Sacco published his comics in the anthology *Yahoo!* (collected as *Notes from a Defeatist*), before traveling to Palestine. He serialized his reporting from the occupied country in the early 1990's, establishing his reputation as one of the most important cartoonists of his generation. Trips to Sarajevo and Bosnia produced a number of works on the break-up of the former Yugoslavia, including *The Fixer: A Story from Sarajevo, Safe Area Goražde,* and *War's End: Profiles from Bosnia 1995-1996.* His 2009 book, *Footnotes in Gaza,* is an attempt to uncover what happened in Khan Younis and Rafah in November, 1956. Sacco's work is defined by his cartoonish figures, photo-realistic backgrounds, intricate cross-hatching, and unconventional page layouts, in which he includes captions as if they were physical objects embedded on the page.

piecing together testimonials and carefully crediting each witness. The resulting narrative is as follows: On November 3, 1956, the IDF entered Khan Younis. IDF members began rounding up adult men (some were killed in their homes) and forcefully instructed them to line up against a wall of a fourteenth-century castle at the center of town. According to the United Nations, the official death toll is 275, but a death toll of "more than a hundred" was reported.

On November 12, 1956, the IDF entered Rafah and began herding Palestinian men toward the town school and school yard. The men were forced to sit for hours, pressed against one another with their heads down, while the IDF implemented a "screening operation" to weed out collaborators with Egypt or other anti-Israeli fighters, such as the *fedayeen*. In the process, according to the United Nations, 111 Palestinians were killed. More survived this ordeal than the previous massacre and were able to testify about the details. Even so, there are many inconsistencies among the stories, which Sacco foregrounds in his efforts to have the reader understand his journalistic ethic. For the most part, he relies on only accounts that were confirmed by two or more witnesses; however, he is careful to point out the subjective nature of oral history even in such cases. In the end, Sacco portrays himself as a desensitized story collector who briefly forgets compassion in his zeal to find details. With a redirection in his final pages, Sacco wordlessly reminds the reader where the real story is, giving the reader close-ups from the perspective of those brutalized in the massacres.

Characters
- *Joe Sacco*, the author and narrator, has prominent round eyeglasses, which are used as a masking devise that allows readers to see events from the author's perspective. He is portrayed as a comically bumbling character, a humble exaggeration of Sacco himself.
- *Abed Elassouli*, Sacco's primary guide and interpreter, is a large Palestinian man who always has a creased brow. He is even-tempered and resourceful and facilitates interviews by convincing potential informants to trust Sacco and his intentions, primarily by taking advantage of

the trust he has established in the community. He shares his memories of the first *intifada*, when he was thirteen or fourteen years old, during which he was shot in the leg by an Israeli soldier.
- *Mohammed Yousef Shaker Mousa* witnessed the massacre at Rafah, survived it, and fled to the coast. He is a key informant for Sacco on the Rafah massacre.
- *Mohammed Atwa El-Najeeli* witnessed and survived the massacre at Rafah, in spite of being shot multiple times in the head. He is another key informant for Sacco.
- *Jemal Abdel Nasser*, a.k.a. *Gamal Abdel Nasser*, the president of Egypt from 1956 to 1970, was a leader idealized by many of Sacco's Palestinian informants.
- *Ariel Sharon* was the controversial commander of the IDF at the time of the Khan Younis and Rafah massacres and is widely considered responsible for others. He was the prime minister of Israel from 2001 to 2006, during which time Sacco made research visits to the country.
- *David Ben Gurion* was a Zionist leader and first prime minister of Israel, serving from 1948 to 1953 and from 1955 to 1963.
- *Moshe Sharett*, a.k.a. *Moshe Shertok*, was the prime minister of Israel from 1953 to 1955, during which time tensions between Israelis and Palestinians escalated.
- *Moshe Dayan* was the chief of staff of the IDF from 1953 to 1958 and, thus, was the leader of the Israeli forces at the time of the Khan Younis and Rafah massacres.
- *Khaled*, who joined the Palestinian political party Fatah at the age of fourteen, tells of detecting and killing Palestinian collaborators with Israel. He becomes a key facilitator of important interviews.
- *The Fedayee*, which is a pseudonym he uses to protect his identity, was a former guerrilla fighter with the *fedayeen*. He tells of some activity by the Palestinian resistance, providing political balance to the narrative.
- *Dr. Abdullah El-Horani* lined up against the wall at the castle with other adult men during the Khan

Younis massacre, but he escaped by running at the last minute.

- *Ashraf*, a.k.a. *the Lion*, a large, mustachioed man, is first seen when his home is threatened by Israeli bulldozers that are leveling Palestinian housing to make way for Israeli settlers. Later, his home is demolished, and he takes a pivotal role in facilitating interviews in Rafah.
- *Awad Mohammed Ahmed* sketches out the herding of Rafah men into a school yard. His map is reproduced by Sacco.
- *Rachel Corrie*, an American activist, was killed in Rafah in 2003 by an Israeli bulldozer while she was protesting to protect Palestinian homes.
- *Yasir Arafat*, a.k.a. *Abu Ammar* to Sacco's informants, was an Arab nationalist, leader of Fatah, and the chairman of the Palestinian Liberation Organization.

Artistic Style

One of the first artistic aspects a reader might notice about *Footnotes in Gaza* is the surprisingly comic, Robert Crumb-like parody of a self-portrait the self-trained Sacco uses to narrate his work. This style belies the earnestness of Sacco's graphic journalism. It demands intense participation from the reader to piece together this narrative of horrific events. Sacco has deft eyes and ears for character and is able to capture body language exactly to convey complex emotional states, which allows the illustration to "speak."

To aid in presenting the intense drama, Sacco often shifts perspective radically and avoids standard panels. Frames are dense, irregular, and often overlapping. Sacco makes use of a masking effect to foreground details that convey the sobering reality of living in an occupied territory. Though his own image is somewhat laughable and vaguely deflecting through his blank eyeglasses, the settings are meticulously detailed: Sudden sweeps to full double-spread layouts show panoramic views of devastation. For instance, after Ashraf's home is demolished and time has passed, the reader sees birds have nested in holes in the remaining wall, and the intricacies of slaughtering a bull for Eid al-Adha, the festival of sacrifice, are documented. The latter is made more effective when juxtaposed with Israeli soldier-turned-journalist Marek Gefen's description of the aftermath of the Khan Younis massacre as a "human slaughterhouse." The images are always shown in black and white, with cross-hatched shadowing.

Themes

The main themes of *Footnotes in Gaza* correspond with the book's primary genre of graphic journalism. The novel focuses on how the genre can be used to redress the political imbalance of the American media, to reveal what traditional, camera-dependent journalism cannot, and to excavate history in a truthful manner in order to reflect on its silence and contemporary relevance, as well as how the politics of a region can teach the reader about the world. Sacco's primary motivation is to correct the imbalance of the American media coverage of the Israeli-Palestinian conflict, as it is often biased in favor of Israeli agendas.

One of Sacco's strengths is to coax members of a community that fears the pro-Israeli forces to speak openly about the massacres; in doing so, he captures the struggle of an occupied people to be represented politically. As is not uncommon in Palestinian testimonies, characters in Sacco's text use the Holocaust as a historical reference point to highlight the hypocrisies of certain tactics of the state of Israel. They ask, essentially, why would a people who have been massacred themselves inflict such violence? One interviewee cries, "Hitler didn't do this to them!" as Israeli forces demolish Palestinian homes. To parallel the experiences of the Palestinian and Jewish people, Sacco uses a recurring image throughout the book: The countless abandoned shoes of the men herded for "screening" and lined-up for execution reminds the reader of a scene from a Nazi concentration camp.

Sacco foregrounds the journalistic challenge of objectivity, making it clear that oral history is powerful but necessarily subjective. This fact becomes apparent when, for example, he realizes that an informant's memory is of 1967 events, not those of 1956, or in instances in which multiple and impossibly conflicting accounts are reproduced. He even includes the embellished touches of his interview subjects, such as with "the legend of the doves," which includes reports of a dove landing on a British soldier's shoulder when he interrupts the unjust proceedings at Rafah. Sacco also mocks the almost gleeful, and therefore inappropriate, detachment he develops in response to some of the best and most harrowing stories he collects, which in itself offers a critique of the journalist's task. Ultimately, however, *Footnotes in Gaza* uses journalistic and graphic technique to further the understanding that oral history can enlighten the reader about the world. Accordingly, many critics comment on the importance of the 1956 massacres to understanding the cyclical cultures of hatred and vengeance.

Impact

Joe Sacco's primary influences were not visual artists but prose writers such as George Orwell, Noam Chomsky, Michael Herr, and Hunter S. Thompson. Like the New Journalists, he utilizes the full expressive potential of reporting. In addition, he uses his power to draw from memory those views he cannot access with a camera, such as the demolishing for defense or resettling of Palestinian homes along borders, where cameras are forbidden. The possibilities for visual detail allow Sacco to do what Harvey Kurtzman of EC Comics envisioned for war comics, to take the reader there and to educate. Furthermore, where conventional documentary methods, such as photographic stills or film, could produce an overwhelming sense of life under Israeli occupation, Sacco's untutored graphic style allows for frequent unexpected lightness.

Sacco will likely influence many comics artists in the future. The positive responses to Sacco's work from critics—who are repeatedly surprised by the graphic novels genre, which has been considered a juvenile medium—attests to the strength of Sacco's impact. That his work has appeared in such mainstream and nongraphic venues as *Harper's Magazine* and that his books have been reviewed in such publications, which rarely give attention to graphic works, signify the magnitude of Sacco's accomplishment.

Susan Honeyman

Further Reading

Al-Ali, Naji. *A Child in Palestine: The Cartoons of Naji al-Ali* (2009).

Folman, Ari, and David Polonosky. *Waltz with Bashir: A Lebanon War Story* (2008).

Modan, Rutu. *Exit Wounds* (2007).

Rall, Ted, ed. *Attitude: The New Subversive Political Cartoonists* (2002).

Sacco, Joe. *Palestine* (2007).

Bibliography

Blincoe, Nicholas. "Cartoon Wars: The Israeli Occupation Gets Hard-Hitting Treatment from the Comic-Book Genius Joe Sacco in *Palestine.*" *New Statesman*, January 6, 2003, p. 26.

Cockburn, Patrick. "They Planted Hatred in Our Hearts." *The New York Times Book Review*, December 27, 2008, BR13.

Hajdu, David. "Joe Sacco and Daniel Clowes." In *Heroes and Villains: Essays on Music, Movies, Comics, and Culture*. Cambridge, Mass.: Da Capo Press, 2009.

Venezia, Antonio. "New New (Graphic) Journalism." *Radical Philosophy* 161 (May/June, 2010): 58-60.

See also: *Fax from Sarajevo; The Fixer; Palestine; Maus: A Survivor's Tale; Pyongyang; Burma Chronicles*

FRANK BOOK, THE

Author: Woodring, Jim
Artist: Jim Woodring (illustrator)
Publisher: Fantagraphics Books
First serial publication: 1991-2001
First book publication: 2003

Publication History

The Frank Book comprises stories that originally appeared in a variety of publications between 1991 and 2001, including "BUZZ", "Dramatis Personae", "Heavy Metal", "Hyena", "Measles", "The Millennium Whole Earth Catalog", "Pictopia", "PULSE!", "Snake Eyes", and "The Stranger". Frank, the central character of the stories, debuted on the cover of Jim Woodring's autojournal, *JIM*, Volume 1, issue 4 (1990). He appears prominently in Volume 2 of *JIM* as well as in *Tantalizing Stories* and *FRANK*.

Fantagraphics Books released a two-volume set entitled *Frank* (1994) and *Frank* Volume 2 (1997) and released *The Frank Book*, a single-volume collection, in 2003. The new collection contains all previously published Frank stories, with the exception of "Frank and Monty in Forever Hungry" (*Tantalizing Stories*, issue 6), co-created with Mark Martin. Notably, some of the story titles have been expanded to reflect the content and, presumably, to avoid confusion, as many stories were previously published under the title "Frank." One of these, for example, concerns an invitation Frank receives to attend a party; in *The Frank Book*, it is titled "Frank in the House of the Dead." An appendix containing some additional comic art and the dramatis personae of the *Frank* series ends the volume.

Plot

The Frank stories share no common plot; rather, there are common thematic elements that signify, most prominently, mood and mythology. No one speaks, and text, when it appears, is minimal and serves only to move the story forward. Characters, including Frank, are often killed, only to reappear in a new incarnation. Thus, continuity between stories and overall character development are not features of this imaginary world,

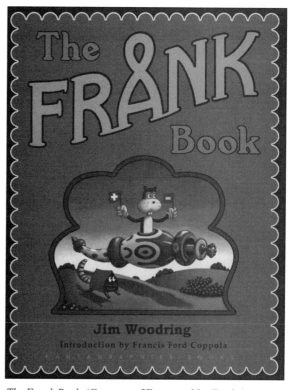

The Frank Book. (Courtesy of Fantagraphics Books)

which is called the Unifactor. Indeed, the stories truly concern the ostensibly mysterious machinations of the Unifactor, so powerfully impressive is the imagined realm.

Similar to the manner in which Charles Schulz's character Charlie Brown prominently inhabits the world of *Peanuts*, Frank occupies the Unifactor. Stories often begin with Frank observing his surroundings, giving rise to the critical observation that Frank possesses childlike wonderment and, at times, might be considered a stand-in for a reader trying to make sense of this world. Frank usually encounters or sets in motion conflicts that often have no clear resolution; the motivations of various characters regularly seem strange or outright baffling.

As the impulse or reasoning behind characters' actions in the Unifactor is, at times, known only to Woodring, it becomes plausible to suggest that Woodring, consciously or not, works against interpretation. He displaces a critical emphasis on "plot" in favor of fueling a subjective appreciation of the comic's aesthetics and the energies contained therein.

Characters

- *Frank*, the protagonist, is an anthropomorphic creature who appears in most of the stories and is, by turn, uncomplicated and cunning. He solicits comparison to George Harriman's slapstick, ambiguously gendered Krazy Kat, as Woodring has stated that the bumbling Frank is sexless, despite his male name and the common use of the male pronoun to describe him; Frank, though, does not possess Krazy's lack of guile. He appears to suffer from a form of anterograde amnesia, in that he evinces constant forgetfulness.
- *Manhog*, the antagonist, is Frank's nemesis. Part man and part hog, Manhog suffers a good deal and exhibits base and basic desires.
- *Whim* is typically depicted as a thin entity with a grinning, devilish face. He is able to manipulate other beings and materials in the Unifactor, often through the use of his Whim-Grinder.
- *Pupshaw* and *Pushpaw* are Frank's "pets," both of whom jealously guard their benefactor.
- *Jerry Chickens* are misshapen, chickenlike creatures who are generally malicious.
- *Real Pa* and *Faux Pa* are two versions of Frank's father. They are indistinguishable from one another to the extent that their appearance as two separate entities might be said to constitute an illusion. They are often in the service of Whim.
- *Lucky* is the ironically named, not-quite-human lackey whose life is constant work and drudgery.

Artistic Style

The *Frank* stories are most often drawn in black and white, with boldly lined characters and panels and clear gutters. Color, when used, is saturated, with finely balanced sky blues, pea greens, sage purples, damp yellows, and reddish oranges. Although the Unifactor contains psychotropic substances, reflecting the author's self-admitted usage of the same, the hallucinatory effect is not necessarily displayed in the overall use of color.

The character of Frank was drawn initially with his left eye smaller than his right, though this dissimilarity disappeared early on. He is mostly purple, with a white belly and face, and has two buck teeth. His white boots and gloves recall Disney's Mickey Mouse. Manhog, who goes without clothing like most of the characters, originally and briefly possessed a penis.

A variety of other creatures and things reflect the unpredictable and unknowable nature of the Unifactor. Notably, *jivas*, spiritlike symbols that litter the realm, appear in a multitude of colorful forms. There are occasional humanoid characters and other entities both recognizable, such as frogs, and utterly strange, such as floating "bilats."

The Unifactor's landscape is recognizable to readers, with flora and water; its interior, though, is at

The Frank Book. (Courtesy of Fantagraphics Books)

once solid and pliable. Buildings bespeak an Eastern influence.

Themes

The aesthetics of the Unifactor inspire and evoke a mood concomitant with an alien mythology rather than a knowable, Earth-like existence. Frank wanders the landscape in a state of constant wonder and makes observations, the impetus and true impact of which are rarely fathomable. In Woodring's first full-color *Frank* story, 1992's "Frank in the River," which opens *The Frank Book*, Frank walks through a town empty of other sentient beings, looking at and being passively looked at by objects possessing eyes. The nondual "eye" is symbolic of the unity of the Godhead and indicates conscious awareness. He accidentally knocks over a large urn, breaking it; this action sets up the rest of the story, in which he encounters Manhog in their place of mutual employment. Physical and psychological conflict, strange motivations, competition and manipulation, and the spiritual "rightness" of *jivas* combine in a story that is as open-ended as the random accident that compelled the story's plot. Variations on this episode and its aesthetics color many of the stories. In "Frank in the House of the Dead," Frank is reading, bedecked with a fez, suggesting a philosophical bent; for Frank, this is invariably a pose. A leaf blows in through a window, distracting him. He goes outside to look at his garden and sees a sluglike creature on the ground, a two-dimensional bilat floating by, and the Whim-like face of the garden's scarecrow. He leaves the house with a picnic basket, only to sit under a tree and think about himself; in his reverie, he imagines his death. *Jivas* abound. This pressing theme of the spiritual becomes, more than anything, perhaps the most striking yet subtle aspect of Frank's world, infusing it to the extent that the spiritual principle of animism is the chief philosophical feature of the Unifactor.

This is not surprising, considering Woodring's professed study of Ramakrishna, the nineteenth-century Hindu mystic who embraced Advaita Vedânta, with its emphasis on nondualism and unity. In this light, the name "Unifactor" bears particular potency. If an engagement with the spiritual results fruitfully in one's ostensible betterment, then Frank should experience

change. However, he and his cohorts do not; rather, their frequent transformations reflect, if anything, the violence generated by selfish ends. Spiritual change would be unwarranted. They are in the Unifactor rather than of it, still possessing a material existence that betrays their failure at spiritual transformation. If Frank's constant forgetfulness and self-concern are any indication, a lack of awareness of the world that one is a part of will always present an obstacle to embracing the spiritual and its attendant freedoms.

More directly, "Frank and the Truth about Plenitude" begins with Frank observing a flock of floating *jivas*. He reaches out to touch one, but it evades him. Sneaking up on another, he captures it and uses it as an airship. Ultimately reaching an observatory, he anchors the *jiva* and proceeds to dress up as a kind of swami, after observing the mode of dress in a portrait. However, the self-centered and simple-minded Frank is not a master of himself, as a swami would be, and so his attempts at levitation are limited. He gives up in

---

Jim Woodring

Jim Woodring was working as an animator when he began self-publishing *Jim*, an anthology of dream art. In 1986 he began to be published by Fantagraphics, and he quickly became one of the most unusual cartoonists working at the time. His Frank character was frequently depicted in wordless, surreal stories, and Woodring spun the character off into his own title in 1996, and the adventures of Frank have been Woodring's primary comics work since that time. Frank resides in a nightmarishly bizarre world where seemingly anything is possible. A naif, Frank spends his time with his pets, Pupshaw and Pushpaw, and his adventures have a fairytale quality that is often disturbed by outbreaks of graphic violence, bodily eruptions, and scenes expressing abstract cosmology. Woodring's numerous Frank books include *The Portable Frank*, *Weathercraft*, and *Congress of the Animals*. His visual style is notable for its intricacy, including a quavering black line that lends texture to figures that might otherwise seem at home in Saturday morning cartoons.

frustration, finding peace only after he releases the *jiva*. Woodring suggests that Frank is enamored by surface and style more than the rewarding depths found in a spiritual life that is won by committing to change.

Manhog treads a similar path in "Gentlemanhog." After suffering a Jerry Chicken's prank, he encounters a two-dimensional shadow man in an Edenic garden. The entity educates Manhog in all ways, and Manhog ends up wearing a philosophically inspired fez. His master dies, and Manhog again meets Frank, whom he invites to dinner. To Frank's horror and Manhog's evil delight, the dinner is the Jerry Chicken. Violence, revenge, and, most notably, a return to form—Manhog will never be a "gentleman"—are typical of Woodring's creatures.

Despite the recurring violence and confusion, Woodring's world is not without its playful side. In "Frank's Fish," Frank catches a fish that is replete with a moustache, lipstick, and mascara, which he takes home to eat. While cutting the fish, though, Frank is faced with a series of Chinese boxes: fish inside fish inside fish. The final fish escapes, and its shadow imprint, spattered on the wall, is also imprinted on Frank's face in the final frame. The title is knowingly misleading, then, in that Frank never really possesses the fish; rather, it is the fish that in some way has grasped Frank, leaving a carnivalesque stamp. Frank and fish are herein associated through superficial markings, suggesting that the unity and mutual dependence of the hunter and the hunted are, though serious, sources of inspired play. In that manner, the story achieves almost allegorical heights: Frank attempts to possess something he needs, with the result that the sought-after thing leaves its mark but escapes. Likewise, the reader struggles to comprehend the artist's presentation of the mystery of the Chinese-box fish, with the result that the sought-after meaning leaves its mark and remains elusive. The story has no resolution save the imprimatur of art itself.

Impact

Woodring's *Frank* stories are so individualistic as to defy imitation. However, similarities to Woodring's revival of supposedly dead characters can be found in animated series such as *Animaniacs* and *South Park*. In terms of its nonsensical nature, the *Frank* series has much in common with Kaz's *Underworld*, Archer Prewitt's *Sof'Boy*, and the dreamworld of David Heatley.

Films

Visions of Frank. Directed by Jim Woodring. Press Pop, 2007. This film features eight animated shorts in various styles, including the traditional two-dimensional comic form and claymation. Most of the shorts depict Frank's encounters with Whim and his Whim-Grinder.

Andrew Lesk

Further Reading

Kaz. *Underworld* (1992-   ).
Prewitt, Archer. *Sof'Boy* (1997-   ).
Woodring, Jim. *The Lute String* (2005).

Bibliography

Poodle, Amy. "Jim Woodring's FraAOOOO-OOOOOIIIIink: Detourning the Dream Factory." *Mindless Ones*, May 9, 2008. http://mindlessones. com/2008/05/09/fraaooooooooooiiiiink-detourning-the-dream-factory/#more-224.

Tong, Ng Suat. "A Short Walk Through the Unifactor: Jim Woodring, Frank, and *Weathercraft*." *The Hooded Utilitarian*, July 6, 2010. http://www.tcj. com/hoodedutilitarian/2010/07/a-short-walk-through-the-unifactor-jim-woodring-frank-and-weathercraft.

See also: *The Complete Fritz the Cat; Ed the Happy Clown*

FROM HELL: BEING A MELODRAMA IN SIXTEEN PARTS

Author: Moore, Alan
Artist: Eddie Campbell (illustrator); Pete Mullins (contributing artist)
Publisher: Top Shelf Comics
First serial publication: 1989-1996
First book publication: 1999

Publication History

From Hell began with Alan Moore musing about "writing something lengthy on a murder." Although Moore originally dismissed the Jack the Ripper murders as too obvious and played out, he became intrigued by the story because of the publicity surrounding their centennial. That led him to Stephen Knight's *Jack the Ripper: The Final Solution* (1976), which gave him the idea for the story. Having decided to create the comic as a serial for Steve R. Bissette's horror comic anthology *Taboo*, he contacted artist Eddie Campbell, who agreed to illustrate the story.

From Hell was published serially from 1989 to 1992. Only the first six chapters appeared in *Taboo*, as the anthology ran for only seven issues. Following its demise, Moore and Campbell took the series to Kitchen Sink Press, which published the work in ten volumes between 1991 and 1996. The final appendix, *Dance of the Gull Catchers*, was published in 1998, and Eddie Campbell Comics published the entire series as a trade paperback in 1999. As of 2011, trade paperbacks are published by Top Shelf Comics in the United States and Knockabout Comics in the United Kingdom. In 2001, *From Hell* was the first of Moore's comics work to be adapted to film, though Moore himself had no involvement with the production.

Plot

From Hell is an expansive, extensively researched fictional exploration of the 1888 Jack the Ripper murders. The premise is taken mostly from Knight's book, which posits that the murders were the result of a conspiracy to conceal the birth of an illegitimate royal child in White-chapel. Dr. William Withey Gull, the royal surgeon and a prominent member of the secret

From Hell. (Courtesy of Top Shelf Productions)

society of Freemasons, is asked to silence a group of prostitutes who are threatening to reveal the child's identity if they are not paid a sum of ten pounds.

Gull, who, as a result of a stroke, is either delusional or divinely inspired by an ancient Masonic god, takes the assignment as an opportunity to brutally murder the women. The murders are an occult ritual of his own devising, ostensibly to reinforce the patriarchy within the cultural consciousness and bring about the twentieth century. He finds the prostitutes with the help of coachman John Netley and kills Polly Nicholls first, grotesquely mutilating her body and removing her organs.

Inspector Frederick Abberline is assigned to the first murder case because of his familiarity with the White-chapel area. It becomes clear to him that the case will not be solved easily. Intense sensationalism around the murders has gripped London, stoked by a false letter to the police signed Jack the Ripper. Soon, Scotland Yard is inundated with hundreds of letters, all purporting to be from the murderer. In addition, Abberline must deal with corruption among both his supervisors and his subordinates. Meanwhile, Gull continues his murder spree, and as he kills more prostitutes, he begins to see visions of the future.

Mary Kelly soon realizes that she has been targeted. She becomes distraught, drinking heavily and alienating her live-in partner. She is the fifth and last victim to be murdered. Gull eviscerates her beyond recognition and burns her heart to ashes. During this time, he has an extended vision of the future, in which he sees a modern office full of disaffected people. Afterward, he feels that his life has peaked; having seen the world beneath him, he has nowhere to go but down.

Abberline, for his part, continues his fruitless search for the murderer until Robert Lees, the royal psychic, comes to him claiming to be able to find the address of the White-chapel murderer. Lees is an imposter with a grudge against Gull, and leads Abberline to him simply to embarrass the man. However, much to the shock of Abberline, Lees, and Mrs. Gull, Gull confesses to the murders.

Abberline and Lees are pressured to keep quiet so as not to provoke scandal. The Freemasons hold a secret tribunal in which they declare Gull insane. Gull refuses the judgment of the court, stating that no man among them is fit to judge, as he has surpassed them all. His death is faked and he is taken to a mental facility.

For years, Abberline continues his work for Scotland Yard until, by chance, he discovers the true motivation behind the murders: blackmail and the royal baby. He resigns from the force in disgust, but he remains silent for fear of retribution. He is given a substantial pension and retires to the seaside.

The last chapter of the book is a sequence that occurs moments before Gull's death. In it, he flies as a spirit outside time, influencing other serial killers and causing many events in the nineteenth and twentieth centuries that are peripherally related to his own crimes, before becoming one with God and the infinite and finally dying.

From Hell contains an exhaustive appendix that details which elements of the story were fictionalized and provides a list of references. It also includes a comics essay about the history of "Ripperology" and Moore's own musings about the nature of Jack the Ripper within the cultural consciousness.

From Hell. (Courtesy of Top Shelf Productions)

Characters

- *Sir William Withey Gull*, the antagonist, is the royal family's physician and a prominent Freemason. He has thick white sideburns and usually wears formal clothing and a top hat. Despite being in his eighties, he is strong, intimidating, and wickedly intelligent. He is fascinated with the complexity of nature and displays many characteristics known to be present in serial killers. When Queen Victoria asks him to remove a threat to the crown, he embarks upon a murderous rampage that he believes to be an occult ritual to bring about the twentieth century.

- *Frederick Abberline*, a protagonist, is a middle-aged inspector with the London Metropolitan Police. He is stout, has a dark mustache, and often wears a bowler hat. While quiet, he has a strong sense of duty and honor and does not hesitate to take initiative when required to. He is assigned to investigate the White-chapel murders and becomes increasingly frustrated with the lack of conclusive evidence and the irresponsible, selfish behavior of his superiors and subordinates. When he unexpectedly discovers the identity of the murderer, he is pressured to keep silent.

- *Mary Jane Kelly*, a.k.a. *Marie Jeanette Kelly*, also a protagonist, is a prostitute living in Whitechapel. Dark-haired and alluring, she is strong willed and intelligent but restricted by the social barriers of her class. When she and her friends are required to pay an "insurance" fee to the local mob, she blackmails Walter Sickert, threatening to reveal the identity of Prince Albert Victor's illegitimate child. As her companions are butchered, she becomes increasingly fearful for her own safety and descends into alcoholism. She is the fifth and final victim of the White-chapel murderer, though it is implied that she may have escaped.

- *Robert Lees* is a tall blond man employed by Queen Victoria as the royal psychic. A charming man prone to self-righteous indignation, he claims to have visions and to communicate with the dead. He occasionally suffers violent seizures. In the prologue, he reveals that all of his predictions were made up, but that they came true nonetheless. He pretends to know the identity of the White-chapel murderer and leads Abberline to Gull's home because of a personal grudge, at which point Gull confesses to the crimes.

- *Prince Albert Victor*, a.k.a. *Prince Eddy*, the grandson of Queen Victoria, has soft features, an imperial moustache, and deep, mournful eyes. He is foolish, impulsive, and, by his own admission, weak. Early in the story, he impregnates a shopgirl and marries her, a scandal that leads to the White-chapel murders.

- *Walter Sickert* is an artist active in the White-chapel area and in the bohemian community of Victorian society. While charged with the social education of Prince Eddy, he unintentionally allows the prince to marry a shopgirl and father a daughter. When Kelly blackmails him, he goes to the prince's mother, who reports the incident to Queen Victoria.

- *Sir Charles Warren* is commissioner of the London Metropolitan Police and the grand sojourner of the London Freemasons. He is tall, dresses well, and wears a horseshoe mustache. His militaristic tendencies have made him unpopular in his post. He was the one who originally recommended Gull to Queen Victoria. When Gull begins his rampage, Warren is aware of his crimes; unable to stop him, he becomes complicit in the cover-up.

- *Queen Victoria*, an aged, imposing monarch, is the head of the royal family. While powerful and intelligent, she is also merciless and superstitious. She is in perpetual mourning for her deceased husband, Albert, but trusts Gull, whom she considers strong and dependable. When news of her grandson's scandal reaches her, she dispatches Gull, first to "silence" Prince Eddy's wife and then to eliminate the prostitutes who have blackmailed Sickert.

- *John Netley*, a stagecoach driver with a "shallow brow and closely spaced eyes," is enlisted by Gull to provide transportation and to seek out the various prostitutes he is charged with eliminating. Although he is unsettled by Gull's more demonic inclinations and overcome with fear and guilt over his involvement in the crimes, he maintains his silence.

- *Polly Nicholls* is a prostitute in the White-chapel district and an acquaintance of Kelly, said to look remarkably young for her age. She has an estranged son and former husband who left her, allegedly for her drinking habits and possibly for another woman. She is the first victim of the White-chapel murderer.

- *Annie Chapman* is a prostitute in the White-chapel district and an acquaintance of Kelly. Aging and overweight, she remains fierce and individualistic. She falls ill and feverish before becoming the second victim of the White-chapel murderer.

- *Elizabeth Stride*, a.k.a. *Long Liz*, is a prostitute in the White-chapel district and a friend of Kelly. She is a Swedish immigrant and the third victim of the White-chapel murderer.

- *Catherine Eddowes* is an impoverished woman living in the White-chapel district. She has a lover named John Kelly, with whom she is picking hops in Kent when she decides to return to London because she believes she knows the identity of the White-chapel murderer. Instead, she becomes his fourth victim, accidentally identified as Mary Kelly because of her lover's name.

Artistic Style

Campbell renders the pages of *From Hell* in stark black strokes and furious scribbles, varying his style greatly from page to page. At times, the drawings are astonishingly meticulous, while at others, the pen lines seem almost haphazard. Some pages appear to have been drawn on canvas and shaded with crayon, and a number of scenes are rendered entirely in grayscale watercolor. The different techniques create wildly different moods, with furious slashes of the pen matching the violence and chaos they depict.

The level of detail also varies with each page, as does the level of realism. Backgrounds and architecture are almost invariably photorealistic, and certain architectural structures are depicted in staggering detail. While characters are generally drawn with realistic body structures, facial depictions range from finely detailed to mere sketches. Minor characters often have cartoonishly exaggerated features. Such variation is used to great effect within the story, as expressions are often emphasized at moments of heightened emotion. During events of significance, certain characters are rendered nearly stroke by stroke from their historical depictions. Throughout the story, certain characters' facial features, such as Kelly's, remain ambiguous.

(Colin McPherson/Corbis)

Alan Moore

It is hard to make generalizations about English writer Alan Moore, winner of the Eisner Award and the Hugo Award. His prolific output of comics and graphic novels, spanning more than three decades, covers the gamut from satire and political criticism to traditional superhero adventures. But Moore's works are consistently sophisticated, complex, and mature, geared toward adult audiences rather than younger readers. One of the most celebrated and influential comics writers in the world, Moore offers stories that are intellectually challenging and thought-provoking—though be advised that they often include graphic sex and violence.

Realism is particularly effective within *From Hell* given its semihistorical subject matter, lending authority to some parts and serving to remind readers of the speculative nature of others. Certain historical documents, such as pictures, maps, and news articles, are not drawn by Campbell but rather included directly in the comic, serving to add historical authenticity to the work and underline thematic elements.

Campbell is particularly unforgiving when it comes to depicting violence. The various mutilations carried out on the women in White-chapel are shown with explicit anatomic clarity and historical accuracy, making some sequences difficult to view. These illustrations neither glorify nor exploit the atrocities, but simply and bluntly depict them as the human actions that they are.

Themes

From Hell is not so much a murder mystery as a subversion of traditional "whodunits" into something of a "whydunit." In Moore's own words, it is "a postmortem of Victorian society with fiction as a scalpel." The events of the book, from the murder and investigation to the exploration of various peripheral characters' lives, are a means of exploring the time period. Seemingly every piece of Ripper trivia has been incorporated into the plot, however obliquely, with cameos from historical figures such as the Elephant Man, Oscar Wilde, and William Blake. Even a fourteen-year-old Aleister Crowley makes an appearance. Visual and literary quotations provide context and color to characterize the society in which such an event could take place. The portrayal of Victorian London is bleak, showing a bloated, corrupt upper-class society eviscerating the poverty-stricken underbelly of White-chapel.

With his extensive notes and metafictional approach, Moore winkingly acknowledges the limitations of the fiction. The narrative is an amalgam of numerous different theories of the Ripper murders, a Koch's snowflake of speculation. In the appendix, Moore writes that the mythology of Jack the Ripper is open to the limitless possibilities of fiction but confined to the limitations of what little historical truth is actually known. Within those confines, the Ripper becomes a faceless receptacle for what society fears: a Jew, a doctor, a Freemason, or a wayward royal mad with power.

The events of *From Hell* also present a theory on the nature of myth and the human mind. The murders have a real effect on the society of London, one that resonates throughout history, and the visions that Gull experiences before his death fantastically demonstrate the ways in which a single action can alter history's architecture. While it is never made clear whether or not the events that Gull experiences are in any way "real," the themes and concepts he explores have power, and his statement to the modern age that he "births" is haunting.

Impact

The roots of *From Hell* lie in horror comics, though the work transcends the genre to become something far more epic. The ghastliness of the violence is matched by an equally disturbing existential dread that permeates the work. Moore also expands on the manipulation of time he explored in his earlier texts, namely *Watchmen* (1986-1987). As a work of comics literature, *From Hell* is longer and more exhaustive than anything Moore had produced before. Throughout its publishing run, it received accolades from fans and critics alike, who praised its complexity and its scope.

From Hell is one of the most significant works in Moore's development as a writer and an intellectual. In writing that "the human mind is one place where all of the gods and monsters in human mythology are arguably real," he unintentionally sparked his own interest in magic. Many of his subsequent works, such as *The League of Extraordinary Gentlemen* (1999-), *Promethea* (1999-2005), *Supreme* (2003, book), and *Lost Girls* (2006, book), are clearly influenced by this concept. All of these works explore the edifices of the human mind through fictional narratives, while maintaining an awareness of their constructs. In the years after *From Hell*, Moore became a self-professed magician, further secluding himself and solidifying his role as the mysterious, crazed guru of comics literature.

Films

From Hell. Directed by Albert Hughes. Twentieth Century Fox, 2001. This film adaptation stars Johnny

Depp as Inspector Frederick Abberline, Heather Graham as Mary Kelly, and Ian Holm as Sir William Gull. Abberline is a brilliant yet troubled detective whose career is aided by the psychic visions he experiences while taking opium. As he investigates the Ripper murders, he discovers a conspiracy among the London elite, but the case gets personal when he becomes romantically involved with Kelly. Moore refused any involvement in the film, to its detriment, and it bears little resemblance to the source material.

Sam Julian

Further Reading

Campbell, Eddie. *Bacchus* (1987-1995).

Eisner, Will. *The Plot: The Secret Stories of the Protocols of the Elders of Zion* (2005).

Moore, Alan, and Kevin O'Neill. *The League of Extraordinary Gentlemen* (1999-   ).

Bibliography

Di Liddo, Annalisa. *Alan Moore: Comics as Performance, Fiction as Scalpel*. Jackson: University Press of Mississippi, 2009.

Gravett, Paul. *Graphic Novels: Everything You Need to Know*. New York: Collins Design, 2005.

Moore, Alan. "Alan Moore Interview." Interview by Brad Stone. Comic Book Resources, October 22, 2001. http://www.comicbookresources.com/?page=article&id=511.

_____. *From Hell: The Compleat Scripts*. Falston, Md.: Bordlerlands Press, 2000.

See also: *It Was the War of the Trenches*

FUN HOME: A FAMILY TRAGICOMIC

Author: Bechdel, Alison
Artist: Alison Bechdel (illustrator)
Publisher: Houghton Mifflin
First book publication: 2006

Publication History

Alison Bechdel's memoir *Fun Home* was first published in hardcover by Houghton Mifflin in June, 2006, and spent two weeks on *The New York Times* best-sellers list for nonfiction hardcovers between June and July. That same summer, the French journal *Liberation* serialized a French translation by Corinne Julve and Lili Sztajn. This translation was published in book form by Éditions Donoel in October, 2006. In September, 2006, *Fun Home* was published in the United Kingdom by Jonathan Cape. In 2007, an Italian translation and a Brazilian Portuguese translation appeared, followed by a German translation in 2008. Subsequent translations have been published in Hungarian, Korean, Polish, and Chinese.

The release of *Fun Home* did not occur without controversy. In October, 2006, a citizen of Marshall, Missouri, petitioned to have *Fun Home*, as well as Craig Thompson's *Blankets*, removed from the shelves of the public library, complaining that the two books were "pornography" and would be harmful to young readers. Amy Crump, the director of the library, defended their presence on the shelves but organized a committee to deliberate the matter. The books were suspended from circulation during the deliberation, but on March 17, 2007, the library's board of trustees voted to reinstate them. Bechdel referred to the incident as "a great honor" and "part of the whole evolution of the graphic novel form."

A similar controversy occurred at the University of Utah in 2008, when *Fun Home* appeared on the syllabus for a class titled "Critical Introduction to English Literary Forms." A student protested the book's inclusion in the class and was given an alternative assignment. Although she also formed the group "No More Pornography" to continue the protest against the book and others like it, *Fun Home* was not removed from the

Fun Home: A Family Tragicomic. (Courtesy of Mariner Books)

syllabus, and the chair of the English Department defended the decision.

Plot

Fun Home addresses the defining moments of Alison Bechdel's early life. She describes the events from her childhood in rural-industrial Beech Creek, Pennsylvania, to her departure for college, where the revelation of her father Bruce's homosexuality, her parents' divorce, her own coming out, and Bruce's death occur within a span of months. Structurally, however, the book is nonlinear, jumping back and forth in time and narrating important events as they become relevant to the theme being developed. Each chapter focuses on one or two main themes regarding her relationship with her father and thus includes memories that best illustrate them.

The first chapter, titled "Old Father, Old Artificer," mainly deals with the Bechdel house itself and Bruce's obsession with its decor, often at the expense of familial happiness. The second chapter, "A Happy Death," begins with Bruce's death, which may have been a suicide or just a roadside accident. (This is questioned throughout the book, with emotional consequences for Alison.) The rest of the chapter fills in details of Bechdel's early life as well as the story of how her parents came to run the Bechdel Funeral Home (which the children nicknamed the "fun home") and live in the family house. The chapter ends with a college-aged Alison learning of her father's death and returning home with her partner, Joan, for his funeral.

Chapter 3, titled "That Old Catastrophe," begins with Alison coming out to her parents in a one-sentence letter and the near immediate revelation from her mother of Bruce's own homosexuality. The chapter dives back into history to uncover more evidence of his homosexuality in his excessive attention to aesthetic details and interest in high school boys. The importance of literature to both Bruce and Alison is introduced, in the form of Bruce's intense identification with F. Scott Fitzgerald and Fitzgerald's novel *The Great Gatsby* (1925). The chapter eventually doubles back to Alison's discovery of her own homosexuality and her first homosexual experience.

"In the Shadow of Young Girls in Flower," the fourth chapter, begins with a more abstract speculation on the causes of Bruce's death while gardening. This leads to a lengthy depiction of his obsession with the family garden, as an opportunity both to express his feminine side and to recruit local young men to do the heavy lifting. Subsequent parts of the chapter address family trips with these "babysitters," one to New York City and one camping in Pennsylvania, both of which provided important emotional epiphanies to the near pubescent Alison.

Chapter 5, titled "The Canary-Colored Caravan of Death," begins with a rare tender moment between Alison and Bruce, in which they encounter a sunset while walking in the woods. This leads to a discussion of Bruce's relative rootedness in Beech Creek. The rest of the chapter deals with the artistic inclinations of each member of the Bechdel family and the irony that this inclination creates familial separation instead of bonding. Of particular interest is the evolution of Alison's diary from an initial struggle with verbal conveyance into an embrace of the visual mode as her primary means of expression. She recalls her final disavowal, at quite a young age, of color in her work.

Chapter 6, "The Ideal Husband," continues in this artistic vein, with a focus on Alison's mother, Helen. While Helen struggles with Bruce's arrest for providing alcohol to a young boy and his subsequent psychiatric treatment, she juggles finishing her master's thesis in literature and her performance in a local production of Oscar Wilde's play *The Importance of Being Earnest* (1899). Until this point, Helen is not given much of a voice, but her faltering strength, often manifesting itself in distant coldness, is on full display here, with results both tragic and triumphant. Her thesis is destroyed in a rainstorm, and she falls behind in her rehearsals. However, she rewrites the paper in one night and delivers a superior performance in the end. Meanwhile, young Alison continues to explore the limits of her femininity in her journal and daily life, culminating in her first period.

Alison and Bruce's divergent trajectories come to a head in the final chapter, titled "The Antihero's Journey," which focuses on the brief aftermath of Alison's coming out before her parents' divorce and Bruce's death. The chapter begins as Alison reflects on a trip to New York City with her father in 1976, four years before she came out. There, she awoke to gay life and to her father's curious comfort in it. The middle of the chapter depicts her struggles with literature, especially James Joyce's novel *Ulysses* (1922), and her father's concurrent encouragement. Her course readings occur parallel to her independent reading of lesbian literature, culminating in her fateful letter to her parents.

The rest of the chapter depicts one of Alison's visits home and her last days with her father. Helen confides her unhappiness to Alison, and in a private conversation with Alison in the car on the way to the movies, Bruce begins to unveil his sense of identity as a homosexual and the history behind it. However, the conversation is brief, stilted, and ultimately unfinished. After the film, they stop by a gay bar, where the bouncer rejects them because Alison is still underage. They then return home in silence. The emotional core of the ending resembles that of the entire book; namely, Alison finds happiness with her father only in memory. The book closes with an image of a young Alison suspended in midair jumping off a diving board, her father, with open arms, waits below.

Characters

- *Alison Bechdel* is the author, narrator, and protagonist of the memoir. Her life from her early childhood to her college years is documented; intensely private moments highlight the difficulty and confusion of her early life. Readers watch as she experiences her first period and orgasm, questions her gender and sexuality, develops artistically and intellectually, explores all forms of literature, and has her first homosexual encounter.
- *Bruce Bechdel* is Alison's father and Helen's husband. He is depicted as distant, cold, effeminate, and intrusively and overbearingly aesthetically minded. A high school English teacher and funeral home director, he had his first homosexual experience at fourteen and was closeted his entire life, often at the expense of his wife and three children. In lieu of authentic sexual expression, he manifests his homosexuality primarily in his obsessive upkeep of his family's home and the funeral home. The interactions between father and daughter waver

between tense and tender, but the two identify most clearly over their mutual love of literature: Bruce introduces Alison to important classics and helps her refine her reading practices at college. He died when he was hit by a semi on the side of the road, where he had been gardening. He is described as having jumped backward into the truck's path. Alison considers it a suicide on a literal level but explores the deep emotional

Fun Home: A Family Tragicomic. (Courtesy of Mariner Books)

causes of his death, many of which she sees as coming from her.

- *Helen Bechdel* is Alison's mother and Bruce's wife. Relatively voiceless for the first half of the book, she quietly, though tensely, tolerates Bruce's idiosyncrasies, emotional neglect, and homosexual affairs. She and Bruce used to be urbane intellectuals, with high hopes of thriving in literary, academic, and theatrical spheres. Their marriage seemed to be doomed from the start, when their engagement began with Bruce verbally abusing her and abandoning her to spend time with a friend later revealed to be his lover. She opens up to Alison after the latter comes out, and they have brief moments of bonding in the final part of the book.

Artistic Style

Bechdel's emotional growth goes hand in hand with her artistic development. In the course of *Fun Home*, she makes two important declarations: She abandons linear storytelling and color. *Fun Home* exhibits the ultimate outcome of both of these realizations, as it is told in a series of recursive and circular set pieces and is rendered in black and white over a blue-green wash.

Her decision to eschew color by no means limits her. While the dark colors provide what she called a "bleak, elegiac quality," they also facilitate clean, acutely detailed depictions of myriad visual forms. She often composed drawings by photographing herself in the poses she wanted each of her family members to hold in the frame, often dressing in the costumes she wanted them to wear. She would then draw what the photographs yielded in a hybrid realistic-cartoonish mode. Human figures in the re-creations of actual photographs that appear within the text are given a more lifelike appearance (such photographs occupy the title pages of some chapters). The most artistically striking elements of *Fun Home* are the frequent representations of these actual photographs, as well as pages of novels, book covers, newspapers, posters, maps, handwritten and typewritten letters, television and film screens, children's drawings and diaries, calendars, and other textual forms. These vivid and realistic renderings reflect the near total pervasiveness of literature in

Bechdel's life and her relationship to and understanding of her father. The reader consequently has a feeling of immersion in her life and outlook. This is most clearly illustrated in frames in which Bechdel's hand holds a photograph up to the reader. Critics have pointed to these moments as pleas from Bechdel to the reader to fully enter her experience and share her trauma, to see these images as she sees them.

Themes

The various and important themes of *Fun Home*—among them, family, suicide, grief, homosexuality, coming-of-age, coming out, and artistic development—can be encapsulated under two main headings: identity and identification and the role of literature in everyday life. The predominant emotional arc of the story consists of Bechdel's attempt to identify with her father. This process evolves into a discovery of her own identity as a homosexual. This discovery, and her subsequent declaration of it, is accompanied by the revelation of her father's own homosexuality. Bechdel is thus able to remap her entire upbringing and her various levels of identification with her father through her new understanding of their shared sense of identity outside familial and social norms. In short, her struggle to identify with her father partly leads to a discovery of her real identity, which in turn facilitates a deeper sense of identification with her father, who had ironically (and perhaps tragically) shared a similar identity all along.

Bechdel's discovery of her identity develops alongside with her extensive reading, much of which was encouraged by her father. *Fun Home* is saturated with references to and lengthy discussions and interpretations of Greek mythology, classics of Western literature, and a wealth of lesbian and feminist writings. The title of each chapter is a literary reference of some sort, and its content somehow addresses a character's sense of identity as it relates to a work of literature. Early in the narrative, Bechdel claims, "I employ these allusions . . . not only as descriptive devices, but because my parents are most real to me in fictional terms," a concept to which she remains faithful, as the main characters' true identities are, for the most part, subjugated to their fictional public masks. The most prominent example of this literary influence is novelist James

Joyce, whose *A Portrait of the Artist as a Young Man* frames the early parts of *Fun Home* and whose *Ulysses* serves as the main locus of identification between father and daughter, on both literal and symbolic levels.

Impact

Fun Home won near immediate critical and popular praise. In addition to the many awards for which it was nominated and won, it has garnered a broad and diverse wave of academic interest. The first bit of large-scale attention came in January, 2007, when the Anglophone Studies Department at Université François Rabelais at Tours hosted a conference devoted entirely to the book. Such issues as the use of drag as a metaphor, paratextuality, and paradoxical tensions were addressed in professional academic papers delivered in both Tours and Paris. American critics have subsequently addressed aspects ranging from *Fun Home*'s homosexual identity politics to its reliance on modernist literary texts, its modernist sentiment and form, its status as a harbinger of a genre of "serious" graphic narratives, and the effect it has had on the way critics and popular audiences read memoir. It has been lauded far and wide as a revolutionary piece of art that sparks reflection on the very nature of literature and narrative.

Brian Chappell

Further Reading

Clowes, Daniel. *Ghost World* (1997).
Satrapi, Marjane. *Persepolis* (2003).
Spiegelman, Art. *Maus: A Survivor's Tale* (1986).
Thompson, Craig. *Blankets* (2003).

Bibliography

Bechdel, Alison. "An Interview with Alison Bechdel." Interview by Hillary L. Chute. *Modern Fiction Studies* 52, no. 4 (2006): 1004-1013.
Freedman, Ariela. "Drawing on Modernism in Alison Bechdel's *Fun Home*." *Journal of Modern Literature* 32, no. 4 (Summer, 2009): 126-140.
Lemberg, Jennifer. "Closing the Gap in Alison Bechdel's *Fun Home*." *Women's Studies Quarterly* 36, nos. ½ (2008): 129-140.
Pearl, Monica B. "Graphic Language: Redrawing the Family (Romance) in Alison Bechdel's *Fun Home*." *Prose Studies* 30, no. 3 (2008): 286-304.
Watson, Julia. "Autographic Disclosures and Genealogies of Desire in Alison Bechdel's *Fun Home*." *Biography* 30, no. 1 (2008): 27-57.

See also: *Blankets; Ghost World; Persepolis; Maus: A Survivor's Tale*

G

GEMMA BOVERY

Author: Simmonds, Posy
Artist: Posy Simmonds (illustrator)
Publisher: Pantheon Books
First serial publication: 1999
First book publication: 1999

Publication History

In the late 1970's, Posy Simmonds began drawing a weekly comic strip for *The Guardian* called *The Silent Three of St. Botolph's.* This led to other strips and, in 1981, a full-fledged book entitled *True Love*, which can be considered her first attempt at a graphic novel. Her penchant for satire and literary adaptation led naturally to her most celebrated work, *Gemma Bovery*, which, in the tradition of the nineteenth-century novel, was serialized in *The Guardian*, appearing every Monday through Saturday in 1999. The success of the series prompted its publication in book form the same year. The book quickly garnered critical interest and attention and was even nominated for the celebrated Prix de la Critique Award for the best comic published in France, organized by the Association des Critiques et des Journalistes de Bande Dessinée. Though Alan Moore's *From Hell* took the award, the resulting critical interest helped *Gemma Bovery* find an American publisher in 2004.

Gemma Bovery. (Courtesy of Pantheon Books)

Plot

The book loosely follows the general plot of Gustave Flaubert's *Madame Bovary* (1857; English translation, 1886), though acquaintance with the novel is not necessary to appreciate Simmonds's story. *Gemma Bovery* opens in the French town of Bailleville, Normandy, where the local baker, Raymond Joubert, consoles Charles Bovery, still mourning the death of his wife. Raymond admits to the reader that "the blood of Gemma Bovery is on my hands" and jumps at the

chance to snatch her recently discovered diaries, which Charles has been too distraught to examine. Spiriting them away one by one, Raymond fills in the gaps of the tragic story he both witnessed and played a significant role in creating.

In the aftermath of a failed relationship and suffering from the flu, Gemma Tate attaches herself to disheveled divorcé Charles, who nurses her back to health. Though Gemma secretly hopes to win back her former lover, a recently married restaurant critic named Patrick, she finds life seductively comfortable with Charles. However, a lack of money and the demands of Charles's ex-wife and children lead her to contemplate a simpler life in a place where "Culture and style go hand in hand, where the business of living is taken seriously, where food isn't full of chemicals. Where property is dirty cheap"—in other words, France. Though Charles initially has little interest in France, he is carried away by Gemma's enthusiasm and promises of a happy life, much to the chagrin of his former wife, who accuses him of betraying his children and his financial responsibilities.

In France, the couple settle into a life similar to one they shared in London. Charles becomes content in his country existence, restoring old furniture for British vacationers, while Gemma feels trapped in a rotting, leaking, vermin-infested hovel. Their neighbor, Raymond, follows her at a distance, eager to be a modern-day Flaubert. To this end, he "wills" her to strike up a romance with a local landowner and law student, Hervé de Bressigny. When the relationship becomes too serious, he decides to intervene, sending Gemma a breakup letter plagiarized from Flaubert. Though Gemma suspects the letter is inauthentic, the breakup is confirmed when Hervé writes his own letter, far less literary, canceling their planned elopement to London. To make matters worse, Hervé's mother is planning to sue Gemma over a piece of furniture that she promised to have Charles restore, which has since disappeared.

Heartbroken, Gemma is left to face Charles's wrath (who learns about the affair from Madame de Bressigny) and tremendous debt. In a plot twist that surprises even Raymond, Gemma enlists his help to draft a letter to the Bressignys' lawyers, but when she goes to collect the letter from him, she is shocked to find a copy of *Madame Bovary* in his kitchen. She notes his guilty reaction and banishes him from her house. Nevertheless, Raymond feels that he, alone, can save her from the same fate as Madame Bovary. He writes letters to Charles, the Rankins (Gemma's English friends who live nearby), and Patrick, warning them that "something was closing in on her, something was going to happen to her. . . . An accident of some sort." Again, his

Gemma Bovery. (Courtesy of Pantheon Books)

authorial pretensions fail him, as she dies mysteriously a few days later.

Characters

- *Raymond Joubert*, a former book editor, has returned to Bailleville to manage his family's bakery. Full of literary pretensions, he loves gossip and enjoys dissecting the lives of his customers. Though at times a bit of a caricature, as when he derides the English for preferring the French countryside to the French themselves, he emerges as the most psychologically realized creation in the novel, revealing his own character through the intimate confessions of the novel's heroine.
- *Gemma Bovery*, a successful magazine illustrator prior to meeting Charles, is the novel's tragic heroine, modeled on Flaubert's Emma Bovary. Like her, Gemma is too passionate for the squalid realities of daily existence. She is an artist who simply works in the wrong medium: men. No relationship can sustain her artistic vision of a pastoral, Antoine Watteau-like world in which art and love are intertwined and immortal. Bills, betrayals, and nosy neighbors will always intrude.
- *Charles Bovery*, a divorced furniture restorer, lives a comfortable, if bohemian, lifestyle before meeting Gemma. Lost in his own world, he avoids the messier side of life, preferring to tinker away in his studio. He lives in fear of his former wife, who perpetuates their married existence through a series of threatening calls and letters. Nonetheless, he is a passionately devoted father, indulging his children in the same way he indulges Gemma's whims and fancies.
- *Hervé de Bressigny* is a young law student whose well-to-do family owns an estate in the Bailleville area. He has returned to the ancestral home to cram for his law exams, which he already failed once, so he can establish a respectable life with his bride-to-be, Delphine. A man ruled by powerful women, he quickly falls under Gemma's sway, all the while knowing that his mother would never approve of such relations.
- *The Rankins*, a.k.a. *Mark* and *Wizzy*, are an English couple who have a house near the Boverys'. They are well off and employ both Charles and Gemma in various restoration tasks. The couple represents a broad satire of English couples who settle in France for such amenities as the culture, the wine, and the landscape, but are otherwise distrustful of the French and do not mix in their society.

Artistic Style

Perhaps the most unique aspect of *Gemma Bovery* is its storytelling. To call it a graphic novel is in some ways misleading, since this has become synonymous with a single approach: a comic book novel. Whereas many traditional comics rely heavily on artwork, using text simply for dialogue or narration, Simmonds strikes a closer balance between the two. Essentially, *Gemma Bovery* is a self-contained novella with an accompanying visual text. The art itself follows a loose comic book format, though it occasionally adds fine details such as a montage, a setting, or an impressionistic detail. The effect is like reading several different works at once, each one adding a different perspective or interpretation to the story line.

A typical example of this occurs on page 27, when Raymond reads about Gemma's escape from London. The reader observes Gemma's dislike of the children, who are too wrapped up in sports, television, and pizza, instead of such things as the wildflowers that interested her as a youth. It concludes sparely, "Gemma had soon had enough of it." This text is not included in the comic strip frame or in a traditional narration box but rather exists in the blank space of the page itself, as a self-contained novel, seemingly oblivious to its comic book companion. The text even appears in book font, as if to call attention to itself as the story. Indeed, Raymond's narration is concocted solely from his own observations and Gemma's diaries; he cannot know what really happened, which the author provides in comic strip asides (though these, too, may be Raymond's imagination).

Beneath the text, a more traditional comic follows, several small frames detailing Charles and Gemma's argument over his children and former wife. The style of the drawings is quite at odds with the text: Whereas the text is sharp, spare, and matter-of-fact, the black-and-white drawings are soft, at times sketchlike or simply unfinished. They have the look of half-remembered or improperly realized visions of what may have been. This in itself is a brilliant commentary on the novel, which claims authoritative knowledge by one or more of its narrators.

The story line of the comic strip also adds insights to Gemma's character that Raymond could never know, revealing her as more self-aware than the fatalistic narrator believes her to be. For example, in her argument with Charles, the two are drawn in the style of a Sunday cartoon, with deft characterizations and a simple back-and-forth that is mostly portrayed as two talking heads in the frame. In the last frame, however, Charles retreats to the background, while Gemma, in the foreground, assumes a more detailed, slightly more portraitlike appearance. In this frame, she is no longer a modern stand-in for Madame Bovary, but a sympathetic, realistic modern woman, lamenting, "S--t . . . s--t. . . . I chose bloody Quality of Life . . . now I've made myself poor."

Themes

With *Madame Bovary* as its inspiration, *Gemma Bovery* is an understandably rich and complex work. Its chief motivating concepts are the relationship between life and art (or reality and illusion) and the satirization of middle-class life and values. With regard to the former, the novel itself is a profound meditation on the question, "What is art?" Do the great works of art, such as *Madame Bovary*, provide mirrors into the human soul as timeless critiques of modern society, or are they ideals dreamed up by artists that, even in their disappointments, far surpass people's mundane achievements? Raymond is clearly in love with the past, as demonstrated by his dropping out of a career in Paris to resurrect his family's bakery, and pines for the fictional Madame Bovary. He hopes, foolishly, to consummate his love of art through Gemma and, by the end of the novel, to save her from her fateful demise. Raymond is disappointed time and again by the reality, particularly when Gemma loves men he feels superior to, and she rejects him as a snoop and voyeur. In the end, he can only cling to the illusion that he has "created" her story and seeks validation in her discovered diaries—which, ironically, say little about him at all. In this sense, *Gemma Bovery* is as much his story as hers, as he tries to emerge as a modern-day Flaubert, rather than a character in his own tangled plot.

Simmonds set out to do much more than translate *Madame Bovary* into the graphic novel form; her work demonstrates a keen eye for satire and caricature, a gift she honed with her satirical portraits in *The Guardian* and one that she brings chiefly to bear on the pretensions of the vacationing Brits. The Rankins, in particular, represent a class of well-to-do suburbanites who view France as a kind of European Disneyland, hawking a quaint brand of nineteenth-century culture unavailable at the shops. Wizzy Rankin adores the superficial aspects of France, but when it comes to the people themselves, she demurs, "Oh God, they're *frightfully* difficult to know. . . . I mean, they're jolly friendly in shops . . . and our builders are sweet . . . but other frogs, they aren't bothered . . . well, why *should* they?" This attitude is shared by most of the English, and even, to some extent, by Gemma herself.

The satire, however, is double edged, for most of the French deplore the uncultured, commercialized English. Hervé's mother dismisses Charles as a "repulsive anglais," and Raymond, when confronted with Patrick's charm and polished French, can only remark, "All this was said with the most perfect French accent I have ever heard in a foreigner. . . . Absolutely *repellent*." Neither side can ever truly know the other, since conventional stereotypes and cartoon reality get in the

Posy Simmonds

Posy Simmonds's cartoons and illustrations have been featured in magazines and newspapers around the world. She is also acclaimed for her various children's books. Her most acclaimed work, however, has come from a series of prose/comic hybrid graphic novels that combine large blocks of text with sequential art, including *Gemma Bovery* and *Tamara Drewe*. These works often update classic works of literature to the modern day, while satirizing British middle-class values.

way. Fittingly, it is a comic book that exposes this cultural ignorance, allowing the reader to see both sides as they truly are.

Impact

Gemma Bovery's success has challenged American assumptions of what a graphic novel can be and should do. Major figures such as Michiko Kakutani, Elaine Showalter, and Eric Griffiths have enthusiastically supported the book, with the latter encouraging talk of a Booker Prize. Though no prize was forthcoming, the implications were clear: Here was a work that could not be dismissed as simply a "comic" or "children's book." Indeed, in Mick Imlah's *Times Literary Supplement* review of Simmonds's second book, he scarcely even refers to it as a graphic novel. Instead, he declares, "its single most impressive attribute is the brilliant management of what would be termed, in a purely literary context, the plot." This does not downplay Simmonds's amazing artwork, but, rather, reminds the reader that the art is scarcely distinguishable from the text; the two blend seamlessly together in service of the story.

Gemma Bovery has subsequently appeared in nearly every survey of the modern graphic novel, including Paul Gravett's authoritative anthology *Graphic Novels: Everything You Need to Know* (2005). On the strength of this single work, Simmonds became one of the leading graphic novelists in England, a reputation that her next book, *Tamara Drewe* (2008), has ably confirmed.

Joshua Grasso

Further Reading

Bechdel, Alison. *Fun Home* (2006).
Simmonds, Posy. *Tamara Drewe* (2008).
Thompson, Craig. *Blankets* (2005).
Tomine, Adrian. *Shortcomings* (2007).

Bibliography

Constable, Liz. "Consuming Realities: The Engendering of Invisible Violences in Posy Simmonds's *Gemma Bovery*." *South Central Review* 19/20 (Winter, 2002): 63-84.

Durrant, Sabine. "Posy Simmonds: The Invisible Woman." *The Telegraph*, October 21, 2007. http://www.telegraph.co.uk/culture/books/3668684/Posy-Simmonds-the-invisible-woman.html.

Gravett, Paul. *Graphic Novels: Everything You Need to Know*. New York: Collins Design, 2005.

_____. "Posy Simmonds: A Literary Life." *The Comics Journal* 286 (November, 2007): 26-67.

Kakutani, Michiko. "A Romantic Like Emma, Trapped in the Bourgeoisie." *The New York Times*, January 28, 2005. http://www.nytimes.com/2005/01/28/books/28book.html.

See also: *Fun Home; Tamara Drewe; Blankets; Shortcomings*

GET A LIFE

Author: Berberian, Charles; Dupuy, Philippe
Artist: Charles Berberian (illustrator); Philippe Dupuy (illustrator)
Publisher: Les Humanoïdes Associés (French); Drawn and Quarterly (English)
First serial publication: *Monsieur Jean*, 1991-2005
First book publication: 2006 (English translation of first three volumes)

Publication History

Get a Life is an English translation (by Helge Dascher) of the first three volumes of the *Monsieur Jean* series by Philippe Dupuy and Charles Berberian. Dupuy and Berberian began their collaborative career in 1983 when they met while working on the French comics fanzine *Plein la gueule pour pas un rond* (full mouth treats), also known as *PLG*. They created *Monsieur Jean* in 1990 and published a few strips about the character in the monthly comic book *Yéti*.

In 1991, Dupuy and Berberian released their first graphic novel depicting the life of Monsieur Jean, *Monsieur Jean: L'amour, la concierge*, with the French comics publisher Les Humanoïdes Associés. They published the second volume, *Monsieur Jean: Mes nuits les plus blanches*, in 1992, and the third volume, *Monsieur Jean: Les femmes et les enfants d'abord*, in 1994, also with Les Humanoïdes Associés. The *Monsieur Jean* series ran through 2005 and comprises seven volumes.

The Canadian company Drawn and Quarterly published *Get a Life* in 2006. An English translation of Dupuy and Berberian's graphic novel *Journal d'un album* (2002), which recounts the creation of the *Monsieur Jean* series, was also published by Drawn and Quarterly in 2006 under the title *Maybe Later*. Drawn and Quarterly continues to publish English versions of Dupuy and Berberian's work, with *Haunted*, an English version of Dupuy's solo work *Hanté* (2005), appearing in 2008.

Plot

The *Monsieur Jean* stories in *Get a Life*, derived from Dupuy's and Berberian's own experiences, portray

Get a Life. (Courtesy of Drawn and Quarterly)

the life of a young Parisian man as he advances in his career and, with maturity, leaves bachelorhood to become a husband and father. The stories, which are intended for an adult audience, recount the daily life of Monsieur Jean, a successful novelist. They include stories of his annoying encounters with his concierge, Madame Poulbot, who is referred to as "my beloved concierge." Madame Poulbot distrusts the quiet, reclusive young man who lives upstairs and is visited by strange-looking friends. He does not leave for work each day, and she believes he is living a dissolute life at the expense of his parents. When she sees him on a television program discussing his successful novel *The Ebony Table*, she changes her opinion of him, but this discovery does not really ease their relationship. A typical French concierge, she continues to pry into his life and take offense at the smallest complaints.

Felix, Monsieur Jean's best friend, is a constant source of frustration, frequently imposing on Jean while bemoaning his fear that someday Jean will abandon him in disgust. Felix is always late and never has any money, but he is always ready to take Jean out for a meal. He asks Jean to help him write and illustrate product-

information copy but falls asleep and leaves Jean to do all of the work. At the last minute, as he is about to leave for several days, he brings his demanding cat, Theo, to stay with Jean. When Felix asks Jean to help him move a few items from his parents' home, everything, including large boxes of books and a kitchen stove, turns out to be cumbersome and almost impossible to carry up to Felix's apartment.

Jean's friend Clement is sympathetic but critical, playing the role of devil's advocate. When Theo stays with Jean, Clement tells him what a nightmare awaits him. Clement always has opinions and criticisms regarding Jean's love affairs, his social life, and almost every other aspect of his existence.

Jean's love affairs frequently go astray. He falls in love at first sight with a woman he does not know, then watches as her significant other arrives. When he does establish a relationship with a woman, he has problems communicating with her, is afraid of commitment, and loses her. In such cases, he often encounters his former girlfriends again in the company of their husbands. Jean also innocently gets involved in his friends' marital problems and suffers for his attempts to help.

In his professional life, Jean is also besieged with problems, as he deals with negative literary critics, demanding publishers, the bumbling agents who arrange his appearances and book signings, and unscrupulous movie producers. Intermingled with the episodes of Jean's daily life are his dreams and daydreams, many of which place him in combative situations. At times, he is a medieval warrior in a castle; at others, he is a military commander fighting a battle against a pizza-firing enemy.

Get a Life. (Courtesy of Drawn and Quarterly)

Characters

- *Monsieur Jean*, the protagonist, is a successful novelist who lives in Paris. He is tormented by loneliness, self-doubt, unsuccessful relationships, and the daily challenges of life.
- *Felix* is Jean's best friend, with whom he occasionally works on advertising copy. He is also Jean's nemesis, as he is perpetually late, broke, and planning grandiose projects that require Jean's help.
- *Theo* is Felix's cat who stays with Jean when Felix is gone. Jean is very uncomfortable with Theo.
- *Clement* is Jean's other friend, always supportive but also critical.
- *Madame Poulbot*, Jean's concierge, is his major antagonist, suspecting him of all sorts of disreputable activities.
- *Chantal* is one of Jean's former girlfriends. When he meets her again at an art exhibit, she is with her oversolicitous husband, Michel, and expecting a baby. She reminds Jean of how he destroyed their relationship.
- *Veronique* and *Jacques* are married friends of Jean who have trouble finding time for each other and embroil Jean in their marital difficulties.

Artistic Style

Dupuy and Berberian maintain a consistent drawing style throughout *Get a Life*. The visual style of the first volume of *Monsieur Jean* established certain expectations for the subsequent novels in the minds of readers, and Dupuy and Berberian have emphasized that the series' popularity has restricted their creativity and opportunities for experimentation in that area. Since the publication of Dupuy's solo graphic novel *Haunted*, they have become interested in exploring different drawing styles and have indicated that when they publish another volume of *Monsieur Jean*, it will not be done in the style of the previous ones, even though many readers will be upset.

Get a Life makes extensive use of color. The everyday world in which the stories are set is realistically colored, with soft tones that stress the mundane, repetitive nature of Jean's world. Dupuy and Berberian also use color to signal a change of setting from Jean's real-world life to his mental life. Dreams, daydreams, and thoughts are imbued with a reddish-brown coloration. When Jean is angry during these sequences, the color changes from a reddish-brown to a more intense red.

Dupuy and Berberian use a page layout that mixes panel sizes and shapes, with framed and unframed panels that often crowd the pages. The layout reflects Jean's jumbled, confusing, and difficult daily life. Because *Get a Life* anthologizes three volumes of the *Monsieur Jean* series, it is divided into three sections. Between the stories that demarcate volumes 2 and 3, there are two pages, each of which depicts an unframed character. On the first page, the concierge, Madame Poulbot, is depicted as having devil horns, flying with red wings, and drawing a bow armed with a "broom arrow." The following page features a blue image of Jean seated in an armchair, with a cat perched on the back of the chair, a girlfriend sitting on the floor, and a record player spinning a vinyl record. The second image represents Jean's

---

Charles Berberian

One half of the famed cartooning duo Dupuy-Berberian, Charles Berberian first published work in the French fanzine scene of the early-1980's before releasing *Petit peintre* in 1985. Responsible for both writing and drawing (with Philippe Dupuy) the *Henriette* series and the *Monsieur Jean* series, the duo became important figures in the 1990's, pushing French comics toward greater psychological realism in the humor comics genre. Their conjointly produced autobiographical *Get a Life* detailed the creation of one of their *Monsieur Jean* graphic novels. In 2008 they launched a new series, *Boboland*, which aggressively parodies the lives of an international bohemian class. Independent of Dupuy, Berberian has published several books of illustration and comics, including *Cycloman* (with Gregory Mardon) and *Les Gens* (with his wife, Anna Rozen). *Sacha* is his extended comic portrait of a cat. His visual style was defined early in his career by its updating of the Belgian Marcinelle school, influenced by André Franquin and Yves Chaland. When he switched to a brush pen in the 1990's, his style became more open and free.

dream life, contrasting sharply with the adventures he has in the second volume. The third image, colored in red and green, depicts a child-sized Jean surrounded by items from his life that symbolize his ongoing frustration with his existence.

Get a Life contains little author commentary; the text is presented almost entirely in dialogue bubbles. Much of the humor of *Get a Life* derives from its depiction of the characters, each of whom has a distinctive and often-exaggerated feature. Jean has a large nose and a sad-looking face; Felix has a sharp nose and a small face that radiates optimism; Madame Poulbot always has an expression of mischievous delight.

Themes

Get a Life is the humorous story of a young man experiencing life, with all its problems, puzzlements, successes, and failures. Monsieur Jean is a solitary individual in the process of forming relationships, discovering himself, and developing his ideas about what is important and possible in life. He has much to learn about himself and about interaction with other people. The episodes of *Get a Life* create a portrait of an individual who is by nature pessimistic, sensitive, self-doubting, well meaning, and likable. Jean finds life difficult despite his success as a novelist.

A second major theme of *Get a Life* is the little tragedies and negative serendipity of everyday life. For example, Jean's attraction to the woman taking a survey in the supermarket results in his having to buy identical groceries twice. Felix insists on going to the Matisse exhibit, intending to meet a girlfriend, but leaves when he does not find her, while Jean meets his former girlfriend Chantal and her husband there. Forgetting to feed Theo and listening to Clement's horror stories about the cat's temper result in Jean being arrested while Theo is peacefully waiting at the apartment.

Daydreaming and dreaming as a means of coping with life is another recurring theme. Jean escapes from boring situations and disappointing events by fantasizing, although at times his dreams also intensify his bad experiences.

Impact

Dupuy and Berberian have brought a new dimension to the creation of graphic novels with their close collaboration on the *Monsieur Jean* series and its English-language version, *Get a Life*. The two writers/artists share every aspect of their work, so much so that it is impossible to assign certain characters, story lines, or a specific artistic style to one or the other. Typical of the experimental Modern Age of graphic novels, *Get a Life* departs from traditional formats, instead emphasizing Monsieur Jean's psyche. The story line of *Get a Life* contrasts sharply with the earlier, more traditional French graphic novels, such as René Goscinny and Albert Uderzo's *Asterix* (1961-1979) and Hergé's *The Adventures of Tintin* (1929-1976), which depict characters in historical contexts and focus on action. *Monsieur Jean* has been immensely popular in France, and Dupuy and Berberian were recognized as major French graphic artists in 2009 when they were awarded the Grand Prix de la Ville d'Angoulême at the Angoulême International Comics Festival. *Get a Life* has enjoyed an excellent reception in the world of English-language graphic novels and has been instrumental in introducing Dupuy and Berberian's work to English-speaking countries, especially the United States.

Shawncey Jay Webb

Further Reading

Dupuy, Philippe. *Haunted* (2008).

Dupuy, Philippe, and Charles Berberian. *Maybe Later* (2006).

Bibliography

Dauncey, Hugh, ed. *French Popular Culture: An Introduction*. London: Arnold, 2003.

Fosdick, Charles, Laurence Groves, and Libbie McQuilan, eds. *The Francophone Bande Dessinée*. New York: Rodopi, 2005.

Groensteen, Thierry. *The System of Comics*. Translated by Bart Beaty and Nick Nguyen. Jackson: University Press of Mississippi, 2007.

See also: *Haunted; Glacial Period; Dead Memory; The Adventures of Tintin*

GHOST WORLD

Author: Clowes, Daniel
Artist: Daniel Clowes (illustrator)
Publisher: Fantagraphics Books
First serial publication: 1993-1997
First book publication: 1997

Publication History

Ghost World first appeared in *Eightball*, issue 11 (June, 1993), an alternative comic book published by Fantagraphics Books and written and drawn by Daniel Clowes. *Eightball* alternated continuing series, such as *Like a Velvet Glove Cast in Iron*, with single stories, such as "Ugly Girls," in which a Clowes's alter ego states his preference for brainy, bespectacled brunettes over blond bombshells. *Ghost World* ran for eight issues, ending in *Eightball*, issue 18 (March, 1997); each chapter was self-contained, yet they work together as a whole.

When *Ghost World* was published as a graphic novel in 1997, the chapters were named, and Clowes added some preliminary drawings hinting at a backstory: In one image, main characters Enid and Rebecca are shown in their graduation gowns, with Enid giving the finger to their old school; in another, the girls, looking twelve or thirteen, are shown visiting a grave. In 1998, *Ghost World* received Ignatz Awards for "outstanding achievement in comics and cartooning" in two categories: Outstanding Graphic Novel or Collection (for the graphic novel) and Outstanding Story (for the original *Eightball* series). *Ghost World* has been reprinted numerous times, including a 2008 hardcover edition combining the original comic with the film screenplay, unused drawings, memorabilia, and an introduction by Clowes.

Plot

In interviews, Clowes has said that he began writing *Ghost World* with the idea of creating characters whose circumstances and experiences were far removed from his, yet who still shared some of his attitudes. While he originally felt that writing about teenage girls would prevent the story from becoming too autobiographical,

Ghost World. (Courtesy of Fantagraphics Books)

Clowes said he was surprised at how much of himself ended up in *Ghost World*. Like his young heroines, he dislikes the slickness and manipulation of modern culture; values the odd, offbeat, and old; and still struggles to define his own identity.

The story opens on a random day in the life of Enid and Rebecca, teenage girls with spare time. They watch a bad comedian on television and delight in his awkwardness. Enid chides Rebecca for reading *Sassy*, a teen magazine, which she derides as fake and pseudo-hip. She describes an encounter with John Ellis, who has befriended a pedophiliac former priest. Enid also tells of meeting Bob Skeetes and a Satanist couple. While little happens in the first chapter, the reader gets a sense of the characters and their offbeat humor.

In the next episode, Enid has a garage sale but decides that her childhood treasures, like "Goofie Gus," a statuette from fifth grade, are too precious to part with. She does sell an eggbeater to Skeetes, who invites her to call him for a psychic reading. She and Rebecca encounter Melorra, a former classmate whom the girls dislike, in a diner and the Satanists in the supermarket. At this point, the girls are so in synch with each other that Rebecca immediately recognizes the Satanist couple, even though she has never seen them.

Enid adopts a retro punk look but is disgusted when an old classmate, John Crowley (formerly known as "Johnny Apes") misinterprets her style choice. Enid talks about wanting to find one perfect, vintage look, but her quest for the perfect style seems as elusive as her quest for the perfect man. She says she wants to meet a sophisticated man, like her favorite cartoonist, "David Clowes," but she is horrified when she sees him in a magazine shop. (Clowes draws himself as a shabby, leering creep.) She and Rebecca discuss their sex lives, or lack thereof. Enid persuades Josh to take her to a sex shop, where she buys a bondage mask. She finds the seedy shop hilarious, but Josh is clearly embarrassed. She narrates this adventure to Rebecca and then reminisces about her first sexual experience. Rebecca is angry that Enid went to the sex shop without her.

As their aimless days continue, Rebecca and Enid visit Hubba Hubba, a fake 1950's diner, and make fun of its inauthentic decor, menu, and waiter, whom Rebecca calls "Weird Al." They amuse themselves by reading personal ads and later play a trick on a man who is trying to reconnect with a woman he once met. Enid calls him, pretending to be the woman, and arranges to meet him at Hubba Hubba. The girls persuade a disapproving Josh to drive back to the diner to see if the man described as a "bearded windbreaker" will show up. The prank succeeds, but it is less fun than they expected.

Enid and Rebecca discuss "Norman," a man who sits and waits for a bus that was rerouted years ago. They see Melorra and some of her obnoxious show business friends in a diner, briefly torment Josh, and then wander around town, where they see the Satanist woman apparently on her own after a fight with her husband. Feeling forlorn, the girls clasp hands. Enid promises not to leave for college. Later, the girls look through old pictures, including one of the graffiti "Ghost World" Enid took years ago, and Enid becomes obsessed with finding a record from her childhood. They argue about Enid's college plans. Enid, angry at Rebecca, tries to seduce Josh but leaves in tears when he confesses he really cares about her. When she returns home, she sees her father has left her a box of old records in her room. She falls asleep listening to the song "A Smile and a Ribbon."

As the story concludes, Rebecca tries to accept that Enid may go away if she passes her college entrance exam. She and Enid discuss Enid's encounter with Josh and if she should pursue a relationship with him. Enid jokes that when she gets tired of Josh, Rebecca can have him as a hand-me-down. Late that night, Rebecca knocks on Josh's door. They have sex, but she still suspects that Josh likes Enid more. In an attempt to revisit a rare happy childhood memory, the girls go to "Cavetown, USA," a cheesy tourist attraction. Rebecca talks about going with Enid when she leaves for college. She wants everything to be like it was in high school, while Enid wants to change everything, especially herself. Enid dreams of one day getting on a bus and going to some distant city, where she can create a new identity.

Enid fails her college exam. As autumn sets in, she has a final encounter with Rebecca, now working in a bagel shop; they are polite, but it is clear they are no longer close, and Rebecca seems to be hiding tears. In the final scene, Enid walks through town carrying a 1950's-style round suitcase. She finally sees the graffiti artist painting "Ghost World." She calls to him, but he runs away. As she walks by, Enid sees Rebecca and Josh through a restaurant window. She says a silent goodbye to her old friend, gets on the bus, and leaves.

Volumes

- *Chapter 1, "Ghost World"* (1993). This volume introduces Enid, Rebecca, and some of the eccentric characters they encounter, including John Ellis, Bob Skeetes, and the Satanists.
- *Chapter 2, "Garage Sale"* (1993). Enid has trouble letting go of childhood treasures; more

encounters with Skeetes and the Satanists are featured.

- *Chapter 3, "Punk Day"* (1994). This covers the girls' angst about clothes, boys, and sex; Enid has a disappointing glimpse of cartoonist "David Clowes."
- *Chapter 4, "The First Time"* (1994). This includes the first appearance of Josh and Enid's story about the loss of her virginity.
- *Chapter 5, "Hubba Hubba"* (1995). Enid and Rebecca play a phone prank; Josh disapproves.
- *Chapter 6, "The Norman Square"* (1995). As Enid considers college, the girls experience the beginnings of separation anxiety.
- *Chapter 7, "A Smile and a Ribbon"* (1995). The girls experience nostalgia for their childhood and a romantic triangle.
- *Chapter 8, "October"* (1997). In this long concluding chapter, friendship ends as Enid and Rebecca take their lives in different directions.

Characters

- *Enid Coleslaw*, the protagonist, is a smart and sarcastic eighteen-year-old girl with a black bob hairstyle, glasses, and a quirky sense of style. On impulse, she may dye her hair green and adopt a retro 1977 punk look or wear go-go boots or a leather bondage mask she finds in a sex shop. As the series begins, Enid has just graduated high school, lives with her father, and has no particular plans for the future. She and her friend Rebecca spend their time hanging around diners, making fun of the odd characters they see. She is critical of contemporary popular culture and of people she deems trendy and pretentious, but she has sympathy for those she considers true outsiders. While she appears knowing and self-assured, she has moments of self-doubt.

- *Rebecca Doppelmeyer*, Enid's best friend, is a teenage girl with blond hair who shares Enid's sarcastic sense of humor but is slightly more conventional in her style and outlook. She lives with her elderly grandmother. Although the more traditionally attractive of the two girls, Rebecca is quieter and less confident, allowing Enid to take the lead in their activities. Like Enid, she is interested in Josh, but she is sure he prefers Enid. When Enid flirts with the idea of attending

Ghost World. (Courtesy of Fantagraphics Books)

college, Rebecca feels resentful that her friend has made this major life decision without her, and this creates a rift that ultimately ends their friendship.

- *Josh* is a friend and semi-serious love interest for both Enid and Rebecca. Tall, blond, and unassuming, he seems to be around the same age as the girls—he may be slightly older. He is more serious and mature than they are and has a car and his own apartment. While disapproving of the girls' pranks and schemes, he is, as Enid says, easily manipulated into going along with them. Josh clearly has a crush on Enid, but he is also attracted to Rebecca.
- *Bob Skeetes* is an eccentric, middle-aged astrologer and psychic. His gaunt face and prominent teeth lead Enid, who keeps running into him at odd moments, to compare him to actor Don Knotts. Enid suspects Skeetes is a con man, but she finds him fascinating.
- *John Ellis* is an obnoxious, confrontational acquaintance of Enid, obsessed with serial killers, child molesters, and Nazis. Nerdy and unattractive, he seems to have a crush on Rebecca, who ignores him.
- *Enid's Father*, whose first name is never revealed, apparently changed his last name from Cohn to Coleslaw. Ellis interrupts Enid when she is about to explain why he changed his name, but since Enid refers to her father's political activism, it may have been a protest against right-wing lawyer Roy Cohn. Enid's father is balding, slightly rotund, and well meaning but a little overwhelmed by his role as a single father.
- *Melorra* is a perky, overly earnest former classmate of Enid and Rebecca and a symbol of everything they hate. She works for Greenpeace but takes an acting role in a commercial for a right-wing political candidate.

Artistic Style

Ghost World is notable for its clean black-and-white lines and distinctive use of one accent color, pale blue. This melancholy, twilight shade gives the panels an appropriately "ghostly" feeling and mimics the look of a dark room lit by television (an image Clowes uses throughout the series). Clowes told an interviewer that he used Rubylith overlays to add the blue tones to *Ghost World*, a technique he learned in art school in the late 1970's.

Clowes's earlier work was often grotesque and hyperdetailed, showing the influence of underground comics legend Robert Crumb and *MAD* magazine artist Basil Wolverton, but with *Ghost World*, he moved toward a more simplified, stylized look, reminiscent of 1950's commercial artwork or old newspaper cartoon strips. He also uses classic cinematic techniques to striking effect, alternating close-ups with medium and long shots and sometimes showing his characters through unusual perspectives, framed in a window or looked down on from far above. The almost wordless final page of *Ghost World*, for example, echoes the look, if not the mood, of film noir: a full view of Enid walking, the restaurant in the background; a closer view, over Enid's shoulder, of two figures in the restaurant window; a close-up of Rebecca, seen through the window; Enid's reaction, at medium distance; a bird's-eye view of her walking down the street; Enid outlined in black against the open door of the bus; a long view of the empty street. As he does throughout the story, Clowes uses alternating panel sizes and perspective to frame the action and emphasize key moments. While *Ghost World* is known for its quirky characters and sharp, funny dialogue, scenes such as this one show that Clowes can tell a story using purely visual elements.

Themes

Coming of age, identity, friendship, and loss are major themes in *Ghost World*. Over the course of a single summer, Enid and Rebecca grow up, try to figure out who they are, and ultimately grow apart.

Initially, Enid and Rebecca, like the two teenage heroines of the film *The World of Henry Orient* (1964), to which Clowes refers in a drawing, live in an ordinary world made extraordinary through imaginative projection. Thus, the strange, sun-shunning couple glimpsed in a diner must be Satanists. Cheap and seedy places such as the Hubba Hubba diner and the sex shop are imbued with a mysterious glamour. Though some reviewers described Enid and Rebecca as "bored teen-agers," Clowes says he sees them as the opposite of bored, because they always have something they can get excited about. Yet as the summer ends and adult responsibilities draw nearer, that sense of excitement is being drained away by the banality of the real world.

Both Enid and Rebecca struggle to define their identities throughout the series. Rebecca is the less flamboyant of the two girls, more of a follower than a leader. Tall, thin, and blond, she would be a natural fit for the role of popular girl, but she resists this stereotype. While Enid wears an eclectic mix of vintage fashions, Rebecca's clothes are plain and generic. She lacks confidence and feels inferior to Enid, and when she learns Enid has applied to college, she feels threatened and becomes defensive. While the prospect of losing her best friend scares Rebecca, there is a sense that the break may ultimately be good for her, allowing her to come into herself. Enid, meanwhile, attempts to define herself in opposition to mass culture. She despises the sameness of strip-mall America and tries to re-create an older, more glamorous world through clothing, culture, and artifacts, although she worries about seeming pretentious. She dreams of running away, losing her past, and becoming a different person, and the ending hints she is on this path.

Ghost World presents an amazingly honest and intimate portrait of female friendship. Enid and Rebecca mirror each other in many ways, and each serves as a repository for the other's past. They can be casually foul-mouthed and insulting with each other but will defend each other against criticism from outside. The closeness of their friendship is, ironically, what dooms it: Neither girl can grow into a new identity when the other is a constant reminder of their shared past. The inevitability of lost friendship dominates the final chapters of *Ghost World*, but other losses permeate the work, beginning with childhood. Enid speaks of two stepmothers, but her mother is never mentioned. Did she die, or simply leave? Rebecca lives with her grandmother; her parents are also mysteriously absent. The graffiti "Ghost World," scrawled on Enid's garage door and other places throughout the city, underscores a sense of loss and emptiness. The final panel, showing Enid's bus disappearing into a tunnel, may mean a new

beginning for Enid, but the image of a deserted street and empty bench are also suggestive of death.

Impact

Ghost World is a rare example of a modern "alternative" comic that achieved relatively wide popular success without compromise. The second of Clowes's longer stories to be serialized in *Eightball*, it showed the maturing of his talent beyond satire, hate rants, and crude humor and featured fully developed characters who were more than stand-ins for the author. Although Enid and Rebecca share some of their creator's opinions—Enid's distaste for reggae and the Grateful Dead, for example, is pure Clowes—they are also completely believable as teenage girls.

Reviewers praised *Ghost World* for its pitch-perfect dialogue and authentic portrayal of teen life, comparing Clowes to *Catcher in the Rye*'s (1951) author J. D. Salinger. It was popular among both teen and adult readers and, especially in graphic novel format, reached readers not normally interested in comic books.

The popularity of *Ghost World* and the subsequent film brought Clowes into the mainstream spotlight; he is one of a few comics creators asked to do a strip for *The New York Times*. In 2009, *Ghost World* was named one of the "Twenty Best Graphic Novels of the Decade" by *Paste Magazine* and was ranked number 10 in a list of "The Twenty-Five Greatest Gen X Books of All Time" in *Details* magazine.

As a pioneer of independent comics in the late 1980's and 1990's, Clowes, especially in his focus on realistic characters and settings and introspective themes, has influenced such younger creators as Craig Thompson and Adrian Tomine. In an interview, Clowes acknowledged his influence on Tomine, saying that Tomine grew up reading his work, much as Clowes grew up reading *MAD* magazine and Crumb.

Films

Ghost World. Directed by Terry Zwigoff. United Artists, 2001. Screenplay by Clowes and Zwigoff. This film adaptation stars Thora Birch as Enid and Scarlett Johansson as Rebecca. The film differs from the novel in that it develops a third major character,

Seymour (played by Steve Buscemi), not featured in the book, although he somewhat physically resembles Skeetes and contains elements of the unnamed man Enid and Rebecca trick into coming to the diner to meet his dream woman. Zwigoff, director of the documentary *Crumb* (1994), and Clowes shared an Academy Award nomination for best screenplay.

Kathryn Kulpa

Further Reading

Burns, Charles. *Black Hole* (1995-2005).

Friedman, Aimee, and Christine Norrie. *Breaking Up* (2007).

Thompson, Craig. *Blankets* (2003).

Tomine, Adrian. *Optic Nerve* (1995-1998).

_____. *Summer Blonde* (2002).

Bibliography

Booker, M. Keith. *May Contain Graphic Material: Comic Books, Graphic Novels, and Film*. New York: Praeger, 2007.

Clowes, Daniel, Ken Parille, and Isaac Cates. *Daniel Clowes: Conversations*. Jackson: University of Mississippi, 2010.

Clowes, Daniel, and Terry Zwigoff. *Ghost World: A Screenplay*. Seattle: Fantagraphics, 2001.

Hajdu, David. "Joe Sacco and Daniel Clowes." In *Heroes and Villains: Essays on Music, Movies, Comics, and Culture*. Cambridge, Mass.: Da Capo Press, 2009.

Hignite, Todd. "Daniel Clowes." *In the Studio: Visits with Contemporary Cartoonists*. New Haven, Conn.: Yale University Press, 2006.

Schwartz, Ben, ed. *The Best American Comics Criticism*. Seattle: Fantagraphics, 2010.

Taylor, Craig. "Girls' World." *The Guardian*, November 3, 2001, pp. 60-67.

See also: *Black Hole; Blankets; Like a Velvet Glove Cast in Iron; David Boring*

GIVE IT UP! AND OTHER SHORT STORIES

Author: Kafka, Franz; Kuper, Peter
Artist: Peter Kuper (illustrator)
Publisher: NBM
First book publication: 1995

Publication History

Give It Up! And Other Short Stories is one of several comic book adaptations of literary works illustrated by Peter Kuper. Kuper also illustrated an adaption of Franz Kafka's novella *Die Verwandlung* (1915; *The Metamorphosis*, 1936), which was published by Crown Comics in 2004. *Give It Up!* was published by Comics-Lit, an imprint of NBM, which is known as an "alternative" comics publisher for the simple reason that it does not publish superhero comics. ComicsLit titles include adaptations of Marcel Proust's seven-volume novel *À la Recherche du temps perdu* (1913-1927; *Remembrance of Things Past*, 1981) and Upton Sinclair's novel *The Jungle* (1906), also illustrated by Kuper. Kuper's work frequently addresses and confronts humanitarian issues, and *Give It Up!* is no exception.

The stories featured in *Give It Up!* were all written by Kafka in the 1920's. Most are flash-fiction pieces that Kuper repeats verbatim. "A Fratricide" and "A Hunger Artist" are abridged and adapted. "A Hunger Artist" is one of Kafka's most famous short stories and is frequently anthologized. Of the nine stories, only "A Fratricide" and "A Hunger Artist" were published during Kafka's lifetime. The rest of the stories, including the title story, were published posthumously. These stories survived thanks to Max Brod, Kafka's friend and literary executor; Kafka asked Brod to burn his unpublished manuscripts after his death, but Brod not only preserved them but also published them. Kafka was a compulsive perfectionist and dismissed most of his works as mediocre and unworthy of publication, an assessment shared by few contemporary or modern critics.

Give It Up! And Other Stories was first published by ComicsLit in 1995, and a hardcover version was reissued in 2003. The first paperback version came out in 2005.

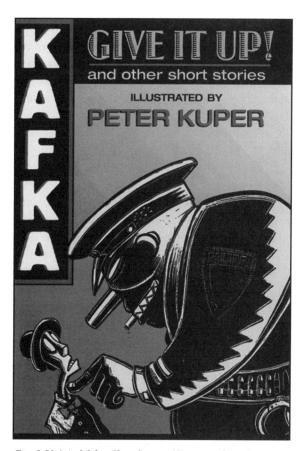

Give It Up! And Other Short Stories. (Courtesy of Nantier Beall Minoustchine Publishing)

Plot

Give It Up! contains nine short stories by Franz Kafka: "A Little Fable," "The Bridge," "Give It Up!," "A Hunger Artist," "A Fratricide," "The Helmsman," "The Trees," "The Top," and "The Vulture." Each tale has its own set of characters, most of whom remain unnamed.

The collection opens with "A Little Fable," wherein a mouse scurries through a maze. The mouse recalls a time when the world seemed overwhelmingly big and how he found the maze comforting in contrast; now, however, the ever-shrinking maze is just as terrifying. The mouse reaches a cul-de-sac, and there is nowhere left to go but straight into a mousetrap. A cat, watching from above the maze, offers a solution: "You only need to change your direction." The mouse turns around, and the cat promptly eats it.

In "Give It Up!," the title story, a narrator/protagonist is rushing to work and has forgotten the way. He is relieved to see a police officer, whom he hopes will give him directions. Instead, the police officer yells "Give It Up!" and shoves the narrator against the wall, pushing his finger into the narrator's neck, until it twists and contorts.

"A Hunger Artist" is the longest story in the collection. The protagonist, a "hunger artist," starves himself in a cage for the entertainment of the public. His "act" is orchestrated by an impresario, who also serves as his agent and makes most of the decisions. The impresario publicizes the hunger artist's "performances" and sets a forty-day limit to the fast, which is as long as an audience will remain interested. The hunger artist resents this limit and wants to fast for much longer. It is only when fasting acts become less popular and the impresario consequently loses interest in being his agent that the hunger artist gets his wish.

The hunger artist then freelances with a circus, where he fasts himself nearly to death, without attracting the notice of the spectators or even the circus staff. One day, the circus overseer passes the hunger artist's cage and, not seeing anything or anyone in it, complains about the cage being unused. When the circus staff open the cage, they discover the neglected hunger artist, who has now almost perished. The hunger artist explains that he had always wanted people to admire him for fasting but that they should not admire it; fasting is easy for him, since he could never find the food he craved. With this confession, the hunger artist dies, is buried, and is replaced by a panther, who knows what food he desires and devours it exuberantly, a spectacle far more popular for the circus crowds than that of the hunger artist.

The collection begins and ends with blood. In the story "The Vulture," a vulture tortures the narrator by attacking his feet. A bystander offers to shoot the vulture and goes home to fetch his gun, whistling as he saunters off. The narrator realizes from the malicious, knowing look on the vulture's face that the latter understood everything. The vulture then swoops high into the air, plunges into the mouth of the narrator, and drowns in its victim's blood.

Characters

- *A first person narrator* is the protagonist of "The Bridge," "Give It Up!," "The Helmsman," and "The Vulture." It is unclear whether this narrator represents a coherent, single personality. However, the narrators of all four stories share some key elements. They are all underdog figures: alienated, tortured both physically and psychologically, and victimized by authority figures. They invariably undergo traumatic transformations, often ending in death.

- *The hunger artist* is the protagonist of "A Hunger Artist." He is a meek and emaciated figure. Unassertive by nature, he is easily controlled and subdued by the impresario, although he is given to fits of anger whenever he is forced to end his fast. He is quiet and reclusive and does not reveal his motives for fasting until the very end. Critics of Kafka's work believe that this character is meant to represent Kafka himself, and thus the story is a kind of self-portrait.

- *A police officer* appears in three of the nine stories as a thematic antagonist. The police officer is always large and looming, with a wide, menacing face and jagged teeth. He is impatient and easily angered and makes great autocratic displays of intimidation to assert his power.

Artistic Style

Many readers will recognize the stylistic similarity between the art of *Give It Up!* and that of the macabre *Spy vs. Spy* strip in *MAD* magazine. This is no accident: Kuper has been illustrating Antonio Prohías's *Spy vs. Spy* since 1997. As in *Spy vs. Spy*, in *Give It Up!* there are no shades of gray, either literally or figuratively. The sharp contrasts of white and black mirror the starkness of the stories themselves.

Give It Up! is full of juxtapositions. Diminutive, anxious protagonists are dwarfed by grotesque and massive villains, such as the police officer and the vulture. The background images are surreal and distorted. Panels, when they are used at all, are usually arranged in skewed diagonal angles, enhancing the dystopian images contained within their frames.

Kuper takes full advantage of the interpretive potential of visual illustration. Indeed, his pictures add "a thousand words" to Kafka's terse, minimalist narratives. The art contains numerous subtle cues that suggest particular readings and link the nine stories thematically. The cat, the panther, and the police officer, which appear in three separate stories, all have similar serrated teeth, thus putting a common face on the archetypal villain. In "The Fratricide," the onlookers have large eyeballs growing out of their necks instead of their heads, echoing the story's implication that people are frequently more interested in watching human tragedy than preventing it. Kuper is particularly innovative in his illustration of the story "The Trees." The original story is a one-paragraph commentary about how tree trunks in the snow seem easily movable, although they are stuck to the ground. Kafka's "story" is more of an observation than a narrative, but Kuper gives the plot action and shape through his illustrations of a street person being pushed and prodded by a police officer.

Kuper's drawings contain numerous nuances that transpose Kafka's works into modern times. For example, the mouse of "A Fable" wears a suit, carries a briefcase, and seems to be rushing to work. Thus, his confinement in the maze and his consumption by the cat serve as commentary on the modern-day corporate world.

The limbs of the characters are often elongated and contorted. Kuper likely took inspiration from not only Kafka's stories but also his drawings. Kafka was fond of doodling black-and-white stick figures, whose limbs are stretched and twisted, as though they were trapped in societies and environments that restrain and deform both their bodies and minds.

Themes

Although the stories are not explicitly linked by either Kafka or Kuper, the plots share similar elements. In almost all the stories, a diffident and alienated male protagonist is victimized or preyed upon by a predator or an authority figure. The protagonist is usually isolated in his plight, without supporters or defenders. Each protagonist has little or no possibility of "winning" against his opponent, and his only options are futile resistance or surrender. The protagonist usually resists, at least for a while, but his perseverance is rendered pointless when he is ultimately annihilated by opposing forces.

Kafka suggests that we are not in control of our destiny, and our destiny is invariably bleak. Beginning with "A Little Fable," the protagonists frequently find themselves "out of the frying pan and into the fire." The words of the police officer in the title story "Give It Up!" sum up what seems to be the only rational response to this predicament: giving up. Despite the inevitability of defeat, the protagonists are nonetheless compelled to resist; their sense of justice will not allow them to do otherwise.

Despite the nihilism inherent in the narratives, the protagonists still yearn for salvation and release. Only in the last story, "The Vulture," is there a possibility of redemption, but it is bought at the cost of the protagonist's death. When the vulture flings itself into the narrator's mouth, the narrator says, "I was relieved to feel him drowning irretrievably in my blood which was filling every depth, flooding every shore."

The protagonist is always alone in his struggle, but that is not for lack of people around him. Almost every story has one or several witnesses, who seem utterly indifferent and unsympathetic to the protagonist's plight. There is a sense that all the bystanders form a single, monolithic entity, which is invariably apathetic or voyeuristic.

Impact

Adapting literary works to the comic book medium is a long tradition in the industry. The first such series was *Classic Comics*, later *Classics Illustrated*. The series, started by Lewis Kanter in 1941, published more than 150 adaptations of literary classics until it folded in 1971. *Classics Illustrated* titles include *Frankenstein*, *A Tale of Two Cities*, and *Moby Dick*, but nothing as dark or avant-garde as the works of Kafka.

Give It Up! differs from many other comic book adaptations in that the artist not only illustrates but also interprets the work through innovative techniques that cast the timeless stories into new contexts. As Jules Feiffer notes in his introduction to the collection, Kuper's drawings are not so much illustrations as "riffs, visual improvisations."

Give It Up! received excellent reviews from *The New York Times*, *Publisher's Weekly*, *Kirkus Review*, and many other publications. Critics have commented on the sophistication of Kuper's interpretations and his success in capturing the mood and themes of Kafka's work. There is general assent that Kuper's expressionist artistic style corresponds well with Kafka's moody, terrifying prose.

The same year that the *Give It Up!* reprint appeared on shelves, Totem Books published *Introducing Kafka* as part of its "Introducing" comic book series. *Introducing Kafka* also contains adaptations of Kafka's "A Hunger Artist" and *The Metamorphosis*.

Bettina Grassmann

Further Reading

Hernandez, Gilbert, Jaime Hernandez, and Mario Hernandez. *Love and Rockets* (1982-1996).

Kuper, Peter, and Franz Kafka. *The Metamorphosis* (2003).

Mairowitz, David Zane, and Robert Crumb. *Introducing Kafka* (1993).

Bibliography

Celayo, Armando, and David Shook. "Comic Adaptations of Literary Classics." *World Literature Today* 81, no. 2 (March/April, 2007): 33-36.

Josipovici, Gabriel. Introduction to *Collected Stories*, by Franz Kafka. New York: A. A. Knopf, 1993.

Kafka, Franz. *The Great Wall of China, and Other Short Works*. Edited and translated by Malcolm Pasley. London: Penguin Books, 2002.

See also: *The Curious Case of Benjamin Button; Gemma Bovary; Introducing Kafka; The System*

GLACIAL PERIOD

Author: Crécy, Nicolas de
Artist: Ortho (letterer)
Publisher: Musée du Louvre (French); NBM (English)
First book publication: *Période glaciaire*, 2005 (English translation, 2006)

Publication History

Glacial Period is the English translation (translator Joe Johnson) of Nicolas De Crécy's *Période glaciaire*, the first of four graphic novels commissioned by the Louvre Museum and showcasing the museum's art collection. As part of the Louvre's campaign to bring contemporary art into the museum and to attract younger individuals, Fabrice Douar, deputy director of the publishing department of the museum, envisaged the creation of a series of graphic novels about the art collection in the Louvre. In discussing his project, Douar has also emphasized the aesthetic aspect of bringing two different worlds of art together. The artists chosen for the project were Crécy, Marc-Antoine Mathieu, Eric Liberge, and the collaborative team of Bernard Yslaire and Jean Carrière.

Because the graphic novels genre was one in which the Louvre's publication department had no experience, the museum brought Futuropolis, a major publisher of alternative and experimental graphic novels, into the project. Crécy's original French work was produced as a co-edition by the Musée du Louvre Éditions and Futuropolis and published in collaboration in 2005. The English translation was published in 2006 by NBM under the corporation's imprint ComicsLit. In 2007, *Glacial Period* published by NBM earned Crécy a Will Eisner Comic Industry Award nomination for Best Painter/Multimedia Artist (interior art).

Plot

Officials at the Louvre Museum set only one criterion for the graphic novels that they commissioned. The museum required that the novel focus its story line on the museum and its art collection and not simply use the museum as a setting for a novel. Each novelist commissioned to write for the series was given a day to conduct research in the museum and find the topic of his novel. Crécy found the museum's collection overwhelming. As he viewed the breadth of the collection and the diverse cultures, art, civilizations, and artistic styles represented, he was acutely aware of his own inability to comprehend so much art and culture about which he had incomplete knowledge.

In *Glacial Period*, he portrays a group of individuals confronted with the art of past civilizations with which they are unfamiliar. The story is set thousands of years in the future after Earth has experienced a long glacial period that has separated human beings from their history. Crécy presents a team of archaeologists composed of human academics and genetically engineered dogs, who have time-sensitive noses capable of dating artifacts and who speak human language; the team is exploring Europe, known as the frozen continent, to find evidence of the pre-ice age civilization.

There is considerable discord among the team members as they battle the freezing temperatures and cross wide expanses of frozen wasteland. A series of confrontations among Gregor, the team leader, and other team members, including the historian Paul, Hulk, Juliette, and Joseph, occur on the journey. The confrontations are motivated by professional jealousy and competition, by discriminatory disdain for other species, and by romantic interests in Juliette. The group discovers the Rungis wholesale food market covered with graffiti and mistake it for a temple and the graffiti for religious inscriptions. Gregor leaves Paul and part of the team to study the "temple," while Paul, Juliette, Esteban, and Joseph, accompanied by the three dogs, continue their trek.

Hulk gets lost, finds the museum, and discovers rooms full of statues. The statues begin to talk to him. They eventually tell him that the museum is about to collapse into a subterranean chasm. The statues see him as their savior sent to help them escape. Hulk devises a plan for escape. The art is to make a transgenerational effort, creating one large piece of art and thus acquiring the necessary force of propulsion to flee. Meanwhile, Gregor, Juliette, Joseph, and Esteban have reached the Louvre and entered the rooms housing the paintings. They speculate about the meaning of the art and come up with all sorts of wrong ideas.

The ground begins to break up, and the group members are separated. Gregor encounters Harmenz, the creature of *The Skinned Ox* painting; he kills Gregor. Hulk sends the Bes statue to get Juliette and Joseph. They escape on the back of the art beast, which is a large dog. Paul, the historian, has arrived and is surrounded by artistic representations of Jesus that have fled the museum because of the pagan deities. The novel ends with Paul watching the art beast running off into the distance, to a new life for the art.

While the plot of Crécy's novel deals with serious issues, he enriches it with humor through both the dialogue and the drawings. Much of the humor comes from the misinterpretations of the archaeologists. They believe the museum is a private mansion belonging to artist Eugène Delacroix when they find the *Smoking Turk* painting with the nameplate "Delacroix." Esteban

---

Nicolas de Crécy

Having graduated from the comics school in Angoulême, France, Nicolas de Crécy worked briefly as an animator for Disney before publishing his first graphic novel *Foligatto* (written by Tjoyas) in 1991. His series with writer and later filmmaker Sylvain Chomet, *Léon la came*, was serialized in *(À Suivre)* and collected in three volumes, the second of which was awarded the prize for best album at the Angoulême Festival in 1998. That same year he collaborated with Chomet on the short film *La vieille dame et les pigeons*, which was nominated for an Academy Award. De Crécy has worked in a variety of visual styles, including fully painted art (*Foligatto* and *Bibendum céleste*), black-and-white pen drawings (*M. Fruit*) and pen drawings with watercolor wash (*Léon la came*). In 2009 he published *Période glaciaire* conjointly with the Louvre Museum in Paris, which also exhibited his original art. He is one of the most distinctive draftsmen working in comics, with a tremblingly thin line and often grotesque or bizarre human figures.

Glacial Period is one of four graphic novels commissioned by the Louvre Museum in Paris, France, showcasing the museum's art collection. (Mario Goldman/AFP/Getty Images)

believes the pyramid in the Louvre courtyard is an igloo. They speculate that the paintings and other icons were intended for them. The squabbling among the art pieces also adds humor, as do the commentaries of Hulk and the other dogs about being hungry and about being ill-adapted for distance trekking on skis in frigid weather.

Characters

- *Hulk*, the protagonist, is a genetically engineered pig-dog with a time-sensitive nose. He is essential to the mission. He is in love with Juliette but realizes that their being members of different species prevents a relationship between them. He is highly aware of Gregor's disdain for nonhumans and resents the way he treats him and orders him about.
- *Juliette*, a.k.a. *Ma'am*, a member of the archaeology team and daughter of the financial backer of the mission, is fond of Hulk and values him for both his friendship and his expertise.
- *Gregor*, the team leader, is an abrasive, dictatorial individual with little respect for others.
- *Joseph* is a team member extremely concerned about his future glory and is eager to publish.
- *Paul* is the team historian and believes himself to be essential to the mission.
- *Esteban*, another team member, discovers the pyramid in the courtyard of the Louvre.
- *Firedog* is the first artwork to speak to Hulk. He thinks Hulk is a pig. He frightens him at first.
- *Rhyton*, an ancient Cretan vase in the shape of a bull's head, explains the screaming Hulk heard.
- *Pig*, a.k.a. *Vattier de Bourville*, is another of the artifacts involved in the initial conversation with Hulk.
- *Pierre Séguier*, chancellor of France, painted by Charles Le Brun, recounts the Nazi invasion and how the works were saved. He says they were more valued than the lives of the human populace.
- *The Cat Goddess Bast* tells Hulk he is the savior of the artifacts and must get them to safety.
- *Harmensz* is the subject of the painting *The Skinned Ox*. It is his screams that Hulk hears.

Harmensz kills Gregor and then returns to his canvas to find peace.

Artistic Style

In *Glacial Period*, Crécy masterfully brings together two different worlds of art, that of the Louvre and that of the graphic novel, by interspersing panels featuring reproductions of the museum's paintings with panels of his own work and by creating panels that feature the museum's paintings and statues and also characters drawn by him. The contrast among the art styles serves to emphasize the theme of his story, that the civilization trapped in the frozen continent of Europe is far removed from that of the team of explorers.

Crécy uses almost no author commentary to impart information to the reader. Physical location, time lapse, and relationships between one event and another are all expressed either in the dialogue among the individuals or in the use of color to indicate night or day, atmospheric conditions, and physical surrounding, such as the museum interiors or the chasm into which Juliette and Joseph fall. The only author commentary that he uses is to indicate the cracking and settling of the land and buildings surrounding the characters. Crécy uses a murky, muted mixing of color, which reflects the frozen wasteland in which the characters find themselves and the confused state of mind of the explorers as they confront the Louvre and its artworks.

Crécy relies heavily on the drawing of facial expressions to convey much of the intrigue of his story. The character of Gregor is depicted with a variety of facial expressions, including arrogance, anger, a state near dementia, and fear. Hulk is also given a wide range of both facial expression and body language in his depiction. In true dog fashion, Hulk's ears reveal his interests, anger, and fear. The visual humor of the novel also results primarily from the depiction of the dogs. They have a strong resemblance to pigs, especially when portrayed from the rear or lying on their sides or stomachs. In addition, the use of a light pink coloring further emphasizes their genetic altering with pig genes.

Themes

The major theme of the novel deals with the function of art. Crécy questions the notion that art can be preserved by and transmitted from one civilization to another. The misinterpretations and assumptions made by the team of archaeologists, who apply their own prejudices and reactions to the art they discover in the Louvre, suggest strongly that only the civilization that created the art understands its meaning. They are certain the paintings they find are evidence of an oral culture that lacked a writing system and used images to communicate. Viewing a number of nude paintings, Joseph is certain the museum was a brothel.

This theme is related to a second theme of the graphic novel. The art becomes alive and speaks only to the dog Hulk, with the exception of Bes, who speaks with Juliette and Joseph when he is sent to find them. Hulk's reaction to the art is different from that of the human beings. He sniffs and investigates but does not immediately begin to impose his interpretation. If this is the result of his lack of human arrogance and sense of superiority, it is not definitely stated. However, tension between species and barriers between the human species and others are both themes explored by Crécy.

From the beginning of the novel, Crécy portrays an antagonistic relationship between Hulk and Gregor. To Gregor, Hulk is a dog to be ordered about, disdained, and used. Hulk confronts Gregor about his attitude and reminds him of his importance to the mission, which is, in his and Juliette's opinion, equal to or greater than Gregor's. Hulk and Juliette have a close friendship; however, Hulk is bothered by the limitation on their relationship caused by his appearance. Juliette cannot fully love him because he is not human. Once inside the Louvre, Hulk comments on the violence and cruelty of human beings to animals, as he views statues of *The Rustic Skinner* and *Child with Goose*. Hulk hears horrible screams and eventually is told that it is Harmensz, subject of *The Skinned Ox*, being skinned alive. Harmensz has his vengeance as he leaves his canvas and kills Gregor.

The academic propensity to self-centeredness and self-aggrandizement is the third theme explored by Crécy. Paul, Esteban, and Joseph are preoccupied with publishing their findings and theories and gaining recognition.

Impact

Crécy's *Glacial Period* has had a significant impact on the acceptance of the graphic novel in the greater art world as an alternate art form with an aesthetic quality and value of its own. The work has enjoyed immense public success, especially in France, and has validated the Louvre's decision to bring the graphic novel into its collections and exhibits. Crécy's novel is the first of the graphic novels to ally the popular art form, the *bande dessinée*, with the high art of the museum.

In conjunction with the other three novels of the series—*The Museum Vaults—Excerpts from the Journal of an Expert*, *On the Odd Hours*, and *The Sky over the Louvre*—the novel has brought the Louvre into the field of graphic novel publication. In addition to the four graphic novels originally commissioned by the museum, Musée du Louvre Editions has also published Japanese graphic novelist Hirohiko Araki's manga novel *Rohan at the Louvre*.

Shawncey Jay Webb

Further Reading

Carrière, Jean-Louis, and Bernard Yslaire. *The Sky over the Louvre* (2011).

Crécy, Nicolas de. *Salvatore* (2011).

Liberge, Eric. *On the Odd Hours* (2010).

Mathieu, Marc-Antoine. *The Museum Vaults: Excerpts from the Journal of an Expert* (2007).

Bibliography

Dauncey, Hugh, ed. *French Popular Culture: An Introduction*. New York: Oxford University Press, 2003.

Fosdick, Charles, Laurence Grove, and Libbie McQuilan, eds. *The Francophone Bande Dessinée*. New York: Rodopi, 2005.

McKinney, Mark, ed. *History and Politics in French Language Comics and Graphic Novels*. Jackson: University Press of Mississippi, 2008.

See also: *Embroideries; Epileptic; The Adventures of Tintin*

GOLEM'S MIGHTY SWING, THE

Author: Sturm, James
Artist: James Sturm (illustrator)
Publisher: Drawn and Quarterly
First book publication: 2001

Publication History

The Golem's Mighty Swing was first published in paperback and cloth in 2001 by Drawn and Quarterly in Montreal. It was reprinted in 2003. Four years later, Drawn and Quarterly republished it along with two other of James Sturm's graphic novellas, *The Revival*, originally published in 1996, and *Hundreds of Feet Below Daylight*, originally published in 1998. These three novels were collected in a single volume entitled *James Sturm's America: God, Gold, and Golems*. *The Golem's Mighty Swing* has been translated into Spanish, French, and Polish editions.

Plot

The Golem's Mighty Swing tells the story of a barnstorming Jewish baseball team, the Stars of David, that travels throughout the Midwest in the early 1920's. The plot is told primarily, but not exclusively, through the narrative voice of Noah Strauss, a former outfielder for the Boston Red Sox who left the major leagues because he could not obtain a starting job and because of his weak knees. The Stars of David play approximately 160 baseball games a year, traveling 20,000 miles annually in their old, beat-up, and unreliable bus.

The members of the team are routinely subjected to anti-Semitic comments and discrimination from fans, townspeople (including children), and even umpires. When the team members eat in restaurants, they often must sit in the back of the establishment because they are Jewish. The only one who does not experience this discrimination is the team's sole black player, Henry Bell, who, because of his celebrity status among black fans, eats free in their homes. The team wins a majority of its games but flounders financially because of low attendance and unfavorable business deals. Although they do not make much money, they get to play the game they love, and, as

The Golem's Mighty Swing. (Courtesy of Drawn and Quarterly)

Strauss stresses, it is better to play baseball for a living than be a pushcart peddler or a sweatshop tailor like his father.

When the team's bus breaks down in Cedar Falls, Iowa, and Strauss realizes that he has difficulty affording the repairs, thus endangering the team's ability to show up at future games (such as the upcoming games in Putnam and Rockford), he reluctantly resorts to enlisting the help of baseball promoter Victor L. Paige. After an earlier game, Paige had offered to promote the Stars of David baseball games in exchange for a cut and suggested that Bell dress as a golem (a huge, dangerous supernatural figure from Jewish mysticism) to draw bigger crowds. A large first baseman formerly of the Negro Leagues, Bell agrees to dress as a golem for higher pay.

The advertisements featuring a Jewish team with a golem player work both for and against the team: The stadium in Putnam is packed, but the advertisements also incite fear, ethnic hatred, and even hysteria in the townspeople. The *Putnam Post Bugle* claims that the Jews must be defeated for the good of the soul of the United States. Hoping to attract more fans to the Stars of David game, Paige publishes an article in the Putnam newspaper warning the male citizens to hide their women. Paige fails to realize or does not care that his article, coupled with rampant anti-Semitism, will lead to a riot. The mean-spirited fans attack the Jewish players, who are saved by Bell as the golem and then by a torrential downpour, which cancels the game and allows the team to escape to another town.

The story ends ten years after the Putnam game. Strauss mentions that the Stars of David played another four years before disbanding. Strauss has retired from baseball because his knees gave out, and his brother Mo has moved to Tarrytown and gotten married. While in Greenville, North Carolina, Strauss learns of a baseball game between professional athletes, called the Big Leagues, and amateurs, dressed in rural farmer costumes, who call themselves the Hay Seeds. Moonshine Mullins, the Hay Seeds's alcoholic manager, entertains the fans by getting drunk and attacking umpires. During the game, a fan is brought onto the field to play. This is yet another spectacle put on by Paige. Strauss is disgusted by how Paige's antics make a mockery of baseball, yet he finds himself attracted to the buffoonery.

Characters

- *Noah Strauss*, a.k.a. *the Zion Lion*, the main character and narrator, is the third baseman and manager for the Stars of David. A former member of the Boston Red Sox, he is emotionally strong and calm, but his knees hurt him so badly that he can barely run.
- *Moishe Strauss*, a.k.a. *Mo*, Strauss's sixteen-year-old brother, is a talented second baseman but overly emotional. He wears shoe polish on his face to pretend he has a beard. Children attack him after the game in Forest Hills.
- *Buttercup Lev*, a slow-ball pitcher for the team, throws sidearm and relies on guile and location

James Sturm

In the 1990's, James Sturm was known as the creator of *The Cereal Killings*, a work serialized by Fantagraphics but never collected in book form. While working as the artistic director of Seattle's weekly newspaper *The Stranger*, he turned his attention to comics detailing American history, publishing *The Revival* with his own Bear Bones Press in 1996. *Hundreds of Feet Below Daylight* (1998) and *The Golem's Mighty Swing* (2001) completed his American history trilogy, with books about mining and a Jewish barnstorming baseball team, respectively. In 2003 he wrote the acclaimed Fantastic Four miniseries *Unstable Molecules* for Marvel Comics, positing a connection between the fictional Storm family and the real-life Sturms. In 2004 he founded the Center for Cartoon Studies in White River Junction, Vermont, a master's degree program teaching comics. For that institution he wrote *Satchel Paige: Striking Out Jim Crow* (2007), which was drawn by Rich Tommaso. In 2010 he published *Market Day*, a work set in eastern Europe during the early 1900's about the collision of old world values and increasing industrialization.

to compensate for his lack of a fastball. He is an alcoholic and gets beaten up by anti-Semites before a game against the Putnam All-Americans.
- *Henry Bell*, a.k.a. *Hershl Bloom*, is an African American pretending to be a Jew from the lost tribes of Israel to play with the Stars of David. He is a first baseman and pitcher. A favorite among the black fans, he played for twenty years in the Negro Leagues for the Chicago Unions. He plays the golem and saves the team during the Putnam game.
- *Victor Paige*, an unscrupulous promoter, works for the Big Inning Promotional Agency, a sports-marketing company based in Chicago. He compliments Strauss for having a talented team yet knows little about baseball. His agency procured the golem costume worn in the 1915 German silent film *Der Golem* (the golem), and he persuades Strauss to dress Henry Bell as a golem to attract more fans.

Artistic Style

The artwork in *The Golem's Mighty Swing* is simple, clean, and sparse, but not necessarily minimalist. The focus of Sturm's graphic novel is squarely on the prose, with artwork supporting but not detracting from the text. Sturm's drawings primarily use black and white, with a sepia-tinted color for background. This use of color helps create the environment or set the mood, which constitutes a significant part of the baseball game and eliminates the need for shading.

As would be expected, many panels are devoted to the baseball games, particularly the relationship between the batter and the pitcher. The drawings of the baseballs differ markedly in size, showing the distance the ball has been hit, its trajectory, and the perspective of the character viewing the ball. This is especially true when Bell bats. Sturm devotes ten panels to a Bell

home run to show different perspectives, including the reactions of the fans, Strauss, Paige, and Bell himself. From the home-plate perspective, the ball realistically appears large when it leaves the bat (in fact, it is above the clouds in one panel) but seems far smaller when it drops over the fence. When Strauss hits the ball against Putnam pitcher Mickey McFadden, Sturm places the baseball inside the "O" in "WHOP," cleverly indicating the strength with which Strauss hit it and giving the panel a cartoonish feel. Sturm also shows how slowly Lev pitches by drawing a large baseball with clearly delineated seams, indicating that the ball seems large to the batter because of its lack of velocity.

When an anti-Semite in Putnam rails against the Jews playing, Sturm draws him as a caricature, with his large mouth wide open in every panel, showing only four teeth. His hair stands up, and his ears are large.

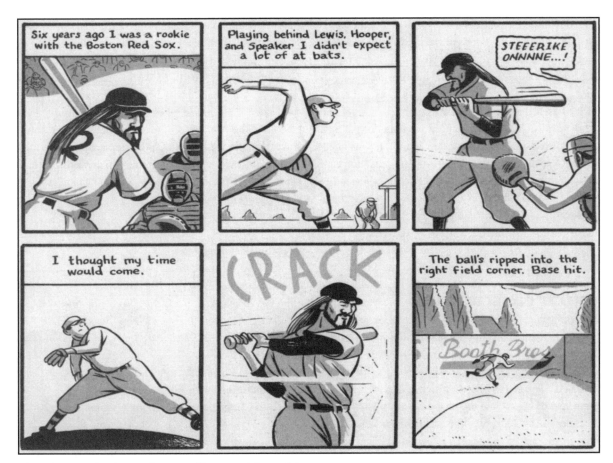

The Golem's Mighty Swing. (Courtesy of Drawn and Quarterly)

Sturm draws the character as almost half man, half gorilla; through this caricature, Sturm demonstrates that anti-Semitism is a subhuman characteristic.

Themes

A tribute to the dedicated but largely unrewarded barnstorming teams of the 1920's and the talented Negro League teams that persevered through great hardships, *The Golem's Mighty Swing* is notable for its treatment of racism and prejudice against both Jews and African Americans and for its consideration of spectacle in sports.

The Golem's Mighty Swing is also concerned with Jewish identity and anti-Semitism. Strauss, an ethnic and cultural Jew, struggles with his identity as a Jewish baseball player. He loves the game and expresses happiness that he is not a sweatshop tailor like his father, yet he believes that he has betrayed his Jewish faith by playing baseball, particularly on the Sabbath. Similarly, the Jewish players wear beards to look like religious Jews; even the youngest, Mo, must wear a beard, but because he is only sixteen, his beard consists of shoe polish. The beards are a gimmick, as is Paige's idea of Bell masquerading as a golem. This ploy can work because, according to the story, many of the fans in the Midwest had not seen a Jew before; for instance, Forest Grove resident Hetty Douglas does not care about baseball but attends the game so that she can see what Jews look like. Boys in Forest Grove throw rocks at Mo to knock off his cap so they can see the horns they believe grow on the heads of Jews. Through these characters and their actions, Sturm illustrates the anti-Semitic prejudice that was rampant in the Midwest at this time.

Because the Stars of David are a barnstorming team, all their games are away games; they are never the home team. This may be an allusion to the "wandering Jew," a nomadic person who is never at home or at peace, or a reference to Philip Roth's *The Great American Novel* (1973), in which a Jewish baseball team spends all its time on the road.

Sturm also addresses the issue of spectacle. Although the act of the team members wearing beards seems fine on the surface, Sturm shows how spectacle can go too far, with the concept of the golem. Sturm employs this religious mysticism effectively when the concept of the golem incites the anti-Semitism in Putnam. A game that would ordinarily contain mean-spirited racial and ethnic epithets transforms, because of the spectacle, into a riot that might have caused someone to be killed if not for divine intervention (the torrential downpour). Sturm concludes with his objection to spectacle in the third and last section, in which Paige has successfully turned a pure sport into an unworthy sideshow, thereby debasing the game.

Impact

The Golem's Mighty Swing (2001) brought a focus on baseball, Jewish culture, and historical fiction to the graphic novel. Artist Rich Tommaso claims that this novel influenced him a great deal when he prepared to collaborate with Sturm on their graphic novel about Satchel Paige, a record-setting African American pitcher who played for the Negro Leagues.

As the last part of a trilogy, *The Golem's Mighty Swing* reflects elements of Sturm's two preceding graphic novellas. All three works are about desperate times in American history, from 1801 (in *The Revival*) to 1886 (in *Hundreds of Feet Below Daylight*) to the 1920's. The themes of the American pioneer spirit, thirst for money, racism, and dreams of success permeate all three works by Sturm, which were gathered into the 2007 collection *James Sturm's America: God, Gold, and Golems*.

Eric Sterling

Further Reading

Gotto, Ray. *Cotton Woods: The Comic Strip Adventures of a Baseball Natural* (1991).

Stamaty, Mark Alan. *Too Many Time Machines: Or, the Incredible Story of How I Went Back in Time, Met Babe Ruth, and Discovered the Secret of Home Run Hitting* (1999).

Sturm, James. *James Sturm's America: God, Gold, and Golems* (2007).

_____. *Satchel Paige: Striking Out Jim Crow* (2007).

Bibliography

Arnold, Andrew D. "Out of the Ballpark." Review of *The Golem's Mighty Swing* by James Sturm. *Time,*

August 17, 2001. http://www.time.com/time/arts/article/0,8599,171550,00.html

Badman, Derik A. "The Golem's Mighty Swing." Review of *The Golem's Mighty Swing* by James Sturm. *MadInkBeard*, March 3, 2008. http://madinkbeard.com/archives/the-golems-mighty-swing

Goodman, George. "The Golem's Mighty Swing." Review of *The Golem's Mighty Swing* by James Sturm. *NINE: A Journal of Baseball History and Culture* 13, no. 1 (Fall, 2004): 149-151.

Harde, Roxanne. "'Give 'Em Another Circumcision': Jewish Masculinities in *The Golem's Mighty Swing*." In *The Jewish Graphic Novel: Critical Approaches*, edited by Samantha Baskind and Ranen Omer-Sherman. New Brunswick, N.J.: Rutgers University Press, 2008.

See also: *Maus: A Survivor's Tale; A Jew in Communist Prague; The Jew of New York*

GOOD-BYE, CHUNKY RICE

Author: Thompson, Craig
Artist: Craig Thompson (illustrator)
Publisher: Top Shelf Comics
First book publication: 1999

Publication History

The genesis of *Good-Bye, Chunky Rice* was a series of short, autobiographical sketches that Thompson wrote to relieve his own homesickness after moving to Portland. Thompson worked on what would become his first book while doing illustrations for Dark Horse Comics and Top Shelf Productions, among other publishers. The final work, strongly influenced by his childhood love for Jim Henson and Dr. Seuss, was published by Top Shelf in 1999, quickly earning him critical, if not commercial, success. It was only after the success of his second book, *Blankets* (2005), that *Chunky Rice* became better known; it was then acquired by Pantheon Books.

Plot

As the story opens, Chunky Rice, a small turtle, is preparing to leave home and his love, the glassy-eyed deer mouse Dandel. Chunky Rice clearly has misgivings about moving on but reluctantly tells Dandel that "my home is on my back." For unknown reasons, he has decided to venture to the "Kahootney Islands" on a ship chartered by a local seaman, Captain Chuck. Chuck's brother, Solomon, cheerfully helps Chunky Rice carry his belongings to the ship, telling stories of his childhood that soon become significant to the story. While Chunky Rice is preparing to abandon Dandel, Solomon hastens to return to his own "love," a pet bird named Merle. After Chunky Rice departs, Captain Chuck convinces him to abandon all his useless belongings (though he ends up pocketing them himself) and ushers him aboard.

On board, Chunky Rice meets his fellow travelers Ruth and Livonia. The sisters are conjoined twins, though Ruth is a little person and Livonia is of average height (Ruth perches awkwardly in a high chair beside Livonia). They are clearly running away from

Good-Bye, Chunky Rice. (Courtesy of Pantheon Books)

problems of their own, though nothing of their history is revealed to Chunky Rice.

As a paying passenger, Chunky Rice is given the "privilege" of doing chores for Captain Chuck, and while working in the hold, he finds all his abandoned belongings. While Chunky Rice is reading old comics and reminiscing about Dandel, the ship is hit by a terrible storm that floods the decks and nearly capsizes the vessel. The storm subsides, and Chunky Rice emerges shaken, but only until he hears the radio belting out a Motown tune. For the first time in the novel, Chunky Rice abandons himself to the bliss of the moment and dances with the twins. After dancing, he finds a live fish, which has been washed on the deck by the storm; encouraged to throw it overboard, he watches the sea swallow it up. The frame pans out, and the sea becomes a bottle of water, which Dandel is holding as she prepares to send a "message in bottle" to Chunky Rice.

The substories of the book, artfully connected to the main narrative, follow Dandel's attempts to lure Chunky Rice home and Solomon's search for his missing bird, Merle. The reader also learns the story behind Chuck's curious indifference to Solomon. As children, Chuck blamed his younger brother for allowing their father to drown their dog's puppies in a river. Solomon went his own way, marrying himself to the sea, while Solomon remained home, finding companionship with an injured bird. In a parallel to Chunky Rice, Merle's wings heal, and she momentarily joins a flock of seagulls. She ultimately returns, perhaps suggesting Dandel's last words in the novel, "There is no good-bye, Chunky Rice." Indeed, in the last panel, one of Dandel's bottles "clunks" against the bow of the ship, having already found Chunky Rice.

Good-Bye, Chunky Rice. (Courtesy of Pantheon Books)

Characters

- *Chunky Rice*, in appearance a childlike "man turtle," is an artistic, highly sentimental character, whose chief dialogue is internal. In some ways, he resembles a character in a silent film, who speaks more with his gestures and eyes. Only around Dandel does he express himself verbally, though these passages are relatively brief, as they occur in his reminiscences aboard the ship.

- *Dandel*, Chunky Rice's romantic interest, is a small white "woman mouse" in appearance, with large, marblelike eyes. She often speaks for Chunky Rice and knows how to get him talking. Though obviously deeply in love with Chunky Rice, she is unable to follow him on his journey, even when he asks her to do just that. Nevertheless, she encourages his quixotic adventure of self-discovery to the Kahootney Islands.

- *Solomon* is a profound character in his own right (though initially providing comic relief) and a "double" to Dandel and Chunky Rice. Physically, he resembles a grizzled dockworker, with a large head (on which he always wears a cap), slightly oversized clothing, and a T-shirt that seems to read "Jesus Saves" (the script is always cut off by his jacket). Solomon's most pronounced characteristic is his quaint "pirate" speech, which hides his clever insights behind a veil of buffoonery.

- *Captain Chuck*, a lifelong seaman, is like his brother in that his gruff, lusty exterior hides the pain beneath. Only to the sea can he open his heart and express his true wonder for life, love, and creation.

- *Ruth and Livonia*, conjoined twins, are seemingly ill-matched in every way possible: They are different sizes, have different tastes (one smokes, one does not), and even sleep at different times. As a counterpoint to Chunky Rice, they are content with their lot and are no longer searching for meaning; they have found it in each other.

Artistic Style

There is no mistaking Thompson's work for that of another artist, and yet, the style of *Good-Bye, Chunky Rice* differs strikingly from his more famous work, *Blankets*. Perhaps in homage to childhood itself, the characters conjure up a world of talking animals and grotesque humans, part dream, part reality. As characters, Chunky Rice and Dandel could inhabit any Sunday morning comic strip, minus the clichéd punch lines. There is an overriding sense of cuteness and sentimentality in Thompson's work that is entirely appropriate in this context.

Perhaps the most refreshing element of Thompson's style is his courage to explore the metaphor of "cuteness," or what might more appropriately be called the icons of childhood. *Chunky Rice* can be read as a grown-up *Peanuts*, perhaps; a story of what Charlie Brown does when he falls in love and decides to make it in the outside world.

Cuteness aside, the most striking quality of Thompson's artwork is its sumptuousness; flipping to any random page reveals sweeping vistas of black and white, embellished throughout with striking details that repay several readings. A typical example occurs on pages 118-119, where the reader sees Chuck and Chunky leaning against the railing of the ship, taking in the grandeur of the ocean. The clean "white" space of the ship and the characters is contrasted vividly by the dramatically dark rolling waves all around them. Page 118 is a splash page, which is foiled by the following page (the two pages connect, as if to suggest one unified image), which has three long frames, each one slowly zooming out to show the immensity of the water. The waves are drawn with incredible detail, as if to suggest the reality that peeks behind the "cartoon" metaphor.

Aesthetically, the drawings are quite beautiful, but Thompson never settles for surface charm; with each pan out, the story comes into clearer focus. On the following pages, the ship has become a mere embellishment on the shifting, volatile pattern of the ocean, until it disappears entirely by the second frame. Here Thompson plays with impressionism itself, suggesting that the ocean is as much within as without. On page 121, the ocean assumes an oval shape, becoming smaller and smaller, until it fits in a single bottle of water—the water carried by Dandel as she prepares to send a new message to Chunky. These illustrations are entirely wordless, which attests to the power of Thompson's imagery. His metaphors speak clearly through his sharp, though seductive drawings, always lifting the cartoon mask to peer at the people beneath.

Themes

The central theme of the book is the experience of loss, both when something one loves is taken away and when one has to choose to leave something behind, for whatever reason. Though Chunky seemingly has everything he needs, he is built for adventure and travel (his home is on his back, after all). In essence, can one ever appreciate home (and those one loves) without ever leaving it and them? Is home a physical place or a state of being? Clearly Dandel, Solomon, and Captain Chuck have all found this sense of home; the harder part is finding someone with whom to share it. Chuck has lost his wife, Glenda, and his new wife lacks his appreciation of the sea (she seems to stay below deck most of the time, emerging only to cook dinner). Dandel realizes that her sense of self is drained of meaning without Chunky; the sea reflects isolation rather than comfort, which she vainly tries to fill up with bottles. Even Solomon needs the comforting chirps of Merle to fill his days. Does life go on without the very thing that makes it worth living?

The book never reaches a definitive conclusion, nor does Chunky ever reach the Kahootney Islands (a name which sounds suspiciously like "hooey," perhaps suggesting their illusory quality). Each stage of his brief voyage is punctuated by the baggage he brings along. Even when his belongings are more or less stolen from him by Captain Chuck, they all come back to him, reminding him of who he is and what he has left behind. As a young "man," Chunky feels that the voyage out will be forever, turning his back once and for all on his former life. Dandel knows better, as her persistent bottles attest. Chunky's mythic adventure to unknown lands will ultimately lead him back home, or at least to those elements of home that will always be part of him.

The sense of homecoming is echoed by other characters in the book, most notably in the twins. Indeed, despite their forced connection, they are still able to maintain separate identities and lives. In one passage, as Ruth falls asleep, Livonia calmly lights a cigarette and explains that Ruth always dozes off a few hours earlier than she does, providing Livonia with some peace and quiet. Each person in a relationship needs time alone. For Ruth and Livonia, it lasts a few hours; for Chunky, a few months or years. Every hero, from Odysseus onward, has to return home, and the bottle Chunky finds in the last panel foreshadows this conclusion. Nothing ends, whether in life or death; the world is continually made new through relationships and discoveries.

Impact

Following its publication, *Good-Bye, Chunky Rice* won considerable critical acclaim, with a Harvey Award and an Ignatz Award nomination. Even Alan Moore, one the most discerning critics on the comic books scene, in a quote found in the jacket of the novel, called the work "both funny and genuinely touching . . . an affecting meditation upon friendship, loneliness, and loss, all delivered with a real feel for the musicality of the comic strip form." It took the subsequent success of *Blankets*, however, to make *Chunky Rice* a commercial success. After several printings of the book by Top Shelf, Pantheon acquired the rights to the novel and published a lavish new edition, clearly positioning it in the context of *Blankets*. However, the critical success alone was sufficient to open many doors for Thompson, and while writing *Blankets* (which took several years), he worked for *Nickelodeon* magazine and pursued other projects for Top Shelf. The ambitious artwork and storytelling of *Good-Bye, Chunky Rice* foreshadows *Blankets* and *Habibi*, forthcoming as of 2011.

Joshua Grasso

Further Reading

Blain, Christophe. *Isaac the Pirate: To Exotic Lands* (2003).

Smith, Jeff. *Bone: The Complete Cartoon Epic in One Volume* (2004).

Thompson, Craig. *Blankets* (2005).

_____. *Carnet de Voyage* (2004).

Bibliography

Gravett, Paul. *Graphic Novels: Everything You Need To Know*. New York: Collins Designs, 2005

Thompson, Craig. "Interview with Craig Thompson, Parts 1 and 2." Interview by Brian Heater. *The Daily Cross Hatch*, May 28, 2007.

See also: *Blankets; Ghost World*

H

HARD BOILED

Author: Miller, Frank
Artist: Geof Darrow (illustrator); Claude Legris (colorist); John Workman (letterer)
Publisher: Dark Horse Comics
First serial publication: 1990-1992
First book publication: 1993

Publication History

Originally serialized as three separate volumes, *Hard Boiled* was published by Dark Horse Comics. *Hard Boiled,* issue 1, was released in September, 1990, followed by *Hard Boiled,* issue 2, in December, 1990. The series was not completed until the release of *Hard Boiled,* issue 3, in March, 1992. The work was a collaborative effort between author Frank Miller and artist Geof Darrow.

Miller was best known for his successful runs at both Marvel Comics and DC Comics, revolutionizing the superhero genre with his 1979-1983 work on Marvel Comics' *Daredevil* and on DC Comics' *The Dark Knight Returns* (1986). Darrow was previously known for his work with French comics writer Moebius, who inspired much of his highly detailed style and influenced his cyberpunk flourishes. Although Miller initially scripted the work, Darrow took liberties with the script in his illustrations. Miller then reinterpreted his script for the final product. The gap between issues is partially attributed to Miller's work from 1991 to 1992 on *Sin City* (1991-2000) and to Darrow's European-influenced artistic work ethic, taking months at a time to produce his illustrations. Following Miller's departure from DC Comics in 1988 over a censorship dispute, Miller and Darrow came together at Dark Horse Comics with the purpose of pushing the boundaries of what could be depicted in mainstream comics.

Geoff Darrow with Jada Pinkett Smith. (Getty Images)

Geoff Darrow

Though he has produced only a small amount of comics art, Geoff Darrow is among the most distinctive artists working in the field. After publishing a series of stories featuring *Bourbon Thret* in France, Darrow undertook two collaborations with writer Frank Miller. *Hard Boiled*, about a homicidal cyborg tax collector, reveled in gratuitous violence, while *Big Guy and Rusty the Boy Robot* parodied the conventions of Japanese monster movies and manga. After collaborating on the *Matrix* films, Darrow worked with the Wachowski brothers on the seven-issue *Shaolin Cowboy* series. Darrow's art is renowned for its ridiculously high levels of detail, in which images are packed solid with characters and backgrounds. He draws figures with extremely thin, clean lines that highlight his compositional skills, while also downplaying the distinction between characters and their settings. Despite his fascination with outrageous violence, Darrow's art is characterized by a very elegant sense of design.

Plot

Hard Boiled tells the story of Nixon, an assassin android working for Willeford Home Appliances in a futuristic Los Angeles. The graphic novel begins as Norman, a member of the Willeford group, panics over Nixon's most recent assassination attempt, one that has quickly escalated out of control. Nixon is causing a wave of public destruction as he attempts to take down his target. He is rammed by a car but continues to fight despite his intense injuries, killing his target in the process. Norman sends a repair crew to Nixon, which brings him back to the Willeford building and operates on him with a combination of human medical and mechanical-repair techniques. Nixon awakens in his Burbank home lying next to his wife, thinking that the previous experience had been a dream. He returns to sleep, continuing to have nightmares about the experience he is unsure he had.

In the morning, Nixon drives across Los Angeles, referring to himself as Carl Seltz, an insurance investigator. He pursues a car that he believes holds a person committing insurance fraud. Following a chase and a series of crashes, both cars become unusable, and Nixon continues to pursue his target on foot. Nixon sees that the person he is pursuing is an elderly woman, later revealed to be named Blanche, who is holding a child captive. The child claims to be Christie, an innocent girl in need of help. Nixon eventually retrieves Christie and creates an explosion to serve as a cover for his escape from Blanche. He steals a police car and drives away with Christie, only to be ripped out of the car by Blanche. The two engage in hand-to-hand combat. Nixon detonates a grenade in her body and escapes again.

Nixon walks to a junkyard, where Blanche and Christie find him. Blanche removes her human vestiges and reveals herself to be an android. She tells Nixon that he is also an android, which he refuses to believe. She conveys her disdain for the human race and implores him to join her in her cause against their makers at Willeford. He responds by destroying her. Christie makes clear that she too is an android and that their race is doomed because of his refusal to accept reality. A watchdog from Willeford destroys Christie to silence her. After an attempt to make himself appear human proves futile, Nixon takes a train home.

While sitting on the train, he sees the Willeford brand marking on his left arm and finally acknowledges his android self. The watchdog shows him the way to Willeford Home Appliances, where he kills all people present except for Mr. Willeford and his assistant. Mr. Willeford captures Nixon and begins to disassemble him. However, Nixon agrees to continue to be Willeford's assassin if he can have his mind returned to his previous ignorance as an android believing he is human. Nixon returns home to his family, reformatted and unaware of the graphic novel's events.

Characters

- *Nixon*, a.k.a. *Carl Seltz*, the protagonist, is an assassin android built by Willeford to murder the corporation's competitors. Although other androids refer to him as Nixon, he is programmed to believe that he is insurance investigator Carl Seltz, married, a father of two children, and living in Burbank. A malfunctioning unit, he continuously shifts his identity in name and occupation. His only constant is a belief that he is and desires to be human. He is also referred to as Harry Burns and Unit Four.
- *Blanche*, the antagonist, is the previous year's model android built by Willeford. She has defected from the company. Initially appearing as an overweight, elderly woman, she engages Nixon in combat in an attempt to make him realize he is an android and to join her cause to destroy Willeford. She is also known as Unit Two.
- *Barbara* is an android working for Willeford. She is fully cognizant of her status as an android and only wears human clothing on the lower half of her body. She is secretly working in support of Blanche's cause to overthrow Willeford's corporation.
- *Mr. Willeford* is the owner of Willeford Home Appliances and the creator of Nixon and his fellow androids. He is obese to the point of having almost no independent motor control over his own body. He relies on the use of mechanized

devices to perform all tasks. He lives in the Willeford Home Appliances building.

- *Becky Seltz* is Nixon's wife and the mother of his two children. She is aware that her husband is actually an android, and it is suggested that she is employed by Willeford as well. She uses her sexuality to prevent Nixon from recalling or pondering his android state.
- *Christie* is an android built by Willeford. She appears as a blond-haired child, playing a part in Blanche's plan by luring Nixon in as she pretends to be held captive by Blanche.

Artistic Style

Hard Boiled draws upon Ridley Scott's 1982 cyberpunk film *Blade Runner* as well as on themes from the hard-boiled pulp fictions popularized during the 1920's and 1930's. With the cyberpunk aesthetic, Darrow's Los Angeles is a combination of ever-present consumer culture in streets filled with the grime of industrialism. A majority of the panels are filled with hordes of consumer objects, futuristic technologies, symbols, cars, and people. This is countered with Darrow's attention to the hard-boiled noir aesthetic; he clothes his protagonist in a trench coat and makes his home a divided space between the light and the dark. Together, these influences form a vision of Los Angeles in which there is only escape from the crowd in the domestic space, yet even there, the presence of the outside world creeps in.

Darrow makes use of contrastingly sprawling and confining paneling to create his futuristic Los Angeles. On many pages he uses half-page, full-page, and two-page canvases to paint portraits of the enormity of the city, filling these spaces with details designed to suffocate the characters in the mass. Crinkles on the clothing of the dead can be found in all portions of his wide-angle shots with expression penciled onto every face and symbols of the mechanized world, as graffiti covers every inch of many of the walls in his full-page and two-page scenes. In contrast, he uses smaller panels in sequence to provide close-ups and allow even more finely inked expressions to come through, such as wrinkles on foreheads above lips curled with enticement. The city becomes a space dominated by finely

detailed excess, yet Darrow's domestic spaces have an impressionistic quality, providing characters a softer, sleeker look in comparison with the jagged horror of the city. Yellows, blues, and reds dominate Claude Legris's color scheme, evoking the noir elements of Golden Age comics while injecting them into a Modern Age dystopia.

Themes

Identity is among *Hard Boiled*'s central themes. Nixon constantly wars between his own self-perception and the perceptions of other characters, managing to maintain any one identity for only brief periods of time. Initially, he identifies himself as Nixon the tax collector. However, another character refers to him as Unit Four, stripping Nixon of even his programmed individuality. He is identified as Dad by his son and is a tortured soul unable to drift to sleep as visions of his bifurcated self haunt him in his dreams. As Dad, he can be comforted only by domestic life and sexual gratification from his wife. When he goes into Los Angeles during the daytime, however, he imagines himself in a variety of identities: Carl Seltz, an insurance investigator; Harry Seltz, investigator for the Benevolent Assurance Corporation; Harry Burns; and Carl Burns. He cycles through these identities while struggling to keep his humanity that can only be bestowed upon him by his creator, Mr. Willeford.

Another central theme in *Hard Boiled* is consumerism. A majority of Darrow's panels and pages are layered with the presence of corporate structures and consumer products. Consumerism is present in objects ranging from signs and advertisements inhabiting the Los Angeles landscape to beer bottles lining the streets, candy bars connected with fetuses in medical and mechanical equipment, and giant cans of soda in grocery stores with screens constantly advertising new products. Humans are reduced to consumer products as well, conveyed through the pastiche of human and android prostitution and by symbols of popular culture icons presented as dolls and figures on t-shirts.

Impact

Hard Boiled was initially met with critical and popular responses ranging from disgust to delighted applause.

Some viewed it as borderline pornography, and its publication created moral uproar and legal problems. A Gainesville, Florida, comic-store owner was charged and acquitted for selling mature content to a minor; an Oshkosh, Wisconsin, retailer had his stock of *Hard Boiled* seized until he would agree to put an in-store censor over the material after allegedly selling it to a minor. Ultimately, it was decided that the material, although offensive, could be sold as long as it was to adult audiences.

In *Hard Boiled,* issue 3, Dark Horse Comics printed a variety of reader responses, and although many expressed sentiment similar to those found in the Florida and Wisconsin court cases, many were positive analyses of the nature of such a project. Many lauded the extreme nature of the work as a statement about the medium's abilities, while others simply reveled in the pure excess of the work and its visual complexity. *Hard Boiled*'s success was assured when Miller and Darrow won an Eisner Award for Best Writer/Artist in 1991.

Although underground comics had previously depicted violence, sexuality, and other taboo subjects to equal extremes, *Hard Boiled* served as an introduction of hyperviolence and hypersexuality to mainstream comic books. In this regard, many of the increasingly violent and pessimistic works of the Modern Age during the 1990's and 2000's can be traced to *Hard Boiled*. Mark Millar, J. G. Jones, and Paul Mounts's *Wanted* (2003-2004) is an example of a comic influenced by *Hard Boiled* that infuses hyperviolence and mature language into mainstream comics; it was even developed into a major film released in 2008. The introduction of these mature, adult themes can even be extended to manga works such as Atsushi Kaneko's *Bambi and Her Pink Gun* (1998-2001) series that explores intense violence and is grounded in American pulp culture. Additionally, Darrow's European,

Moebius-inspired artwork and increasingly layered, heavily populated landscapes introduced sensibilities from European comics to the American mainstream. The influence of his art can be seen in Miller's later works such as *300* (1998).

Shaun T. Vigil

Further Reading

Dick, Philip K., and Tony Parker. *Do Androids Dream of Electric Sheep?* (1968)

Giraud, Jean. *Moebius 4: The Long Tomorrow and Other Science Fiction Stories* (1988).

Kaneko, Atsushi. *Bambi and Her Pink Gun* (1998-2001).

Millar, Mark, J. G. Jones, and Paul Mounts. *Wanted* (2007).

Miller, Frank, and Geof Darrow. *Big Guy and Rusty the Boy Robot* (1996).

Bibliography

Cavallaro, Dani. "The Brain in a Vat in Cyberpunk: The Persistence of the Flesh." *Studies in History and Philosophy of Biological and Biomedical Sciences* 35 (2004): 287-305.

DuBose, Mike S. "Holding Out for a Hero: Reaganism, Comic Book Vigilantes, and Captain America." *Journal of Popular Culture* 40, no. 6 (2007): 915-935.

Wandtke, Terrence R. "Frank Miller Strikes Again and Batman Becomes a Postmodern Anti-Hero: The Tragi(Comic) Reformulation of the Dark Knight." In *The Amazing Transforming Superhero! Essays on the Revision of Characters in Comic Books, Film, and Television*. Jefferson, N.C.: McFarland, 2007.

See also: *Sin City*

HARUM SCARUM

Author: Trondheim, Lewis

Artist: Lewis Trondheim (illustrator); Brigitte Findakly (colorist); Jeremy Eaton (letterer)

Publisher: Editions Dargaud (French); Fantagraphics Books (English)

First book publication: *Walter*, 1996 (English translation, 1997)

Harum Scarum. (Courtesy of Fantagraphics Books)

Publication History

Harum Scarum is the English translation of *Walter*, the third volume of French cartoonist Lewis Trondheim's comic book series *Les Formidables Aventures de Lapinot* (1993-2003), rendered as *The Spiffy Adventures of McConey* in English. French comics publisher Editions Dargaud published the original French edition of this title in 1996. In 1997, Seattle-based Fantagraphics Books published comics editor, translator, and publisher Kim Thompson's English-language version of Trondheim's work. Though *Walter* represented the third volume of Trondheim's original series, Fantagraphics marketed *Harum Scarum* as the first volume of *The Spiffy Adventures of McConey*.

In 1998, Fantagraphics published *The Hoodoodad* (French title *Pichenettes*, 1996) as the second volume in the McConey series. German, Dutch, Finnish, and Swedish editions of *Harum Scarum* have also been published. Series numbering among translated editions is inconsistent, a detail that is in keeping with the loose thematic connections between volumes, all of which treat stand-alone stories featuring an ensemble cast of recurring animal-like characters.

The stories in the series center on the exploits of an anthropomorphic rabbitlike character known as Lapinot in the original French and McConey in the English versions. In total, Trondheim has published fifteen Lapinot comic books, ten of which belong to the *Les Formidables Aventures de Lapinot* series. German publisher Carlsen Comics has published German translations of all ten volumes in the series. Trondheim's first Lapinot story, *Un Intérieur d'artiste*, appeared in 1991 and is the only Lapinot story to reveal the character's first name (Antonio). The volumes in the Lapinot series were published between 1993 and 2003, and all feature the work of noted comics colorist Brigitte Findakly, Trondheim's wife.

Since 1997, Trondheim has published four volumes in a companion series entitled *Les Formidables Aventures sans Lapinot*. Also colored by Findakly, these comics feature characters and environments featured in the Lapinot series, but the title character is absent.

Plot

As the first volume of *Les Formidables Aventures de Lapinot* to appear in English, *Harum Scarum* introduces English-language readers to one of France's most beloved and recognizable comics characters as well as to Trondheim's unique and influential cartooning and storytelling style. It also marks a departure from other volumes in the series with its evocation of a nineteenth-century Paris inhabited by mad scientists, political agitators, and monsters. As such, it calls to mind the adventure stories of Jules Verne, H. G. Wells, and John Buchan, as well as the earlier popular fiction of Sir Arthur Conan Doyle. In contrast, most Lapinot stories occur in various contemporary settings, though a few volumes pay homage to specific literary genres (such as Westerns and Romantic literature) and antiquated settings (such as the Wild West and nineteenth-century England) as evinced in *Harum Scarum.*

Harum Scarum. (Courtesy of Fantagraphics Books)

The story opens with McConey screaming in terror at the sight of a sinister, crooked silhouette of a monstrous reptile and bounding out of a Parisian townhouse. Figures resembling a cat and dog follow, yelling all the while. The three retreat to a café to collect their wits over a couple of bottles of wine. During the course of the trio's conversation, readers discover that the cat is a wisecracking journalist and the dog is a detective. After the detective leaves to file his report, McConey and the journalist decide to return to the scene of the monster sighting. After running into the detective once again, McConey fills in the backstory preceding the shocking event that opens the book.

The previous day, one of McConey's fellow medical school students, Bertrand Walter, asked him to visit his father the following day. Familiar with the elder Dr. Walter's research into animal behavior, McConey agrees to Bertrand's request. McConey's neighbor, the journalist, tags along. Hearing what sounds like a violent struggle from inside Dr. Walter's home, McConey and the journalist race to the police station, which brings readers up to speed with the detective's role in the extraordinary caper.

From this point, *Harum Scarum* moves quickly through a series of remarkable events. The journalist vanquishes the monster at Dr. Walter's house, and Bertrand Walter reappears only to narrowly escape the Chief Inspector's dragnet. Meanwhile, McConey and his partners urgently search for Dr. Walter and, in turn, are hunted by the Chief Inspector, the head of the Secret Service, the ambassador of Jakkanstan and his thugs, a gang of Czekovian communists, and a pack of monsters. Ultimately, they prevail against mad Dr. Walter, who has created a powder that alters people and animals into monstrous manifestations of their aggressions and fears.

Characters

- *McConey* is the sensible and good-natured main protagonist. Rabbitlike in appearance with buck teeth, long ears, and enormous feet, he is the only character in the story that does not wear shoes or have a nose. McConey studies medicine and once worked for Dr. Walter as a research assistant. His even temper and cool intelligence

provide a notable contrast to the excitable nature of almost all the other characters in the book.

- *Cat* remains unnamed in this particular book; however, he appears in most of the Lapinot stories as Richard. Here, he is a journalist who lives next door to McConey. Cat has a smart remark for every situation, and he often courts danger with his back talk and verbal barbs. He continuously quests for the perfect headline. The Jakkanstanis and Czekovians insist his ubiquitous cap is a time machine.

- *Inspector Ruffhaus*, his canine appearance aside, resembles a classic noir detective in his trench coat and peaked hat. Anxious to solve crimes and preserve justice "by the book," he initially betrays Bertrand Walter to the Chief Inspector. Once he realizes that his boss is an accomplice to a criminal conspiracy, Ruffhaus becomes a worthy ally for McConey and Cat.

- *Bertrand Walter*, crocodilian in appearance, hopes to enter the medical profession in his father's footsteps. His potential theft and sale of his father's mind-controlling formula to the totalitarian regimes of Jakkanstan and Czekovia may have driven Dr. Walter over the edge. Bertrand comes to a tragic and ironic end.

- *Dr. Walter* looks like a wrinkled, bespectacled version of his son. Once a great animal behaviorist, he has become a paranoid megalomaniac who believes his creation of a volatile formula that mutates all living creatures that come in contact with it into violent monsters, is a divine gift.

- *Chief Inspector* of police possesses a crooked beak and continually squints and scowls. He uses his title and rank to manipulate his underlings and enforce his sinister will.

- *Grimaldi*, the lion, is the head of the Secret Service. He is in cahoots with the Chief Inspector as they attempt to steal Dr. Walter's formula.

- *Stanislav Khambehl* is a despot from Jakkanstan. Bearish and pompous, Khambehl is an avid chess player and aspires to rule the world. He plans on using Dr. Walter's time machine to achieve this end.

- *Mister Vincente*, like the Chief Inspector, has an enormous hooked bill as his most prominent facial feature. A communist leader from Czekovia, he vies with Stanislav Khambehl for possession of Dr. Walter's time machine. Once the device is in his hand, Vincente plans to crush the capitalist regimes once and for all.

Artistic Style

A self-taught cartoonist, Trondheim has a loose, confident, and deceptively simple drawing style. His renderings of his animal characters seem almost childlike in their exaggeration of characters' features, but his accurate depiction of period clothing, vehicles, and furniture reveals a deliberate eye for detail and subtlety. Trondheim's signature gift for convincingly evoking complete, coherent worlds in which readers can readily immerse themselves is most evident in his astonishing drawings of architecture, city streets, and domestic and public interiors.

In *Harum Scarum*, Trondheim's intelligent illustration is devoid of drawing techniques such as cross-hatching to suggest depth and contrast. Instead, these visual qualities are evoked through Findakly's extraordinary coloring work. She is a prolific and influential colorist who has worked with several comics artists, most notably Trondheim's frequent collaborator Joann Sfar. Findakly's work is characterized by a sophisticated encompassing of bold primary shades and subtle pastels. Most effective in *Harum Scarum* is her rendering of light from direct sources such as shaded light bulbs and fires burning in drawing-room hearths and the shadows they cast. Her work in this regard lends an eerie yet warm film-noir mood to the work.

Trondheim hews to a traditional page layout in *Harum Scarum*, arranging multiple small panels on each page. Beyond this conventional arrangement of images, Trondheim does not observe a regular or consistent placement of panels per page. Wider and horizontal panels sometimes break up the presentation of small square panels as the story requires, and Trondheim treats readers to a variety of perspectives, from eye-level to three-quarter view, to zoom into and out of action, emphasizing the story's action-packed pace.

Themes

One of the characteristic features of Trondheim's work in general is an improvisational storytelling style that allows his characters to free associate or "riff" on topics. *Harum Scarum* is no different, with its juxtaposition of Cat's lame wisecracks with McConey's thoughtful psychological and philosophical insights. Between these extremes, Trondheim seems to be exploring the theme of human vanity expressed as a will to dominate others in *Harum Scarum*.

What makes this particular idea so poignant in *Harum Scarum* is Trondheim's treatment of it in what appears to be a funny animal story. Trondheim's anthropomorphized animal characters provide an ironic frame in which to consider human ambitions and their most sinister expressions. Trondheim further underscores this irony by placing an examination of these ideas in the context of a literary genre, detective fiction, in which truth ultimately prevails, though it is always complicated by false impressions and misleading clues.

Lewis Trondheim

One of the most prolific cartoonists in the world, Lewis Trondheim is also among the most celebrated comics artists to have emerged from the French "nouvelle bande dessinée" movement of the 1990's. Initially noted for his writing, Trondheim legendarily taught himself to draw comics by producing a five-hundred-page graphic novel, *Lapinot et les carrotes de Patagonie*. His Lapinot character was featured in a ten-volume series from Dargaud in the 1990's and 2000's. He has worked in a number of genres, including humor-fantasy (the *Dungeon* series, with Joann Sfar and others), autobiography (*Little Nothings*, *Approximate Continuum Comics*), and experimental comics. His visual style is highly cartoony and the preponderance of his work—including his autobiographical comics—feature anthropomorphic characters. At the end of the 1990's he was producing new comics at the rate of more than a dozen books per year and though he has since scaled back his production, he still releases books much more quickly than his peers.

Harum Scarum, on the other hand, concludes on an ambiguous note, leaving readers to consider the questions raised in the story.

Ultimately, Trondheim invites readers to consider how noble intentions such as serving the common good can become perverted by prejudice, ideology, and greed. McConey, Cat, and Ruffhaus demonstrate the antidote to these temptations by working together in an effort to preserve their shared interest in one another's survival as they face and escape one danger after another.

Impact

Trondheim's Lapinot stories enjoy a wide readership in Europe. The publication of *Harum Scarum* in English is significant for many reasons. First, while many Trondheim titles have been translated into English, Fantagraphics Books' editions of *Harum Scarum* and *The Hoodoodad* remain the only examples of his work in the Lapinot comics universe in English. These stories offer yet another view into Trondheim's prolific art and serve as an example of a small-press comic book achieving mainstream status with comics readers of all ages.

In addition, *Harum Scarum* provides an example of how Trondheim's work often seeks to challenge literary and comic traditions and conventions. Even though *Harum Scarum* contains recognizable comic book features such as panels and conversation bubbles, Trondheim uses these elements to juxtapose themes, images, and texts that may seem discordant, such as his almost childlike characters roaming the streets of a realistically drawn city street or dialogue about complex ideas interspersed with puns and jokes. The overall effect of these disparate qualities merging on the pages of *Harum Scarum* is a delightful dissonance rooted in tradition that surpasses the arbitrary limitations of conventions reinforcing reader's expectations.

Greg Matthews

Further Reading

Guibert, Emmanuel, and Joann Sfar. *The Professor's Daughter* (2007).

Jason. *Werewolves of Montpellier* (2010).

Trondheim, Lewis. *The Hoodoodad* (1998).

Bibliography

Beaty, Bart. "The Strange Case of Lewis Trondheim." In *Unpopular Culture: Transforming the European Comic Book in the 1990's*. Toronto: University of Toronto Press, 2007.

Chaney, Michael A. "Animal Subjects of the Graphic Novel." *College Literature* 38, no. 3 (Summer, 2011): 129-149.

Miller, Ann. *Reading Bande Dessinée: Critical Approaches to French-Language Comic Strip*. Chicago: Intellect Books, 2007.

See also: *The Rabbi's Cat; Mouse Guard; Maus: A Survivor's Tale*

HARVEY KURTZMAN'S JUNGLE BOOK:
OR, UP FROM THE APES! (AND RIGHT BACK DOWN)

Author: Kurtzman, Harvey
Artist: Harvey Kurtzman (illustrator)
Publisher: Ballantine Books; Kitchen Sink Press
First book publication: 1959

Publication History

After leaving *MAD* magazine in 1957, Harvey Kurtzman, who had helped to found the magazine in 1952, supported himself primarily through freelance work. He developed an idea for a book of stories for Ballantine Books, which had previously published collections of *MAD* comics. Despite his misgivings, Ian Ballantine offered Kurtzman a contract.

The full title of the collection is *Harvey Kurtzman's Jungle Book: Or, Up from the Apes! (and Right Back Down)—In Which Are Described in Words and Pictures Businessmen, Private Eyes, Cowboys, and Other Heros All Exhibiting the Progress of Man from the Darkness of the Cave into the Light of Civilization by Means of Television, Wide Screen Movies, the Stone Axe, and Other Useful Arts*. In addition to the book's four stories, Kurtzman worked on a parody of science-fiction movies to be included in a second volume. However, the book was a commercial failure, and no second volume appeared. Nonetheless, it became a much-desired collector's item. In 1986, Kitchen Sink Press republished the book in hardcover and released a softcover version in 1988.

Plot

All four stories parody popular fiction and nonfiction works of the 1950's. The inspiration for "Thelonius Violence" was *Peter Gunn* (1958-1961), a television series about a hip, sophisticated private investigator who dresses stylishly and loves cool jazz; the show is best remembered for its jazzy theme music by Henry Mancini. Violence, in a parody of hipster dialogue, tells about a young woman blackmailed for cheating at school. At different points in the story, he is pummeled by a thug who wants him to back off and surrounded by shapely women. It is revealed that Violence and the

Harvey Kurtzman's Jungle Book. (Courtesy of Kitchen Sink Press)

thug are partners and extortionists, and he ends the story as a professional wrestler.

The title of "The Organization Man in the Grey Flannel Executive Suite" is an amalgamation of the titles of three best sellers of the 1950's. Cameron Hawley's novel *Executive Suite* (1952) concerns success and succession in a business setting; a film version was released in 1954. Sloan Wilson's novel *The Man in the Gray Flannel Suit* (1955) deals with the search for meaning in a materialistic, business-oriented United States, while William H. Whyte's *The Organization Man* (1956) studies management practices in major American corporations. Kurtzman's story, an autobiographical treatment of his experience working at Timely Publications in the 1940's, satirizes the venality of business in general and the publishing industry in particular through the initial naïveté and gradual corruption of Goodman Beaver. He begins working for Shlock Publications with high hopes but gradually comes to resemble the cynical editors he at first cannot comprehend. Like the others, he begins groping the secretary and, at the end, steals from the company.

"Compulsion on the Range" parodies the television Western *Gunsmoke* (1955-1975). Marshal Matt Dollin, obsessed with besting outlaw Johnny Ringding in a gunfight despite Ringding's superior skills, trails Johnny to American Indian country. Despite Dollin's incompetence, the chief swears Ringding will face "Indian revenge." Dollin pursues his nemesis to Los Angeles, where Zorro argues in favor of a nonviolent approach. Lacking a worthy opponent, Ringding leaves the country, and Dollin is counseled by a Freud-influenced doctor who helps him resolve his psychological issues. The story concludes with Ringding experiencing Indian revenge—in India.

Kurtzman claimed "Decadence Degenerated" was based on his experiences in Texas while in the military, but it also reads as a parody of certain southern writers such as Erskine Caldwell and Tennessee Williams. A group of ignorant men in Rottenville pass the time by complaining of boredom and mentally undressing the alluring Honey Lou as she walks by. Her rather masculine sister tries to protect her from the men and from Si Mednick, a bookworm whom the men criticize for his unmanly ways. When Honey Lou is murdered, the sheriff arrests the "queer" Mednick, who falls prey to a lynch mob despite the efforts of a journalist. The townspeople are abashed to learn that Mednick had been working on gifts for them, and the story ends with the revelation that the gifts were actually bombs.

Characters

- *Thelonius Violence* is a good-looking and muscular private detective who believes himself to be more intelligent and capable than he truly is. His first name evokes jazz pianist Thelonious Monk, despite the alternative spelling, and relates to his

love of jazz, while his last relates to the violence in which television character Peter Gunn was involved.

- *Lolita Nabakov* is the young woman being blackmailed for cheating on an exam in "Thelonius Violence." Her name derives from Vladimir Nabokov's novel *Lolita* (1955). She is blond, curvaceous, and vapid.

- *Goodman Beaver*, the protagonist of "The Organization Man in the Grey Flannel Executive Suite," is a young man with blond hair and a wide grin. He is a good man at the beginning of the story, though a naïve and overambitious "eager beaver," but he is corrupted by his work environment. Kurtzman later featured the hopeful, naïve version of the character in stories published in *Help!* magazine.

- *Mike Verifax* is the secretary at Shlock Publications in "The Organization Man in the Grey Flannel Executive Suite." She is young, blond, and shapely, and she takes constant sexual harassment in stride. She admires Goodman's idealism in the beginning and is saddened by how he changes.

- *Lucifer Shlock* is the older, slovenly head of Shlock Publications in "The Organization Man in the Grey Flannel Executive Suite." Unscrupulous and concerned chiefly with the bottom line, he finds Goodman's idealism strange. As Goodman becomes more like him, he grows to admire the young man.

- *Matt Dollin*, the protagonist of "Compulsion on the Range," is a parody of Matt Dillon, the protagonist of the television series *Gunsmoke*. He is a confident but incompetent gunfighter obsessed with outdrawing Johnny Ringding. Later, with a doctor's help, he realizes that his obsession derives from his failure as a youth to hide from his father a racy picture of a woman that he kept in his dresser—he was unable to beat his father to the drawer.

- *Johnny Ringding* is an outlaw in "Compulsion on the Range." Faster on the draw than Dollin, he at first gleefully and then reluctantly bests him in gunfights. His crimes in American Indian country and abduction of the chief's daughter earn him the threat of "Indian revenge." Before this happens, however, he travels to Los Angeles and is confronted by Zorro, whose refusal to fight him drives Ringding out of the country.

- *Zorro* is the "Marshallero" of Los Angeles in "Compulsion on the Range." Older and heavier than in his prime, he proclaims he is a modern

lawman, using words rather than violence to keep the peace. He attempts to subdue Ringding by appealing to his conscience and staring him down, taking Ringding's abuse until the gunfighter departs in frustration.

- *Honey Lou* is an attractive young blond in "Decadence Degenerated." She pays no attention to the men who mentally undress her but appears

Harvey Kurtzman's Jungle Book. (Courtesy of Kitchen Sink Press)

interested in the more sophisticated Si Mednick, despite her sister's protectiveness. Her murder prompts Mednick's arrest and lynching, despite his innocence

- *Sam* is Honey Lou's beefy older sister in "Decadence Degenerated." Wearing masculine clothing and a bandana, she easily intimidates the men who leer at Honey Lou. She later confesses to her sister's murder, claiming she wanted to teach her not to run around with men.
- *Si Mednick* is a shy man in "Decadence Degenerated" who eschews his peers' rural attire in favor of glasses, a beret, and a parasol. He offers a present to Honey Lou, which prompts the anger of Sam and the town's suspicions when Honey Lou is murdered. He protests his innocence but is lynched anyway. The journalist who defends him says Mednick loved his fellow citizens, as demonstrated by the clocks he was working on as gifts; when the townspeople take the gifts home, however, they explode.
- *Chief Beeferman* is a corrupt sheriff in "Decadence Degenerated" who allows an innocent man to be taken by a lynch mob while he focuses on "fund-raising."
- *Etaoin Shrdlu* is a reporter from Fayetteville in "Decadence Degenerated." He is taken for a Yankee outsider by Chief Beeferman, even though he hails not from the North but from the northern part of the state. He tries to fight the ignorance and bigotry of Rottenville but also reveals his own self-interest in his desire for a good story.

Artistic Style

The four stories of *Jungle Book* share a consistent artistic style, an exaggerated cartoonish approach to the human figure. Rounded, elongated figures prevail, suggesting fluidity in the characters' movements. Except for Sam, the women are ridiculously voluptuous. Shading and lines suggest shape, texture, and lighting, but the images tend to be spare and clean. Kurtzman's characters' faces are caricatures, expressing emotional states and vacuity. Often the eyes are blank circles, and the women lack noses except in profile.

Harvey Kurtzman

One of the most celebrated cartoonists in American history—and a man for whom an industry award is named—Harvey Kurtzman is best remembered as the original editor of *MAD*, the generation-defining humor comic book. Working initially as a freelance creator of fill-in material and as a cartoonist for the *New York Herald Tribune*, Kurtzman made his reputation as the editor of EC Comics' war titles, *Frontline Combat* and *Two-Fisted Tales*. In 1952, he launched *MAD*, the satirical magazine that would become one of the biggest sensations in comics for several decades. After leaving the magazine in 1956, Kurtzman launched a short-lived rival, *Trump*, with Hugh Hefner, then *Humbug* and *Help!* In the latter, he produced the *Goodman Beaver* strips that brought him the ire of Archie Comics. Starting in 1962, he and Will Elder began publishing Little Annie Fannie in *Playboy Magazine*, a feature that ran for twenty-six years. Kurtzman is among the most influential humor cartoonists of all time, ushering in a new era of sophisticated satire in American comics.

The black-and-white artwork has a range of gray tones, both to suggest color and to create shading and lighting effects. In addition, in most images, thin horizontal lines are detectable. As an experiment, Kurtzman drew the artwork on lined paper, with assurances from the printer that the lines would disappear in the finished product. The fact that they did not, he said later, indicates the low-budget nature of the original paperback book.

Kurtzman's lettering, unlike that of many comics, is not all in capital letters and evokes a personal handwriting style rather than type. Like many letterers, he employs boldface for emphasis and symbols for curse words. Speech balloons convey dialogue, and, because many of the panels are tall due to the vertical orientation of the book, words are frequently hyphenated to fit the balloons.

Themes

The title *Jungle Book* and the first part of the subtitle, *Up from the Apes! (and Right Back Down)*, suggest one of the major themes of the book: For all of human-kind's vaunted achievements, it is hardly the pinnacle of civilization. Kurtzman presents this theme through satire. Characters who think they are intelligent are shown to be idiots, characters proud of their skills are revealed as incompetent, and characters thought to be virtuous are shown as corrupt or corruptible. In addition, the books and television shows that inspired Kurtzman's parodies, most of them from the 1950's, have in common a middlebrow sensibility that he also mocks. While not aspiring to the highest levels of art, his targets set themselves above lowbrow forms of entertainment; in poking fun at this middlebrow sensibility, Kurtzman ridicules its pretentions. Humanity in *Jungle Book* is depicted as fallen, not theologically but ontologically, perhaps resulting from humanity's root brutishness or its perpetual tendency toward delusion.

The objectification of women is also a prominent theme. Except for the masculine Sam in "Decadence Degenerated," whose imagined unclothed form is depicted as repulsive, the women's exaggerated curves are ogled and groped repeatedly in the four stories. Kurtzman himself objectifies these women through the hypersexualized way he draws them, yet the men who harass them are depicted as fools, creeps, and villains, pointing toward a critique of lewd masculine behavior.

Impact

The commercial failure of *Harvey Kurtzman's Jungle Book* meant that the book itself did not make much of an impact, but Kurtzman's larger influence is enormous. While he was best known for his contributions to *MAD*, those who admired his work and sought it wherever they could find it embraced his keen satiric sense as well as his comically exaggerated artwork and rhythmic progressions from panel to panel, all of which are found in *Jungle Book*. It is little wonder, then, that in his introduction to the 1986 republication of *Jungle Book*, Art Spiegelman noted that his copy of

the original 1959 edition had literally fallen apart from repeated reading. Indeed, Kurtzman inspired the next generation of satirical cartoonists, many of whom, such as Robert Crumb and Gilbert Shelton, were associated with the underground comics of the 1960's and beyond. Although such cartoonists developed their own individual styles, Kurtzman's influence is evident in their work and throughout the industry. The Harvey Awards, given to comics creators by their fellow professionals since 1988, are named in his honor.

Darren Harris-Fain

Further Reading

Crumb, Robert. *The Complete Crumb Comics* (1987).

Gonick, Larry. *The Cartoon History of the Universe* (1977-1992).

Kurtzman, Harvey. *Playboy's Little Annie Fanny* (2000).

Bibliography

Harvey, Robert C. "The Comic Book as Individual Expression: Harvey Kurtzman and the Revolution." In *The Art of the Comic Book: An Aesthetic History*. Jackson: University Press of Mississippi, 1997.

Hoberman, J. "Harvey Kurtzman's Hysterical Materialism." In *Masters of American Comics*, edited by John Carlin, Paul Karasik, and Brian Walker. Los Angeles: Hammer Museum and the Museum of Contemporary Art, 2005.

Kitchen, Denis. "'Man, I'm Beat': Harvey Kurtzman's Frustrating Post-*Humbug* Freelance Career." *Comic Art* 7 (Winter, 2005): 3-16.

Kitchen, Denis, and Paul Buhle. *The Art of Harvey Kurtzman: The Mad Genius of Comics*. New York: Abrams ComicArts, 2009.

See also: *A Cartoon History of the Universe; The Book of Genesis; The Complete Fritz the Cat; Ghost World*

HATE

Author: Bagge, Peter

Artist: Peter Bagge (illustrator); Jim Blanchard (inker); Eric Reynolds (inker); Jeff Johnson (colorist); Mary Woodring (colorist)

Publisher: Fantagraphics Books

First serial publication: 1990-1998

First book publication: 1993-2001

Publication History

Hate began as a black-and-white comic book written and drawn by Peter Bagge and published by Seattle-based Fantagraphics Books. In his previous series for the same publisher, the magazine-format *Neat Stuff* (1985-1990), Bagge had chronicled the angst-ridden adventures of the Bradley family, with teenage son Buddy as his semiautobiographical hero. Having concluded *Neat Stuff*, Bagge wanted to launch a new series with the look and feel of 1960's underground comics that would focus on a single character in a standard-sized comic book format. Initially considering titles such as *Hey, Buddy* and *The Adventures of Buddy Bradley*, Bagge provisionally titled the series *Hate*, and the name stuck.

Hate picks up Buddy's story in Seattle as a twenty-something slacker. Bagge also used the series as an opportunity to provide an outlet for up-and-coming alternative comic book creators by including their work as backup features. Beginning with issue 16, Bagge introduced color and employed an inker, Jim Blanchard, to streamline his artistic style, as the story line shifted from Seattle to New Jersey, Buddy's home state. *Hate* ran for thirty issues, and the Buddy Bradley material was later reprinted in a series of six trade paperback collections as well as two digest-sized editions, all published by Fantagraphics Books.

Plot

Hate follows the trials and tribulations of hard-drinking, cynical Buddy Bradley as he wanders aimlessly through life from one coast to the other, has a variety of sexual and other misadventures, and occasionally searches for love, or at least some small

Hate: Buddy's Got Three Moms! (Courtesy of Fantagraphics Books)

measure of happiness. In the first half of the series, Buddy is living in Seattle, the epicenter of a growing cultural movement of the early 1990's in the United States. Readers first meet Buddy as he speaks to them and gives them a tour of his apartment, which he shares with his scheming friend Stinky and their reclusive roommate George.

Buddy begins a relationship with the stuck-up, sex-obsessed Val, a friend of his former girlfriend Lisa. Their attempts at romance are often thwarted by interference from Buddy's friends, and Buddy refuses to allow Val to move in with him. Buddy's brother, Butch, a racist Navy washout, visits and causes chaos, while his sister, Babs, suffers as a single mom with two hellish children and a sleazy, deadbeat former husband named Joel.

At the start of the series, Buddy is working at a used bookstore. He later agrees to co-manage a grunge band with Stinky, but he soon gives it up. Buddy reluctantly gets Lisa a job at the bookstore and slowly resumes a relationship with her. George moves in with a wealthy female benefactor and publishes a "zine" that paints an unflattering portrait of Buddy.

Val reenters Buddy's life, having gathered her own bizarre collection of friends. Stinky returns from the road after the band falls apart. Soon, everyone has converged at Buddy's place and wants to move in, leaving Buddy on the couch and ultimately prompting him to leave Seattle.

Buddy and Lisa head to his parents' home in New Jersey for the second half of the series. Adjusting to suburban life is difficult, as is dealing with Buddy's dotty mother and abrasive, often-ill father. Buddy and his old friend Jay reconnect and open a collectibles store together, B and J's Collector's Emporium, while Lisa settles into domestic life with the help of Buddy's mother. Buddy buys a distinctive monster truck with tiny back wheels and dubs it the "Poliomobile."

Jay's heroin addiction and tendency to use the store funds for drugs put him at odds with Buddy, while the family struggles with traditional gender roles as the Bradley men face off against Lisa and the Bradley women. Lisa grows attached to Buddy's father, and his sudden death in a traffic accident sends her into another period of depression and detachment. She finds solace in Joel's arms and begins an affair with him. Meanwhile, Buddy finds himself attracted to a colleague's wife, a wholesome girl named Doris.

Hate: Buddy's Got Three Moms! (Courtesy of Fantagraphics Books)

Lisa's depression leads her to therapy and Prozac. When she disappears, Buddy tracks her down in New York, where she has shaved her head and moved in with her Goth punk friend Elizabeth. As Buddy's mother becomes more involved with a man named George and plans to sell the house, Buddy's local friends and a newly arrived Stinky, now working a postal route with an Uzi hidden in his truck, contemplate turning the suburban location into a crack house. When Butch joins Stinky on a deserted beach to shoot guns, Stinky blows his own brains out, leaving Butch traumatized and everyone wondering whether Stinky intended to commit suicide or simply made a drunken mistake. They leave Stinky buried in an unmarked grave and agree never to tell anyone.

Butch starts working at Buddy's store as Buddy begins a relationship with an assertive woman named Sally. He also sees an Asian American woman named Nicole, but he is not happy with either relationship.

As the series ends, Buddy's mother moves to Florida with her new boyfriend; Babs reunites with Joel; Val and Buddy's former roommate George have become a couple; and Sally becomes extremely upset when she discovers that Buddy has gotten back together with Lisa, who has left Elizabeth in New York. Sally winds up with Butch as Buddy proposes to Lisa, who is pregnant with his baby. The series closes as the couple plans its future as a new family.

Volumes

- *Hey, Buddy* (1993). Collects issues 1-5. Buddy Bradley lives in Seattle, surrounded by a grotesque collection of friends, acquaintances, and losers. He begins dating a stuck-up rich girl named Val, but complications ensue.
- *Buddy the Dreamer* (1994). Collects issues 6-10. Buddy's friend Stinky becomes a rock-star sensation, while Buddy finds himself drawn into a depressing relationship with his former girlfriend Lisa.
- *Fun with Buddy and Lisa* (1995). Collects issues 11-15. As tensions mount in Seattle, Buddy and Lisa decide to abandon their friends and start their lives over on the East Coast.
- *Buddy Go Home!* (1997). Collects issues 16-20.

Buddy embarks on a career as a collectibles-store manager, as he and Lisa adjust to life in a New Jersey suburb with Buddy's bizarre family.
- *Buddy's Got Three Moms!* (1999). Collects issues 21-25. After the death of Buddy's father, Buddy faces suburban life surrounded by three domineering women, until Lisa decides to flee and significantly alters her lifestyle.
- *Buddy Bites the Bullet!* (2001). Collects issues 26-30. Stinky commits suicide, sending shock waves through Buddy's circle of friends. Everyone is facing the realities of adulthood, and Buddy and Lisa decide to get married.

Characters

- *Harold William Bradley, Jr.*, a.k.a. *Buddy,* the protagonist, is a twentysomething cynic with a large nose and shaggy black hair that often obscures his eyes. Paradoxically, he has little self-esteem but thinks he is right about everything. He professes to be a dedicated bachelor but longs for love.
- *Lisa Leavenworth* is Buddy's on-again, off-again girlfriend and, by the end of the series, the mother of his child. She is a fiery redhead with a variety of psychological problems, including self-hatred, suicidal tendencies, and a predisposition to bad hygiene.
- *Leonard "Stinky" Brown* is Buddy's roommate, modeled on singer Iggy Pop. He is lanky, has a tuft of blond hair, wears round sunglasses, has personal-hygiene issues, and is addicted to drugs and hard living. He is constantly concocting elaborate get-rich schemes that inevitably fail.
- *Jay*, Buddy's friend and business partner, is a tall, thin thirty-six-year-old with short hair and a crooked nose. He is a heroin addict and is prone to taking advantage of the business by lifting money for his own use.
- *Valerie "Val" Russo* is a trendy brunet who is always dressed stylishly and exerts emotional control over her boyfriends and social circle. She enjoys violent sex in odd places, perhaps as a reaction to her strict, wealthy upbringing.
- *George Cecil Hamilton III* is one of Buddy's

roommates, an African American geek with a penchant for conspiracy theories, social isolation, and self-publishing zines. By the end of the series, he has begun a relationship with Val, despite his apparent lack of interest in or understanding of women.

- *Jimmy Foley* is Buddy's New Jersey neighbor, a blond stoner who is on parole and attending Alcoholics Anonymous meetings. He sits around all day playing video games and coming up with often-illegal schemes for making money.
- *Butch Bradley* is Buddy's younger brother, a hulking young man with a crew cut, a violent streak, and a host of racist and fascist beliefs. He had some Navy experience, but now hangs out with Buddy's friend Jimmy until finally finding work at Buddy's collectibles store.
- *Babs Bradley* is Buddy's blond sister, a heavy drinker and the long-suffering mother of two undisciplined children, Tyler and Alexis. She turns to religion after the departure of her husband, Joel, with whom she eventually reunites.
- *Betty Bradley*, Buddy's mother, has perfectly coiffed dark hair. Although overbearing and opinionated, she is resigned to her domestic role. Like everyone else in the family, she drinks heavily. After the death of Buddy's father, she begins the next chapter in her life by moving away with her new boyfriend.
- *Brad Bradley*, Buddy's father, is a gruff old man with glasses and little hair. Certain that he is dying most of the time, he sleeps often and expects the rest of the family to cater to him. He dies suddenly when hit by a truck while out on a stroll.
- *Joel* is a sleazy, long-nosed lecher who is Babs's former husband and the father of her two children. He has a short affair with Lisa but goes back to Babs.
- *Tom Kaufman* is an old friend of Buddy, a mustached blond who becomes a cop with a pleasant, normal home life.
- *Yahtzi Murphy* is a violent, stringy-haired bootlegger who sells illegal video tapes and torments Buddy and Stinky.

- *Elizabeth Mizell* is a Jewish Goth punk with piercings and purple hair. She has no respect for Buddy and tries to protect Lisa from him. While Lisa is living with her in New York, the two have an occasionally sexual relationship.

Artistic Style

One of the most distinctive elements of *Hate* is Bagge's extraordinarily exaggerated drawing style, influenced by 1960's underground comics creators such as Robert Crumb and by some Japanese manga traditions. Bagge's spaghetti-limbed funhouse figures capture the chaotic mood of their off-kilter lives and their resilience in the face of daily setbacks and tragedies. When experiencing extreme emotions, especially rage, Bagge's already-grotesque characters often transform into even more abstract distortions of humanity that only vaguely resemble their usual selves, with enormous faces eclipsing the rest of their bodies and twisting into nightmarish shapes.

The muddy, manic dirtiness of the imagery during the series' black-and-white period, with its cluttered,

---

Peter Bagge

One of the key figures in the development of the American alternative comics sensibility in the late-1980's and 1990's, Peter Bagge's *Hate* was a signature comic series for an entire generation of readers. Bagge broke into comics after dropping out of the School of Visual Arts, working on magazines like *Punk*, *Screw*, and, with Robert Crumb, *Weirdo*. His *Neat Stuff* series for Fantagraphics brought him recognition in the 1980's, but it was with *Hate* that he made his reputation. The chronicle of slacker Buddy Bradley and his exploits in Seattle's burgeoning grunge culture, *Hate* parodied alternative culture and made Bagge a star. Since cancelling *Hate* in 1999, Bagge has worked with Marvel and DC Comics on titles including *Yeah!*, *Sweatshop*, and a Spider-Man story. Bagge's art is extremely cartoony, with grossly exaggerated characters and a busy aesthetic. His stories tend toward sharp satire and frequently reflect the artist's libertarian philosophy.

heavily shadowed settings and layouts, gives way after issue 16 to a sharper, more streamlined style, thanks to the presence of inker Blanchard and Bagge's desire to tone down his own artwork and brighten the mood of the series. Although expressive distortion still happens in the title's latter half, there is a much smoother delineation overall, with more fluid lines and the addition of full color. The series settles into a relatively consistent, cartoonlike approach for the remainder of its run that slightly obscures its grungy, "comix"-inspired origins.

Themes

Throughout the series' thirty-issue run, Bagge uses Buddy Bradley to embody much of the alienation and disenfranchisement he experienced as a white, suburban young adult. Buddy is confused and consumed by paranoia, racist and misogynistic opinions, and a tendency toward self-destructive behavior in the forms of drug and alcohol abuse and torturous romantic relationships. While not all of the unsavory aspects of Buddy's character can or should be attributed to the author, clearly Bagge feels that a specific type of young, lower- to middle-class Caucasian American in the early 1990's faced challenges that too often stemmed from within as much as from the world without.

The rapidly changing world serves as another target for Bagge's acerbic wit, with the expansion of homogenous franchised consumerism and the advent of the Internet as a retreat for the lonely and obsessed also coming under fire. Buddy's devotion to right-wing radio and rampant use of empty sex, drinking, and drugs as an escape from the monotony of a meaningless existence and Lisa's frequent psychotic breaks and periods of depressive self-loathing are all symptoms of what Bagge sees as an utter breakdown of culture at the end of the twentieth century.

Bagge depicts sex itself as comical and ugly and romance as a gender game that masks more basic, primal desires. His choice for Lisa's last name, Leavenworth, suggests that he might be equating some relationships with a kind of spiritual incarceration. That even death, often shown as sudden and senseless, is shaken off by his characters with so little emotional response is indicative of their detachment from reality and their own feelings.

The series' sarcastic finale, in which Buddy and Lisa decide to deal with her pregnancy by getting married because it just seems like the thing to do, neatly subverts the Hollywood-style happy ending upon which it plays. Rather than deal with all of their personal and shared issues, Buddy and Lisa are going through the motions, doing what society expects. Despite Bagge's cynical tone, however, it is possible that Buddy and Lisa will find a kind of happiness with their own crazy adaptation of the American Dream.

Impact

Bagge's work is often credited as helping to define the "grunge" movement of the early 1990's, a phenomenon of popular culture that grew out of the alternative rock scene in the Pacific Northwest and included the rise of bands such as Nirvana to the national stage. The two-part story "Follow That Dream" in issues 8 and 9, in which Buddy becomes co-manager of a band that eventually employs his friend Stinky as lead singer, became one of the series' most popular tales, summing up much of Bagge's thoughts on the rock-music scene in Seattle and the clash between creative integrity, corrupt business practices, and celebrity idolatry. Issue 12 features a story called "Collector's Scum!" that allows Bagge to comment on the comic book collecting world and the American obsession with mindless consumption.

The series gained further notoriety with a sudden, shocking plot twist in its final issues, in which Stinky commits suicide in front of Butch. The incident is enveloped in Bagge's usual dark humor, but Stinky's motivations are kept intentionally unclear. The death of Stinky not only continues to haunt Buddy and Butch for the rest of the series but also remained a topic of discussion in the comics press for many months.

Arnold T. Blumberg

Further Reading

Bagge, Peter. *The Bradleys* (2004).

_____. *Everybody Is Stupid Except for Me, and Other Astute Observations* (2009).

Clowes, Dan. *Eightball* (1989-2001).

Bibliography

Moffett, Matthew L. "Buddy Does Seattle." *School Library Journal* 51, no. 9 (September, 2005): 242.

Nashawaty, Chris. "Comix Trip." *Entertainment Weekly* 239 (September, 1994): 47.

True, Everett. Introduction to *Buddy Does Seattle*, by Peter Bagge. Seattle: Fantagraphics Books, 2005.

See also: *Black Hole; Box Office Poison; Life Sucks; Love and Rockets*

HAUNTED

Author: Dupuy, Philippe
Artist: Philippe Dupuy (illustrator)
Publishers: Cornélius (French); Drawn and Quarterly (English)
First book publication: *Hanté*, 2005 (English translation, 2008)

Publication History

Hanté, the original French version of *Haunted*, was published in 2005 by the French alternative graphic novel publisher Cornélius, which had published *New-York: Carnet*s (1996), created by Philippe Dupuy with Charles Berberian, chronicling their trip to the city. The cover of *Hanté* used a drawing of Dupuy wearing a white jogging suit and running through a tangle of arteries and tendons. In 2006, Dupuy received a nomination for the Best Comic Book at the Angoulême International Comics Festival. *Hanté* was the first graphic novel that Dupuy published without the collaboration of Berberian. Since forming his partnership with Berberian, Dupuy had worked independently only once before. In 1994, addressing issues related to their work and revealing aspects of their personal lives, each author wrote sections of *Un Journal d'un album*; this technique was in sharp contrast to their usual working method of jointly creating all aspects of a text.

In 2008, *Haunted*, the English version, translated by Helge Dascher, was published by the Canadian publishing house Drawn and Quarterly. This version used a different cover, featuring the head of Dupuy with a brain and blood vessels emerging from the back. Drawn and Quarterly has also published English versions of *Le Journal d'un album* entitled *Maybe Later* (2006) and a collection of the Monsieur Jean stories entitled *Get a Life* (2006). *Haunted* is also available through Drawn and Quarterly as an e-book.

Plot

In *Haunted*, Dupuy explores his own mind and psyche. As he jogs, his mind takes him into a fantasy world, where he encounters a diverse group of characters. Several times, the trip through his mind leads to

Haunted. (Courtesy of Drawn and Quarterly)

interpolated stories in which he does not participate with characters. Dupuy begins his graphic novel with a dream he has had about paintings of faces with no eyes. He follows this with the first "Run Movie 1—Jogging" in which he is jogging, explaining that with each stride the jogger has a thought. This leads to the first story about a dog who chews off his leg when he is caught in a leg-hold trap. The dog struggles to survive but dies. A bird discovers the carcass and plucks out an eye.

The second "Run Movie 2—Hands" recounts another incident in which a missing body part is featured as he recalls his horror at seeing a boy in his class who had no hands. Dupuy returns to stories dealing with loss of body parts in two of the later stories, "Labyrinth" and "Forest Friends." In "Labyrinth," a creature with a human body and an animal head is emasculated by worms or maggots and experiences horror, rage, and finally, despair, ending in suicide. The plot of "Forest Friends" is more complex. The forest friends are a group of male buddies. One of the group loses his arm; his friends wrestle with the problem of commitment, of "being there" for someone, and of trying to understand someone else's pain.

Between "Hands" and "Labyrinth," Dupuy includes five stories. In "The dReam" he portrays himself watching a catastrophe from his window, failing to call for help since he does not know the phone number. In "The Museum," as he runs, his mind takes him into a museum where he talks with a dog about having a private place and about creativity. "Empty" deals with an artist named Hamfist who attempts to discover the meaning of empty space. In "The Old Lady and the Turtle," the jogging Dupuy's mind creates an old woman who has a turtle companion and helps him explore his inner self. In "The Rats," Dupuy is remodeling a house, and rats come out of the structure and invade his body; he vomits them, but they return in his dreams. He eventually leaves the house.

Haunted. (Courtesy of Drawn and Quarterly)

Between "Labyrinth" and "Forest Friends," the jogging Dupuy's mind involves him in a conversation with his deceased mother, whom he meets while jogging in "Mom," and to an encounter with a sort of renaissance-man duck who has collected so many objects and learned so much that he has lost himself and is trying to find himself. There are two stories after "Forest Friends," "Lucha Libre" and "The Finish Line." In "Lucha Libre," a wrestler defeats all challengers and brags about his lack of compassion and his violence. Then a female wrestler with whom he is in love appears to challenge him and renders him helpless. The final story, "The Finish Line," returns to Dupuy jogging and thinking about knowing when to stop, to not cross the line between everyday reality and the world of the mind. The final scene shows Dupuy descended into the chasm of his mind, residing with his cartoon characters.

Characters

- *Philippe Dupuy*, the author, appears as the main character in most of the stories.
- *A dog*, who is caught in a leg hold trap, chews off his leg.
- *A boy without hands* successfully performs a variety of tasks but inspires horror in a twelve-year-old Dupuy.
- *A dog*, who is a museum guard, guides Dupuy through his own museum or mind.
- *Hamfist* is an artist in search of emptiness.
- *An old lady* guides Dupuy on a search for self.
- *Escarole* is the old lady's turtle.
- *A male creature* with a human body and an animal head rejoices in being alive. He enters a labyrinth, is emasculated, becomes desperate, murders a couple engaged in sex, and commits suicide by running into a wall.
- *Dupuy's mother*, who is dead, jogs with him to discuss what is important in life and how to live.
- *A duck*, a collector of everything, has tried to learn every skill and all the information available in the world. He has realized that he has lost himself.
- *A group of forest friends* is composed of a reindeer, a rabbit, a creature who may be a beaver, and a creature who appears to be a wolf. The wolf has lost his arm. The friends fail to give the wolf the support he needs; he goes to the city. The friends philosophize and worry about him. The wolf returns, and they drink a toast to his arm.
- *A male Lucha Libre wrestler* sporting an "M" on his mask, brags that he is the murderer, the minotaur. He defeats all challengers.
- *A female Lucha Libre wrestler* is the downfall of the Lucha Libre wrestler M. She challenges him, and he is unable to fight her.

Artistic Style

In *Haunted*, Dupuy uses a style of drawing that contrasts sharply with that of the works done in collaboration with Berberian. The motif of running, of hurrying along, is reflected in his characters, which have much in common with sketchbook characters or images doodled on the margins of a page. They convey a sense of quickness, of fleeting time, and of the momentariness of life. There is no time for elaborate, detailed depiction. The entire graphic novel is done in black and white. The themes of transparency, weakness, inability, and emptiness are portrayed by Dupuy's use of characters drawn without color or substance. The drawings of a cross section of his body and the images of him, and often other characters (such as the old woman or the forest friends), either within his own organs or in a hole that has suddenly opened reinforce the motif of his run through his own mind.

Dupuy uses a wide variety of formats, ranging from full-page layouts to unframed multi-images per page and series of panels on a page. In addition, he uses combinations of framed and unframed drawings. This technique adds to his theme of running, of moving quickly, and of searching for himself and the meaning of living. His use of dialogue and author or character commentary is varied from story to story. The text begins and ends with Dupuy addressing himself or the implied reader with a commentary on running. Three of the stories— "The Dog," "The Rats," and "Labyrinth"—rely totally on drawings to convey meaning; there is neither dialogue nor commentary. "Empty" and "Forest Friends" use dialogue bubbles almost

Philippe Dupuy

One half of the famed cartooning duo Dupuy-Berberian, Philippe Dupuy broke into the French fanzine scene of the early 1980's before releasing *Petit peintre* in 1985. Sharing writing and drawing duties with Charles Berberian, Dupuy produced the *Henriette* series and the *Monsieur Jean* series. Their jointly produced graphic novel *Maybe Later* detailed the production of a volume in the *Monsieur Jean* series and the rise of the French small press scene in the 1990's. In 2008 they launched a new series, *Boboland*, which aggressively parodies the lives of an international bohemian class. Independent of Berberian, Dupuy published the autobiographical reflection *Haunted* in 2008, a series of discontinuous and dreamlike fragments drawn in a sketchy style. With Berberian, his visual style was defined early in his career by updating the Belgian Marcinelle school style, influenced by André Franquin and Yves Chaland. When he switched to a brush pen in the 1990's, his style became much more open and free.

exclusively; Dupuy does not appear as a character in either of these stories.

In "Lucha Libre," Dupuy relies almost exclusively on the drawings in the first half of the story, then he adds character commentary and eventually ends with a dialogue bubble when the girl speaks to the wrestler. In "Hands" and "The dRcam," only author commentary accompanies the drawings. In "The Museum," "Mom," and "The Duck," Dupuy uses a combination of dialogue bubbles and author or character commentary. In "The Museum" the preponderance of the written text is the conversation between the dog and Dupuy; however, when he recalls the pictures he made as a child, Dupuy switches to author commentary. "Mom" is framed in author commentary, as Dupuy remarks when he is running alone. When Mom is present he uses bubbles. "The Duck" uses dialogue bubbles primarily but contains some commentary by the duck. This mixing of pictorial and text formats enhances the sense of *Haunted* being a compilation of thoughts both connected and unconnected that run through Dupuy's mind as he jogs.

Themes

Dupuy explores the effects of loss or lack of body parts, of solitude and its resulting loneliness and introspection, and of interpersonal relationships and the creation of self. With the dog that self-mutilates to free itself from the trap, the boy without hands, the emasculated fantasy creature, and the forest friend who has lost his arm, Dupuy examines the gamut of outcomes of amputation. Only the boy truly succeeds in adjusting to his disability. Although the dog struggles desperately to survive, it dies. Emasculation plunges the fantasy creature into an intense despair, resulting in suicide. The forest friend experiences a lesser degree of despair and resigns himself to the loss of his arm.

The cartoons of the boy with no hands and of the forest friend also address the problems associated with interaction with others. Lacking hands, the boy is perceived as different. His handicap isolates him from other people. No matter how much he overcomes his handicap, he always remains other than normal. In "Forest Friends," Dupuy concentrates more on the reaction of the friends than on that of the friend who has experienced the loss. The friends want to help, but they do not know how to do so. During the period of absence of the injured friend, they vacillate between worrying about him and going on with their lives. Dupuy portrays strongly the fact that each individual remains alone, as the friends discover and accept the fact that they cannot really share in either the emotional or physical pain of their friend. For Dupuy, each individual is a unique entity surrounded by solitude, or the empty space, whose meaning Hamfist attempts to discover in "Empty."

As Dupuy runs through the pages of his graphic novel, he penetrates deeper into his own mind and even in to his subconscious. His encounters with the dog in the museum, the old lady with the turtle, his mother, and the collector duck all provide opportunities to explore life, its meaning, and the finding or creation of one's true self. The dog in the museum and the old lady point out the creative possibilities of the mind. During his brief run with his mother, he considers the need to distinguish and preserve the important and meaningful events and aspects of life while letting go of the rest.

The discussion between Dupuy and the collector duck develops the same theme.

Impact

Haunted has enlarged the scope of Dupuy's career as a graphic novelist. Writing *Haunted*, he experimented with a different writing style, a different approach to creating a graphic novel, and even the concept of what constitutes a graphic novel. Dupuy was actually running when he started writing *Haunted*. Thus, the work emanated from thoughts and observations that he hurriedly sketched and wrote on small notepads while sitting in cafés in Paris.

In addition, *Haunted* has opened a new direction for the team of Berberian and Dupuy. The long-running *Monsieur Jean* had confined them to presenting their characters and story line in a certain way, because readers expect certain traits and elements in *Monsieur Jean*. Both Dupuy and Berberian have stated in interviews that they feel what Dupuy did in *Haunted* is something they want to incorporate into their collaborative work. Although they are aware that many readers will be upset to see the *Monsieur Jean* stories taking a new direction, they are eager to use the innovations and ideas that Dupuy developed in *Haunted* as a springboard to give *Monsieur Jean* a new direction and attract new readers.

Shawncey Jay Webb

Further Reading

Abouet, Marguerite. *Aya* (2007-2009).

Delisle, Guy. *Burma Chronicles* (2008).

Dupuy, Philippe, and Charles Berberian. *Get a Life* (2006).

_____. *Maybe Later* (2006).

Bibliography

Dauncey, Hugh, ed. *French Popular Culture: An Introduction*. London: Arnold, 2003.

Forsdick, Charles, Laurence Grove, and Libbie McQuillan, eds. *The Francophone Bande Dessinée*. New York: Rodopi, 2005.

Groensteen, Thierry. *The System of Comics*. Translated by Bart Beaty and Nick Nguyen. Jackson: University Press of Mississippi, 2007.

See also: *Aya of Yopougon; Burma Chronicles; Get a Life*

He Done Her Wrong:
The Great American Novel—And Not a Word in It

Author: Gross, Milt
Artist: Milt Gross (illustrator)
Publisher: Doubleday; Fantagraphics Books
First book publication: 1930

Publication History

The title of the book *He Done Her Wrong* is taken from a line in the ballad "Frankie and Johnny," which had been popular in various versions since the beginning of the 1900's. In the song, which was loosely based on an actual murder case, Frankie kills her man, Johnny, because he "done her wrong." The plot of Gross's story, however, has little or nothing to do with the song, and Gross's subtitle (*The Great American Novel—And Not a Word in It*) indicates his intention to produce a visual novel with no text. It was first published in 1930, and, as such, it is often regarded as the second American graphic novel. The more serious *God's Man: A Novel in Woodcuts* (1929) by Lynd Ward is widely considered to be the first; indeed, *He Done Her Wrong* can be viewed as a reaction to the deeply serious tone of Ward's novel.

He Done Her Wrong was reprinted in 1963 by Dell, with an introduction by the cartoonist Al Capp. It was then reprinted in 1971 by Dover Books, with what were seen as offensive racial stereotypes removed, and later in a 1983 edition from Abbeville Press retitled *Hearts of Gold*. A more faithful reprint was published in 2005 by Fantagraphics Books, with an introduction by Craig Yoe and an appreciation by Paul Karasik.

Plot

He Done Her Wrong is 260 pages, and though it does not have formal chapters, it is divided into eight sections, usually separated by a blank page followed by a small vignette. The opening section has no title, but using the subject matter of the vignettes, the following seven sections are effectively titled: "The Big City," "The Bloodhound," "The Rich Widow," "No Help Wanted," "The Pampered Dog," "The Hospital," and "The Mouse."

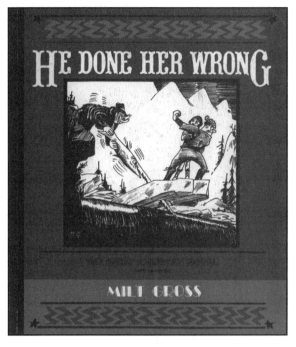

He Done Her Wrong. (Courtesy of Fantagraphics Books)

In the introductory section, readers meet the hero and heroine. The female protagonist is a young, pretty singer in a rough bar, set in a snowy landscape that looks like the Yukon. Her singing is so beautiful that she can reduce hardened men to tears. The hero is a hulking hunter who, even within the conventions of broad cartooning, cannot be described as handsome. When the heroine is the object of unwanted attention in her dressing room, the hero comes to her rescue. A villainous businessman then persuades him to form a partnership hunting for furs. After a tearful farewell with the heroine, the hero earns a huge amount of money for his new partner. However, the villain persuades the heroine that the hero has died, then marries her and takes her to the big city.

As the hero begins to search for his lost love, the villain becomes obsessed with a vending machine and loses his entire fortune trying to get it to work. While the heroine and her two children are thrown into the street, the villain strikes up a relationship with a rich widow, much to the dismay of the widow's pampered dog.

The hero makes his way to the big city, where, after a series of slapstick adventures, he narrowly misses the heroine when a sign advertising a play called *Fate* is lowered between them as they pass in the street. Finally, he tracks down the villain and, knife in hand, interrupts his marriage to the rich widow. The hero gives chase, and the villain, trying to escape with some of the widow's belongings, falls into a coal chute. In the joke that was censored in the mid-twentieth-century editions, the hero, having followed the villain, finds that

he is strangling a black character rather than the villain covered in coal dust.

Meanwhile, the heroine is desperately searching for work. In a long sequence, she is shown going through a series of meetings, pleading her case so she can finally get a job scrubbing floors. The villain has also fallen on hard times; the widow's butler tracks him down in order to throw him into the street, much to the amusement of the widow's dog. While robbing a barbershop, the villain is discovered by the hero, and a huge fight ensues.

The hero is rushed, unconscious, to the hospital where the heroine is now working. Unfortunately, in the fight, he acquired a photograph of the widow

He Done Her Wrong. (Courtesy of Fantagraphics Books)

inscribed with "To my beloved intended husband," which the heroine now finds. Distraught, she packs her bags and leaves. When the villain is brought to the same hospital, the hero literally drags him back to the wilderness in search of the heroine, but the villain has a gun and is able to turn the tables.

Just as the villain has the hero tied to a log in a sawmill, in a double parody of the conventions of melodrama, the heroine coincidentally happens to be walking past the mill with her two children. The hero, the heroine, and her children are all rescued when what appears to be a stuffed moose's head hanging in the mill turns out to be a real moose sticking its head through a hole in the wall. The moose attacks the villain and saves the day.

In the final parody of the excesses of melodrama, a birthmark on the hero's bottom reveals him to be the long-lost son of a timber magnate. The villain is condemned to shotgun marriages to a series of women, while, in the final frame, the hero and heroine share an embrace as a loving grandfather plays with their five children in the background.

Characters

Because they inhabit a wordless novel, the main characters do not have names, but they can be identified by their roles in the narrative.

- *The heroine*, as is typical of her origins in melodrama, is beautiful, virtuous, and virginal. Her looks change slightly when she moves to the big city and starts wearing fashionable clothes. However, by the end of the novel, she has reverted to her more traditionally feminine appearance.
- *The hero* is a large, simple-looking hunter with almost superhuman strength. He wears buckskins and a coonskin hat until the end of the story, when, newly rich, he is seen wearing natty plus fours.
- *The villain*, with his fur coat, top hat, and moustache, is based on the model from melodrama. He is totally ruthless, driven by lust for both money and the heroine, but he is not exceptionally clever, as demonstrated by the complete collapse of all his schemes.

- *The heiress* is a large, aging dowager with a hooked nose, pandered to by her butler and devoted dog.

Artistic Style

Even in an era of loose, fluid draftsmanship in American newspaper strips, Gross's artwork in *He Done Her Wrong* stands out as particularly gestural. Every page, even the most detailed ones, seems to have been drawn at great speed, as if in a frenzy of creativity. To work in this way is not simply a matter of haste, as it requires a great surety of touch.

Gross's skill in design also comes to the fore, with the layout of the pages varying dramatically, from intensely detailed double-page spreads through multiple-panel action sequences to small, simple single images surrounded by the white expanse of the page. There are often no panel borders, and the story flows at a varying pace, sometimes frenetic, sometimes leisurely. The lack of dialogue means that Gross has to be particularly inventive in some of his storytelling. He rarely falls back on the obvious, although at one point, the trapper who tells the hero of the villain's evil scheme has a drawing of an eye and a saw above his head to indicate "I saw." More typically, Gross's solutions to the challenge of wordlessness are original and ingenious; when the villain tells of the "death" of the hero, the headstone has a likeness of the hero on it, and readers see the coffin underground with a dummy in it.

Gross uses heavily blacked pages for moments of high drama, as when the heroine is threatened in her dressing room. There, the leering face of her would-be assailant is surrounded by total blackness; later, after the hero has left, she is shown silhouetted three times in a doorway, each time looking a little sadder. When action scenes are required, Gross's swift drawing style becomes even more frenetic. As the hero and villain fight in the barbershop, an entire page is taken up by a whirling mass of circular lines in which fragments of faces, hands, and feet can be seen, surrounded by equipment flying in all directions. Gross also uses action sequences to develop complex slapstick scenes. When the villain leaves the barbershop, he is kicked out while tied to a chair, the springs of which send him bouncing halfway across the city. He bounces to a window where the wealthy widow is taking a bath, and her attempts to attack him merely result in him bouncing back to her window, where he shrugs helplessly as she hits him again.

At other times, the slapstick can be less hectic, as when the villain confronts the vending machine. Across two pages, in twelve drawings without panel borders, he gradually descends from cool assurance to wild frustration. The effect is to create a slow buildup of humor similar to that of the 1920's *Punch* cartoons by English social satirist H. M. Bateman.

The majority of Gross's pages are sparse, yet elegantly designed; however, sometimes he fills panels with incidental humorous detail. When the hero drags the villain back into the wilderness, they pass through a city scene depicting first-floor stables; people hanging off the back of an elevated railway car; a holdup in an automobile; and a mother, with her children, balancing on her head on a seesaw.

Themes

Although the subtitle of *He Done Her Wrong* was meant as an ironic joke by Gross and although the characters and the events of the story are relentlessly humorous, it is still a novel that has to deliver its narrative without recourse to dialogue or even sound effects. The only text in the story is diegetically contained, and even then it is only sporadic, mostly delivered in the form of street signs or fragments of handwriting. Therefore, *He Done Her Wrong* is a formal experiment in the nature of visual storytelling.

The story is mainly a parody of the kind of melodramas that were well established in the nineteenth century and still popular in theaters and cinemas in the 1920's. As such, it plays with the rigid stereotypical roles of melodrama: the beautiful, virginal heroine; her faithful, strong suitor; and the rich, evil villain who has designs on the (usually impoverished) heroine. Despite being a parody, however, underneath Gross's comic treatment, *He Done Her Wrong* is a story of love, lust, and greed. For such a broad comedy, there are many serious undertones in the novel, including the contrast between the innocent wilderness and the evil city. The twenty-six-page-long sequence in which the heroine searches for work also struck a chord with

Milt Gross

Born in 1895, Milt Gross began producing comic strips for the *New York Journal* when he was only twenty years old. His first success was *Gross Exaggerations*, an illustrated column in the *New York World* that featured his distinctively comical blend of English and Yiddish phrasings. His 1930 epic, *He Done Her Wrong*, was a three-hundred-page wordless graphic novel parodying the work of Lynd Ward. The next year, Gross went to work for the Hearst chain, producing syndicated strips. His comic book work from the 1940's was collected in 2010 as *The Complete Milt Gross Comic Books and Life Story*. Gross's visual style was exceptionally cartoonish, colorful, and dynamic. His characters feature extremely exaggerated features and body types, and his work holds a strong appeal for young children. Gross has been extremely influential on a generation of cartoonists and animators interested in slapstick humor, from *MAD* magazine to *Ren and Stimpy*.

contemporary audiences, who by 1930 were suffering the effects of the Great Depression.

Impact

When the reputation of American newspaper artists and writers began to be rehabilitated in the 1960's and 1970's, Gross was left behind. As Winsor McCay, George Herriman, E. C. Segar, and others reemerged as household names, Gross was comparatively neglected. Despite his memorable characters and his zany humor, which remained easily accessible to audiences in the latter part of the twentieth century, it was not until 2009 and 2010 that major texts specifically devoted to Gross began to appear.

Some of Gross's most memorable work appeared in book form, and with titles like *Nize Baby* (1926) and *Dunt Esk* (1927), it may be that the use of Yiddish slang and phonetic spellings kept these works less accessible to later audiences. However, *He Done Her Wrong*'s wordless quality is what makes it both international and timeless in its appeal. Some critics maintain that it is still imbued with Jewish humor, but given the success of American Jewish humor across a wide range of media, if this is true, it should be construed as praise and not criticism.

The immediate and, indeed, short-term impact of Gross's work on the development of the graphic novel was minimal. Perhaps unsurprisingly, no other artists tried to emulate him by creating a wordless novel. Even Gross's subsequent works, such as *Dear Dollink* (1945), belong to the field of illustrated books rather than graphic novels. His more general influence on other cartoonists and comic artists has been vast, however. Figures as diverse as Matt Groening, Jules Feiffer, and Robert Crumb have acknowledged their admiration for Gross; in fact, Crumb used Gross's famous catchphrase "Is dis a system?" in a panel from *Despair* comics in 1969. The various reprints of *He Done Her Wrong* have kept his work alive, and in the twenty-first century, it appears that the nature of his work and his contributions to the development of the putative graphic novel have finally been recognized.

David Huxley

Further Reading

Gross, Milt. *Famous Fimmales: Witt Odder Ewents from Heestory* (1928).

_____. *I Shoulda Ate the Eclair* (1946).

Gross, Milt, and Henry Wadsworth Longfellow. *Hiawatta: Witt No Odder Poems* (1926).

Bibliography

Gross, Milt, and Ari Y. Kelman. *Is Dis a System? A Milt Gross Comic Reader*. New York: New York University Press, 2009.

Gross, Milt, and Craig Yoe. *The Complete Milt Gross Comic Books and Life Story*. San Diego, Calif.: IDW, 2010.

Harvey, R. C. "Milt Gross: *Banana Oil* and the First Graphic Novel?" *The Comics Journal*, November 10, 2010. http://classic.tcj.com/top-stories/milt-gross-banana-oil-and-the-first-graphic-novel.

Heer, Jeet. "The Incomplete Milt Gross." *The Comics Journal*, April 12, 2010. http://classic.tcj.com/history/the-incomplete-milt-gross.

See also: *The Complete Fritz the Cat; Nat Turner; The Adventures of Tintin*

HEY, WAIT...

Author: Jason (pseudonym of John Arne Sæterøy)
Artist: Jason (illustrator)
Publisher: Jippi Forlag (Norwegian); Fantagraphics Books (English)
First serial publication: *Vent Lint*, 1998-1999
First book publication: 2002 (English translation, 2001)

Publication History

Hey, Wait... was first published in 1998 by Jippi Forlag in Norway in the comic book *Mjau Mjau*, issues 3 and 4. It was edited and translated from the Norwegian by Kim Thompson and published by Fantagraphics Books in 2001 and later in 2010 in the collection *What I Did*, which includes *Sshhh!* and *The Iron Wagon*, also by Jason. It was published in book form in Norwegian in 2002 as *Vent Lint*.

Plot

Part 1 is a story of two anthropomorphized animals, Bjørn and Jon, who, as close friends, share the innocent joys of childhood. Like all boys from any culture, they create mischief, fly kites, read comics, talk about girls, and consider what they want to be when they grow up—Bjørn a journalist and Jon a comic book artist. They decide to form a Batman club, the membership initiation of which consists of swinging out on a limb over a cliff and then falling back safely on land. Jon performs this feat successfully, while Bjørn waits for another time.

Later, when walking to school, Jon meets a ghoulish creature who waves and smiles at him as he rides by on a bicycle. Later that day, after school, the two boys meet at the cliff for Bjørn's initiation. Jon sees how frightened Bjørn is and hollers out, "Hey, Wait!" —but not in time to stop Bjørn from jumping out for the limb. Unable to grasp the limb, Bjørn falls to his death. Jon attends Bjørn's funeral, at the request of his father. As they leave the cemetery, Jon's mother comments that the accident was not his fault. Jon sneezes and suddenly grows into an adult who walks home alone to an empty apartment.

Hey Wait... (Courtesy of Fantagraphics Books)

In part 2, Jon lives an isolated and lonely life as an adult. He lives apart from his wife and their child and works a boring factory job, something that he and Bjørn swore they would never do. His empty life is one of menial activities such as brushing his teeth, walking to work, eating alone, looking out his kitchen window into emptiness, standing at a drill press all day and drilling a hole into cubes, undressing at night before going to bed alone, watching the television game show *Jeopardy!*, playing tennis, having a short romantic relationship, drinking, and complaining about work (despite staying in the job year after year).

Jon has a dream in which he falls to his death off the cliff where Bjørn died. Death looks down at him and laughs. During one of Jon's blackouts, after a night of heavy drinking, Death appears before him. They sit at his kitchen table, and Jon describes his life. "Anyway . . . my life didn't exactly turn out like I expected . . . now if I was being punished that would make sense to me . . . if I was a bad person . . . but I'm not." There is no reply from Death. He merely stares as Jon bows his head. Death asks Jon to close his eyes and count to three. When Jon opens his eyes, he comes face-to-face with his childhood self who plays ball with Bjørn as though the accident on the cliff never happened. In the last sequence, Jon steps on a bus filled with ghoulish figures and sits down calmly as the bus moves down the road.

Characters

- *Jon*, the main protagonist, is a dog-like character whose life is reflected in a series of short sequences, from childhood to his lonely adult existence that ends in early death.
- *Bjørn*, with long rabbit-like ears, is Jon's best friend who accidentally falls off the cliff as part of an initiation.
- *Death*, who appears like a ghoulish figure with blackened eyes and wearing a suit, passes Jon the

day that Bjørn falls accidentally to his death and later when Jon awakes from a blackout before his life ends.

Artistic Style

In this tale, told in pen and ink, Jason draws each character and object with the same even line, free of shading and cross-hatching. This style is best described as "clear line." The cartoonist Joost Swarte originally used this term ("ligne claire") in 1977 to describe Hergé's style in the comic series *The Adventures of Tintin* (1929-1976). By using the same even lines, each object and character inside the panels is given an equal amount of concentration. In addition to these consistent lines, Jason provides large portions of white space to focus audience attention on important scenes and objects, such as the tree on the cliff where Bjørn falls to his death. In this example, the white space in the background concentrates the reader's attention on the tree and the cliff.

Another element of Jason's style is his unemotional rendering of feelings. Rather than using cartoon gestures or exaggerated facial expressions, which are a trademark in superhero comics, Jason presents his

Hey Wait... (Courtesy of Fantagraphics Books)

characters with plain expressions no matter the emotion. These unemotional expressions leave characters' feelings open to interpretation, which involves the audience more intimately with the story. Jason's simple, static style produces a contemplative reaction to the unfolding narrative of familiar events in the lives of the characters. His effective style—using even lines, white space, and fixed emotional expressions—makes Jason's story plausible, even when he mixes the real with the fantastic, such as when Jon and Bjørn fly a kite and a dinosaur snatches it from the sky. Jason's style ensures the narrative is both relatable and surprising, as when surreal incidents unfold.

In the front matter, Jason previews the style he uses throughout the book. In this wordless page with six panels, he shows Jon and Bjørn passing an apartment door. Bjørn looks around cautiously before Jon rings the doorbell. The boys run away quickly before the door opens and a monster, similar to the one from the horror film *Creature from the Black Lagoon* (1954), stares directly at the reader. The reader is a witness to the prank, which is a common one played by children, but is not prepared to see a monster behind the door. What is even more puzzling is that instead of looking around for the perpetrators of the prank, the monster looks directly at the reader. Thus, the simple panel-to-panel transition not only immediately involves the reader in the action but also cautions the reader to expect the unexpected in this tale of Magical Realism.

Jason's style shies away from any panel experimentation, though his use of various devices produces a visually stimulating narrative within traditional panels. The artistic style is secondary to the narrative. The way in which the story is disseminated remains consistent throughout, with six bold, bordered panels per page.

Jason's black-and-white panels have plenty of white space with the simplest of details and little dialogue. Every third page in part 1 and more than two-thirds of the pages in part 2 are wordless. His later completely wordless strips and stories in *Sshhhh!* display a skillful use of the genre of wordless comics. Most of the book is told in single, one-page events that together form an album of childhood and adult lives. Jason admits the most important influences on the creation of *Hey, Wait…* were the stories of French comic artist Fabio Viscogliosi

(known as Fabio), who uses simple characters and situations to present hapless events in the life of a vagabond cat that first appeared in *L'oeil du Chat* (1995).

Jason uses word balloons creatively. One example involves Jon's teacher. In what appears to be a history lesson, the teacher delivers a lecture; however, from the limited, telescopic portion of text captured inside a round word balloon, the lecture makes no sense. Not only is this effective in relating the nonsensical nature of the lecture, but also it presents Jon's complete lack of interest. As his teacher delivers the lecture, Jon draws a Batman figure in his notebook.

Jason repeats panels on a page to heighten awareness of certain events in the story. For example, Jason does not show Bjørn's death. Instead, a page of six all-black panels follow the previous panel in which Bjørn is shown jumping out for the tree limb on the edge of the cliff. The page of black panels is followed by a panel of a skull and a candle on a bookcase that strongly implies Bjørn's death before it is confirmed in a funeral scene.

In another series of panels, in order to show Jon losing consciousness during a drunken stupor, Jason masks more and more of the panels as Jon sits on the couch drinking, until he is shown with only the simplest of lines. The next panels are entirely white before a sketch of a toilet appears; the lines become bolder as Jon is shown falling on his knees before he vomits in the toilet.

Jason

Norwegian cartoonist John Arne Sæterøy, known by his pen name "Jason," has earned international acclaim for his minimalist comics, which often combine real-world historical and pop-cultural figures with animal-headed protagonists. His clean-line artistic style, along with his minimal use of dialogue, makes him primarily a visual cartoonist, requiring the reader to pay close attention to each panel in order to gain the full effect of the story. His tales often combine both humor and profound sorrow.

Duplicating panels are also used when Jon is dead and then opens his eyes. The tree is shown in all six panels on the page between when Jon sees his childhood self and when Jon and Bjørn are playing soccer, suggesting what could have been if they had not played on the cliff. The last panel on the page with the boys playing soccer shows Bjørn, who scores a goal. He jumps into the air, with his hands held high in triumph, much like his pose before he jumped for the tree limb. Jon is left with a warm memory of Bjørn.

Themes

Friendship and guilt are the major themes in this work. The friendship between Jon and Bjørn in part 1 is heartfelt and innocent. Jason provides numerous examples of the boys playing and enjoying each other's company before Bjørn's accidental death, which leaves Jon alone with an overwhelming feeling of guilt.

In part 2, the negative effects from guilt permeate Jon's adult life. He lives a lonely life with low self-esteem, dealing with resentment, isolation, depression, and alcoholism. Jon is unable to forgive himself because he feels responsible for Bjørn's death. Like his repetitious job in the factory, Jon's life is uneventful and mechanized. He is divorced, cannot keep a steady relationship, and spends his evenings drinking until he falls asleep in a blackout. When Death arrives, Jon does not plead for his life. For Jon, Death is the only end to his misery. As a concession, Death offers Jon a glimpse of what his life could have been if the accident had not occurred.

Impact

Hey Wait… has been favorably received and is considered a representative piece of the European (especially French) comics of the 1990's and early 2000's. As part of the "new comics" scene burgeoning in France in the early 2000's, Jason joined fellow artists such as Joann Sfar and David B. in presenting graphic novels that deal with highly personal, often autobiographical, subject matter. As Jason's first book to be translated into English, *Hey Wait…* introduced the Norwegian artist to a new level of success and had an influence on both European and American graphic novels that came after it.

David A. Beronä

Further Reading

B., David. *Epileptic* (2005).

Brown, Chester. *I Never Liked You: A Comic-Strip Narrative* (1991-2002).

Jason. *The Living and the Dead* (2006).

Bibliography

Jason. "Interview with Jason." Interview by D. J. Douresseau. *Comic Book Bin*, June 15, 2004. http://www.comicbookbin.com/charlie32.html.

_____. "The Jason Interview." Interview by Matthias Wivel. *The Comics Journal* 294 (December, 2008): 28-77.

_____. "A Short Interview with Jason." Interview by Tom Spurgeon. *The Comics Reporter*, January 27, 2007. http://www.comicsreporter.com/index.php/resources/interviews/7393.

See also: *The Frank Book; I Never Liked You; Harum Scarum; Epileptic*

HICKSVILLE

Author: Horrocks, Dylan
Artist: Dylan Horrocks (illustrator)
Publisher: Drawn and Quarterly
First serial publication: 1992-1996
First book publication: 1998

Publication History

Dylan Horrocks originally serialized the majority of *Hicksville* across issues 1-10 of his comic book *Pickle* between 1992 and 1996. Though Horrocks had previously published works in New Zealand, Australia, and England, *Pickle* was significant in introducing him to North American audiences. *Pickle*'s publisher, the defunct Canadian company Black Eye Books, issued a complete version of the novel in 1998 that included around fifty pages of previously unserialized content. Drawn and Quarterly published a new edition of the collected version in 2001.

Despite the generally high regard in which readers and critics held *Hicksville*, this edition soon fell out of print. A new edition arrived in 2010, also from Drawn and Quarterly, with new cover art and an expanded glossary, though it lacked the two-page introduction by the mononymic cartoonist Seth that had graced previous editions. Most notably, this edition opens with a thirteen-page introduction in comics form in which Horrocks traces his relationship to the medium and discusses the experience of creating *Hicksville*.

Plot

Because Horrocks employs a nonlinear, discontinuous, and fragmentary style of storytelling in *Hicksville*, the book's narrative resists easy paraphrase. At the novel's heart, however, is the story of Leonard Batts, a North American journalist for the fictional *Comics World* magazine, who travels to the town of Hicksville on the East Cape of New Zealand. Seeking information about Dick Burger—a newly minted mainstream comics superstar whose work has revitalized the superhero genre—Batts finds himself in a rural community where, inexplicably, everyone reads and admires comics of all kinds. Despite this, few of the town's

Hicksville. (Courtesy of Drawn and Quarterly)

residents speak to Batts about their distinguished former citizen, and many treat Batts with open contempt for merely mentioning Burger's name. Even the few who speak to him at all offer little more than obtuse allusions to Burger's past misdeeds, along with suggestions that only Kupe, the mysterious and unseen lighthouse keeper, can tell the full story.

Provoked by the otherwise friendly townspeople's aggressive disdain for his research, Batts makes an ill-advised attempt to provoke them at their annual Hogan's Alley party, to which all are supposed to come as a favorite comics character. As Batts runs away from the party in pursuit of a vision that has haunted him throughout the prior chapters, he accidentally plunges off of a cliff and into the sea.

Batts wakes up the next day in the previously inaccessible lighthouse, where he meets Kupe, who had fished Batts out of the water the night before. Kupe at last explains Burger's crime: In the basement of the lighthouse is a secret library that contains comics for which the world was not yet ready, many of them works of great genius, but none of them available elsewhere. As a young man, Burger became fascinated with an unpublished graphic novel about the Superman analogue Captain Tomorrow that was meant to provide an elegant end to the long-lived hero's story. Violating the taboo around the library, Burger stole the originals of this tale and fled to the United States, where he published the work as his own after updating the art and changing the ending to leave Captain Tomorrow's fate open. On learning all this, Batts flies to the United States and confronts Burger who returns the original novel in exchange for Batts's silence. At *Hicksville*'s end, Batts returns to New Zealand, ready to explore the histories of comics that might have been.

Horrocks weaves a host of other stories into and around Batts's narrative. Many are told in the form of comics read by characters within the novel itself. Most notable is an enigmatic tale in which three figures from different points in the history of New Zealand investigate a puzzling cartographic and topological phenomenon. Also important are Hicksville native Sam Zabel's minicomics—titled, like Horrocks's original serial, *Pickle*—that take over much of the novel's second and sixth chapters. These comics, which offer visions of Zabel's life in the years he was away from home, also contain comics within them—selections from Zabel's canceled newspaper strip. The novel also regularly takes tangents into the lives of the town's other

Hicksville. (Courtesy of Drawn and Quarterly)

residents, especially Grace, whose tortured love triangle with Kupe and the tearoom operator Danton led her to flee from home for some time. Grace's story, like almost all the others that crop up throughout the book, begins and ends in medias res, a fragment of something larger. Like the books in Kupe's library, these glimpses into other lives are hints of other histories, of stories that sit beside those that are known.

Characters

- *Leonard Batts* is a journalist for *Comics World* magazine who comes to New Zealand in search of information about Burger. Though originally from Newfoundland, Batts claims to be a U.S. citizen out of a sense of embarrassment about his origins.
- *Dick Burger* is a media mogul and comics superstar about whom little is known. Despite his deep sense of entitlement and self-involvement, Burger is haunted by his past.
- *Sam Zabel* is a recently unemployed cartoonist who returns home to Hicksville, where he offers some assistance to Batts. In a comic within the comic, Zabel recounts the story of his childhood friend Burger's attempt to bribe him with a job in the mainstream American comics industry.
- *Grace* is a botanist who, like Zabel, returns to Hicksville after time abroad. She is romantically entangled with both Kupe and Danton and possesses a deep distaste for Burger, with whom she grew up.
- *Mrs. Hicks* is the benevolent matriarch of Hicksville. She runs the Hicksville Book Shop and Lending Library, which seems to own one or more copies of almost every comic book ever published. Additionally, she operates a small printing press and provides Batts with a bed.
- *Danton* is the operator of Hicksville's Rarebit Fiend Tea Rooms and is one of Grace's former partners.
- *Emile Kópen* is a comics artist, cartographer, and magician from the mysterious country of Cornucopia.
- *Cincinanti Walker* is a film star who takes a liking to Zabel during his brief reunion with Burger.

- *Kupe* is the keeper of Hicksville's lighthouse and the protector of its taboo library of secret comics.

Artistic Style

Throughout *Hicksville*, Horrocks, who serves as the book's sole illustrator, employs a rough and cartoony style. Working exclusively in black and white, he relies heavily on thickly inked lines that give his story's characters and locales a strong sense of presence, even as they efface most of the subtle intricacies of real bodies and places. Though he maintains this commitment to minimalism throughout, Horrocks varies his style slightly in each of the embedded comics and stories that interrupt the main narrative. Excerpts from Burger's superhero comics, for example, rely heavily on cross-hatching to give the illusion of texture and tone—a technique popularized during the 1980's and 1990's by mainstream artists such as Todd McFarlane. By contrast, segments about Grace's past make extensive use of deeply inked black shadows, conveying a sense of her emotional turmoil. Horrocks's work grows sketchiest in the excerpts from Zabel's minicomics that occasionally appear throughout the text. Here, he employs a style clearly meant to evoke the rough-and-tumble cartooning of self-published, photocopied comics.

While *Hicksville* itself is slightly larger, the actual content of most of the book's pages is exactly the size of a sheet of photocopier paper folded in half. This too calls up the minicomics tradition in which Horrocks was an active participant.

Though many of its pages contain up to nine panels, most of *Hicksville*'s layouts are linear and clear. For much of the book, Horrocks surrounds his panels and the space around them in black rather than white, encouraging his readers both to take their time with each individual image and to contemplate carefully the relation of each new panel to those that precede and follow it. The resultant sense of care and precision gives the book a cartographic feel that is surely no accident, as Horrocks has frequently remarked on the relationship between comics and maps. This connection between the temporal cartography of the comics page and the real spaces represented on maps finds a correlate in the care Horrocks takes in depicting the landscapes of rural

New Zealand. Scholars such as Hammish Clayton and Mark Williams have called special attention to this element of *Hicksville*, noting the ways in which it visually quotes elements of the New Zealand tradition of fine-arts landscape painting.

Themes

If a single concern cuts through *Hicksville*'s various competing narrative layers, it is the status of the comics medium itself. The book as a whole can be read as a meditation on both the troubled public perception of the medium and its largely untapped formal potential. These concerns become especially apparent in the novel's final chapters, when Batts finds himself in the town's secret library.

The larger story of Burger also stages the historical dominance of the superhero genre over the comics industry throughout much of the twentieth century. *Hicksville* suggests that work such as that which Burger produces tends to obscure the other possibilities that the medium is capable of exploring. In this light, Batts's story might be read as a hopeful allegory about the discovery that comics can do more than tell tales of costumed crusaders.

Critics tend to connect *Hicksville*'s interest in comics and its preoccupation with New Zealand. Just as the comics medium has traditionally been marginalized in conversations about art, New Zealand is a country that often seems to exist at the limits of the known world. Batts in particular continually reasserts the frustrations of a life lived at the limits of normalcy, from his resistance to his Newfoundlander heritage to his irritation at being the sole coffee enthusiast in a town that drinks nothing but tea. These and other such moments might be read as attempts to gain new perspective on the questions of marginalization that *Hicksville*'s ironically central subjects pose. In this context, the town of Hicksville itself functions as a sort of redemptive fantasy, taking something ostensibly strange—the practice of reading comics—and turning it into something ordinary and essential.

Impact

Hicksville derives from a period when many independent cartoonists were struggling to reconcile their own

---

Dylan Horrocks

Best known for the graphic novel *Hicksville*, originally serialized in *Pickle*, Dylan Horrocks has developed a reputation as one of the deepest thinkers about issues pertaining to comics. *Hicksville*, which tells a story of betrayal in the American comic book industry set in New Zealand, was widely praised for its imaginative depiction of comics as a neglected art form. Following the completion of that work, Horrocks went to work for DC Comics, writing *Hunter: The Age of Magic* for their Vertigo imprint and *Batgirl*. He began serializing *Atlas* with Drawn and Quarterly in 2002, but has produced only three issues in total. He now serializes a number of stories on his website. Horrocks's comics are characterized by a visual style that defines a sort of cartoonish realism, in which characters and images depart from strict naturalism but are clearly drawn from life. His stories have a strongly romantic and utopian sensibility.

---

interests and investments in the mainstream American comics industry and its favored genre, the superhero. To this extent, Horrocks's work is similar to otherwise different texts such as Alex Robinson's *Box Office Poison* (2001) and Chris Ware's *Jimmy Corrigan* (2000). It is thus no accident that though *Hicksville*'s narrative opens with a parodic pastiche of superhero action, it proceeds to explore an array of alternative approaches to comic art.

Horrocks himself frequently cites a broad range of influences on his work, from the precise draftsmanship of Hergé's *Adventures of Tintin* (1929-1976) serials to Charles M. Schulz's long-running newspaper strip, *Peanuts* (1950-2000). The embedded comics that frequently appear throughout *Hicksville* allow Horrocks to experiment with and restage many of these influences. These intratexts also point to the importance of the postmodernist metafictional gamesmanship of non-comics writers such as Jorge Luis Borges to Horrocks's creative process.

Despite the implicit challenge that *Hicksville* offers to mainstream comics publishers, Horrocks found himself on the receiving end of job offers from DC Comics and its adult-oriented imprint Vertigo in the wake of his novel's initial book publication. This association was short lived, but it speaks to the resonance of *Hicksville* beyond the relatively small audience of independent comics. In the subsequent years, *Hicksville* has remained in high regard, garnering strongly favorable reviews upon its republication in 2010. Nevertheless, Horrocks's personal output since *Hicksville*'s completion has been relatively minimal.

Hicksville is important for the way it calls attention to the fundamentally transnational status of comics. In portraying the tension between the glamorous corporate entertainment capitals of Burger's America and the quiet beauties of rural New Zealand, it encourages its readers to seek out and explore comics from more unfamiliar locales. In this regard, it has arguably helped influence comics publishers, as they have turned to previously neglected regions of the world as they search for new material. Along similar lines, *Hicksville* has been received as a significant contribution to the literature and art of New Zealand, suggesting its ability to reach beyond conversations about comics as such, even as it remains grounded in Horrocks's medium of choice.

Jacob Brogan

Further Reading

Campbell, Eddie. *The Fate of the Artist* (2006).

Seagle, Steven T., and Teddy Kristiansen. *It's a Bird . . .* (2004).

Bibliography

Clayton, Hamish, and Williams, Mark. "Smoke at Anchor: Dylan Horrocks' *Hicksville*." In *Floating Worlds: Essays on Contemporary New Zealand Fiction*, edited by Anna Jackson and Jane Stafford. Wellington, New Zealand: Victoria University Press, 2009.

Horrocks, Dylan. "Sweeping Out the Lighthouse: An Interview with Dylan Horrocks." Interview by Tom Spurgeon. *The Comics Journal* 243 (May, 2002).

Jackson, Anna, and Jane Stafford. "Introduction: The Gaming Halls of the Imagination." In *Floating Worlds: Essays on Contemporary New Zealand Fiction*, edited by Anna Jackson and Jane Stafford. Wellington, New Zealand: Victoria University Press, 2009.

Lister, Sam. "Playgrounds, Gardens, Communities, Worlds: Dylan Horrocks's *Hicksville*." *Journal of New Zealand Literature* 25 (2007): 138-163.

See also: *Jimmy Corrigan; It's a Bird; Box Office Poison*

HISTORY OF VIOLENCE, A

Author: Wagner, John
Artist: Vince Locke (illustrator); Robert Lappan (colorist)
Publisher: DC Comics
First book publication: 1997

Publication History

Originally serialized as three ninety-six-page volumes, *A History of Violence* was published by Paradox Press, a relatively short-lived imprint of DC Comics. Paradox was created to release graphic novels that did not feature superheroes or fantasy and science-fiction elements, as those were the genres most clearly associated with DC Comics and their successful Vertigo imprint, respectively. John Wagner, an American writer raised in Scotland, was best known for having created the Judge Dredd character for the British magazine *2000 AD* in the 1970's. Vince Locke was not widely known as an artist when the graphic novel was serialized, his best-known work being the *Deadworld* (1987) series for Arrow Comics and *American Freak* (1994) for Vertigo. Unusually for DC Comics, the Paradox titles were released in black and white.

Plot

A History of Violence tells the story of Michigan diner owner Tom McKenna, a retiring man who is thrust into the national spotlight after he defends his eatery from an attempted robbery. Shortly thereafter, three members of a New York organized crime family arrive in town. The leader of the gangsters, John Torrino, believes that Tom is really a man named Joey Muni, who, some twenty years prior, had injured Torrino's eye in a fight. Like Joey, Tom is missing a finger on his left hand. While Torrino is initially unsure of whether Tom is really Joey, his henchmen make vague threats to the McKenna family. Torrino is convinced of Tom's real identity only when he sees Tom's son, Buzz, who bears a strong resemblance to his father at a younger age. The gangsters abduct Buzz and confront Tom on his farm. In the ensuing shoot-out, Tom kills Torrino's men and

A History of Violence is one of the notable works of comics writer John Wagner, and one of a few works of Wagner's to be adapted into film. (Michael Germana/SSI Photo/Landov)

is himself wounded. His wife, Edie, saves his life when she shoots Torrino.

The second chapter is almost entirely composed of a flashback set in Brooklyn two decades earlier. Joey and his best friend, Richie Benedetto, are teenagers living in a part of New York controlled by organized crime. When Richie's brother Steve is assassinated by mob hit man John Torrino, Richie wants to avenge his death, but Joey is reluctant. Later, when Joey realizes that his grandmother, with whom he lives, needs an operation that the family cannot afford, he agrees to help Richie steal from the mob. The duo pulls off a daring midday robbery of Lou Manzi's family, killing several men in the process. Richie is ultimately captured by Torrino, after he carelessly begins to spend the money stolen in the robbery. Joey seeks to escape from New York and the Manzi family, and he does so only after a fight in an alley where he blinds Torrino and loses a finger.

The final chapter returns to the present day. Tom confesses to the police his role in the robbery of Lou Manzi and the death of his men, but he is released because he had not been read his Miranda rights. Later, Tom receives a phone call from someone he recognizes to be Richie, begging for help. When Torrino is killed in his hospital bed by a hired killer, Tom receives a second call, threatening his family. He and Edie fly to New York to cooperate with the police regarding the murders from twenty years earlier. While in New York, Tom realizes that he cannot protect his family from the gangsters except by taking matters into his own hands. Learning that Manzi's operations are now run by his son, Little Lou Manzi, he surrenders to two of his men. After being taken to a warehouse, he kills the mobsters and engages in an elaborate shoot-out with various henchmen. Ultimately, Tom discovers his friend Richie, armless and legless, dangling from a meat hook, where he has been tortured for two decades by Little Lou. Little Lou surprises Tom and chains him to the ceiling before torturing him with an electric drill. Tom escapes and kills Little Lou with a chainsaw, ending the threat to his family. He then ends the life of his friend, Richie, when the badly injured man begs for his own death.

Vince Locke

Artist Vince Locke made a name for himself in the late-1980's independent comics scene as the artist on the cult hit *Deadworld*, a post-apocalyptic series featuring zombies. In the 1990's he began working for DC Comics' Vertigo imprint, including work on *Sandman* and *American Freak*, a limited series written by Dave Louapre. In 1997 he published, with writer John Wagner, *A History of Violence*, a noir-inspired crime comic with strong horror overtones that was later adapted for the screen by filmmaker David Cronenberg. Locke's art is characterized by its emphasis on cross-hatching and shading done with thin pen lines. His figures are largely realist, with a tendency toward the grotesque. His drawings are often sketchy, with unpolished lines that are intended to make them seem dashed off. His framing and page designs are classical, and he only occasionally uses widescreen visual effects.

Characters

- *Joey Muni*, the protagonist, is a married, middle-aged father of two, who runs a diner in a small Michigan town. He is living under the alias of Tom McKenna because he fears that members of a New York organized crime family wish him dead.
- *Richie Benedetto* is Joey's best friend from childhood. A teenage boy living in Brooklyn, he attempts to avenge the death of his brother by robbing the Manzi organized crime family. After successfully pulling off the crime, Richie is captured by the Manzi family when he is indiscrete with the stolen cash.
- *John Torrino* is an elderly hit man in the Manzi organized crime family. In the aftermath of the crime committed by Joey and Richie, he is wounded by Joey and loses an eye. The main action in the book is motivated by Torrino's desire to hunt down and kill Joey. He is the primary antagonist in the first part of the book.
- *Little Lou Manzi* is the son of Lou Manzi, the organized crime leader who is robbed by Joey and Richie. After his father's death, he takes control of the Manzi crime family. He is an unrelenting sadist who tortures Richie, and later Joey, with construction tools. He is the antagonist in the final part of the book.
- *Edie McKenna* is a middle-aged mother of two, married to Tom McKenna. Edie supports her husband throughout the course of the story, even after learning that he has been lying about his past during the entirety of their relationship.

Artistic Style

A History of Violence was serialized as three black-and-white, undersized volumes, a format that was not frequently used by DC Comics. The smaller page size forced artist Locke to place fewer panels on each page than is common in other comics of this period, providing a relatively open page design that complements and underscores the rural setting of the book's first chapter. Over time the story becomes increasingly dark and violent, moving from subtle threats of harm to scenes of elaborate and gratuitous torture. This narrative development is supported by Locke's art, which moves toward higher concentrations of black as the story unfolds.

Locke is known for a realistic style that is defined by his scratchy penmanship and frequent use of cross-hatching. The figure drawing throughout the book tends toward a minimalist representational style that often looks sketched rather than fully polished. At the same time, Locke makes extensive use of detailed backgrounds to establish a sense of place, and, on occasion, he will foreground a single visual element, such as a gun, by rendering it in greater detail than the other visual elements on the page. The rough lines of the drawings contribute to the chaotic and disorderly feeling created by the story.

In keeping with the book's realist approach, thought balloons are not used and all communication takes place through dialogue. Captions are used in the second chapter, which is a flashback to Joey's youth told from Tom's point of view. A notable weakness of the book stems from the use of clichéd dialogue during the fight sequences that stretches the level of realism found in the work. Additionally, the characterization of the McKenna family is not a strong point of the work, with each of the members of the supporting cast being one-dimensional rather than fully fleshed out with problems or subjectivities of their own.

Themes

A History of Violence is notable for its use of elements of noir crime fiction in the graphic novel form. Wagner introduces quotidian realism in the first chapter, only to have it disrupted by elements of danger. Throughout the course of the book the quiet life of the McKenna family is disrupted by increasingly more dangerous outbreaks of violence, which suggest that the family may be fated to a bleak future. The initial confrontation in the diner seemingly occurs randomly, but the national attention paid to Tom's actions creates the opportunity for Torrino to reenter his life. The showdown with Torrino and his men at the McKenna farm results in serious injury to Tom and reveals the full extent of the threat to his family. It is only by acting to preempt retaliation by Little Lou Manzi that Tom can protect his own life and the lives of his family.

Centrally, the book addresses the relationship of the past to the present through the figure of Tom/Joey. When the sins of the past are revisited on the quiet diner owner in the present, the question of what kind of man Tom is rises to the surface. Additionally, the book asks the reader to consider the merits of preemptive violence as a moral course of action. Ultimately, *A History of Violence* makes readers consider to what degree people are shaped in the present by their actions in the past. To this end, the book evinces a high degree of fatalism.

Impact

A History of Violence might not be remembered were it not for the success of David Cronenberg's 2005 film adaptation. Like most books in DC's short-lived Paradox Press series, the graphic novel was serialized to remarkably little fanfare in 1997 and was eventually allowed to fall out of print before being republished in conjunction with the film. The book found an appreciative audience with fans of crime comic books, a genre that had been generally neglected since the end of the 1940's, and it, alongside *Road to Perdition* (1998) and *Stray Bullets* (1995), was one of the key works that helped spark a renewed interest in the crime comics genre. The book is remembered now for the striking grotesquerie of its conclusion, with the horribly mutilated Richie Benedetto hung from meat hooks. Writer Wagner has a background in satire and a tendency to push the boundaries of taste to extremes, which can be seen in the gradually escalating levels of horror and brutality found in this book. The legacy of *A History of Violence* and *Road to Perdition* can be found in DC's *100 Bullets* (1999-2009), a noir/fantasy hybrid developed in 1999, and more contemporary crime comic books such as *Criminal*.

Films

History of Violence, A. Directed by David Cronenberg. New Line Productions, 2005. This film adaptation stars Viggo Mortensen and Maria Bello as Tom and Edie Stall, Ed Harris as Carl Fogarty, and William Hurt as Richie Cusack. The film differs from the graphic novel in many ways. Notably, the names of the characters have been altered, the entire second chapter has been eliminated, and Tom and Richie are brothers and Richie is a successful gangster. The film was nominated for Academy Awards in the categories for Best Adapted Screenplay (Josh Olson) and Best Supporting Actor (William Hurt).

Bart Beaty

Further Reading

Azzarello, Brian, and Eduardo Risso. *100 Bullets* (1999-2009).

Brubaker, Ed, and Sean Phillips. *Criminal* (2006-   ).

Collins, Max Allan, and Richard Piers Rayner. *Road to Perdition* (1998).

Grist, Paul. *Kane* (1993-   ).

Lapham, David. *Stray Bullets* (1995-2005).

Bibliography

Beaty, Bart. *David Cronenberg's "A History of Violence."* Toronto: University of Toronto Press, 2008.

Locke, Vince. "Interview by Will Colling for The Nexus," August 5, 2005. http://insidepulse.com/2005/08/05/39887.

_____. *Visions: Drawings and Paintings*. Plymouth, Mich.: Caliber Press, 1992.

Wagner, John. "Interview by La Placa Rifa and W. R. Logan for The Class of '79." http://www.2000ad.nu/classof79/jw_interview.htm.

See also: *Kane; Road to Perdition; Stray Bullets*

HOUDINI: THE HANDCUFF KING

Author: Lutes, Jason
Artist: Nick Bertozzi (illustrator)
Publisher: Hyperion Paperbacks for Children
First book publication: 2007

Publication History

The writer of *Houdini: The Handcuff King* is Jason Lutes, who is a cartoonist from Seattle, a winner of multiple Harvey and Ignatz Awards, and the author of the acclaimed *Jar of Fools*, released in 1997 by Black Eye Books. He developed the thumbnail sketches for *Houdini: The Handcuff King* in his role as an instructor at the Center for Cartoon Studies in White River Junction, Vermont, which was established in 2005, and is the only college-level training program of its kind in the United States and concentrates on the creation and marketing of comics and graphic novels.

Illustrator Nick Bertozzi, from New York, considers Lutes to be one of his favorite cartoonists. Once Lutes's pacing and imagery of the book were in place, Bertozzi was hired by James Strum to flesh out the art in the penciling stage, along with inking, gray-toning, and lettering in the book. While Bertozzi already had a graphic novel in process, *Houdini: The Handcuff King* took precedence, especially since he was working under a cartoonist of such high esteem.

In early 2005, Hyperion Books announced in *Publishers Weekly* its plans to partner with the Center for Cartoon Studies to publish a series of graphic novels for younger readers. This partnership was conceived after the exchange of ideas between Brenda Bowen, vice president and editor-in-chief of Hyperion Books for Young Readers, and many artists she had met during the 2004 Comic-Con International: San Diego. James Strum produced the books with acclaimed cartoonists and students from the comics program; he also acted as series editor. In April, 2007, *Houdini: The Handcuff King* became the first book in the series to be published. Due to popular demand, a paperback edition was released in July, 2008. The second book in the series, *Satchel Paige: Striking Out Jim Crow* by Sturm and Rich Tomasso was released in December, 2007. The

---

Nick Bertozzi

Nick Bertozzi emerged as one of the most important new cartoonists in the 2000's when his series *Rubber Necker* won two Harvey Awards in 2003. His 2007 graphic novel, *The Salon*, was originally serialized online before being collected by St. Martin's Press. It tells the fictional story of the birth of Cubism as a reaction to a series of murders in Paris, where various real-life historical figures—including Pablo Picasso, Georges Braque, and Gertrude Stein—unite to solve the crime. That same year, Bertozzi illustrated *Houdini: The Handcuff King*, based on a script by Jason Lutes. He is one of the founders of the ACT-I-VATE comics blog, where he serializes two Web comics: *Persimmon Cup* and *Pecan Sandy*. Bertozzi's art tends toward a representational minimalism, with thick, rounded lines used to draw his figures.

---

series produces two graphic biographical installments a year.

Plot

World famous escape artist, Harry Houdini is chronicled through this biographical sketch of his famous jump from the Harvard Bridge into the Charles River, in May, 1908. This work provides an "eyewitness" account of a single event in history while being entertaining and educational to middle school and adult readers.

The story begins with Harry in his room at the Charles Hotel in Boston as he times himself picking a lock, while his wife, Bess, is nearby. The two of them practice kissing each other as Bess passes the lock pick to Harry. Harry then leaves his room at 6:00 A.M. to go over his final preparations for the stunt he is to perform later that morning. While running to the bridge, he greets men he has compensated to pay him homage at the event. Harry then meets his assistants at the Charles River and has an unfriendly exchange of words with the police officer on duty. While the police will not allow Harry to make a practice jump from the bridge, he does so anyway.

Upon his return to the hotel, Harry is hounded by the press. He brags about his success to the reporter who is interviewing him and reveals that he has studied every form of entrapment and how to extricate himself, while giving credit to his wife for his fame. During the interview, Harry is appalled by the interviewer's mockery, and he retreats to his room, sulking.

Bess comforts Harry and gives him the reassurance and emotional support he needs to prepare mentally for his death-defying jump. He then meets up with Mr. Beatty, his newly hired man, and exits the hotel to greet the waiting photographers and spectators. When Harry enters his jumping-off point on the bridge, the men he compensated earlier bow and tip their hats to him. Harry then interacts with the crowd and exhibits himself as the police search him for keys and lock picks. The police then bind him with handcuffs and shackles.

Meanwhile, Bess is getting ready to meet up with Harry. As she enters the hotel lobby, she is mobbed by the press; Mr. Beatty protects her and escorts her to a taxi. When she arrives at the bridge, she is stopped by police and told she is unable to get through the crowd of spectators. One officer asks for proof that she is really Harry's wife, and she produces her marriage license from her purse. It is critical that she meets up with Harry, as the success of his stunt depends on her presence.

While Harry is on a podium ready to jump, he is greeted by Bess. The two of them exchange kisses (and the lock pick) as the crowd cheers. Harry then takes his dive into the nearly freezing river as one of his assistants keeps time. After one minute and nineteen seconds, Harry emerges from the water unbound, and the crowds go wild.

Characters

- *Harry Houdini*, the protagonist, is the famous escape artist, who is strong and muscular and believes pompously that he can escape any sort of snare. He thinks that he is better than the local police and that they should allow him to do whatever he pleases. He is obsessed with fame and popularity, which he feeds off.

- *Bess* is Harry's beloved wife and is a fashionable woman in her early twenties. She and Harry have a close bond, and her adoration for him is obvious. She sticks up for him whenever he is criticized, and he believes he would be nothing without her. She is always smirking at people who think Harry is a fraud. She is later escorted to Harry's jump and kisses him good luck.

- *Seven Bowing Bystanders* are the men whom Harry pays to give homage to him prior to his jump. They are seen later in the story tipping their hats and bowing to Harry as he makes his entrance to his bridge jump. Each man places a letter of Harry's last name on their balding scalps to spell out "H-O-U-D-I-N-I."

- *Officer Hogan* is the first Boston police officer to guard the Harvard Bridge in the morning of Harry's jump. This plump man is also responsible for examining Harry's body seconds before his jump for any contraptions. He is certain that his handcuffs are the best and does not want criminals to believe they can escape from them. He is against Harry making a practice jump.

- *Mr. Kukol* is one of Harry's personal assistants and is responsible for checking the temperature of the Charles River; he reports that it is just shy of being frozen.

- *Mr. Vickery* is another of Harry's personal assistants. He is responsible for timing Harry's escape from the Charles River. He is present when Harry is making his practice jump in the morning.

- *Mr. Smith* is the newspaper reporter who interviews Harry at the Charles Hotel during breakfast. Harry finds him to be bothersome and feels the reporter has little respect for him. After the interview, he is seen making a call to his editor. He waits for Bess to enter the hotel lobby on her way to Harry's jump and harasses her. Mr. Beatty stops him, and he gets thrown into the street.

- *Mr. Collins* is Harry's most trusted man. Harry introduces him to Mr. Beatty. He is responsible for running the stop clock while Harry is submerged. He is seen as a bold and competent man.

- *Mr. Daniel Beatty*, a.k.a. *the New Man*, is a skilled detective and a robust man and is Harry's newest hired man. He is responsible for protecting Bess when Mr. Smith harasses her. He punches Mr. Smith and keeps him in a headlock as Bess proceeds to her taxi. He misses Harry's jump, as he was busy protecting Bess and stopping Mr. Smith.

- *Police Officer Fields* greets Harry outside the Charles Hotel on his way to the Boston Bridge. He escorts Harry through the crowd of spectators and secures him with regulation handcuffs. He examines Harry after he has been handcuffed and shackled.
- *Officer Hemphill* is responsible for offering Officer Fields the handcuffs Harry will use during his jump.
- *Mr. Gustavson* is another of Harry's hired men. He sits in a rowboat on the Charles River and waits for Harry to emerge from the water. He then rows Harry back to shore.

Artistic Style

Bertozzi's black-and-white line drawings are clear and not overly detailed. Depth and color is added to the illustrations with grayish-blue shading. The boldness in the artwork in the foreground of many panels effectively depicts various emotions seen throughout the plot, such as nervousness and excitement. Speech bubbles are consistently placed at the top of each panel, allowing for easy reading flow, and the caption writing is consistent in size. The illustrations mimic the time period and setting of Boston, Massachusetts, in 1908, while the drawing style is consistent throughout and maintains the mood.

The open and airy page layout contributes to the clear organization of the work as seen through appropriately sized panel sequencing and surrounding white space. A majority of the panel transitions feature action-to-action progressions, such as when Houdini is picking locks. Subject-to-subject panel transitions are also apparent, as when Houdini is underwater picking his locks while his assistants and the crowd are waiting.

A number of wordless panels are used throughout the story and help to progress the plot. Some wordless panels are placed between panels with speech bubbles to depict characters' facial emotions. Visual clues in the panels also extend the plot, as when Bess is pushing her way through the crowd to get to Harry prior to his bridge jump. More than a dozen pages contain wordless panels, which provide clues to readers throughout the book.

Themes

Houdini: The Handcuff King is notable for setting the trend for graphic novel biographies of famous individuals. Throughout the book, Harry displays his arrogance and egoism as an insecure man obsessed with fame. This attitude is displayed through his conversations and displayed emotions. His competitive streak is shown through his obsession with improving his tricks and tactics.

Harry researches and studies ways to extricate himself from handcuffs, straight jackets, and sealed containers and continually proves his abilities. The combination of his work ethic, ego, and skill creates a legendary, inimitable character.

Harry has a passionate and loving relationship with his wife, Bess, who acts as his supporter. Throughout the book, she is shown as his equal partner. She follows him wherever he goes. She is always on his mind, which is made apparent in the book through thought bubbles.

Impact

Houdini: The Handcuff King was the first published collaboration between the Center for Cartoon Studies and Hyperion Books. It was also the first book to portray Harry Houdini in graphic novel format. It set the precedent for other titles in the series, such as *Satchel Paige: Striking Out Jim Crow*; *Thoreau at Walden* (2008), by John Porcellino; and *Amelia Earhart: This Broad Ocean* (2010), by Sarah Stewart Taylor and Ben Towle. The series allows students at the Center to work on and gain experience in publishing graphic novels. These titles set the bar for graphic biographies.

An introduction to the book is provided by Glen David Gold, who is the author of *Carter Beats the Devil* (2001). He gives a thorough background history on Houdini's life. The book ends with panel discussions highlighted with thumbnails of images from the story with detailed explanations, historical facts, and

Harry Houdini is pictured here with chains. (Apic/ Getty Images)

light commentary. These discussions allow for additional reader insight and provide an avenue for classroom studies. These attributes, as well as a bibliography and short author and artist backgrounds, are included in the other titles in the series. Each book introduction is written by a prominent person in a field related to the title.

The series publication has set the standard for quality graphic biographies, which has resulted in other publishers following suit. After its publication, *Houdini: The Handcuff King* was named a 2008 Young

Adult Library Services Association (YALSA) Great Graphic Novel for Teens. Hyperion has also produced a discussion guide for *Houdini: The Handcuff King*.

In 2010, Bertozzi's artwork was featured at the "Monsters and Miracles: A Journey Through Jewish Picture Books" show at the Skirball Cultural Center in Los Angeles. The art show then traveled to the Eric Carle Museum of Picture Book Art in Amherst, Massachusetts, where it was on display through January, 2011.

Janet Weber

Further Reading

Burns, Jason M. *Hat Trick* (2010).
Gaiman, Neil. *The Books of Magic* (1993).
Lutes, Jason. *Jar of Fools: A Picture Story* (2003).
Naifeh, Ted. *Courtney Crumin* series (2003-2009).
Rocks, Misako. *Biker Girl* (2006).

Bibliography

Baxter, Kathleen. "We're Just Wild About Harry: Master Magician Harry Houdini Still Fascinates and Mystifies Kids of All Ages." *School Library Journal*, April, 2010, p. 21.
Milliken, Joe. "Just Like Magic: The Center for Cartoon Studies Publishes Its First Graphic Novel." *Vermont Guardian*, April 27, 2007. http://www.vermontguardian.com/culture/042007/CartoonStudies.shtml.
Reed, Calvin. "More Comics from Disney—Duh." *Publishers Weekly* 252, no. 9 (February 28, 2005).

See also: *Jar of Fools; The Golem's Mighty Swing*